THE
ANTITRUST
IMPULSE

COLUMBIA UNIVERSITY SEMINAR SERIES

The University Seminars at Columbia University welcomes this study of The Antitrust Impulse: An Economic, Historical, and Legal Analysis by Theodore P. Kovaleff to the Columbia University Seminars Series. The study has benefited from Seminar discussions and reflects the advantages of scholarly exchange provided by the Seminar Movement.

Aaron W. Warner
Director, University Seminars
Columbia University

THE FUTURE OF AMERICAN BANKING
James R. Barth, R. Dan Brumbaugh, Jr., and Robert E. Litan

THE EVOLUTION OF U.S. FINANCE, VOLUME I
Federal Reserve Monetary Polity: 1915–1935
Jane D'Arista

THE EVOLUTION OF U.S. FINANCE, VOLUME II
Restructuring Institutions and Markets
Jane D'Arista

THE ANTITRUST IMPULSE, Volume I and Volume II
An Economic, Historical, and Legal Analysis
Theodore P. Kovaleff

FROM MALTHUS TO THE CLUB OF ROME AND BACK
Problems Of Limits to Growth, Population Control, and Migrations
Paul Neurath

THE ANTITRUST IMPULSE

Volume II

An Economic, Historical, and Legal Analysis

Theodore P. Kovaleff
Editor

M.E. Sharpe
Armonk, New York
London, England

Library of Congress Cataloging-in-Publication Data

The Antitrust impulse: an economic, historical, and legal analysis /
[edited by] Theodore P. Kovaleff.
p. cm. — (Columbia University seminar series)
Includes index.
ISBN 1-56324-180-3 (V. 1)   1-56324-181-1 (V.2)   1-56324-085-8 (set)
1. Antitrust law—United States.
I. Kovaleff, Theodore Philip, 1943–
II. Series.
KF1649.A2A419 1994 v. 2
343.73'0721—dc20
[347.303721]
94-5618
CIP

Printed in the United States of America

The paper used in this publication meets the minimum requirements of
American National Standard for Information Sciences—
Permanence of Paper for Printed Library Materials,
ANSI Z 39.48-1984.

BM (c)   10   9   8   7   6   5   4   3   2   1

Contents

VOLUME II

PART II

Philosophical Perspective

PART III

Economic Perspective

List of Tables and Figures

Contributors

WALTER ADAMS / JAMES BROCK

A member of the economics faculty of Michigan State University since 1947, Walter Adams also served as its President (1969–1970). A prodigious writer, he quickly became known for his work on the theory of competition and monopoly; as a result, he was appointed to the Attorney General's National Committee to Study the Antitrust Laws (1953–1955). He is the author of *Monopoly in America* and an editor and contributor to *The Structure of American Industry*. Recently, with James W. Brock (see below), he has written *The Bigness Complex: Industry, Labor, and Government in the American Economy*; *Dangerous Pursuits: Mergers and Acquisitions in the Age of Wall Street*, and a devastatingly satirical play, *Antitrust Economics on Trial: A Dialogue on the New Laissez-Faire*.

James Brock has been a member of the economics faculty of Miami University (Ohio) since 1979. Promoted to full professor in 1989, the following year, he was named to the prestigious Moeckel professorship. In addition to the aforementioned coauthored books with Walter Adams, he has writtten *Antitrust, the Market and the State: The Contributions of Walter Adams*.

DONALD DEWEY

Donald Dewey has been a member of the Economics faculty at Columbia University since 1960. He is the author of many scholarly works, including *The Theory of Imperfect Competition*; *Monopoly in Economics and Law*; *Modern Capital Theory*; and *The Antitrust Experiment in America*.

ELEANOR M. FOX / LAWRENCE A. SULLIVAN

Since 1976 Eleanor M. Fox has been a Professor at the School of Law, New York University, where she has taught courses in all aspects of antitrust law. The author of several widely used texts, many articles, and a number of books, including *Industrial Concentration and the Market System: Legal, Economic, Social and Political Perspectives*, she served as a member of President Jimmy Carter's National Committee for the Review of Antitrust Laws and Procedures and is a member of the Advisory Board of *The Antitrust Bulletin*.

Lawrence A. Sullivan has taught courses on antitrust, international transactions, and patents at the University of California Law School, Boalt Hall since 1967. He coauthored *Cases and Materials on Antitrust* with Eleanor Fox. He, too was a member of the Carter committee to review the antitrust laws.

ERNEST GELLHORN / CHARLES A. JAMES / RICHARD POGUE / JOE SIMS

Before becoming a partner in the Cleveland law firm of Jones Day Reavis & Pogue, Ernest Albert Eugene Gellhorn had been a Professor of Law at Duke University and the University of Virginia. Subsequently, he was Dean at the law schools of Arizona State University, Case Western University, and the University of Washington. An expert in the administrative and regulatory fields, he is the author, with Glen O. Robinson, of a casebook on the topic. He is a member of the Advisory Board of *The Antitrust Bulletin*.

Charles A. James received his law degree in 1979 from the National Law Center of George Washington University. He spent six years at the Federal Trade Commission in the Bureau of Competition. He then entered private practice in the Washington office of Jones, Day, Reavis & Pogue where he remained until joining the Antitrust Division as Deputy Assistant Attorney General. In early 1992, he was appointed Acting Assistant Attorney General in Charge of the Antitrust Division. With the change of administrations, he rejoined his former law firm where he chaired the Antitrust and Trade Regulation Section of the Government Regulation Group.

Richard Pogue has been a partner specializing in antitrust enforcement in Jones, Day, Reavis & Pogue since 1961. He chaired the American Bar Association's Antitrust Section. (1983–1984) and is a member of the Advisory Board of *The Antitrust Bulletin.*

Joe Sims began his legal career with the Antitrust Division of the Department of Justice in 1970, starting as a trial attorney but quickly being advanced to Special Assistant and then Deputy Attorney General for Policy Planning and Legislation. In 1979 he left his last governmental position, Deputy Attorney General for Regulated Industries and Foreign Commerce, to become a partner at the law firm of Jones, Day, Reavis, & Pogue. He has remained professionally active, having chaired the Sherman Act Section 1 (1988–90) and the Civil Practice and Procedure committees (1990 to the present) of the Antitrust Section of the American Bar Association. With William Kovacic, he is the author of *The Antitrust Government Contracts Handbook.*

MILTON HANDLER

Immediately after being graduated from the School of Law at Columbia University in 1926, Milton Handler was invited to join its faculty; he remained there until his retirement in 1972. Starting with his stint as General Counsel to the National Labor Board (1933–1934), he was active in government service. He served as Special Assistant to the General Counsel of the Treasury Department (1938–1940), as Assistant to the General Counsel, Lend Lease (1942–1943), as a member of the Attorney General's National Committee to Study the Antitrust Laws (1953–1956) and as Chair of the Special Committee to Study the New York State Antitrust Laws (1953–1956). Intricately involved with the Temporary National Economic Committee and its investigation of the concentration of economic power, he wrote *A Study of the Construction and Enforcement of the Federal Antitrust Laws.* In addition to having written a number of case books, he is the author of *Reforming the Antitrust Laws; Antitrust in Perspective;* and *Antitrust in Transition*, a three-volume collection of his most important articles.

THOMAS EUGENE KAUPER

Thomas Eugene Kauper interrupted a teaching career that had begun in 1964 at the University of Michigan Law School to join the Department of Justice in 1969. His first assignment was in the Office of Legal Council, where he held the rank of Deputy Assistant Attorney General. From 1972 until 1976, he was Assistant Attorney General in Charge of the Antitrust Division of the Department of Justice. Since that time he has been a member of the University of Michigan Law School faculty specializing in antitrust and trade regulation.

THEODORE P. KOVALEFF

After having taught economic and legal history at St. John's University, New York University, and Barnard College, Theodore P. Kovaleff was Assistant Dean at the Columbia University School of Law from 1977 to 1992. He is the author of *Business and Government During the Eisenhower Administration: A Study of the Antitrust Policy of the Antitrust Division of the Justice Department*. He is a member of the Advisory Board of *The Antitrust Bulletin* and was Guest Editor of its volume marking the centennial of the Sherman Act.

ROBERT H. McGUCKIN, III

Robert H. McGuckin, III, served with the Antitrust Division of the Department of Justice from 1974 to 1986, rising to Director of Research, Economic Analysis Group before leaving to become the Chief of the Center for Economic Studies of the Bureau of the Census. Editor of a special issue of *The Antitrust Bulletin* celebrating the tenth anniversary of the Economic Policy Office of the Antitrust Division and author of *Empirical Methods in Economic Analysis: An Innovative Approach to Statistical Techniques*, he has also been been recognized by the Justice Department with its "Award of Distinction" and with the "Unusually Outstanding Award" given by the Bureau of the Census.

STEPHEN A. RHOADES / JIM BURKE

While working on his doctorate in economics at the University of Maryland, Stephen A. Rhoades served as a staff economist at the Federal Trade Commission. Upon receipt of the degree, he joined the Federal Reserve Board. He is currently Chief of the Financial Structure Section of the Division of Research and Statistics. His research is primarily directed in the fields of industrial organization, banking, and antitrust. He is the author of *Power, Empire Building, and Mergers*.

Jim Burke received a Ph. D. in economics from the University of Maryland in 1973. Since that time, he has been primarily involved with regulatory policy matters in the Division of Research and Statistics at the Federal Reserve Board. His research has been related to the structure and performance effects of consolidation in banking.

JAMES FRANKLIN RILL

James Franklin Rill spent the first thirty years of his legal career in private practice with the firm of Collier, Shannon, Rill & Scott. During this period he was instrumental in founding the Antitrust Law Section of the American Bar Association, which he subsequently chaired. In 1989 President George Bush appointed him as the Assistant Attorney General in Charge of the Antitrust Division of the Department of Justice. He served in that position until early 1992, when he returned to his law firm. He is a member of the Advisory Board of *The Antitrust Bulletin*.

CHARLES F. RULE / DAVID L. MEYER

After graduating from the University of Chicago Law School and serving as law clerk to Daniel M. Friedman, chief judge of the United States Court of Claims (now the Court of Appeals), Charles F. Rule joined the Antitrust Division of the Department of Justice in 1982. Starting as a Special Assistant to Assistant Attorney General William F. Baxter, he was soon appointed Deputy Assistant Attorney General, first being responsible for Policy Planning and Legislation and then Regulatory Affairs. After a stint as Acting Assistant Attorney General in charge of the Antitrust Division, he was confirmed to the post in September 1987; he remained until the end of the Reagan administration. He is now a partner in the law firm of Covington & Burling in Washington, D.C.

David L. Meyer is also an attorney with Covington & Burling, where he has practiced since 1989. Between 1987 and 1989 he was Special Assistant to the Assistant Attorney General in Charge of the Antitrust Division. After graduating from the Yale Law School, he clerked for the Honorable Ralph K. Winter, on the United States Court of Appeals for the Second Circuit.

LOUIS B. SCHWARTZ

Louis B. Schwartz began his career serving on the staffs of the Securities and Exchange Commission and the Criminal and Antitrust Divisions of the Department of Justice. He joined the faculty of the University of Pennsylvania Law School in 1946, remaining there until he became a member of the 65 Club at the University of California, Hastings College of Law in 1984. A member of the Attorney General's National Committee to Study the Antitrust Laws (1953–1955), and Director of the National Committee on Reform of Federal Criminal Laws (1967–1971), he is the author of *Antitrust and Regulatory Alternatives* (with John J. Flynn and Harry First).

JOHN J. SIEGFRIED / MICHELLE MAHONY

John J. Siegfried has been Professor of Economics at Vanderbilt University since 1972. An economist with the Federal Trade Commission, a Senior Staff Economist for the Council of Economic Advisors, and member of the Board of Editors of *Review of Industrial Organization*, *The Quarterly Review of Economics and Business*, and *Journal of Economic Education*, he is also the author of *Empirical Studies in Industrial Organization* (with David Audretech), *Economic Analysis and Antitrust Law* (with Terry Calvani), and of nearly 100 articles.

Michelle Mahony is working on her doctoral dissertation in economics at Northwestern University.

JERROLD G. VAN CISE

An internationally respected authority on the administration and enforcement of the antitrust corpus, Jerrold G. Van Cise was a member of the Attorney General's National Committee to Study the Antitrust Laws (1953–1955). With fellow Cahill, Gordon & Reindel partners, William T. Lifland and Laurence T. Sorkin, he is author of *Understanding the Antitrust Laws; The Antitrust Laws from the Point of View of a Private Practitioner*, (with Sigmund Timberg); *The Federal Antitrust Laws*, and *Understanding the Antitrust Laws*.

JAMES R. WITHROW, Jr.

A member of the law firm of Donovan Leisure Newton & Irvine for a career which lasted from 1935 to 1987, James R. Withrow, Jr., specialized in the areas of antitrust and management.

EDWIN MORTON ZIMMERMAN

After graduating from law school in 1959, Edwin Morton Zimmerman was appointed to the faculty of the Stanford Law School. In 1965 he took a leave of absence to join the Department of Justice. Subsequently, President Lyndon B. Johnson appointed him Assistant Attorney General in Charge of the Antitrust Division in 1968, where he remained until the end of the administration. He has been a partner in the Washington law firm of Covington & Burling since 1969.

VOLUME II

DOMINICK T. ARMENTANO

Dominick T. Armentano is Professor of Economics at the University of Hartford, where he specializes in antitrust, industrial organization, and the relationship between business and society. He is the author of *Antitrust and Monopoly: Anatomy of a Policy Failure*; *Antitrust Policy: The Case for Repeal*; and *Myths of Antitrust: Economic Theory and Legal Cases*.

TERRY CALVANI / MICHAEL L. SIBARIUM

Terry Calvani has been a member of the faculties of Law at Stanford University, Vanderbilt University, and the University of Virginia. The Chair of the American Bar Association's Special Committee to Study Antitrust Penalties and Damages from 1979 to 1982, he then worked as a Commissioner on the Federal Trade Commission until 1990, serving as Acting Chairman from 1985 to 1986. Thereafter, he joined the Washington D. C. office of the law firm of Pillsbury, Madison, & Sutro. With John Siegfried, he is the author of *Economic Analysis and Antitrust Law*. He is a member of the Advisory Board of *The Antitrust Bulletin*.

Michael L. Sibarium served as an Attorney Advisor to Terry Calvani from the time Calvani became acting chairman until 1990. He is presently a member of the Washington law firm of Winston and Straun, specializing in business litigation, antitrust, and trade regulation; he is also a faculty member of the National Law Center, George Washington University.

WILLIAM J. CURRAN III

William J. Curran III was an attorney in the Antitrust Division of the Department of Justice from 1969 to 1975 and has continued to specialize in the field since then. He has served as Editor of *The Antitrust Bulletin* since 1983.

JOEL DAVIDOW

Joel Davidow is a partner in the Washington D.C. law firm Ablondi, Foster, & Sobin where he specializes in the fields of antitrust, international trade, technology transfer, and unfair competion law. He has held various positions at the Federal Trade Commission and is a former Director of Policy Planning and Chief of the Foreign Commerce Section of the Antitrust Division of the Department of Justice. He is Foreign Antitrust Editor of *The Antitrust Bulletin* and a Member of the Advisory Board of the *BNA Antitrust and Trade Regulation Reporter*.

HAMILTON FISH, Jr.

Hamilton Fish, Jr., has been a member of the U.S. House of Representatives since 1969. He is Vice Chairman of the House Judiciary Committee and member of the House-Senate Joint Economic Committee.

JOHN J. FLYNN

John J. Flynn has been a faculty member of the University of Utah College of Law since 1963, specializing in antitrust and business organization. He has served as a consultant to the U.S. Senate Antitrust and Monopoly Subcommittee of the Judiciary Committee and the Bureau of Competition of the Federal Trade Commission and as President of the Section on Antitrust and Economic Regulation of the Association of American Law Schools. He is the author of *Federalism and State Antitrust Regulation*; *Antitrust and Regulatory Alternatives* (with Louis B. Schwartz); *Free Enterprise and Economic Organization: Antitrust* (with Louis B. Schwartz and Harry First); and *Free Enterprise and Economic Organization: Government Regulation* (with Louis B. Schwartz and Harry First). He is a member of the Advisory Board of *The Antitrust Bulletin*.

RALPH H. FOLSOM

With the exception of a stint at the Federal Trade Commission in the late 1970s, Ralph H. Folsom has been a faculty member of the University of San Diego School of Law since 1975, where he specializes in antitrust and law in the People's Republic of China. He is author of *State Antitrust Law and Practice; Antitrust Laws and Trade Regulation, Corporate Competition Law in the European Communities*; and *International Business Transactions* (with Michael Wallace Gordon and John A. Spanogle).

DOUGLAS GINSBURG

In 1983 Douglas Ginsburg left Harvard Law School to become Deputy Assistant Attorney General for Regulatory Affairs. Before being appointed Assistant Attorney General in Charge of the Antitrust Division of the Department of Justice in 1985, he served in the Office of Management and Budget. In 1986

President Ronald Reagan appointed him to the Court of Appeals, District of Columbia Circuit. He is the author of a number of books, including *Antitrust, Uncertainty, and Technological Innovation* and *Regulation of the Electronic Mass Media: Law and Policy for Radio, Television, Cable and the New Video Technologies.*

VALENTINE KORAH

Valentine Korah is Professor of Competition Law at University College, London; she has visited at the Fordham University School of Law on several occasions. She is a member of the Advisory Board of *The Antitrust Bulletin* and the author of *Competition Law of Britain and the Common Market*; *Franchising and the EEC Competition Rules: An Introductory Guide to EEC Competition Law And Practice*; and *Know-how Licensing Agreements and the EEC Competition Rules: Monopolies and Restrictive Practices.*

WILLIAM E. KOVACIC

William E. Kovacic has experience in government, private practice, and teaching. He served as a Legislative Assistant to the Antitrust Subcommittee of the Senate Judiciary Committee, in the Federal Trade Commission in the Planning Office of the Bureau of Competition, and as Attorney-Advisor to Commissioner George W. Douglas, and then joined the law firm of Bryan, Cave, McPheeters & McRoberts in Washington, D.C. In 1986 he was appointed to the faculty of the George Mason University School of Law, where he specializes in antitrust and government contracts. He has been Chair of the Antitrust and Trade Regulation Section of the Federal Bar Association since 1990. With Joe Sims, he is the author of *The Antitrust Government Contracts Handbook.*

WILLIAM H. PAGE

William H. Page joined the Antitrust Division of the Department of Justice under the Attorney General's Honors Program after graduating from the University of New Mexico School of Law. After three years in the Chicago office he was appointed to the faculty of Boston University School of Law. Since 1981 he has been a member of the faculty of Mississippi College School of Law, where he was named J. Will Young Professor of Law in 1991.

ALMARIN PHILLIPS

Almarin Phillips has taught Economics at the University of Pennsylvania since 1948, specializing in the regulatory process. Codirector of the President's Commission on Financial Structure and Regulation (1970–1971), he also has been a member of the Board of Governors of the Federal Reserve System (1962 –1973). He is the author of *Market Structure, Organization and Performance: An Essay on Price Fixing and Combinations in Restraint of Trade* and *Promoting Competition in Regulated Markets*; and, with Oliver Williamson, he edited *Perspectives on Antitrust Policy*. He is a member of the Advisory Board of *The Antitrust Bulletin*.

PETER WALLACE RODINO, JR.

A member of the U.S. House of Representatives from 1949 to 1989, Peter Wallace Rodino, Jr., was Chairman of the influential House Committee on the Judiciary. After leaving government service he entered private practice, joining the New Jersey law firm of Rodino and Rodino. He served as a member of President Jimmy Carter's National Committee for the Review of Antitrust Laws and Procedures.

WILLIAM G. SHEPHERD

William G. Shepherd is Chair of the Department of Economics at the University of Massachusetts in Amherst. In 1967–1968, he was Economic Advisor to Assistant Attorney General Donald F. Turner. He has served as President of the Transportation and Public Utilities Group of the American Economic Association (1976) and the Industrial Organization Society (1990) and is a member of the Advisory Board of *The Antitrust Bulletin*. He is the author of *The Treatment of Market Power*; *Public Enterprise: Economic Analysis of Theory and Practice*; *Public Policies Toward Business*; and *Market Power and Economic Welfare*.

RICHARD M. STEUER

Richard M. Steuer has been a partner in the New York City law firm of Kaye, Scholer, Fierman, Hayes & Handler since 1973. He is the author of *A Guide to Marketing Law*.

HANS B. THORELLI / JAMES M. PATTERSON

The publication of his doctoral dissertation, *The Federal Antitrust Policy—Origination of an American Tradition*, in 1955 established Hans B. Thorelli as an authority in the field. Since then, however, most of his work has been in the fields of business planning, marketing, and consumer rights in the North Atlantic Community of nations. His current research efforts are concentrated in the area of strategic planning and structure-strategy-performance relationships in international as well as domestic business. Since 1964 he has been Professor of Business Administration at Indiana University. He served as a member of the President's Advisory Council (1975–1977) and has represented the United States in a number of international negotiations.

James M. Patterson has been Professor of Marketing at the School of Business, Indiana University since 1960. An expert on the structure and performance of the petroleum industry, he is the author of *Marketing: The Firm's Viewpoint* (with S. F. Otteson and W. G. Panschar); *Competition, Ltd.: The Marketing of Gasoline* (with Fred C. Allvine); and *Highway Robbery: An Analysis of the Gasoline Crisis* (with Fred C. Allvine).

DONALD F. TURNER

After a stint in private practice, Donald F. Turner joined the faculty of Harvard Law School in 1954. With the exception of his tenure as Assistant Attorney General in Charge of the Antitrust Division of the Department of Justice (1965–1968), he remained there until his retirement in 1987. Subsequently, he taught at the Georgetown University Law Center (1987–1988) and was a Senior Fellow at the Brookings Institution (1988–1989). With Carl Kaysen, he is the author of *Antitrust Policy*.

Introduction

BY MILTON HANDLER*

In 1982 in an article in the *Columbia Law Review*[1] I urged that, in anticipation of the Sherman Act's centennial, our antitrust jurisprudence be intensively examined in an effort to develop a consensus "on such clarifications and revisions as might be necessary for antitrust to cope with the changing conditions of the remaining years of this and the ensuing ones of next century."[2] In 1987, under the aegis of my lectureship at the Association of the Bar of the City of New York, I arranged a symposium consisting of two sessions, each of which ran an entire day. The addresses delivered at the first session by a galaxy of antitrust luminaries were published in the May 1987 issue of the *California Law Review*.[3] The second session took place in November 1987.

---

* Senior Partner, Kaye, Scholer, Fierman, Hays & Handler.

[1] Handler, *Reforming the Antitrust Laws*, 82 COLUM. L. REV. 1287 (1982); N.Y.L.J., April 5-13, 1982, at 1, col. 2.

[2] Handler, *Foreword to Symposium: Anticipating Antitrust's Centennial*, 75 CAL. L. REV. 787 (1987).

[3] *Symposium: Anticipating Antitrust's Centennial*, 75 CAL. L. REV. 787 (1987). The participants and the titles of their addresses are set

This time the papers were published in the March 1988 issue of the *Cardozo Law Review*.[4]

---

forth in the Table of Contents of the CALIFORNIA LAW REVIEW as follows: *Foreword*, Milton Handler; *The Durability, Relevance, and Future of American Antitrust Policy*, Donald F. Turner; *Comment: Antitrust in the Next 100 Years*, Robert Pitofsky; *The Viability of the Current Law on Horizontal Restraints*, Lawrence A. Sullivan; *Comment: The Sullivan Approach to Horizontal Restraints*, Thomas E. Kauper; *Comment: The Battle for the Soul of Antitrust*, Eleanor M. Fox; *Comment: Horizontal Restraints in Antitrust: Current Treatment and Future Needs*, Harvey J. Goldschmid; *The Viability of Vertical Restraints Doctrine*, William F. Baxter; *Comment: Vertical Restraints and the Secularization of Antitrust*, Earl E. Pollock; *Comment: The Future Viability of the Current Antitrust Treatment of Vertical Restraints*, Sanford M. Litvack; *Monopolization, Mergers, and Markets: A Century Past and the Future*, Phillip Areeda; *Comment: Comparative Advantage and Antitrust Law*, Frank H. Easterbrook; *Comment: Market as Mirage*, Frederick M. Rowe; *Comment: Some Thoughts on Monopoly, Markets, and Mergers*, Michael Malina; *Antitrust, Deregulation, and the Newly Liberated Marketplace*, Stephen G. Breyer; *Comment: Some Additional Safeguards for the Newly Liberated Marketplace*, Louis B. Schwartz; *Comment: Deregulatory Schizophrenia*, Alfred E. Kahn.

   4   *Symposium: Anticipating Antitrust's Centennial*, part II, 9 CARDOZO L. REV. 1135 (1988). The participants and the titles of their addresses are set forth in the Table of Contents of the CARDOZO LAW REVIEW as follows: *The Proper Role for Antitrust in a Not-Yet-Global Economy*, Donald I. Baker; *Antitrust in Today's World Economy*, Barry E. Hawk; *The Coexistence of Antitrust Law and Trade Law With Antitrust Policy*, Harvey M. Applebaum; *The Role of Antitrust in an Age of Technology*, Ira M. Millstein; *The Insignificance of Macroeconomics in Patent Antitrust Law: A Comment on Millstein*, Richard A. Posner; *Complex Tradeoffs in Patent Antitrust Law: A Comment on Millstein*, F. M. Scherer; *Balancing the Benefits and Detriments of Private Antitrust Enforcement: Detrebling, Antitrust Injury, Standing, and Other Proposed Solutions*, David Klingsberg; *Federal and State Antitrust Enforcement: Constitutional Principles and Policy Considerations*, Daniel Oliver; *The Appropriate Role of the Antitrust Enforcement Agencies*, Douglas H. Ginsburg; *The Appropriate Enforcement Role of the Government Antitrust Agency*, Sanford M. Litvack; *Open Letter to the New President of the United States*, John H. Shenefield; *Where Do We Go From Here—An Overview*, Milton Handler.

In my overview, which was entitled "Where Do We Go From Here,"[5] I stated:

> Our aim in the symposium was a modest one. The last word has not and cannot be said about any subject which is as pliable and responsive to changing conditions as is our specialty. A law which has been on the books for almost a century—particularly one regarded as part of our unwritten Constitution—is entitled to celebratory proceedings. But it is more important for us to appraise its pluses and minuses—its accomplishments and its shortcomings—its virtues and its deficiencies. Ours is just a beginning. As we approach the centennial, it is to be hoped that the bar associations and universities will place antitrust under the microscope and help in the restatement of its purposes and doctrines so as better to advance the public interest.

I am thus delighted that Dean Kovaleff, my Columbia colleague, has organized the present volume in which a constellation of outstanding specialists and scholars have placed antitrust under the microscope and have endeavored to restate its purposes, its doctrines, and its future. From these and other studies that have been undertaken in the past several years, there should emerge the consensus that I hoped would develop on what antitrust goals should be preserved and what role antitrust should be expected to play in the years ahead.

As well as peering into the future, it is desirable and illuminating to turn to the past to take account of the vicissitudes encountered by antitrust as well as to note its singular accomplishments. The contrast of where antitrust stood five or six decades ago and its situation today helps to put our present inquiry into proper perspective.

The first case book on trade regulation did not appear until 1923.[6] While my own teaching materials were initially circulated in mimeograph form in the late twenties, it was not until 1937 that my *Cases and Materials on Trade Regulation* was published. For years my and Oppenheim's case books were the only two on

---

[5] Handler, *Where Do We Go From Here—An Overview*, 9 CARDOZO L. REV. 1305 (1988).

[6] H. OLIPHANT, CASES ON TRADE REGULATION (1923).

the market.[7] This is to be contrasted with the increased number of case books that are now in active use in the law school world.[8]

Although there were some studies of the various aspects of antitrust,[9] there was no handbook until Sullivan's work came out in 1977[10] and no authoritative treatise until the publication of the various volumes of the Areeda-Turner and Areeda-Hovenkamp treatise starting in 1978. For some years my TNEC No. 38 was the only available brief study of our antitrust doctrines.[11] The first symposium occurred in December 1931 at Columbia.[12]

---

[7] M. HANDLER, CASES AND OTHER MATERIALS ON TRADE REGULATION (1st ed. 1937, Supp. 1947; 2d ed. 1951; 3d ed. 1960, Supps. 1965; 4th ed. 1967, Supps. 1968, 1970). S. C. OPPENHEIM, CASES ON TRADE REGULATION (1936).

[8] M. HANDLER, H. BLAKE, R. PITOFSKY, H. GOLDSCHMID, CASES AND MATERIALS ON TRADE REGULATION (2d ed. 1983); S. C. OPPENHEIM & G. WESTON, CASES AND MATERIALS ON UNFAIR TRADE PRACTICES (4th ed. 1983); L. SCHWARTZ, J. FLYNN, H. FIRST, FREE ENTERPRISE AND ECONOMIC ORGANIZATION: ANTITRUST (6th ed. 1983); S. C. OPPENHEIM & G. WESTON, FEDERAL ANTITRUST LAWS, CASES AND COMMENTS (4th ed. 1981); P. AREEDA, ANTITRUST ANALYSIS (3d ed. 1981); R. POSNER & F. EASTERBROOK, ANTITRUST CASES, ECONOMIC NOTES, AND OTHER MATERIALS (2d ed. 1981).

[9] *See, e.g.,* H. B. THORELLI, THE FEDERAL ANTITRUST POLICY (1954); M. S. MASSEL, COMPETITION AND MONOPOLY (1962); C. KAYSEN & D. F. TURNER, ANTITRUST POLICY (1959); A. D. NEALE, THE ANTITRUST LAWS OF THE UNITED STATES OF AMERICA (1959); H. KRONSTEIN, J. T. MILLER & I. E. SCHWARTZ, MODERN AMERICAN ANTITRUST LAW (1958); E. S. MASON, ECONOMIC CONCENTRATION AND THE MONOPOLY PROBLEM (1957); G. W. STOCKING & M. W. WATKINS, CARTELS OR COMPETITION? (1948).

[10] L. A. SULLIVAN, HANDBOOK OF THE LAW OF ANTITRUST (1977).

[11] TEMPORARY NATIONAL ECONOMIC COMMITTEE, INVESTIGATION OF CONCENTRATION OF ECONOMIC POWER, A STUDY OF THE CONSTRUCTION AND ENFORCEMENT OF THE FEDERAL ANTITRUST LAWS, 76TH CONG., 3d SESS. (Senate Comm. Print, Monograph No. 38, 1941).

[12] *The Columbia Symposium on the Anti-Trust Laws,* 18 A.B.A.J. 265 (1932).

Let us pause for a moment to compare the situation today. Abundance has superseded scarcity. There has been a virtual explosion of writings and symposia, the number of which is almost incalculable. Our library shelves are now crowded with books, pamphlets, brochures and articles dealing with the almost infinite combinations and permutations of antitrust rules. No aspect of this corner of the law has escaped the most minute scholarly inquiry. The four issues of the present volume are thus a fitting culmination of the stream of publications that have flowed from the pens of antitrust scholars and practitioners.

In addition to noting this vast explosion of knowledge, it is worth pausing to review the evolution of our antitrust jurisprudence and the cycles of enforcement during its first century. There was meager enforcement in the early years. During the Coolidge administration, the staff of the Justice Department's Antitrust Division was about the size of a corporal's guard. As late as President Roosevelt's first term, when antitrust was temporarily abandoned by the enactment of the National Industrial Recovery Act, there were only a handful of lawyers in the Division whose task then was to enforce the New Deal regulatory measures. It was only with the advent of Thurmond Arnold as Assistant Attorney General in 1938 that antitrust enforcement became a reality. Appropriations increased in almost geometric progression and the size of the staff of both the Antitrust Division and the Federal Trade Commission multiplied to the point where a veritable army has replaced the earlier corporal's guard.[13]

Notwithstanding the sparseness of public enforcement and the fact that the private action did not come into its own until the middle of this century, by 1911 a remarkable *corpus juris* had been developed by the Supreme Court. We normally think of the

---

[13] The annual appropriations for the Antitrust Division in the twenties hovered around $250,000, W. HAMILTON & I. TILL, ANTITRUST ACTION 23 (T.N.E.C. Monograph No. 16, 1940), while that for 1988 was $44,937,000. Dept. of Justice Appropriation Act of 1988, Pub. L. No. 100-202, 101 Stat. 1329, 1329-9 (1987).

period prior to 1911 as having been concerned primarily with the initial rejection and ultimate adoption of the rule of reason in the interpretation of section 1. But by that time there were the following solid and substantial contributions to our substantive antitrust law. Horizontal arrangements amongst sellers or buyers fixing prices, dividing markets, or allocating customers had been declared unlawful; concerted boycotts had been outlawed; vertical price agreements had been forbidden; stock acquisitions by major competitive factors lacking any monopoly power had been condemned; the recovery of the overcharge in private treble damage actions based on price-fixing had been upheld; price restrictions in patent license agreements were held permissible and restrictive conduct permitted by the laws of foreign lands in which the act occurred had been excluded from the purview of antitrust.[14]

In subsequent years, these bare-bone rulings were greatly amplified. It is estimated that by 1945 (the year that Chief Justice Stone's tenure ended) the number of Supreme Court antitrust rulings aggregated 156. From that time until the end of the most recent term of Court, the number of decisions had mounted to 396.

In my article on the Supreme Court and the antitrust laws[15] I divided the work of the Court into five periods: (1) the period before 1911; (2) from 1911 to 1920; (3) the years of normalcy and inaction; (4) the New Deal days through the forties; and (5) the years 1950–1967. I noted the important doctrinal developments during these periods which I do not pause to repeat here.

---

[14] This paragraph is taken bodily from my paper, *The Supreme Court and the Antitrust Laws: a Critic's Viewpoint*, 1 Ga. L. Rev. 339 (1967), *reprinted in* volume I of my Twenty-Five Years of Antitrust, 89 (1973). In the first chapter in my Antitrust in Perspective (1957), entitled *The Judicial Architects of the Rule of Reason*, I list all of the antitrust decisions either written or participated in by Justice Peckham, Chief Justices White and Taft, and Justices Holmes, Brandeis and Stone.

[15] *Id.*

As to section 1, modern antitrust law begins with Justice Stone's seminal opinion in *Trenton Potteries v. U.S.*[16] Justice Douglas built upon that decision in *Socony-Vacuum.*[17] These two cases provide the basis for effectively ridding the economy of classic cartel-types of restraints. There is a vast literature on the varieties of conduct that have been challenged and condemned, based on the invigorated principles derived from these landmark rulings on horizontal collusion.

A word, however, is warranted about the Court's position in regard to vertical restraints. It has stood steadfast in its outlawry of vertical price agreements.[18] The ingenious devices by which businessmen sought to evade the Court's rulings, encouraged at times by its decisions, have ultimately been unsuccessful.[19] The other vertical restraints have had a more checkered history. At first the Court felt that it lacked the information necessary to pass judgment on their validity.[20] Then it applied a strict rule of illegality.[21] Finally, realizing the error of its ways, it put vertical restraints on a sound footing, subjecting them to a rigorous rule of reason of inquiry to determine whether, in point of fact, the restrictions had a serious anticompetitive impact.[22] The Antitrust

---

[16] United States v. Trenton Potteries Co., 273 U.S. 392 (1927).

[17] United States v. Socony-Vacuum Oil Co., 310 U.S. 150 (1940).

[18] *See, e.g.,* Dr. Miles Medical Co. v. John D. Park & Sons Co., 220 U.S. 373 (1911); Monsanto Co. v. Spray-Rite Serv. Co., 465 U.S. 752, 761–762 (1984).

[19] *See, e.g.,* United States v. General Elec. Co., 272 U.S. 476 (1926); United States v. Line Material Co., 333 U.S. 287 (1948); Simpson v. Union Oil Co., 377 U.S. 13 (1964); Monsanto Co. v. Spray-Rite Serv. Co., 465 U.S. 752 (1984).

[20] United States v. White Motor Co., 372 U.S. 253, 261 (1963).

[21] United States v. Arnold, Schwinn & Co., 388 U.S. 365, 379 (1967).

[22] Continental T.V., Inc. v. GTE Sylvania, Inc., 433 U.S. 36, 59 (1977).

Division has carried this trend even further with its vertical restraints guidelines.[23]

The merger story is quite different. Before 1950, the Court shifted from one theory to another, leaving the law of mergers under the Sherman Act and original section 7 of the Clayton Act in shambles.[24] Its final decisions before the enactment of the Antimerger Act of 1950, permitted acquisitions with a market share of as much as 65%. This led to the enactment of the Celler-Kefauver Act in 1950.[25] Here again we have a rather sorry spectacle of judicial extremism, best summarized by Justice Stewart's famous pronouncement that the only thing consistent about the Court's merger jurisprudence was that the government always won.[26]

In general terms, the Court initially developed a per se interpretation of the Antimerger Act, holding unlawful any substantial increase in concentration.[27] As a result, this act became an anticoncentration statute rather than an act forbidding mergers that were likely to substantially lessen competition.[28] Since the Court's reading imposed undue fetters on the merger process, a reaction was inevitable. Without overruling its earlier

---

[23]   U.S. Dep't of Justice Vertical Restraints Guidelines, 50 Fed. Reg. 6263 (Feb. 14, 1985), *reprinted in* 48 Antitrust & Trade Reg. Rep. (BNA) No. 1199, at 3 (Special Supp. Jan. 24, 1985).

[24]   Handler, *Industrial Mergers and the Antitrust Laws*, 32 COLUM. L. REV. 179, 183 (1932).

[25]   Celler-Kefauver Act of December 29, 1950, Ch. 1184, 64 Stat. 1125 (codified as amended at 15 U.S.C. § 18 (1982 & Supp. III 1985)).

[26]   United States v. Von's Grocery Co., 384 U.S. 270, 301 (1965) (Stewart, J., dissenting) ("The sole consistency that I can find is that in litigation under § 7, the Government always wins.").

[27]   United States v. Pabst Brewing Co., 384 U.S. 546 (1966); United States v. Von's Grocery Co., 384 U.S. 270 (1966).

[28]   United States v. Philadelphia National Bank, 374 U.S. 321 (1963).

decisions or qualifying its conclusions as to the purposes of the legislation, the Court in due course liberalized the statutory prohibitions in favor of a more realistic assessment of the anticompetitive potential of the mergers that it was called upon to review.[29]

With the advent of the Reagan administration, a 180-degree change in merger enforcement policy occurred. The Turner Guidelines were replaced by those drafted by Assistant Attorney General Baxter. Then those guidelines, which ostensibly codified the new Supreme Court approach, were applied by Prof. Baxter's successors to sanction integrations that plainly contravened Supreme Court precedents that have never been overruled. The pendulum swung from one extreme to another, thus encouraging a merger movement of unprecedented dimension. The test was not whether competition was seriously compromised but whether efficiency was affected. The Celler-Kefauver amendment was thus converted from an anticoncentration to a proefficiency measure, and the public was given the feeling that anything goes.

In their emphasis on efficiency and the absence of any barriers to entry, the enforcement authorities ignored the fact that the statute had as one of its purposes the preservation of small business. When considering the effect of an acquisition on horizontal competition, the plight of suppliers, customers, and the small competitor was disregarded. After all, the small businessman, when competing against the members of a tight oligopoly, may be seriously disadvantaged even though not subjected to unlawful predatory competition. A supplier, again without any illegality, may be put at a substantial disadvantage when his principal customers are four oligopolists in a market depleted of small units. The choices available to consumers can be seriously limited when there are only a handful of suppliers. The legislative history of Celler-Kefauver plainly indicates that these kinds of oligopolistic structures were not what Congress meant to favor, while the atomization of industry, which some of the Black-Douglas decisions encouraged, were likewise not what Congress had in mind.

---

[29]   United States v. General Dynamics Corp., 415 U.S. 486 (1974).

In my recent annual lecture I inveighed against the present policy of nonenforcement, which I cannot justify either as a matter of policy or under the constitutional principle of the separation of powers.[30] In my view, the executive branch of the government has no veto power over the laws of Congress after their enactment or the decisions of the High Court once they are promulgated. Rather, it is its constitutional duty to enforce both, whether or not they are to its liking.

There was a time when we heard only paeans of praise of antitrust's virtues although to be sure there was always a vocal minority that ascribed all of our economic ills from inflation to our loss of foreign markets to that piece of legislation.

Today, the critics, encouraged by the disfavor with which the Reagan administration held antitrust, now assert that the anti-trust laws are obsolete and ought to be repealed. They claim that the fear of antitrust liability within the business community has inhibited the ability of American industry to compete effectively in global markets. We hear that overseas companies, unfettered by antitrust constraints, operate at a distinct advantage over their American counterparts.

The facts do not support these criticisms. There is no question that American firms increasingly face international competition, both in domestic markets and abroad. This does not mean, however, that markets in this country no longer need protection from anticompetitive or monopolistic practices. The antitrust laws are designed to protect markets, and if they are not doing the job effectively, they should be improved. That is what this volume and the symposia that preceded it are all about.

---

[30] Handler, *Antitrust Review—1988*, N.Y.L.J., Dec. 15, 1988, at 1, col. 1. My general assertions are documented in a forthcoming paper by James M. Clabault, *Hang Fire: Criminal Antitrust Enforcement 1981–1988.*

I do not burden this introduction with my own views of the adjustments that should be made of our antitrust policies and doctrines. I refer merely to *Reforming the Antitrust Laws, supra,* note 1, and my *Foreword and Overview* in the symposia above referred to.

The critics' refrain that foreign companies enjoy the advantages of antitrust-free legal systems is something of a myth. Antitrust enforcement has become more vigorous than ever in the European Community and in Canada, and to a lesser degree in other parts of the world. Most of the foreign companies that have thrived in international competition have done so not because they belong to cartels, but because they have learned to compete in the rough and tumble of rivalry at home and worldwide.

The answer is to insure that antitrust forbids only those practices that threaten competitive markets without discouraging conduct and arrangements that allow American companies to improve their performance and thus to compete to the best of their ability. This in a word is the consensus we are striving to achieve.

I end as I began: A good doctrine has been given to us by Congress and the courts. Following the Biblical injunction, we should not forsake it. The executive branch has the tools to enable our Nation to enjoy the fruits of a viable and salutary *corpus juris* that is designed to safeguard our economic liberties. What is needed is fair, vigorous and effective enforcement.

Dean Kovaleff and his associates have rendered a singular service to the Nation by their vital contribution to our antitrust learning. I salute them and hope that their efforts will bear good fruit.

Part II

Philosophical Perspective

17
Philosophical perspective: an introduction

BY WILLIAM E. KOVACIC*

At an academic conference in 1984, Donald Dewey and Robert Bork participated in a program to discuss Bork's contributions to antitrust. Dewey concluded that antitrust had offered few gains, but he doubted Bork's view that misguided antitrust policy had hurt the economy. "[I]f the welfare loss of antitrust was substantial," Dewey said, "it would be visible to the naked eye."[1] Bork replied that observable proof of antitrust's costs was readily obtainable. The harm, Bork observed,

> *is* visible to the naked eye—every year at the annual banquet of the Antitrust Section of the American Bar Association. Tables of very highly paid antitrust lawyers stretch far into the distance. Many of them are not visible only because of the curve of the earth.[2]

For Bork, the vast assemblage of prosperous counselors was a reliable sign that "antitrust has been an expensive policy."[3]

The spectacle featured in Bork's remarks portrayed the world of

---

* Professor, George Mason University School of Law, and Of Counsel to Bryan Cave, Washington, D.C.

[1] Dewey, *What Price Theory Can—and Cannot—Do for Antitrust*, 3 CONTEMP. POL'Y ISSUES 3, 7 (1984–1985).

[2] Bork, *Economics and Antitrust: Response*, 3 CONTEMP. POL'Y ISSUES 35, 35 (1984–1985) (emphasis in original).

[3] *Id.* at 35–36.

the 1960's and 1970's—a gold rush of antitrust practice spurred by expansive Supreme Court interpretations of antitrust's strictures[4] and ambitious government assaults against concentrated industries.[5] Through the 1980's, however, antitrust's feedbag grew progressively less bountiful. Filings of new private antitrust cases plunged,[6] and the federal government abandoned traditional enforcement areas such as attempted monopolization, monopolization, and vertical restraints.[7] In

---

4 *See* G. E. GARVEY & G. J. GARVEY, ECONOMIC LAW AND ECONOMIC GROWTH—ANTITRUST, REGULATION, AND THE AMERICAN GROWTH SYSTEM 68–70 (1990); Kovacic, *The Antitrust Paradox Revisited: Robert Bork and the Transformation of Modern Antitrust Policy*, 36 WAYNE L. REV. 1413, 1423–26 (1990).

5 *See, e.g.*, United States v. AT&T Co. [1970–1979 Transfer Binder], Trade Reg. Rep. (CCH) ¶ 45,074 (D.D.C. filed Nov. 20, 1974) (complaint alleging monopolization, attempted monopolization, and conspiracy to monopolize), *consent decree entered*, 552 F. Supp. 131 (D.D.C. 1982), *aff'd sub. nom. Maryland v. United States*, 460 U.S. 1001 (1983); United States v. IBM Corp. [1961–1970 Transfer Binder], Trade Reg. Rep. (CCH) ¶ 45,069 (S.D.N.Y. filed Jan. 17, 1969) (complaint alleging monopolization and attempted monopolization), *dismissal aff'd*, 687 F.2d 591 (2d Cir. 1982); Kellogg Co. [1970–1973 Transfer Binder], Trade Reg. Rep. (CCH) ¶ 19,898 (No. 8883, filed Apr. 26, 1972), (complaint alleging maintenance of highly concentrated, noncompetitive market structure and shared monopolization), *complaint dismissed*, 99 F.T.C. 8 (1982); Exxon Corp. [1973–1976 Transfer Binder], Trade Reg. Rep. (CCH) ¶ 20,388 (No. 8934, filed July 17, 1973) (complaint alleging agreement to monopolize and maintenance of noncompetitive market structure), *complaint dismissed*, 98 F.T.C. 453 (1981); Xerox, 86 F.T.C. 364 (1975) (consent decree settling charges of monopolization, attempted monopolization, and maintenance of noncompetitive market structure).

6 *See* Salop & White, *Private Antitrust Litigation: An Introduction and Framework*, in PRIVATE ANTITRUST LITIGATION—NEW EVIDENCE, NEW LEARNING 3–4 (L. J. White ed. 1988).

7 From 1980 through 1988 the federal government initiated fewer attempted monopolization and monopolization cases than in any 8-year period since 1900. *See* Kovacic, *Failed Expectations: The Troubled Past and Uncertain Future of the Sherman Act as a Tool for Deconcentration*, 74 IOWA L. REV. 1105, 1140 (1989) (hereinafter *Failed Expectations*). After Reagan appointees assumed the leadership of the federal enforcement agencies in 1981 through 1988, the federal government initiated no vertical restraints enforcement matters. *See* Kovacic, *Federal Antitrust Enforcement in the Reagan Administration: Two Cheers for the Disappearance of the Large Firm Defendant in Nonmerger Cases*, 12 RES. IN L. & ECON. 173, 177 (1989).

the 1980's standard antitrust fare consisted mainly of an austere mix of horizontal restraints cases and occasional challenges to large horizontal mergers.[8] From 1980 to 1990 membership in the American Bar Association's Section of Antitrust Law—the host of the annual feast mentioned in Bork's comments—fell from over 15,000 to roughly 10,000. By the end of Ronald Reagan's presidency in 1988, antitrust policy and doctrine largely had embraced the once-heretical agenda that Bork had proposed ten years earlier in *The Antitrust Paradox*.[9]

The swings in litigation and enforcement patterns over the past 30 years are impressive but not unexpected. The dramatic adjustments since 1960 are only the latest in a series of periodic upheavals in a century of experience with the federal antitrust laws. Among the few certainties that antitrust affords is the confounding of commentators who predict that the doctrine and policy of the moment are sure to endure.[10]

---

[8] Changes in the case mix of the federal enforcement agencies in the 1980's are documented in American Bar Association, Section of Antitrust Law, *Report of the ABA Antitrust Law Section Task Force on the Antitrust Division of the U.S. Department of Justice*, 58 ANTITRUST L.J. 737 (1990); American Bar Association, Section of Antitrust Law, *Report of the American Bar Association Section of Antitrust Law Special Committee to Study the Role of the Federal Trade Commission*, 58 Antitrust L.J. 43 (1989). Shifts in the focus of private litigation in the 1980's are reviewed in Salop & White, *supra* note 6, at 37–39.

[9] R. H. BORK, THE ANTITRUST PARADOX: A POLICY AT WAR WITH ITSELF (1978). Jonathan Baker makes this point as follows:

> Over the past fifteen years, the courts and enforcement agencies have created Robert Bork's paradise. Antitrust has adopted the Chicago School's efficiency analysis and the Chicago School's conclusions about the effects of business practices.

Baker, *Recent Developments in Economics That Challenge Chicago School Views*, 58 ANTITRUST L.J. 645, 655 (1989).

[10] For example, in 1928, after 8 years of permissive antitrust policies during the presidential administrations of Warren Harding and Calvin Coolidge, one commentator asserted that "[t]his is the day of big business. . . . The day of the blatant trust-buster is definitely over." Marx, *New Interpretations of the Anti-trust Law as Applied to Business, Trade, Farm and Labor Associations*, 2 U. CIN. L. REV. 211, 222–23 (1928). Not only did the 1929 crash soon destroy the aura of legitimacy that "big business" had attained in the 1920's, but the 1930's featured far-reaching statutory "trustbusting" measures such as the Public Utility Holding Company Act of 1935 and culminated with filing of the Justice Department's monopolization case against Alcoa. *See* Kovacic, *Failed Expectations*, *supra* note 7, at 1116–17.

Subsequent events frequently belie forecasts that extend short-term vectors of antitrust retreat or expansion infinitely into the future.[11]

Antitrust's equilibria are inherently unstable for several reasons.[12] The goals of the antitrust system are indeterminate, leaving the direction of policy to be set substantially by the political and social currents of the moment. Antitrust adjudication is highly decentralized, with decision-making authority spread across 13 federal courts of appeals, over 90 district courts, and the Federal Trade Commission (FTC). Unorthodox perspectives can gain a foothold in the adjudication system through one well-reasoned opinion by a single federal judge or court of appeals panel. No single ideological gatekeeper determines access to these fora, for the antitrust laws confer standing upon the Department of Justice, the FTC, state attorneys general, private companies, and consumers. Given the porosity of the antitrust system to new ideas and its malleability in the face of changing societal perceptions about the correct content of national economic policy, it is no wonder that antitrust's center of gravity shifts greatly over time.

By the time of the Sherman Act's centennial in 1990, antitrust had achieved a comparatively permissive equilibrium, influenced substantially by Chicago School precepts. The transformation of antitrust from the 1960's to the 1990's raises two fundamental questions: What forces animated the realignment of antitrust doctrine and enforcement policy? and Will the equilibrium of the 1980's endure? As a group, the chapters in this section offer answers to both.

Terry Calvani and Michael Sibarium analyze the sources of the conservative redirection of antitrust since the mid-1970's.[13] Al-

---

11   In 1932, Gilbert Montague cautioned that one of the Sherman Act's most impressive features was that "its periods of greatest growth have always immediately followed the periods when its critics have been most firmly convinced that the Act is hopelessly inadequate." Montague, *Proposals for the Revision of the Anti-trust Laws*, in THE FEDERAL ANTI-TRUST LAWS 23, 62 (M. Handler ed. 1932).

12   *See* Kovacic, *The Influence of Economics on Antitrust Law*, 30 ECON. INQUIRY 294, 295–96 (1992).

13   Calvani & Sibarium, *Antitrust Today: Maturity or Decline*, 35 ANTI-TRUST BULL. 123 (1990).

though commentators have lavished attention on the role of the Reagan antitrust agencies in recasting antitrust policy, Calvani and Sibarium conclude that "the most significant changes have been in the case law, influenced by work done in the academy in the fields of law and industrial organization economics, much of which predates the Reagan era."[14] The judicially driven retrenchment of doctrine was indispensable to the well-publicized changes in public and private enforcement patterns that emerged in the 1980's.[15]

In interpreting the open-ended language of the antitrust statutes, federal judges enjoy broad discretion to determine the outcome of specific disputes.[16] No other system of federal economic regulation gives the judiciary so powerful a role in establishing the substantive content of the legislature's commands. From 1962 through 1972 the Supreme Court exercised this extraordinary intrepretive power to expand the scope of antitrust's net and to tighten its mesh. In defining liability standards, the Court established stringent limits on horizontal mergers,[17] distribution practices,[18] and single-firm pricing conduct.[19] In applying these standards, the Court endorsed the expansive use of per se tests[20] and disfavored grants of summary judgment to dismiss antitrust dis-

---

[14]   *Id.* at 174.

[15]   *Id.* at 175–88.

[16]   *See* Kovacic, *Reagan's Judicial Appointees and Antitrust in the 1990s*, 60 FORDHAM L. REV. 49, 51–52 (1991).

[17]   *See* United States v. Pabst Brewing Co., 384 U.S. 546 (1966); United States v. Von's Grocery Co., 384 U.S. 270 (1966); Brown Shoe Co. v. United States, 370 U.S. 294 (1962).

[18]   *See* Fortner Enters., Inc. v. United States Steel Corp., 394 U.S. 495 (1969); Albrecht v. Herald Co., 390 U.S. 145 (1968); United States v. Arnold, Schwinn & Co., 388 U.S. 365 (1967); FTC v. Brown Shoe Co., 384 U.S. 316 (1966).

[19]   *See* Utah Pie Co. v. Continental Baking Co., 386 U.S. 685 (1967).

[20]   *See* United States v. Topco Assocs., Inc., 405 U.S. 596 (1972); Fortner Enters., Inc. v. United States Steel Corp., 394 U.S. 495 (1969); Albrecht v. Herald Co., 390 U.S. 145 (1968); United States v. Arnold, Schwinn & Co., 388 U.S. 365 (1967).

putes.[21] Animating these results was the Court's acceptance of a multidimensional goals structure that emphasized the achievement of nonefficiency objectives.[22]

Calvani and Sibarium describe how the revolution in antitrust since the mid-1970's flowed from the Supreme Court's repudiation of many Warren-era precepts.[23] In some instances, the retrenchment took the form of adjustments in or narrowed applications of liability standards, as the Court adopted a far less hostile view toward distribution practices[24] and single-firm pricing conduct.[25] Equally important developments included the Court's retreat from broad use of per se standards,[26] its endorsement of summary judgment to eliminate frail claims,[27] the reinforcement of the duality requirement in conspiracy cases,[28] and the imposition of more severe standing requirements to limit the field of litigants who might press antitrust

---

21   *Compare* Poller v. CBS, Inc., 368 U.S. 464 (1962) (summary judgment disfavored in antitrust disputes in which motive and intent are significant factors) *with* First Nat'l Bank v. Cities Service Corp., 391 U.S. 253 (1968) (summary disposition deemed appropriate when circumstantial evidence is so weak or so strong that reasonable jurors could reach but one conclusion).

22   *See* FTC v. Proctor & Gamble Co., 386 U.S. 568 (1967); Brown Shoe Co. v. United States, 370 U.S. 294 (1962).

23   Calvani & Sibarium, *supra* note 13, at 126–75.

24   *See* Business Elecs. Corp. v. Sharp Elecs. Corp., 485 U.S. 717 (1988); Monsanto Co. v. Spray-Rite Serv. Corp., 465 U.S. 752 (1984); Falls City Indus., Inc. v. Vanco Beverage, Inc., 460 U.S. 428 (1983); J. Truett Payne Co. v. Chrysler Motors Corp., 451 U.S. 557 (1981); Continental T.V., Inc. v. GTE Sylvania, Inc., 433 U.S. 36 (1977); United States Steel Corp. v. Fortner Enters., Inc., 429 U.S. 610 (1977).

25   *See* Cargill, Inc. v. Monfort of Colorado, Inc., 479 U.S. 104 (1986); Matsushita Elec. Indus. Co. v. Zenith Radio Corp., 475 U.S. 574 (1986).

26   *See* NCAA v. Board of Regents of Univ. of Okla., 468 U.S. 85 (1984); Broadcast Music, Inc. v. Columbia Broadcasting Sys., Inc., 441 U.S. 1 (1979); Continental T.V., Inc. v. GTE-Sylvania, Inc., 433 U.S. 36 (1977).

27   *See* Matsushita Elec. Indus. Co. v. Zenith Radio Corp., 475 U.S. 574 (1986).

28   *See* Copperweld Corp. v. Independence Tube Corp., 467 U.S. 752 (1984).

claims.[29] As the authors point out, the Court's treatment of these and other issues reflected a strong efficiency orientation, with no heed paid to egalitarian values.[30]

Although they generally approve of trends in judicial antitrust analysis since the mid-1970's, Calvani and Sibarium note areas for further doctrinal refinement and identify forces that might unsettle antitrust's current efficiency-based equilibrium in the future. The authors warn that state enforcement policies favoring comparatively restrictive controls on horizontal mergers and vertical restraints could retard, or partially reverse, continued movement toward a national, efficiency-based antitrust policy.[31]

Calvani and Sibarium also propose that the Supreme Court revisit and clarify standards for certain forms of conduct. A major suggested candidate is tying, where the Court's subsequent jurisprudence has clumsily tried to account for the modern economic literature on tying without abandoning remnants of the longstanding per se prohibition of certain conditional sales agreements.[32] On this score the authors will not be heartened by the Court's recent decision in *Eastman Kodak Co. v. Image Technical Services, Inc.*[33] In *Kodak*, the Court not only declined to address the standard for tying liability but also rejected the defendant's argument that summary judgment against the plaintiff's tying claim was warranted because the defendant's lack of market power in the tying product precluded the possibility of material anticompetitive effects in the tied product market.[34] *Kodak* narrows the broad license to grant summary judgment that some

---

[29] *See* Atlantic Richfield Co. v. USA Petroleum Co., 495 U.S. 328 (1990); Cargill, Inc. v. Monfort of Colorado, Inc., 479 U.S. 104 (1986); Associated General Contractors v. California State Council of Carpenters, 459 U.S. 519 (1983); Brunswick Corp. v. Pueblo Bowl-O-Mat, Inc., 429 U.S. 477 (1977).

[30] Calvani & Sibarium, *supra* note 13, at 126–30.

[31] *Id.* at 208–16.

[32] *Id.* at 194–97.

[33] 112 S. Ct. 2072.

[34] S. Ct. at 2079–89.

courts had distilled from *Matsushita Industrial Electronics Co. v. Zenith Radio Corp.*[35]—a cornerstone of the judicially-driven rightward trend that Calvani and Sibarium discern in antitrust analysis.[36]

Like the Calvani and Sibarium paper, John Flynn's contribution to this volume[37] emphasizes the centrality of the courts in antitrust's modern evolution. While Calvani and Sibarium endorse the rightward retrenchment, Flynn sees little to applaud in the post-Warren era of Supreme Court antitrust jurisprudence governing private rights of action. Flynn disapprovingly observes that "court-imposed barriers to private suits" have raised "the possibility that the second century of antitrust enforcement might see the demise, in practice if not in express repeal, of private enforcement or the creation of a hiatus in private actions much like that which prevailed from the 1920's through the 1940's."[38] He welcomes a return to the antitrust jurisprudence of the 1960's, when a "generally receptive Supreme Court . . . gave considerable encouragement and the means to the bar to specialize in the bringing of antitrust suits through the expansion of favorable judge-made doctrine and procedures facilitating private enforcement."[39]

Flynn focuses on three hurdles that confront a future restoration of robust private enforcement. The most formidable obstacle is a series of decisions that have denied standing to litigants who either failed to assert the requisite proximity to the challenged conduct[40]

---

35   475 U.S. 574 (1986).

36   *Cf.* Rule, *Back to the Dark Ages of Antitrust*, Wall Street Journal, June 17, 1992, at A17 ("In a dramatic departure from the economic enlightenment apparent in most of its recent antitrust decisions, the Supreme Court ignored Kodak's common sense defense, and resorted instead to that old bugaboo from the 1960s, 'market failure.' ")

37   Flynn, *Which Past Is Prolog? The Future of Private Antitrust Enforcement*, 35 ANTITRUST BULL. 879 (1990).

38   Flynn, *supra* note 37, at 880.

39   *Id.*

40   *See* Kansas v. Utilicorp United, Inc., 497 U.S. 199 (1990); Associated General Contractors v. California State Council of Carpenters, 459 U.S. 819 (1983); Illinois Brick Co. v. Illinois, 431 U.S. 720 (1977).

or asserted injury by reasons other than the anticompetitive aspects of the defendant's conduct.[41] For Flynn, the flaws and dangers of this trend are vivid in *Atlantic Richfield Co. v. USA Petroleum Co.*,[42] which refused standing to a petroleum retailer who failed to show that the defendant-refiner's maximum resale price-fixing scheme resulted in a predatory maximum fixed price. Particularly troublesome to Flynn is the *Arco* majority's implicit suggestion that "the only purpose of antitrust policy is the protection of 'consumer welfare' as that concept is defined by neoclassical economic theory."[43] Unless the Court substantially lowers standing barriers, Flynn predicts that "the future of private antitrust enforcement is indeed bleak."[44]

The second major impediment to a private enforcement revival is *Matsushita*'s encouragement to lower courts to grant summary judgment to dismiss antitrust claims that lack "economic sense."[45] As with recent standing cases, Flynn criticizes the Court for its "implicit adoption of static neoclassical price theory as the sole guide to antitrust policy."[46] The author notes that ' "[e]conomic sense' is apparently to be determined by neoclassical price theory and the defendant's version of it to determine whether the plaintiffs' case makes 'economic sense.' "[47] Among other implications, the Court's emphasis on economic rationality as a criterion in assessing the propriety of summary disposition "points up the importance of a private plaintiff's attorneys being fully conversant with the economic theory relevant and not relevant to the dispute and presenting their case in a compelling fashion."[48]

---

[41] *See* Atlantic Richfield Co. v. USA Petroleum Co., 495 U.S. 328 (1990); Cargill, Inc. v. Monfort of Colorado, Inc., 479 U.S. 104 (1986); Brunswick Corp. v. Pueblo Bowl-O-Mat, Inc., 429 U.S. 477 (1977).

[42] 495 U.S. 328 (1990).

[43] Flynn, *supra* note 37, at 914.

[44] *Id.* at 917.

[45] *Matsushita*, 475 U.S. at 587.

[46] Flynn, *supra* note 37, at 919.

[47] *Id.*

[48] *Id.* at 923–24.

Flynn indicates that the summary judgment hurdle is not insuperable. In cases such as *McGahee v. Northern Propane Gas Co.*,[49] plaintiffs have succeeded in persuading courts that assessments of competitive harm should be informed by economic learning from schools other than Chicago. Although *Matsushita*'s discussion of predatory pricing quoted liberally from scholars who have endorsed permissive predatory pricing standards,[50] the Supreme Court did not foreclose reliance on arguments provided by economists with more expansive enforcement preferences. For the defense bar, the Achilles heel of *Matsushita*'s economic rationality test is that it can be satisfied by the work of economists who operate within an efficiency framework but find anticompetitive hypotheses for conduct that Chicago School scholars deem procompetitive or benign.[51] The Court's decision in *Kodak* bears out Flynn's view that plaintiffs who build favorable economic theories into their cases can defeat summary judgment motions in a post-*Matsushita* world.[52]

---

49   858 F.2d 1487 (11th Cir. 1988), *cert. denied*, 490 U.S. 1084 (1989).

50   *See Matsushita*, 475 U.S. at 589–90 (citing Philip Areeda, Robert Bork, Frank Easterbrook, Roland Koller, John McGee, and Donald Turner).

51   *See* DeSanti & Kovacic, *Matsushita: Its Construction and Application by the Lower Courts*, 59 ANTITRUST L.J. 609, 649–53 (1991).

52   The *Kodak* majority offered the following interpretation of *Matsushita*'s economic rationality standard:

> The Court's requirement in *Matsushita* that the plaintiffs' claims make economic sense did not introduce a special burden on plaintiffs facing summary judgment in antitrust cases. The Court did not hold that if the moving party enunciates *any* economic theory supporting its behavior, regardless of its accuracy in reflecting the actual market, it is entitled to summary judgment. *Matsushita* demands only that the nonmoving party's inferences be reasonable in order to reach the jury, a requirement that was not invented, but merely articulated, in that decision. If the plaintiff's theory is economically senseless, no reasonable jury could find in its favor, and summary judgment should be granted.

Kodak, 112 S. Ct. at 2083 (emphasis in original; footnote omitted). In several instances, the *Kodak* majority's opinion cited the work of non–Chicago School economists in accepting the plaintiff's argument that Kodak caused competitive harm by price-discriminating between knowledgable and unsophisti- cated customers in offering packages consisting of original copier equipment, parts, and service. *See id.* at 2086–87 & n.22.

The third doctrinal barrier to private enforcement is what Flynn terms "the gradual destruction of private treble damage actions in the area of vertical restraints and the erosion of the distinction between per se rules and the rule of reason."[53] Although Flynn believes that the per se ban on nonprice vertical restraints in *United States v. Arnold, Schwinn & Co.*[54] was ill conceived, he finds little redeeming virtue in the Supreme Court's vertical restraints decisions of the past 15 years:

> The Supreme Court ... seems to be drifting further and further in the direction of relying upon a rigid version of neoclassical thought with its simplistic assumption that all vertical restraints save those masking a cartel or designed by a firm with monopoly power to exclude competition should be considered per se lawful.[55]

As the latest demonstration of "a nonreflective application of neoclassical theorizing,"[56] Flynn criticizes *Business Electronics Corp. v. Sharp Electronics Corp.*,[57] which said that resale price maintenance remains per se illegal but toughened the evidentiary standard that plaintiffs must satisfy to prove an agreement to set resale price levels.

In assessing the doctrinal obstacles described above, Flynn observes that recent jurisprudence governing standing, summary judgment, and vertical restraints does not preclude the reemergence of robust private enforcement. The strength and durability of noninterventionist doctrine depend on several variables. One is the willingness of Congress to reassert the centrality of considerations other than neoclassical economics in antitrust decisionmaking.[58] "The future of private antitrust enforcement," Flynn observes, "will remain impossible to predict without a clear mandate for its continua-

---

53 Flynn, *supra* note 37, at 924.

54 388 U.S. 365 (1967).

55 Flynn, *supra* note 37, at 925.

56 *Id.* at 931.

57 485 U.S. 717 (1988).

58 Flynn, *supra* note 37, at 893, 937–39.

tion or its demise from Congress."[59] However, Flynn's assessment of recent congressional behavior provides slim basis for expecting a legislative reaffirmation of private enforcement:

> It must be noted . . . that Congress has not been a bastion of pro-antitrust fervor. . . . Congress has shown itself remarkably responsive to special interest legislation chipping away at antitrust policy generally and treble damage actions in particular.[60]

"The hard truth," Flynn concludes, "is that Congress' antitrust record has been more anti-antitrust than proantitrust."[61]

A second major variable is the continuing evolution of state antitrust enforcement. Unlike Calvani and Sibarium, who view much recent state enforcement as a blight, Flynn endorses the willingness of state attorneys general to challenge mergers and attack vertical restraints that federal enforcement authorities ignored in the 1980's.[62] However, Flynn warns that unless federal enforcement officials adopt "a more realistic, flexible and less ideological approach to vertical restraints," states may rely increasingly on costly franchise regulation as an inferior, second-best response to perceived instances of market failure in distribution.[63]

A third prominent variable in Flynn's predictive calculus is the composition and attitudes of the federal courts. Flynn foresees that the Bush administration's appointments to the federal bench

> will have a great influence over the next decade in determing whether antitrust policy will remain a significant element in determining economic policy and the rights of consumers and competitors or whether it will become a curious backwater largely of historical interest like it was in the 1920's; of little interest until the next economic disaster such as the Great Depression of the 1930's undermines the economy.[64]

---

59   *Id.* at 893.

60   *Id.* at 890–91.

61   *Id.* at 891.

62   *Id.* at 893–95.

63   *Id.* at 895.

64   *Id.* at 886.

Recent experience underscores Flynn's evaluation of the importance of judicial appointments. By the end of 1992, Presidents Bush and Reagan accounted for roughly 65% of all active judges on the federal courts.[65] In general, the Bush and Reagan appointees have displayed relatively more conservative antitrust preferences than their counterparts nominated by President Carter.[66] Among the prices that Bill Clinton secured in the 1992 presidential election was the power to choose judges who will reinforce or reject the largely conservative orientation in antitrust that the federal courts have embraced since the mid-1970's.

In his article for this volume,[67] Hamilton Fish, Jr. examines congressional antitrust policy making in the 1980's. As the Ranking Minority Member of the House Judiciary Committee and its Monopolies Subcommittee since 1983, Fish focuses on the Judiciary Committee's response to requests for new antitrust exemptions and immunities. The issue is a timely one, for Congress has recently approved a relaxation of antitrust scrutiny for collaborative ventures designed to facilitate the production of new products, processes, and services.[68] Fish is one of several legislators who, during the 102d Congress, introduced bills to extend the protections of the National Cooperative Research Act of 1984[69] (NCRA) to include joint production activities.[70]

---

[65] *See* Goldman, *The Bush Imprint on the Judiciary: Carrying On a Tradition*, 74 JUDICATURE 294, 306 (1991).

[66] *See* Kovacic, *supra* note 16, at 72–82; Kovacic, *Judicial Appointments and the future of Antitrust Policy*, 7 ANTITRUST 8 (Spring 1993).

[67] Fish, *Antitrust Relief and the House Judiciary Committee*, 35 ANTITRUST BULL. 219 (1990).

[68] The new legislation was adopted as The National Cooperative Production Amendments Act of 1993. For a discussion of the rationale for providing antitrust immunity for certain cooperative production activity, *see* Jorde & Teece, *Innovation, Cooperation, and Antitrust*, in *Antitrust, Innovation, and Competitiveness* 47 (T. M. Jorde & D. J. Teece eds. 1992).

[69] 15 U.S.C. §§ 4301–05.

[70] Fish's bill was H.R. 27, The Cooperative Productivity and Competitiveness Act of 1991. This bill would have amended the National Cooperative Research Act to include joint production (but not marketing or distribution) activities.

In the 1980's individual legislators introduced dozens of antitrust-related bills.[71] Of these proposals, Congress ultimately enacted five measures providing important dispensations from the operation of the antitrust laws: the Soft Drink Competition Act of 1980,[72] the Export Trading Company Act of 1982,[73] the Shipping Act of 1984,[74] the Local Government Antitrust Act of 1984,[75] and the NCRA. Whereas John Flynn sees these initiatives as proof of unseemly legislative responsiveness to special interests,[76] Fish views the output as "a mixed bag that does contain some economically logical and desirable law."[77]

In considering legislative proposals, Committee members "have taken a cautious, conserving approach to efforts to provide exemptions or other relief from the antitrust laws for particular industries or situations."[78] Fish states that the Monopolies Subcommittee "has responded to such proposals with restraint, and when its members have decided to act, they have generally sought to amend the original proposal in order to limit the scope of the immunity extended."[79] He explains that "some of the most valuable work done by the subcommittee lies in the careful shaping and narrowing process that seeks to retain the important protections of existing law against competitive abuses."[80]

The Committee's review of exemption and immunity propos-

---

71   Fish, *supra* note 67, at 223–24.

72   15 U.S.C. §§ 3501–03.

73   18 U.S.C. §§ 61–65.

74   46 U.S.C. App. §§ 801 et. seq.

75   15 U.S.C. §§ 34–36.

76   Flynn, *supra* note 37, at 891.

77   Fish, *supra* note 67, at 222.

78   *Id.* at 248.

79   *Id.* at 219. Fish later adds that "[a] predisposition against antitrust exemptions . . ., although more pronounced and consistently held by some Members than others, should be understood to be the point of departure for subcommittee review."(*Id.* at 223).

80   *Id.* at 228.

als can be divided into three parts. In some instances, Fish and his Committee colleagues succeeded in derailing immunity bills. The author recounts the Committee's role in helping to block the Malt Beverage Intrabrand Competition Act, which would have shielded exclusive territorial arrangements for beer distribution from most antitrust scrutiny upon a showing that distributors faced effective interbrand rivalry.[81] Despite enjoying enormous congressional backing in the early 1980's,[82] the beer distribution exemption gradually lost support, even though variants of the bill were introduced in each session of Congress in the 1980's. Fish observes that an important factor in the demise of the beer exemption was "intense counter-lobbying" by commercial concerns whose interests the measure would have undercut.[83]

Fish's description of the beer bill episode is consistent with recent scholarship that explains the introduction of legislation as a product of rent-seeking by members of Congress.[84] The introduction of each bill affords legislators an opportunity to elicit contributions from economic actors who would be affected by the proposed statute. In effect, a member of Congress can extort payments from a specific group by threatening to adopt a position adverse to the group's well-being unless the group contributes to her reelection. The mere fact that a bill appears to be under serious consideration is enough to start the flow of payments. Measured against the legislator's rent-seeking objectives, whether the bill ultimately is enacted is relatively unimportant. The best rent-seeking possibilities emerge in measures that receive serious consideration over a period of years without enactment. In the 1980's the beer bill was such a vehicle, in that it provided

---

[81] *Id.* at 229–30.

[82] During the 97th Congress (1981–1982), the Malt Beverage Intrabrand Competition Act (H.R. 3269) had 280 cosponsors. *Id.* at 229.

[83] Fish explains that "a trade association representing 1,500 firms in the food marketing industry began to lobby most vigorously at the grassroots level and through contacts with every member of Congress against what became known, somewhat disparagingly, as "the beer bill." Fish, *supra* note 67, at 230.

[84] *See* McChesney, *Rent Extraction and Rent Creation in the Economic Theory of Regulation*, 16 J. LEGAL STUD. 101 (1987).

repeated occasions for members of Congress to test the generosity of commercial forces arrayed for and against the exemption.

In a second category of cases, the Committee functioned essentially as a damage-control party, seeking to ensure that the final legislation incorporated only narrow dispensations from the antitrust laws. This category embraces the Shipping Act of 1984, which immunized certain collective rate-making agreements, and the Soft Drink Intrabrand Competition Act of 1980, which provided antitrust immunity for certain exclusive territorial franchise arrangements for soft drink bottlers. In both instances, Fish describes a reluctant Judiciary Committee, yielding to irresistible political forces which supported the measures but using its influence to water down competition-suppressing provisions.[85]

For antitrust historians, the soft drink bottlers exemption is the more interesting of the two damage control episodes, for it offers an intriguing glimpse of antitrust lawmaking and congressional oversight of federal antitrust enforcement. As Fish explains, the soft drink bill counteracted FTC initiatives in the 1970's to challenge the bottlers' use of exclusive distribution territories.[86] The FTC began the bottlers' cases in the early 1970's in response to congressional criticism that the Commission had ignored serious competitive problems in the food industry.[87]

---

[85]   Fish states that the Monopolies Subcommittee reported a soft drink exemption bill only when "confronted . . . with the inevitable." Fish, *supra* note 67, at 228. Fish describes the Subcommittee's consent to the 1984 Shipping Act in similar terms:

> The Shipping Act serves as an example of immunity legislation emanating from another committee whose ultimate passage was perhaps inevitable. The Monopolies Subcommittee sought, however, with persistence and eventual success, to rewrite and refine it in order to preserve and guarantee as much competitive activity as possible.

Id. at 234.

[86]   *Id.* at 225–26; *see* Coca-Cola Co., 91 F.T.C. 517 (1978), *remanded*, 642 F.2d 1387 (D.C. Cir.), *complaint dismissed*, 97 F.T.C. 257 (1981).

[87]   *See* Kovacic, *The Federal Trade Commmission and Congressional Oversight of Antitrust Enforcement: A Historical Perspective*, in PUBLIC CHOICE AND REGULATION: A VIEW FROM INSIDE THE FEDERAL TRADE COMMISSION 63, 82–88 (R. J. MacKay, J. C. Miller III & B. Yandle eds. 1987); Kovacic, *The Federal Trade Commission and Congressional Oversight of Antitrust Enforcement*, 17 TULSA L.J. 587, 636–51 (1982).

By the decade's end, Congress accused the FTC of overreaching in this area, heeded the bottlers' complaints, and enacted the 1980 statute. The sequence shows how Congress uses its relationship with the FTC to extract rents (in the form of campaign contributions and other electoral resources) from regulated firms: It urges the FTC to undertake a law enforcement program, and, as the program unfolds, it protects firms that are subject to FTC suits.[88]

In the final category of matters, the Judiciary Committee helped to fine-tune proposals that provided what most Committee members regarded as justifiable limits on antitrust exposure. This grouping includes the Export Trading Company Act of 1982, the Local Government Antitrust Act of 1984, and the NCRA. In reviewing these measures, Fish observes that the Committee was generally sympathetic to the underlying aims of the legislation and saw its role as ensuring that the correct means were used to accomplish legitimate ends.[89] The author is least pleased with the Committee's performance concerning the Export Trading Company Act. Rather than simply clarify what the Committee believed to be adequate existing protection for collaborative foreign sales activities, the Committee consented to a certification procedure that enables the Department of Commerce, with the consent of the Department of Justice, to shield certain arrangements from treble damage suits. Fish concludes that the Monopolies Subcommittee may not have been "sufficiently skeptical" about the bill's certification apparatus.[90]

The author is more sanguine about the outcome with the Local Government Antitrust Act and the NCRA. Each measure addressed what the Committee perceived to be a genuine need for reform, and the Committee succeeded in ensuring that immunity was no more expansive than necessary. The NCRA addressed concerns that existing antitrust doctrine and enforcement practice discouraged

---

[88]   *See* Kovacic, *Congress and the Federal Trade Commission*, 57 ANTI-TRUST L.J. 869, 887–88 (1989).

[89]   Fish, *supra* note 67, at 234–48.

[90]   *Id.* at 248.

American firms from pursuing useful cooperative research and development (R & D) projects. The Monopolies Subcommittee's recommendations provided the essential framework for the final bill—notification of the joint R & D ventures to the FTC and the Justice Department, mandated application of the rule of reason to covered activities, and limitation of monetary relief to single damages.[91]

The Local Government Antitrust Act responded to fears that a recent Supreme Court decision limiting the availability of the state action doctrine for a state's political subdivisions[92] would expose local jurisdictions to crippling treble damage litigation.[93] Fish describes how the Monopolies Subcommittee deflected proposals for complete local government immunity and obtained approval for the preclusion of damages in suits challenging conduct not authorized by the state.[94] Thus, the enacted version of the bill barred damage actions but permitted aggrieved parties to obtain injunctions to attack behavior by political subdivisions and their employees falling outside the scope of state action protection.

Beyond inspiring passage of the Local Government Antitrust Act of 1984, judicial interpretations of the content of the state action doctrine supply the subject for William Page's contribution to this volume.[95] Developments in the state action area constitute an important exception to the modern trend, emphasized in the Calvani/Sibarium and Flynn articles, of retrenchment in the antitrust system. Since the mid-1970's, cases presenting the issue of government involvement have increased substantially.

---

91   *Id.* at 244–48.

92   *See* Community Communications Co. v. City of Boulder, 445 U.S. 40 (1982). In *Boulder*, the Court ruled that a municipality does not enjoy state action immunity unless its conduct constitutes the sovereign action of the state or is authorized by a clearly articulated state policy that supplants competition with regulation.

93   Fish, *supra* note 67, at 239–42.

94   *Id.* at 242–44.

95   Page, *State Action and "Active Supervision": An Antitrust Anomaly*, 35 ANTITRUST BULL. 745 (1990).

Skirmishes along the boundaries of state action immunity promise to figure prominently in antitrust disputes well into the Sherman Act's second century.

The state action doctrine originated in 1943 with the Supreme Court's decision in *Parker v. Brown*,[96] which, as Page explains, "left the question of the desirability of state intervention in markets largely to the state political process."[97] The Court left the elaboration of *Parker* mainly to the lower courts until 1975, when *Goldfarb v. Virginia State Bar*[98] signaled the Court's interest in revisiting and narrowing *Parker*'s broad protection. In 1980 the Court set the basic framework for modern state action analysis in *California Retail Liquor Dealers Association v. Midcal Aluminum, Inc.*[99] The *Midcal* Court established "two standards for antitrust immunity" under the *Parker* doctrine: first, the challenged restraint must be "one clearly articulated and affirmatively expressed as state policy" and second, the policy must be "actively supervised" by the state itself.[100]

Page's paper criticizes the second of these tests—the "active supervision" requirement. The author recommends dispensing with the active supervision criterion and refocusing the state action doctrine "on the nature of the state's legislative choice."[101] Under Page's reformulation, the availability of state action immunity would hinge entirely upon the existence of a clearly articulated legislative decision to displace competition with other strategies for organizing the state's economic affairs. The adequacy of state machinery to oversee implementation of the legislature's competition-suppressing choice would be deemed irrelevant.

Page levels three principal arguments against the active supervi-

---

96   317 U.S. 341 (1943).

97   Page, *supra* note 95, at 748.

98   421 U.S. 773 (1975).

99   445 U.S. 97 (1980).

100   *Id.* at 105.

101   Page, *supra* note 95, at 770.

sion requirement. First, he rejects the view of decisions such as *Hallie v. City of Eau Claire*[102] and *Patrick v. Burget*[103] that active supervision ensures the legitimacy of the state's action by providing evidence that the state's program of regulatory intervention genuinely advances state policy rather than purely private interests. Page states that "the relative probability that public or private actors will follow the legislative mandate should not determine whether they have in fact done so in a particular case."[104] For state action immunity to apply, "[i]t should be sufficient . . . that the challenged action, public or private, is within the state's clearly articulated policy, regardless of the probability *ex ante* that it would be so."[105]

Page's second concern with the active supervision criterion is that it "mistakenly assumes that unsupervised private action pursuant to state law cannot enforce a public policy."[106] The author explains that "[t]he absence of regulatory review does not indicate an illegitimate purpose; indeed the whole point of the state action exemption is to accept the definition of the public interest that the state adopts through its constitutional legislative processes."[107] In *324 Liquor Corp. v. Duffy*,[108] the Supreme Court denied immunity for a liquor resale price maintenance program on the ground that the state merely authorized the actions of private wholesalers without either setting prices or reviewing their reasonableness.[109] By making immunity depend on the existence and operation of a regulatory bureaucracy, *Duffy* wrongly makes liability depend "upon a formal distinction . . . that is unrelated to any valid federal concern."[110]

---

102   471 U.S. 34 (1985).

103   486 U.S. 94 (1988).

104   Page, *supra* note 95, at 753.

105   *Id.*

106   *Id.* at 755.

107   *Id.* at 756–57.

108   479 U.S. 335 (1987).

109   *Id.* at 344–45.

110   Page, *supra* note 95, at 757.

Nor, Page observes, is it apparent why states should be compelled to employ "cumbersome command-and-control regulation" in place of "market-based, permissive regulation" of the type at issue in *Duffy*.[111]

The author's third objection is that the active supervision inquiry deflects judicial attention away from the fundamental question of whether the conduct in question is consistent with a clearly articulated state policy. Page warns that the active supervision requirement threatens to swallow *Midcal*'s clear articulation command by lulling courts into assuming that the existence of seemingly robust state supervisory machinery, without more, provides assurance that the supervised conduct was authorized by a legislative decision to displace competition.[112] In *Patrick*, for example, the Supreme Court denied immunity to a hospital peer review process because no state agency had "power to review private peer review decisions and overturn a decision that fails to accord with state policy."[113] Page concludes that the Court need not have reached the active supervision issue. Rather, rigorous application of the clear articulation test by itself would have precluded immunity, as the state statute that delegated authority to the peer review committee did not authorize the committee to restrict competition in the market for medical services.[114]

Since *Patrick*, judicial interpretations of the state action doctrine have raised additional questions about whether the active supervision requirement is administrable. To insist that states install and operate supervisory machinery forces one to define what form and quality of oversight are sufficient. Such an inquiry can enmesh courts in problematic assessments about whether state regulatory authorities in practice have exerted adequate effort to apply nominal powers to review the conduct of private parties. Several recent decisions have expressed considerable wariness over making judgments

---

[111] *Id.* at 758.

[112] *Id.* at 758–64.

[113] *Patrick*, 486 U.S. at 102.

[114] Page, *supra* note 95, at 761–62.

about whether the state has made effective use of its oversight apparatus.[115]

The Supreme Court's decision in *Federal Trade Commission v. Ticor Title Insurance Co.*[116] provides little helpful guidance in this respect. The *Ticor* majority stated that the purpose of the active supervision inquiry

> is to determine whether the State has exercised sufficient independent judgment and control so that the details of the rates or prices have been established as a product of deliberate state intervention, not simply by agreement among private parties. . . . The question is not how well state regulation works but whether the anticompetitive scheme is the State's own.[117]

Where private parties propose a rate that takes effect unless the state vetoes it, the Court held that "the party claiming the immunity must show that state officials have undertaken the necessary steps

---

115   For example, in New England Motor Rate Bureau, Inc. v. FTC, 980 F.2d 1064 (1st Cir. 1990), the First Circuit considered the preparation and filing by private rate bureaus of collective tariffs for motor carriers. The FTC had found that the collective rate-setting did not enjoy state action immunity because the state regulators' exercise of their nominal authority to review suggested rates had been deficient. The First Circuit concluded that the FTC improperly had chosen to second-guess policy decisions reserved for state officials:

> The FTC's position, at bottom, seems to be that the "active supervision" prong necessitates an inquiry by the FTC as to whether a particular state's regulatory operation demonstrates satisfactory zeal and aggressiveness. The FTC would, in effect, try the state regulator. We think this goes too far. . . . It is not the province of the federal courts nor of federal regulatory agencies to sit in judgment upon the degree of strictness or effectiveness with which a state carried out is own statutes. It is sufficient that a meaningful scheme of regulation is in existence and that there are sufficient indications that active regulation under this scheme is taking place.

908 F.2d at 1075–76. The First Circuit ruled that *Patrick*'s requirement that nominal oversight power be exercised was satisfied because the state's monitoring instrumentality (1) was staffed, funded, and operational; (2) gave state overseers adequate power to monitor compliance with state regulatory policies; (3) was enforceable in the state's courts; and (4) showed a "basic level of activity" toward ensuring that private parties "carry out the state's policy and not simply their own policy." *Id.* at 1071.

116   112 S. Ct. 2169 (1992).

117   112 S. Ct. at 2177.

to determine the specifics of the price-fixing or ratesetting scheme."[118]

The *Ticor* Court went on to sustain an FTC finding that state insurance commissioners had exercised inadequate oversight by checking filings only for mathematical accuracy and failing to insist that rate bureaus submit information that state regulators had requested years before.[119] *Ticor*'s requirement that courts determine whether state authorities have taken "the necessary steps" to monitor private actors may force courts to make difficult, imponderable judgments about the enthusiasm and skill with which state agencies execute their oversight responsibilities. Problems that arise in evaluating the earnestness with which state officials apply monitoring tools may yet lead the courts to reassess, as Page has proposed, the usefulness of an active supervision requirement.

State action litigation was not antitrust's only growth industry during the conservative retrenchment since the late 1970's. As the Calvani/Sibarium and Flynn papers indicate, state antitrust enforcement grew substantially during the 1980's, particularly in fields such as merger control that once had been the exclusive province of the federal antitrust agencies and private litigants.[120] Ralph Folsom's contribution to this volume[121] examines the causes of the modern resurgence of state enforcement and distills lessons for state antitrust officials from the "laboratories" of individual state enforcement experience. Folsom presents extensive statistical data on recent state enforcement patterns and supplements his narrative discussion with extensive indices that compile state legislation for controlling restrictive business practices.

Following a period of vigorous activity from 1890 until 1918,[122]

---

[118] *Id.* at 2179.

[119] *Id.* at 2179–80.

[120] *See* Lande, *When Should States Challenge Mergers: A Proposed Federal/State Balance*, 35 N.Y. L. Sch. L. Rev. 1047 (1990).

[121] Folsom, *State Antitrust Remedies: Lessons from the Laboratories*, 35 Antitrust Bull. 941 (1990).

[122] *See* May, *Antitrust Practice and Procedure in the Formative Era: The Constitutional and Conceptual Reach of State Antitrust Law, 1880–1918*, 135 U. Pa. L. Rev. 495, 501–03 (1987).

state antitrust enforcement grew dormant for the next half-century. As Folsom recounts, the seeds of the recent revival were planted in the 1970's. Twenty-one jurisdictions enacted new antitrust statutes, and federal law enforcement assistance grants enabled state governments to create new, or to expand existing, antitrust enforcement bureaus.[123] Even as states bolstered their statutes and increased prosecutorial resources in the 1970's, the virtually exclusive focus of state enforcement consisted of applying state and federal prohibitions on horizontal restraints such as bid-rigging. The notion that state governments might assume an important role in controlling mergers was largely alien to state antitrust authorities.[124]

The diversification of state antitrust enforcement in the 1980's can be told as a story of unintended consequences.[125] Among other goals, the Reagan administration sought to decentralize political power by emphasizing federalism and to reduce government intervention in the marketplace. In retrenching antitrust policy, the Reagan leadership at the FTC and the Justice Department gave little evident thought to how state attorneys general—many of them hostile to Reagan administration political and economic preferences—would respond to the federal government's relaxation of merger standards and its abandonment of vertical restraints enforcement. To Reagan

---

123   Folsom, *supra* note 121, at 950–53, 955–59.

124   In a speech in 1974, Michael Zaleski, the Assistant Attorney General for the State of Wisconsin, described the following division of labor between federal and state antitrust officials:

> [T]he federal Department of Justice is geared up to handle the larger investigations and actions which the states are [not] now, and probably never will be, able to handle because of the economics of the situation. The types of cases to which I am referring are the monopoly and merger cases. . . . We have to concentrate on the hard-core violations and leave the complex economic cases . . . to the federal government.

Michael Zaleski, Utilization of State Laws in Anti-Trust Prosecutions (Presentation to the National Association of Attorneys General Organized Crime Control Seminars, March 19–June 12, 1974), *quoted in* National Association of Attorneys General, Committee on the Office of the Attorney General, State Antitrust Laws and Their Enforcement 45 (Oct. 1974).

125   *See* Kovacic, *Comments and Observations*, 59 ANTITRUST L.J. 119, 124 (1990).

administration officials, what emerged from the state antitrust laboratories was Frankenstein's monster, free to prosecute merger and vertical restraints cases that the federal enforcers disdained.[126]

States gradually occupied enforcement terrain that the Reagan enforcement agencies had abandoned.[127] For the most part, the expansion of state enforcement received reinforcement from judicial interpretations of state antitrust authority. The states have failed to persuade the Supreme Court to allow parens patriae suits under the federal antitrust statutes on behalf of indirect purchasers,[128] but the Court has upheld the validity of state statutes that permit state governments to seek treble damages on behalf of indirect purchasers.[129] In a development that greatly solidified the states' importance in merger enforcement, the Court also sustained the ability of states to obtain divestiture to remedy violations of the federal antitrust laws.[130]

Folsom draws several conclusions from his review of recent state enforcement experience. He emphasizes the diversity of state approaches in statutory design and enforcement practice.[131] In doing so, he attempts to address a concern posed by the Calvani/Sibarium paper:[132] Will state merger enforcement lead to a Balkanization of merger control in the United States? Folsom acknowledges the possibility of fragmentation, but he anticipates that the coordinating

---

[126]   In a speech in 1988, FTC Chairman Daniel Oliver called the National Association of Attorneys General a "group of counter-revolutionaries" that "seeks to undo our progress through a process that poses a serious threat not only to consumers but to our basic constitutional scheme as well." Oliver, *Statement of Chairman Oliver*, 57 ANTITRUST L.J. 235, 242 (1988).

[127]   *See* Constantine, *An Inside Look at Current Trends in State Antitrust Enforcement*, 1 ANTITRUST 6 (1987); Moore, *New Cops on the Beat*, National Journal, May 23, 1987, at 1338.

[128]   *See* Kansas v. Utilicorp United, Inc., 497 U.S. 199 (1990); Illinois Brick Co. v. Illinois, 431 U.S. 720 (1977).

[129]   *See* California v. ARC America Corp., 490 U.S. 93 (1989).

[130]   *See* California v. American Stores Co., 495 U.S. 271 (1990).

[131]   Folsom, *supra* note 121, at 959–62.

[132]   *See* Calvani & Sibarium, *supra* note 13, at 211–16.

activities of the Antitrust Division of the National Association of Attorneys General will "provide uniformity and predictability" to state merger enforcement.[133]

Folsom devotes extensive attention to the effect of state remedial schemes. He finds that the principal determinant of levels of private enforcement of state antitrust statutes is the nature of monetary relief. State codification of per se offenses has had little apparent effect on private enforcement activity, but Folsom identifies a strong positive relationship between the availability of mandatory treble damages and the filing of private cases.[134] State enforcement agencies, which account for about one-third of all reported state antitrust litigation, appear to rely principally on civil penalty remedies and rarely invoke state-based criminal sanctions.[135] Folsom attributes the latter pattern to weaknesses in state criminal penalty schemes, which tend to treat antitrust offenses as misdemeanors rather than as felonies.[136]

Folsom's statistical study also confirms an impression that antitrust practitioners have derived from well-publicized episodes of state enforcement—that California and New York have been the most active state antitrust jurisdictions.[137] Among other variables, Folsom attributes the standing of these two states to shared characteristics such as the existence of active state and local public prosecution units and automatic trebling of damages. The author points out that while California's public enforcement programs rely chiefly on civil penalty actions, New York has resorted with increasing frequency to criminal sanctions to punish and deter violations.[138]

---

133   Folsom, *supra* note 121, at 960–62.

134   *Id.* at 962–64.

135   *Id.* at 964–65.

136   *Id.* at 965.

137   *Id.* at 966. Folsom's data indicate a second tier of active jurisdictions consisting of Arizona, Connecticut, Illinois, New Jersey, Ohio, and Washington. Somewhat surprisingly, this second group omits Maryland and Massachusetts, which Folsom places in a third group of moderately active states. *Id.* at 966–67.

138   *Id.* at 967.

Almarin Phillips's contribution to this volume[139] treats a third area (along with state action litigation and state enforcement) in which antitrust's horizons have expanded amid the general recent retrenchment of doctrine and enforcement policy. With the Justice Department's successful prosecution of the Otter Tail Power Company in the early 1970's,[140] antitrust discovered regulated industries with a vengeance. The government's success in attacking Otter Tail's refusal to wheel power to municipally owned distribution companies lent considerable impetus to the Justice Department's decision to file its massive monopolization suit against AT&T[141] and inspired numerous private plaintiffs to attack the conduct of regulated firms in the electric power, telecommunications, and natural gas industries.[142] Today it is unusual to find a firm that is currently subject to extensive public utility regulation or, owing to deregulation, was recently subject to extensive regulatory oversight that has not spent time in an antitrust courtroom over the past 25 years.

Phillips documents the emergence of a post-World War II consensus among academics and policy makers supporting moves to rely more heavily on competition (and antitrust enforcement) to motivate regulated firms.[143] In the 1970's and 1980's, this consensus helped to prompt a shift in governance strategies from comprehensive controls to market-based incentives in the telecommunications, transportation, financial services, and electric power industries. As the Justice Department's successful effort to compel the restructuring of the Bell System dramatically shows, antitrust litigation provided an important tool for change.

---

[139]   Phillips, *Antitrust Principles and Regulatory Needs*, 35 ANTITRUST BULL. 631 (1990).

[140]   United States v. Otter Tail Power Co., 410 U.S. 366 (1973).

[141]   *See* P. TEMIN, THE FALL OF THE BELL SYSTEM 108–09 (1987).

[142]   *See* S. COLL, THE DEAL OF THE CENTURY: THE BREAKUP OF AT&T 22–23 (1986); Flynn, *Discussion: Legal Approach to Market Dominance: Assessing Market Power in Antitrust Cases*, in TELECOMMUNICATIONS DEREGULATION— MARKET POWER AND COST ALLOCATION ISSUES 28, 38–41 (J. R. Allison & D. L. Thomas eds. 1990).

[143]   Phillips, *supra* note 139, at 632–50.

Phillips's aim is to assess whether the decisive swing away from regulation toward competition-based approaches has been wise, to determine whether it is "possible that there is now a full turn of the screw—that deregulation and antitrust have been applied in areas in which they are the inappropriate remedy."[144] Phillip's effort to evaluate institutional comparative advantage (regulation versus competition with supervision by antitrust courts) leads him to conclude that recent policies exaggerate the curative powers of unencumbered market rivalry and undervalue the usefulness of traditional regulation. He explains that the reversal of earlier reliance on regulation "has gone to the extreme that now regulatory needs tend to be ignored."[145]

To illustrate his concerns, Phillips focuses on recent experience with commercial aviation, electric power, and telecommunications. Contrary to preregulation assumptions about contestability in commercial aviation, Phillips observes that experience has shown that "[e]ntry is not as easy as had been thought, and exit is far from costless."[146] Structural features of the airline industry "imply that a substantial degree of market power remains in some unregulated airline markets."[147] These features, coupled with other industry characteristics, "make questionable the existence of a stable, multi-firm, competitive equilibrium."[148] The author does not seek a return to the preregulation regime of the Civil Aeronautics Board, but he cautions that "the experiments in fully market-determined results" may have failed in ways that dictate reconsideration of the correct mix of regulatory and market strategies.[149]

In reviewing experience with the electric power industry, Phillips offers a negative appraisal of the application of antitrust principles to solve disputes over wheeling obligations and price squeezes.

---

144   *Id.* at 650.
145   *Id.* at 674.
146   *Id.* at 653.
147   *Id.*
148   *Id.* at 654.
149   *Id.* at 656.

Brute force application of essential facility theories to mandate wheeling tend to overlook rent-seeking motives that sometimes animate requests for wheeling and to underestimate technical obstacles to providing transmission access.[150] Courts that use traditional attempted monopolization and monopolization analysis to evaluate price-squeeze allegations are prone to underestimate the capacity of public utility regulatory commissions to prevent an investor-owned utility from recouping losses incurred to eliminate a downstream rival.[151] Given a choice between alternative governance structures, the author concludes that "the competitive problems of the electric power industry seem better left to the regulators than to the antitrust courts."[152]

Phillips' third example—telecommunications—treats problems that have arisen in the course of implementing the Bell System divestiture and in executing related, procompetitive telecommunications policies over the past 20 years. He observes that continued emphasis on procompetitive policies "will not result in intolerable inefficiencies in plain old telephone service"[153] but may impose serious costs in other important respects:

> The big problems will emerge in connection with new telecommunications technologies. If the policies continue to insist and enlarge on competitive solutions, including competitive solutions to problems of standardization, and if the services and pricing policies of local exchange carriers continue to be restricted as they now are, a public network for new services operation on common carrier principles for the benefit of the nation at large will not become available.[154]

Phillips concludes that "[p]utting AT&T back together again is not the answer," but he urges recognition that the current mix of governance strategies fails to acknowledge the limits of competition and the inevitability of greater application of traditional regulatory methods.

---

150   *Id.* at 659–60.

151   *Id.* at 660–61.

152   *Id.* at 661.

153   *Id.* at 674.

154   *Id.*

Although the evidence to date is limited, there are signs that other antitrust system participants share Phillips's view about the need for a reassessment of the relative strengths and weaknesses of competition and regulation.[155] In particular, recent judicial decisions dealing with antitrust challenges to the conduct of integrated electric utilities have shown greater confidence in the efficacy of traditional public utility regulation and a heightened skepticism about the ability of antitrust courts to intervene in ways that improve the welfare of consumers.[156] As a group, such decisions are consistent with Phillips's call for greater humility about the value of antitrust as a preferred substitute for traditional regulation.

---

[155]   *See* Kovacic, *The Antitrust Law and Economics of Essential Facilities in Public Utility Regulation,* in ECONOMIC INNOVATIONS IN PUBLIC UTILITY REGULATION. 1 (M. A. Crew ed. 1992).

[156]   *See* City of Anaheim v. Southern California Edison Co., 955 F.2d 1373 (9th Cir. 1992); City of Vernon v. Southern California Edison Co., 955 F.2d 1361 (9th Cir.), *cert. denied,* 113 S. Ct. 305 (1992). Town of Concord v. Boston Edison Co., 915 F.2d 17 (1st Cir. 1990), *cert. denied,* 111 S. Ct. 1337 (1991).

18
Antitrust today:
maturity or decline

BY TERRY CALVANI* and MICHAEL L. SIBARIUM**

I. Introduction

The development of antitrust law has been nothing short of revolutionary over the past 15 years. Not long ago there was considerable academic discussion of the purposes of antitrust.[1]

---

* Commissioner, Federal Trade Commission; Adjunct Professor of Management, Owen Graduate School of Management, Vanderbilt University.
** Attorney Advisor to Commissioner Terry Calvani, Federal Trade Commission.

AUTHORS' NOTE: *The views expressed herein are the authors' and do not necessarily reflect the views of the Federal Trade Commission or any other Commissioner.*

[1] *Compare* Elzinga, *The Goals of Antitrust: Other Than Competition and Efficiency, What Else Counts,* 125 U. Pa. L. Rev. 1191 (1977), with Sullivan, *Economic & More Humanistic Disciplines: What Are the Sources of Wisdom for Antitrust?* 125 U. Pa. L. Rev. 1214 (1977). This debate was in some sense a replay of the Bork-Bowman/Blake-James

Some were concerned with the preservation of small business; or as Justice Peckham stated in *United States v. Trans-Missouri Freight Association*, with "the small dealers and worthy men whose lives have been spent therein, and who might be unable to readjust themselves to their altered surroundings."[2] Others believed that there was a significant positive correlation between accumulation of economic size and political power, and thus saw antitrust as necessary to the preservation of a democratic system of government.[3] Still others viewed antitrust as a system of business ethics: certain commercial practices, *e.g.*, price discrimination or pricing below "cost," affront commonly held views of proper conduct and ought to be forbidden. And some saw antitrust as a vehicle for preserving competition (usually defined in terms of efficiency[4]). Others yet espoused additional goals.[5]

---

exchange of 1965. *Compare* Bork & Bowman, *The Crisis in Antitrust*, 65 COLUM. L. REV. 363 (1965) *with* Blake & Jones, *In Defense of Antitrust*, 65 COLUM. L. REV. 377 (1965).

2   166 U.S. 290, 323 (1897).

3   S.600, 96th Cong., 1st Sess. (1979) is a good example of proposed legislation owing its existence at least in part to this objective. This legislation generated volumes of hearings and numerous papers. *See, e.g., Mergers and Economic Concentration: Hearings on S.600 Before the Subcomm. on Antitrust, Monopoly and Business Rights of the Senate Comm. on the Judiciary*, 96th Cong., 1st Sess. (1979). *Cf.* Salamon & Siegfried, *Economic Power and Political Influence: The Impact of Industry Structure on Public Policy*, 71 AMER. POL. SCI. REV. 1026 (1977).

4   The most prominent of the works urging an efficiency based antitrust policy are R. POSNER, ANTITRUST LAW (1976), and R. BORK, THE ANTITRUST PARADOX (1978). Professor Posner sits on the United States Court of Appeals for the Seventh Circuit to which he was appointed in 1981. Robert H. Bork served on the United States Court of Appeals for the District of Columbia Circuit from 1982 until his resignation in 1988.

5   For a discussion of the menu of possible antitrust policies, *see* Calvani, *The Mushrooming Brunswick Defense*, 50 ANTITRUST L.J. 319, 340–45 (1981). *See also* Calvani, *Consumer Welfare Is Prime Objective of Antitrust*, Legal Times 14 (Dec. 1984), *reprinted in part in* ECONOMIC ANALYSIS AND ANTITRUST LAW 7–14 (Calvani & Siegfried 2d ed. 1988).

Today, we think it fair to say that the debate—if not over—is in the "fourth quarter" with the preservation of competition the clear winner.[6] This development was presaged in the economic and legal literature; indeed, it was born and nurtured in the academy.[7] Although discussion of the so-called Reagan Antitrust Revolution has been commonplace—with enforcement appointees proclaiming its virtue while critics lamented the work of Reagan-appointed officials[8]—the real battle has been in the courts, and it is there that this consensus has been firmly established. This article seeks to explore the antitrust revolution; not in the normative approach of the academy, but rather in what the courts have actually done.

The discussion will proceed in four parts. First, we briefly explore the pronouncements of the Supreme Court on the purpose of antitrust. Second, we discuss changes in various antitrust

---

[6] Yet, scholars continue to debate the issue. For briefs that advocate the traditional wisdom, *see* Fox, *The Politics of Law and Economics in Judicial Decision Making: Antitrust as a Window*, 61 N.Y.U.L.Rev. 554 (1986), and Fox, *Consumer Beware Chicago*, 84 Mich. L.Rev. 1714 (1986).

A few have recently proposed that the elimination of wealth transfers are the underlying predicate of antitrust. *See*, Lande, *Wealth Transfers as the Original & Primary Concern of Antitrust: The Efficiency Interpretation Challenged*, 34 Hastings L.J. 65 (1982); *see also* Clark, *Antitrust Comes Full Circle: The Return to the Cartelization Standard*, 38 Vand. L.Rev. 1125 (1985). There is no significant practical difference in case selection and outcome between this standard and that of efficiency. The classic case producing a different result would be a cartel or monopoly that was able to engage in perfect price discrimination. Such cases are as common as unicorns. *See*, Calvani, *Rectangles & Triangles: A Response to Mr. Lande*, 58 Antitrust L.J. 657 (1989).

[7] Although numerous individuals participated in the debate and scholarship, perhaps none was more important in the evolution of antitrust learning than Aaron Director of the University of Chicago. Interestingly, Professor Director's medium of communication was his teaching rather than his publication. *But cf.* Director & Levi, *Law and the Future Trade Regulation*, 51 Nw. U.L. Rev. 281 (1956). For a description of these developments, *see* Posner, *The Chicago School of Antitrust Analysis*, 127 U. Pa. L.Rev. 925 (1979).

[8] *See infra* note 223 and accompanying text.

doctrines. In the third part, we seek to describe the changes in the quantity and quality of government—and more importantly, private—litigation. Lastly, we hope to make some predictions for the future.

II. Antitrust and Supreme Court rhetoric

During its near 100-year exposition on the Sherman Act and subsequent antitrust legislation, the Supreme Court has not voiced a consistent statement of the purpose of the antitrust laws. The Court's various formulations of antitrust's objectives are not unlike the differing views that have been expressed in the academic debate.[9] Yet, the rhetoric of antitrust decisions has undergone important change in recent years. Today, the Court's language is consistent with its analysis in moving away from nonefficiency-oriented objectives toward the protection of the competitive environment as the predicate for antitrust. An understanding of these "first principles" may shed light on the result reached by the Court in a number of cases through the years.

Historically, much of the Court's rhetoric has focused on very general, nonspecific, principles. In *Northern Pacific Railway Co. v. United States*, the Sherman Act was described as "a charter of economic liberty."[10] This theme was echoed by the Court, albeit more fully, in *United States v. Topco Associates, Inc.*:

> Antitrust laws in general, and the Sherman Act in particular, are the Magna Carta of free enterprise. They are as important to the preservation of economic freedom and our free-enterprise system as the Bill of Rights is to the protection of our fundamental personal freedoms. And the freedom guaranteed each and every business, no matter how small, is the freedom to compete—to assert with your vigor, imagination, devotion, and ingenuity whatever economic muscle it can muster.[11]

---

9   *See supra* notes 1-8.

10   356 U.S. 1, 4 (1958).

11   405 U.S. 596, 610 (1972). The antitrust laws are seen by these judicial writers as playing a fundamental role in preserving our free enterprise system. *See also*, Associated Gen. Contractors of Cal., Inc. v. California State Council of Carpenters, 459 U.S. 519, 538 n.13 (1983).

Such pronouncements tend to elevate the antitrust laws to constitutional significance, but are woefully short on policy prescription in any meaningful sense.

Several more specific purposes of antitrust can, however, be gleaned from Supreme Court decisions. One such purpose of the Sherman Act emphasized early by the Supreme Court was the concern that efficient business combinations might restrain competition by driving small dealers out of business. In *United States v. Trans-Missouri Freight Association*, for example, the Court explicitly recognized that the preservation of competitors (even the inefficient), rather than the preservation of competition, was an appropriate antitrust objective.[12]

A second and related objective has been the preservation of atomistic industrial organization. In *Brown Shoe Co. v. United States*,[13] the Court observed that the "dominant theme pervading congressional consideration of the . . . [Celler-Kefauver] amendments was a fear of . . . a rising tide of economic concentration in the American economy." Perhaps the clearest rendition of this populist theme was offered by the Court in its 1966 decision in *United States v. Von's Grocery Co.*:

> From this country's earliest beginning there has been an abiding and widespread fear of the evils which flow from monopoly—that is the concentration of economic power in the hands of a few . . . . Congress passed the Sherman Act . . . in an attempt to prevent further concentration and to preserve competition among a large number of sellers . . . . Like the Sherman Act of 1890 and the Clayton Act in 1914, the basic purpose of the 1950 Celler-Kefauver Act was to prevent economic concentration in the American economy by keeping a large number of small competitors in business.[14]

---

[12]   166 U.S. at 323. *See supra*, note 2 and accompanying text.

[13]   370 U.S. 294, 315 (1962).

[14]   384 U.S. 270, 274-77 (1966). The populist theme was stressed by the Federal Trade Commission in its decision in Brown Shoe Co., Inc., 62 F.T.C. 679, 720 (1963) ("historically one of the purposes of the antitrust laws, over and above purely economic considerations, has been to preserve '. . . an organization of industry in small units which can effectively compete with each other. . . .' ").

These populist overtones of the antitrust laws were also recognized by Judge Learned Hand in the famed *ALCOA* case:[15]

[A]mong the purposes of Congress in 1890 was a desire to put an end to great aggregations of capital because of helplessness of the individual before them . . . . Throughout the history of these statutes it has been constantly assumed that one of their purposes was to perpetuate and preserve, for its own sake and in spite of possible cost, an organization of industry in small units which can effectively compete with each other.[16]

Other decisions cast the populist antitrust rhetoric in somewhat different, but related tones.[17]

During the past 15 years the Court has focused increasingly on maximizing consumer welfare by the protection of competition as the proper objective of antitrust. Indeed, in 1975 the Court went so far as to assert that "the sole aim of antitrust legislation is to protect competition."[18] Two years later the Court held that windfall profits that would have inured to one competitor but for another's acquisition of yet a third failing firm did not constitute cognizable "antitrust injury." In the words of the Court: "It is

---

15   United States v. Aluminum Co. of America, 148 F.2d 416, 421 (2d Cir. 1945) (sitting as the court of last resort due to the absence of a quorum of the Supreme Court due to recusal).

16   148 F.2d at 428–29 (emphasis added).

17   *See, e.g.*, United States v. Falstaff Brewing Co., 410 U.S. 526, 541 (1973), where Justice Douglas emphasized the labor dislocation and absentee ownership effects that can result from mergers: "Control over American business is being transferred from local communities to distant cities where men on the 54th floor with only balance sheets and profit and loss settlements before them decide the fate of communities with which they have little or no relationship. As a result of mergers . . . states are losing major corporations and their local communities are becoming satellites of distant corporate control."
Douglas continued: "A case in point is Goldendale in my native state of Washington. It was a thriving community and the ideal place to raise a family—until the company that owned the sawmill was bought by an out of state giant. In a year . . . auditors in far away New York City, who never knew the glories of Goldendale, decided to close the local mill. . . . Goldendale became . . . . crippled." 410 U.S. at 543.

18   Gorden v. New York Stock Exchange, Inc., 422 U.S. 659 (1975).

inimical to the purposes of these laws to award damages for the type of injury claimed here."[19]

The Court's opinion in *Broadcast Music, Inc. v. Columbia Broadcasting System* is more instructive yet.[20] There the Court considered an arrangement for the blanket licensing of music copyrights by competitors. The Court focused on the purpose of the statute in holding that the arrangement at bar must be evaluated by considering whether its effect

> facially appears to be one that would always or almost always tend to *restrict competition and decrease output . . . or instead one designed to increase economic efficiency* and render markets more rather than less competitive.[21]

Here the Court equates the restriction of competition with the restriction of output, and discusses increased competition in terms of economic efficiency. Thus, antitrust policy is defined in economic terms.[22]

---

[19] Brunswick Corp. v. Pueblo Bowl-O-Mat, Inc., 429 U.S. 477, 488 (1977), discussed *infra* at notes 197–99 and accompanying text. *See also* R. POSNER & F. EASTERBROOK, ANTITRUST 154 (2d ed. 1981).

[20] 441 U.S. 1 (1979).

[21] *Id.* at 19–20 (emphasis added).

[22] In Connell Constr. Co. v. Plumbers & Steamfitters Local Union No. 100, 421 U.S. 616, 623 (1975), the message was more focused: "competition based on efficiency is a positive value that the antitrust laws strive to protect." *Cf.* Northern Natural Gas Co. v. Federal Power Commission, 399 F.2d 953 (D.C. Cir. 1968) (basic goal of antitrust law is "to achieve the most efficient allocation of resources").

This is not to say that the focus on economic efficiency is altogether novel. Long before the antitrust revolution emerged, the Supreme Court recognized the economic theory of the antitrust laws. In *Apex Hosiery v. Leader*, for example, the Court recounted the purpose of the Sherman Act as: "The end sought was the prevention of restraints to free competition in business and commercial transactions which tended to restrict production, raise prices or otherwise control the market to the detriment of purchasers or consumers of' goods and services, all of which had come to be regarded as a special form of public injury." 310 U.S. 469, 493 (1940).

(footnote 22 continued)

In the next part, we demonstrate how the Court's holdings—rhetoric aside—tip the scales in favor of an antitrust law whose principal purpose appears aimed at promoting competition.

III. Changes in doctrine

In this section we will explore several antitrust doctrines and the changes in those doctrines that have taken place within recent memory. Our goal is to set forth major areas in which the Supreme Court has reversed its previous rulings or otherwise chartered a new course. We begin with the topic of price predation, an area in which the influence of the academy on the development of the law can be readily traced.

A. Predatory pricing

The Court has spoken three times within the last 20 years on the subject of price predation. The first occasion was the Court's 1967 opinion in *Utah Pie Co. v. Continental Baking Co.*[23] There new entrants into the market confronted a well-entrenched dominant, albeit local, firm. In an effort to garner market share the new firms priced below average total costs. Finding that defendants had contributed to a "deteriorating price structure," the Court seemed to condemn prices below average total costs. It is noteworthy that the plaintiff continued to hold significant market share, increased sales and remained profitable during the period of alleged price predation.

In *Northern Pacific Railway Co.*, the Court endeavored to reconcile these efficiency goals of the statute with other objectives previously recognized by the Court. "It rests on the premise that the unrestrained interaction of competitive forces will yield the best allocation of our economic resources, the lowest prices, the highest quality and the greatest material progress, while at the same time providing an environment conducive to the preservation of our democratic political and social institutions. But even were that premise open to question, the policy unequivocally laid down by the Act is competition." 356 U.S. 1, 4 (1958).

[23]   386 U.S. 685 (1967).

In the decade before *Utah Pie* and the more than two decades since, the economic and legal communities have been locked in debate over the prevalence of predatory pricing practices and their effects on competition. Simplistically, two camps have emerged; those that see predatory pricing as a serious threat to competition and those that view the threat as too remote to be the concern of antitrust. To see how the debate has developed and where it is going, we briefly visit the university.

1. THE DEBATE[24] As with much of the antitrust revolution, the seeds of this doctrinal change were sowed within the academy. In the first half of this century, few economists doubted the efficacy of predatory pricing. An academic model of the classic predator arose during that period that went unchallenged until the late 1950's. The classic predator was a firm of such unequaled size and financial strength that a drastic cut in price in some small part of its territory, sustained with monopoly profits earned elsewhere, could eliminate a smaller competitor, leaving the predator to raise its prices and recoup its losses in that local market.[25]

In 1958, Professor McGee published his famous analysis of the *Standard Oil* case,[26] challenging the classic theory.[27] The Standard Oil trust had always been considered the paradigm of the classic predator. McGee attacked that notion, postulating that below-cost pricing to drive out competitors is an irrational course of action for a dominant firm and that mergers or collusion will always be more efficient means of monopolization. In his empirical study of the trial record, he found no evidence of attempted

---

[24] This section relies on and excerpts liberally from Calvani & Lynch, *Predatory Pricing Under the Robinson & Patman & Sherman Acts: An Introduction*, 51 ANTITRUST L.J. 375 (1986).

[25] A classic exposition of this perspective is contained in I. TARBELL, THE HISTORY OF THE STANDARD OIL COMPANY (abr. ed. D.M. Chalmers ed. 1969).

[26] Standard Oil Co. v. United States, 221 U.S. 1 (1911).

[27] McGee, *Predatory Price Cutting: The Standard Oil (N.J.) Case*, 1 J.L. & ECON. 137 (1958).

predation by Standard Oil. Commentaries that followed reinforced and expanded the McGee hypothesis through both theoretical and empirical analysis.[28]

The apparent consensus in the literature that developed as a result—that predatory pricing should be a minor concern of the antitrust law, if any concern at all—had no effect on the case law. As evidenced by the *Utah Pie* decision, courts continued on the course set in motion by the early Sherman Act cases, and judicial findings of predatory pricing were much more common than the McGee theory would have allowed.[29] Evidently, the courts were not yet ready to accept such a radical contravention of the conventional wisdom.

Then, in 1975, professors Areeda and Turner offered a cost-based rule for determining whether or not a pricing strategy is "predatory."[30] To oversimplify a bit, Areeda and Turner hold that any price at or above short-run marginal cost (or, as a more easily ascertainable surrogate, average variable cost) is nonpredatory, while a price below short-run marginal (or average variable)

---

[28] *See, e.g.*, Elzinga, *Predatory Pricing: The Case of the Gunpowder Trust*, 13 J.L. & Econ. 223 (1970) (concluding that predatory pricing by the Powder Trust, if it existed at all, was not nearly as prevalent as believed); Koller, *The Myth of Predatory Pricing: An Empirical Study*, 4 Antitrust L. & Econ. Rev. 105 (Summer 1971) (examining data on 26 findings of liability for predatory pricing and discovering only three instances of sales below cost with predatory intent that caused a misallocation of resources); Stigler, *Imperfections in the Capital Market*, 75 J.Pol.Econ. 287 (1967).

[29] *See* Calvani & Lynch, *supra* note 24, at 378.

[30] *See* Areeda & Turner, *Predatory Pricing & Related Practices Under Section 2 of the Sherman Act*, 88 Harv. L. Rev. 697 (1975). This article in turn spawned a host of commentary. Much of the literature has been collected in Symposium, *Predatory Conduct and Empirical Studies in Collusion*, 10 J. Reprints in Antitrust L. & Econ. 7 (1980). For a critical review of this literature, see Calvani & Lynch, *supra* note 24.

cost is predatory.[31] Areeda and Turner designed their rule around the notion, offered by McGee, that predatory pricing is comparatively rare and that any policy on predation should minimize deterrence to competitive pricing. Nevertheless, they reject the McGee argument that predatory pricing is "irrational." They contend that McGee's hypothesis loses force when mergers and collusion to create monopolies are illegal, and that the legal impediments to anticompetitive mergers and collusion are far greater today than they were in the days of the Standard Oil trust. Absent those alternatives, they argue, predation may be an efficient means of monopolization.[32]

Since publication of the Areeda-Turner article a decade ago, the courts have relied almost exclusively on economic analysis to evaluate predatory pricing allegations.[33] As Hurwitz and Kovacic note, the Areeda-Turner rule "has provided either the analytical foundation or the point of departure" for most post-1975 predatory pricing decisions.[34] The substantial reliance by courts on cost-based presumptive rules[35] to determine whether a price is "predatory" has made antitrust violations dependent upon a showing of predatory pricing extremely difficult for plaintiffs to prove.[36]

---

[31] Areeda & Turner, *supra* note 30, at 733. For a brief but more complete discussion of the Areeda-Turner rule, see Calvani & Lynch, *supra* note 24, at 380-81.

[32] 3 P. AREEDA & D. TURNER, ANTITRUST LAW ¶ 711(b) n.6 (1978). Richard Posner also rejects the notion that predatory pricing is patently irrational, citing the potential profitability of predatory pricing conducted in one geographic market when that predation deters entry into other markets. Posner, *Exclusionary Practices and the Antitrust Laws*, 41 U. CHI. L. REV. 506, 516-17 (1974).

[33] *See, e.g.*, Hurwitz & Kovacic, *Judicial Analysis of Predation: The Emerging Trends*, 35 VAND. L. REV. 63, 94 (1982).

[34] *Id.* at 78. For a discussion of case law, *see id.* at 78, 97, 99-112, 149-50; Calvani & Lynch, *supra* note 24, at 394-96.

[35] *See* Hurwitz & Kovacic, *supra* note 33, at 99-110, 149-50.

[36] *See id.* at 139-49 & n.1.

Although virtually all predatory pricing plaintiffs face substantial obstacles in the post-Areeda-Turner era, courts have been reticent to apply the marginal cost rule too rigidly.[37] This lack of complete confidence in Areeda-Turner apparently stems from the tremendous controversy in the literature sparked by the two scholars' article. Some commentators attacked their short-run marginal cost rule as too permissive of predation and others claimed that the rule was yet too restrictive of procompetitive pricing behavior.[38] The subsequent retreat by the courts from stout adherence to a pure marginal cost standard for determining whether a price is "predatory" has resulted in a somewhat varied judicial treatment of cost-based standards.[39] The pervasive reliance by the courts upon Areeda-Turner as a common point of reference, however, reflects the notion held by Areeda and Turner and others in the literature that predatory pricing, if uncommon, is not irrational and hence is a proper subject for antitrust scrutiny.

Disagreeing with that commonly held presupposition, adherents of the early McGee philosophy rejoined the debate in the literature.[40] If predatory pricing is not theoretically "irrational," they argue, at least it will be so rare that any law restricting price

---

[37] *See, e.g.*, William Inglis & Sons Baking Co. v. ITT Continental Baking Co., 668 F.2d 1014 (9th Cir. 1981), *cert. denied*, 459 U.S. 825 (1982).

[38] For a summary of this literature and the alternative predation rules offered by the various commentators, *see* Calvani & Lynch, *supra* note 24, at 381-94.

[39] *See, e.g.*, McGahee v. Northern Propane Gas Co., 858 F.2d 1489, 1495 (11th Cir. 1988) ("The Areeda & Turner test is like the Venus de Milo; it is much admired and often discussed, but rarely embraced. Perhaps this reluctance to embrace is due to the substance from which it is formed. The Areeda & Turner test is carved from economic assumptions, not from antitrust statutes and judicial precedents."). *See also*, Hurwitz & Kovacic, *supra* note 33, at 99-112 & n.83, 149-50.

[40] *See* R. BORK, *supra* note 4, at 144-60 (1978); McGee, *Predatory Pricing Revisited*, 23 J.L. & ECON. 289 (1981); and Easterbrook, *Predatory Strategies and Counterstrategies*, 48 U. CHI. L. REV. 263 (1981).

competition will do more social ill than good. Thus, the "problem" of predatory price-cutting warrants no legal proscriptions.[41] Robert Bork was the first to state his argument in the post-Areeda-Turner literature,[42] but McGee himself[43] and then-professor Easterbrook[44] subsequently entered the fray as well.

The importance of their analysis to the development of the law is that the Supreme Court adopted much of it in *Matsushita*. In its decision, the Court went to great pains to avoid addressing the substantial controversy in the literature and case law surrounding the use of the Areeda-Turner or other cost-based rules to determine when pricing behavior is "predatory." Faced with a summary judgment determination in the context of an alleged "conspiracy" to price predatorily, the Court was able to leapfrog consideration of substantive rules of liability for price-cutting and instead wrote the McGee-Bork-Easterbrook reasoning into the law of predatory pricing through its enumeration of the summary judgment standard.

2. THE *MATSUSHITA* CASE[45] The Supreme Court decided *Matsushita Electric Industrial Co. v. Zenith Radio Corp.*[46] during its 1986 term. Plaintiffs in *Matsushita* were American television manufacturers Zenith and National Union Electric Corporation (hereinafter collectively referred to as Zenith). Zenith claimed that defendants, 21 Japanese-controlled corporations that manufactured or sold television sets, had illegally conspired to drive U.S. firms from the American television market. The gist of this conspiracy allegedly was a scheme to raise and maintain artifi-

---

[41]   *See* R. Bork, *supra* note 4, at 154; Easterbrook, *supra* note 40, at 318; and McGee, *supra* note 40, at 317.

[42]   R. Bork, *supra* note 4, at 154.

[43]   McGee, *supra* note 40, at 317.

[44]   Easterbrook, *supra* note 40, at 318–38.

[45]   This section relies on and excerpts liberally from Calvani & Lynch, *Predatory Pricing After Matsushita*, 7 ANTITRUST 22 (June 1986).

[46]   475 U.S. 574 (1986).

cially high prices for television receivers sold by defendants in Japan and, at the same time, to fix and maintain low prices for television receivers exported to and sold in the United States. Zenith alleged that these low prices were at levels that produced substantial losses for defendants. They asserted violations of §§ 1 and 2 of the Sherman Act and § 2(a) of the Robinson-Patman Act, and various trade law violations.[47]

After several years of discovery, defendant Japanese television manufacturers filed motions for summary judgment, claiming that the alleged conspiracy was economically irrational and practically infeasible.[48] The district court found that the admissible evidence did not raise a genuine issue of material fact as to the existence of the alleged conspiracy, in large part because the evidence that bore directly on the alleged price-cutting conspiracy did not rebut the more plausible inference that the Japanese firms were cutting prices to compete in the American market and not to monopolize it. Summary judgment was entered against Zenith on all of its antitrust claims, as the court found they were functionally indistinguishable.[49]

The Court of Appeals for the Third Circuit reversed the district court, determining that a factfinder reasonably could find a conspiracy to depress prices in the American market in order to drive out American competitors, a conspiracy which was funded by excess profits obtained in the Japanese market. The court relied on expert opinion suggesting that the Japanese firms sold televisions in the United States at substantial losses and on evidence of agreements among them to set supracompetitive prices in Japan and minimum prices for televisions exported to the American market, as well as evidence that the firms limited the number of distributors of their products in the United States.[50]

---

[47]   *Id.* at 578.

[48]   *See id.* at 578, 588.

[49]   *See id.* at 579.

[50]   *See id.* at 580–81.

The Supreme Court reversed the denial of summary judgment. The Court held that "if the factual context renders respondents' claim implausible—if the claim is one that simply makes no economic sense respondents must come forward with more persuasive evidence to support their claim than would otherwise be necessary."[51] The Court thus enumerated the summary judgment standard to include a consideration of the "plausibility" of Zenith's claim, opening wide the door to application of the McGee-Bork-Easterbrook hypothesis that predatory pricing is, at least in practical terms, almost always irrational for profit-maximizing businessmen.

"A predatory pricing conspiracy is by nature speculative," the Court wrote.[52] For predatory pricing to be a rational course of action, the conspirators must have a "reasonable expectation" of recovering, through later monopoly profits, more than the losses suffered during the price war.[53] Yet, the Court concluded, "the success of such schemes is inherently uncertain: the short-run loss is definite, but the long-run gain depends on successfully neutralizing the competition," a costly and uncertain outcome.[54]

Moreover, the Court wrote, driving out one's rivals is not a sufficient condition for earning future monopoly profits adequate to cover short-term losses; the predator must have some assurance that its anticipated monopoly pricing will not "breed quick entry by new competitors eager to share in the excess profits."[55] The success of any predatory scheme thus "depends on *maintaining* monopoly power for long enough both to recoup the predator's losses and to harvest some additional gain."[56] Because the predator must have this elusive assurance that its monopoly can be sustained for a significant period of time, "there is a consen-

---

51   *Id*. at 587.

52   *Id*. at 588.

53   *Id*. at 589.

54   *Id*.

55   *Id*.

56   *Id*. (emphasis in original).

sus among commentators that predatory pricing schemes are rarely tried, and even more rarely successful."[57]

Furthermore, the Court contended, the foregoing analysis shows that the adequate returns to predatory pricing are highly speculative even for a single firm seeking monopoly power. The charge in *Matsushita* was that a large number of firms conspired over a period of many years to charge low prices in order to stifle competition. Extremely high costs of coordination among numerous firms make a conspiracy to price predatorily "incalculably more difficult to execute than an analogous plan undertaken by a single predator," the Court wrote.[58]

Applying this chiefly McGee-Bork-Easterbrook framework to the facts before it, the Court concluded that the prospects for the Japanese firms of attaining monopoly power seemed slight. Two decades after their conspiracy was allegedly commenced, they appeared to be far from achieving monopoly power; the two largest shares of the retail market in television sets were held by RCA and Zenith, and not by any of the defendant Japanese electronics companies. Moreover, the market shares of RCA and Zenith, which together accounted for approximately 40% of sales, had not declined appreciably during the 1970's.[59] Yet, after two decades, Zenith contended that the Japanese firms were "still artificially *depressing* the market price" in order to drive the larger and well-established Zenith out.[60]

In view of the failure of the alleged predatory pricing scheme after two decades, the prospects of maintaining monopoly power long enough in the American television market to recoup such substantial losses appear especially dim, the Court reasoned.[61] Moreover, the Court found no basis to conclude that entry into the market is especially difficult, yet without barriers to entry it

---

[57]   *Id.*

[58]   *Id.* at 590.

[59]   *Id.* at 591.

[60]   *Id.* (emphasis in original).

[61]   *Id.* at 592.

"would presumably be impossible to maintain supracompetitive prices for an extended time."[62] Maintaining supracompetitive prices would also depend upon the continued cooperation of the conspirators, and on the numerous competitors' ability to escape antitrust liability for price-fixing. Each of these factors, the Court contended, weighs more heavily as the time needed to recoup losses grows.[63] The Court thus concluded that "[t]he alleged conspiracy's failure to achieve its ends in the two decades of its asserted operation is strong evidence that the conspiracy does not in fact exist."[64]

The Court even considered and rejected the expert study offered by Zenith suggesting that defendants had sold their products in the American market below cost. The study, the Court asserted, was not based upon actual cost data, but was an expert opinion based on a mathematical construction that in turn rested upon assumptions about petitioners' costs. The Court found the study implausible and that its probative value was far outweighed by the "economic factors . . . that suggest that such conduct is irrational."[65] The Court apparently found the McGee-Bork-Easterbrook reasoning so compelling that even an expert study, albeit one that did not use actual cost data, could not make Zenith's predatory pricing story credible enough to raise a genuine issue of fact for trial. The Court summarized thus:

> [P]redatory pricing schemes require conspirators to suffer losses in order eventually to realize their illegal gains; moreover, the gains depend on a host of uncertainties, making such schemes more likely to fail than to succeed. These economic realities tend to make predatory pricing conspiracies self-deterring: unlike most other conduct that violates the antitrust laws, failed predatory pricing schemes are costly to the conspirators.[66]

---

[62] *Id.* at 592 n.15.

[63] *Id.* at 592.

[64] *Id.*

[65] *Id.* at 594 n.19.

[66] *Id.* at 594–95.

True to the McGee-Bork-Easterbrook argument, the Court also noted the dangers of chilling price competition by imposing liability for price-cutting. The Court wrote that "cutting price in order to increase business often is the very essence of competition."[67] Thus, mistaken inferences in cases attacking price-cutting are especially costly, "because they chill the very conduct the antitrust laws are designed to protect."[68] While any concern about discouraging procompetitive conduct must be balanced against the desire that illegal conspiracies be identified and punished, "[t]hat balance is . . . unusually one-sided in cases such as this one."[69]

The Court thus reversed the Third Circuit, asserting that "petitioners had no motive to enter into the alleged conspiracy"[70] and that the court of appeals in denying summary judgment "failed to consider the absence of plausible motive to engage in predatory pricing."[71] In fact, "as presumably rational businesses, [the Japanese firms] had every incentive *not* to engage in the conduct with which they are charged, for its likely effect would be to generate losses for [them] with no corresponding gains."[72] The absence of a plausible motive was especially significant to the Court in view of the ambiguousness of the evidence relied upon by the court of appeals to raise an inference of "predatory pricing conspiracy." For example, evidence of agreements concerning minimum price-setting and limitations on numbers of distributors in the U.S. was more consistent with a conspiracy by the Japanese firms to raise prices than to price predatorily. Likewise, evidence that the Japanese firms priced at levels that succeeded in taking away business from the larger and better established Zenith was more consistent with an inference of

---

67   *Id*. at 594.

68   *Id*.

69   *Id*.

70   *Id*. at 595.

71   *Id*.

72   *Id*. (emphasis in original).

competitive behavior than an agreement among 21 companies to price predatorily.[73] The Court remanded the case, stating that "in light of the absence of any rational motive to conspire, neither petitioners' pricing practices, nor their conduct in the Japanese market, nor their agreements respecting prices and distribution in the American market, suffice to create a genuine issue for trial."[74]

3. AFTER *MATSUSHITA* The *Matsushita* Court went far toward adopting the McGee-Bork-Easterbrook conviction that any danger a rule against price-cutting may remedy is far outweighed by the danger such a rule poses to price competition. In articulating the summary judgment standard in *Matsushita* to include consideration of the "plausibility" of a claim, and then asserting so forcefully on a theoretical level the implausibility of any predatory pricing scheme, the decision appears to provide a broad basis for lower courts virtually to write predatory pricing out of the law.

Most of the Court's analysis of the irrationality of predation is broad enough to apply to all predatory pricing claims, as is the literature upon which the Court so heavily relies. Therefore, the same analysis that made an allegation of conspiracy to price predatorily "implausible" in *Matsushita* could be used to nullify an inference of "predatory" or "anticompetitive" intent from evidence of price-cutting in single-firm predator cases. The "no rule" adherents advocate removing price-cutting entirely as an element of antitrust offenses; after *Matsushita*, the lower courts have a firm basis for carrying out that wish, and for doing so at the summary judgment stage.

It remains to be seen to what extent the courts will rely upon *Matsushita* as authority for discarding predatory pricing claims directed at single-firm behavior. While the Supreme Court has declined to foreclose all predatory pricing theories,[75] its decision

---

[73]   *Id.* at 597.

[74]   *Id.* (citation omitted).

[75]   In Cargill, Inc. v. Montfort of Colorado, Inc., 479 U.S. 104, 107 S. Ct. 484 (1986), the Court continued its assault on predatory pricing;

in *Matsushita* can only have the effect of deterring predatory pricing litigation and further insulating price cutting from the reaches of antitrust law. Plaintiffs alleging predatory pricing already face significant hurdles in attempting to meet the demands of Areeda-Turner and its variants. After *Matsushita*, their future looks yet dimmer.

B. Nonprice vertical restraints

The change in the law here has been nothing short of cataclysmic. In *United States v. Arnold, Schwinn & Co.*,[76] the Court addressed the issue of vertically imposed nonprice restraints. In that case a manufacturer had forbidden its distributors and franchised dealers from selling outside their assigned territories. The Court found such restrictions to be per se illegal, and announced that resellers may sell wherever they choose to do so: "it is unreasonable without more for a manufacturer to restrict and confine areas or persons with which an article may be traded after the manufacturer has parted with dominion over it."[77]

---

this time in the merger context. Holding plaintiff's failure to adequately allege and prove price predation was fatal to its claim of antitrust injury, the Court denied plaintiff standing under § 16 of the Clayton Act, 15 U.S.C. § 26, to enjoin a merger of two of its rivals. 107 S. Ct. at 495. Significantly, the Court declined an invitation by the United States to adopt a per se rule "denying competitors standing to challenge acquisitions on the basis of predatory pricing theories" based on the McGee-Bork-Easterbrook reasoning. The Court made clear that "predatory pricing is an anticompetitive practice forbidden by the antitrust laws. While firms may engage in the practice only infrequently, there is ample evidence suggesting that the practice does occur." *Id*. Finally, as if to signal that the gateway to predatory pricing claims will remain slightly ajar, the Court said, "nothing in the language or legislative history of the Clayton Act suggests that Congress intended this Court to ignore injuries caused by such anticompetitive practices as predatory pricing." *Id*. See discussion *infra* at notes 211–22 and accompanying text.

[76]   388 U.S. 365 (1967).

[77]   *Id*. at 379. Three aspects of the decision are particularly interesting. First, the Court had only 4 years earlier addressed a similar

The per se rule of *Schwinn* was expressly overruled some 10 years later in *Continental T.V., Inc. v. GTE-Sylvania, Inc.*[78] Try as the Court might—and as the Ninth Circuit did, the Court was "unable to find a principled basis for distinguishing Schwinn."[79] In the Court's words, "we conclude that the *per se* rule stated in *Schwinn* must be overruled."[80]

As with price predation, the influence of academic scholarship was featured prominently. Justice Powell's opinion is literally filled with citations to the antitrust economics literature.[81] Professor Posner's work is cited with approval several times. Indeed, the opinion contains a discussion of the economic effects of vertical restraints.

> Vertical restrictions promote interbrand competition by allowing the manufacturer to achieve certain efficiencies in the distribution of his products. These "redeeming virtues" are implicit in every decision

---

question in White Motor Co. v. United States, 372 U.S. 253 (1963). There the trial court had found the territorial restrictions to be per se violations, and the Supreme Court reversed remanding for a rule of reason analysis. The Court reasoned that it knew too little of the actual impact of such restrictions to judge them illegal per se. Obviously, the period 1963-67 must have been a period of learning!

Second, the Court distinguished between such restrictions where Schwinn had imparted title to its customers from those where it had entered into consignment arrangements with resellers and retained title. The former were proscribed as per se illegal, while the latter were to be judged under the rule of reason.

Third, the "without more" language quoted above gave rise to considerable debate and speculation. Could the Court have meant that additional factors would remove the conduct in question from the per se category? The lower courts were divided with some applying a per se rule to territorial and customer restrictions, while others declined to apply a per se rule where other factors distinguished the cases before them from *Schwinn*. *See* ABA, Antitrust Law Developments, 68-69 & nn.464, 465 (2d ed. 1984); S.C. Oppenheim, G.E. Weston, & J.T. McCarthy, Federal Antitrust Laws 599-601 (4th ed. 1981).

[78]   433 U.S. 36 (1977).

[79]   *Id.* at 46.

[80]   *Id.* at 58.

[81]   *Id.* at 48 n.13, 51 n.18.

sustaining vertical restrictions under the rule of reason. . . . [N]ew manufacturers and manufacturers entering new markets can use the restrictions in order to induce competent and aggressive retailers to make the kind of investment of capital and labor that is often required in the distribution of products unknown to the consumer. Established manufacturers can use them to induce retailers to engage in promotional activities or to provide service and repair facilities necessary to the efficient marketing of their products. . . . The availability and quality of such services affect a manufacturer's good will and the competitiveness of his product. Because of market imperfections such as the so-called "free rider" effect, these services might not be provided by retailers in a purely competitive situation, despite the fact that each retailer's benefit would be greater if all provided the services than if none did.

The Court also noted that " '[g]enerally a manufacturer would prefer the lowest retail price possible, once its price to dealers has been set, because a lower retail price means increased sales and higher manufacturer revenues.' "[82] Furthermore, "a manufacturer is likely to view the difference between the price at which it sells to its retailers and their price to the consumer as his 'cost of distribution,' which it would prefer to minimize."[83] Indeed, the Court was sufficiently confident of its conclusion that it critiqued those who took a different view. In response to Professor Commanor's argument that the promotional activities encouraged by vertical restraints resulted in increased product differentiation and therefore less interbrand competition, the Court observed:

> This argument is flawed by its necessary assumption that a large part of the promotional efforts resulting from vertical restrictions will not convey socially desirable information about product availability, price, quality, and services. Nor is it clear that a *per se* rule would result in anything more than a shift to less efficient methods of obtaining the same promotional effects.[84]

Thus, the Court reversed its earlier application of the per se rule to vertical nonprice restrictions. The rule of reason would

---

[82] *Id.* at 56 n.24, *citing* Note, 88 HARV. L. REV. 635, 641 (1975).

[83] *Id.* at 56 n.24, *citing* R. POSNER, *supra* note 4.

[84] *Id.* at 56.

henceforth govern.[85] In one case the Court made a very significant decision that virtually revolutionized antitrust law. And again the influence of the academy and the scholarly literature played a prominent role.[86]

C. Horizontal price restraints

Although less dramatic, the Court's decisions in *Broadcast Music, Inc. v. Columbia Broadcasting Sys., Inc.*[87] and *NCAA v. Board of Regents of Univ. of Okla.*[88] herald very significant changes in antitrust analysis. Generations of lawyers have cited

---

[85] Having treated nonprice restrictions, what of their sister—vertically imposed restrictions on pricing? Although the majority in *Sylvania* almost ignored the issue, Justice White, concurring, did not. Citing Professor Posner on several occasions, Justice White observed that there was no principled distinction between price and nonprice restrictions. In his words: "The effect, if not the intention, of the Court's opinion is necessarily to call into question the firmly established *per se* rule against price restraints." 433 U.S. at 70.

In the wake of *GTE-Sylvania*, the courts of appeals rendered conflicting decisions "regarding the proper dividing line between the rule that vertical price restraints are illegal *per se* and the rule that vertical nonprice restraints are to be judged under the rule of reason." Business Electronics Corp. v. Sharp Electronics Corp., 108 S.Ct. 1515, 1517 & n.1 (1988). The Supreme Court resolved the conflict in *Sharp*, holding "a vertical restraint is not illegal *per se* unless it includes some agreement on price or price levels." *Id.* at 1525. *See infra* at notes 315-34.

[86] Two commentators have noted that since the Supreme Court's decision in *GTE-Sylvania*, almost every circuit has held that market power is an essential element of the plaintiff's vertical nonprice case. *See* Popofsky & Goodwin, *The Hard-Boiled Rule of Reason Revisited*, 56 ANTITRUST L.J. 195 (1987). This is consistent with the analysis proposed by Professor Easterbrook in *Vertical Arrangements and the Rule of Reason*, 53 ANTITRUST L.J. 135, 153 (1984). There and elsewhere Easterbrook has urged that market power is a necessary screen that ought be employed in all antitrust cases.

[87] 441 U.S. 1 (1979).

[88] 468 U.S. 85 (1984).

United States v. Socony-Vacuum Oil Co.[89] for the proposition that a combination that has "the effect of raising, depressing, fixing, pegging, or stabilizing the price of a commodity . . . is illegal per se."[90]

In *BMI*[91] the Court remanded for rule of reason analysis an agreement among a group of composers to issue a blanket license to CBS to perform the composers' songs. The Court concluded that a pricing arrangement that is essential to a legitimate purpose is not within the per se rule. In doing so the Court observed that the arrangement at bar increased the availability of the compositions and therefore served a legitimate purpose in the marketplace. Most noteworthy were the Court's instructions as to how courts should determine whether to apply rule of reason or per se analysis: A court should analyze whether the practices before it "facially . . . tend to restrict competition and decrease output . . . or instead are designed to increase economic efficiency and render markets more, rather than less, competitive."[92]

In *NCAA*[93] the Court refused to apply the per se rule to allegations that the NCAA had fixed prices for telecasts of collegiate football games and that the exclusive network contracts were tantamount to a group boycott of all other broadcasters. The Court stated that although the use of exclusive contracts to limit the number of televised games constituted horizontal price-fixing and limits on output, it would be inappropriate to apply the per se rule to "an industry in which horizontal restraints on competition are essential if the product is to be available at all."[94] Nevertheless, the Court, after a rule of reason analysis, concluded that the arrangements were an unreasonable restraint on competition.

---

89   310 U.S. 150 (1940).

90   *Id.* at 223.

91   441 U.S. 1 (1979).

92   *Id.* at 19 (emphasis added).

93   468 U.S. 85 (1984).

94   *Id.* at 101.

Several points flow from the Court's pronouncements. First, the Court expressly stated that there is often no bright line that separates per se from rule of reason analysis,[95] thus destroying another taxonomy that characterized the outlines of many casebooks. Second, the Court went on to say that the essential inquiry under both is the same, *i.e.*, "whether or not the challenged restraint enhances competition."[96] Thus the Court has explicitly recognized the breakdown of the tidy rules that at least superficially characterized much of the traditional wisdom.

There are perhaps, four ways to view the *NCAA* and *BMI* decisions. First, one may assert that the cases are sui generis and really not that important. The facts were quite complicated, and bore no reasonable resemblance to garden-variety horizontal restraints. A second, and polar opposite, approach is to say that the decisions herald a new rule of reason: A truncated or "quick look" rule of reason. A third view is that these cases stand for the very simple proposition that rule of reason analysis is appropriate in cases where a desired good or service could not be produced absent the restraint. Yet another approach is to say that the cases simply rehash—in more glorified dress—the law of ancillary restraints. Old wine in new bottles; nothing more.

The first approach is clearly wrong. The recent case law clearly demonstrates that *NCAA* and *BMI* problems are hardly unique. The second, third and fourth approaches may be variations on the same theme. One important—perhaps the most important—result of the cases is that the utility of the conventional labelling exercise has been called into question.

A good example of the conventional wisdom antedating *NCAA* is the Seventh Circuit's 1982 decision in *Marrese v. American Academy of Orthopaedic Surgeons*[97] where the Seventh

---

[95]   *Id*. at 104 n.26.

[96]   *Id*. at 104.

[97]   692 F.2d 1083 (7th Cir. 1982), *vacated on other grounds*, 1982-83 Trade Cas. (CCH) ¶ 65,214 (7th Cir.), *opinion replaced*, 706 F.2d 1488 (7th Cir. 1983), *on rehearing*, 726 F.2d 1150 (7th Cir. 1984), *rev'd*, 470 U.S. 373 (1985).

Circuit, per Judge Posner, stated that the "great watershed of the [antitrust] law is the distinction between *per se* illegality and illegality under the Rule of Reason."[98] Yet, as Professor Timothy J. Muris has observed:

> Litigants and courts have taken positions that distort *both* ends of this dichotomy—saying that conduct must be condemned automatically, without regard for any redeeming competitive virtues, if it can be categorized as falling into a *per se* category; while conduct falling into the residual rule of reason category cannot be condemned at all until all aspects of its marketplace context are examined (including market definition, market power, intent, and net competitive effect).[99]

The result of all this, Muris reminds us, is: "plaintiffs hoping to win quickly through application of the *per se* epithet, and defendants hoping to wear down (or scare away) the opposition with the rigors of an elaborate rule of reason analysis."[100]

Importantly, the Court has reminded us that the essential quality of both per se and rule of reason analysis is the same—does the challenged restraint enhance competition or restrict output. In *BMI* the Court explained that the inquiry focuses on two questions. First, "whether the practice facially appears to be one that would always or almost always tend to restrict competition and decrease output."[101] Second, and in the alternative, the Court asked whether the practice is "instead designed to 'increase economic efficiency and render markets more, rather than less, competitive'?"[102] Thus, the neat simple outline, under which

---

98   692 F.2d at 1093.

99   T. J. Muris, Bureau of Competition's Approach to Applying the Rule of Reason 3 (unpublished manuscript) (emphasis in original).

100   *Id.* at 4. Professor Muris has characterized the "neat simple outline approach," referred to above, as "long on labels and short on both analysis and flexibility." *Id.* at 5.

101   441 U.S. at 19-20, *quoting* United States v. United States Gypsum Co., 438 U.S. 422, 436 n.13 (1978).

102   441 U.S. at 20.

conduct, such as price-fixing or tie-ins, is placed under either a per se or rule of reason heading which such dictates the result, is outmoded—if it ever had vitality.

Recently, the Federal Trade Commission has had occasion to apply the *NCAA/BMI* reasoning in the *Massachusetts Board of Registration in Optometry* case.[103] There the Commission found that the state regulatory board had violated section 5 of the Federal Trade Commission Act[104] by restricting the ability of optometrists to engage in commercial practices. While the case posed a good number of interesting and novel issues, the Commission used the decision to apply the teachings of the *BMI/NCAA* decisions to the case at bar. The Commission's analysis borrowed liberally from Professor Muris's work.

The Commission first inquired whether the restraint in question was "inherently suspect";[105] that is, whether the "practice is the kind that appears likely, absent an efficiency justification, to 'restrict competition and decrease output'?"[106] This question determines "whether defendants must come forward with a procompetitive explanation for their conduct to avoid summary condemnation, or whether the plaintiff must instead present a theory of competitive harm and proof of the defendants' market power to avoid losing the case."[107] If the conduct is not inherently suspect, then it is analyzed under the conventional rule of reason with the attendant market definition, power assessment, etc.[108] If it is inherently suspect, then the court (or the Commission, as the case may be) proceeds to pose a second question: "Is there a

---

[103]   5 Trade Reg. Rep. (CCH) ¶ 22,555 (1988).

[104]   15 U.S.C. § 15 (1982).

[105]   Naked horizontal price fixing and market allocation are examples of inherently suspect behavior.

[106]   5 Trade Reg. Rep. (CCH) ¶ 22,555, at p. 22,243.

[107]   T.J. Muris, *supra* note 99.

[108]   5 Trade Reg. Rep. (CCH) ¶ 22,555, at p. 22,243.

plausible efficiency justification for the practice?"[109] If the efficiency justification appears plausible,[110] further inquiry is needed to determine whether the justification is really valid. However, if there is no plausible efficiency, the inherently suspect conduct is per se unlawful.[111] There are simply no likely benefits to offset its inherent threat to consumer welfare. If the efficiency is valid, the practice must then be assessed under the full-blown rule of reason.[112] If invalid, the practice is unreasonable and unlawful under the rule of reason without further inquiry.[113]

---

[109]   To determine whether an efficiency justification exists the Commission asks whether the practice seems capable of creating or enhancing competition (*e.g.*, by reducing the costs of producing or marketing the product, creating a new product, or improving the operation of the market). *Id. See also* T.J. Muris, *supra* note 99.

It might be anticipated that participants in "naked" price fixing agreements might be able to establish a plausible efficiency sufficient to avoid per se treatment by asserting that their agreement eliminated the transaction costs associated with negotiating individual sales, etc. The Supreme Court rejected this sort of claim in Catalano, Inc. v. Target Sales, Inc., 446 U.S. 643, 649 (1980), and Arizona v. Maricopa County Medical Soc'y, 457 U.S. 332, 353-54 (1982). *See also* T.J. Muris, *supra* note 99.

[110]   An efficiency justification is plausible "if it cannot be rejected without extensive factual inquiry." 5 Trade Reg. Rep. (CCH) ¶ 22,555, at p. 22,243.

[111]   *Id*.

[112]   *Id*.

[113]   *Id*. Application of this mode of analysis is easier to follow in the context of a hypothetical case. Suppose a local hardware dealer and 15 of its competitors—all small independently owned hardware stores in the same geographic market—met last month in a hotel suite and agreed to fix the price of a standard shovel that they will all sell next spring. The dealers believe their conduct was reasonable.

Utilizing a labelling approach, *i.e.*, price-fixing by competitors is illegal per se, the reasonableness of the conduct is irrelevant; but under the approach set forth above, the dealers may be able to prove the plausibility and validity of an efficiency.

(*footnote 113 continued*)

The *Massachusetts Board of Registration in Optometry* case provides a road map of the Commission's view of the state of the law of horizontal restraints. More importantly, *NCAA* and *BMI* reveal the poverty of the dated rhetoric of Socony-Vacuum and similar cases.

D. The duality requirement

It is axiomatic that § 1 of the Sherman Act does not proscribe unilateral conduct.[114] There have been two important developments—one substantive and the other procedural—that have circumscribed the universe of impermissible conduct. First, the Court has rejected the availability of "bathtub" conspiracies.[115] In *Copperweld Corp. v. Independence Tube Corp.*,[116] the Court held that "the coordinated activity of a parent and its wholly owned subsidiary must be viewed as that of a single enterprise for purposes of § 1 of the Sherman Act."[117] The Court reasoned that a "parent and a wholly owned subsidiary *always*

Suppose the dealer and its competitors wanted to jointly purchase some advertising in a major newspaper that would be too expensive for each of them individually. They needed to fix the price of the shovel, so that they could advertise the shovel as being on sale at any of their convenient locations on Saturdays throughout the summer for the same low price.

By demonstrating that absent the agreement on price none of the hardware stores could have advertised the sale in a medium as effective as the newspaper, the dealers may be able to show that output may be enhanced and escape liability.

[114]   15 U.S.C. § 1 (1982).

[115]   "Bathtub conspiracies" are "conspiracies" between parents and wholly owned subsidiaries or between wholly owned subsidiaries themselves.

[116]   467 U.S. 752 (1984).

[117]   *Id.* at 771. Prior to *Copperweld* a good number of courts held that separate incorporation did not preclude commonly owned business entities from conspiring with one another. For a collection of cases so holding, see ABA, ANTITRUST LAW DEVELOPMENTS 11-14 (2d ed. 1984).

have a 'unity of purpose or a common design,' "[118] so that an "agreement" between such entities involves "no sudden joining of economic resources that had previously served different interests . . . ."[119] Thus, *Copperweld* effectively restricts the reach of the antitrust laws by denominating a class of agreements which, as a matter of law, do not satisfy the duality requirement.[120]

While repudiating application of the so-called intraenterprise conspiracy doctrine[121] to parents and their wholly owned subsidiaries, the Court expressly reserved the question of "under what circumstances, if any, a parent may be liable for conspiring with an affiliated corporation it does not completely own."[122] In the wake of *Copperweld*, most courts have followed the lead of the Department of Justice[123] in holding that a parent that controls a subsidiary corporation by virtue of a majority stock interest therein cannot be liable under § 1 for conspiring with such an

---

[118] 467 U.S. at 771 (emphasis in original).

[119] *Id.* The Court also referred to the well-settled rule that "coordinated conduct of a corporation and one of its unincorporated divisions" cannot constitute the requisite duality under § 1. *Id.* at 770. To hold that the same conduct can give rise to liability because a business, for reasons wholly unrelated to competitive effects, chose to separately incorporate a division as a wholly owned subsidiary, is to "look to the form . . . and ignores the reality." *Id.* at 772.

[120] The Court paid homage to the avalanche of academic criticism that paved the way for *Copperweld*. *See* 467 U.S. at 766 n.12.

[121] The intraenterprise conspiracy doctrine "provides that § 1 liability is not foreclosed merely because a parent and its subsidiary are subject to common ownership." 467 U.S. at 759. Although the doctrine tends to be defined in terms of § 1 of the Sherman Act, the debate surrounding it may be relevant in the § 2 context as well. Indeed, the original complaint in *Copperweld* included a count under § 2 that was dismissed before trial. Nevertheless, the reasoning of the Supreme Court would likely preclude any conspiracy to monopolize claims premised on the coordinated activities of parents and wholly owned subsidiaries.

[122] *Id.* at 467.

[123] Brief for the United States as Amicus Curiae at 21 n.31. *See* Copperweld Corp. v. Independence Tube Corp., 467 U.S. at 766.

entity.[124] The question remains open, however, as to whether common ownership will preclude a finding of conspiracy between subsidiaries of the same parent.[125]

Once again the courts have by judicial construction reduced the number of possible antitrust cases. And again the result is consistent with economic analysis. The "bathtub conspiracy" of yesteryear is but a remnant of antitrust history.

Second, and perhaps more importantly, the Court has dramatically curtailed the ability of plaintiffs in vertical restraint cases to establish a cognizable contract, combination or conspiracy. Prior to the Court's decision in *Monsanto Co. v. Spray-Rite Service Corp.*,[126] many commentators questioned the continued vitality of the *Colgate*[127] doctrine, which held that a manufacturer may announce a resale price maintenance [RPM] policy and thereafter refuse to deal with retailers who fail to comply with that policy. The courts of appeal were divided over the showing a terminated dealer must make in order to establish the existence of an agreement to maintain resale prices.[128] Indeed, in *Russell*

---

[124] *Compare* Computer Identics Corp. v. Southern Pac. Co., 756 F.2d 200, 205 (1st Cir. 1985) (51% ownership renders coordinated conduct outside proscription of § 1) *with* Sonitrol of Fresno, Inc. v. Amer. Tel. & Tel. Co., 1986-1 Trade Cas. (CCH) § 67,080, at 62,566–67 (D.D.C. 1986) (ownership interests of 23.9% and 32.6% respectively in affiliated corporations insufficient to create "unity of purpose or common design" as to insulate agreements between parent and affiliates from § 1 liability). For additional annotations of cases interpreting *Copperweld*, *see* ABA, ANTITRUST LAW DEVELOPMENTS I-17 n.91m (2d ed., Supp. 1988).

[125] For a compendium of the cases, *see* ABA, ANTITRUST LAW DEVELOPMENTS I-17 n.91n, 91o & 91p (2d ed., Supp. 1988).

[126] 465 U.S. 752 (1984). For a discussion of the decision, *see* Calvani & Berg, *Resale Price Maintenance After Monsanto*, 1984 DUKE L.J. 1164, 1187–1204.

[127] United States v. Colgate & Co., 250 U.S. 300 (1919).

[128] *See* Monsanto v. Spray-Rite Service Corp., 465 U.S. at 752 & n.5. The theory of these cases is typically that the plaintiff-dealer was terminated in furtherance of a conspiracy between the manufacturer and

Stover Candies[129] the FTC brought what can only be described as a test case to confirm that little, if anything, remained of the *Colgate* doctrine.[130] On appeal, the Eighth Circuit reversed the Commission's finding of liability, holding that any pronouncement of the continued vitality of *Colgate* should be left to the Supreme Court.[131]

Less than 6 months later, the Supreme Court in *Monsanto* breathed new life into the *Colgate* doctrine.[132] Focusing on the importance and difficulty of distinguishing in dealer-termination cases between concerted action to set prices and concerted action on nonprice restraints (the former illegal per se while the latter subject to scrutiny under the rule of reason),[133] the Court cautioned that "[i]f an inference of such an [RPM] agreement may be drawn from highly ambiguous evidence, there is a considerable danger that the doctrines enunciated in *Sylvania* and *Colgate* will

---

other dealers to fix resale prices. The Seventh Circuit in *Monsanto*, for example, held that "an antitrust plaintiff can survive a motion for a directed verdict if it shows that a manufacturer terminated a price-cutting distributor in response to or following complaints by other distributors." *Id.* at 752. The court of appeals' opinion is reported at 684 F.2d 1226, 1238 (7th Cir. 1982).

[129] 100 F.T.C. 1 (1982). For a more detailed discussion of the case *see* Calvani & Berg, *supra* note 126, at nn.112–18 & accompanying text.

[130] The Commission, per Commissioner Pertchuck, held that while the mere announcement of a policy to terminate dealers that fail to comply with suggested resale prices, *standing alone*, does not *automatically* create an illicit combination, such a policy coupled with widespread dealer compliance with or without actual terminations "should be adequate to support an inference that there is unwilling compliance and, here, that there are agreements." *Id.* at 40–41. Chairman Miller dissented from the Commission majority.

[131] Russel Stover Candies, Inc. v. FTC, 718 F.2d 256 (8th Cir. 1983).

[132] "Under *Colgate* a manufacturer can announce its resale prices in advance and refuse to deal with those who fail to comply. And a distributor is free to acquiesce in the manufacturer's demand in order to avoid termination." 465 U.S. at 752.

[133] 465 U.S. at 761–63.

be seriously eroded."[134] Since manufacturers and dealers "have legitimate reasons to exchange information about the prices . . . of their products in the market,"[135] particularly where the manufacturer attempts to further a particular marketing strategy through nonprice restrictions, and since complaints about price-cutters by their rivals are unavoidable from the manufacturer's perspective,[136]

> Permitting an agreement to be inferred merely from the existence of complaints, or even from the fact that termination came about in response to complaints, could deter or penalize perfectly legitimate conduct.[137]

In rejecting the standard employed by the Seventh Circuit the Court held, "something more than evidence of complaints is needed."[138]

> The correct standard is that there must be evidence that tends to exclude the possibility of independent action by the manufacturer and distributor. That is, there must be direct or circumstantial evidence that reasonably tends to prove that the manufacturer and others had a conscious commitment to a common scheme designed to achieve an unlawful objective.[139]

Despite the Court's rhetoric, it affirmed the finding of liability against *Monsanto* on this new standard. The evidentiary basis of the Court's decision, however, has come under attack as being inconsistent with the tenor of the opinion.[140] Not surprisingly,

---

134   *Id.* at 763.

135   *Id.* at 762.

136   *Id.* at 763.

137   *Id.*

138   *Id.* at 764.

139   *Id.* at 768.

140   The criticism generally is threefold. First, the Court characterized as "plainly relevant and persuasive as to a meeting of the minds," 465 U.S. at 765, testimony by a Monsanto district manager that 5 months *after* Spray-Rite was terminated Monsanto approached *other* price-

lower courts struggled to find the balance between that which the Supreme Court said and that which it did in *Monsanto*.[141]

In *Matsushita Electric Industrial Co., Ltd. v. Zenith Radio Corporation*,[142] the Court expressly adopted the reasoning of *Monsanto* in the context of allegations of a horizontal conspiracy, holding that

> antitrust law limits the range of permissible inferences from ambiguous evidence in a § 1 case. . . . To survive a motion for summary judgment or for a directed verdict, a plaintiff . . . must present evidence that tends to exclude the possibility that the alleged conspirators acted independently.[143]

Thus, while *Monsanto* spawned a procedural vehicle by which courts may, should they choose to, permit defendants to escape trial in all but the most egregious cases under § 1, *Copperweld* effected a substantive limitation on the universe of cognizable antitrust claims.

---

cutting distributors and their parent entities and threatened to retaliate against them if they did not adhere to suggested retail prices. Second, the Court referred to an "arguably more ambiguous" newsletter prepared by a distributor reporting on a meeting with Monsanto officials 4 weeks before the Spray-Rite cut off which discussed Monsanto's efforts to "ge[t] the market place in order" and "maintain a minimum market price level." *Id.* at 766. The third criticism leveled against the decision is that the Court stretched to find circumstantial evidence of a causal link between the inferred agreement and Spray-Rite's termination, and may have effectively read a causation requirement out of the prima facie case by holding "it would be reasonable to find [the termination of Spray-Rite was pursuant to an RPM agreement], since it is necessary for competing distributors to know that those who do not comply will be terminated." *Id.* at 767. For a more detailed critique of the Court's evaluation of the evidence in *Monsanto*, see Calvani & Berg, *supra* note 126, at 1195-97.

[141]   Lower court cases interpreting *Monsanto* are compiled at ABA, ANTITRUST LAW DEVELOPMENTS I-10 to I-12 & n.48g, 48h (2d ed., Supp. 1988).

[142]   475 U.S. 574 (1986).

[143]   *Id.* at 588.

E. The Poller *doctrine*[144]

Rule 56 of the Federal Rules of Civil Procedure provides in essence that a court may grant summary judgment if there is no genuine issue of material fact and the moving party is entitled to judgment as a matter of law.[145] In its 1962 decision in *Poller v. CBS*,[146] the Court reversed the trial court's grant of defendant's motion for summary judgment. In doing so Justice Clark, writing for the Court, used language that was to haunt lower courts for years: "summary procedures should be used sparingly in complex antitrust litigation."[147] The Court reasoned that

> motive and intent play leading roles, the proof is largely in the hands of the alleged conspirators, and hostile witnesses thicken the plot. It is only when the witnesses are present and subject to cross-examination that their credibility and the weight to be given their testimony can be appraised.[148]

As a result of the Court's choice of language, many came to regard summary judgment as virtually unavailable in antitrust proceedings.[149]

---

[144] For a recent, quality discussion of the use of summary judgment in an antitrust context, *see* Calkins, *Summary Judgment, Motions to Dismiss, Other Examples of Equilibrating Tendencies in the Antitrust System*, 74 Geo. L. J. 1065, 1104–39 (1986), and Schwarzer, *Summary Judgment and Case Management*, 56 Antitrust L.J. 213, 215 (1987).

[145] Fed. R. Civ. P. 56.

[146] 368 U.S. 464 (1962).

[147] *Id.* at 473.

[148] *Id.*

[149] *See* Calkins, *supra* note 144, at 1120 for a discussion of commentators who held this view. For a collection of cases citing *Poller* as authority in denying motions for summary judgment, *see* Silverman, *Summary Judgment in Antitrust Litigation* in 2 PLI, 27th Annual Antitrust Law Institute 245 (1986).

Of course the Court's language in *Poller* may be read differently. One may persuasively argue that the Court was addressing the use of

Then in 1968, the Court seemed to backtrack when it declined to embrace the plaintiff's argument that "Rule 56(e) should, in effect, be read out of antitrust cases" in *First Nat'l Bank of Arizona v. Cities Serv. Co.*[150] The Court's language there became a common weapon in defense counsel's sparse arsenal to obtain summary judgments.

But most importantly, the Court recently in *Matsushita Electric Industrial Co. Ltd. v. Zenith Radio Corp.*[151] had occasion to consider the use of summary judgment in an antitrust context. Recall that plaintiffs, domestic manufacturers of electronic products, had alleged that Japanese competitors had violated the federal antitrust laws by conspiring to sell their products in the United States below cost.[152] Most importantly the Court held that where plaintiff's evidence may be properly interpreted in accord with either a legal or an illegal scheme, it was insufficient as a matter of law to thwart defendant's motion for summary judgment. The Court placed considerable reliance on its earlier decision in *Monsanto Co. v. Spray-Rite Service Corp.*[153] There the Court had held that a jury could not be permitted to find the existence of a price-fixing conspiracy on the basis of a dealer termination that followed the manufacturer's receipt of complaints from other dealers of price cutting by the terminated dealer. Rather, there must be evidence tending to exclude the possibility that the manufacturer had acted independently.

Of course, these developments cannot be considered in isolation and must be analyzed in the context of other summary

---

summary procedures in cases where "motive and intent play leading roles," that is, where they are important unsolved issues of material fact. *See* 2 P. AREEDA & D. TURNER, ANTITRUST LAW ¶ 3166 at 62 (1978). Obviously, summary procedures are inappropriate in cases where "motive & intent play leading roles."

[150]   391 U.S. 253, 289 (1968).

[151]   475 U.S. 574 (1986).

[152]   For a discussion of the case, see *supra* notes 45–74 and accompanying text.

[153]   465 U.S. 752 (1984).

judgment decisions.[154] Nonetheless, it is clear that lower courts need no longer be hampered by the rhetoric of the *Poller* doctrine.[155] Indeed, an influential panel of the Seventh Circuit in *Collins v. Associated Pathologists, Ltd.,*[156] recently referred to *Matsushita* as one of a "trilogy of cases in which the Supreme Court made clear that, contrary to the emphasis of some prior precedent, the use of summary judgment is not only permitted but encouraged in certain circumstances, including antitrust cases."[157] The court read *Matsushita* as relying on "a seemingly new evidentiary standard for summary judgments"[158]—"whether sufficient evidence exists in the pre-trial record to allow the non-moving party to survive a motion for directed verdict."[159]

The *Poller* doctrine takes its place in antitrust history.[160]

---

[154] *See* Schwarzer, *supra* note 144.

[155] *See generally,* Schwarzer, *supra* note 144; Childress, *A New Era for Summary Judgments: Recent Shifts at the Supreme Court,* 116 F.R.D. 183 (1987).

[156] 1988-1 Trade Cas. (CCH) ¶ 67,971, at 57,951 (7th Cir. 1988) (JJ. Cummings, Coffey and Easterbrook).

[157] *Id.* The other two cases referred to by the *Collins* court were Celotex Corp. v. Carlett, 477 U.S. 317 and Anderson v. Liberty Lobby, Inc., 477 U.S. 242 (1986). For a discussion of those cases *see* Schwarzer, *supra* note 144, at 215–17.

[158] *Id.*

[159] *Id.* Richards v. Neilsen Freight Lines, 810 F.2d 898 (9th Cir. 1987), is an excellent example of the application of the new summary judgment principles by a lower court. *See* Schwarzer, *supra* note 144, from which this discussion borrows heavily. There the plaintiff was a local short-haul trucking company that delivered shipments provided it by defendant long-haul carriers. Plaintiff filed suit against defendants alleging that they had conspired to boycott him and other local carriers that had solicited back orders from their customers. There was testimony that one of defendants' chief executive officers had testified that there was a "gentlemen's agreement that we won't back solicit." 810 F.2d at 903; *see* Schwarzer, *supra* note 144, at 225. The trial court granted defendants' motion for summary judgment, and the court of

(footnote 159 continued; footnote 160 appears on following page)

F. Robinson-Patman Act

Three changes in the Robinson-Patman[161] case law merit attention. First, and perhaps most important, was the Court's clarification of the interstate commerce jurisdictional requirements of the Act. The interstate commerce requirements of Robinson-Patman are somewhat different from, and more narrow than, those of its sister antitrust laws.[162] While the jurisdiction of the Sherman Act[163] is coextensive with the commerce power of the United States Constitution, § 2(a) of the Robinson-Patman Act applies only to persons (1) "engaged in commerce," (2) who engage in otherwise proscribed discrimination "in the course of such commerce," (3) "where either or any of the purchases involved in such discrimination are in commerce."[164]

---

appeals affirmed. The courts reasoned that each defendant had a legitimate reason to terminate a local delivery concern that attempted to obtain its customers' back haul. More importantly, the court found that "there was no evidence from which a jury could find that it was more likely that the termination was the result of an unlawful conspiracy than of legitimate independent action." Schwarzer, *supra* note 144, at 225.

160   *See, e.g.,* Miller v. Indiana Hosp., 843 F.2d 139, 143 (3d Cir. 1988) ("The summary judgment standard is no different in antitrust litigation than in any other"). For a discussion of other recent cases upholding the use of summary judgment in antitrust contexts, *see* Schwarzer, *supra* note 144, at 222–28. *See also* Popofsky & Goodwin, *supra* note 86.

161   15 U.S.C. § 13 (1982).

162   Indeed one may argue that the Robinson-Patman Act has little in common with antitrust generally. While antitrust is concerned with the protection of competition, the Robinson-Patman Act seeks to protect some *from* competition. For a discussion of the legislative history of the statute and its protectionist mission, *see In re* General Motors Corp., 103 F.T.C. 691 (1984). Thus, it is not surprising that the Supreme Court has held § 3 of the Robinson-Putnam Act *not* to be an antitrust law within the meaning of § 4 of the Clayton Act. *See* Nashville Milk Co. v. Carnation Co., 355 U.S. 373 (1958).

163   15 U.S.C. § 1 et seq. (1982).

164   The three jurisdictional commerce requirements discussed in the text are contained only in § 2(a) of the Act. Sections 2(c) (the "dummy

In its 1954 opinion in *Moore v. Mead's Fine Bread Co.*,[165] the Court, per Justice Douglas, announced what came to be known as the "interstate treasury" theory.[166] Following *Mead's*, a num-

---

brokerage" provision) and 2(d) (the promotional services provision) contain only the first two jurisdictional requirements of § 2(a). Some courts have held that § 2(c) imposes lower interstate commerce jurisdictional requirements than § 2(a), *see, e.g.*, Rangen, Inc. v. Sterling Nelson & Sons, Inc., 351 F.2d 851, 860–61 (9th Cir. 1985), *cert. denied*, 383 U.S. 936 (1966); Thurman Indus., Inc. v. Pay 'N Pak, Inc., 1987-1 Trade Cas. (CCH) ¶ 67,591 (W.D. Wash. 1987); while others have held the requirements of 2(c) are similar to those of § 2(a), *see, e.g.*, Rohrer v. Sears, Roebuck & Co., 1975 Trade Cas. ¶ 60,352 (E.D. Mich. 1975). Most courts have held the commerce requirements of § 2(d) are more lax than those for § 2(a). *See, e.g.*, Shreveport Macaroni Mfg. Co. v. F.T.C., 321 F.2d 404, 408–09 (5th Cir. 1963), *cert. denied*, 375 U.S. 971 (1964), and cases cited at ABA, ANTITRUST LAW DEVELOPMENTS 221 n.19 (2d ed. 1984); *but see, contra* Zoslaw v. M.C.A. Distrib. Corp., 693 F.2d 870, 881 (9th Cir. 1982), *cert. denied*, 460 U.S. 1085 (1983). Although § 2(e) contains no reference to commerce, courts have read a commerce requirement into the provision similar to that of § 2(d). Under § 2(f), plaintiff must satisfy all of the jurisdictional prerequisites of § 2(a), and also demonstrate that defendant "engaged in commerce, in the course of such commerce," knowingly induced or received the unlawful discount. Thus, § 2(f) arguably contains greater jurisdictional hurdles than § 2(a), but at least one court has declined to give § 2(f) this expansive reading. Great Atl. & Pac. Tea Co. v. F.T.C., 557 F.2d 971, 979 (2d Cir. 1977), *rev'd on other grounds*, 440 U.S. 69 (1979). For a detailed discussion of the interstate commerce requirements of § 2(a), (c), (d), (e) and (f), *see* 3 E.W. KINTNER & J.P. BAUER, FEDERAL ANTITRUST LAW §§ 21.2–21.5, 27.4, 28.4 (1983).

[165]   348 U.S. 115 (1954).

[166]   In *Mead's Fine Bread*, defendant produced and sold bread in New Mexico in competition with the plaintiff-baker at a lower price than defendant sold like bread in Texas. Although the lower priced sales that caused the competitive injury were purely "intrastate," the Court held it sufficient that the higher priced sales were "in commerce" and that profits derived from them were used to finance the lower priced sales. The expansive reading of the case, and the "interstate treasury" label, are derived from dicta in the opinion that "the treasury used to finance the warfare is drawn from interstate, as well as local, sources. . . . If this method of competition were approved, the pattern for growth of monopoly would be simple. As long as the price warfare was strictly interstate, interstate business could grow and expand with

ber of courts held that the jurisdictional commerce requirement of the statute may be met (at least in primary line cases)[167] with evidence that profits from interstate sales underwrite the losses of local price-cutting.[168] Since the defendant in *Mead's* actually did make its higher priced sales in a different state than the lower priced sale, however, it is questionable whether the holding was as far-reaching as dicta in the opinion suggests.[169]

The Court rejected this "underwriting" or "interstate treasury" theory 20 years later in favor of the so-called state line approach in *Gulf Oil Co. v. Copp Paving Co.*[170] In *Copp*, defendant oil companies, producers of liquid asphalt for interstate highway construction, were alleged to have engaged in illegal price discrimination. Although the sales were intrastate, plaintiff, relying in part on *Mead's Fine Bread*, urged that the sales were in reality interstate because of the interstate nature of highway construction. In rejecting that argument, the Court also rejected the thesis that the interstate jurisdiction of Robinson-

---

impunity at the expense of local merchants. . . . Congress, as guardian of the Commerce Clause, certainly has power to say those advantages shall not attach to the privilege of doing an interstate business." 348 U.S. at 119–20.

[167] Primary line, or seller level injury, is that which occurs at the level of competitors of the discriminating seller. Geographic price discrimination is a common variety. Secondary line, or buyer level injury, relates to that injury which occurs at the level of competing purchasers from the discriminating seller.

[168] *See, e.g.*, Littlejohn v. Shell Oil Co., 456 F.2d 225, 227–29 (5th Cir. 1972), *rev'd en banc*, 483 F.2d 1140, 1143-45 (5th Cir.), *cert. denied*, 414 U.S. 1116 (1973).

[169] *See* E.W. KINTNER & J.P. BAUER, *supra* note 164, § 21.3 at 147–48; *see also* S.C. OPPENHEIM, G.E. WESTON, P.B. MAGGS & R.E. SCHECHTER, UNFAIR TRADE PRACTICES AND CONSUMER PROTECTION 772 (4th ed. 1983). *Mead's* is still cited for the proposition that it is sufficient if either the higher or lower priced sale being compared crosses state lines. S.C. OPPENHEIM, G.E. WESTON & J.T. MCCARTHY, *supra* note 77, at 745.

[170] 419 U.S. 186 (1974).

Patman was coextensive with that of the Sherman Act.[171] The Court reiterated that "at least one of the two transactions [must] cross a state line."[172] Thus, the "interstate treasury" theory was laid to rest.[173] In the process, the universe of possible Robinson-Patman Act claims was significantly curtailed.

Second, the Court in *J. Truett Payne Co. v. Chrysler Motors Corp.*[174] rejected the "automatic damages" rule[175] that had been adopted by several lower courts.[176] Thus a simple showing that the plaintiff was disfavored vis-à-vis a competing buyer is no longer sufficient to mandate the award of damages. Rather there must

---

[171] It is noteworthy that the Court did not expressly overrule *Mead's Fine Bread* in *Copp*. Rather, it distinguished *Mead's* as follows: "The Court [stated in *Mead's*] that Congress clearly has power to reach the local activities of a firm that finances its predatory practices through multi-state operations. This language, however, spoke to the commerce power rather than to jurisdiction under § 2(a). In fact, Mead's did have interstate sales and its price discrimination thus fell within the literal language of the statute." 400 U.S. at 200–201 n.17.

[172] 419 U.S. at 200.

[173] In the years since *Copp Paving*, most courts that have considered the question have followed its more stringent jurisdictional commerce requirements. *See, e.g*, William Inglis & Sons Baking Co. v. ITT Continental Baking Co., 668 F.2d 1014, 1043 (9th Cir. 1981); Delta Marina, Inc. v. Placquemine Oil Sales, Inc., 644 F.2d 455, 457 (5th Cir. 1981); McGoffin v. Sun Oil Co., 539 F.2d 1245, 1248 (10th Cir. 1976); Holleb & Co. v. Produce Terminal Cold Storage Co., 532 F.2d 29, 35 (7th Cir. 1976).

[174] 451 U.S. 557 (1981).

[175] Under the "automatic damages" rule, a plaintiff was entitled to recover the amount of the price discrimination without any necessary showing of actual injury.

[176] The leading case approving of "automatic damages" was Fowler Manufacturing Co. v. Gorlick, 415 F.2d 1248, 1252–53 (9th Cir. 1969), *cert. denied*, 396 U.S. 1012 (1970). *But see contra* Enterprise Industr., Inc. v. Texas Co., 240 F.2d 457 (2d Cir.), *cert. denied*, 353 U.S. 965 (1957). Additional cases are cited in J. Truett Payne Co. v. Chrysler Motors Corp., 451 U.S. at 561 n.557.

be a demonstrable nexus between the price discrimination and plaintiff's injury.[177]

Lastly, the Court addressed the meeting competition defense in *Falls City Industries, Inc. v. Vanco Beverage, Inc.*[178] There the seller charged all Indiana wholesalers a lower price than that charged to plaintiff, a Kentucky wholesaler that operated in the same geographic market as an Indiana wholesaler just over the Ohio river.[179] Plaintiff alleged that it was injured because the price differences were reflected in the retail prices charged to customers who came from Indiana to Kentucky to purchase beer, thereby reducing sales from plaintiff to Indiana retailers.[180] The district court rejected defendant's meeting competition defense on the ground that Falls City did not create the price difference by lowering its price to Kentucky wholesalers but by raising it to Indiana wholesalers more than it raised it to Kentucky wholesalers; thus, the higher Indiana price was not set in good faith.[181] The court held the defense was available only where the seller "adjusted prices on a customer to customer basis to meet competition from other brewers" rather than where prices are raised statewide "for the sole reason that it followed the other brewers . . . for its profit."[182] The court of appeals affirmed.

The Supreme Court used the case to expand the availability of the meeting competition defense on several fronts. First and

---

[177]   451 U.S. at 562 *quoting* Perkins v. Standard Oil Co., 395 U.S. 642, 648 (1969).

[178]   460 U.S. 428 (1983).

[179]   *Id.* at 432.

[180]   *Id.* at 433. Indiana law required Falls City to charge all Indiana wholesalers the same price. It also prohibited Indiana wholesalers from selling to out of state retailers, and Indiana retailers from purchasing from out of state wholesalers.

[181]   *Id.* at 434.

[182]   *Id.*

foremost, the Court resolved a conflict among the circuits[183] in holding that § 2(b) permits a seller to adopt reasonably well-tailored area-specific price differences in response to competitive conditions and does not require "customer by customer" responses.[184] Finding nothing in the legislative history requiring the narrower construction, the Court reasoned that where a seller has good reason to believe a competitor is charging lower prices throughout a region, customer-by-customer negotiations would not only be unlikely to yield different prices but may actually make "meaningful price competition unrealistically expensive for smaller firms. . . ."[185]

The Court also rejected the argument that the defense was unavailable because the price difference was achieved by raising, rather than lowering prices. While the defense requires that the "seller offer the lower price in good faith *for the purpose* of meeting the competitor's price,"[186] it does not require "a seller to *lower* its price in order to meet competition."[187] The Court dismissed the contention that the seller's good faith is impugned if the prices raised "respond to competitors' prices and are set with the goal of increasing the seller's profits."[188] Nothing in § 2(b) requires that a seller who in good faith meets a competitor's price to retain a customer must forego profits he may earn by raising prices to other customers. Finally, while § 2(b) must be asserted in a defensive manner, *i.e.*, the lower price must be

---

[183] The conflict arose from the various courts of appeals interpreting F.T.C. v. A.E. Staley Mfg. Co., 324 U.S. 746 (1945). For a survey of the positions of the circuits pre-*Falls City*, see Falls City Industries, Inc. v. Vanco Beverage, Inc., 460 U.S. at 447–48 n.14.

[184] *Id.* at 447–48, 450.

[185] *Id.* at 449.

[186] *Id.* at 439 (emphasis in original).

[187] *Id.* at 444 (emphasis in original). The court noted: "the seller is not required to show that the [price] difference resulted from subtraction rather than addition. . . . In a period of generally rising prices, vigorous price competition for a particular customer or customers may take the form of smaller price increases rather than price cuts." *Id.*

[188] *Id.* at 427.

calculated to "meet not beat" the competitor's price, the Court held it may be invoked to justify lower prices offered either to retain existing customers or to obtain new ones.[189]

Before concluding our discussion of the Act, it must be noted that the Court has gone to great lengths to reconcile the purposes of the price discrimination law with those of antitrust more generally. In *Great Atlantic & Pacific Tea Co. v. FTC*,[190] the Court admonished against interpretations of the Robinson-Patman Act which "extend beyond the prohibitions of the Act and, in so doing, help give rise to a price uniformity and rigidity in open conflict with the purposes of other antitrust legislation . . . ."[191] Similarly, in *United States v. United States Gypsum Co.*,[192] the use of interseller price verifications as a means of conforming with the good faith requirement of § 2(b) was rejected as a defense to criminal price-fixing charges. In short, the policy concerns underlying the Sherman Act are of paramount importance, and liberal interpretations of the price discrimination law that conflict with those policies will not be countenanced.

G. Standing

Recent years have seen a dramatic increase in the willingness of courts to invoke the doctrines of "antitrust standing" and "antitrust injury" to dismiss private antitrust claims. The effect of both doctrines is to limit the class of potential plaintiffs for antitrust violations, based on the nature of the relationship between the injury alleged and the violation asserted.[193] While academicians have argued that these doctrines are theoretically

---

[189]   *Id.*

[190]   440 U.S. 69 (1979).

[191]   *Id.* at 80 *quoting* American Canteen Co. of America v. FTC, 346 U.S. 61, 63 (1953).

[192]   438 U.S. 422 (1978).

[193]   *See* Page, *The Scope of Liability for Antitrust Violations*, 37 STAN. L. REV. 1445, 1447 (1985).

distinct,[194] many courts continue to treat antitrust injury as an element of antitrust standing.[195] This section examines the development of both these doctrines in the Supreme Court.

The statutory root of both antitrust standing and antitrust injury analysis in most private cases is § 4 of the Clayton Act which provides a treble-damages remedy to "any person who shall be injured in his business or property by reason of *anything*

---

[194] *See, e.g., id.*, at 1483–85. Professor Page argues that while the policy of "optimal deterrence" should underlie both doctrines, they are distinguishable by the nature of their respective inquiries. "Antitrust injury, by requiring a causal relationship between the plaintiff's harm and the inefficient aspect of a practice, gives a first approximation of one component of the optimal penalty and so avoids many of the costs of overdeterrence. Antitrust injury analysis alone, however, may lead to an inappropriately broad scope of liability because, for example, the sum of the individual harms caused by the anticompetitive aspect of the violation may clearly exceed the optimal penalty. In that event, standing analysis must confine recovery to a narrower group of plaintiffs. . . . In essence, then, the object of standing is to identify the most efficient plaintiff or plaintiffs from among those who have suffered antitrust injury." *Id.* at 1484.

He continues: "The relationship between the doctrines implies both that antitrust injury analysis must precede standing analysis, and that rules of standing should be formulated in terms of the practices and the forms of antitrust injury at issue." *Id.* at 1484–85.

[195] *See, e.g.,* Chrysler Corp. v. Fedders Corp., 643 F.2d 1229, 1234–35 (6th Cir.), *cert. denied*, 454 U.S. 893 (1981) (antitrust injury is the element which is added to traditional notions of standing to produce antitrust standing); F. Buddie Contracting, Inc. v. Seawright, 595 F. Supp. 422, 431 n.6 (N.D. Ohio 1984) (same); John Lenore & Co. v. Olympia Brewing Co., 550 F.2d 495 (9th Cir. 1977). For a discussion of decisions implicitly treating antitrust injury as an element of standing, *see, e.g.,* Page, *Antitrust Damages and Economic Efficiency; an Approach to Antitrust Injury*, 47 U. CHI. L. REV. 467, 497–500 (1980).

Although the Supreme Court cited Professor Page for his distinction between antitrust injury and antitrust standing, the Court speaks of the distinction in confusing terms, noting: "*A showing of antitrust injury is necessary*, but not always sufficient, *to establish standing under § 4*, because a party may have suffered antitrust injury but may not be a proper plaintiff under § 4 for other reasons." (Emphasis added.)

forbidden in the antitrust laws."[196] The concept of antitrust injury was first announced by the Supreme Court in *Brunswick Corporation v. Pueblo Bowl-O-Mat, Inc.*[197] Respondent Pueblo alleged that Brunswick violated § 7 of the Clayton Act by acquiring certain failing bowling centers in markets in which respondent operated. Pueblo sought damages in the amount of three-fold the profits it claimed it would have earned had the acquired bowling centers gone out of business. The Court rejected this proof, noting that its essence was that the acquisitions "depriv[ed] respondents of the benefits of increased concentration. The damages respondents obtained are designed to provide them with the profits they would have realized had competition been reduced."[198] Thus, the Court held "that for plaintiffs to recover treble damages on account of § 7 violations, they must prove more than injury causally linked to an illegal presence in the market. Plaintiffs must prove antitrust injury, which is to say

---

[196]   15 U.S.C. § 15 (1982) (emphasis added).

[197]   429 U.S. 477 (1977). Prior to *Brunswick*, the Supreme Court recognized that not all injuries that flow from antitrust violations are compensable to every plaintiff under § 4. In Hawaii v. Standard Oil Co., 405 U.S. 251 (1972), for example, the Court held that while a state is "a person" under § 4 whether it sues in its proprietary capacity or as parens patriae, it may not recover treble damages for injury to its "general economy" allegedly attributable to violations of the antitrust laws. Noting that much of this injury to the general economy is essentially a reflection of injuries to the "business or property" of consumers, for which they may recover themselves, the Court reasoned "Even the most lengthy and expensive trial could not . . . cope with the problems of double recovery inherent in allowing damages for harm both to the economic interests of individuals and for the quasi-sovereign interests of the State." *Id.* at 264.

[198]   429 U.S. at 488. The Court questioned whether "the loss of windfall profits that would have accrued had the acquired centers failed even constitutes 'injury' within the meaning of § 4," *id.* at 487, and observed that "[r]espondents would have suffered the identical 'loss'— but no compensable injury—had the acquired centers instead obtained refinancing or been purchased by 'shallow pocket' parents." *Id.*

injury of the type the antitrust laws were intended to prevent and that flows from that which makes defendants' acts unlawful.''[199]

---

[199] *Id.* at 489. Remarkably, the *Brunswick* decision made no reference to the doctrine of "standing." Lower courts had long limited the universe of potential plaintiffs under § 4 by using a variety of formulations under the rubric of antitrust standing. *See* ABA, ANTITRUST LAW DEVELOPMENTS 395-99 (2d ed. 1984) & (2d Suppl. 1983-1988 VII-10-VII-13 (1988)). It was 5 years before the Court explicitly addressed the issue for the first time in Blue Shield of Virginia v. McCready, 457 U.S. 465 (1982). There it was held that a subscriber of a prepaid group health plan had standing to sue the plan and a psychiatric society for an alleged conspiracy to exclude clinical psychologists from receiving insurance reimbursements for "psychotherapy" services covered by the plan. Although it eschewed choosing from among the various standing formulations adopted in the lower courts, the Court specifically rejected defendant's arguments that the facts of the case warranted denial of standing based on those previous decisions.

Specifically, the Court rejected arguments that a finding of standing would expose defendant to the risk of duplicative recovery and that damages would be difficult to calculate as in Hawaii v. Standard Oil Co., 405 U.S. 251 (1972) and Illinois Brick Co. v. Illinois, 431 U.S. 720 (1977) (indirect purchasers generally barred from recovering treble damages); that McCready's injury was too "fortuitous," "incidental" or "remote," holding instead that her harm "was clearly foreseeable" and "a necessary step in effecting the ends of the alleged illegal conspiracy," 457 U.S. at 478; and that plaintiff was not an "economic actor" in the market that was restrained, stating that "as a consumer of psychotherapy services entitled to financial benefits under the [defendant's plan]," plaintiff was "within that area of the economy . . . endangered by [that] breakdown of competitive conditions." *Id.* at 48.

The *McCready* Court recognized that antitrust injury "as analyzed in *Brunswick*, is one factor to be considered in determining the redressability of a particular form of injury under § 4," 457 U.S. at 483 n.19. The Court found subscribers of the Blue Shield plan faced a "Hobson's choice"—forego the practitioner of their preference and receive reimbursement under the plan, or see the practitioner of their choice and forego reimbursement. In the latter case, the Court found that foregoing reimbursement and thereby incurring higher net cost for a psychologist's services would constitute direct antitrust injury to the subscribers. *Id.* at 483. In the former, injury in the first instance would be borne by competitors of the conspirators, "and inevitably—though indirectly— by the customers of the competitors." *Id.* at 483. Either way, the Court held plaintiff's injury " 'flows from that which makes defendants' acts unlawful' within the meaning of *Brunswick*, and falls squarely within the area of Congressional concern." *Id.* at 484.

In *Associated General Contractors of California v. California State Council of Carpenters*,[200] the Supreme Court outlined a case-by-case approach based on "well accepted common-law rules applied in comparable litigation" to be followed in determining whether a plaintiff has standing to recover antitrust damages.[201] Plaintiff Union alleged, *inter alia*, that defendant coerced owners of land and others who let construction contracts to hire nonunion firms. The Supreme Court reversed a Ninth Circuit ruling that conferred standing on the Union, stating that the determination of whether a plaintiff in a given antitrust action has standing to sue depends on a number of factors including: (1) the causal connection between the antitrust violation and harm to the plaintiff and whether that harm was intended to be caused; (2) the nature of the plaintiff's alleged injury including the status of the plaintiff as a consumer or competitor in the relevant market; (3) the directness or indirectness of the injury and the related inquiry of whether the damages are speculative; (4) the potential for duplicative recovery or complex apportionment of damages; and (5) the existence of more direct victims of the antitrust violation.[202] The Court held that "the Union is not a person injured by reason of a violation of the antitrust laws within the meaning of § 4 of the Clayton Act."[203]

---

200 459 U.S. 519 (1983).

201 *Id.* at 533. The Court examined the Sherman Act in light of its common law background, noting that in 1890 "a number of judge-made rules circumscribed the availability of damages recoveries in both tort and contract litigation—doctrines such as foreseeability and proximate cause, directness of injury, certainty of damages, and privity of contract." *Id.* at 532–33. It noted "a similarity between the struggle of common-law judges to articulate a precise definition of the concept of 'proximate cause' and the struggle of federal judges to articulate a precise test to determine whether a party injured by an antitrust violation may recover treble damages." *Id.* at 535–36.

202 459 U.S. at 537–43. The Court stated "In our view, courts should analyze each situation in light of the factors set forth in the text . . . ." *Id.* at 536 n.33.

203 *Id.* at 546.

The Court returned to the doctrine of antitrust injury in *Matsushita Electric Industrial Co., Ltd. v. Zenith Radio Corp.*[204] It rejected plaintiff's claim that a conspiracy by Japanese electronics manufacturers to depress prices in the American market in order to drive out U.S. competitors could be inferred from evidence that defendants engaged in "a whole host of [other] conspiracies in restraint of trade."[205] These conspiracies included defendants' alleged agreements to fix minimum prices for products exported to the American market,[206] to distribute products in the United States according to a "five company rule,"[207] and to fix prices at artificially higher prices in Japan.[208] Citing *Brunswick*, the Court held that any conspiracy to charge higher than competitive prices for products shipped to the U.S. market could only benefit plaintiff, and thus provides no basis for the recovery of damages.[209] Similarly, respondents could not recover for a "conspiracy to impose nonprice restraints," such as the five-company rule or the check-price agreement, "that have the effect of either raising market price or limiting output. Such restrictions, though harmful to competition, actually benefit competitors by making supracompetitive pricing more attractive."[210]

Most recently, in *Cargill, Inc. v. Montfort of Colorado, Inc.*,[211] the Court addressed the applicability of the doctrines of antitrust standing and antitrust injury to cases brought under

---

[204]   475 U.S. 574 (1986). For a discussion of the case see *supra*, notes 50–79 and accompanying text.

[205]   *Id.* at 586.

[206]   The parties referred to these price-fixing agreements as the "check price agreements." 475 U.S. at 581.

[207]   The court of appeals held that a reasonable factfinder could conclude that under the rule each Japanese producer was permitted to sell only to five American distributors. *Id.*

[208]   475 U.S. at 580, 584 & n.7.

[209]   *Id.* at 582–83.

[210]   *Id.* at 583.

[211]   107 S. Ct. 484 (1986).

§ 16 of the Clayton Act.[212] Section 16 provides that private parties "shall be entitled to sue for and have injunctive relief . . . against threatened loss or damage by a violation of the antitrust laws." Although § 4, unlike § 16, requires proof of actual injury to "business or property," the Court endorsed the view that under either statute plaintiff "must still allege an injury of the type the antitrust laws were designed to prevent."[213] The Court reasoned

> It would be anomalous, we think, to read the Clayton Act to authorize a private plaintiff to secure an injunction against a threatened injury for which he would not be entitled to compensation if the injury actually occurred.[214]

In *Cargill*, the nation's fifth largest meat packer brought suit under § 16 to block a merger between two of its larger competitors. At trial, plaintiff's theory of injury was that after the merger defendants would engage in a "price-cost 'squeeze' " by simultaneously bidding up the price of cattle and reducing the price at which it sold boxed beef. The district court held the allegation that the squeeze would " 'severely narro[w]' Montfort's profit margins constituted an allegation of antitrust injury."[215] The court of appeals affirmed, deeming Montfort's claimed injury "to be a form of predatory pricing in which [defendant] will drive other companies out of the market by paying more to its cattle suppliers and charge less for boxed beef that it sells to institutional buyers and consumers."[216]

---

212   15 U.S.C. § 26 (1982).

213   107 S. Ct. at 490.

214   *Id.*

215   *Id.* at 488, *quoting* 591 F. Supp. at 691-92.

216   *Id. quoting* 761 F.2d 570, 575 (10th Cir. 1985). The Supreme Court's decision in *Cargill* has been criticized for focusing solely on theories of injury flowing from defendant's postmerger pricing, and failing to recognize that plaintiff's assertion that defendants would bid up the price of inputs may have been properly analyzed as a nonprice predation theory. Krattenmaker & Salop, *Analyzing Anticompetitive Exclusion*, 56 ANTITRUST L.J. 71, 73-74 (1987).

The Supreme Court observed that plaintiff's allegations give rise to two possible theories of injury.[217] First, Montfort claimed that it would suffer injury in the form of lower profits occasioned by competing with defendant's postmerger prices that would be set at or slightly above defendant's costs in order to increase its market share.[218] Its alleged injury was the threat of lost profits resulting from the lower prices Montfort would be able to command for the boxed beef it sold in competition with defendant. Relying on *Brunswick*, the Court held "that the threat of loss of [such] profits due to possible price competition following a merger does not constitute threat of antitrust injury."[219]

Alternatively, Montfort argued that after the merger defendant would attempt to drive Montfort out of business by engaging in sustained predatory (below-cost) pricing. The Court characterized such predatory pricing as "capable of inflicting antitrust injury."[220] Finding that plaintiff neither raised nor proved predatory pricing before the district court, however, the Supreme Court reversed on this theory as well.[221]

---

[217] 107 S. Ct. at 491.

[218] *Id.*

[219] *Id.* at 493.

[220] *Id.*

[221] *Id.* at 494. Having concluded that plaintiff had not established antitrust injury, it was unnecessary to reach the broader question of standing. Nevertheless, the Court addressed two aspects of the standing issue that warrant mention. First, the opinion confirms that standing analysis under § 16 will not always be identical to standing analysis under § 4. The Court noted that some factors considered under § 4 analysis such as the risk of duplicative damage recoveries and multiple lawsuits are not relevant under § 16. *Id.* at 490 n.6. Second, the Court declined an invitation by the United States, appearing as amicus curiae, to adopt a per se rule denying competitors standing to challenge acquisitions on the basis of predatory pricing theories. *Id.* at 495. While the practice may occur only infrequently, the Court found ample evidence that it does exist, and could identify no reason to "deny standing to a party seeking an injunction against a threatened injury merely because such injuries rarely occur." *Id. Cargill* has become the

The growing importance of antitrust standing—and particularly antitrust injury—in private litigation is reflected in the sheer volume of reported decisions turning on these issues in recent years.[222] By requiring private plaintiffs to establish antitrust injury, and further limiting the ability of more remote victims to maintain damage actions, the Supreme Court has furnished an important new weapon for exercising spurious antitrust claims from an overburdened judicial system.

H. Conclusion

Both supporters and critics of the Reagan years have attributed the dramatic changes in antitrust to the policies ushered in by the 1980 change in administrations.[223] Both are wrong. William F. Baxter, Reagan's first Assistant Attorney General in charge of the Antitrust Division, and his counterpart James C. Miller III, former Chairman of the Federal Trade Commission, brought a coherent antitrust philosophy to their official duties and were very articulate spokesmen for injecting economic analysis into antitrust. Nevertheless, the most significant changes have been in the case law, influenced by work done in the academy in the fields of law and industrial organization economics, much of which predates the Reagan era. While not minimizing the importance of President Reagan's appointments to the enforcement agencies, these men and women really reflected the acceptance of

---

battleground in cases in which a firm seeks to preliminarily enjoin a merger between two of its competitors. *Compare* Phototron Corp. v. Eastman Kodak Co., 842 F.2d 95 (5th Cir.), *cert. denied*, 108 S. Ct. 1996 (1988) (standing denied) *with* R.C. Bigelow, Inc. v. Unilever N.V., 56 Antitrust & Trade Reg. Rep. (BNA) 160 (2d Cir. 1989) (standing conferred).

[222] For annotations of recent cases, *see* ABA, Antitrust Law Developments VII-14 to VII-16 (standing cases) & VII-16 to VII-19 (injury cases) (2d ed. Supp. 1988).

[223] Many of the papers delivered at the Arlie House Conference on Antitrust Policy in the spring of 1987 took this view. *See, e.g.*, Fox & Sullivan, *Antitrust—Retrospective and Prospective: Where Are We Coming From? Where Are We Going?* 62 N.Y.L. Rev. 936 (1987).

the "new learning." The decisions discussed above well illustrate this point and cannot be ignored.

IV. Antitrust enforcement

In this section we describe the effects of these doctrinal changes on public and private antitrust litigation. Since treble damages litigation has accounted for the great majority of antitrust cases, we begin our study there.

A. *Private enforcement*

The principal incentive for victims of antitrust violations to pursue private remedies is the potential recovery of "threefold of the damages sustained by him, and the cost of suit, including a reasonable attorney's fee."[224] In creating a private enforcement mechanism, Congress sought to "deter violators and deprive them of the fruits of their illegal violations."[225] The private right

---

[224] 15 U.S.C. § 15(a) (1982). Treble damages actions were first authorized by § 7 of the Sherman Act, 26 Stat. 210 (1890). The Supreme Court has described the Senate floor discussions as indicating the provision "was conceived of primarily as a remedy for [t]he people of the United States as individuals, 'especially consumers.' " (citations omitted). Brunswick Corp. v. Pueblo Bowl-O-Mat, Inc., 429 U.S. 477, 486 n.10 (1977). *But see* Mandville Island Farms, Inc. v. American Crystal Sugar Co., 334 U.S. 219, 236 (1948).

The incentive to sue may be even greater given that the award of an attorney's fee is mandatory even if the "successful" plaintiff recovers only nominal damages. *See, e.g.*, Home Placement Serv. v. Providence Journal Co., 819 F.2d 1199, 1210 (1st Cir. 1987) (award of nominal damages is a factor that may be considered in deciding on amount of fee award, but fee award need not be nominal). For additional citations *see* ABA, ANTITRUST LAW DEVELOPMENTS 478 n.729 (2d ed. 1984) & (2d Suppl. 1983–1988 VII-62 (1988)).

Section 16 of the Clayton Act, 15 U.S.C. § 26, also provides that the court "shall award" to a plaintiff who "substantially prevails in an injunctive suit the cost of the suit including a reasonable attorney's fee."

[225] Blue Shield of Virginia v. McCready, 457 U.S. at 472.

of action, coupled with the treble damages and attorney's fees provisions, theoretically reduces the cost to the taxpayer of vigilant federal antitrust enforcement.[226] As the Supreme Court put it in *Reiter v. Sonotone Corp.*[227]

> Congress created the treble-damage remedy of sec. 4 precisely for the purpose of encouraging private challenges to antitrust violations. These private suits provide a significant supplement to the limited resources available to the Department of Justice for enforcing the antitrust laws and deterring violations.

The following table sets forth the number of private antitrust actions filed in the federal courts over the past three decades.

In the early years of the Sherman Act, private antitrust litigation took a back seat to government enforcement. Familiar

---

[226]   The actual impact of private antitrust cases on overall enforcement is complex, and some scholars have even argued that the harshness of the treble damages remedy has prompted courts to dispose of more cases before trial, effectively limiting the reach of substantive antitrust laws. *See* Calkins, *supra* note 144. For a detailed analysis of private antitrust litigation and its relationship to federal enforcement, *see* *Symposium*, 74 Geo. L.J. 999 (1986), for four articles based on papers delivered at the Georgetown Conference on Private Antitrust Litigation, November 8-9, 1985.

[227]   442 U.S. 330, 334 (1979). The relationship between private actions and public law enforcement was again recognized by the Court in Brunswick Corp v. Pueblo Bowl-O-Mat, Inc., 429 U.S. 477 (1977). In reviewing the legislative history of the Clayton Act of 1914, H.R. Rep. No. 627, 63d Cong., 2d Sess. 14 (1914), the Court noted: "The initial House debates concerning provisions related to private damages actions reveal that these actions were conceived primarily as 'open[ing] the door of justice to every man, whenever he may be injured by those who violate the antitrust laws, and giv[ing] the injured party ample damages for the wrong suffered.' 51 Cong. Rec. 9073 (1914) (remarks of Rep. Webb) . . . . The House debates following the conference committee report, however, indicate that the sponsors of the bill also saw treble-damages suits as an important means of enforcing the law. . . . In the Senate there was virtually no discussion of the enforcement value of private actions, even though the bill was attacked as lacking meaningful sanctions . . . ." 429 U.S. at 486 n.10 (citations omitted).

Table 1
Private Antitrust Cases

Year	Private cases
1960	228
1965	472*
1970	877
1975	1,375
1976	1,504
1977	1,611
1978	1,435
1979	1,234
1980	1,457
1981	1,292
1982	1,037
1983	1,192
1984	1,100
1985	1,052
1986	838
1987	758
1988	654

* Includes 26 electrical equipment industry cases.

SOURCE: Annual Report of the Director of the Administrative Office of the U.S. Courts, 1983, 1984, 1985, 1986, 1987 and 1988 (preliminary edition).

---

cases from this era such as *Standard Oil Co. v. United States,*[228] *Chicago Board of Trade v. United States*[229] and *United States v. Colgate & Co.*[230] remain cornerstones of antitrust jurisprudence today. Although the number of private filings increased somewhat after World War II, it was the 1960's that brought explosive growth in antitrust litigation. While much of this activity was attributable to the cascade of price-fixing cases filed in connec-

---

[228] 221 U.S. 1 (1911).

[229] 246 U.S. 231 (1918).

[230] 250 U.S. 300 (1919).

tion with the Electrical Equipment conspiracies,[231] we must turn to other forces to understand the surge in filings in the 1970's, and their corresponding decline in the past decade.[232]

The growth in private filings in the 1960's and 1970's can be attributed to a variety of factors. The allure of treble damages and attorney's fees grew ever more attractive in our increasingly litigious society.[233] Moreover, the national mood, highly suspicious of corporate concentration and power, no doubt influenced the thinking of lawyers and even judges in ways that we would not attempt to quantify.[234] But it was the law itself, the breadth of the per se rules, the reluctance of courts to employ summary proceedings, the relative ease of establishing duality of conduct, and the lack of sophisticated economic analysis that stacked the deck in plaintiffs' favor.

As discussed in part III, *supra*, recent years have seen important substantive and procedural changes in antitrust laws, some of which have peculiarly affected the private plaintiff. Table 1 indicates that the number of private filings peaked in 1977, and has been in relatively steady decline ever since. In that same year, the Supreme Court issued two landmark decisions largely responsible for the antitrust implosion to follow. The first, *GTE-*

---

[231]   During the 1961-1964 period approximately 1,900 suits were filed against 19 producers of electrical equipment following criminal convictions in Philadelphia. Electrical Equipment cases accounted for 1,739 of the 2,005 private antitrust actions filed in 1962 which explains the dramatic drop in filings in 1963 to 380. *See* S.C. OPPENHEIM, G.E. WESTON & J.T. MCCARTHY, *supra* note 77, at 1062-63 & n.95, 99.

[232]   In contrast to the early years, private antitrust filings have accounted for more than 95% of all civil antitrust cases in recent years. *Compare* table 1, *supra, with* tables 2 and 3, *infra; accord* ABA, ANTITRUST LAW DEVELOPMENTS 385 n.1 (2d ed. 1984).

[233]   The growth of private antitrust filings from the 1960's to 1970's was not unlike the recent growth in filings under the civil RICO statute that also provides for treble damages.

[234]   *See, e.g.,* United States v. Von's Grocery Co., 384 U.S. at 274-77 *quoted supra* note 14 and accompanying text.

Sylvania,[235] signalled the Court's reluctance to invoke per se rules and its willingness to inject principles of industrial organization economics in antitrust analysis. The second, *Brunswick*,[236] announced the doctrine of antitrust injury which limits the universe of potential plaintiffs in private suits.[237] Together, these cases marked the beginning of a litany of Supreme Court decisions—*BMI, NCAA, Copperweld, Monsanto, Matsushita, AGCC, Cargill, Sharp*—that have virtually closed the courthouse door, or at least the jury box, on many private antitrust claims that might have prevailed in an earlier era.

B. *Public enforcement*

1. FEDERAL ENFORCEMENT   Public enforcement is dispersed. Since both the federal and state governments have antitrust laws, public enforcement takes place on both levels. Federal enforcement is, for the most part,[238] vested in two agencies: The Federal Trade Commission and the Antitrust Division of the Department of Justice. After a brief look at the total level of federal enforcement, we consider the activities of the two principal agencies in reverse order.

---

[235]   *See supra* notes 85–94 and accompanying text.

[236]   *See supra* notes 225–27 and accompanying text.

[237]   A third 1977 decision, Illinois Brick Co. v. Illinois, 431 U.S. 720 (1977), further restricted the number of cognizable antitrust damage claims by barring suits by indirect purchasers.

[238]   To be precise, a good many federal agencies share antitrust authority. For example, the Federal Reserve Board considers antitrust issues in its review of bank merger applications. Prior to January 1, 1989, the Department of Transportation was responsible for assessing the competitive effects of airline mergers. On November 14, 1988, however, the Federal Trade Commission, with the concurrence of the Antitrust Division of the Department of Justice, announced that the effect of the CAB Sunset Act, 49 U.S.C. § 1551(a)(7), would be to require that any airline merger or acquisition after January 1, 1989 be reviewed under the Hart-Scott-Rodino notification program regardless of whether it has been approved by the Department of Transportation.

The following table reflects the total of civil and criminal antitrust cases commenced by the Department of Justice in recent years.

Table 2
DOJ Antitrust Division Antitrust Cases Commenced in U.S. District Court During Fiscal Years 1960, 1965, 1970 and 1975–1988

Year	DOJ Civil	DOJ Criminal	Total DOJ
1960	59	27	86
1965	33	10	43
1970	54	5	59
1975	37	35	72
1976	45	20	65
1977	34	37	71
1978	27	31	58
1979	31	27	58
1980	28	55	83
1981	25	71	96
1982	18	94	112
1983	10	98	108
1984	14	100	114
1985	11	47	58
1986	6	53	59
1987	15	92	107
1988	11	87	98

SOURCE: United States Department of Justice, Antitrust Division, Workload Statistics FY 1960, 1965, 1970 and 1975–1988.

Rather obviously, table 2 illustrates that while recent years have seen a decrease in the number of civil filings in the federal courts, that trend has been offset, in sheer numbers, by the sharp increase in criminal cases that have been brought. The Carter administration brought an average of approximately 67.5 cases each year, 30 civil and 37.5 criminal. William Baxter and his Reagan administration successors, in contrast, brought some 94 cases annually, 14 civil and 80 criminal.

Clearly, the statistics do reflect differences in the enforcement priorities of the two administrations. The Reagan Justice Department focused on hard-core criminal violations such as price-fixing, bid-rigging, and horizontal market divisions—per se offenses with demonstrably anticompetitive effects. On the other hand, the relative absence of cases challenging vertical restraints—both price and nonprice—reflected the administration's view that the procompetitive value of such restraints generally outweighs, or at least offsets, any threat to competition they may pose. A review of the Department's workload statistics going back to 1960, however, supports the case that the changes between the Carter and Reagan years may, in fact, have been part of larger trends in public enforcement influenced by the changes in doctrine described in part II, *supra*, which have made it more difficult for the government to establish vertical conspiracies and have substantially eroded the range of per se offenses.

The enforcement activities of the Federal Trade Commission are more difficult to describe than those of the Antitrust Division. Unlike the Division, which initiates all of its civil and criminal challenges in federal court, and files its consent decrees there as well,[239] the Commission typically proceeds by administrative complaint in antitrust actions. Two principal exceptions to this rule are where the Commission invokes the power of the federal judiciary to seek civil penalties or to block anticompetitive acquisitions prior to their consummation. The following table sets forth two measures of Commission enforcement activity—administrative complaints issued and actions that the Commission has authorized its staff to initiate in federal courts or referred to the Department of Justice—for selected years since 1960.

---

[239] The Antitrust Procedures and Penalties Act (Tunney Act), 15 U.S.C. § 16(b)–(h) (1982), sets forth the procedures for district court approval of Justice Department consent decrees.

Table 3

Federal Trade Commission Administrative Complaints Issued and District Court Actions Authorized 1960, 1965, 1970 and 1975–1988

Year	Court actions authorized[1]	Administrative complaints issued[2]	Total
1960	n.a.	214	n.a.
1965	n.a.	65	n.a.
1970	n.a.	36	n.a.
1975	n.a.	30	n.a.
1976	n.a.	39	n.a.
1977	n.a.	24	n.a.
1978	n.a.	12	n.a.
1979	n.a.	37	n.a.
1980	2	34	36
1981	6	23	29
1982	4	7	11
1983	0	10	10
1984	7	22	29
1985	5	20	25
1986	7	14	21
1987	8	6	14
1988	17	21	38

[1] Consistent data before 1980 is unavailable. Data for fiscal years 1980–1988 include all civil penalty actions filed by the Justice Department on behalf of the F.T.C. and all preliminary injunction actions the Commission *authorized* its own staff to file. Transactions are often abandoned after the parties are advised that the Commission authorized staff to seek a preliminary injunction, thereby obviating the need to file the case. *See infra* text accompanying notes 272–73.

[2] Data for 1960, 1965 and 1970 "double counts" administrative complaints issued in cases in which the Commission subsequently (rather than simultaneously with the issuance of the complaint) accepted consent agreements. The *total* number of consent agreements finally accepted by the Commission in those years were 57 (1960), 39 (1965), and 12 (1970). Consents agreements accepted simultaneously with the issuance of complaints are not double counted.

SOURCE: Data is provided for the 12-month periods ending June 30, 1960, 1965, 1970, 1975, the 15-month period ending September 30, 1976 and fiscal years 1977–1988. Data for 1960, 1965 and 1970 based on Annual Report of the Federal Trade Commission. Data for subsequent years compiled by the Office of the Assistant Director for Evaluation, Bureau of Competition, Federal Trade Commission.

Table 3 reflects the extraordinarily high level of Commission activity in the early 1960's, much of which is now widely regarded as having been driven by policies that tended to penalize smaller competitors, particularly in the Robinson-Patman arena. While the number of administrative cases brought in more recent years has ebbed and flowed, the trend since the mid-1960's has been toward more modest enforcement activity. Examination of the Commission's Management Information System [MIS], however, reveals changes in enforcement priorities at the Commission similar to those at the Department of Justice described above, with fewer cases being brought in such areas as vertical restraints, the Robinson-Patman Act, and nonhorizontal mergers.

2. STATE ENFORCEMENT Public antitrust enforcement at the state level is directed by the various states' attorneys general, working independently and in cooperation with one another through the National Association of Attorneys General [NAAG]. Although the first state antitrust laws actually predate the Sherman Act,[240] state enforcement lapsed into retreat in the early 20th century in the face of legislative apathy, lack of public interest, opposition from the business community and a series of constitutional challenges to the statutes themselves.[241] A 1974 NAAG study conducted under the direction of then New Hampshire attorney general and NAAG president-elect, Warren Rudman, noted that only four states made any sustained effort to enforce their antitrust laws throughout this period of decline, and characterized most state statutes as falling into "disuse" after the turn of the century.[242]

---

[240] One recent study reports that 13 states had enacted antitrust statutes before 1890. 1 R.H. FOLSOM, STATE ANTITRUST LAW AND PRACTICE xxvii (1988).

[241] *Id.*; *see also* THE NATIONAL ASSOCIATION OF ATTORNEYS GENERAL, COMMITTEE ON THE OFFICE OF ATTORNEY GENERAL (Warren B. Rudman, Chairman), STATE ANTITRUST LAWS AND THEIR ENFORCEMENT 4 (1974) (hereinafter NAAG Study).

[242] NAAG Study, *supra* note 241, at 2.

Antitrust at the state level began making something of a comeback in the 1960's and the early 1970's. In 1960, the NAAG Committee on Antitrust became one of only seven NAAG standing committees. By 1961, ten states had antitrust enforcement programs.[243] But the renaissance would be short-lived. The NAAG Study detected no pattern of steady growth in the number of full-time attorneys devoted to antitrust matters in the offices of the states' attorneys general between 1970 and 1974.[244] The NAAG Study found that "relatively few Attorneys Generals' offices are active in enforcing state antitrust laws."[245] In 1968–1969, for example, only eight states plus Puerto Rico reported bringing any antitrust actions under state law (a total of 30-odd cases).[246] In 1972–73, only 10 of 37 states responding to a NAAG questionnaire reported filing antitrust actions, coincidentally a total of 37 cases in all.[247]

Given the relatively modest resources at the disposal of states' attorneys general, their cases tended to focus on local, rather than interstate investigations, and on per se offenses where the problems of proving a violation are minimized as is the need for the extensive economic analysis.[248] Often, the cases consisted of "tag along" suits following federal price-fixing actions.[249] In short, the states' attorneys general had carved out a discrete niche in the topography of public antitrust enforcement, nothing more.

---

[243]   *Id.* at 2.

[244]   *Id.* at 42. Interestingly, a 1987 NAAG survey reported that only 17 of the 39 states responding had one or more attorneys working on antitrust enforcement full time—suggesting that the growth in state antitrust enforcement has been concentrated in a fewer than half the states. 18 J. OF REPRINTS FOR ANTITRUST L. & ECON. (1988).

[245]   *Id.* at 45.

[246]   *Id.* at 46.

[247]   *Id.* at 45.

[248]   *Id.* at 45, 47.

[249]   Ewing, *Overview of State Antitrust Law*, 56 ANTITRUST L.J. 103 (1987).

All this began to change in the late 1970's. Ironically, the modern ascendance of state antitrust enforcement may owe its genesis to the federal agencies. The Crime Control Act of 1976[250] authorized the grant of federal "seed money" to assist states in establishing antitrust enforcement programs. In 1978 Congress sought to give the Antitrust Division a significant increase in its budget. Then Assistant Attorney General Donald I. Baker responded that the proposed increase was so large that he could not wisely spend the money. He further opined that he could not increase the size of the Division that dramatically because he did not have the personnel to supervise and train that many additional entry-level staff attorneys. Congress was adamant; more federal monies were to be spent in the antitrust enforcement effort. The result was that a series of federal grants were made available to state attorneys general to establish or augment their state antitrust agencies.[251]

The new and newly expanded state entities began to work. Fueled by the federal grants, state attorney general antitrust enforcement programs were begun in 24 states,[252] and the number of public prosecutions almost doubled from 206 in 1977 to 400 in

---

[250] 42 U.S.C. § 3739. The Act was an amendment to the Omnibus Crime Control and Safe Streets Act of 1968, Pub. L. 90-351, Sec. 309, 82 Stat. 197 (1968).

[251] Baker originally requested a $29,785,000 appropriation for FY78. *Fiscal Year 1978 Appropriations for State, Justice, and Commerce Departments, the Judiciary, and Related Agencies: Hearings on H.R. 7556 Before the Subcomm. on State, Justice, Commerce and the Judiciary of the Senate Committee on the Judiciary*, 95th Cong., 1st Sess. 723, 724, 726, 730 (1977) (statement of Donald I. Baker, Assistant Attorney General for Antitrust, Department of Justice). Ultimately, Congress appropriated $39,785,000 for the Antitrust Division, including $10,000,000 for antitrust enforcement grants to the states. Departments of State, Justice and Commerce, the Judiciary, and Related Agencies Appropriation Act of 1978, Pub. L. No. 95-86, 91 Stat. §§ 419, 425 (1977).

[252] S.C. OPPENHEIM, G.E. WESTON & J.T. McCARTHY, *supra* note 77, at 1060.

1979.[253] Although other factors contributed to the increase in state enforcement activities, most notably the express grant of parens patriae authority to states by the Hart-Scott-Rodino Antitrust Improvements Act of 1976,[254] some growth may be related to the changes in federal antitrust doctrine. In some instances state law may enable the attorney general to avoid obstacles posed by federal precedents limiting the availability of damages to indirect purchasers (*Illinois Brick*[255]), erecting stringent evidentiary requirements to establish vertical conspiracies (*Monsanto*[256]), or sheltering bathtub conspiracies from attack (*Copperweld*[257]). Such forum shopping has been acknowledged by state antitrust prosecutors.[258]

Other factors credited with spurring the growth of state enforcement activities include (1) a plethora of "modern" state antitrust statutes enacted since 1971 that are free from constitu-

---

[253]   J.O. von Kalinowski, *Antitrust Laws and Trade Regulation*, 16L Business Organizations § 132.01 n.7 and accompanying text; S.C. OPPENHEIM, G.E. WESTON & J.T. MCCARTHY, *supra* note 77, at 1059-60; R.H. FOLSOM, *supra* note 240, at xxviii.

[254]   Codified at 15 U.S.C. § 15c-h (1982).

[255]   Illinois v. Illinois Brick Co., 431 U.S. 720 (1977). Following *Illinois Brick*, at least 11 states and the District of Columbia enacted legislation effectively repealing the decision under their state antitrust laws. *See* J.O. von Kalinowski, *supra* note 253, § 132.01, at pp. 132–33. In California v. ARC America Corp., 109 S. Ct. 1661 (1989), the Supreme Court held that § 4 of the Clayton Act as interpreted in *Illinois Brick* did not preempt indirect purchaser claims under state antitrust laws.

[256]   Monsanto Co. v. Spray-Rite Service Corp., 465 U.S. 752 (1984).

[257]   Copperweld Corp. v. Independence Tube Corp., 467 U.S. 752 (1984).

[258]   *See* Constantine, *An Inside Look at Current Trends in State Antitrust Enforcement*, 1 ANTITRUST 6, 7 (1987). Lloyd Constantine is New York Assistant Attorney General in charge of the Antitrust Bureau. *See also* Wilson, *Defending an Antitrust Action Brought by a State AG*, 1 ANTITRUST 10 (1987). Thomas M. Wilson III was chief of Maryland's Antitrust Division from 1974–1978.

tional doubt;[259] (2) increased cooperation between states through what has amounted to the NAAG Antitrust Division; (3) the proliferation of "revolving funds" which make state antitrust enforcement appear financially self-sustaining; and (4) the perceived inaction by the Reagan administration in policing certain types of antitrust violations.[260]

It is unclear whether the rate of public prosecutions has increased in the 1980's. Data compiling the number of public prosecutions by the various states is not generally available, and we have not endeavored to make such calculations for this article. A survey of the available literature, however, does not yield a clear picture. A recently published treatise on state antitrust laws purports to tally all litigation brought under state antitrust laws reported in 1980 Trade Cas. (CCH) through 1986 Trade Cas. (CCH).[261] Extrapolating from the data in that study, there appears to have been an average of less than 32 prosecutions annually, both civil and criminal, including public consent agreements, over a 7-year period.[262] The study may understate the actual level of enforcement activity, however, since some cases may not be reported until a judicial opinion is rendered or a settlement announced, if at all. A 1986 NAAG study reportedly found the states' attorneys general had 140 antitrust cases "pending," 30 of which were criminal, in state and federal courts.[263] Interestingly this figure, if accurate, falls below the 400 prosecutions reported in 1979.

---

[259] Of the 50 states only Arkansas, Pennsylvania and Vermont do not have antitrust statutes of general applicability. J.O. von Kalinowski, *supra* note 259, § 132.01 n.12.

[260] *See generally* R.H. Folsom, *supra* note 240, at xxvii–xxxiv; J.O. von Kalinowski, *supra* note 253, § 132.01.

[261] R.H. Folsom, *supra* note 240.

[262] The study found a total of only 661 reported cases, 66.27% of which were either private state actions or pendent private claims under state law in federal court, and these figures include public consent agreements.

[263] 18 J. of Reprints for Antitrust L. & Econ. 3 (1988).

Regardless of whether the number of state prosecutions is up, it is clear that the states are pursuing larger cases with greater impact on interstate commerce than ever before. Recent activities of the state attorneys general and our predictions for the future, are discussed near the end of the following section.

V. The future of antitrust

In this section we attempt to focus our crystal ball. In doing so we examine three areas of antitrust doctrine where the revolution is still inchoate, *i.e.*, where the Supreme Court has yet to conform the law with the approach advocated by most followers of the Chicago school: merger law, tying agreements, and resale price maintenance. Following that discussion we will explore the important question of whether antitrust is in a decline, and in doing so will explore two areas of growth—nonprice predation, and, perhaps more importantly, the rise of state antitrust law and enforcement.

A. Inchoate doctrines

1. MERGER LAW   In *United States v. Von's Grocery Co.*,[264] Justice Potter Stewart, dissenting, observed:

> the Court pronounces its work consistent with the line of our decisions under § 7 since the passage of the 1950 amendments. The sole consistency that I can find is that . . . the government always wins.[265]

He was correct. Merger cases decided during the mid-1960's produced what might be described as a per se rule against horizontal mergers of any significant size.

The facts of *Von's* are instructive. There the Court found that a merger between two grocery chains holding a 7.5% market

---

264   384 U.S. 270 (1966).

265   *Id.* at 301.

share in Greater Los Angeles to be illegal.[266] The high-water mark in the evolution of this per se standard was not *Von's*, however, but the Court's decision in *United States v. Pabst Brewing Co.*[267] There the Court found objectionable a merger between two brewers who held a combined market share of 4.49%.[268] Thus, Justice Stewart's comment was a succinct statement of the law.

The tide began to turn with the publication of the 1968 Merger Guidelines by the Department of Justice.[269] The principal reflection of change in the Supreme Court to date, however, remains its 1974 decision in *United States v. General Dynamics Corp.*[270]

The law of mergers has not received much attention from the Supreme Court simply because not many such cases have reached the Court on their merits in recent years. This is a result of fewer Government merger prosecutions. While the great bulk of all antitrust litigation has been and continues to be private litigation,[271] merger law enforcement has traditionally been the domain of the federal authorities. Less merger activity by the Department of Justice and the Federal Trade Commission means fewer merger cases are likely to make their way to the Supreme Court.

---

[266]   In reaching its result the Court observed that as the number of single stores had declined, the number of chain-owned locations had increased, and that concentration was increasing within the industry.

[267]   384 U.S. 546 (1966).

[268]   As in *Von's Grocery*, the Court noted a decline in the number of firms and growing concentration within the industry.

[269]   49 Fed. Reg. 26,823 (1984).

[270]   415 U.S. 486 (1974). Merger law has continued to mature in the lower courts, many of which now examine supply-side substitutability in defining product markets. See Baker, *The Antitrust Analysis of Hospital Mergers and the Transformation of the Hospital Industry*, 51 L. & CONTEMP. PROBS. 93 (1988).

[271]   *See* ANNUAL REPORT OF THE DIRECTOR OF THE ADMINISTRATIVE OFFICE OF THE U.S. COURTS, 1983–1988 (Preliminary Edition).

Why have there been fewer public prosecutions? The answer is twofold. First, the passage of the Hart-Scott-Rodino Antitrust Improvements Act of 1976[272] dramatically changed the procedure of merger enforcement. The law generally requires that parties provide advance notice of large mergers to both the F.T.C. and the Antitrust Division, and await a statutorily proscribed period before consummating such transactions. While previously the agencies would file suit after the consummation of an objectionable merger, the agencies today have an opportunity to make their objections known to the parties before the "eggs have been scrambled."[273] This often results in objectional mergers being aborted prior to consummation, or in the restructuring of such transactions to eliminate the Government's concerns, *e.g.*, by divesting horizontal overlaps.

A second reason for the change in Government activity is the recognition that mergers that would have been challenged in an earlier day, do not pose sufficient anticompetitive problems to warrant challenge. Our economic sophistication has improved over time. While our ability to define product and geographic markets has been refined, recognition of the importance of barriers to entry is perhaps the most significant development.

While there has been little merger action in the Supreme Court, there have been important cases at the Federal Trade Commission. In *B.F. Goodrich*,[274] the Commission set forth a taxonomy of merger analysis. It began by defining the relevant

---

[272]   15 U.S.C. § 18a (1982).

[273]   For an analysis of the problems associated with obtaining effective relief in a § 7 case after consummation of an acquisition, *see* Elzinger, *The Antimerger Law: Pyrrhic Victories?* 12 J.L. & Econ. 43 (1969). Professor Elzinger noted that in some cases "the firm to be restored [as part of the § 7 relief], quite literally, no longer exists." *Id.* at 53. He also observed that "[m]arket conditions may so change during a prolonged adjudicatory proceeding that, at its conclusion relief negotiations may seem almost unnecessary," *id.* at 75, *i.e.*, the market may have corrected itself.

[274]   *In re* The B.F. Goodrich Co., 5 Trade Reg. Rep. (CCH) ¶ 22,519 (1988).

product and geographic markets, using the analysis first set forth in the Merger Guidelines and then adopted by the Commission in *Hospital Corporation of America.*[275] It then proceeded to a discussion of barriers and impediments to entry using the analysis set forth in *Echlin Manufacturing Co.,*[276] to which we will turn later. From there the Commission turned to the subject of concentration levels.[277] Finally, the Commission turned its attention to other structural factors. These included (1) product homogeneity,[278] (2) price elasticity of demand,[279] (3) cost func-

---

[275]   106 F.T.C. 361 (1985), *aff'd sub nom.* Hospital Corp. v. America v. F.T.C., 807 F.2d 1381 (7th Cir. 1986), *cert. denied*, 481 U.S. 1038 (1987).

[276]   105 F.T.C. 479 (1985).

[277]   Had the *Goodrich* decision been written 15 years earlier, the Commission—and the courts, for that matter—would have probably begun and ended the discussion there. Concentration levels tended to be determinative.

[278]   As the Commission put it: "The extent to which products in a given industry are homogeneous helps to determine the likelihood of anticompetitive effects from an acquisition. As the DOJ Guidelines indicate 'In a market with a homogeneous . . . product, a cartel need establish only a single price—a circumstance that facilitates reaching consensus and detecting deviation. As the products . . . become more . . . heterogeneous . . . the problems facing a cartel become more complex. Instead of a single price, it may be necessary to establish and enforce a complex schedule of prices corresponding to gradations in actual or perceived quality attributes among the competing products.'

"Two dimensions of product heterogeneity are particularly relevant. First, differences in product quality may make price differentials necessary to produce a stable market equilibrium, and achieving a consensus on such differentials is likely to be difficult. Moreover, maintaining a consensus becomes more difficult when it must cover full lines of products of varying qualities, because a firm can disguise its efforts to cheat more easily. Second, if transportation costs represent a substantial proportion of total product value, and if firms are located substantial distances from one another, coordination efforts must minimize or eliminate the competitive impact of these differences." 5 Trade Reg. Rep. (CCH) ¶ 22,519, at p. 22,152 (citations omitted).

(footnote 279 appears on following page)

tions,[280] (4) size distribution of purchasers,[281] (5) transaction characteristics,[282] (6) stability and predictability of demand and supply conditions,[283] and (7) significance of vertical integration.[284]

---

[279] Here the Commission's analysis was fairly traditional. The Commission observed: "As the price elasticity of demand for a product declines, the degree to which an increase in that product's price can be sustained without losing a significant number of sales increases, for two reasons. First, industry firms will find it easier to collude profitably, because an effort to raise prices to supracompetitive levels will not induce as many buyers to switch their purchases to alternative products. Second, industry firms will have a greater incentive to collude, because the additional revenue that any given price increase produces will increase." *Id*. at p. 22,154 (citations omitted).

[280] The Commission stated: "The similarity of cost functions among industry firms also affects the likelihood of anticompetitive effects from an acquisition. If cost functions vary widely from one firm to another, each will prefer a different industry price level, and developing a collusive consensus price will consequently be more difficult. If there are only a few firms in the industry, cost differences nevertheless may not prevent firms from accepting price or input levels somewhat different from their optimal levels." *Id*. at p. 22,156 (citations omitted).

[281] "The size distribution of purchasers . . . may also affect the likelihood of anticompetitive effects. . . . If a small number of buyers accounts for a large percentage of total product purchases, that may constrain the pricing discretion of product manufacturers to some degree." *Id*. at p. 22,158.

[282] In the Commission's view: "The manner in which sales are typically made . . . also affects the likelihood of anticompetitive effects . . . for two reasons. First, if most firms make only a few sales each year, their incentives to cheat are likely to be high. Each additional sale contributes substantially to income, and the risk of effective retaliation from competitors is correspondingly reduced. On the other hand, if the typical firm makes many sales each year, the value of cheating on a given transaction is not substantial and the prospect of effective retaliation may be correspondingly greater. Second, when sales are made openly, cheating can be detected quickly and easily, and retaliation by rival firms is consequently more likely. On the other hand, when sales are made through private negotiations, it is much more difficult to detect and punish secret price concessions." *Id*.

(footnotes 283 and 284 appear on following page)

Under *Goodrich*, once the relevant markets are defined, the next inquiry is into the existence of entry barriers. In *Echlin*, the Commission essentially adopted the so-called Stiglerian approach to entry barriers—named for Professor George Stigler—who defines them as "additional long-run costs that must be incurred by an entrant relative to the long-run costs faced by incumbent firms."[285] Entry barriers may take any variety of forms including necessary governmental approvals, licenses, patents and the like. The Commission also introduced the term "impediments" to entry, those conditions which necessarily delay entry into a market for a "significant period of time and thus allow[s] market power to be exercised in the interim."[286] In the absence of entry barriers so defined, any attempt to exercise market power would eventually be met by the entry of new firms seeking to reap supracompetitive profits, and sooner or later the resulting increased supply would drive prices back to competitive levels.[287]

---

[283]   "Greater stability and predictability make it easier to create and sustain a collusive arrangement. By contrast, shocks that suddenly alter demand or supply conditions may complicate collusion. In industries in which fixed costs are a high percentage of total costs, the presence of substantial excess capacity—as a result of a sudden decline in demand— may place strong downward pressure on prices." *Id.* at p. 22,159 (citations omitted).

[284]   *Id.* at pp. 22,161–22,166.

[285]   105 F.T.C. at 485. *See* G. STIGLER, THE ORGANIZATION OF INDUS- TRY 67 (1968). "The relevant costs are economic costs measured at the time of entry. . . . The economic cost to incumbents is the opportunity cost of retaining a factor of production, not the original price that was paid for it." 105 F.T.C. at 486. But analysis of comparative costs is tricky, where, for example, the lower costs an incumbent firm enjoys relative to a new entrant merely reflect the greater risk facing new firms—risks that the incumbent previously incurred and is now being compensated for in the form of lower costs. *Id.*

[286]   105 F.T.C. at 486.

[287]   *Id.* at 484.

Whether the Supreme Court will ultimately embrace a more economic approach to merger analysis cannot be said with certainty. The subject remains inchoate until the Court has had an opportunity to address cases presenting these issues.

2. TYING AGREEMENTS   The Supreme Court's treatment of tying law well-illustrates the tension between the doctrine of judicial restraint and the ability of courts to inject the "new learning" into well-established antitrust principles.

In its 1984 decision in *Jefferson Parish Hospital Dist. No. 2 v. Hyde*,[288] the Court flirted with abandoning the per se rule of illegality for tying arrangements, and blinked. With a deep bow to stare decisis, Mr. Justice Stevens, writing for the Court in an

---

[288]   466 U.S. 2 (1984). Hyde was an anesthesiologist who was denied admission to the medical staff of East Jefferson Hospital because the hospital had a contract with Roux & Associates, a professional medical corporation, to provide all of its anesthesiological services for patients. The district court denied relief on the ground that the anticompetitive consequences of the contract were outweighed by the benefits of improved patient care. The Fifth Circuit reversed holding the contract was per se illegal. It defined the relevant geographic market for the tying product as hospitals on the East Bank of Jefferson Parish, and held that the hospital possessed sufficient market power in the tying product to coerce purchasers of the tied product. Although the Supreme Court was unanimous in reversing the result, the case produced three different opinions.

The Supreme Court held that East Jefferson Hospital lacked sufficient market power to invoke the per se rule. Since 70% of the patients residing in Jefferson Parish entered hospitals *other than* East Jefferson, evidence that residents of East Parish preferred to go to East Jefferson, the closest hospital, did "not establish the kind of dominant market position that obviates the need for further inquiry into actual competitive conditions." *Id.* at 26–27. Having dismissed the per se theory, the Court had little difficulty disposing of the case under the rule of reason.

Since *Jefferson Parish*, a number of lower courts have treated a 30% market share as a minimum requirement to establish market power, effectively limiting the number of per se cases that might arise. *See e.g.*, Will v. Comprehensive Accounting Corp., 776 F.2d 665, 672 (7th Cir. 1985), *cert. denied*, 475 U.S. 1129 (1986). *See also* ABA, ANTITRUST LAW DEVELOPMENTS I-79 n.590c (2d ed. Supp. 1988).

opinion joined by two other Justices, began by noting, "[i]t is far too late in the history of our antitrust jurisprudence to question the proposition that certain tying arrangements pose an unacceptable risk of stifling competition and therefore are unreasonable *'per se'.*"[289] Rather than merely parrot the traditional tests of per se illegality for tying arrangements espoused by lower courts,[290] the Court explained:

> Our cases have concluded that the essential characteristic of an invalid tying arrangement lies in the seller's exploitation of its control over the tying product to force the buyer into the purchase of a tied product that the buyer did not want at all, or might have preferred to purchase elsewhere on different terms. When such "forcing" is present, competition on the merits in the market for the tied item is restrained and the Sherman Act is violated.[291]

The Court emphasized that the per se rule "is only appropriate if the existence of forcing is probable."[292] Such cases would include those where the Government has granted the seller a patent or similar monopoly over a product, or where the existence of market power is probable, such as where the seller has a high market share or offers a unique product that competitors are not able to offer.[293]

---

[289]　466 U.S. at 9.

[290]　Under pre-*Jefferson Parish* case law, tying arrangements were per se unlawful where it was established that (1) two separate products or services were involved; (2) the sale of one product or service was conditioned on the purchase of the other; (3) the seller had sufficient economic power in the market for the tying product to restrain trade in the market for the tied product; and (4) a not insubstantial amount of interstate commerce in the tied product was affected. *See* ABA, ANTITRUST LAW DEVELOPMENTS 77 (2d ed. 1984).

[291]　466 U.S. at 12. The statement appears to address a division in the case law as to whether proof that the buyer was forced or coerced to purchase a product he did not want is required to establish a per se violation and, if so, what type of proof will suffice. *See e.g.*, ABA, ANTITRUST LAW DEVELOPMENTS 82 nn.56, 58 and accompanying text.

[292]　466 U.S. at 15.

[293]　*Id.* at 16–17.

In a separate concurring opinion, Justices Brennan and Marshall threw their weight behind the opinion of the Court to form a majority in favor of adhering to the per se rule. Noting the Court had long held tying arrangements subject to per se scrutiny, they reasoned, "[w]hatever the merit of policy arguments against this longstanding construction of the Act might have, Congress, presumably aware of our decisions, has never changed the rule by amending the Act."[294] Therefore, they saw no reason to depart from their usual practice of standing by such a settled statutory interpretation and leaving the task of modifying the statute's reach to Congress.

Although concurring in result, a formidable minority led by Justice O'Connor[295] argued that the contract at issue should be judged under the rule of reason whether viewed as an exclusive dealing agreement or as a tying arrangement. Unlike other per se offenses, Justice O'Connor noted that tying arrangements had never been condemned by the Court without proof of market power or anticompetitive effect.

> [T]ying doctrine incurs the costs of a rule of reason approach without achieving its benefits: the doctrine calls for the extensive and time-consuming economic analysis characteristic of the rule of reason, but then may be interpreted to prohibit arrangements that economic analysis would show to be beneficial.
>
> . . . .
>
> The time has therefore come to abandon the "per se" label and refocus the inquiry on the adverse economic effects, and the potential economic benefits, that the tie may have. The law of tie-ins will thus be brought into accord with the law applicable to all other allegedly anticompetitive economic arrangements, except those few horizontal or quasi-horizontal restraints that can be said to have no economic justification whatsoever. This change will rationalize rather than abandon tie-in doctrine as it is already applied.[296]

---

294   *Id.* at 32.

295   Justices Burger, Powell, and Rehnquist joined in the opinion of Justice O'Connor.

296   466 U.S. at 34–35. The minority went on to identify three "threshold requirements," the presence of which would be required to

The unusual candor with which four Justices pronounced the per se rule dead on arrival suggests the very real possibility that changes in the Court's composition may create a majority willing to bury the doctrine once and for all.

3. RESALE PRICE MAINTENANCE[297]   Probably no area of antitrust, with the possible exception of merger policy, has generated the attention garnered by the debate surrounding resale price maintenance.[298] The history of RPM has been treated extensively elsewhere,[299] but a brief recap is probably in order. The Supreme Court's decision in *Dr. Miles Medical Co. v. John D. Park & Sons*[300] is a convenient point of departure. There the Court held

---

subject the challenged restraint to full rule of reason analysis: "[T]ying may be economically harmful primarily in the rare cases where power in the market for the tying product is used to create *additional* market power in the market for the *tied* product. . . . But such extension of market power is unlikely, or poses no threat of economic harm, unless the two markets in question and the nature of the two products tied satisfy three threshold criteria.

. . . .

"First, the seller must have power in the tying product market. . . . Second, there must be a substantial threat that the tying seller will acquire market power in the tied-product market. . . . Third, there must be a coherent economic basis for treating the tying and tied products as distinct." *Id.* at 36–39 (emphasis in original).

Under the rule of reason, a tie-in that satisfies all three threshold requirements may nevertheless entail economic benefits that outweigh the attendant economic harms, and warrant upholding the arrangement. *Id.* at 41.

[297]   This section draws heavily on and excerpts from Calvani & Berg, *supra* note 126, and Calvani & Langenfeld, *An Overview of the Current Debate on Resale Price Maintenance*, 3 CONTEMP. POLICY ISSUES 1 (1985).

[298]   Antitrust issues are seldom fare for publications of general interest. Resale price maintenance is different. Not only has the subject been covered in the legal literature, it has been treated in such diverse publications as airline magazines and general interest news periodicals. *See* Calvani & Berg, *supra* note 126.

[299]   *Id.*

[300]   220 U.S. 373 (1911).

that a distribution plan under which a seller and its authorized distributors had entered into contracts that established resale prices was an invalid restraint on alienation: "agreements or combinations between dealers, having for their sole purpose the destruction of competition and the fixing of prices, are injurious to the public interest and void."[301] The Court's opinion rested upon its conclusion that the restraint upon alienation was unreasonable under common-law principles. Antitrust played a very minor role in the Court's decision, and might be characterized as dictum. Thus, the antitrust significance of the *Dr. Miles* decision has been greatly overestimated by subsequent courts and commentators.[302] Nonetheless, the case has come to stand for the proposition that resale price maintenance is a per se violation of the antitrust laws.

The Court's decision in *United States v. Colgate & Co.* some 7 years later was the next opinion of note. There the Court addressed the lawfulness of Colgate's unilateral refusal to sell to distributors that did not honor resale prices set by Colgate. The Government did not allege nor did it seek to prove that there were agreements obligating distributors to maintain the minimum prices set by Colgate. The Court dismissed the indictment finding no violation of § 1 of the Sherman Act[303] absent any allegation of an illegal agreement. Thus the distinction between RPM imposed and enforced by contract and the suggestion of resale prices coupled with a unilateral refusal to deal received Supreme Court recognition.

The decades between 1919 and the Court's decision in *Monsanto Co. v. Spray-Rite Service Corp.*,[304] with their several relevant Supreme Court decisions and the rise and subsequent demise of state fair trade laws, are interesting but need not trouble us

---

301   220 U.S. at 408.

302   *See* Calvani & Berg, *supra* note 126, at 1168.

303   15 U.S.C. § 1 (1982).

304   465 U.S. 752 (1984).

here.[305] However, *Monsanto* merits our consideration. The defendant, a herbicide manufacturer, held a 15% market share in the late 1960's, while its principal competitor possessed some 70% of the market. In an effort to increase market share, Monsanto changed its distribution policy. Moving to a 1-year distributor contract, Monsanto predicated renewal on the success of distributors in implementing educational programs and on maintaining defendant's products as the primary line. Market share doubled in a 4-year period.

In 1968 the defendant informed plaintiff, a discount distributor who principally sold Monsanto's competitors' products, that its contract would not be renewed. Plaintiff sued alleging that it was terminated for failing to abide by defendant's RPM policy. The trial court instructed the jury that defendant's conduct was per se unlawful if it was in furtherance of a conspiracy to fix prices. The jury, in response to special interrogatories, found that the termination was pursuant to a conspiracy between defendant and one or more of its distributors to set resale prices. The court of appeals affirmed holding that "proof of termination following competitor complaints is sufficient to support an inference of concerted action."[306] As the Supreme Court later phrased the rule announced by the court of appeals, "an antitrust plaintiff can survive a motion for a directed verdict if it shows that a manufacturer terminated a price-cutting distributor in response to or following complaints by other distributors."[307] Because that holding brought the Seventh Circuit into direct conflict with several other courts of appeals, the Supreme Court granted certiorari.[308]

The case is important in an antitrust context for several reasons, including its discussion of the contract, combination, or

---

[305] *See* Calvani & Berg, *supra* note 126, at 1167–79.

[306] Monsanto Co. v. Spray-Rite Serv. Corp., 684 F.2d 1226, 1233 (7th Cir. 1982), *aff'd*, 465 U.S. 752 (1984).

[307] 465 U.S. at 759.

[308] For a review of the conflicts within the circuits, *see* Calvani & Berg, *supra* note 126, at 1189 n.99.

conspiracy requirement of § 1 of the Sherman Act.[309] It is also important for what it did not say about the per se quality of RPM. Despite the arguments of the Antitrust Division in its briefs, the Supreme Court eschewed the opportunity to squarely address the per se issue. Rather, the Court in a footnote observed that the case did not present an "occasion to consider the merits of this argument."[310] The Court noted that neither party had argued the per se issue in either the district court or on appeal. Moreover, neither party pressed the argument urged by the Antitrust Division in the Supreme Court. Accordingly, the Court "declin[ed] to reach the question."[311] Interestingly, the Court did seem to accept the Division's argument that the distinction reflected in the case law between price and nonprice restrictions did not make economic sense.[312]

The existence of a separate concurring opinion underscores the Court's failure to affirm *Dr. Miles.* Noting that *Dr. Miles* had stood for 73 years and that Congress had "never enacted legislation to overcome the interpretation of the Sherman Act adopted in that case,"[313] Justice Brennan found it necessary to express his view that the Court's opinion adhered to the rule in *Dr. Miles.* Several years ago there was speculation that "Justice Brennan sought—unsuccessfully—to have Dr. Miles clearly affirmed in the opinion of the Court."[314] Ultimately, the *Monsanto* Court left the question of the continued viability of the per se rule prohibiting resale price maintenance for another day.

The Court again eschewed the opportunity to resolve the debate over the per se rule in *Business Electronics Corporation v.*

---

[309]   15 U.S.C. § 1 (1982). *See supra* notes 126–41 and accompanying text.

[310]   465 U.S. at 762 n.7.

[311]   *Id.*

[312]   *Id.* at 761–63.

[313]   *Id.* at 769.

[314]   Calvani & Berg, *supra* note 126, at 1190–91.

Sharp Electronics Corporation.[315] Sharp published a list of suggested minimum retail prices for electronic calculators sold primarily to businesses, but its written dealership agreements did not require its dealers to charge these or any other specific price.[316] Petitioner became Sharp's exclusive distributor in the Houston, Texas area in 1968.[317] In 1972, Sharp appointed Hartwell as a second retailer in the Houston area.[318] Petitioner's retail prices were often below those suggested by Sharp, and generally below those of Hartwell.[319] Hartwell complained to Sharp about the petitioner's low prices several times, and in June 1973 presented Sharp with an ultimatum that Hartwell would resign its dealership unless Sharp terminated petitioner's dealership within 30 days.[320] Sharp did so in July 1973.[321]

Petitioner alleged that Sharp and Hartwell conspired to terminate petitioner and that such conspiracy was per se unlawful under § 1. The district court instructed the jury as follows:

> A combination, agreement or understanding to terminate a dealer because of his price cutting unreasonably restrains trade and cannot be justified for any reason.
>
> . . . .
>
> If a dealer demands that a manufacturer terminate a price cutting dealer, and the manufacturer agrees to do so, the agreement is illegal if the manufacturer's purpose is to eliminate the price cutting.[322]

The Fifth Circuit reversed, holding that per se treatment for vertical agreements between manufacturer and dealer to termi-

---

[315]   108 S.Ct. 1515 (1988).

[316]   *Id.* at 1518.

[317]   *Id.* at 1517.

[318]   *Id.* at 1517–18.

[319]   *Id.* at 1518.

[320]   *Id.*

[321]   *Id.*

[322]   *Id.*

nate a second dealer was appropriate only where the first dealer expressly or impliedly agreed to set its prices at some level.[323]

The Supreme Court, per Justice Scalia, forcefully affirmed: "a vertical restraint is not illegal *per se* unless it includes some agreement on price or price levels."[324] Building on *Sylvania* and *Monsanto*, the Court recalled that departures from the rule of reason standard must be based on "demonstrable economic effect, . . . rather than formalistic distinctions."[325] The foundation now firmly established, the Court cast what may prove to be the mortal blow to the classic RPM claim arising from a dealer termination.

> There has been no showing here that an agreement between a manufacturer and a dealer to terminate a "price cutter," without a further agreement on the price or price levels to be charged by the remaining dealer, almost always tends to restrict competition or reduce output.[326]

The Court noted that such an agreement cannot be distinguished from vertical nonprice restraints with respect to assisting cartelization.[327] Absent an agreement on price with the remaining dealer, "the manufacturer both retains its incentive to cheat on any manufacturer-level cartel (since lower prices can still be passed on to consumers) and cannot as easily be used to organize and hold together a retailer-level cartel."[328]

Although the opinion expressly rested upon "economic analysis,"[329] it also considered the common-law precedent that consti-

---

323   *Id., quoting* 780 F.2d at 1218.

324   *Id.* at 1525.

325   *Id.* at 1520–21.

326   *Id.* at 1521.

327   *Id.*

328   *Id.*

329   *Id.* at 1523. The Court emphasized that "[c]artels are neither easy to form nor easy to maintain. Uncertainty over the terms of the

tuted restraint of trade at the time the Sherman Act was enacted.[330] As in *Monsanto*, the Court recognized that "vertical agreements on resale prices have been illegal per se since *Dr. Miles*."[331] The Court went on to emphasize that the basis for *Dr. Miles* was that the resale restriction at issue in that case was "an unlawful restraint on alienation."[332] Noting the jury below found "no agreement on resale price or price level, and hence no restraint on alienation," the Court held that the common-law rationale of *Dr. Miles* was inapplicable to the case at bar.[333]

Writing for the majority, Justice Scalia's opinion provides insight into how the Court may ultimately reverse, not only *Dr. Miles*, but other antitrust precedents that may be inconsistent with the consumer welfare model of antitrust.

> The Sherman Act adopted the term "restraint of trade" along with its dynamic potential. It invokes the common law itself, and not merely the static content that the common law had assigned to the term in 1890. . . . If it were otherwise, not only would the line of *per se* illegality have to be drawn today precisely where it was in 1890, but also case-by-case evaluation of legality (conducted where

---

cartel, particularly the prices to be charged in the future, obstructs both formation and adherence by making cheating easier." *Id.* at 1521.

Focusing on the difficulty of distinguishing price from nonprice vertical restraints, the Court noted "all vertical restraints . . . have the potential to allow dealers to increase 'prices' and can be characterized as intended to achieve just that. In fact, vertical nonprice restraints only accomplish the benefits identified in *GTE Sylvania* because they reduce intrabrand price competition to the point where the dealer's profit margin permits provision of the desired services." *Id.* at 1521–22. Thus, the Court declined to impose the per se rule across the board on vertical agreements "that contain the word 'price,' or that affect the 'prices' charged by dealers." *Id.* at 1521.

[330]   *Id.* at 1523.

[331]   *Id.* This statement, together with the absence of any footnote reserving the question of per se illegality for RPM, may explain Justice Brennan's decision to join the majority in *Sharp*.

[332]   *Id.* at 1524.

[333]   *Id.*

per se rules do not apply) would have to be governed by 19th-century notions of reasonableness. It would make no sense to create out of the single term "restraint of trade" a chronologically schizoid statute, in which a "rule of reason" evolves with new circumstances and new wisdom, but a line of *per se* illegality remains forever fixed where it was.[334]

The public policy underlying the debate cries out for a reconsideration of *Dr. Miles.* A practice ought not be deemed a per se violation unless it is always, or almost always, anticompetitive. We tolerate such proscription only when the costs of ferreting out the infrequent procompetitive or benign conduct are sufficiently high to warrant a general prohibition. RPM, however, may be employed for both procompetitive[335] and anticom-

---

[334]   *Id.* at 1523-24.

[335]   Several potentially procompetitive explanations have been advanced in defense of RPM. Perhaps best known is the concern that absent RPM discount retailers will "free ride" off of advertising and services performed by full price retailers. *See* S. OSTER, *The FTC v. Levi Strauss: An Analysis of the Economic Issues*, in IMPACT EVALUATION OF FEDERAL TRADE COMMISSION VERTICAL RESTRAINT CASES 48, 61 (1984). Even this use of RPM has been questioned in some quarters. *See Oversight of FTC Law Enforcement: Hearing Before the Subcomm. on Commerce, Transportation and Tourism of the House Comm. on Energy and Commerce*, 98th Cong., 2d Sess. 52 (1984) (statement of former Federal Trade Commissioner Bailey).

A second procompetitive use of RPM, particularly in the apparel industry, is quality certification. Customers regard some dealers as capable of certifying product quality. Some manufacturers would prefer to market their product through these "leading stores." Manufacturers may choose to refuse to sell to discounters in an attempt to insure the margin necessary to finance the desired ambience. Admittedly, the consumer welfare implications of this use of RPM is ambiguous.

Finally, RPM has the potential for assuring an efficient number of retail outlets. Theoretically, resale price maintenance would be utilized when additional outlets produce gains that exceed the costs of reduced demand resulting from the higher prices of protected resale margins. The first necessary condition under this explanation is that there must be at least two types of retail establishments, each with a different cost structure. Second, availability of the product through a variety of retailers must induce more demand than the lower unprotected prices of fewer outlets. Third, each type of outlet must have customers who

petitive[336] purposes, suggesting that rule of reason analysis may be a more appropriate standard for evaluating such restraints. The Supreme Court has implicitly recognized this in *Monsanto* and *Sharp* in severely limiting the availability of the per se rule, but to date has declined to expressly overrule *Dr. Miles* and its progeny. Whether it will be prepared to do so in the near future, however, remains to be seen.

---

regularly patronize it as well as customers who price-shop. Under these circumstances, higher-cost retailers would lose sales to those price sensitive customers who overlap both high- and low-cost sellers. If higher-cost sellers would lose sufficient numbers of customers to warrant dropping the product, a manufacturer would have an efficiency-enhancing rationale for employing resale price maintenance. In other words, resale price maintenance may be employed to purchase display space in higher-cost outlets. *See generally* Telser, *Why Should Manufacturers Want Fair Trade?* 3 J.L. & Econ. 86, 86–87 (1960); Bowman, *The Prerequisites and Effects of Resale Price Maintenance*, 22 U. Chi. L. Rev. 825, 832–43 (1955).

[336] Manufacturers can use RPM to police cheating by participants in a manufacturers' cartel. The presence of a manufacturers' cartel does not necessarily mean that resellers will employ uniform pricing. Where some retailers discount, it may simply reflect a local, individualized pricing policy harmless to the cartel; but, alternatively, it might indicate that the resellers' supplier has discounted to the reseller in violation of the cartel agreement. Interpretation of retail discounting may be difficult, and while the imposition of RPM does not eliminate a cartel member's incentive to cheat, it does eliminate a variable that would otherwise complicate cartel surveillance.

Another improper use of RPM is as the "cat's paw" of a dealers' cartel. Dealers with monopsony power may induce manufacturers to impose RPM in an effort to enhance the ability of dealers to police cheating by recalcitrant cartel members. Manufacturers' agents or participating retailers could then monitor dealer adherence to the set price. Note that the manufacturer in this situation is coerced to establish and maintain as the set price the dealers' cartel price, rather than the price that yields the optimum distribution margin to the manufacturer. For an empirical study of how the various procompetitive and anticompetitive uses of RPM are reflected in the case law, *see* Ippolito, *Resale Price Maintenance: Economic Evidence From Litigation*, Bureau of Economics Staff Report (Federal Trade Commission 1988).

B. Areas of growth?

Much of the discussion above has focused on what might be characterized as the waning of antitrust's influence in the United States. Certainly there are many cases that would have been brought 20 years ago that would not be brought today. Areas of conduct that were previously characterized as per se violations are today examined under the rule of reason, and this has also meant that some previously thought good cases will not be filed. What then is the future of antitrust?

There are those who question whether antitrust ought not be relegated to the courses in legal history.[337] Obviously, the previous discussion of federal criminal antitrust prosecutions illustrates one area of growth.[338] Are there others? In the following sections we discuss two such areas.

1. NONPRICE PREDATION[339]   The very term ''nonprice predation'' has been within the antitrust lexicon a short time. Some definition is perhaps in order. Simply put, nonprice predation is strategic behavior designed to raise rivals' costs.[340] While nonprice predation can arise in numerous contexts, abuse of the regulatory and legal process provides a fertile environment for this variety of anticompetitive practice. The firm that opposes the application of a competitor for a license or certificate of need without any basis is an excellent example. Another example would be the firm that invokes the federal import relief statutes in an effort to stem the flow of unwanted competition without any evidence that the

---

337   *See, e.g.*, Addresses of Stephen Sussman before the Antitrust Section, Ohio State Bar Association, Columbus, Dec. 5, 1986, and Antitrust Section, Texas State Bar Association, Houston, Oct. 14, 1986. Suffice it to say that Mr. Sussman does not believe that the future holds much for antitrust.

338   *See supra* table 2 and the paragraph following it.

339   This discussion draws heavily on Calvani, *Non-Price Predation*, 54 ANTITRUST L.J. 409 (1985).

340   For a rather complete survey of the literature on this subject, *see generally, Nonprice Predation*, 16 J. REPRINTS IN ANTITRUST L. & ECON. 403 (1987).

underlying statutory predicate, *e.g.*, dumping, is present.[341] Even if the respondent ultimately prevails in such a proceeding, the predator firm may succeed in heaping costs upon the respondent in the form of legal fees and expenses as well as the cost of posting any bond required by statute in connection with respondent's defense.

Nonprice predation is important from a policy perspective. It is more anticompetitive than its cousin price predation because it is both less risky and less expensive. As discussed earlier,[342] predatory pricing is expensive. It requires the expenditure of present resources in the hope of capturing future monopoly rents. Since these rents are both future and uncertain they must be discounted in value. Moreover, absent significant entry barriers there is no guarantee that the presence of supracompetitive profits will not itself lure new entry into the industry, thereby precluding not only the capture of monopoly rents but also the recoupment of resources spent during the period of predation. Indeed, the very presence of salvage assets (from the predated victim) at distress prices may itself lure new entry into the industry, with the result that the new entrant may face lower cost functions than the established predator. If the predator is a dominant firm, as is usually alleged, then the predator may have to sacrifice profits across a much larger product and geographic range. Thus, the losses encountered by the predator may be much greater relative to those of its prey. All of this is to suggest that price predation is both expensive and risky.

Nonprice predation is different. It does not require a significant sacrifice of present profits in the hope of recouping them together with monopoly profits in the future. If the strategy involves abuse of the regulatory process (as is often the case), then the principal costs are legal and related fees. These can be expected to rise less significantly than would the costs, *i.e.*, lost

---

[341]   The very filing for such relief may discipline the foreign competitor and alter its pricing practices. *See generally*, Calvani & Tritell, *Invocation of U.S. Import Relief Laws as an Antitrust Violation*, 31 ANTITRUST BULL. 527 (1986).

[342]   *See* the discussion of predatory pricing *supra* notes 23–75 and accompanying text.

revenues, associated with across the board price cutting. Moreover, such nonprice predation involving regulatory abuse may be protected from antitrust scrutiny by the *Noerr-Pennington* doctrine.[343]

The subject is not insignificant. The F.T.C. has indicated its interest in bringing nonprice predation cases.[344] Indeed, it has successfully concluded the first.[345] Moreover, a reading of the case law indicates that there are a good number of such cases even though the litigants and the courts may not utilize the term "nonprice predation" to describe them.[346] It is a doctrine that is likely to become important grist for the mill of antitrust counsel.

2. STATE ANTITRUST ENFORCEMENT   The growing importance of state antitrust enforcement can be readily seen in the antitrust literature.[347] While the reasons for this resurgence in

---

[343]   The doctrine takes its name from two important Supreme Court cases: Eastern Railroad President's Conference v. Noerr Motor Freight Inc., 365 U.S. 127 (1961), and United Mine Workers v. Pennington, 381 U.S. 657 (1965).

[344]   *See, e.g.*, Calvani, *supra* note 339 at 410.

[345]   *See In re* AMERCO, 109 F.T.C. 135 (1987).

[346]   *See, e.g.*, *In re* Burlington Northern, Inc., 822 F.2d 518 (5th Cir. 1987), *cert. denied*, Union P.R. Co. v. Energy Transp. Sys., Inc., 108 S. Ct. 701 (1988). There plaintiffs alleged defendant railroads conspired to prevent construction of a coal slurry pipeline by, among other things, filing lawsuits to invalidate a water contract between plaintiffs and the United States Department of Interior and defending suits brought by plaintiffs to establish certain easements under the railroads' tracks. The reported decision concerned a discovery dispute arising from plaintiffs' efforts to obtain documents concerning the underlying lawsuits. *See also*, Outboard Marine Corp. v. Pezetel, 474 F. Supp. 168 (D. Del. 1979).

[347]   At the 1987 Annual Spring Meeting of the Antitrust Section of the American Bar Association, for example, three papers were presented addressing state antitrust enforcement activities, and a panel discussion was held focusing on state enforcement. *See, Current Trends in State Antitrust Enforcement*, 56 ANTITRUST L.J. 99-153 (1987). The Section's periodic magazine has also focused on the emergence of state enforcement in recent years. *See, e.g.*, State Enforcement: Putting the Pieces

state enforcement are diverse,[348] the political potential that comes with the office of attorney general in many states is a matter of historical record.[349] Not surprisingly, a number of AGs have indicated that they have no intention of curtailing their high profile enforcement presence even if federal activity increases in the future.[350] Four areas of state activity warrant our attention here: (a) local investigations, (b) multistate investigations, (c) merger activity, and (d) multistate efforts to establish uniform enforcement guidelines and to influence the direction of antitrust in the courts.

Traditionally, local investigations of per se offenses have comprised the bulk of state enforcement efforts. State activity continues in this area, focusing on cases that involve the greatest citizen and government expenditure, and on commercial activity most vital to the state's economy.[351] The attorneys general are increasingly conducting their own investigations and claim to be stepping up criminal prosecutions.[352] The increased role of states

---

Together, Antitrust (Winter 1987). *See also State Antitrust Enforcement*, 18 J. OF REPRINTS FOR ANTITRUST L. & ECON. (1988).

[348] *See supra* notes 250–60.

[349] Indeed one lobbyist has reportedly suggested that the attorneys general rename their group the National Association of Aspiring Governors. Barrett, *Attorneys General Flex Their Muscles*, Wall St. J., July 13, 1988, at 25.

[350] Lloyd Constantine, New York Assistant Attorney General for Antitrust, has commented that the states are no longer interested in preserving antitrust law for federal antitrust enforcers of the future, but "to enforce it themselves, singly, in ad hoc collective efforts, and through an evolving antitrust division staffed by the states." Constantine, *Current Antitrust Enforcement Initiatives by State Attorneys General*, 56 ANTITRUST L.J. 111 (1987). *See also* Ewing, *Overview of State Antitrust Law*, 56 ANTITRUST L.J. 103, 109 (1987).

[351] Constantine, *supra* note 350, at 112. As noted earlier, the existence of so-called *Illinois Brick* repealers provide added incentive for private parties as well as state attorneys general to pursue remedies under state law. *See supra* note 255 and accompanying text.

[352] Constantine, *supra* note 350, at 112–14. Some attorneys general also claim to be using antitrust laws to pursue other types of criminal activity such as fraud, official corruption, and extortion. *Id.* at 115.

as purchasers of goods and services provides an incentive for states to sue in their proprietary capacity,[353] and has prompted an attempt by 24 states to monitor highway construction bids by purchasing computer programs necessary to analyze bid data.[354]

While local enforcement may be the stalwart of state antitrust activity, the coordinated efforts of the states to conduct interstate antitrust investigations have attracted widespread attention. NAAG's Multistate Antitrust Task Force is a core group of assistant attorneys general that acts as the coordinator for some of these cooperative activities.[355] Among the more highly touted victories by the attorneys general have been the settlements obtained in resale price maintenance investigations such as *Minolta*[356] and, more recently, *Panasonic*.[357] Horizontal restraints

---

[353] *See, e.g.*, State of South Dakota v. Kansas City Southern Industries, Inc., Civ. 83-5046 (judgment on jury verdict filed April 12, 1988) (State of South Dakota won $600 million in treble damages from a railroad that interfered with the construction of a coal slurry pipeline project. The jury found that the railroad conspired with competitors to thwart the project, thereby restraining trade in the coal transportation market. Actual damages were calculated as state's loss of profits in a water sale contract cancelled after the project was abandoned).

[354] Brockmeyer, *State Antitrust Enforcement*, 57 ANTITRUST L.J. 169, 173 (1988).

[355] 18 J. OF REPRINTS FOR ANTITRUST L. & ECON. 6 (1988).

[356] The *Minolta* camera resale price-fixing investigation, spearheaded by Maryland and New York, ultimately led to settlements in 37 states. *See, e.g.*, Maryland v. Minolta Corp., B86-613 (S.D.N.Y. 1986); New York v. Minolta Corp., 86 Civ. 1605 (S.D.N.Y.); Pennsylvania v. Minolta Corp., Civ. No. 86-2063 (E.D. Pa. 1986). A settlement fund in the amount of $4 million was reportedly established. Barrett, *supra* note 349. All 37 state actions were consolidated in the Federal District Court for the District of Maryland.

[357] Maryland and New York again teamed up to investigate allegations of vertical price-fixing in electronics products by Panasonic. That investigation resulted in a settlement that provides for Panasonic to reimburse up to $16 million to as many as 665,000 consumers nationwide. 56 Antitrust & Trade Reg. Rep. (BNA) 89 (January 19, 1989).

California has reportedly joined New York and Maryland to investigate retail pricing in the luggage industry. *See* Brockmeyer, *supra* note

of trade have also been the subject of joint investigations by the states, perhaps the most notable being the pending reinsurance litigation in San Francisco.[358]

The most controversial area of state growth has been in the merger arena. A number of states have attempted to block mergers under their own antitrust laws with mixed success.[359] The states have also challenged acquisitions under § 7 of the Clayton Act in federal court.[360] Few cases have actually been litigated to judgment, however, since the costs and the risks involved in

---

354, at 173. The investigation initially focused on RPM, but reportedly widened to cover horizontal activity. Interestingly, two attorneys in the Maryland Antitrust Division were designated as Special Assistant Attorneys General for New York in that case. *Id.*

[358] The suit was originally filed in San Francisco by the attorneys general of New York, West Virginia, Wisconsin, Minnesota, Massachusetts, Alabama and California in March 1988. A related complaint was filed in state court in Austin by the Texas attorney general. OFFICE OF THE ATTORNEY GENERAL OF THE STATE OF CALIFORNIA, FACT SHEET ON THE MULTISTATE PROSECUTION OF ANTITRUST VIOLATIONS IN THE INSURANCE INDUSTRY (Mar. 22, 1988). The suit alleges that four U.S. insurance companies conspired with others to reduce the coverage of the standard "commercial general liability" policy. Some have questioned whether the attorneys general will be able to muster sufficient evidence to prevail. Labaton, *Business and the Law*, The New York Times, April 4, 1988, D-2. Also of note is the Task Force's investigation into the joint development of a debit card by Visa and Mastercard. Brockmeyer, *supra* note 354, at 172.

[359] *See, e.g.,* Texas v. Coca-Cola Bottling Co. of the Southwest, 1985-2 Trade Cas. (CCH) ¶ 66,765, upholding the constitutionality of the Texas antitrust law that substantially tracks the language of § 7 of the Clayton Act. *But see* State *ex rel.* Van De Kamp v. Texaco, Inc., 252 Cal. Rptr. 221, 762 P.2d 385 (Cal. 1988). By a 4 to 3 vote, the court held that the Cartwright Act's prohibition on "a combination of capital" did not permit the attorney general to attack Texaco's $10.1 billion purchase of Getty Oil in 1984. *See* Hager, *State Supreme Court Foils Van de Kamp's Challenge to Getty's Merger with Texaco*, Los Angeles Times, Oct. 21, 1988.

[360] *See, e.g.,* City of Pittsburgh v. The May Department Stores, Inc., 1986-2 Trade Cas. (CCH) ¶ 67,304 (W.D. Pa. 1986); California v. American Stores Co., 872 F.2d 837 (9th Cir.), *stay granted*, 110 S. Ct. 1, *cert. granted*, 110 S. Ct. 275 (1989).

litigation often exceed those attendant to making divestitures that satisfy an attorney general.[361] Thus, the fact that a firm agrees to make additional divestitures after completion of federal review to satisfy an aggressive attorney general is no indication that the additional relief was necessary to preserve competition. Moreover, in some instances states' attorneys general have insisted on settlement terms that bear little relationship to the consumer welfare model of antitrust.[362] Indeed, the federal agencies may demand additional relief even after a state has settled with the merging parties.[363]

The increased merger activity of the states raises important legal and policy issues.[364] The question of federal preemption with respect to merger challenges under state law looms large and is

---

[361]   This is particularly true where there are competing bidders for the target company waiting in the wings.

[362]   For example, in West Point-Pepperill's recent acquisition of J.P. Stevens, the attorneys general of North Carolina, South Carolina and New York agreed not to challenge the acquisition in return for West Point's commitment "not to close plants for two years and to make good faith efforts not to reduce employment levels; to provide preferential consideration to former Stevens managers, and to use and maintain present contracts with local vendors." Stevens, Financial News (AP, wire) (May 5, 1988).

[363]   The settlement in Texas v. Coca-Cola Bottling Co. of Southwest, 1986-2 Trade Cas. (CCH) ¶ 67,169 (Tex. D. Ct. 1986), required the respondent, *inter alia*, to divest the acquired bottler's vending machines to the owners of property on which said machines were located and imposed other restrictions for a period of 7 years. Two years later the Federal Trade Commission issued an administrative complaint alleging that the acquisition violated § 7 of the Clayton Act. The notice of contemplated relief states that if respondent is found to have violated § 7 the Commission could require divestiture and prior approval for future acquisitions of soft drink assets in the relevant areas of the country for up to 10 years. 55 Antitrust & Trade Reg. Rep. (BNA) 215 (Aug. 11, 1988).

[364]   For additional background on the relationship between state and federal antitrust laws, *see, e.g.*, Hovenkamp, *State Antitrust in the Federal Scheme*, 58 INDIANA L.J. 375 (1983).

largely unresolved.[365] While federal antitrust law has been held not to preempt state law in a number of other contexts, mergers that attract the attention of the federal agencies tend, by their very nature, to implicate a most substantial share of interstate commerce. Thus, merger challenges by the states will likely impose greater burdens on interstate commerce than will most other state enforcement actions. While several courts have permitted states' attorneys general to proceed under § 16 of the Clayton Act to challenge an acquisition under § 7, the scope of that authority, assuming it exists, has yet to be defined.

There are sound policy reasons for limiting the standing of states' attorneys general under § 16. Mergers often involve transfers of assets in several states, and may be motivated in part by efficiencies that may not be recognized if the acquisition is permitted to proceed in some states but not others. Moreover, the threat of multiple public prosecutions may create substantial and prolonged uncertainties that complicate corporate planning, postpone the realization of efficiencies, and discourage parties from settling without litigation.[366] The policy considerations recognized

---

[365] In State *ex rel.* Van De Kamp v. Texaco, Inc., 252 Cal. Rptr. 221, 762 P.2d 385 (Cal. 1988), the court did not reach the question of whether a consent agreement previously reached with the Federal Trade Commission preempted an action by the California attorney general brought under state law. *Id.* at 386. *See supra* note 359. The courts below held that the state action was preempted. California v. Texaco, Inc., 1984-2 Trade Cas. (CCH) ¶ 66,253 (Cal. Super. Ct. 1984), *aff'd*, 219 Cal. Rptr. 824.

[366] Assuming for the sake of argument that both the states and the federal authorities will adhere to their respective published guidelines and policy statements, they may reach different conclusions about the competitive impact of a given transaction, and what divestitures may be necessary to remedy any antitrust concerns. In such cases, the merging parties may agree to one package of divestitures to satisfy one enforcement entity (in the case of HSR matters generally the federal agency), only to find that another public entity, *i.e.*, a state, will insist on additional or different divestitures to satisfy its competitive concerns. Thereafter, the parties may be left with a less valuable, and less efficient, operation as a result of the sequential divestitures than may

in *Lieberman v. FTC*[367] and *Mattox v. FTC*,[368] courts affirmed the Commission's determination that it may not share Hart-Scott-Rodino materials with the states, are pertinent here. In *Lieberman* the court observed:

> We doubt if Congress would have intended to have the staffs of fifty state attorneys general sitting as oversight committees reacting to Commission or Justice Department decisions whether to block large-scale mergers of national or international significance.[369]

The same policy concerns were echoed by the Fifth Circuit in *Mattox v. FTC*:[370]

> [b]ecause HSR only covers transactions likely to affect the entire national economy, Congress may have wanted to centralize regulation of such mergers in the FTC and the Justice Department. Disclosure to state attorneys general would tend to balkanize that needed centrality.[371]

As Ky Ewing has put it:

> Bluntly put, whenever jobs are threatened in any locality, by reallocation of resources by the proper functioning of active, open, free markets, you will find many people who will urge antitrust enforcement action. The clothing will be antitrust, even if the motivation is more political.[372]

---

have been necessary had all enforcement authorities voiced their concerns before any divestitures took place. Parties may ultimately elect to litigate a preliminary injunction rather than settle with any government entity absent assurances that other enforcement entities will not bring suit after the first settlement is concluded; assurances which the federal agencies cannot presently provide.

367   771 F.2d 32 (2d Cir. 1985).

368   752 F.2d 116 (5th Cir. 1985).

369   *Id.* at 40. On the other hand, the *Lieberman* court did add that "a state official can seek a preliminary injunction against an illegal merger under federal antitrust law. . . ." *Id.* at 39.

370   752 F.2d 116 (5th Cir. 1985).

371   *Id.* at 122.

372   Ewing, *supra* note 249, at 109.

He adds, "I am not entirely certain in my own mind that that's all bad."[373] We tend to disagree.

Recognizing this danger of "balkanization" and in an effort to avoid it, the attorneys general, through NAAG, issued their own Horizontal Merger Guidelines in December 1987.[374] Effective state enforcement in the merger field has been frustrated, however, by the decisions in *Lieberman* and *Mattox*. NAAG reacted to these decisions by creating the NAAG Voluntary Pre-Merger Disclosure Compact.[375] The Compact provides that no signatory state will seek precomplaint discovery from a merging party if the parties required to make an HSR filing provide a copy of such filing to the "designated" state as provided in the Compact. In December 1987 NAAG adopted a resolution urging states to adopt uniform "little Hart-Scott-Rodino Acts" if federal legislation requiring that such information be provided to the states is not forthcoming.[376]

Among the other efforts states have made to establish uniform approaches to shaping and enforcing the law are: (a) The December 1985 NAAG Vertical Restraints Guidelines (adopted by all NAAG members); (b) 46 states signed NAAG's amicus brief to the Supreme Court in *Monsanto*; (c) 20-odd members teamed up to argue that the Texaco-Getty merger was unlawful;

---

[373] *Id.*

[374] While the NAAG Guidelines generally resemble the Justice Department's 1984 Merger Guidelines, they differ in a variety of ways including market definition, entry barrier analysis, concentration trends, and the efficiencies defense. *See* Ewing, *supra* note 249, at 107.

[375] As of April 1988, 44 states and territories had adopted the Compact. The Compact became effective as of March 15, 1988. Query whether the Compact runs afoul of the Compact Clause of the Constitution which states in pertinent part: "No State shall, without the Consent of Congress, . . . enter into any Agreement or Compact with another State . . . ." U.S. Const. art. I, § 10, cl. 3. Recently, NAAG's Air Travel Industry Enforcement Guidelines were challenged on this and other grounds by several major carriers. Trans World Airlines, Inc. v. Mattox, C.A. No. A89-CA0067 (W.D. Tex.)

[376] Brockmeyer, *supra* note 354, at 172.

(d) in *Sharp*, 44 states joined in an amicus brief written by Maryland and Ohio; (e) the states jointly submitted comments in Department of Transportation proceedings concerning the proposed Eastern Air/Texas Air and USAir/Piedmont acquisitions; and (f) NAAG has developed a comprehensive series of positions on pending legislative proposals.

It is still too soon to tell how significant a force NAAG will be in the long term. Unresolved questions of preemption, varying state funding levels, changing public support or apathy, and congressional sentiment to NAAG's legislative positions in the future are impossible to predict with reasonable certainty. For now, at least, NAAG is holding out the promise of new life for the private antitrust bar. Antitrust violations do occur at the local level, and states will often have a distinct advantage over the federal authorities in pursuing these violations in a cost-effective manner. Whether the states will ultimately prove to be champions of competition on a wider scale, through sensible and successful enforcement initiatives rather than mere rhetoric, remains to be seen.

VI. Conclusion

The past 15 years have seen dramatic changes in the direction of antitrust. Spurred by the academy, but driven by the courts, antitrust is maturing into a coherent body of law dominated by a concern for maximizing consumer welfare. While antitrust has been used in the past to advance other political values, the great body of case law which has developed in recent years makes it unlikely that courts will tolerate efforts to use the federal antitrust laws to advance unrelated social goals in the future.

To say that antitrust has matured, however, is not to deny that new areas of activity lie ahead. Not only has the Court yet to address a number of important issues, but much fine tuning remains to be done in the areas in which it has spoken. The growing activism of the states' attorneys general will pose challenges to both the local and the national practitioner. The wave of deregulation set in motion by the Reagan era will bring many industries under the watchful eye of antitrust that have not previously been exposed to its pitfalls. Empirical studies await to be done that will validate, or critique, the analytic framework for federal merger enforcement. In short, changes in economic conditions and the demise of per se rules may generate new and complex antitrust problems.

Through the years, antitrust has often found itself as the political ball bantered about by players with vastly different agendas. Recently, the Supreme Court has gone far to define the rules of the game such that the ultimate winner is always the consumer. Whether enforcement will increase or decline in coming years will depend largely on the ability of advocates for or against particular enforcement actions to fashion arguments within these rules.

19
Which past is prolog? the future of private antitrust enforcement

BY JOHN J. FLYNN*

I. Introduction

For the past four decades, and despite doubts voiced 100 years ago by the principal draftsmen of the Sherman Act,[1] the primary enforcement of the federal antitrust laws has occurred through private litigation.[2] Many of the leading cases carving out new

---

* Hugh B. Brown Professor of Law, College of Law, The University of Utah, Salt Lake City.

1 Klingsburg, *Balancing the Benefits and Detriments of Private Antitrust Enforcement: Detrebling Antitrust Injury, Standing and Other Proposed Solutions*, 9 CARDOZO L. REV. 1215 (1988) (summarizing remarks of Senators Sherman and George expressing doubts about the ability of private plaintiffs to surmount the financial and legal obstacles to maintaining private suits).

2 Salop & White, *Private Antitrust Litigation: An Introduction and Framework*, in PRIVATE ANTITRUST LITIGATION: NEW EVIDENCE, NEW LEARNING 3-4 (L. White, ed. 1988). Private suits have outnumbered public enforcement from a ratio of 6 to 1 to a ratio of 20 to 1 over the

standards of antitrust legality and illegality are ones that have resulted from private litigation. There is no doubt that the attraction of treble damages and attorneys' fees have provided a major incentive for the great increase in private antitrust actions over the past four decades. A generally receptive Supreme Court in the 1960's to the early 1970's gave considerable encouragement and the means to the bar to specialize in the bringing of antitrust suits through the expansion of favorable judge-made doctrine and procedures facilitating private enforcement.

Thereafter, judicial hostility to private antitrust enforcement began a noticeable rise. In the late 1970's and the 1980's, that hostility was manifested in the development of technical barriers to maintaining suits by doctrines such as "standing" and the intraenterprise conspiracy rule; by the increased use of summary judgment at a preliminary stage in private antitrust cases; and, by the shift in judicial and enforcement attitudes in favor of the legality of vertical market restraints. By the late 1980's, changes in several doctrines and the shift in attitudes in the enforcement agencies have led to outright proposals to abolish or severely limit private antitrust enforcement, while court-imposed barriers to private suits continued to mount. The trend has been running against private enforcement of antitrust policy, raising the possibility that the second century of antitrust enforcement might see the demise, in practice if not in the express repeal, of private enforcement or the creation of a hiatus in private actions much like that which prevailed from the 1920's through the 1940's. If the past is prolog, which past is the prolog to the future of private antitrust enforcement—the relative absence of private antitrust enforcement in the first six decades or the activism of the last four decades of antitrust law?

---

period measured. While many private suits were actions following federal enforcement, the sheer number of private suits has consistently exceeded those filed by the federal government. The added deterrence of disgorging treble damages has added significantly to the deterrent effect of the antitrust laws through reliance upon rational self-interest to protect one's own interest without the necessity of direct government intervention.

Predicting the future of private antitrust, let alone the future of the economy or who will win the World Series next year, is a matter of weighing several variables—some known, and many more, not known. The task puts one in mind of the late Arthur Leff's reformulation of the economist's special theory of the second best into a general theory of the second best: "If a state of affairs is the product of *n* variables, and you have knowledge of or control over less than *n* variables, if you think you know what is going to happen when you vary 'your' variables, you're a booby."[3] To minimize the risk of violating Leff's general theory of the second best, this article reviews some of the key variables relevant to determining the future of private antitrust enforcement—passive or active, after listing variables one simply cannot make predictions about at this point in time.

II. Unknown variables

A. *The ideology of enforcement officials and judges*

One set of unknown variables of central significance to a prediction of the future of antitrust generally, is the approach to antitrust policy by the appointments President Bush will make to the enforcement agencies and the courts. It is not difficult to imagine that the appointment of moderates and realists to the enforcement agencies and the courts will have a significant impact on antitrust enforcement. Following 8 years of what many have seen as Reagan administration nonenforcement of the antitrust laws[4] and the appointment of judges with strong-minded, if

---

[3] Leff, *Economic Analysis of Law: Some Realism About Nominalism*, 60 VA. L. REV. 451 (1974).

[4] *See, e.g.*, Adams & Brock, *Reaganomics and the Transmogrification of Merger Policy*, 33 ANTITRUST BULL. 309 (1988); Krattenmaker & Pitofsky, *Antitrust Merger Policy and the Reagan Administration*, 33 ANTITRUST BULL. 211 (1988); Litvak, *The Appropriate Enforcement Role of the Government Antitrust Agency*, 9 CARDOZO L. REV. 1291 (1988); Pitofsky, *Does Antitrust Have a Future?* 76 GEO. L.J. 321 (1987); Shennefield, *Open Letter to the New President of the United States*, 9 CARDOZO L. REV. 1295 (1988).

not rigidly ideological, beliefs in the wisdom of a policy of extreme laissez faire, the appointment of experienced lawyers rather than theorists to the agencies and courts can have a profound effect on antitrust enforcement. If that were to occur, perhaps we will see the end to enforcement guidelines issued for advocating judicial nonenforcement of the laws Congress passed or for legislating the views of enforcement officials of what the law ought to be rather than leaving to Congress the primary law-making power. Government intervention in private litigation to prevent private enforcement might also subside. Court decisions dealing with the reality of cases and the practical procedural problems of litigation might even become the norm. We might even see the Justice Department stop trying to inflate its enforcement statistics by bringing the same case over and over in each federal district court in the Union! There are, after all, only so many road builders one can charge with bid rigging and soft drink bottlers one can charge with price fixing. And, judges might begin to analyze the reality of cases in light of the values underlying the law instead of deductively applying the conclusions of a theoretical model in light of its unrealistic assumptions to a reality not before the court.

There are a few aspects of the Reagan administration policies one can applaud and hope the Bush administration will continue. For example, the increased emphasis upon criminal sanctions for hard-core antitrust violations and support for a significant increase in criminal fines[5] should continue to be a major emphasis of the Bush administration's antitrust policy. The continuation of the Carter administration's more stringent examination of the regulated industries has also produced worthwhile results by questioning the on-going need for regulation in rapidly changing areas of the economy. Beyond that however, it is difficult to identify positive benefits of 8 years of Reaganomics on antitrust policy, let alone the economy generally, unless one simply assumes that nonaction, a decline in staff morale at the enforcement agencies, and the shrinking of enforcement budgets are, ipso facto, benefits.

---

[5]   *See* Starling, *Criminal Antitrust Enforcement*, 57 ANTITRUST L.J. 157 (1988).

B. The use and misuse of enforcement guidelines

One unpredictable variable of public enforcement in need of review by both Congress and the new administration is the expanded use made of enforcement "guidelines."[6] Many commentators are troubled by the expansive use of enforcement guidelines by the Antitrust Division beyond the merger area. The practice of an executive branch law enforcement agency issuing guidelines stating what the policy should be on a law adopted by Congress and committed to the courts for interpretation is inconsistent with the functions of a law enforcement agency, the Congress and the courts. While the FTC does have rule-making power subject to appropriate administrative law constraints, the Justice Department should confine its rule making to the only area where Congress has conferred a similar type of administrative authority—the administration of merger policy as a result of the Hart-Scott-Rodino Act.[7] Even in that instance, a serious reexamination of the practice should be undertaken since the Antitrust Division engages in a wide range of informal law making when issuing "guidelines" and negotiating settlements with Hart-Scott-Rodino applicants without sufficient legal constraints upon the process or independent review of the standards adopted or the procedures followed.

The Merger Guidelines of both the FTC and the Antitrust Division also should be reviewed in the name of complying with the law Congress enacted[8]—rather than some law the agency

---

[6] For an interesting review of the use of enforcement guidelines in the merger area and the conversion of the Antitrust Division from a law enforcement agency to an administrative one, *see,* Sullivan, *The Antitrust Division as a Regulatory Agency: An Enforcement Policy in Transition,* 64 WASH. U.L.Q. 997 (1986).

[7] 15 U.S.C. § 18a.

[8] The underlying assumption of the Guidelines is to judge mergers by static neoclassical price theory rather than the dynamic structural standard implied by an incipiency standard and the legislative history of the Act. In effect, the Guidelines apply pre-1950 Sherman Act standards (1920's Sherman Act standards) to mergers. A major goal of the 1950's amendment was, of course, to overturn the application of Sherman Act

believes Congress should have enacted. If there is a problem with that law, appropriate legislation should be presented to Congress for its consideration[9]—a process mandated by the Constitution despite claims made for unilateral law-making powers implicit in some of the other executive branch practices of the Reagan administration. At a very minimum, considerable thought should be given to lowering the level of the Herfindahl index triggering merger challenges by the enforcement agencies. At a minimum, consideration should be given to enforcing the standards adopted, rather than an undisclosed set of standards adopted for in-house use.[10] Actions should be brought or inaction should be thoroughly explained where the agency's own standard for when a merger should be challenged is violated by a particular merger.

Other "guidelines" issued by the Antitrust Division do not appear to be for providing guidance—but are for advocacy. There are few who believe that the Antitrust Division's Vertical Guidelines were intended to be a fair summary of what the law is on vertical restraints, let alone what Congress intends the enforcement agencies should do about vertical restraints.[11] The

---

standards to mergers. *See,* Schwartz, *The New Merger Guidelines: Guide to Governmental Discretion and Private Counselling or Propaganda for Revision of the Antitrust Laws,* 71 CALIF. L. REV. 575, 576 (1983): "[U]nder the guise of regularizing discretion, the antitrust laws are being amended without benefit of congressional action."

9   *See,* The Merger Modernization Act, H.R. 4247, 99th Cong., 2d Sess. (1986), the Reagan administration's proposal for a change in the Clayton Act § 7 standards to require that a merger's effect "will be" to increase the ability of one or more firms profitably to maintain prices above a competitive level for a significant period of time. The proposal would abandon the incipiency standard of the present law and rely solely on neoclassical price theory to determine the legality of a merger—a policy course it would appear the 1984 Guidelines and the current administration of them is adopting in fact if not in law. It is a policy course Congress never adopted.

10   *See* Lande, *The Rise and (Coming) Fall of Efficiency as the Ruler of Antitrust,* 33 ANTITRUST BULL. 429, 453 (1988).

11   *See,* Note, *The 1980's Amendment to the Sherman Antitrust Act and the Revitalized Per Se Illegality of Resale Price Maintenance,* 9 CARDOZO L. REV. 1435 (1988).

Vertical "Guidelines" are an advocate's brief for a particular belief of what the law ought to be rather than what Congress intends. As such, they should be withdrawn by the Bush administration.[12] Similar claims are made about the Guidelines for International Operations and those too should be withdrawn since they read like draft judicial opinions instead of a fair summary of what the courts have decided the law is.[13] Antitrust Division authorities should be limited to advocating their beliefs through briefs in government cases in court where they can be challenged before an impartial judge and in independently refereed law review articles, unless we are willing to give the agency law-making powers heretofore left to the judiciary or Congress and law review footnote checkers.

C. Judicial appointments

Another unknown variable of great significance to the future of private antitrust enforcement concerns what types of judicial appointments the new administration will make. Judicial appointments are, of course, crucial to the future evolution of antitrust policy. Congress has entrusted wide discretion to the courts in defining the direction and meaning of antitrust policy. While the Warren Court era judges may have gone too far in their concern for populist values in cases like *Von's Grocery*[14] and

---

[12] The vertical restraint guidelines and the international operations guidelines are "nothing more than a large *amicus* brief" and should be withdrawn. 55 ANTITRUST & TRADE REG. REP. (BNA) 799 (Nov. 3, 1988) (Remarks of T. Kauper).

[13] For a contrary view, *see* Hawk, *The Proposed Revisions of the Justice Department's Antitrust Guidelines for International Operations and Recent Developments in EEC Competition Law*, 57 ANTITRUST L.J. 299 (1988).

[14] United States v. Von's Grocery Co., 384 U.S. 270 (1966). The problem with the Court's opinion is not necessarily the result, but the way the Court got there. The Court's opinion is primarily a factual one without establishing predictable standards by which a merger ought or

Schwinn,[15] it appears that the Burger and Rehnquist era of judicial activism is going too far in the direction of embracing a simplistic static version of neoclassical economic ideology without regard for reality or the goals of antitrust policy in cases like *Matsushita*[16] and *Business Electronics v. Sharp*.[17] The direction taken by the Bush administration in its judicial appointments and congressional reaction to them will have a great influence over the next decade in determining whether antitrust policy will remain a significant element in determining economic policy and the rights of consumers and competitors or whether it will become a curious backwater largely of historical interest like it was in the 1920's; of little interest until the next economic disaster such as the Great Depression of the 1930's undermines the economy.

---

ought not to be judged pro- or anticompetitive. The subsequent adoption of premerger notification and the examination of a proposed merger by the enforcement agencies prior to its consummation, may have mitigated the dilemma of the courts in establishing workable guidelines for judging the legality of mergers under the broad incipiency standards of the Clayton Act by limiting the number of litigated cases. But it has not eliminated the problem of adopting and making known workable standards implementing the policies of Congress—it has simply shifted it to those administering premerger notification.

[15]   United States v. Arnold, Schwinn & Co., 388 U.S. 365 (1967) (drawing the line between lawful and unlawful dealer restrictions on resale between consignment and sales transactions on the basis of the common law doctrine of restraints on alienation; a knowable and predictable rule, but one easily circumvented and one that failed to grapple with all of the normative goals underlying the doctrine of restraints on alienation and the purposes of antitrust policy). *See* Flynn, *The Function and Dysfunction of* Per Se *Rules in Vertical Market Restraints*, 58 WASH. U.L.Q. 767 (1980).

[16]   Matsushita Electric Industrial Co. Ltd. v. Zenith Radio Corp., 475 U.S. 574 (1986). *See* Flynn, *An Antitrust Allegory*, 38 HASTINGS L.J. 517 (1987).

[17]   Business Electronics Corp. v. Sharp Electronics Corp., 108 S. Ct. 1515 (1988). *See*, Flynn, *The "Is" and "Ought" of Vertical Restraints After* Monsanto Co. v. Spray-Rite Service Corp., 71 CORNELL L. REV. 1095, 1114 (1986) (criticizing the Fifth Circuit's analysis in *Business Electronics* subsequently followed by the Supreme Court).

A key to the reflective development of antitrust policy through new appointments to the courts is that the Senate exert responsibly its coequal authority in the appointment of judges. Serious Senate evaluation will insure that we have judges who are reflective about the values they hold; open minded to challenges to those values and contrary statements of values; aware of the reality and facts of cases they must decide; skillful in the use of legal reasoning rather than the manipulation of definitions and deductive logic; experienced in the practical problems of litigation; and, sensitive to the congressionally mandated values underlying the laws they must enforce instead of the implementation of their own closed-minded and ideological beliefs.[18]

D. *Overcoming barriers to entry in the private antitrust litigation market*

Another unpredictable variable affecting the future of private antitrust enforcement concerns the willingness of the private bar and their clients to invest the resources necessary to bring credible private antitrust cases. From my conversations with members of both the plaintiffs' and defendants' bars around the country, it is apparent that many are cautiously gearing up for an increased level of federal antitrust enforcement—particularly in the merger area and in the area of horizontal restraints.

There is a growing chorus of concern about the merger movement claiming that it is driven primarily by promoters and deal makers interested in fees rather than the rational and efficient organization of the merging firms.[19] That perception is gaining the upper hand in Congress, among the public and even on Wall Street. There is more and more academic writing suggesting that the hypermerger movement is not in our national eco-

---

[18] *See* Flynn, *The Reagan Administration's Antitrust Policy, "Original Intent" and the Legislative History of the Sherman Act*, 33 ANTITRUST BULL. 259 (1988).

[19] *See* Krattenmaker & Pitofsky, *supra* note 4; Adams & Brock, *supra* note 4.

nomic interest, creates a debt-heavy corporate America posing fundamental economic risks in the event of a recession, detracts from economic efficiency and capital investment by draining off capital to nonproductive ends, and creates unmanageable firms that soon find themselves spinning off parts of the acquired firm.[20]

Another explanation for the belief that merger enforcement will increase may be the result of the past 8 years of merger mania with little or no stringent section 7 enforcement.[21] One wit commenting on the passing antitrust scene suggested that the relaxed triggering level of the Herfindahl index is reached in just about every merger that now takes place after 8 years of merger fever and the general nonenforcement of section 7. Art Buchwald's cynical column about the inconclusive debate in the Justice Department over whether to challenge the merger of the Sampson Securities Company owning the stock of all companies west of the Mississippi and the Delilah Corporation owning all companies east of it, attached as an appendix to Justice Douglas' concurring opinion in *United States v. Pabst Brewing Co.*,[22] no longer seems so far-fetched.

Eight years of lax enforcement, sanctioned and encouraged by some judges, also may explain why there appears to be a likelihood of an increase in both public and private enforcement in other areas of antitrust as well. The business community, like everyone exceeding the speed limit on the highway at 3:00 a.m. because no police are on the scene, can soon lose its fear of antitrust. Those subject to the law begin to engage in activities coming closer and closer to the line of illegality. For example, parties to a merger recently attempted to circumvent the ability of the FTC to have a court issue a preliminary injunction to stop the

---

[20]   *See,* W. ADAMS & J. BROCK, THE BIGNESS COMPLEX (1986); D. DAVENPORT & F. SCHERER, MERGERS, SELL-OFFS AND ECONOMIC EFFICIENCY (1987); R. WILLS, J. CASWELL & J. CULBERTSON, ISSUES AFTER A CENTURY OF FEDERAL COMPETITION POLICY (1987).

[21]   *See* Adams & Brock, *supra* note 4.

[22]   384 U.S. 546, 553–55 (1966).

merger by moving up the date of acquisition after receiving notice the Commission intended to seek the injunction.[23] It is an example of increased antitrust activity because of the Reagan era of low visibility enforcement policy encouraging high-risk conduct by those subject to the law. Such conduct is encouraged by the tendency of the last administration to seek a justification for whatever someone wished to do in terms of the neoclassical model—save horizontal price fixing—without asking whether the competitive process might be damaged on a long- or short-term basis, whether other schools of economic and political thought ought to be heard from or even whether the reality of particular cases should be considered.

Perhaps the enforcement agencies have finally recognized the unduly permissive climate they have created. Startling things have begun to happen. The FTC staff has even filed a Robinson-Patman Act proceeding against major book publishers charging price discrimination in favor of large book store chains over their smaller competitors.[24] Most antitrust practitioners have come to believe that mentioning the Robinson-Patman Act within the confines of the Federal Triangle was at least a misdemeanor; suggesting that a case be filed to enforce the Act was a felony.

E. Confused congressional antitrust attitudes

Adding to the possibility that there may be more vigorous and wide-ranging antitrust enforcement by the federal agencies generating additional private enforcement, is the prospect that Congress will continue to exert pressure for such a course of conduct. It is doubtful that Senator Metzenbaum will be any more sympathetic to moves to relax antitrust standards than he has been in the past. It is likely that Congressman Brooks, chairperson of the House Judiciary Committee, will be similarly inclined. One

---

[23]   FTC v. Elders Grain, Inc., 1989-1 Trade Cases ¶ 68,411 (7th Cir. 1989).

[24]   *In re* Harper & Row, Publishers, Inc., Dkt. Nos. 9317–9222 (FTC Dec. 22, 1988).

observer has classified Congressman Brooks as a cross between Congressman Celler and Congressman Rodino. Consequently, I expect we will see continued pressure for more active merger enforcement, the aggressive investigation of a broader range of horizontal restraints, continued calls to pursue vertical price-fixing cases[25] and concerns expressed about enforcement policy dealing with other questionable practices. For the Washington bar, there would appear to be plenty of Hill work ahead with the reintroduction of resale price maintenance legislation, moves to repeal the McCarran-Ferguson Act, battles over legislation modifying *Illinois Brick* and proposed legislation designed to eliminate the presumption of economic power with regard to intellectual property.[26]

It must be noted however, that Congress has not been a bastion of proantitrust fervor. Despite a general proantitrust reputation, a PAC-dominated Congress has not managed in the past decade to enact an activist antitrust agenda by passing bills such as those designed to overturn the *Illinois Brick* decision or come to grips with standards to govern vertical restraints. Instead, it has enacted such questionable legislation as the One House Veto of agency rule making later invalidated by the Supreme Court;[27] the reincarnation of the unused Webb-Pomerene Act through export trade cartels under the Export Trading Act of 1982;[28] legislation authorizing joint research

---

[25]   *See, Brooks Offers Bill on Standards in Resale Price Maintenance Suits*, 56 ANTITRUST & TRADE REG. REP. (BNA) 363 (March 9, 1989).

[26]   *See, Few Surprises Expected as Congress Focuses on Competition, Deception Issues*, 56 ANTITRUST & TRADE REG. REP. (BNA) 86 (Jan. 19, 1989).

[27]   Pub. L. No. 96-252, 94 Stat. 374 (1980), held unconstitutional in Consumer's Union, Inc. v. F.T.C., 691 F.2d 575 (D.C. Cir. 1982), *aff'd sub nom.*, Process Gas Consumers Group v. Consumer Energy Council of America, 463 U.S. 1216 (1983). *See also*, I.N.S. v. Chada, 462 U.S. 919 (1983).

[28]   15 U.S.C. §§ 4001 *et seq.*

ventures and limiting private treble damage actions with respect to them;[29] legislation limiting treble damage remedies for peer review activities in the health care field;[30] legislation sanctioning exclusive territories in the soft drink bottling business;[31] and legislation eliminating damage actions, but not injunction actions, for anticompetitive activity by local governments.[32] When all is said and done, Congress has shown itself remarkably responsive to special interest legislation chipping away at antitrust policy generally and treble damage actions in particular. The hard truth is that Congress' antitrust record has been more anti-antitrust than proantitrust, making it another unpredictable variable in predicting the future of private antitrust activity.

A significant anti-antitrust bill that has materialized in the 101st Congress, is a move to permit production and commercialization joint ventures along lines similar to the immunity provided by the Export Trading Company Act of 1982 and the National Cooperative Research Act of 1984.[33] Playing on concerns about foreign competition, it is argued that U.S. firms need immunity to form production and distribution cartels for the purposes of coordinating production and marketing activities in competition with foreign firms or cartels. Although the Attorney General and Secretary of Commerce have voiced early support for such a measure,[34] the proposal has sparked widespread debate and oppo-

---

[29]   15 U.S.C. §§ 4301–05.

[30]   The Health Care Quality Improvements Act of 1986, 42 U.S.C. §§ 11101, *et seq.*

[31]   Soft Drink Interbrand Competition Act, 15 U.S.C. §§ 3501–03.

[32]   Local Government Antitrust Act of 1984, 15 U.S.C. §§ 34–36.

[33]   The Joint Manufacturing Opportunities Act of 1989, H.R. 423, 101st Cong., 1st Sess. (1989); National Cooperative Innovation and Commercialization Act of 1989, H.R. 1024, 101st Cong., 1st Sess. (1989). *See generally, Witnesses Declare That Antitrust Law Discourages Formation of Joint Ventures*, 56 ANTITRUST & TRADE REG. REP. (BNA) 319 (March 2, 1989).

[34]   56 ANTITRUST & TRADE REG. REP. (BNA) 9 (Jan. 5, 1989).

sition from both the right and the left in academia. Hearings on the bill will find all the heavyweights of antitrust trooping to the Hill to debate what would be the most fundamental reorientation of antitrust policy since the NRA of the 1930's.

Giving rebirth to a form of the National Recovery Act of the 1930's[35] should provoke an interesting debate. Blaming America's competitive ills on the antitrust laws, after a sustained period of nonenforcement and the creation of significant judicial limitations on private enforcement, is a bit disingenuous if not hypocritical. Doing so through unnecessary legislation permitting joint production and commercialization ventures cuts out the heart of antitrust policy—preserving a competitive process as the best way to allocate resources, control undue accumulations of private economic power, insure innovation and insure equality of access to the market. United States trade policy should be seeking ways to break open Japan's domestic market to foreign competition, rather than gradually eliminating competition in our own in a vain attempt to emulate Japan's culture and system. As James Fallows recently observed, if we must imitate Japan to best Japan in the marketplace we also must be prepared to do the following if we expect to see it work:

> First, we rig politics so that one party is always in power and big-city votes don't count. Then we double the cost of everything else but hold incomes the same. Then we close the borders and start celebrating racial purity. Then we reduce the number of jobs for women by 70 to 80 percent. Then we set up a school system that teaches people not to ask questions. After a while, we can have a trade surplus too.[36]

In order to make such a system work like Japan's, we also must implement like Japan a system of economic and political feudal-

---

[35]   Held unconstitutional in Schechter Poultry Corp. v. United States, 295 U.S. 495 (1935).

[36]   Fallows, *For Those Who Have a Yen for the Japanese Way: Think Twice*, Washington Post (weekly ed. Feb. 20–26, 1989), at 23, 24. *See also*, Fallows, *The Hard Life*, THE ATLANTIC MONTHLY, March 1989, at 16.

ism, markets closed to foreign competition, and manufacturing and distribution cartels designed to raise domestic consumer prices about 70% higher than those prevailing in the United States.

The time has come for Congress to stop chipping away at antitrust policy piecemeal by flirting with each competitive crisis—real or imagined—as it comes along. We need another T.N.E.C. study or exhaustive and fundamental hearings of the type that the late Senator Philip Hart endured to establish whether America's competitive ills in the world economy are due to the failure to enforce antitrust policy in our domestic and foreign trade, rather than the existence of antitrust laws that are too rigid for our national economic survival in a more competitive world economy. The price we pay in abandoning antitrust policy as the basic means for regulating our economy and relationships within it are of wide-ranging and long-term economic, political and social dimensions.[37] The present tendency of Congress to ad hoc antitrust policy to pieces, has left both the public's understanding and Congress' understanding of the broader social, political and economic purposes of competition policy confused and disorganized. It is time for Congress to go beyond the ad hoc and fad of the moment and take a much broader, deeper and long-term look at what our commitment to a competitive process means and what it ought to mean— politically, socially and economically for the immediate and long-term future. The future of private antitrust enforcement will remain impossible to predict without a clear mandate for its continuation or its demise from Congress.

F. A rebirth of state antitrust enforcement?

Another variable that is difficult to gauge concerns a little-noticed development in Washington, D.C. but not among law

---

[37]   For some idea of the implications *see* M. Sklar, The Corporate Reconstruction of American Capitalism 1890–1916 (1988), a review of the economic, social and political issues involved in the process of institutionalizing antitrust policy at the turn of the last century.

firms elsewhere in the country. It is the continued growth and increased vitality of state antitrust enforcement.[38] State antitrust enforcement has become institutionalized with committed bureaucracies in many states devoted to its expansion. State antitrust officials do not fear to tread where federal enforcement officials believe the law should not tread. For example, states are becoming more active in merger enforcement[39] and favor more vigorous antitrust review of vertical restraints.[40] Both California and New York have been active in merger enforcement and state attorneys general in other states are interested as the result of significant mergers in their states such as the recent merger between Utah Power & Light Company and Pacific Corp.[41] creating a large regional electric utility and significant antitrust and regulatory issues in a basic public service for the local economies of several states.

In the vertical restraints area, state enforcement officials remain the major enforcers of traditional antitrust policy. For example, the state antitrust offices of New York and Maryland recently settled resale price maintenance cases for $16 million against Panasonic.[42] In addition, many states have been particularly active in franchise regulation, either under state antitrust

---

[38] A collection of recent significant articles reviewing state antitrust enforcement is reprinted in 28 J. REPRINTS FOR ANTITRUST L. & ECON. #2 (1989).

[39] State attorneys general have found it necessary to become involved in the "guidelines" game in the merger field. *See, National Association of Attorneys General Merger Guidelines*, 50 ANTITRUST & TRADE REG. REP. 1306 (Spec. Supp., March 12, 1987).

[40] With respect to vertical restraints, the National Association of State Attorneys General has also issued a set of "guidelines" in 1985. *See*, 5 Trade Reg. Rep. (CCH) ¶ 50,478.

[41] *Re* Utah Power & Light Co., 45 Fed. Energy Reg. Comm'n Rep. (CCH) ¶ 61,095, 96 P.U.R.4th 325 (1988).

[42] *See, Panasonic Will Refund $16 Million to Settle New York, Maryland RPM Cases*, 56 ANTITRUST & TRADE REG. REP. (BNA) 89 (Jan. 19, 1989).

and securities laws or under special state franchise statutes. In any current trade regulation index, state franchise cases consume pages of citations. In many instances, state franchise regulation is a response to the vacuum of sensible federal regulation of vertical market relationships under federal antitrust law. It should be noted also, that some of the state regulatory responses are anticompetitive and are not necessarily in the public interest. Rapidly multiplying state franchise regulations have been creating a confusing patchwork of regulation as well, which many national franchisors are finding increasingly difficult and expensive to comply with. Anticompetitive and unnecessary state regulations are a cost of the failure of federal enforcement officials to adopt a more realistic, flexible and less ideological approach to vertical restraints, leaving a vacuum where state and local officials are pressured to adopt regulatory approaches to fill in the gap; regulations that are not always in the public interest.

The consequences are that many law firms and courts around the country find themselves involved with a rapidly growing field of state antitrust enforcement—either states enforcing federal antitrust laws as consumers or in the enforcement of state antitrust and related laws in their own courts regulating vertical marketing and other practices. This is one of those variables one can predict will continue and that it probably will expand despite the recently announced effort of the FTC to adopt franchise rules designed to preempt state franchise regulation.[43] It is also reasonable to predict that such action by the FTC will be vigorously resisted and will be viewed as an attempt to get rid of significant state and *federal* regulation of the sale, enforcement and termination of franchises. It will not be viewed as the adoption of a responsible, effective and fair uniform federal standard to govern franchising and other vertical market abuses, but the further abandonment of federal responsibility to adopt a more realistic and pragmatic antitrust approach to vertical market restraints.

---

[43] *FTC's Advance Notice of Proposed Rulemaking on Amendment of Trade Regulation Rule Governing Franchises*, 56 ANTITRUST & TRADE REG. REP. (BNA) 307 (Feb. 23, 1989).

G. The deregulation movement

Another difficult to gauge variable of significance to private antitrust enforcement is the continued evolution of deregulation of presently or previously regulated industries. As a general proposition, one might expect to see antitrust policy involved in both generating pressure to deregulate and in "regulating" industries after they are "deregulated." For example, the natural gas transmission industry is now going through the confusion of ad hoc deregulation—deregulation imposed by the Federal Energy Regulatory Commission [FERC] converting pipelines from being brokers of natural gas to being common carriers of gas. It is a jurisdictionally questionable exercise of power by FERC[44] and an area that Congress should be addressing through legislation. Deregulation of gas purchases and sales by pipelines is nonetheless underway and it is a process that is generating private treble damage litigation by sellers and buyers of gas and is likely to cause more private litigation in the future.[45] Common carrier status for transmission pipelines and other developments in the industry are expected to lead to mergers in the industry—mergers likely to generate significant competitive questions about the activities of merged firms postmerger, and arrangements leading up to or entered into in conjunction with a particular merger.

In the electric power industry, FERC has begun to use its authority over mergers in the industry to impose common carrier obligations similar to those it is imposing in the gas transmission business on the merging parties where the merger has anticompetitive features. The leading case is *Utah Power & Light Co.*,[46]

---

[44]   *See, e.g.*, Watkiss, *Deregulatory Myopia: Sacrificing the Filed Rate Doctrine and Rule Against Retroactive Ratemaking to Promote Competition in Gas Markets*, 42 Sw. L.J. 711 (1988).

[45]   *See, e.g.*, James River Corp. v. Northwest Pipeline Corp., Civ. No. 87-1141 RE (D. Ore. 1987); State v. Panhandle Eastern Pipeline Co., 852 F.2d 891 (7th Cir.), *cert. denied*, 109 S. Ct. 543 (1988).

[46]   45 Fed. Energy Reg. Comm'n Rep. (CCH) ¶ 61,095 (Oct. 26, 1988).

and the conditions imposed are already generating complex regulatory issues. The conditions also may spark antitrust disputes in the future because of the considerably more complex nature of the electric utility industry as compared with the natural gas industry.[47] It is generally agreed in the industry that it is on the edge of a large number of mergers seeking to rationalize the transmission system and competing sources of power generation. Such mergers are likely to raise substantial competitive issues and cause significant private antitrust litigation before the dust finally settles and the industry is more sensibly structured both horizontally and vertically. Once again, it is an area in urgent need of congressional action,[48] rather than an ad hoc regulatory response by conditions placed on mergers that happen to come along.

Another regulated industry likely to breed significant private antitrust work is the telephone industry. The breakup of A.T. & T. is only part of the problem. The more significant and longer term problem, one where the Justice Department, the operating companies and Judge Greene have a considerable difference of opinion, concerns the question of the scope of businesses the divested Bell operating companies will be allowed to enter. State regulatory schemes also have a considerable interest in the matter. State action or nonaction in response to operating company moves into related businesses is the source of complex antitrust issues of interest to the private bar as well.

The seven Bell operating companies have total assets of $151 billion plus and revenues of $69.7 billion in 1987; they are among the largest and most powerful entities in our society and hold monopoly control over a key segment to the future evolution of

---

[47] *See* Russo, *Transmission Access—A Crucial Issue for an Industry*, 123 PUB. UTIL. FORT. 18 (Feb. 16, 1988).

[48] Among other things, Congress should consider adopting a law permitting private power companies access to low-cost public power if the private power companies agree to open up their transmission systems on a common carrier basis subject to FERC rate and service regulation. We can no longer afford the wasteful and environmentally harmful duplication of generation and transmission resources caused by the long-standing war between public and private power.

communications technology and policy in our society. They are seeking the end to restrictions in the A.T. & T. consent decree limiting the kinds of related businesses they may engage in, including the manufacture of telephone equipment, the providing of long distance service and the providing of information services, including cable TV and enhanced computer services. Judge Greene is resisting on the ground that the operating companies still have a bottleneck monopoly over switching and the local loop and that permitting the operating companies to engage in related lines of business will only be inviting the anticompetitive abuses that required the breakup of A.T. & T. in the first place. Former Assistant Attorney General Rule to the contrary notwithstanding,[49] Judge Greene obviously has the better of the debate. Moreover, the advent of fiber optic cable on the local loop is likely to strengthen and expand the bottleneck monopoly over switching and the local loop by taking over such fields as the delivery of cable television and computer services to the home. Many of the operating companies are also seeking the relaxation or abolition of local rate regulation under the banner of "incentive" or "revenue sharing" rate regulation; the conferring of

---

[49]   Rule, *Antitrust and Bottleneck Monopolies*, 5 TELEMATICS 16 (Dec. 1988). Former Assistant Attorney General Rule's basic objection is that antitrust courts are not capable of regulating pricing decisions by the bottleneck monopolist and that economic theory (based on unrealistic factual and normative assumptions) dictates that it is in the bottleneck monopolist's best interest to insure maximum use of the bottleneck at the lowest possible cost. Consequently, it is assumed that even where the bottleneck monopolist drives out competitors in related markets the consumer will be better off since there is no way to determine whether they will be worse off. Like other policy pronouncements of Mr. Rule, this one appears to be the product of abstract economic theorizing detached from reality and inconsistent with the congressionally mandated goals of antitrust policy. *See*, Flynn, *supra* note 18. The implication of Rule's analysis that bottleneck monopolies create no antitrust problems because the theoretical conclusions of a model deductively derived from its unrealistic assumptions says so, implies that the original A.T. & T. should be put back together again. Several of the operating companies seem to be bent upon that path with respect to their own operations and apparently with the academic support of former Assistant Attorney General Rule.

monopoly pricing discretion on the operating companies that will leave only antitrust policy as a control over the potential abuse of the otherwise unchecked bottleneck monopoly power and profits conferred.

These developments generate a classic circumstance inviting private antitrust actions if deregulation at the state or federal level comes to pass. There are already some possible suits in the wind as the result of attempts by the operating companies to obtain greater pricing discretion over local rates and permission to enter related businesses. One type of suit illustrating the connection between bottleneck pricing discretion and entry into related business activity is private antitrust litigation challenging the use of negative options for inside wiring.[50] Many local phone companies sent consumers a notice that their phone company would take care of any inside wiring problems they might have unless the consumer sent in a notice to the contrary. A monthly charge was to be assessed to all those not opting out of the so-called contract.[51] Using monopoly power over captured customers and potentially deceptive sales practices to entrap customers for a service they probably need once in a couple of generations is not an enhancement of consumer welfare.

Another deregulated industry ripe for antitrust concern is the airline business. The Department of Transportation has permitted a large number of mergers in the industry to go through— Herfindahl notwithstanding—without significant challenge. The results have been predictable and probably would not have happened if the initial review of mergers in the industry had been committed even to the Reagan antitrust enforcement agencies

---

[50] *See*, Sollenbarger v. Mountain States Telephone Co., 121 F.R.D. 417 (D.N.M. 1988).

[51] This information is based upon a study of documents released by the FCC pursuant to a Freedom of Information Act request addressed to the Commission by the author. *See*, *In re* John Flynn, FOI Cont. No. 88-188 (FCC, March 10, 1989).

upon the phasing out of regulation rather than to the Department of Transportation.[52]

As a result of mergers taking place after deregulation, TWA has 83% of the market at St. Louis and fares have gone up 22% in the past 3 years; Delta has 77% of the Salt Lake hub and fares have gone up 26% in that market over the past 3 years; and, in Detroit, Northwest has 62% of the market and fares have gone up 27% in that market. During the same time period, the airline component of the consumer price index has gone up 11.1%. A private survey of 18 hubs where one carrier controls more than 50% of the market found that in 15 of those hubs consumers pay significantly higher fares than the industry norm.[53] It would appear that there is strong evidence of monopoly pricing going on—activity the Antitrust Division should be—but appears not to be—deeply concerned about, apparently in the belief that supposed perfect competition coupled with supposed free entry will take care of a supposed problem. Perhaps some imaginative private attorney can figure out an antitrust theory on behalf of an appropriate plaintiff for what appear to be monopoly overcharges as the result of several mergers that should not have been allowed to take place in the first instance in an industry characterized by significant entry barriers in reservations systems, airport landing rights and airport gate restrictions.

Several other industries, such as health care and emerging high tech industries developing difficult to classify intangible intellectual property values, present unique challenges to both antitrust and regulatory schemes seeking to curb practices suggesting abuses of economic power take place often in the industry

---

[52] Under the Civil Aeronautics Board Sunset Act, 49 U.S.C. App. §§ 1551, *et seq.*, DOT authority over airline mergers under the old Act ceased on January 1, 1989, thereby leaving them subject to regulation under the antitrust laws at the instance of the antitrust enforcement agencies and private parties.

[53] The highlights of several recent studies are summarized in Hamilton, *The Hubbub Over Airline Hubbing,* Washington Post (national weekly ed., Feb. 13–19, 1989), at 21.

in a manner inconsistent with the normative goals underlying antitrust policy. Such industries are, and are likely to continue to be, a fruitful source of private antitrust challenges. Like those industries now undergoing deregulation, these emerging areas of complex economic activity continue to generate significant private antitrust litigation in both federal and state courts. As such, they are new frontiers challenging the imagination and creativity of the legal process to deal constructively with the issues they raise in the context unique to the activity involved and compatible with the underlying social, economic and political values we hold in common.

How a mixed system of private and public health care shall be regulated where third-party payment governs economic incentives and deep ethical issues and government financing effect access and availability, remains an unpredictable variable in estimating the future role of private antitrust in health care. Private and public efforts to protect emerging new technologies in high technology industries not neatly fitting traditional patent and copyright protections, also raise unpredictable variables that hold unknown implications for the future vitality of private antitrust enforcement in significant areas of newly emerging technological activity.

III. Predictable variables

If the Bush administration continues along the antitrust path chartered by the Reagan administration, there are several identifiable variables that must be changed if private antitrust enforcement is to have a significant future as the most important form of antitrust enforcement and a check upon public nonenforcement of the laws Congress has adopted. These are variables that largely reflect a current judicial hostility to private antitrust enforcement, despite section 4 of the Clayton Act vesting a cause of action in "any person who shall be injured in his business or property by reason of anything forbidden in the antitrust laws."[54]

---

[54]   15 U.S.C. § 15(a).

A. "Standing"

The first predictable variable influencing the future of private antitrust enforcement concerns access to the courts for private parties seeking to enforce the rights the law has given them. Over the past several years a particularly strange and pernicious doctrine called "standing" has been growing like a noxious weed. It is a confused and confusing doctrine, like "proximate cause" in torts and "privity" in contracts, limiting access to the courts in many areas of law without revealing the underlying reasons for doing so. It is an offshoot of the doctrine of justiciability; a doctrine more than one writer has pointed out is a myth. It is a myth because a finding that a particular dispute is not justiciable or that a party does not have "standing," outside the case or controversy doctrine, is to say something about the meaning or scope of the underlying law without saying so.[55] Masking or hiding what is being said about the underlying law behind a concept called "standing," obscures the substance of what is said about the underlying law and greatly confuses what the law is, how it should be pleaded considering the facts in a particular case and at what point in the litigation process it is appropriate to deal with the underlying substantive issues involved. Like the old doctrine of "substantive due process," standing doctrine allows courts to litigate the merits of disputes and the meaning of the law on abstract paper motions without saying so by pretending that a claimant lacks a right to bring the suit in the first instance.[56]

---

[55] McCormack, *The Justiciability Myth and the Concept of Law*, 14 HASTINGS CONST. L.Q. 595 (1987). *See also*, Fletcher, *The Structure of Standing*, 98 YALE L.J. 221, 229 (1988): "The essence of a true standing question is the following: Does the plaintiff have a legal right to judicial enforcement of an asserted legal duty? This question should be seen as a question of substantive law, answerable by reference to the statutory or constitutional provision whose protection is invoked."

[56] The analytical methodology of many standing cases resembles that followed in United States v. Butler, 297 U.S. 1 (1936), the classic substantive due process case. The majority repeatedly denied it was making any value choice when it set the Agricultural Adjustment Act down beside the Due Process clause to see if the former "squared" with the latter. The methodology is similar to that followed by economic

Use of the myth called "standing" is particularly pernicious since it is invoked at the preliminary stages of the dispute and involves a paper minitrial on both the facts and law *via* motion practice without any of the constraints of a normal trial or a full record on which the court can make an informed judgment. Understanding the basis of the decision and its substantive implications for both the field of law involved and future disputes under that law is often impossible and contributes to further litigation to establish the boundaries of what is not being said. Moreover, the doctrine generates substantial confusion over the constitutionally mandated different roles of judge and jury in the litigation of a private suit—no matter what the field of law infected by the virus called "standing."

These realities are particularly apparent in the antitrust field, where standing holdings have served as a mask for hiding decisions on causation issues, damage issues and issues about the substantive meaning and scope of the law. Saying one thing while deciding another, is scarcely an informed and artful use of legal analysis and has generated considerable confusion over what one must allege and prove in the early stages of antitrust litigation to avoid being summarily dismissed from court.

Elsewhere, I have suggested that private antitrust litigation should adopt the following analytical framework to both escape the bog of standing and more clearly define the distinction between judge and jury functions in private antitrust litigation:

1. Is there a factual connection between the plaintiff's claimed injury and the defendant? (an issue not often contested);

---

ideologues who measure the legality of a practice in a particular case by seeing if the deductively derived conclusions of the model square with the unrealistic assumptions of the model. Many standing cases also pretend not to be making a value judgment concerning the underlying law when they examine whether the plaintiff is the proper person to maintain the particular suit. How one can make that judgment without also making judgments concerning the scope of the protections offered by the underlying law, causation or damage issues and the normative values underlying these issues is difficult to discern.

2. Do the policies of the law and its system of protection extend to the interest that the plaintiff seeks to vindicate; and if some protection is afforded, what standard of care does the legal system impose upon the defendant? (questions of law for the judge);

3. Was the standard of care breached by the defendant? (a question of fact for the jury); and

4. What are the damages? (questions of fact for the jury).[57]

Such a system of analysis delineates the line between judge and jury functions and avoids the substantive confusion over duty, causation and damage issues generated by the courts' use of the shifting, changing and meaningless concept of antitrust standing. Confronting most "standing" issues as ones concerning the scope of the duties imposed by the antitrust laws, causation problems or damage questions, would also require that the factual, normative and legal basis for the decision be identified and confronted, that it be done at an appropriate time and place in the litigation, that it be done in light of the constitutional division of judge and jury functions and that it be done in light of all the congressionally defined goals for antitrust policy.[58]

---

[57] Flynn, *Rethinking Sherman Act Section 1 Analysis: Three Proposals for Reducing the Chaos*, 49 ANTITRUST L.J. 1593, 1610–11 (1980); Flynn, *supra* note 15; Flynn, *supra* note 17, at 1124; Flynn & Ponsoldt, *Legal Reasoning and the Jurisprudence of Vertical Restraints: The Limitations of Neoclassical Economic Analysis in the Resolution of Antitrust Disputes*, 62 N.Y.U. L. REV. 1125 (1987).

[58] Direct suits by shareholders, employees or suppliers of corporations injured by an antitrust violation, for example, should be treated as damage issues, not "standing" issues. Requiring the suit to be maintained by the corporation in most but not all cases avoids complex damage issues, the risk of multiple recoveries, prejudice to creditor rights and the undue consumption of court time by a multiplicity of lawsuits. While the end result of such an approach would often be similar to the end result in using "standing" doctrine, the process by which the determination would be made would differ significantly and the issue considered would be narrowed down to a damage issue and not be confused with or become the vehicle for determinations on the scope

The most recent antitrust pure "standing" case in the Supreme Court is *Associated General Contractors v. California State Council of Carpenters.*[59] In that case the Court upheld the dismissal before trial of an antitrust complaint charging that the defendant contractors had engaged in a conspiracy to cause third-party contractors to hire subcontractors not signatory to the collective bargaining contract between the plaintiff union and the defendant contractors. The Court held that the right to bring an antitrust treble damage action—so-called standing—was to be interpreted in light of common law limitations like foreseeability, proximate cause, privity, directness of injury, and certainty of damages and that the antitrust laws should not be held to extend a remedy to everyone injured by every ripple of an antitrust violation. The Court then sought to structure a test for determining whether the plaintiff union was within the class of persons the antitrust laws were designed to protect by an examination of a complex of factors such as the directness of the injury alleged, whether the plaintiff was in the area of the economy claimed to be damaged by a breakdown of competitive conditions, whether the plaintiff was within an identifiable class of persons with an incentive to bring the action and whether damages were speculative.

Issues of the substantive meaning of the law, causation and proof of damages are confusingly mixed by the Court's approach

---

of the duties imposed under the antitrust laws without saying so. Treating the issue as a damage issue would also leave room for unusual cases where a right to maintain an action should be recognized and would permit a more understandable distinction to be drawn between the damage requirements for injunctive actions and damage actions. *See* Flynn, *Rethinking the Sherman Act Section 1 Analysis, supra* note 57, at 1593.

[59]   459 U.S. 519 (1983). The decision in Atlantic Richfield v. USA Petroleum Co., 110 S. Ct. 1884 (1990) might also be considered a standing decision. It is not a pure standing decision because the majority opinion, confused and confusing as it is, purported to be analyzing the case on the issue of what evidence is sufficient to prove "injury."

in the name of standing, and one required to be decided before a full record of the claim is presented to the Court without clearly identifying which issue is being decided, at what point in the litigation it must be decided or how the recipe of factors to decide it should be blended. If the Court wished to hold section 1 of the Sherman Act should not apply to a vertically induced boycott in labor markets where a competitive process is distorted by private contract (a substantive ruling on the scope of the duties imposed by the antitrust laws in the circumstances), it should have said so rather than decide the substantive duty issue behind a fog of standing doctrine leaving ambiguous the basis of the decision. The opinion reads like a common law judge's analysis of whether someone has stated a claim within the common law forms of action, rather than a lucid explication of the scope of the duties imposed on the defendant by the antitrust laws, the standards of proof for finding a breach of the duty, the factors necessary to prove the element of causation or the considerations underlying the issue of what damages are and are not recoverable.

The consequences are apparent. The opinion is a confused and confusing mishmash further hampering the intelligent pleading of a private treble damage action; our understanding of what violates the law and what does not; the meaning and scope of the constitutional right to jury trial in treble damage actions; what facts are relevant to the analysis of the issue and at what point in the trial they become relevant; and, the structuring of an orderly process for the motion stage and the trial stage of a private antitrust case. Apparently, in a certain class of cases where a conspiracy is claimed to deny a plaintiff access to a market governed by a competitive process, it will be necessary to hold a minitrial on the pleadings to determine whether the law is violated, whether the violation caused the plaintiff damage and whether a plaintiff has a right to recover for the damages claimed in the circumstances to satisfy something called standing. If a plaintiff survives that process at the motion stage of the case, then the plaintiff can have a trial to determine whether the defendant has violated duties owed the plaintiff under the antitrust laws, whether that violation has caused the plaintiff injury and whether the injury claimed constitutes measurable damages under the antitrust laws. In philosophy, circular reasoning of this sort is called a tautology; in law it is called standing; and, in reality it should be called a form of unnecessary analytical chaos.[60]

The Court's opinion in *Associated Contractors* also relied upon the much debated and related rule of *Illinois Brick*,[61] denying recovery of damages by indirect purchasers. *Illinois Brick*, whatever its merits, was not a standing decision but one that drew the line around the duties imposed on an antitrust defendant at liability to the first in the chain of distribution in the name of avoiding undue complexity in damage calculations and the risk to defendants of multiple liability beyond that permitted by the statute. Instead of seeking a less drastic remedy for these legitimate concerns in indirect purchaser cases like mandatory joinder of all claimants, the Court simply barred indirect purchaser claims. Ever since the decision, confusion has reigned over issues like who are indirect purchasers and whether the concerns underlying *Illinois Brick* are present where overcharges caused by an antitrust violation are passed through to an indirect plaintiff down the line of distribution.

Two recent cases illustrate some of the confusion that now abounds: In *County of Oakland v. City of Detroit*,[62] the Sixth Circuit reversed dismissal of a claim on standing grounds and held that the plaintiffs who passed on alleged overcharges as the result of an upstream conspiracy should not be denied standing because they passed through the overcharges. In *In re Wyoming Tight Sands Antitrust Cases*,[63] the Tenth Circuit denied parens patriae standing, in direct conflict with a Seventh Circuit decision

---

[60] For more colorful descriptions of standing doctrine see the summary listed in Fletcher, *supra* note 55, at 221.

[61] Illinois Brick Co. v. Illinois, 431 U.S. 720 (1977).

[62] 866 F.2d 839 (6th Cir. 1989), *cert. denied*, 110 S. Ct. 3236 (1990).

[63] 866 F.2d 1286 (10th Cir. 1989), *aff'd, sub nom.*, Kansas & Missouri v. Utilicorp United, Inc., 110 S. Ct. 2807 (1990).

upholding standing in similar circumstances. Standing was denied[64] to states suing on behalf of consumers allegedly the victims of a price-fixing conspiracy in the natural gas business even though the enhanced prices had been directly passed on to the state's consumers. The Tenth Circuit did so because it read *Hanover Shoe*[65] as requiring a preexisting cost plus contract in order to invoke the pass-through exception to the *Illinois Brick* rule barring indirect purchasers from maintaining an antitrust suit.

The Supreme Court affirmed[66] the Tenth Circuit's overly technical and narrow reading of the pass-through exception to *Illinois Brick*. The Supreme Court speculated that the utility passing on the overcharge may be injured independently of an injury to its customers and that timing problems caused by state rate regulation might raise complex issues of apportionment of the amount passed on.[67] The majority further speculated that

---

[64]   State v. Panhandle Eastern Pipe Line Co., 852 F.2d 891 (7th Cir.), *cert. denied*, 109 S. Ct. 543 (1988).

[65]   Hanover Shoe, Inc. v. United Shoe Machinery Corp., 392 U.S. 481 (1968).

[66]   Kansas & Missouri v. Utilicorp United, Inc., 110 S. Ct. 2807 (1990).

[67]   The Court's hypotheticals can easily be changed to support the opposite result of permitting a recovery. More likely than not, over-charges for gas sold to the utilities for resale to consumers would have been included in utility rates as a recoverable expense for which consumers must pay. Regulatory lag in discovering the inflated charges for gas would mean the utilities would retain earnings reflecting the overcharge for a substantial time. In addition to the possibility of utilities keeping the float for overcharges because of regulatory lag, the "filed rate" doctrine might preclude a retroactive recovery of all of the excessive charges for a basic cost input to a utility like gas purchase costs. Ratemaking is generally said to be prospective. Past errors in rates may not generally be recovered in future rates. At the federal level, the filed rate doctrine precludes a regulated entity from charging rates other than those on file with the regulatory commission and has been held to

there remained a risk of double recoveries due to the complexity of apportioning the damages between the utility and its customers, even though the Court had held that state courts acting under state antitrust laws were free to adopt a policy of permitting indirect purchaser suits in *California v. Arc America Corp.*[68] State courts are apparently considered capable of sorting out the complexities of indirect purchaser suits while federal courts are not.

The twisting and turning of the federal courts on the right of indirect purchasers to maintain a damage action is an example of the undue confusion generated by both antitrust standing doctrine, other judicially created limitations on the right to maintain damage actions like the *Illinois Brick* decision and the detachment of antitrust rules from the underlying purposes of the law. It also bespeaks of a judicial hostility to private antitrust enforcement by the creation of abstract and hypothetical complications to avoid giving effect to the congressional grant of a right to "*any* person who shall be injured in his business or property by

---

preclude a court or regulatory commission from altering a rate retroactively. The doctrine is said to be based on the need to preserve the stability of rates and protect the primary jurisdiction over ratemaking in the regulatory commission. *See*, Arkansas Louisiana Gas Co. v. Hall, 453 U.S. 571, 101 S. Ct. 2925, 69 L. Ed. 2d 856 (1981); Square D Co. v. Niagara Frontier Tariff Bureau, Inc., 476 U.S. 409, 106 S. Ct. 1922, 90 L. Ed. 2d 413 (1986); L. Schwartz, J. Flynn & H. First, Free Enterprise & Economic Organization: Government Regulation 355–57 (1985). The same day the Court decided the *Kansas* case, it decided a case where the filed rate doctrine was invoked to strike down a negotiated rate by truckers lower than the filed rate with the ICC. *See*, Maislin Industries, U.S., Inc. v. Primary Steel, Inc., 110 S. Ct. 2759 (1990). Consequently, if the utility is the only party able to recover for the overcharge, it is likely that the utility will be able to retain the overcharge and consumers would not recover anything for the higher prices they paid and state regulatory policy would preclude a regulatory commission from recouping the overcharge for consumers by retroactive ratemaking.

68   109 S. Ct. 1661 (1989).

reason of *anything* forbidden in the antitrust laws"[69] to bring a private damage action. It is also a warning to any antitrust plaintiff to hire a specialist in geometry or metaphysics before filing a treble damage action where potential standing or *Illinois Brick* problems may be lurking in the vicinity.

Standing type confusion has not stopped there. The states have stepped into the *Illinois Brick* controversy by passing state laws permitting indirect purchaser suits in some circumstances for a violation of their own state antitrust laws. In *California v. ARC America Corp*,[70] the Ninth Circuit held that state antitrust law provisions permitting suits by indirect purchasers found in the Alabama, California and Minnesota antitrust laws are preempted by federal antitrust policy because they stand "as an obstacle to the accomplishment of the full purposes and objectives of federal antitrust law." The Supreme Court granted certiorari and the Solicitor General—surprisingly—came into the case on the side of the states. In a unanimous opinion, the Court reversed the Ninth Circuit and held that federal law does not preempt state antitrust laws from granting indirect purchasers the right to maintain a state antitrust suit seeking damages for injuries they may claim.[71] Now, rather than confronting the complexity of sorting out damage proofs in a single federal action, defendants will be confronted with doing so in an array of state cases involving varying state laws authorizing indirect purchaser suits under state antitrust laws.

An analogous line of standing type cases has been evolving in the merger field as a result of the Supreme Court's standing decision in *Cargill, Inc. v. Monfort of Colorado*.[72] In *Cargill*, the Court required a plaintiff competitor seeking to enjoin a merger to prove an injury of the type the antitrust laws were designed to

---

[69] Clayton Act § 4, 15 U.S.C § 15 (emphasis added).

[70] 1987-1 Trade Cas. (CCH) ¶ 65,575 (9th Cir. 1987).

[71] California v. Arc America, 109 S. Ct. 1661 (1989).

[72] 479 U.S. 104 (1986).

prevent. While rejecting an amicus argument by the Justice Department arguing that competitor suits to enjoin a merger should be denied standing as a matter of course because of the danger that the suit would be used to curb competition rather than foster it, the Court's opinion left confused and confusing just what a private plaintiff must prove to maintain a private action challenging a section 7 violation. The Court held that a private antitrust plaintiff seeking standing to maintain an injunction action is required to show threatened loss from an antitrust violation as opposed to loss due "merely to an increase in competition."

Where the injunction sought is a preliminary injunction, the issue becomes even more complex since the plaintiff is faced with having to prove a form of double incipiency—that the plaintiff is likely to prevail on the merits where the merits require a showing of a threatened—rather than actual—loss of competition or tendency to a monopoly. Treating the issue as a standing issue rather than a duty, damage or causation issue, once again forces a plaintiff to prove a case in chief at the preliminary stages of the litigation in order to be able to go on to prove the case in chief—a substantial barrier to private actions for injunctive relief and a result that significantly alters the express language of section 16 of the Clayton Act.[73]

Some lower courts have read *Cargill* as denying competitors standing to bring injunctive actions to enforce section 7 of the Clayton Act in just about any circumstances imaginable. For example, in *Phototron Corp. v. Eastman Kodak Co.*[74] the Fifth Circuit held that a competitor challenging a merger resulting in a

---

[73] Section 16 provides that any person "shall be entitled to sue" for injunctive relief for "threatened loss or damage. . . ." Requiring proof of actual loss or damage is inconsistent with this express language. Any fear of a misuse of the right to seek a private injunction for anticompetitive purposes should be more than remedied by the costs of filing such suits in the first place and the express requirement for posting a bond to cover the costs of an improvidently granted injunction.

[74] 842 F.2d 95 (5th Cir.), *cert. denied*, 108 S. Ct. 1996 (1988).

66%-85% market share in the wholesale photo-finishing market lacked standing to challenge the merger. In the course of effectively repealing section 16 of the Clayton Act, the court held that a competitor lacked standing to challenge a merger creating a monopolist as a result of the Supreme Court's *Monfort* decision. The *Phototron* court's standing holding appears to result in barring a private plaintiff from maintaining a suit where the merger results in a potential violation of section 2 of the Sherman Act and a clear violation of section 7 of the Clayton Act.

The Second Circuit parted company from the Fifth in the recent case of *R.C. Bigelow v. Unilever N.V.*,[75] a private suit challenging a merger that would have resulted in a single firm with 84% of the herbal tea market. *Bigelow* involved a merger that the FTC had studied for 6 months without action or an explanation for its nonaction. The Second Circuit upheld the plaintiff's standing, finding that an 84% market share not only justified a finding that the merger created a monopoly, but that it also raised a presumption of antitrust injury for purposes of a private injunction action under sections 7 and 16 of the Clayton Act. The *Bigelow* case raises another conflict in the circuits over antitrust standing and one demanding clarification of the doctrine by either the Court or Congress.

Cargill, Illinois Brick, Associated Contractors and their progeny, have generated an even more confused standing, injury and causation type of controversy in the context of a vertical price-fixing case. In *USA Petroleum Co. v. Atlantic Richfield Co.*,[76] a panel of the Ninth Circuit reversed dismissal on standing grounds of a competitor's claim that the defendant oil company had engaged in a conspiracy to set maximum prices with the purpose and effect of injuring the plaintiff independent gasoline marketer. The trial court held the plaintiff had no standing to complain without a showing that the maximum price fixed was a

---

[75]   56 Antitrust & Trade Reg. Rep. (BNA) 160 (2d Cir. 1989).

[76]   1988-2 Trade Cas. (CCH) ¶ 68,255 (9th Cir. 1988). *Contra,* Jack Walters & Sons Corp. v. Morton Building, Inc., 737 F.2d 698 (7th Cir. 1984).

predatory price—since by definition the plaintiff could not claim that it suffered the type of injury the antitrust laws prohibit absent proof of below-cost pricing; the plaintiff's injury was caused by "competition" not the displacement of it. The court of appeals rejected the simplistic cliche that the antitrust laws were enacted to protect competition, not competitors—how can you have competition without competitors—and held that the plaintiff was entitled to its day in court to determine whether it suffered antitrust damage. In effect, the court held that the plaintiff should not be thrown out of court at the preliminary stage of the litigation by a combination of cliches and economic theorizing inconsistent with the congressionally defined goals of antitrust policy and the procedural demands of a sensible litigation process.

On its face the complaint presented a clear claim that the law was violated, despite what some may think about the per se prohibition of maximum price fixing. Whether the alleged violation caused damages to the plaintiff and whether they were measurable damages were issues that could not be determined on a paper motion at preliminary stages of the litigation and must await further discovery and trial on the merits.

The Supreme Court reversed,[77] and held:

> Antitrust injury does not arise for purposes of § 4 of the Clayton Act . . . until a private party is adversely affected by an *anticompetitive* aspect of the defendant's conduct; . . . in the context of pricing practices, only predatory pricing has the requisite anticompetitive effect. . . . Low prices benefit consumers regardless of how those prices are set, and so long as they are above predatory levels, they do not threaten competition. Hence, they cannot give rise to antitrust injury.[78]

The majority went on to observe that the "antitrust injury requirement ensures that a plaintiff can recover only if the loss stems from an competition-*reducing* aspect or effect of a defen-

---

[77]   Atlantic Richfield Corp. v. USA Petroleum Co., 110 S. Ct. 1884 (1990).

[78]   110 S. Ct. at 1892 (emphasis in original).

dant's behavior.''[79] Since the conduct involved a vertical maximum price-fixing agreement reducing prices, the Court held the conduct was not a "competition-reducing" form of behavior because consumers were benefited and not harmed by the practice.

The opinion further complicates a treble damage plaintiff's ability to bring a damage action since it is not clear whether the majority is changing the meaning of what it is that violates the law, holding that "causation" is not present, or defining as a matter of law what will constitute "injury" for purposes of section 4. Implicitly, the majority opinion appears to be suggesting that the only purpose of antitrust policy is the protection of "consumer welfare" as that concept is defined by neoclassical economic theory. A vertical maximum price-fixing agreement lowering prices to consumers "benefits" consumers under this line of thinking since the only purpose of antitrust policy is to insure the lowest possible price absent predatory pricing—which cannot happen or last long under the artificial assumptions of the model. Consequently, the opinion can be read as saying that nonpredatory vertical maximum price fixing is not a violation of the law, per se or otherwise, since by definition consumers are not injured by a reduction in price. Implicitly, and despite claims to the contrary in the majority opinion, the decision overrules the *Albrecht* decision[80] except where a maximum price-fixing conspiracy raises prices. If, of course, one takes the views that the goals of antitrust policy are broader than the neoclassical concept of "consumer welfare," that courts should take account of facts unique to the industry involved in the dispute before the court and that the law is designed to protect competition as a process rather than an abstract two-dimensional ideal based upon theoretical assumptions which seldom exist in reality,[81] the conduct could well be found to violate the law.[82]

---

[79]   110 S. Ct. at 1894 (emphasis in original).

[80]   Albrecht v. The Herald Co., 390 U.S. 145 (1968).

[81]   The most succinct and accurate summary of the goals of antitrust policy mandated by Congress and enforced by the courts until recently,

Or the majority opinion can be read as saying that competitors have no standing to complain about a vertical maximum price-fixing conspiracy because the antitrust laws only protect consumers and not competitors. If this is the holding of the majority, then it is difficult to see who might maintain a suit since—in the absence of below cost predatory pricing—a vertical maximum price-fixing conspiracy setting prices below that which would pertain in the absence of the conspiracy, would benefit consumers (at least "benefit" under the assumptions of the model if not the law and in reality) and not harm them. Consequently, consumers could not maintain a suit since they are not injured.

A government suit, logically, should meet the same fate, if "consumer welfare" is the sole goal of antitrust policy. And, despite statements in the opinion to the contrary, it would appear that the logical upshot of the opinion is to reduce the per se status of vertical maximum price fixing where the maximum price is a nonpredatory reduction in price to a violation that no one could sue to redress since there would by definition be no antitrust injury. Indeed, the opinion might even be read as wiping out competitor suits generally unless it is first shown that the practice

---

neoclassical theory notwithstanding, is that suggested by Professor Eleanor Fox: "There are four major historical goals of antitrust, and all should continue to be respected. These are: (1) dispersion of economic power, (2) freedom and opportunity to compete on the merits, (3) satisfaction of consumers, and (4) protection of the competition process as market governor." Fox, *The Modernization of Antitrust: A New Equilibrium*, 66 CORNELL L. REV. 1140, 1154 (1981). *See also*, Flynn, *The Misuse of Economic Analysis in Antitrust Litigation*, 12 Sw. U.L. REV. 335 (1980); Flynn, *supra* note 18.

These are political goals, values, and "ought" propositions. They call for tools of analysis capable of implementing a more subtle concept of competition, competition as a process, rather than the mechanically measured quantitative concept advocated by neoclassical theorists. It is clear that Congress intended to regulate commerce and to prohibit private commercial practices that interfered with the competitive process, regardless of the wealth-enhancing quality of those practices. *See*, Flynn & Ponsoldt, *supra* note 57.

[82]   *See*, Flynn & Ponsoldt, *supra* note 57.

in question raised prices to consumers. Then, of course, it will be argued that competitor suits are really derivative of consumer rights and are "indirect" actions that must be dismissed since they violate the policy of *Illinois Brick* by generating too much complexity for federal courts to handle.

The majority opinion may also be read as an interpretation of the causation requirement or of the injury requirement for maintaining a treble damage action. If read as a "causation" decision, one elaborating on the euphemistic requirement that for an injury to be an "antitrust injury" it must be one that "flows from" an antitrust violation, the opinion raises the endless metaphysical debates surrounding causation that can be spun out of the *Brunswick*[83] and *Cargill*[84] decisions and their progeny. And, if the opinion be viewed as an interpretation of the "injury" requirement, it generates great confusion over the scope of the function of a jury to determine both the fact and amount of damage only after a full trial, rather than by judicial speculation in the preliminary stages of litigation.

If private antitrust litigation is to play an important role in the future, this growing morass of standing decisions and the confusion between (1) what duties the antitrust laws create and what evidence is necessary to show a breach, (2) what evidence is sufficient to show a factual connection between the breach and injury to the plaintiff, and (3) what evidence is sufficient to prove injury, are in need of a substantial overhaul. These issues are also in need of considerable clarification in view of the significant issue of how they relate to who is constitutionally required or entitled to decide which question—on what standards and at what point in a trial—judge or jury. It is an area to which the private bar, the administration and Congress should all address their attention and find a solution to what has become a most significant barrier to private antitrust enforcement—the mythology

---

[83]   Brunswick Corp. v. Pueblo Bowl-O-Mat, Inc., 429 U.S. 477, 489 (1977) (damage claimant in a § 7 merger case must show the "injury is casually linked to an illegal presence in the market").

[84]   Cargill, Inc. v. Monfort of Colorado, 479 U.S. 104 (1986).

of standing to sue and the procedural and substantive morass it has created.

Antitrust policy also would benefit by preventing the undermining of antitrust policy by substantive decisions made about the scope of duties created by the antitrust laws, causation issues and the meaning of and method for proof of damages behind the mask of standing, indirect injury and injury. Like the doctrines of proximate cause in torts and privity in contracts, the doctrine of standing should be relegated to the attic of legal history—there to gather dust as one of the curiosities of the past designed to provide certainty while only generating massive confusion and depriving litigants of their appropriate day in court on the merits of their claims.[85] If the doctrine of antitrust standing is not reigned in, then the future of private antitrust enforcement is indeed bleak.

B. The role of summary judgment

Another predictable variable of great significance to the future of private antitrust enforcement is the substantial change in the role of summary judgment in antitrust litigation and the startling decision of *Matsushita Electric Industrial Co., Ltd. v. Zenith Radio Corp.*[86] In *Matsushita* the Supreme Court held that the Third Circuit did not apply the proper standard in reversing a trial court's grant of summary judgment in a private suit alleging that several Japanese consumer electronics manufacturers had engaged in a predatory pricing scheme. The plaintiffs claimed the defendants had conspired to drive them from the market by a longstanding conspiracy to keep prices high in Japan and low in the United States—prices often so low that they were 20%–25% below cost.[87] Ever vigilant for protecting the geometric symmetry

---

[85] *See generally*, Cohen, *Transcendental Nonsense and the Functional Approach*, 35 COLUM. L. REV. (1935).

[86] 106 S. Ct. 1348 (1986).

[87] *See*, Sussman, *Business Judgment vs. Antitrust Justice*, 76 GEO. L.J. 337, 341 (1987).

of neoclassical price theory even at the expense of the facts of actual cases, the Antitrust Division filed an amicus brief on the side of the defendants relying on an earlier law review article commenting on the case by a newly appointed federal judge who did not try the case, review the record or hear the appeal.[88]

The Court's opinion upholding the trial court's grant of summary judgment did several things of great significance for private antitrust litigation:

1. It substantially changed the standard by which summary judgment motions are to be weighed thereby altering the traditional test and the balance between a court's law making and a jury's fact finding functions in private antitrust litigation;

2. It looked only at the defendant's theory of the case to determine whether the plaintiff stated a claim, thereby making the defendant's "plausible" theoretical explanation of its conduct the test for summary judgment rather than the plausibility of plaintiff's facts and allegations of a violation of its rights the test for whether the motion should be granted;

3. It appeared to buy hook, line and sinker the application of abstract neoclassical price theory to judge the validity of an antitrust claim despite alternative economic and other frameworks for understanding the facts of the dispute and Congressional policy to the contrary;[89]

4. It ignored or tried to explain away the facts of the dispute and the plaintiff's interpretation of them in reaching its decision; and

---

[88]   Matsushita Electric Industrial Co., Ltd. v. Zenith Radio Corp., 106 S. Ct. 1348, 1359 n.10 (1986), citing the "sensible assessment" of Easterbrook, *The Limits of Antitrust*, 63 Texas L. Rev. 1 (1984). For a "sensible assessment" of the Court's majority opinion, *see*, Flynn, *supra* note 16.

[89]   For a persuasive examination of the facts—as opposed to abstract theory detached from the reality of the dispute before the court—explaining what was occurring in the case, *see* Note, *Below Cost Sales and the Buying of Market Share*, 42 Stan. L. Rev. 695 (1990).

5. It tipped the balance in judging summary judgment motions decidedly against—rather than in favor of—the party moved against.[90]

If the majority was seeking to straighten out the standards to govern summary judgment motions in antitrust cases, the opinion is a classic demonstration of G.K. Chesterton's cynical observation: "If a thing is worth doing, it is worth doing badly."

Perhaps the most significant parts of the Court's decision are those establishing a new standard for summary judgment motions and the implicit adoption of static neoclassical price theory as the sole guide to antitrust policy and the standard to be used for summary judgment motions in antitrust cases. Any attorney involved in private litigation will have no doubt encountered the new summary judgment standard in just about every case they bring or defend: "[I]f the factual context renders respondent's claim implausible—if the claim is one that simply makes no economic sense—respondents must come forward with more persuasive evidence to support their claim than would otherwise be necessary."[91]

"Economic sense" is apparently to be determined by neoclassical price theory and the defendant's version of it to determine whether the plaintiffs' case makes "economic sense." Since neoclassical price theory dictates that predatory pricing is seldom tried and rarely successful, reality to the contrary notwithstanding,[92] the Court's opinion requires a "respondent to a motion for

---

[90] *See*, Flynn, *supra* note 16; Ponsoldt & Lewyn, *Judicial Activism, Economic Theory and the Role of Summary Judgment in Sherman Act Conspiracy Cases: The Illogic of* Matsushita, 33 ANTITRUST BULL. 575 (1988).

[91] 106 S. Ct. at 1357.

[92] One study of the data compiled by the Georgetown study of private antitrust litigation, PRIVATE ANTITRUST LITIGATION: NEW EVIDENCE, NEW LEARNING (L. White ed. 1988), suggests that 20% of all private cases with a settlement rate of over 90% were predatory pricing

summary judgment in an antitrust case to show that the predictions of The Model do not follow from the assumptions of The Model."[93] While tautologies may serve academics in the course of befuddling their students, they scarcely serve legal reasoning and the fair resolution of lawsuits in accord with the underlying purposes of the law and the practical requirements of a sensible procedural system. With all due respect, the majority opinion's method of analysis is logically absurd, inconsistent with the historical purposes of the Federal Rules of Civil Procedure, an impingement upon the constitutional right to jury trial, contrary to the goals of antitrust policy, and potentially devastating to all private antitrust litigation if it is to be rigidly followed in the future.

In recent years, summary judgment motions are granted in whole or in part in over 50% of private antitrust cases; a factor contributing heavily to the 47% decrease in private suits in the past 10 years.[94] The widespread and growing use of summary judgment in private antitrust suits is testimony to either the

---

cases. *See, Forward: The Cases, the Judges, and Economic Research in U.S. Antitrust Policy*, 13 WAGE-PRICE L. & ECON. REV. 1, 17 (1989).

In Cargill, Inc. v. Monfort of Colorado, 479 U.S. 104, 121 (1986), the Court observed: "While firms may engage in the practice [predatory pricing] only infrequently, there is ample evidence that the practice does occur." In this author's experience, predatory pricing does occur with more frequency than is generally believed or an abstract economic theory based on a world of perfect competition and rational maximization would suggest. The problem is one of proving the conduct has taken place. Determining cost information and the standard by which pricing is to be deemed "predatory" are often insuperable barriers to bringing a suit on this basis. Where a case is brought the battle can be long, complex and expensive. *See, e.g., Inglis Wins $13.3 Million Judgment in 17-Year-Old Predatory Pricing Case*, 56 ANTITRUST & TRADE REG. REP. (BNA) 369 (March 9, 1989). The problem becomes impossible where courts begin with an assumption the practice simply could not happen and, after *Matsushita*, utilize that assumption to measure a plaintiff's case on a motion for summary judgment.

93   Flynn, *supra* note 16.

94   55 ANTITRUST & TRADE REG. REP. (BNA) 797 (Nov. 3, 1988).

baseless nature of many such suits, to the growing use of summary judgment motions by trial judges to cut off lawsuits they do not like or to the increasing influence of ideology to resolve lawsuits detached from the reality of the lawsuit and the congressionally mandated goals of the law. While some of this increased use of summary judgment is no doubt due to baseless or poorly pleaded lawsuits, my review of the cases over the past 10 years suggests that a far greater share of it is attributable to judges getting rid of lawsuits they do not like or cases they mistakenly believe will consume too much time on a busy docket and increased reliance on the ideology of neoclassical theorizing dictating what the law ought to be rather than the policies of Congress and the facts of cases determining what the law ought to be.

Those cases that are baseless lawsuits can be readily dealt with by the use of rule 11 sanctions, rather than distorting the standards for summary judgment to deal with the imagined problem of countless baseless lawsuits filed by dishonest or incompetent lawyers or competitors seeking to misuse the antitrust laws. *Matsushita*'s standard for determining whether summary judgment should be granted can only accelerate the trend demonstrated by the standing and *Illinois Brick* doctrines of prematurely deciding antitrust cases on the pleadings and before trial. *Matsushita* establishes a bad process for legal decision making whatever one might think of private litigation to enforce antitrust policy. Moreover, as the important Georgetown study of private antitrust litigation shows, it is an unnecessary trend if one views the issue solely from the perspective of the light burden private antitrust litigation imposes on the courts.[95]

Procedural issues to one side, the substantive standards for weighing predatory pricing cases announced by *Matsushita*, that predatory pricing is seldom tried and rarely successful as determined by neoclassical theorizing, has come under increased scru-

---

[95] PRIVATE ANTITRUST LITIGATION: NEW EVIDENCE, NEW LEARNING, *supra* note 92, at 8–10.

tiny and attack. For example, Oliver Williamson has argued that the neoclassical approach paints too simplistic a picture of predatory pricing and that the enforcement agencies and the courts should also evaluate the practice from the newly emerging economic perspective of offensive strategic behavior—or conduct aimed at actual or potential competitors to discipline or otherwise deter competitive behavior.[96] Although Williamson expressed reservations about the plaintiff's theory of the case in *Matsushita*, in part because of an economist's grave reservations about the efficacy of conspiracy doctrine, he found that the dissenting opinion in *Matsushita* adheres more closely to the standards that ought to be followed in summary judgment cases—a conclusion supported by an extensive study of the record in the case.[97]

In other words, the majority overturned decades of summary judgment law and cut off a full and fair analysis of the plaintiff's theory of the case and the record facts, a theory based on economic insights suggesting that a 15-year predatory pricing campaign by Japanese firms may well have been for strategic anticompetitive purposes. The Court did so because the ma-

---

[96]   Williamson, *Delimiting Antitrust*, 76 GEO. L.J. 271 (1987). *See also*, Krattenmaker, Lande & Salop, *Monopoly Power and Market Power in Antitrust Law*, 76 GEO. L.J. 241 (1987). Among the difficulties critics of the neoclassical school of economic thought have had in arguing for alternative analytical methods for assessing conduct claimed to violate antitrust policy is the penchant lawyers and judges pretending to be economists have for models to define legal rules and dictate what the facts of specific cases are and mean. Such an approach to the legal analysis of disputes is a long discredited method of analytical positivism. *See* Flynn, *Legal Reasoning, Antitrust Policy and the Social "Science" of Economics*, 33 ANTITRUST BULL 713 (1988). Unfortunately, the methodology has become attractive to judges and requires critics of the current state of antitrust analysis to come up with alternative models, one hopes empirically based rather than abstract models, providing a scientific analytical framework for decision making that will always produce the right answer and eliminate discretion in decision making. Unfortunately, several hundred years of legal decision making have proven such a standard of certainty to be an illusion, and a dangerous one at that.

[97]   Ponsoldt & Lewyn, *supra* note 90.

jority's view of the case and the realities of predatory pricing practices were captured by a belief in the religion of static neoclassical price theory—proof of Stendhal's observation that "all religions are founded on the fear of the many and the cleverness of the few."

Some lower courts, not overwhelmed by the superficial logic of the model and a temptation to clear their docket of cases by a freewheeling use of summary judgment and *Matsushita*'s invitation to do so, have found grounds for believing that predatory pricing is more often attempted, can be successful and requires a trial of the facts underlying predatory pricing claims where they are alleged—"economic" plausibility to the contrary notwithstanding. In *McGahee v. Northern Propane Gas Co.*,[98] the 11th Circuit reversed dismissal of a Sherman Act and Robinson-Patman Act claim of predatory pricing despite *Matsushita*. The court noted that the Areeda-Turner test for predatory pricing, drawing the line of illegality at average variable cost,[99] "is like the Venus DeMilo: it is much admired and often discussed, but rarely embraced." In conflict with decisions from other circuits and the abstract theoretical test for summary judgment the majority adopted in *Matsushita*, the court held: "when an antitrust defendant moves for judgement as a matter of law, the test for predatory pricing must consider subjective evidence and should use average total cost as the cost above which no inference of predatory intent can be made."

The *McGahee* case was a well prepared appeal; one pursued by lawyers intimately familiar with economic theorizing and the goals of antitrust policy. It is also a case decided by a judge concerned about the facts of the dispute before him; facts carefully and fully documented by the plaintiff's attorneys. It points up the importance of a private plaintiff's attorneys being fully conversant with the economic theory relevant and not

---

[98]   858 F.2d 1487 (11th Cir. 1988), *cert. denied*, 109 S. Ct. 2110 (1989).

[99]   Areeda & Turner, *Predatory Pricing and Related Practices Under Section 2 of the Sherman Act*, 88 HARV. L. REV. 697 (1975).

relevant to the dispute and presenting their case in a compelling fashion. Great care should be taken by a plaintiff's attorneys before filing a case—care to think out carefully the theory of their case, to retain competent and thoughtful economic advice and to be prepared to confront judges who may place a heavy burden on a plaintiff to sustain his or her case at the preliminary stages of the litigation. Until the narrow and closed-minded ideological approach of *Matsushita* is overcome or ignored however, careful drafting of a well thought out complaint in much greater detail than normally required and with the assistance of an economist—not a lawyer pretending to be an economist—is the only hope for overcoming what is a bad and unwise Supreme Court standard for summary judgment motions in the antitrust field and a significant nail in the coffin of the future of private antitrust enforcement.

C. *Vertical market restraints and the meaning of per se and the rule of reason*

A final and significant variable that private antitrust enforcement must confront is the gradual destruction of private treble damage actions in the area of vertical restraints and the erosion of the distinction between per se rules and the rule of reason. In the past, a large percentage of private cases involved vertical market restraints, an area that neoclassical ideology suggests should be of little or no antitrust concern. Twenty years ago the *Schwinn* decision's rigid per se rule prohibiting any restraint on alienation after title had passed made vertical market restraints of great antitrust concern.[100] The private bar responded by attempting to overregulate vertical marketing restraints through a legion of private treble damage actions challenging many aspects of vertical marketing relationships and doing so pursuant to a wooden application of a rule of per se illegality. In response to these developments, the *Sylvania* decision[101] put a considerable

---

[100]   United States v. Arnold, Schwinn & Co., 388 U.S. 365 (1967).

[101]   Continental T.V., Inc. v. GTE Sylvania, Inc., 433 U.S. 36 (1977).

damper on the use of private antitrust suits to regulate anything other than vertical price fixing.[102]

Elsewhere, I have written extensively about vertical restraints suggesting that the appropriate standard by which they should be governed lay somewhere between the two extremes of the legal formalism of *Schwinn* and the unrealistic ideological theorizing of neoclassical thought relied upon in part by the *Sylvania* Court to overturn *Schwinn*. I have been suggesting for the past 10 years that the per se rules in antitrust ought to be viewed as evidentiary presumptions of varying levels of rebutability,[103] in part to avoid the rigidity of the two extremes represented by *Schwinn* and by the neoclassical approach—extremes incapable of taking account of the facts unique to individual cases and all the policies underlying the antitrust laws. The Supreme Court, however, seems to be drifting further and further in the direction of relying upon a rigid version of neoclassical thought with its simplistic assumption that all vertical restraints save those masking a cartel or designed by a firm with monopoly power to exclude competition should be considered per se lawful. The irony that the rigidities of both the *Schwinn* and neoclassical approaches suffer from the same analytical faults, a failure to capture fully the values underlying antitrust policy and an inability to take account of facts unique to individual cases, seems to have escaped the Court.

A good illustration of the wisdom of treating per se rules as evidentiary presumptions subject to well defined defenses and justifications is demonstrated by the confused and confusing state of the tying doctrine in antitrust. In the not too distant past, tying arrangements were treated harshly by the courts—a seemingly absolute rule of per se illegality governed conduct once it was

---

[102]   *See* Flynn, *supra* note 17, at 1095.

[103]   *See* Flynn, ANTITRUST L.J., *supra* note 57. The suggestion has subsequently been proposed by others. *See,* 7 P. AREEDA, ANTITRUST LAW, chap. 15 (1986).

defined as "tying" after cases like *Northern Pacific*[104] and *International Salt*.[105] There is reason for treating tying arrangements with suspicion, because Congress has singled out tying arrangements for special treatment under an incipiency standard in section 3 of the Clayton Act[106] and tying can impinge upon fundamental values underlying the Sherman Act if the congressional goals of that Act are respected by the courts. Sorting out those tying arrangements that impinge on antitrust goals from those that do not can be a challenge from one unique factual circumstance to another. The analytical method for doing so is, therefore, crucial to the development of a predictable tying doctrine—one that sensibly handles the facts of cases, respects the goals for antitrust established by Congress and provides a knowable and predictable standard for those subject to the law.

A rigid per se approach is incapable of doing these things where it subsumes all the issues to be determined under the initial analysis of whether a particular transaction is or is not a tying arrangement.[107] The per se approach traditionally followed in tying cases reached new heights of legal formalism in the first *Fortner* decision categorizing a financing arrangement for goods as a tying arrangement and suggesting it was per se unlawful if there is "power" in the tying product market.[108] On a second appeal of the same case, much backing and filling was required to explain why the particular financing arrangement was not an

---

104   Northern Pacific Ry. Co. v. United States, 356 U.S. 1 (1958).

105   International Salt Co. v. United States, 332 U.S. 392 (1947).

106   15 U.S.C. § 15.

107   Bauer, *A Simplified Approach to Tying Arrangements: A Legal and Economic Analysis*, 33 VAND. L. REV. 283, 284 (1980): "Notwithstanding . . . extensive Supreme Court attention, there is as much heat as light in this area. The doctrine which has developed is often unpredictable and frequently irrational, and the applicable rules make the analysis far more complicated than necessary. A simpler and more direct approach is long overdue."

108   Fortner Enterprises, Inc. v. United States Steel Corp., 394 U.S. 495 (1969).

illegal tying arrangement[109]—an inference left by the first *Fortner* decision. Although the two decisions generated considerable confusion, is was thereafter widely believed that tying arrangements remained per se illegal where there were two separate products and "power" was shown in the tying product market. For tying cases, the translation of the Latin phrase "per se" must be amended from "in itself" to "in itself along with a few other mushy things."

In 1984, the Supreme Court once again stepped into what had become a growing morass of tying cases in the lower federal courts, and added to the morass, in *Jefferson Parish Hospital v. Hyde*.[110] In that case, the Court recognized tying arrangements were per se illegal, but only where it was shown that there were two separate products and there was power in the tying product. The Court then proceeded to hold what was labeled below a "tying arrangement," a lawful tying arrangement. The plaintiff, an anesthesiologist, claimed that a hospital had refused certification for him to practice in the hospital because it had a contract with a group of anesthesiologists to provide all necessary anesthesiology services at the hospital. The court of appeals held that the arrangement was a tying arrangement because consumers not wishing to have surgery "cold turkey" were forced to buy one product to get another—the tying product being the hospital operating room and the tied product being anesthesiology services. The lower court found power in the tying product and a not insubstantial amount of commerce involved, and therefore held the tie per se illegal.[111]

It is fair to suggest that the Supreme Court struggled unsuccessfully with the analysis of both the facts and the law on review; attempting to sort out what appeared to the Court at least as a square peg—the facts of the case and the reality of the

---

[109] United States Steel Corp. v. Fortner Enterprises, Inc., 495 U.S. 610 (1977).

[110] 466 U.S. 2 (1984).

[111] Jefferson Parish Hosp. v. Hyde, 686 F.2d 286 (5th Cir. 1982).

hospital and medical businesses—that did not fit a round hole—
the per se pigeonhole the record below labeled as the antitrust
offense of "tying." Viewed from the defendant hospital and
plaintiff doctor's point of view, the contract was an exclusive
dealing arrangement with a competing supplier of the service;
viewed from the patient's perspective, the arrangement was a per
se illegal tying arrangement requiring the patient to purchase one
product in order to have another.

Not surprisingly, the Court's analysis unraveled once the
confines of the seemingly rigid per se rule of tying analysis
captured the Court's thinking and method for analyzing the case.
The opinion wanders back and forth between arguments that
there were not two separate products to the issue of whether there
was sufficient power in the tying product market to the issue of
whether the power that did exist was the "kind" of market power
necessary to prove the arrangement illegal. *Jefferson Parish* left
tying analysis in further disarray, while also leaving the plaintiff
doctor excluded from providing service in the defendant hospital.
Patients in the hospital were left with little or no choice in the
selection of the physician to provide them with anesthesiology
services.

Think of how much simpler and more clear cut the analysis
might have been if the Court had simply held that if the
arrangement was to be labeled a tying arrangement, it was
presumptively illegal subject to some affirmative defenses[112]—
defenses proving a justification or excuse for the arrangement
under the circumstances of the case. Instead of the analysis being

---

[112]   The level of rebutability should vary from one category of per se
illegality to another. For example, the presumption of per se illegality
for horizontal price fixing should be nearly conclusive, although some
circumstances might justify recognition of a narrow justification or
excuse, particularly where other regulation is present. *See*, Broadcast
Music, Inc. v. C.B.S. System, Inc., 441 U.S. 1 (1979); F.T.C. v. Indiana
Federation of Dentists, 476 U.S. 447 (1986). On the other hand, only a
moderately presumptive level of illegality would be appropriate in the
case of tying arrangements. *See*, Data General Corp. v. Digidyne Corp.,
734 F.2d 1336 (9th Cir. 1984), *cert. denied*, 473 U.S. 409 (1985).

deflected into arcane epistemological debates over the existence of one or two products and metaphysical distinctions between various types of market power, the analysis could have addressed in a straightforward way whether the displacement of a competitive process in anesthesiology services was justified in the circumstances unique to the case and by means within those permitted by the congressional goals of antitrust policy.

The majority of subsequent tying cases dismissed at some early stage of the proceeding, cite one or more of the inconsistent holdings one may read into the *Jefferson Parish* decision. This state of affairs may be pleasing to those who believe the tying doctrine should be done away with altogether—out of a naive belief that tying arrangements simply do not matter despite what Congress has said about them, the facts and circumstances of individual cases and the underlying goals of antitrust policy tying arrangements can impinge in many circumstances. Real judges deciding real cases brought by real lawyers and dealing with the messy world of real facts however, need something better than the rigid but unknowable standards of per se tying doctrine at the one extreme and the unrealistic approach of neoclassical theorizing, unconcerned about the facts and the law, at the other extreme.

Some tying cases continue to be brought, particularly in the area of intellectual property rights, where claims of tying still benefit from a presumption of power in the tying product. For example, in *Digidyne Corp. v. Data General Corp.,*[113] Chief Judge Browning of the Ninth Circuit held that a computer manufacturer's refusal to license its popular copyrighted computer operating system unless licensees of the program also purchase the computer system from it constituted a per se illegal tying arrangement. On petition for certiorari, Justices White and Blackmun dissented from the refusal to grant certiorari claiming that the decision was inconsistent with whatever the holding was in the *Jefferson Parish* case.[114] In another recent case, *William*

---

[113] 734 F.2d 1336 (9th Cir. 1984).

[114] Data General Corp. v. Digidyne Corp., 473 U.S. 908 (1985).

Cohen & Sons, Inc. v. All American Hero, Inc.,[115] a district court held that the requirement that trademark licensees for a fast food franchise purchase all their beef needs from the franchisor—licensor of the trademark—constituted a tying arrangement and that the existence of the trademark justified an inference of power in the tying product at least for purposes of a motion for summary judgment by the defendant to dismiss the case.

Aside from the particular results in these cases, it is apparent that the rigidity of the per se concept is creating at least two problems: (1) the creation of arcane and confused distinctions to mitigate the per se rule in certain cases where business reality requires without appearing to do so; and (2) the detachment of the legal analysis of the practice from the facts unique to each case and the underlying goals of antitrust policy—particularly the goal of protecting each person's right to succeed or fail in the market as the result of a competitive process.[116]

An understandable application of per se rules instead of a mechanical application of definitions, the avoidance of judicial gymnastics to sidestep a fixed rule in specific cases and the

---

[115] 693 F. Supp. 201 (D.N.J. 1988).

[116] Professor Eleanor Fox has concisely summarized the unique meaning of the *competitive process* as intended by those who drafted the Sherman Act, as distinguished from competition, as follows: "One overarching idea has unified these three concerns (distrust of power, concern for consumers and commitment to opportunity for entrepreneurs): *competition as process.* The competition process is the preferred governor of markets. If the impersonal forces of competition, rather than public or private power, determine market behavior and outcomes, power is by definition dispersed, opportunities and incentives for firms without market power are increased, and the results are acceptable and fair. Some measure of productive and allocative efficiency is a byproduct, because competition tends to stimulate lowest-cost production and allocate resources more responsively than a visible public or private power." Fox, *supra* note 81, at 1184. *See also*, Flynn, *Rethinking the Sherman Act*, *supra* note 57, at 1623–27; Flynn, *supra* note 15; Flynn, *supra* note 18, at 304–06.

muting of ideological criticism of the rules would all take place if the per se rules were understood as evidentiary and functional rules of varying levels of rebutability; an analytical process that avoids the tyranny of labels on the one extreme and the tyranny of the simple minded and lawless application of an abstract economic model not in conformity with the reality of the case and the policies of the law on the other. Both public and private antitrust enforcement suffer when the standards to be applied consist of either rigid definitions detached from modern reality or unrealistic conclusions derived from a model of a world that does not exist.

The most recent decision in the direction of a nonreflective application of neoclassical theorizing, and one that both obscures the law of conspiracy and the law of what constitutes vertical price fixing for purposes of antitrust analysis, is *Business Electronics Corp. v. Sharp Electronics Corp.*[117] In that case, the Supreme Court upheld the Fifth Circuit's reversal of a jury verdict for a plaintiff that complained that the defendant cut it off as a dealer in calculators at the behest of a competing distributor because the plaintiff was consistently cutting retail prices. The Supreme Court upheld the Fifth Circuit's ruling that for a vertical agreement between a manufacturer and a dealer to terminate a second dealer to be found unlawful, the first dealer must expressly or impliedly agree to set its prices at "some level," though not a specific one. The Court justified its affirmance of the reversal for a new trial, however, by holding that the prime vice of vertical price fixing is that it can be used to facilitate cartelization and no evidence of cartelization was present in the case—a conclusion derived from neoclassical price theory rather than the goals of antitrust policy. The Court further stated that any lesser standard would subject a manufacturer agreeing with a dealer to terminate another dealer to treble damage liability with no way for the manufacturer to justify its agreement or for a court to distinguish vertical price fixing from other vertical

---

[117]   108 S. Ct. 1515 (1988).

restraints.[118] Other language in the opinion, particularly references to the imaginary horseman of the neoclassical theorist's
artificial and apocalyptic world of vertical market regulation by
antitrust enforcement—"free rider"[119]—suggests that if the per se

---

[118]   The Court should have held that conduct impinging upon a basic
goal of antitrust policy, in this case "promoting freedom and opportunity to compete on the merits," warrants a presumption of illegality
subject to defenses like a good business justification under the circumstances of the case. *See* Flynn, *supra* note 17, at 1114-15, 1143-47.

[119]   The jargon "free rider" is used as a descriptive definition and a
conclusion, not a functional legal concept, in neoclassical analysis. It is
a form of reductionism that might suit theoretical speculation within the
severe limits of its assumptions, but not a useful method for analyzing
disputes not in conformity with the assumptions of the model or the
normative ends of the law. Where used as a definition and a conclusion,
the concept of "free rider" captures one's thinking by hypostatizing
(thingifying) an abstract assumption—the meaning and scope of the
property rights of the proponent of the restraint. By doing so, the
resulting mental picture deflects the analysis from the normative and
factual issues of concern by assuming the question antitrust analysis is
required to explore in vertical market and other restraints analyzed
under the antitrust laws—the scope of the property rights of the parties
to the restraint and how the conflict in rights should be resolved. One of
the underlying legislative objectives of the Sherman Act was to adopt a
federal law giving federal courts the power to define the scope of private
property and contract rights in order to guarantee the existence of a
competitive process governing the determination of those rights.
Describing distributors who do not follow the demands of suppliers with
regard to price and other aspects of their distribution practices as "free
riders" assumes the question to be asked: What ought to be the scope of
the supplier's and distributor's contract and property rights in light of
the goals of antitrust policy and the facts of the case? *See,* Sklar, *The
Sherman Antitrust Act and the Corporate Reconstruction of American
Capitalism, 1890-1914,* in CORPORATIONS AND SOCIETY: POWER AND
RESPONSIBILITY 65 (W. Samuels & A. Miller eds. 1987).
   Consequently, I have never met or seen "free rider," just as I have
never met or seen "proximate cause" or "privity." The words are not
used as concepts in law are used, to both connote the normative values
underlying the concept and denote its application to the facts of the
particular dispute, but are used solely to label whatever a distributor

prohibition on vertical price fixing is not dead, it is severely wounded.

From an economic point of view, the opinion is a strange one since it appears to justify the result and deny consumers the freedom to buy from discounters in the name of preserving the supplier's freedom to market its goods, in circumstances where the termination was not the product of the supplier's independent decision making.[120] The paternalism of suppliers agreeing with some distributors to impose restraints on other distributors for the best interests of consumers is apparently necessary to protect consumers from the scourge of "free riders"—"consumer welfare" Japan style.[121]

Instead of holding that the manufacturer's conduct was presumptively unlawful subject to proof of an economically justifiable reason within the goals of antitrust policy for the cutoff, the Court remanded for a retrial on the question of whether the

---

does as taking something it is assumed belongs to a supplier—without stating why the legal system ought to assume the right should belong to the buyer in the first instance. The "free rider" explanation of vertical restraints is one of the more blatant misuses of a definition to displace the dynamic and functional use of legal concepts as devices for linking the underlying normative goals of the law to the facts of a dispute. *See*, F. COHEN, ETHICAL IDEALS AND LEGAL RULES: AN ESSAY IN THE FOUNDATIONS OF LEGAL CRITICISM 3–7 (1959). As such, it is a thingification and a definition displacing an empirical and normative analysis that should be banned from the legal analysis of vertical restraints and be relegated to Von Jehring's "Heaven" of other meaningless legalisms, there to join "proximate cause," "standing" and "privity"—concepts that obstruct, rather than advance, the legal analysis of disputes through the use of concepts to link facts and policy. *See* Flynn, *Reaganomics and Antitrust Enforcement, A Jurisprudential Critique*, 1983 UTAH L. REV. 269; Flynn, *supra* note 96.

[120] *See*, 55 ANTITRUST & TRADE REG. REP. (BNA) 803–04 (Nov. 3, 1988) (Remarks of E. Fox).

[121] *See*, Fallows, *supra* note 36, reporting that in domestic markets dominated by cartels and vertical market restrictions, Japanese consumers pay retail prices approximately 70% higher on average than in the United States.

cutoff was for setting prices at "some level." Confusion will reign over whether *Business Electronics* is a decision about the meaning of agreement or conspiracy or a decision about the meaning of "price fixing"—epistemological debates similar to those in tying doctrine—since the evidence to prove the existence of a conspiracy or agreement will often be the same evidence as that relied upon to prove the agreement's objective. What lower courts will do with this decision remains a muddled question, since just about every vertical price-fixing case will be concerned with identification of the conduct, the existence of a conspiracy or agreement and the meaning of the Court's standard that the agreement need not be one to fix a specific price, but that prices be fixed at "some level."

When *Business Electronics* and *Atlantic Richfield* are coupled with *Matsushita*, every vertical price-fixing case is a summary judgment candidate since the combination is an invitation to find the plaintiff's claim that the defendant was motivated by a desire to fix prices is economically implausible since the model's assumptions will dictate what facts can be "facts" for purposes of the model. The dictates of the model presume that rational is whatever a supplier does and whatever a supplier does is rational save the implementation of a horizontal cartel. Cases will be analyzed in a nonexistent world populated by white-hatted rational maximizing distributors preoccupied by consumer welfare as a derivative of their own self interest, and black-hatted "free riders" laying waste to the range of perfect competition populated by ignorant consumers who need to be made to pay for services rational maximizers deem they need.

The only prohibition left by this clear path of analysis set by the Supreme Court is that horizontal price fixing is the only conduct of concern under section 1 of the Sherman Act; a conclusion that is difficult to defend if the only goal of antitrust policy is to protect the rationality and property rights of suppliers. After all, what could be more "rational" for profit maximizers than to conspire to fix prices?[122] The *Business Electronics*

---

[122]   *See*, Flynn, *supra* note 16.

decision, a decision dissented from by only Justices Stevens and White, holds ominous implications for the future litigation of vertical price-fixing cases by private plaintiffs and by the enforcement agencies—particularly when coupled with the implications of *Matsushita* and the simplistic use of neoclassical price theory taught in too many 2-week law and economics courses for bench and bar.

IV. Conclusion

One could go on at great length with other Supreme Court decisions and the decisions of several lower courts and what they mean for the future of private antitrust enforcement. There are several circuit court decisions which, by their own standard of relying on economic analysis to decide the case, do so incorrectly from a mainstream economics point of view.[123] What this suggests for private antitrust enforcement is that the practitioner should be well schooled in the various schools of modern economics and have the expert assistance of an economist—not a lawyer pretending to be one as is often the case with too many lawyers and with too many judges—before filing an antitrust case of any significance. Lawyers gearing up for a new round of antitrust's "faustian pact with economists,"[124] would do well to include a professionally trained economist—preferably one with a legal education as well—on their new antitrust team.

The confusion generated by standing doctrine and the distortion in the use of summary judgment in antitrust cases also must be dealt with if private antitrust enforcement is to have a proper

---

[123] *See Antitrust in the U.S. Circuit Courts of Appeal: 11 Cases of 1987*, 20 ANTITRUST L. & ECON. REV. 21 (1988); *Forward: Antitrust Economics in the U.S. Circuit Court of Appeals* 1, 19 ANTITRUST L. & ECON. REV. 1 (1987); Shepherd, 14 *Recent Antitrust Cases and Mainstream Industrial-Organization Economics Criteria*, 19 ANTITRUST L. & ECON. REV. 35 (1987).

[124] *See* Rowe, *The Decline of Antitrust and the Delusions of Models: The Faustian Pact of Law and Economics*, 72 GEO. L.J. 1511 (1984).

role in developing and implementing antitrust policy. In the early life of the Sherman Act, the use in private antitrust cases of restrictive commerce standards, high proof of damage requirements and extensive reliance on the rule of reason restricted access to the courts by private plaintiffs and ushered in a multidecade era of minimal private enforcement. The current reliance on the "efficiency only" test for proof of a violation, standing doctrine and summary judgment standards reversing the burden against the party moved against have all contributed to a dim future for private antitrust enforcement. If the past is a prolog to the future, the minimal use of private enforcement during the first six decades of antitrust enforcement is a more likely prediction of the future of private enforcement unless steps are taken by both the courts and Congress to rectify an imbalance now significantly tilted against the private antitrust plaintiff.

Those who believe antitrust enforcement should make a come-back in the private arena by dealing with reality and seeking to carry out the goals Congress has mandated for it, must pay greater attention to the overriding issue in antitrust policy today—one that has been around for almost 100 years. As Judge Bork put it: "What is the point of the law—what are its goals? Everything else follows from the answer we give. . . . Only when the issue of goals has been settled is it possible to frame a coherent body of substantive rules."[125] Beneath all the controversy in Congress, academia and the courts over the rules of antitrust and the role of private enforcement, be it standing, the role of summary judgment or the implications of vertical price fixing, the overriding issue is: what are the goals of antitrust policy and what is the role of which theory of economics being followed at any one time in history in both defining those goals and the implications of the facts of a particular case? Judge Bork has argued that the only goal Congress intended for antitrust policy is the technical concept of "consumer welfare" or conduct that restricts output—output as defined by the restrictive assumptions of the neoclassical model.

---

[125]   R. Bork, The Antitrust Paradox: A Policy at War with Itself 50 (1978).

Every other serious reviewer of the legislative history of the antitrust laws disagrees with Judge Bork's reading of that history. I do as well.[126] Those drafting the antitrust laws "were defining the limits upon the exercise of private contract and property rights in order to insure the integrity of the political process, the rights of individuals in their exercise of property and contract rights, and the right of competitors to succeed or fail pursuant to a competitive process."[127] For a host of economic, political and social reasons, antitrust policy in this day and age should continue to be viewed as having these goals as the central goals of antitrust policy.[128]

To insure that they are so construed and to restore the vitality of private antitrust enforcement in the future, Congress must clarify the point of the law. What is antitrust policy for and what values is it intended to protect and promote? Congress should hold extensive hearings on this question; hearings aimed at adopting a preamble to the Sherman Act explaining the goals of

---

[126] Flynn, *supra* note 18.

[127] *Id*. at 303.

[128] Obviously, an entire treatise could be written on what the appropriate balance between individualism and community in the economic sphere should be and how it ought to be expressed through law in the late 20th century. Defining that relationship solely in terms of a narrow libertarian economic model is a form of myopia that not only ignores history and experience, but ignores contemporary reality, political and other institutions and the necessary underlying normative beliefs that tie a society together. Efficiency in the use of common resources must be weighed along with other economic values such as innovation and the social and political beliefs that secure the consent of those subject to the law. That consent is defined and secured by a common commitment to a sense of justice and the institutions that implement that common belief. *See*, J. RAWLS, A THEORY OF JUSTICE chap. 5 (1971). Ignoring these broader constraints upon the choice of rules and normative goals governing economic rights and relationships by exclusive reliance upon a narrow utilitarian model divorced from reality and the society in which it functions is a prescription for economic, political and social disaster.

antitrust policy.[129] It would be a fitting thing to do as antitrust policy enters its second century; it is an essential thing to do if antitrust enforcement—public and private—is to be of any relevance at all to our next century or whether it is to continue down the sorry path toward becoming an irrelevant abstraction, wrapped in the theological shroud of a misused economic theory and encumbered with meaningless legalisms making it impossible to implement.

For those committed to the current fashion of defining antitrust policy solely in terms of static neoclassical price theory, one can only suggest that they remember Mencken's observation, which should be every lawyer's and every judge's motto: "Men become civilized not in proportion to their willingness to believe, but in proportion to their readiness to doubt." It is time to bring a lawyer's skepticism to the indiscriminate use of neoclassical theorizing dictating the goals of antitrust policy, the reality it is being asked to deal with and the methodology by which the goals of antitrust are implemented.[130] The reality of the litigation

---

[129]   A tentative draft bill would look like the following:

> Preamble: The purposes of the antitrust laws are: 1. To insure the dispersion of economic power in order to protect the legal, social and political processes from undue economic power; 2. To promote freedom and opportunity to compete on the merits; 3. To foster the satisfaction of consumers and to protect them in the exercise of their contract and property rights; and 4. To protect the competition process as market governor.

This language is based on a distillation of studies of the legislative history of the antitrust laws found in Fox, *supra* note 81, at 1154; Flynn, *Rethinking the Sherman Act, supra* note 57, at 1623-27; Flynn, *supra* note 15.

[130]   There continues to be a considerable amount of scholarship concerning the historical and contemporary goals of antitrust policy rejecting the neoclassical interpretation of that history and the practical application of neoclassical theory to contemporary reality. *See,* Brietzke, *The Constitutionalization of Antitrust: Jefferson, Madison, Hamilton and Thomas C. Arthur,* 22 VAL. U.L. REV. 275 (1988); Brodley, *The Economic Goals of Antitrust: Efficiency, Consumer Wel-*

process demands it and the art of legal analysis requires the restoration of inductive legal reasoning in lieu of the discredited analytical positivism the presently popular methodology of "economic analysis" seeks to put in place of the legal analysis of antitrust disputes, our common consensus on the meaning of economic justice and the normative goals antitrust policy has served in the past century and should serve in the next.

---

fare, and Technological Progress, 62 N.Y.U. L. Rev. 1020 (1987); Curran, *Beyond Economic Concepts and Categories: A Democratic Refiguration of Antitrust Law*, 31 St. Louis U.L. Rev. 349 (1987); Flynn, *supra* note 18; Fox, *The Battle for the Soul of Antitrust*, 75 Calif. L. Rev. 917 (1987); Fox & Sullivan, *Antitrust—Retrospective and Prospective: Where Are We Coming From? Where Are We Going?* 62 N.Y.U. L. Rev. 936 (1987); Gerla, *A Micro-Economic Approach to Antitrust Law: Games Managers Play*, 86 Mich. L. Rev. 892 (1988); Gjerdingen, *The Politics of the Coase Theorem and Its Relationship to Modern Legal Thought*, 35 Buffalo L. Rev. 871 (1986); Lande, *supra* note 10; Hovenkamp, *Antitrust Policy After Chicago*, 84 Mich. L. Rev. 213 (1985); Hovenkamp, *Rhetoric and Skepticism in Antitrust Argument*, 84 Mich. L. Rev. 1721 (1986); Hovenkamp, *Fact, Value and Theory in Antitrust Adjudication*, 1987 Duke L.J. 897; May, *Antitrust in the Formative Era: Political and Economic Theory in Constitutional and Antitrust Analysis, 1880-1918*, 50 Ohio St. L.J. 257 (1989); May, *The Role of the States in the First Century of the Sherman Act and the Larger Picture of Antitrust History*, 59 Antitrust L.J. 93 (1990); Millon, *The Sherman Act and the Balance of Power*, 61 S. Cal. L. Rev. 1219 (1988); Peritz, *The "Rule of Reason" in Antitrust: Property Logic in Restraint of Competition*, 40 Hastings L.J. 285 (1989); Peritz, *A Counter History of Antitrust Law*, 1990 Duke L.J. 263.

20
Antitrust relief and the House Judiciary Committee

BY HAMILTON FISH, JR.*

In every Congress during the 21 years the author has served, bills have been referred to the House Judiciary Subcommittee on Monopolies and Commercial Law to curtail damages or otherwise limit the application of the antitrust laws with respect to certain industries or activities. As a rule, the Monopolies Subcommittee has responded to such proposals with restraint, and when its members have decided to act, they have generally sought to amend the original proposal in order to limit the scope of the immunity extended. It is the purpose of this article to examine recent legislative experience with antitrust exemptions and immunities and to consider the factors, some of them institutional and others peculiar to the legislation at hand, that have reinforced or relaxed the subcommittee's traditional exercise of caution.

Member of Congress from New York since 1969. Since 1983, Ranking Minority Member on the House Judiciary Committee, as well as its antitrust subcommittee.

I. Institutional considerations

A. Structural factors limiting legislative review

Over a century ago, in *Congressional Government: A Study in American Politics*, Woodrow Wilson described our political system as "government by the chairmen of the Standing Committees of Congress."[1] While this would be an overstatement today, it nevertheless remains true that our committee system has been consciously designed to be a bottleneck to reduce the flood of legislation to an orderly and controlled flow, and that it is the committee chairman who generally determines the committee agenda. In the House of Representatives this winnowing process is further refined by the institution of the Rules Committee, which prescribes the order of business and terms of debate on the House floor for all bills reported by the legislative committees.

There are also factors within the House Judiciary Committee itself that serve as constraints on the progress of antitrust legislation. While the Subcommittee on Monopolies and Commercial Law has always been primarily identified with antitrust concerns, it also has jurisdiction over the bankruptcy laws, the creation of federal judgeships, laws governing the States' power to tax, and proposed constitutional amendments involving the conduct of elections, tax or fiscal matters, and the subcommittee is required to devote appropriate time to such matters. Fourteen days, for example, were consumed in hearings on the balanced budget amendment between 1979 and 1982. In addition, the subcommittee must exercise legislative and oversight responsibility over the Antitrust Division, the Executive Office for United States (Bankruptcy) Trustees and the Office of Legal Counsel, all within the Department of Justice, and the United States Bankruptcy Courts and the Court of International Trade.[2]

---

[1]   W. WILSON, CONGRESSIONAL GOVERNMENT 102 (1885).

[2]   HOUSE COMM. ON THE JUDICIARY, REPORT ON THE ACTIONS OF THE COMM. ON THE JUDICIARY DURING THE 99TH CONG., H.R. Rept. 99-1029, 99th Cong., 2d Sess. 105 (1987).

The seniority of the subcommittee's membership can also be a limiting factor. It has long been customary for the Antitrust Subcommittee to be headed by the chairman of the Judiciary Committee and for the Ranking Minority Member on the full committee to assume that position on the subcommittee. Traditionally, the Monopolies Subcommittee has also attracted a preponderance of the other senior members of the Judiciary Committee, both from the majority and minority. In the 100th Congress (1987–88), for instance, of the eight subcommittee Democrats (beside the chairman), one chaired another standing committee while four chaired other Judiciary subcommittees. The six Republicans were also senior members who were similarly committed in terms of responsibilities and time. Although all Members receive staff briefing memoranda and frequently review prepared testimony, the competing demands of seniority, coupled with the tight schedules under which every Member of Congress functions, have an unavoidable impact on participation in hearings and the activism of the subcommittee.

In a few instances, the rules of the House result in committees other than the Judiciary Committee having jurisdiction over laws granting antitrust immunity. An example of this would be the Committee on Agriculture's jurisdiction over the Capper-Volstead Act, relating to agricultural co-ops. Also, bills with antitrust content may be consciously drafted to avoid referral of the legislation to the Judiciary Committee, and by happenstance or design a bill may also be reported by another committee so late in the Congress that a sequential referral to Judiciary will allow little opportunity for antitrust review. On occasion, however, this may backfire on the committee with primary jurisdiction.

The Telecommunications Act of 1980, H.R. 6121, for example, was reported by the Energy and Commerce Committee very late in the 96th Congress (1979–80), after numerous hearings and extensive markup sessions. At the request of seven members of the Monopolies Subcommittee, Chairman Rodino requested and received a sequential referral of that bill to Judiciary, which lasted just over a month. The Telecommunications Act was a rather complex piece of legislation that employed technical terminology with which our Members were not familiar. It was designed to facilitate the entry of a "fully separated subsidiary" of AT&T into unregulated markets, such as data processing and services. In the course of two subcommittee caucuses and two hearings, at which 17 witnesses testified, it became evident that resolution of cross-subsidization and other significant antitrust problems in the bill would require a number of amendments and a major rewriting of the legislation. It would consume more time than remained available under the terms of the referral. As the time period for the sequential referral ran out, the Monopolies Subcommittee and the full committee ordered H.R. 6121 reported adversely. That negative report effectively ended any realistic prospect for its enactment during the remainder of that Congress.

B. The predisposition against exemptions and immunities

New exemptions and immunities constitute additions to what has been described by one commentator as "truly a ragbag collection covering all kinds of different things from all kinds of different periods, with all kinds of justification, and with great diversity in economic effect."[3] In the opinion of the author, it is a mixed bag that does contain some economically logical and desirable law. But I also share the view of many subcommittee members that any additions to the exemptions list require a convincing prior showing of public interest or compelling economic need. My remarks on the Shipping Act of 1983 are representative:

> As a general rule, I do not look with favor on exemptions to our antitrust laws. There must be compelling evidence based upon unique economic factors to justify such an exclusion. I look upon hearings as an opportunity to gain the necessary information as to whether or not these special circumstances are genuinely present.[4]

---

[3]   *Antitrust Exemptions and Immunities: Hearings Before the Subcomm. on Monopolies and Commercial Law of the Comm. on the Judiciary, House of Rep.*, 95th Cong., 1st Sess. 4 (1977) (testimony of Donald I. Baker).

[4]   *Shipping Act of 1983: Hearings Before the Subcomm. on Monopolies and Commercial Law of the Comm. on the Judiciary, House of Rep.*, 98th Cong., 1st Sess. 2 (1985).

Five senior members of the Monopolies Subcommittee, Representatives Rodino, Edwards, Jordan, McClory and Wiggins, subscribed to a similar declaration in the 1979 report of the National Commission for the Review of Antitrust Laws and Procedures: "Each existing or proposed exemption should be justified in terms of empirically demonstrated characteristics of the specific industry that make competition unworkable. The defects in the market place necessary to justify an antitrust exemption must be substantial and clear."[5] A predisposition against antitrust exemptions, therefore, although more pronounced and consistently held by some Members than others, should be understood to be the point of departure for subcommittee review.

C. Recent experience

In the course of the 100th Congress (1987–88), 142 bills were referred to the Monopolies Subcommittee, 38 of which became the subject of hearings. Seven were reported to the full committee and passed by the House and six were enacted into law. Of the 31 hearings held by the subcommittee during the 2 years, 28 were legislative, including the Antitrust Division budget authorization. The others were oversight hearings on such matters as mergers and concentration in the food industry. No reported bill contained an antitrust exemption or modified damages and only one, the Freedom from Vertical Price Fixing Act, H.R. 585, related to antitrust. During the immediately preceding 99th Congress (1985–86), 183 bills were referred to the Monopolies Subcommittee. Twenty of them were the subject of hearings, and seven bills were reported to the full committee and then to the House. Only one of the seven reported bills, the Railroad Antimonopoly Act (H.R. 1140), dealt with antitrust. Further, it was never considered on the House floor. The remaining six passed the House and three

---

5 REPORT TO THE PRESIDENT AND THE ATTORNEY GENERAL OF THE NATIONAL COMMISSION FOR THE REVIEW OF ANTITRUST LAWS AND PROCEDURES 186 (Jan. 22, 1979).

became law.[6] Only 14 of the 23 hearings held by the subcommittee during these 2 years dealt with proposed legislation. The balance were oversight hearings, ranging in their topics from Sir James Goldsmith's attempted takeover of Goodyear to the competitive aspects of the Conrail sale.

In the 98th Congress (1983–84), 163 bills were referred to the subcommittee, 25 were the subject of hearings, and 6 became law.[7] Among those were three bills providing varying degrees of antitrust immunity, the Shipping Act of 1984,[8] the National Cooperative Research Act of 1984,[9] and the Local Government Antitrust Act of 1984.[10] The subcommittee refused to act on legislation providing antitrust relief for beer distributors, although two hearings were held.

Not to be overlooked or underestimated is the disposition of the chairman of the subcommittee, who is traditionally also chairman of the full committee. Although he may be receptive to suggestions from other Members, the chairman's ultimate responsibility for setting the hearing and markup schedule and the overall subcommittee agenda can be pivotal. The decline in fortunes of the beer distributors' legislation, as will be seen, may be related to this.

The sheer number of bills before the subcommittee, therefore, as well as jurisdictional limitations, an inherent resistance to change, the constraints of time and Member availability and the chairman's priorities, all combine to winnow out the great majority of bills referred to the Monopolies Subcommittee, including those providing antitrust exemptions.

---

6   H.R. Rept. 99-1029, *supra* note 2, at 105.

7   HOUSE COMM. ON THE JUDICIARY, REPORT ON THE ACTIVITIES OF THE COMM. ON THE JUDICIARY DURING THE 98TH CONG., H.R. Rept. 98-1193, 98th Cong., 2d Sess. 106 (1985).

8   46 U.S.C. App. 801 et seq.

9   15 U.S.C. 4301–4305.

10   15 U.S.C. 34–36.

II. Recent Monopolies Subcommittee experience with exemptions and immunities

A. *The Soft Drink Intrabrand Competition Act*

The first antitrust exemption to pass the Congress since the Newspaper Preservation Act of 1970,[11] the Soft Drink Intrabrand Competition Act of 1980,[12] was enacted after almost a decade of lobbying by the syrup manufacturers and soft drink bottlers. The genesis of this legislation was a Federal Trade Commission complaint against seven major soft drink manufacturers filed in July 1971, which alleged that the licensing agreements under which they granted bottlers exclusive geographically defined sales territories were in violation of section 5 of the FTC Act.[13] Four years previously, the *Schwinn* case[14] had held that territorial restraints effectuated through sales to wholesalers and dealers were per se illegal.

Initially, the soft drink industry sought a broad exemption that would specifically shield the soft drink and trademark private food label industries from the antitrust laws. A series of bills introduced in the House and Senate from 1972 to 1975 provided for this. During those years, the Monopolies Subcommittee heard extensive testimony from the antitrust enforcement agencies, among others, vigorously objecting to singling out a particular class of products for unique and special treatment under the antitrust laws.

In 1975, an administrative law judge dismissed the FTC complaint, having concluded that the territorial restraints served to promote intrabrand competition. Thereafter, the soft drink industry endorsed a more modest bill, H.R. 6684, which provided for application of the antitrust laws "on any basis other than a

---

11   15 U.S.C. 1801 et seq.

12   15 U.S.C. 3501–3503.

13   15 U.S.C. 45.

14   U.S. v. Arnold, Schwinn & Co., 388 U.S. 365 (1967).

per se basis that the Commission or the court deems appropriate.'' Even this bill drew testimony from the FTC that its passage would seriously impair effective antitrust enforcement, would severely undermine the establishment of per se rules of law, would not promote legal certainty and judicial economy, and would constitute special-interest legislation that would increase the likelihood that other industries would seek similar favored treatment from the Congress.[15]

H.R. 6684 had been favorably reported by the House Committee on Interstate and Foreign Commerce in June 1976, and sequentially referred to the Judiciary Committee. It was reported by Judiciary at the end of July, which would be relatively late in the Second Session of any Congress and was particularly so in a presidential election year with its usual accelerated congressional time frame. (The 100th Congress, which did not adjourn until October 22, 1988, 17 days before the election, was a rare departure from this.) It made no further progress in the House.[16]

In 1977, the Supreme Court held in *GTE-Sylvania*[17] that the law should return to the rule of reason standard that governed nonprice vertical restraints prior to *Schwinn*.[18] This was precisely what the soft drink industry had sought through legislation the previous year. In 1978, however, the FTC reversed the ALJ decision and ruled that as to nonreturnable containers the bottlers' vertical restraints did violate section 5 of the FTC Act.[19] Perceiving its vulnerability even under the rule of reason, the

---

[15] *Exclusive Territorial and Customer Restrictions: Hearings Before the Subcomm. on Monopolies and Commercial Law of the Comm. on the Judiciary, House of Rep.*, 94th Cong., 2d Sess. 305 (1976) (statement of Alfred F. Dougherty, Jr., Deputy Director, FTC).

[16] For the legislative history of H.R. 6684 and its predecessors, *see generally* EXCLUSIVE TERRITORIAL FRANCHISE ACT, H.R. 6684, REPORT OF THE COMM. ON THE JUDICIARY, H.Rept. 94-1230, pt. 2 (1976).

[17] Continental T.V., Inc. v. GTE-Sylvania, Inc., 433 U.S. 36 (1977).

[18] U.S. v. Arnold, Schwinn & Co., 388 U.S. 365 (1967).

[19] 15 U.S.C. 45.

industry appealed to the U.S. Court of Appeals for the District of Columbia Circuit and at the same time began to promote passage of legislation to amend the antitrust laws to create a special new substantive standard to guide the application of those laws to the soft drink industry, a standard so structured as to virtually guarantee that industry a permanent antitrust law exemption.

In the 96th Congress (1979–80), the Soft Drink Intrabrand Competition Act (H.R. 3567), was introduced with 259 cosponsors, more than enough support to force the bill out of committee and onto the House floor by means of a discharge petition signed by a majority of the House, or 218 members, should the committee fail to act. The bill mandated that the use of exclusive geographical territories in trademark licenses involving the manufacturing, distribution, and sale of trademark soft drink products would be lawful, provided the product was "in substantial and effective competition with other products of the same general class."[20]

The Monopolies Subcommittee held five widely spaced hearings on H.R. 3567 and heard from no fewer than 23 witnesses, including the syrup manufacturers, franchised and independent bottlers, the Department of Justice, cosponsors of the bill, and academic experts.[21] A number of those who testified strongly criticized the FTC's intervention in the industry, and much was made of that agency's reversal of the ALJ "who heard the evidence." The failure to legislate was also said to be anticonsumer, antismall business, and injurious to a distribution system which permitted vigorous intrabrand competition.[22] The Department of Justice, on the other hand, reemphasized its consistent opposition to "unnecessary and unclear special interest legislation

---

[20]   H.R. 3567, 96th Cong., 1st Sess. 2 (1979).

[21]   *Soft Drink Intrabrand Competition Act: Hearings Before the Subcomm. on Monopolies and Commercial Law of the Comm. on the Judiciary, House of Rep., on H.R. 3567 and H.R. 3573*, 96th Cong., 1st and 2d Sess. (1980).

[22]   *Id.* at 208 (testimony of Rep. Thomas A. Luken); at 216 (testimony of J. Lucien Smith, former President of Coca Cola); and at 235 (testimony of Cartha DeLoach, Vice President, Pepsico).

as an impingement on our fundamental national policy of reliance on robust and uninhibited competition."[23] Current law, it was said, afforded intrabrand competition all the weight it deserved, and substituting a "substantial and effective competition" standard for the current standard of liability would promote vagueness and uncertainty in the law.[24] Well aware of the sensitivities of the subcommittee members, the Department repeatedly emphasized that passage of the bill "would create an undesirable precedent for similar special interest legislation applicable to other industries."[25]

While the hearings proceeded at an unhurried pace, one each in October and November 1979, one in March 1980, and two in April, the 1,500-member National Soft Drink Association continued intensive grassroots lobbying in congressional districts, a great many of which contained at least one bottler, and maintained an active presence on Capitol Hill. Ultimately, however, the subcommittee's deliberations proved to be somewhat too leisurely for the bill's prime sponsor, Representative Sam B. Hall of Texas, who lost patience and filed a petition to discharge the committee from further consideration of the bill. By mid-June, Representative Hall had the 218 signatures necessary to force a vote on the discharge petition and then on the bottlers' bill itself.

Confronted, therefore, with the inevitable, the Monopolies Subcommittee reported H.R. 3567 without amendment on June 16, and a substitute bill, worked out in negotiations between proponents and opponents, was ordered reported by the full committee on the following day. This measure provided antitrust

---

[23]   *Id.* at 13 (testimony of Richard J. Favretto, Deputy Assistant Attorney General).

[24]   *Id.* at 15, 18 (Favretto testimony).

[25]   *Malt Beverage Intrabrand Competition Act: Hearings Before the Subcomm. on Monopolies and Commercial Law of the Comm. on the Judiciary, House of Rep., on H.R. 3269,* 97th Cong., 2d. Sess. 23 (letter of Asst. Attorney General Robert A. McConnell to Peter W. Rodino, Apr. 13, 1982).

protection for territorial franchise agreements if the soft drink product were in substantial and effective competition with other products of the same general class "in the relevant market or markets," but it expressly excluded price-fixing agreements, horizontal restraints or boycotts, if otherwise unlawful, from the protection of the Act. It was this measure that ultimately became law.[26] A bitter dispute over its interpretation, however, turning on whether the bill simply restated the rule of reason or extended greater protection to territorial franchise agreements in the soft drink industry, was reflected in the text and in the additional views in the House Judiciary Committee report.[27] This dispute over the exact meaning of the language was also prominent during the House floor debate.[28] Even when granting an antitrust exemption after a protracted struggle that extended for nearly a decade, there were those on the subcommittee who would deny that it had done so.

B. The Malt Beverage Intrabrand Competition Act

As the Department of Justice had predicted, and as some had feared, enactment of the soft drink bill was followed by intense lobbying for similar legislation to protect the beer distributors. In the 97th Congress (1981–82), the Malt Beverage Intrabrand Competition Act, H.R. 3269, attracted 280 cosponsors, which was far more than sufficient for another discharge petition and a rapid repetition of the committee's experience with the soft drink legislation. The first of three hearings on that bill, however, was not scheduled until June 23, 1982, late in the Second Session, and a subcommittee markup was never scheduled.

The proponents of H.R. 3269 argued that their difficulties and need for protection were similar to the soft drink industry's, compounded by the problems of insuring a fresh product. The

---

[26]   15 U.S.C. 3501–3503.

[27]   Soft Drink Intrabrand Competition Act, H.Rept. 96-1118, 96th Cong., 2d Sess.

[28]   126 CONG. REC. H5534–5548 (daily ed. June 24, 1980).

Department of Justice and the FTC argued strenuously that there was no proof that competition was unworkable in the beer industry, that procompetitive territorial restraints were already legal under *GTE-Sylvania*[29] and that the bill would combine with existing governmental barriers to entry to prevent market forces from responding quickly to competitive problems.[30] They were joined in their opposition by the National Association of State Attorneys General and by several economists. At this point, a trade association representing 1,500 firms in the food marketing industry began to lobby most vigorously at the grassroots level and through contacts with every member of Congress against what became known, somewhat disparagingly, as "the beer bill." This intense counter-lobbying, which had not been a problem for proponents of the soft drink bill, has been effective and continues to this day.

In the 98th Congress (1983–84), support for the malt beverage bill declined to 149 House cosponsors and there were two hearings. In the 99th Congress (1985–86), there were but 28 cosponsors and no hearings were held, and in the 100th Congress (1987–88), there were 11 cosponsors and again no hearings. In this instance, therefore, an exemption was blocked by a slowdown that provided time for the emergence of vigorous opposition, a precipitous decline in support and the consequent unlikelihood of a successful discharge petition. This legislation, however, returned in the 101st Congress under the sole sponsorship of Representative Brooks, the new chairman of the Judiciary Committee.

C. Shipping Act amendments

Somewhat different was the fate of another exemption advanced by a single industry, the Omnibus Maritime Act, H.R.

---

[29]   Continental T.V., Inc. v. GTE-Sylvania, Inc., 433 U.S. 36 (1977).

[30]   *Malt Beverage Intrabrand Competition Act, supra* note 25, at 7–31 (statement and testimony of Abbott B. Lipsky, Jr., Deputy Assistant Attorney General); and 96–117 (statement and testimony of Walter T. Winslow, Director, Bureau of Competition, FTC).

6899. As reported by the House Merchant Marine Committee on May 9, 1980, this bill would have effectively eliminated all antitrust limits on the maritime industry and granted blanket approval for all shipping conference agreements. It provided that every agreement filed with the Federal Maritime Commission [FMC] would become effective 60 days after filing unless suspended pending a hearing or rejected for failure to comply with procedural requirements.

Assuming jurisdiction over this bill on a sequential referral, again relatively late in a Second Session, the Monopolies Subcommittee held one hearing and received additional statements from a number of other interested parties.[31] Strongly supporting this legislation as the only means to revitalize the U.S. Flag Merchant Marine were the chairman and Ranking Minority Member of the Merchant Marine Committee as well as a number of maritime industry representatives. The Department of Commerce expressed reservations but was generally supportive, while the Justice Department expressed considerable concern about "removing the antitrust laws from this whole industry,"[32] providing an unusual instance of an openly divided administration position on legislation before the committee.

Independent shippers and independent economists were strongly opposed. Dean Andrew Popper of the American University Law School maintained that it was "difficult to conceive a reason to allow the maritime industry to be given radically different treatment" from other regulated industries with intensive common carrier obligations. He went on to assert that "to eliminate a regulatory structure that has the potentiality of establishing competitive force in a particular industry and then to replace that regulatory force with blanket antitrust immunity is

---

[31] *Omnibus Maritime Regulatory Reform, Revitalization and Reorganization Act of 1980: Hearing Before the Subcomm. on Monopolies and Commercial Law, Comm. on the Judiciary, House of Rep., on H.R. 6899,* 96th Cong., 2d Sess. (1980); and REPORT OF THE COMM. ON THE JUDICIARY, H.Rept. 96-935, pt. 3 (1980).

[32] *Id.* at 82 (testimony of Assistant Attorney General Sanford Litvack).

virtually unheard of in the history of industrial regulation in this country."[33]

Proceeding to amend H.R. 6899, the Monopolies Subcommittee limited the available antitrust exemptions solely to those activities engaged in pursuant to an agreement approved by the FMC, which was the rule provided in the Shipping Act of 1916. The subcommittee also mandated open rather than closed carrier conferences, in order to insure a workable competitive market. Although reported from the Monopolies Subcommittee on June 17 and from the full committee on June 19, H.R. 6899 failed to reach the House floor during the remaining days of the 96th Congress.

In the 97th Congress the pattern was repeated. The Merchant Marine Committee reported a bill, the Shipping Act of 1982, H.R. 4374, which the Monopolies Subcommittee in turn changed substantially "to preserve and reinforce the competitive system in which the maritime industry functions."[34] The Monopolies Subcommittee amendments expanded the list of prohibited anticompetitive acts, strengthened FMC procedural powers to investigate and proscribe such conduct, and redrew the demarcation line between the antitrust laws and FMC regulation. Private treble damage actions were largely eliminated, but in lieu of this a reparations remedy was established for injured persons. Although H.R. 4374 passed the House on September 15, 1982, it was late in the Congress and the Senate took no action.

Another Congress, and for yet a third time the Monopolies Subcommittee sought to protect and promote competition in a bill reported by the Merchant Marine Committee and that largely reflected the interests of the ocean carriers and shippers.[35] As H.R. 1878, the Shipping Act of 1983, came to the subcommittee, it contained provisions that would reinstate and possibly expand

---

[33]   *Id*. at 123–124 (statement of Andrew F. Popper).

[34]   INTERNATIONAL OCEAN COMMERCE TRANSPORTATION, REPORT OF THE COMM. ON THE JUDICIARY ON H.R. 4374, H.Rept. 97–611, pt. 2, 18 (1982).

[35]   *See generally* SHIPPING ACT OF 1983, REPORT OF THE COMM. ON THE JUDICIARY ON H.R. 1878, H.Rept. 98-53, pt. 2 (1983).

antitrust immunity as it existed prior to the 1968 *Svenska* decision.[36] Two days of subcommittee hearings brought a number of recommendations for procompetitive amendments from the administration, scholarly experts and others. In particular, the FTC urged retention of a public interest standard, an end to FMC tariff enforcement, a universal right of independent pricing, a sunset on antitrust immunity, and additional limitations on the use of loyalty contracts. Carrier witnesses supported the bill as it had emerged from the Merchant Marine Committee, the shippers wanted more leverage in dealing with the conferences, and the port authority and marine terminal operators sought antitrust immunity similar to that granted carrier agreements.

The bill as reported by the House Judiciary Committee sought to address these and other significant competitive concerns. On the critical question of allowing a carrier to deviate from the established conference rate, which would provide the shipper with more competitive choices, the subcommittee adopted an amendment (which I cosponsored with Representative Hughes) providing for the right of independent action on 10 days' notice for any carrier in a conference serving a U.S. trade. Some carriers wanted a longer waiting period, as much as 45 days, but the subcommittee characteristically sought to narrow the immunity by voting for greater competitive pricing opportunity and the related possibility of improving American export performance. Another subcommittee amendment was a competition standard requiring inquiry into whether a conference agreement "will substantially lessen competition in the ocean commerce of the United States" and whether it will do so "in a manner that outweighs the public benefits of the agreement." In addition, the Monopolies Subcommittee adopted an amendment offered by the author that removed the tariff filing requirement from the Shipping Act and relieved the FMC of its tariff enforcement responsibility. Although the unique circumstances of the industry might make it necessary to sanction price-fixing, tying agreements and cartel

---

[36] FMC v. Aktiebolaget Svenska Amerika Linien, 390 U.S. 238 (1968).

systems, we were able to argue successfully that it would be inappropriate to employ a Federal regulatory agency, using tax-payers' money, to aid in the enforcement of such practices. Early in 1984, the Shipping Act was signed into law.[37]

The Shipping Act serves as an example of immunity legislation emanating from another committee whose ultimate passage was perhaps inevitable. The Monopolies Subcommittee sought, however, with persistence and eventual success, to rewrite and refine it in order to preserve and guarantee as much competitive activity as possible.

D. *The Export Trading Company Act of 1982*

During this same period the committee also worked on export trading company legislation, which would establish a licensing system for export trading companies to immunize their concerted activities from antitrust scrutiny. From the outset, critics inquired whether these activities could have a spillover anticompetitive effect on domestic commerce, and they also questioned whether the Webb-Pomerene Act[38] was not sufficient, although that statute was limited to the sale of goods and excluded services.

Export trading company legislation, however, was strongly endorsed by the Secretaries of Commerce in both the Carter and Reagan administrations. Secretary Philip Klutznick, for instance, wrote to Chairman Rodino of the House Judiciary Committee in 1980, that "exceptions from the antitrust laws should not be granted except where necessary to attain important national aims. I am convinced that increasing U.S. exports is one such compelling national interest."[39] Secretary Klutznick further argued that while "most, if not all, of the activities in which we expect export trading companies to engage would not result in antitrust liability if judged under current interpretations of the antitrust laws and

---

[37]   46 U.S.C. App. 801 et seq.

[38]   18 U.S.C. 61-65.

[39]   Letter from Philip Klutznick to Peter W. Rodino (August 29, 1980).

in a manner consistent with the enforcement policy of the Department of Justice,'' nevertheless ''legitimate uncertainties have arisen over the 'direct and substantial effects' test on U.S. commerce.'' This pervasive uncertainty, it was suggested, was preventing thousands of companies from engaging in cooperative export activity. A certification system administered by the Department of Commerce, as opposed to a possibly less understanding and sympathetic Department of Justice, would greatly facilitate such ventures.

The prospect of increasing our export trade, of course, was widely popular. But the Monopolies Subcommittee refused to rush to judgment on this issue. At a subcommittee caucus on September 30, 1980, the Members unanimously rejected a request to waive jurisdiction to allow the Export Trading Company Act of 1980, H.R. 7230, already reported by the House Foreign Affairs Committee, to proceed to the floor. Of particular concern to Members was the lack of hard evidence—as opposed to merely anecdotal evidence—that export activity was in fact being impeded by existing law and that immunity would significantly increase our overseas trade. A comprehensive study of export discrimination published in 1980 by the Department of Commerce and the Office of the Special Trade Representative had found that while the antitrust laws were of ''concern'' to exporters, ''no specific instances were shown of these laws unduly restricting exports.''[40] There was also strong objection to the Commerce Department's proposed role in antitrust enforcement and to allowing anyone other than Congress to grant antitrust exemptions. Nor was it clear why the Department of Justice's Business Review Letter procedure, which would provide a response within 30 days regarding antitrust enforcement intentions, would not serve to satisfy the needs of exporters. Since the Judiciary Committee would not waive its jurisdiction, further action on export trading company legislation was deferred to the next Congress and a new administration.

---

[40] REVIEW OF EXECUTIVE BRANCH EXPORT PROMOTION FUNCTIONS AND POTENTIAL EXPORT DISINCENTIVES, DEPARTMENT OF COMMERCE AND OFFICE OF THE U.S. TRADE REPRESENTATIVE (1980).

The 97th Congress (1981–82) brought forth two distinct responses to the export trade issue. Chairman Rodino and the Ranking Minority Member, Representative Robert McClory, proceeded in the belief that the appropriate response to exporters who believed the law was unclear was to clarify the law. They introduced the Foreign Trade Antitrust Improvements Act, H.R. 2326, to codify the existing enforcement practices of the Department of Justice and the Federal Trade Commission by requiring that conduct, if it is to be the basis of an antitrust suit, must "have a direct, substantial, and reasonably foreseeable effect" on the domestic or import commerce of the United States. It was soon evident, however, that nothing less than some sort of certification system would satisfy the members of the business community who came to testify before the subcommittee. They were undeterred by the prospect of complex bureaucratic licensing procedures. The administration's Export Trading Company Act, H.R. 1648, accordingly received equal attention in the subcommittee's hearings and moved ahead on a parallel track.

H.R. 1648 had been referred jointly to four House committees: Banking, Foreign Affairs, Judiciary and Ways and Means. Of concern to the Monopolies Subcommittee were amendments to the Webb-Pomerene Act to establish a certification procedure administered by the Commerce Department, which would grant limited antitrust immunity to export trading companies providing financial, marketing and transportation services for small- and mid-size firms engaged in foreign trade. Consultation with the Department of Justice and the Federal Trade Commission would be required. Similar legislation, S. 734, had passed the Senate by a unanimous 93 to 0 vote on April 4, 1981, early in the First Session.

H.R. 2326 was marked up and unanimously reported by the Monopolies Subcommittee on December 10, 1981. It had attracted 50 cosponsors and the strong support of the administration, the American Bar Association, business spokesmen and academic experts. H.R. 2326 was reintroduced as a clean bill, H.R. 5235, which was reported by the full committee on May 18, 1982 and passed by the House on August 3.

The broad support for the Rodino-McClory bill contrasted sharply in three subcommittee hearings with expressions of concern over the potential complexity and delay inherent in the H.R. 1648 certification procedure. In lieu of that, former Assistant Attorney General John Shenefield suggested a "beefed-up" Business Review Letter procedure that would not only protect the exporter against government suits but would limit liability in private suits to single damages if an antitrust violation involving covered activities could be established.

An export trading company certification bill (H.R. 1799), was ultimately reported from the Judiciary Committee on June 15, 1982, and passed the House on July 27, but it differed from the Senate bill in several respects. Whereas S. 734 provided for an exemption from the antitrust laws, thereby implying that certification is necessary for an exporter to act consistently with those laws, the House bill allowed the Secretary of Commerce to issue a certificate of review when the Secretary had determined that it is not inconsistent with the national interest to do so and the Attorney General has determined that the conduct is not "likely to violate the antitrust laws." The House bill thereby preserved the role of the Department of Justice as final arbiter of the antitrust laws, which was reassuring to those who feared the Department of Commerce might not so vigorously pursue and preserve the consumer interest in antitrust.

The House's binding advisory opinion approach also eliminated the bureaucracy and regulation that many had criticized in the Senate bill, such as the seven specified tests, including an undefined "special need," which had to be satisfied prior to the award of an antitrust exemption. Questions remained regarding the delays that would accompany a certification procedure, however, and whether it would actually confer any benefit on exporters that would not be provided by the Rodino-McClory bill. The Antitrust Section of the ABA, among others, opposed enactment of the Senate certification bill "or any similar legislation." The Commerce Department, meanwhile, reversed an earlier position and urged that injured domestic competitors and consumers be denied all recovery for certified activities. Others argued that this would probably lead courts to interpret any grant of antitrust immunity very narrowly, seeking a result that would place abusive conduct outside of the certificate and thus subject to treble damage recovery.[41]

The House went to conference with the Senate on both H.R. 1799 and H.R. 5235, the Rodino-McClory bill, on September 29, 1982, and on October 1, the conference report passed both Houses.[42] The conferees accepted the Foreign Trade Antitrust Improvements Act, H.R. 5235, as it had passed the House, except for deleting a provision exempting export joint ventures from section 7 coverage. The Sherman Act and section 5 of the FTC Act were not to apply to foreign nonimport-related trade or commerce not having a "direct, substantial and reasonably foreseeable effect" on domestic commerce, import trade, or other U.S. exporters. Although no more than a restatement of existing enforcement policy as set forth in the Justice Department's *Antitrust Guide for International Operations*,[43] this bill provided the clarification of the law that many believed was necessary to provide exporters with the reassurance they had so strenuously sought.

A compromise with the Senate placed the export trading company certification procedure in the Department of Commerce with veto authority in the Department of Justice. The conferees adopted the Senate approach of substituting specific standards for the general "antitrust laws" standard favored by the House, but the antitrust law standard was subsumed within the four standards and taken together they were arguably broader than the antitrust law standard standing alone. The House prevailed in allowing single damages to an injured party, although the Senate wanted zero damages. Retention of single damages reflected the

---

[41]   *See generally* Export Trading Company Act of 1981, Report of the Comm. on the Judiciary on H.R. 1799, H.Rept. 97-637, pt. 2, 8–18 (1982).

[42]   128 Cong. Rec. H8459 (daily ed. Sept. 29, 1982).

[43]   U.S. Dept. of Justice, Antitrust Division, Jan. 26, 1977.

Monopolies Subcommittee's strong conviction that the purpose of the legislation was to promote overall U.S. exports, not to promote or protect one group of U.S. exporters at the expense of others who might be without any remedy in the event of abusive and predatory practices by their competitors.

The Senate argued that actual damages would lessen the certainty conveyed by the certificate, but the House conferees maintained that retention of single damages would serve the dual antitrust purposes of compensation and deterrence. House Members also believed the decision on this bill would influence other pending certification legislation, such as H.R. 6262, a bill that would establish a certification system for joint research and development activity by competitors. Both the Monopolies Subcommittee during hearings and markup and the full committee during markup devoted substantial attention to the question of damages and arrived at the same conclusion.

By February 1990, over 7 years after the Export Trading Company Act of 1982 became law on October 8, 1982, just 114 export trading company certificates have been issued by the Department of Commerce and administration witnesses have on several occasions advised the subcommittee that it has been the House's clarification bill, not the certification procedure, which has provided the antitrust certainty sought by U.S. exporters.

E. The Local Government Antitrust Act of 1984

The remaining two exemptions to be discussed, dealing with municipalities and joint R&D undertakings, enjoyed broad-based support. In both instances the question before the subcommittee was not whether relief should be granted, but rather precisely how it should be.

In the *Boulder* case,[44] decided in January 1982, the Supreme Court refused to extend the full protection of state antitrust

---

[44] Community Communications Company, Inc. v. City of Boulder, 445 U.S. 40 (1982).

immunity, set forth in *Parker v. Brown*,[45] to their political subdivisions—cities, counties, and other units of local government. *Boulder* held that municipal action, even by a home rule city with complete authority in local matters, is not immune from antitrust laws unless it constitutes the sovereign action of the state itself or is authorized by a "clearly articulated and affirmatively expressed state policy" of substituting regulation for competition. Soon after this decision, a number of resolutions adopted by city councils and other local bodies began to arrive at the office of the Clerk of the House and were forwarded to the Judiciary Committee. Members also began hearing from local government officials in their districts, as well as the National League of Cities and the U.S. Conference of Mayors.

Assistant Attorney General William Baxter, testifying before the subcommittee at an Antitrust Division oversight and budget authorization hearing conducted in February 1982, was not convinced at that time that any remedial legislation was needed. He observed that there had never been a case holding that a municipality had violated the antitrust laws. Congress could wait, he suggested, until the meaning of *Boulder* was further explained on a case-by-case basis. According to the Assistant Attorney General, "The way it should be dealt with is by a judicial retreat from these kinds of economically contentless per se rules, because sensible antitrust rules would not interfere with any significant amount of municipal activity."[46]

Many members of the subcommittee felt differently, however, as delay would prolong the uncertainty about the limits of antitrust liability for local governmental actions and perhaps subject certain of them and their officials to costly and protracted litigation that might culminate in treble damage awards. Members were particularly concerned about the deterrent effect *Boul-*

---

[45]   317 U.S. 341 (1943).

[46]   *Antitrust Division of the Department of Justice Oversight Hearings Before the Subcomm. on Monopolies and Commercial Law of the Comm. on the Judiciary, House of Rep.*, 97th Cong., 1st and 2d Sess. 48.

der would have on good faith governmental actions that would otherwise be taken in the public interest.

A number of bills began to be introduced in the House. The first of these, H.R. 2981, was introduced by Representative Henry Hyde of Illinois early in May 1983. It provided that a unit of local government shall be liable under the antitrust laws for authorized conduct only to the extent that a state, if authorized by law to engage in identical conduct, would itself be liable under the antitrust laws. Treble damages would lie for conduct beyond the scope of this immunity.[47] Soon afterward, I introduced my own version of a "Boulder bill," H.R. 3361. This provided local units of government with the same immunity as the parent state, if the action taken is authorized by state law or the state constitution and the parent state would have immunity if it took similar action. Since cities, counties and towns are literally the legal "creatures" of the states in which they are situated, it seemed logical to me that they should share in the antitrust immunity accorded to their "creators." But this immunity should only attach when they are engaged in carrying out legitimate governmental functions, as determined by the law of their states.[48] A third bill, H.R. 3688, introduced by Representative Don Edwards, gave immunity for conduct "which is an exercise of the sovereign power of the State in which the local government is located,"[49] and a Senate bill by Mr. Thurmond, S. 1578, granted immunity to any law or official action in the exercise of local government's regulatory powers, but not the sale of goods or services in competition with private persons. Clearly, it was time for Congress to act to insure that the federal antitrust laws would not unduly restrain legitimate decision making at the municipal level.

---

[47]   129 Cong. Rec. E2176 (daily ed. May 11, 1983), (Extension of Remarks by Rep. Hyde).

[48]   129 Cong. Rec. H4124 (daily ed. June 20, 1983) (remarks of Rep. Fish).

[49]   129 Cong. Rec. E3825 (daily ed. June 28, 1983) (Extension of Remarks by Rep. Edwards).

In September 1983, Assistant Attorney General Baxter testified on *Boulder* legislation for a second time before the subcommittee. He conceded that "the need to avoid substantial antitrust litigation costs is seriously disrupting the processes of local government," and concluded accordingly that "the risk of liability and the costs imposed by antitrust litigation may justify statutory antitrust relief for local governments and, ultimately, for taxpayers."[50]

In March and May 1984, the subcommittee held two hearings exclusively devoted to municipal antitrust legislation, which was endorsed by witnesses representing the U.S. Conference of Mayors, the National League of Cities, the National Association of Counties and others.[51] All of those present were aware of the January 1984, $9.5 million jury verdict, trebled to $28.5 million, that had been awarded against the County of Lake and Village of Grayslake, Illinois, and three local government officials individually for conspiring to restrain competition by denying a sewer connection to a proposed real estate development in a newly annexed area.[52] Indeed, the District Attorney for Lake County was among the witnesses at the May hearing. Professor Thomas J. Campbell of Stanford Law School, however, pointed out to the Subcommittee that

It is unfortunate but true that antitrust violations do occur. It is unfortunate but true that units of local government, cities and states can violate the antitrust laws. Not many of the cases that have been brought . . . have actually gone to judgment. I think that is good

---

[50]   *Joint Research and Development Legislation: National Cooperative Research Act of 1984: Hearings Before the Subcomm. on Monopolies and Commercial Law, Comm. on the Judiciary, House of Rep.*, 98th Cong., 1st Sess. 24 (1987).

[51]   *Municipal Antitrust Legislation: Local Government Antitrust Act of 1984: Hearings Before the Subcomm. on Monopolies and Commercial Law, Comm. on the Judiciary, House of Rep.*, 98th Cong., 1st Sess.

[52]   Unity Ventures v. County of Lake, 631 F. Supp. 181 (N.D. Ill. 1986) (judgment n.o.v.), *aff'd*, 841 F.2d 770 (7th Cir. 1988).

and not a surprise. But there are instances—and you cannot admit to knowledge in the area without admitting of this possibility—where units of local governments have conspired with individuals, violated valuable rights, favored one company over another, or created monopolies where free competition had existed before, and the person who pays for that is the American consumer. It can happen, and in my judgment, it has.[53]

He accordingly proposed that the form of the legislation shift from an antitrust exemption to a limitation on remedies. Other witnesses agreed with Professor Campbell that an outright exemption might be more than the situation warranted and could invite years of litigation before its meaning could be clarified.

Following the subcommittee hearings, accordingly, two alternatives were introduced as bills by the chairman. H.R. 5992 proposed yet another immunity test tied to whether or not the local government conduct was "undertaken to protect or provide for the public health, safety or welfare." H.R. 5993 embodied the injunctive relief/remedies approach, eliminating monetary damages against local governments, to which the Senate had already agreed.

Recognizing political realities and mindful of the fact that the legislative window was rapidly closing on the 98th Congress, the National League of Cities and others seeking protection swung behind the injunctive relief/remedies approach. On July 25, 1984, H.R. 5993 was the subcommittee's markup vehicle, and a clean bill, H.R. 6027, was reported to the full committee. This measure eliminated all damage actions under sections 4, 4A, and 4C of the Clayton Act against a local government for official conduct, or damage actions against a person whose conduct was expressly required by a local government, but the right to injunctive relief was preserved. The federal antitrust laws would continue to apply to activity falling outside the definition of "official conduct" and state antitrust law would continue to be applicable. H.R. 6027 passed the House on August 8, by a 414 to 5 vote.

The conference with the Senate lay ahead, but it would focus on the narrower issues of retroactivity and a Senate amendment

---

[53] *Municipal Antitrust Legislation Hearing, supra* note 51, at 192.

prohibiting FTC enforcement actions against cities. The bill that ultimately became law embodied the "remedies" response preferred by Chairman Rodino. On October 11, the House and Senate agreed to a conference report, and the President signed the Local Government Antitrust Act into law on October 24, 1984.[54]

F. National Cooperative Research Act of 1984

Consideration of legislation to shield jointly conducted R&D activities from antitrust attack paralleled the progress of the *Boulder* bills in the 98th Congress. The appeal for protective legislation in this area had been loud, clear and persistent for several years, if somewhat discordant as to the exact remedy being sought. Some believed that there was nothing in the antitrust laws that would flatly prohibit cooperative research enterprises, even among competitors in the same industry. In the previous 15 years, as Chairman James Miller of the FTC testified before the subcommittee, only three cases had been filed against joint ventures, in each instance not because of the joint venture itself but because of collateral agreements alleged to be anticompetitive. "In short, this is not the sort of enforcement record that should leave would-be joint venturers paralyzed with fear."[55] Corporate general counsels, on the other hand, discouraged their management from such cooperative activity, fearing unknown antitrust consequences.

In November 1980, the Department of Justice had published its *Antitrust Guide Concerning Research Joint Ventures*. This was expected, when coupled with the Business Review Letter procedure, to be sufficient to allay antitrust anxieties. Assistant Attorney General Baxter also sought to offer businessmen certain benchmarks to make it easier for them to ascertain the circum-

---

[54]   15 U.S.C. 34–36.

[55]   *Joint Research and Development Legislative Hearings, supra* note 50, at 48 (testimony of James C. Miller, III).

stances under which joint R&D could be lawfully undertaken.[56] There were others who maintained that the proposals before the subcommittee were largely "psychological" bills directed to an illusory problem. Ultimately, however, Mr. Baxter advised the Monopolies Subcommittee that "Perceptions are real. They may be only perceptions, but they are real and they influence behavior," and the administration, accordingly, forwarded its own R&D legislative proposal to the Congress.[57]

Among the other measures considered by the subcommittee were bills offered by Representative Don Edwards of California (H.R. 108), Representative Mike Synar (H.R. 1952), Representative Jim Sensenbrenner (H.R. 3393), and Representative Dan Lungren (H.R. 3952). The author drafted a "minimalist" approach, H.R. 3641, which won considerable support at the subcommittee hearings. It contained no notification procedure, certification procedure, mandatory licensing requirements, governing guidelines, or membership standards. Instead, it provided actual damages plus interest and costs for antitrust injury, and awarded attorneys' fees to prevailing defendants. It made the careful distinction between R&D programs, which were protected, and the marketing or commercial use of their discovery, which were not.

By the time 3 days of subcommittee hearings commenced in September 1983, there were six pending House bills, each with a different response to the problem. Various proposals combined (1) a "safe harbor" for participants meeting market share test and other criteria; (2) disclosure to the Attorney General, and in some instances in the *Federal Register*, in exchange for a certificate limiting antitrust liability for specified conduct ("affirmative clearance") or for the right to proceed in the absence of adverse agency action ("negative clearance"); (3) detrebling damages, generally to actual damages plus interest and costs; and (4) codification of the application of the rule of reason test to R&D

---

[56] William F. Baxter, speech to the National Association of Manufacturers, Washington, D.C. (May 10, 1983).

[57] *Joint Research and Development Legislation Hearings, supra* note 50, at 51.

joint ventures. Also discussed, but not embodied in proposed legislation, were industry-specific exemptions tied to particular research needs.

The administration proposal was set forth as title 2 of the National Productivity and Innovation Act, H.R. 3878, introduced by Congressman Carlos Moorhead, and provided actual damages under Federal and state antitrust law for joint R&D ventures, conditioned upon full disclosure to the Attorney General and notice in the *Federal Register*. It also provided that no joint R&D program should be deemed illegal per se in any action under the antitrust laws. It left in place the existing substantive antitrust standards for determining the legality of joint R&D programs, and treble damages would apply to marketing or production activity. Title 2 was but one element in a comprehensive administration program that sought to encourage private R&D by improving the economic and legal climate. Other titles in H.R. 3878 dealt with intellectual property licensing, patent and copyright misuse and process patents.

Throughout the subcommittee hearings, witnesses frequently stressed the importance of making the U.S. more competitive in the world marketplace, in which other nations had long encouraged their own businessmen to engage in intensive collaborative efforts in high-technology R&D. The Assistant Secretary of Commerce for Productivity, Technology and Innovation, D. Bruce Merrifield, testified that "joint R&D programs have many procompetitive aspects. They reduce duplicative and redundant R&D; they promote the efficient use of scarce technical personnel; and they help to achieve desirable economies of scale in the conduct of R&D."[58]

Proceeding in the belief that a legislative response by the Congress was justified because perceptions of antitrust obstacles have evident real consequences for R&D, the Monopolies Subcommittee marked up H.R. 4963 on March 1, 1984. This was a

---

[58] *Joint Research and Development Legislation Hearings, supra* note 50, at 98.

fusion of earlier legislative concepts and a rejection of others. It most closely resembled the administration bill, providing actual damages, interest from the date of injury (except to the extent found unjust by the courts) and costs for actions brought under Federal or state antitrust laws for conduct within the scope of a joint R&D enterprise. Sensitive to the possible proprietary nature of the agency submission, publication in the *Federal Register* was carefully specified to require a description only "in general terms" of the area of planned activity and its duration. The limitation on damages was made contingent upon disclosure to the Attorney General and the FTC, and it was provided that no joint R&D program shall be deemed illegal per se. The latter provision did no more than codify existing practice, which has consistently been to apply rule of reason analysis in assessing the legality of such undertakings, but witnesses had testified that such language would provide an important additional measure of reassurance to participants.

The subcommittee made only minor changes in the bill considered for markup, and a clean bill, H.R. 5041, introduced by Chairman Rodino with a bipartisan cosponsorship of 14 other members of the full committee, was introduced. This bill was in turn reported by the full committee on March 20, 1984, with minor amendments. There followed discussions with the House Science and Technology Committee, which had reported its own version of an R&D bill the previous fall. These talks resulted in clarifying language that was chiefly related to defining conduct falling within and outside the joint R&D undertaking. On May 1, 1984, the bill was approved by the House, 417 to 0. The Senate passed similar, though not identical legislation on July 31. A conference report was subsequently approved by both Houses and the President signed the National Cooperative Research Act into law on October 11, 1984.[59]

With the statutory certainty of mandated application of the rule of reason and of single damages for antitrust violations occurring within the scope of the R&D joint venture, the incen-

---

[59] 15 U.S.C. 4301–4305.

tives for cooperative research by American companies were in place.

According to the Justice Department, as of February 1990 there had been 168 filings under the National Cooperative Research Act involving 181 joint ventures. A recent assessment places Microelectronics and Computer Technology Corp. (MCC), a high-tech research joint venture whose members were among the most vocal advocates of protective legislation, among those that have achieved success within the microelectronics industry, "through a series of significant, but not spectacular research achievements."[60] In this instance, the Monopolies Subcommittee and the Congress as a whole appear to have acted wisely and well.

III. Conclusion

It is evident from this examination, as was suggested at the outset, that the House Judiciary Committee and in particular its Monopolies Subcommittee have taken a cautious, conserving approach to efforts to provide exemptions or other relief from the antitrust laws for particular industries or situations.

As has been shown, some of the most valuable work done by the subcommittee lies in the careful shaping and narrowing process that seeks to retain the important protections of existing law against competitive abuses. If there is a single conclusion to be drawn from the cases studied, it is that the collective experience and caution of the subcommittee will allow narrowly drawn antitrust exemptions to be enacted into law only if they are justified by special economic circumstances that are grounded in actual experience. On occasions the subcommittee has acted unwillingly, as with the soft drink legislation. On other occasions, perhaps the subcommittee has not been sufficiently skeptical (*i.e.*, the certification apparatus of the export trading company bill).

---

60   Washington Post, December 27, 1987, at K4, col. 1. The first commercial application of MCC-developed technology is on the market, other new technology is being used internally by member companies, and the consortium is making important advances in superconductivity research.

The R&D and *Boulder* bills illustrate the importance of the breadth and quality of support for particular legislation, and the Shipping Act and the export trading company bill, not to mention the soft drink bill, the importance of persistent advocacy. The beer bill is instructive, on the other hand, of what may happen when opposition has the time and incentive to mobilize. Every one of these bills were subject to the competition for time and attention of the subcommittee.

There is no single pattern. It is the author's view that there is a place for antitrust exemptions if they are narrowly drawn and justified by competitive circumstances.

21
State action and "active supervision": an antitrust anomaly

BY WILLIAM H. PAGE*

Of the many features of contemporary antitrust law that would surprise the drafters of the Sherman Act, perhaps none is more prominent than the state action doctrine.[1] Under the late 19th-century's limited conception of the federal commerce power, states' regulatory actions within their borders were beyond the

---

* Professor of Law, Mississippi College School of Law.

AUTHOR'S NOTE: *I presented a nascent version of this argument at the meeting of the Association of American Law Schools Section on Antitrust and Trade Regulation in January 1988. I thank the participants in that meeting for their comments. I also thank Craig Callen for his careful reading of an earlier draft.*

[1] For recent commentary, *see* Hart, *"Sovereign" State Policy and State Action Antitrust Immunity,* 56 FORDHAM L. REV. 535 (1988); Garland, *Antitrust and State Action: Economic Efficiency and the Political Process,* 96 YALE L.J. 486 (1987); Gifford, *The State Action Doctrine After* Fisher v. Berkeley, 39 VAND. L. REV. 1257 (1986); Jorde, *Antitrust and the New State Action Doctrine: A Return to Deferential Economic Federalism,* 75 CALIF. L. REV. 227 (1987); Lopatka, *The State of "State Action" Antitrust Immunity: A Progress Report,* 46 LA. L. REV. 941 (1986).

constitutional reach of the antitrust laws.[2] True, state regulation could be invalid if it had extraterritorial effects, but that was because it exceeded the states' legislative jurisdiction. Consequently, few members of Congress a century ago could have anticipated the problems posed by the conflict of state economic regulation and antitrust that have followed from the expansion of the commerce power. Still fewer would have predicted that the doctrine formulated to address these conflicts would permit states to displace federal law with frankly anticompetitive systems of regulation.

Under the deceptively simple two-step test of *California Retail Liquor Dealers Ass'n v. Midcal Aluminum*,[3] restraints are immune if they are pursuant to a regulatory program that is clearly articulated by the state's constitutional legislative authority, and are actively supervised by some state regulatory agency. I argued some years ago that the clear articulation requirement is an appropriate and a practical vehicle for effectuating the policies of the state action doctrine, but that the active supervision requirement is inconsistent with those policies.[4] Lately, I have defended my argument in support of the clear articulation requirement at some length in response to a critique by John Wiley.[5] In the present article, after a brief overview of the problem, I will extend that discussion to reexamine and reinforce my criticism of the active supervision branch of the doctrine. My

---

[2]   *See* Hovenkamp & MacKerron, *Municipal Regulation and Federal Antitrust Policy*, 32 UCLA L. REV. 719, 725-28 (1985).

[3]   445 U.S. 97 (1980).

[4]   Page, *Antitrust, Federalism, and the Regulatory Process: A Reconstruction and Critique of the State Action Exemption After Midcal Aluminum*, 61 B.U.L. REV. 1099 (1981).

[5]   Page, *Interest Groups, Antitrust, and State Economic Regulation: Parker v. Brown in the Economic Theory of Legislation*, 1987 DUKE L.J. 618, responding in detail to Wiley, *A Capture Theory of Antitrust Federalism*, 99 HARV. L. REV. 713 (1986). For further development of this dispute, *see* Wiley, *A Capture Theory of Antitrust Federalism: Reply to Professors Page and Spitzer*, 61 S. CAL. L. REV. 1327 (1988), and Page, *Capture, Clear Articulation, and Legitimacy: A Reply to Professor Wiley*, 61 S. CAL. L. REV. 1343 (1988).

analysis here is particularly appropriate in light of the Supreme Court's unfortunate reliance on active supervision in *Patrick v. Burget*.[6]

I. Background

One might attempt to justify the state action exemption on the grounds that state regulation and antitrust really have the same goal of promoting the public interest; antitrust establishing the general competitive rules and the states intervening to displace competition in cases of clear-cut market failure.[7] It would be difficult to argue, on the evidence of the kinds of state regulation that survive scrutiny, that present doctrine has this effect. The more satisfactory justification for the doctrine lies in the parallel between the question of the validity of state economic regulation under the antitrust laws and the question of its validity under the 14th amendment. The conflict between state regulation and antitrust reached the Supreme Court in the wake of the New Deal, at a time when the Court was reevaluating its approach to the constitutionality of state regulation. When *Parker v. Brown*[8] first announced an antitrust exemption for state action, the Court had only recently abandoned its efforts under *Lochner*[9] to limit states' authority to interfere with the market.[10] The plaintiff in *Parker* asked the Court to undertake a similar task under a different rubric. In both contexts, the courts must invoke general

---

[6] 108 S. Ct. 1658 (1988).

[7] Some commentators have suggested that the exemption should be limited to regulation aimed at remedying an instance of market failure. *See, e.g.,* Cirace, *An Economic Analysis of the "State-Municipal Action" Antitrust Cases*, 61 TEX. L. REV. 481 (1982).

[8] 317 U.S. 341 (1943).

[9] Lochner v. New York, 198 U.S. 45 (1905). For a recent interpretation of *Lochner* and the persistence of its viewpoint in modern constitutional law, *see* Sunstein, *Lochner's Legacy*, 87 COLUM. L. REV. 873 (1987).

[10] *See* West Coast Hotel v. Parrish, 300 U.S. 379 (1937).

language to invalidate democratically enacted regulatory programs. Many of the same concerns supporting deference in the 14th amendment sphere—experimentation in regulatory programs and dispersion of political power, for example—also support deference in antitrust cases.[11] True, the Court has specified the terms of antitrust law by a variety of per se rules governing private restraints, but it is not obvious how those rules should apply to state regulatory programs in which the intent is ambiguous and the institutional structures quite different. The *Parker* doctrine thus left the question of the desirability of state intervention in markets largely to the state political process.

Parker governed the state action doctrine for decades, while the Court repeatedly denied certiorari to resolve conflicts among the circuits.[12] But in 1975, the Court began a reevaluation of the doctrine with *Goldfarb v. Virginia State Bar*.[13] In a succession of decisions attended by a host of concurring and dissenting opinions,[14] the Court limited the exemption to regulatory schemes in which the state had made a particularly clear-cut choice in conflict with antitrust. The new cases revealed a willingness to examine the political processes by which regulation was adopted and implemented, a tendency very much in line with the Court's process-based approach to constitutional adjudication.[15] The Court distilled the doctrine of these cases into the familiar two-step test in *Midcal*.

In an article published 9 years ago, I argued that the cases from *Goldfarb* to *Midcal* had developed a doctrine that was half right.[16] The requirement of clear articulation by a sovereign body, I concluded, is correct from the perspectives of both traditional

---

[11]   *See* Jorde, *supra* note 1, at 232–34.

[12]   *See* Handler, *Antitrust—1978*, at 78 COLUM. L. REV. 1363, 1375–75, 1374 n.67 (1978).

[13]   421 U.S. 773 (1975).

[14]   For a review, *see* Page, *supra* note 4, at 1113–22.

[15]   *See generally*, J. ELY, DEMOCRACY AND DISTRUST (1980).

[16]   Page, *supra* note 4.

federalism and economics,[17] but the active supervision require-ment adds nothing constructive to the doctrine and should be abandoned.[18]

My argument in support of clear articulation was this. The requirement insures that state regulatory programs in conflict with antitrust be adopted by the state as sovereign—that is, by the state legislature or supreme court—rather than by administrative agencies or municipalities. This distinction reflects important differences between legislation and administration as political processes.[19] Legislative processes are intrinsically more entitled to deference, since they involve the full range of Madisonian checks on dominance by a single interest. When those processes result in a clear policy in conflict with antitrust, one infers that all affected interests have been considered in framing the policy; consider-ations of federalism thus suggest that action pursuant to that policy should be immune. Where the legislative authorization is ambiguous, however, and the anticompetitive regulation really originates in a nonsovereign governmental body, there is good reason to believe that the policy results from the special influence of the regulated interest in the regulatory process. Invalidation of the policy then submits the issue to the state legislature for reconsideration. The effect of the requirement is therefore to leave the ultimate authority for defining state policy in the hands of its legislative processes.

I argued that the active supervision requirement undermines this policy of deference to state regulatory authority by insisting that state regulation take the conventional command-and-control form.[20] This standard limits the states' ability to intervene in the market, and does so on grounds that are inconsistent with the realistic view of command and control regulation that underlies the clear articulation requirement.

---

17 *Id*. at 1113–25.

18 *Id*. at 1125–36.

19 *Id*. at 1109–13.

20 *Id*. at 1128–36.

In a recent article, *A Capture Theory of Antitrust Federalism*,[21] Professor John Wiley agreed with my focus on state political processes as the basis for immunity, and with my rejection of the active supervision branch of the Court's approach. He disagreed, however, with the distinction between legislative and administrative processes that underlies my defense of the clear articulation requirement. His approach would examine the actual functioning and outcome of the political process that led to each instance of state regulation—legislative, administrative, municipal—and try to determine whether the regulation was the result of "capture." I have recently tried to rejustify my support for the clear articulation requirement and to point out some shortcomings in Professor Wiley's approach.[22] In that article, I rely on the political theory of *The Federalist* as well as the modern economic theory of legislation to show that the distinction, implicit in the clear articulation requirement, between legislative and administrative processes is fully justified.[23] Although in recent years the Court has reduced the degree of clarity it requires in legislative mandates, the clear articulation requirement is still the most appropriate and the most workable indicator of state policy.[24] I argue, moreover, that Professor Wiley's capture approach is inconsistent with the principle of state legislative autonomy and beyond the capability of the courts to administer in a principled way.

In the present article, I would like to extend the analysis in my recent work to reconsider my criticism of the active supervision requirement in light of developments since *Midcal*.[25] The active

---

[21] Wiley, *supra* note 5, at 731–39.

[22] *See*, Page, DUKE L.J. *supra* note 5.

[23] *Id*. at 626–42.

[24] *Id*. at 642–45.

[25] For a different critique, *see* Lopatka, *supra* note 1, at 1038 (supervision should only be evidence of legislative intent, not a separate requirement for immunity).

supervision requirement and its twin, the unilateral governmental restraint doctrine in *Fisher v. Berkeley*,[26] reflect the same error Wiley makes in his capture theory: they measure the legitimacy of a state's action against a concept of the state's public interest that is independent of the collective choice of the state's electorate expressed through constitutional legislative processes. The twin doctrines thus render the state action doctrine incoherent by undermining the clear articulation side of the doctrine. Their reliance on the existence of a bureaucratic regulatory structure as a criterion of legitimacy in regulation threatens to displace the clear articulation requirement as the touchstone of valid state policy.

I will consider two justifications for the active supervision requirement. In the next three sections, I will consider the Court's reasoning in *Hallie v. City of Eau Claire*,[27] and in *Patrick v. Burget* that active supervision advances the same values as the clear articulation requirement. In section V, I will consider Professor Thomas Jorde's argument[28] that active supervision forwards the independent value of citizen participation.

II. Supervision as a criterion of legitimacy

In *Hallie*, the Court explicitly justified the active supervision requirement on the ground that, like clear articulation, it provides evidence that a regulatory program really advances a state policy rather than purely private interests.[29] Similarly, in *Patrick v. Burget*, the Court wrote that active supervision:

> requires that state officials have and exercise power to review particular anticompetitive acts of private parties and disapprove those that fail to accord with state policy. Absent such a program of supervision, there is no realistic assurance that a private party's anticompeti-

---

[26]   475 U.S. 260 (1986).

[27]   471 U.S. 34 (1985).

[28]   Jorde, *supra* note 1.

[29]   471 U.S. at 46.

tive conduct promotes state policy, rather than merely the private party's individual interests.[30]

The extent of actual supervision of private conduct apparently need not be great for this "realistic assurance" to arise, so long as there is some regulatory agency with jurisdiction over the restraint. In *Southern Motor Carriers*, the government did not challenge,[31] and the Court apparently approved,[32] a procedure that permitted private carriers to submit to state agencies collective rate proposals that would go into effect if the agency failed to act to disapprove the proposals. *Patrick*, however, held that where no state agency has ultimate authority to overturn the private anticompetitive decision, and judicial review is extremely deferential,[33] the active supervision requirement will not be satisfied.

One important consequence of this reliance on the vigilance of public officials as the basis for the active supervision requirement is that only private rather than municipal (and, by implication, administrative)[34] action that restrains trade need be supervised.[35] The Court in *Hallie* reached this conclusion by distinguishing public from private action in terms of their respective tendencies to advance purely private interests. The Court found there is no reason to believe that municipalities and agencies need to be

---

30   108 S. Ct. at 1663.

31   471 U.S. at 66.

32   The Court noted with approval that the agencies have "ultimate" authority over rates. 471 U.S. at 51.

33   The Court reserved the question of whether judicial review could ever satisfy the active supervision requirement. 108 S. Ct. at 1664–65. *See also* Pinhas v. Summit Health, Ltd., 880 F.2d 1108, 1113 (9th Cir. 1989); Consolidated Gas Co. of Florida v. City Gas Co. of Florida, 880 F.2d 297, 303, *vacated pending rehearing en banc*, 889 F.2d 264 (11th Cir. 1989). For a useful discussion of this issue, *see* Note, *Judicial Review as Midcal Active Supervision: Immunizing Private Parties from Antitrust Liability*, 57 FORDHAM L. REV. 403 (1988).

34   *Hallie*, 471 U.S. at 46 n.10.

35   *Id.* at 47.

supervised to insure that they act in the public interest; private actors, however, are very likely to act in their own interest and so need to be controlled by some form of administrative review.

One might well dispute the generalization that administrative agencies are more likely to follow a clearly articulated state policy than are private actors. The experiences of federal regulatory agencies since the New Deal suggest that administrative agencies do not reliably exercise their discretion in the public interest and must therefore be constrained by political and judicial devices.[36] The presumption of action in the public interest becomes still more dubious if it is extended, as lower courts have recently done, to entities such as state bars[37] and rural electric cooperatives.[38]

But the more important point is that the relative probability that public or private actors will follow the legislative mandate should not determine whether they have in fact done so in a particular case. It should be sufficient for immunity that the challenged action, public or private, is within the state's clearly articulated policy, regardless of the probability *ex ante* that it would be so. That decision must be made by the antitrust court, on the basis of the legislative language and the challenged conduct. If public or private actors do not act pursuant to a clearly articulated state policy, then their actions would simply

---

[36] *See, e.g.*, S. Breyer & R. Stewart, Administrative Law and Regulatory Policy 127–83 (2d ed. 1985) (collecting assessments of regulatory failure); W. Niskanen, Bureaucracy and Representative Government 42 (1971) (bureaucrats maximize their budgets); Cutler & Johnson, *Regulation and the Political Process*, 84 Yale L.J. 1395 (1975).

[37] Hass v. Oregon State Bar, 883 F.2d 1453, 1459–61 (9th Cir. 1989). *But see id.*, at 1464–68 (Ferguson, J., dissenting).

[38] Fuchs v. Rural Electric Convenience Cooperative, Inc., 858 F.2d 1210 (7th Cir. 1988), *cert. denied*, 109 S. Ct. 1744 (1989). *See also* Interface Group v. Massachusetts Port Authority, 816 F.2d 9 (1st Cir. 1987) (port authority); Ambulance Serv. Co. of Reno v. Nevada Ambulance Service, 819 F.2d 910 (9th Cir. 1987) (charitable corporation formed by county board of health).

not be immune.[39] Yet, under the Court's rationale, even if a federal court finds that unsupervised private actions were within the state's articulated policy, they are nonetheless not immune.[40]

What is more disturbing, if the court finds that the private actions were supervised, it may feel somehow "assured" that the action was within a clearly articulated policy. The Court apparently assumes that the existence of a regulatory structure is an indicium of the legitimacy of the state's articulated policy. The presumption that public officials act in the public interest offers assurance, either that they (or the private actors they supervise) are acting within the legislative mandate—a question the federal courts should determine for themselves—or that the legislative mandate is itself one that is worthy of deference. I would like to address this conclusion by refuting its two principal implications.

The first implication is that the absence of a regulatory structure shows that private conduct is not genuinely state action even if it is pursuant to state policy, since a state policy that purports to authorize unsupervised private conduct is, for that reason alone, illegitimate. I argue, in the next section, that this implication assumes a standard of legitimacy external to the democratically enacted choices of the state's body politic. The clear articulation requirement, however, presumes that a state may make choices in conflict with antitrust rules; its only criterion of legitimacy is the process by which the policy is adopted.

The second implication of the Court's justification of the active supervision requirement is that the existence of a regulatory structure demonstrates that the state's policy is legitimate. In section IV, I argue that this reliance on active supervision as affirmative evidence of the legitimacy of state policy is at best redundant: if the challenged conduct is within a clearly articu-

---

[39]   *See, e.g.,* the dicta in Rice v. Norman Williams Co., 458 U.S. 654, 662 (1982): "The manner in which a distiller utilizes the designation statute and the arrangements a distiller makes with its wholesalers will be subject to Sherman Act analysis under the rule of reason."

[40]   *See, e.g.,* Pinhas v. Summit Health, Ltd., 880 F.2d 1108, 1113–14 (9th Cir. 1989); Shahawy v. Harrison, 875 F.2d 1529, 1534–36 (11th Cir. 1989).

lated state policy, it is irrelevant that the state has created a regulatory structure. Worse, such reliance leads courts to ignore or give only cursory attention to the clear articulation requirement, as the Court itself did in *Patrick*.[41]

III. State action without supervision

The Court's requirement of active supervision mistakenly assumes that unsupervised private action pursuant to state law cannot enforce a public policy.[42] In *Midcal*, the Court invalidated a California law that required liquor wholesalers to file price lists and retailers to adhere to them. Since there was no regulatory review of the reasonableness of the prices set in the list, the program involved nothing more than resale price maintenance.[43] The state's articulation of its policy was clear and there was no indication that it was not being carried out exactly as contemplated by the legislature. But the Court found that the absence of bureaucratic supervision conclusively showed that the state regulatory program was nothing more than a sham, a naked preference for the private actors covered by the program.

The reason for the Court's conclusion is implicit in its frequently quoted statement that "the national policy in favor of competition cannot be thwarted by casting such a gauzy cloak of state involvement over what is essentially a private price-fixing arrangement."[44] Had the state cast a thicker cloak by creating a regulatory agency, then the program would have been approved.

---

[41] "In this case, we need not consider the 'clear articulation' prong of the *Midcal* test, because the 'active supervision' requirement is not satisfied." 108 S. Ct. at 1663.

[42] *See* Cohen & Rubin, *Private Enforcement of Public Policy*, 3 YALE J. ON REG. 167, 190 (1985) (legislature may monitor effectiveness of policy by "structuring compensation so that it is based upon easily observable data").

[43] 445 U.S. at 105–106.

[44] *Id*. at 105–106.

The Court explicitly approved state programs that "completely control the distribution of liquor within their borders."[45] As it stood, though, the program looked too much like something that was a per se violation of the antitrust laws. The state was simply disagreeing with antitrust rather than substituting regulation for it. Like nature, the Court abhors a vacuum.

But fair trade laws do substitute something for antitrust, a market ordered on somewhat different terms, and operating within a frame of state law. The simple granting of an antitrust exemption, in specific circumstances, is a form of regulation—or, perhaps deregulation—that Congress has occasionally used to advance particular policies;[46] there is no reason that states should not be able to make the same choice.[47] There are perfectly good arguments in favor of resale price maintenance and they are so well known they do not bear repeating.[48] The Court itself has accepted the arguments in other contexts, leaving the law governing vertical restraints an artificial maze.[49] States, too, should be free to accept those arguments, or to define their public interest in their own terms.

The absence of regulatory review does not indicate an illegitimate purpose; indeed the whole point of the state action exemp-

---

[45]   *Id*. at 106 n.9.

[46]   *See* Page, *supra* note 4, at 1130 n.175.

[47]   The Court itself has used an argument similar to the one in the text in justifying permissive delegations of regulatory authority to administrative agencies. *See SMC*, 471 U.S. at 60 n.22: "Under the Interstate Commerce Act, motor common carriers are permitted, but not compelled to engage in collective interstate ratemaking [citations omitted]. It is clear, therefore, that Congress has recognized the advantages of a permissive policy. We think it unlikely that Congress intended to prevent the States from adopting virtually identical policies at the intrastate level."

[48]   *See* Page, *supra* note 4, at 1131–34. For recent theoretical analysis, *see* Gilligan, *The Competitive Effects of Resale Price Maintenance*, 17 RAND. J. ECON. 544 (1986).

[49]   *See generally* Hay, *Vertical Restraints after* Monsanto, 66 COR-NELL L. REV. 418 (1985).

tion is to accept the definition of the public interest that the state adopts through its constitutional legislative processes. The Court's view depends upon a formal distinction—the existence of a bureaucratic regulatory structure—that makes a restraint look superficially less like conventional per se antitrust violations, but that is unrelated to any valid federal concern.

324 Liquor Corp. v. Duffy[50] shows the conceptual and economic anomalies that the current definition of active supervision has created. Unlike the fair trade law in *Midcal,* the New York law in *Duffy* did not allow wholesalers to set the retail price directly. Instead, it required liquor retailers to charge 12% over the posted wholesale bottle price. The Court suggested that a simple minimum markup law might survive scrutiny, because its implementation involved no discretion on the part of wholesalers, but a mere arithmetic calculation based on the wholesale price. Such a statute presumably would involve no agreement; even if it did involve an agreement, all the active supervision necessary for its implementation would be *ex post* enforcement, since prior review of prices would accomplish nothing.

For two reasons, however, the Court found that the New York statute was more like the fair trade system in *Midcal* than a simple minimum markup provision. First of all, the State Liquor Authority [SLA] had interpreted the statute to permit wholesalers to post off, or reduce, the case price without affecting the bottle price. That interpretation gave wholesalers practical control over retail markups, since retailers normally buy from wholesalers by the case.[51] Second, even if the SLA's interpretation was wrong, and the statute mandated a fixed relationship between the case price and the bottle price, the statute did clearly allow wholesalers to sell at low prices one month, then raise the bottle prices the next month. By this practice, they were able to control the retail markup.[52]

---

[50] 107 S. Ct. 720 (1987).

[51] *Id.* at 725 n.6, 726.

[52] *Id.* at 725 n.6.

The pointlessness of these distinctions as a basis for immunity demonstrates the artificiality of the active supervision requirement. For the same reasons that regulatory review of retail prices would add nothing to justify further deference to the state regulatory program, a simple mandatory minimum markup system is not preferable to the New York system in any meaningful sense.

The Court's objection to the New York law was the discretion it gave wholesalers over the retail markup of their product. Wholesalers may reduce the price one month, then increase it the next, pegging the retail price more than 12% above the actual sale price. Wholesalers want, however, to maximize their own profits, not those of their retailers; thus there are very predictable limits on the wholesaler's discretion in setting retail prices. It is difficult to see why a state may not rely on market-based, permissive regulation like this to accomplish its objectives rather than on a rigid minimum markup criterion or on a cumbersome system of command-and-control regulation. There is no reason, or at least none relevant to federalism concerns, to prefer these alternate forms of regulation to the New York system.

Exclusionary practices, like the peer review at issue in *Patrick*, pose somewhat different problems, but the same conclusion follows. It is true that private actors in peer review may act in their own interests. If they do, however, the only antitrust concern should be whether such actions are within the state's clearly articulated policy. As I will show below, the peer review actions in *Patrick* itself did not meet this standard. If, however, peer review actions are genuinely pursuant to state policy, they should be immune regardless of the system of review the state establishes.

IV. Supervision without state action

The second implication of the *Hallie* rationale for the active supervision requirement is that the presence of a regulatory structure is evidence that the regulatory restraint at issue advances a legitimate regulatory policy. This implication is flatly inconsistent with the clear articulation requirement, which rests the issue of the legitimacy of state policy on the expressed choice of the state's constitutional legislative authority. Such an expression should be conclusive. To add the requirement of supervision suggests that very good evidence of a regulatory structure may justify immunity even where the regulatory action is not authorized by a clearly articulated legislative policy. In the extreme case, it would justify dispensing with the clear articulation requirement altogether. Recent developments confirm my misgivings on this point.

A. The relationship between articulation and supervision

The Court relaxed the clear articulation requirement in *Hallie* and *Southern Motor Carriers* [*SMC*]. Some of the change was needed, particularly the removal of any requirement that state legislation actually compel the restraint in question; as the Court recognized, compulsion is one indication of a clear articulation, but is not a necessary one, since a state may wish to take advantage of the benefits of permissive regulation.[53] But in reaching this conclusion, the Court relied on the same logic that it used to support the active supervision requirement: the distinction between public and private actors and between regulated and unregulated private conduct. In *Hallie*, the Court explicitly presumed that public action, like that of the City of Eau Claire, is in the public interest and therefore need not be compelled by the statute in question.[54] Similarly, in *SMC* the Court conditioned its reasoning concerning the benefits of permissive regulation on the fact that the permission was extended only to *regulated* private actors.[55]

Both of these moves obscure the central point that a legislature may make its purpose clear regardless of whether the entity

---

[53]   *SMC*, 471 U.S. at 58–61; *Hallie*, 471 U.S. at 45–46.

[54]   471 U.S. at 45.

[55]   Southern Motor Carriers Rate Conf. v. United States, 471 U.S. 48, 60 (1985).

to which the legislation applies is public or private, supervised or unsupervised. Equally important, as the last part demonstrates, the benefits of permissive regulation do not depend on supervision of the regulated actors. The Court's approach, in relying on the dubious presumption that public officials act in the public interest, uses the active supervision requirement to assure the antitrust court that the clear articulation requirement has been satisfied. This approach confuses the clear articulation issue with active supervision in a way that threatens to weaken or eliminate the clear articulation requirement.[56]

The effects of the Court's confusion of purpose are most apparent in the lower courts, which rarely fail to find a clearly articulated state purpose.[57] An example of this unduly deferential interpretation is the Ninth Circuit's opinion in *Patrick v. Burget*.[58] There, staff physicians of a small-town medical clinic began peer review proceedings to suspend the staff privileges of a doctor with whom they had had personal and economic disputes.[59] Before the proceedings were completed, the doctor sued under the Sherman Act, alleging that the peer review process was

---

[56]   For a related argument in support of a stricter clear articulation requirement, *see* Hart, *supra* note 1.

[57]   For rare exceptions, *see* Bolt v. Halifax Hospital Medical Center, 891 F.2d 810 (11th Cir. 1990); Consolidated Gas Co. of Florida v. City Gas Co. of Florida, 880 F.2d 297, *vacated pending rehearing en banc*, 889 F.2d 264 (11th Cir. 1989). More typical is Hass v. Oregon State Bar, 883 F.2d 1453, 1457–59 (9th Cir. 1989), which upheld the state bar's rule requiring members to purchase malpractice insurance from the bar itself. The court found clear articulation in state statutes authorizing the bar to impose mandatory malpractice insurance and to create a malpractice insurance fund. These statutes do not indicate a policy to eliminate competition in the malpractice insurance. The court was clearly influenced by its view that active supervision of the bar was not required as the bar could be trusted to act in the public interest. Interestingly, the dissent disputed the court's reasoning on the active supervision requirement, but ignored the clear articulation requirement entirely.

[58]   800 F.2d 1498 (1986), *rev'd on grounds of lack of active supervision*, 108 S. Ct. 1658 (1988).

[59]   800 F.2d at 1502–04.

a boycott. A jury verdict for the plaintiff was reversed by the Ninth Circuit on grounds of immunity, despite substantial evidence of bad faith by the defendants.[60]

The court found that there was a clear articulation of state policy supporting the peer review process, because a state statute provided that:

> The governing body of each health care facility shall be responsible for the operation of the facility, the selection of the medical staff and the quality of care rendered in the facility. The governing body shall:
>
> . . . .
>
> (d) Insure that physicians admitted to practice in the facility are organized into a medical staff in such a manner as to effectively review the professional practices of the facility for the purposes of reducing morbidity and mortality and for the improvement of patient care.[61]

This provision, the court said, restricted free patient choice of physicians.[62] Moreover, it analogized the scheme to authorizing General Motors, Chrysler, and Ford to review the quality of Toyotas: since it involved regulation by competitors, it implicitly recognized the restriction of competition.[63] In addition, the court found that the peer review process was actively supervised, since decisions to terminate privileges were "reported" to the state's board of medical examiners and were judicially reviewable.[64]

The court's interpretation of the clear articulation requirement in *Patrick* would immunize all actions pursuant to legislative delegations of standard-setting authority since any exercise of state authority necessarily involves replacement of free choice in

---

60 *Id.* at 1504–05.

61 Or. Rev. Stat. § 441.055.

62 800 F.2d at 1505–06.

63 *Id.* at 1506. *See also* Marrese v. Interequal, Inc., 748 F.2d 373 (7th Cir. 1984).

64 800 F.2d at 1506.

the market. But there is no indication in the Oregon statute that the peer review committee's delegated authority includes decisions to limit competition in the market for medical services.[65] The criteria listed are medical; none focuses on questions such as convenience and need typically associated with economic regulation of entry. The statute delegates even less authority than an occupational licensing provision, since it applies only to specific facilities.

The statute authorizes nothing that is inconsistent with antitrust: it establishes procedures of self-regulation for hospitals that all economic ventures must establish as a matter of course. Indeed, even in the absence of legislative authority, a hospital that made staffing decisions based upon peer review reports covering only medical criteria would not violate the antitrust laws at all. If, however, doctors with market power, acting under the guise of peer review, made predatory use of the process to deny others access to a hospital, they would be subject to antitrust sanction. It follows that, since the statute does nothing more than authorize the otherwise lawful use of peer review, it should not be interpreted to immunize the predatory use of peer review.

It is useful to compare the delegation in *Patrick* with the one in *Hallie*. The statute in *Hallie* gave the municipality authority to define the area in which it was to provide sewage services.[66] A state agency was given authority to order the city to provide sewage treatment services to other areas, but only subject to those areas' consent to accept sewage collection and transportation services from the city.[67] Thus, the delegation was to the city in its capacity as an economic actor, and reflected a policy of permitting the cities to impose conditions on the provision of sewage services. The alleged restraint was that the city would provide sewage treatment services to neighboring townships only if the buyer would also accept sewage transportation and collection

---

[65]   *See* Bolt v. Halifax Hospital Medical Center, 891 F.2d 810 (11th Cir. 1990).

[66]   471 U.S. 34, 41–44 (1985).

[67]   *Id.* at 44.

services. While this particular tying arrangement was not mentioned in the statute, the Court properly found that the policy of allowing cities to define their service area contemplated the restraint, even when the neighboring areas claimed to be potential competitors for some aspects of the service. The townships' claim that the authority did not extend to instances in which it was used anticompetitively was rejected, since a general authority to refuse to serve unannexed areas necessarily implied actions that would reduce competition in the way plaintiffs alleged occurred in the case.

The statute in *Patrick* gave no such plenary authority to grant and refuse staff privileges; the authority was specifically limited to insuring the staff's compliance with minimum standards of care, a criterion that does not imply a general authority to control the supply of medical services. True, the regulatory authority was given to competitors; but unlike the delegation to the city as a provider of services, the delegation in *Patrick* was made to doctors not because of their economic interest as competitors but because of their expertise as professionals. True also, it is foreseeable that doctors given peer review authority would use it in violation of the established criteria; but the explicit limitation of their authority to medical criteria necessarily implies that actions on other criteria do not advance the state's policy. The allegation was not that the staff had exercised their authority in an anticompetitive way, as was the case in *Hallie*, but that they had gone beyond the scope of their authority in the guise of exercising it.

One might argue in support of the court's lenient interpretation of the clear articulation requirement that decisions on immunity should be made in categorical terms: if peer review is immune at all, it is immune in all instances. It should, under this view, be left to the state courts or administrative review to determine if the exercise of peer review is within the legislative mandate. Otherwise, all peer review decisions would be subject to review in the federal courts as potential antitrust violations, introducing an intolerable degree of uncertainty into the regulatory process. It is here that active supervision comes into play: the active supervision requirement is engaged to play the role of the clear articulation requirement in identifying which actions are within the state's policy. The federal courts, according to this argument, should abandon any effort to assure that state regulatory actions are contemplated by the legislature, since the state's own review machinery accomplishes the same purpose. Even entirely innocuous statutory provisions, like the one at issue in *Patrick*, may thus be interpreted to contemplate a broad displacement of antitrust, since we may rely on active supervision to constrain actions taken pursuant to that authority.

In the first place, the foregoing logic has no application where the defendant is a municipality or an administrative agency that is alleged to have exceeded its authority, since under *Hallie*, the active supervision requirement has no application to those bodies. Consequently, in such cases, the clear articulation doctrine is thoroughly thwarted if the presumption that public officials act in the public interest effectively immunizes all of their actions pursuant to limited delegations. The governmental body may with impunity interpret a narrowly drawn legislative mandate to authorize anticompetitive conduct, a power virtually equivalent to the power to articulate state policy. The presumption that governmental bodies act in the public interest has no force when the issue is whether the agency has exceeded its statutory authority.[68]

Even where the defendants are private individuals, such an approach is inappropriate, since it abandons the state action doctrine to the active supervision requirement. Whenever a regulatory action is alleged to violate the antitrust laws, the issue of the action's consistency with a neutral state legislative policy

---

[68] This, in essence, was Justice White's point in his dissent from the denial of a petition for certiorari in another Ninth Circuit decision. "Municipal actions that contravene express limits in the state policy would not seem to be taken pursuant to a clearly articulated policy and thus would not seem to be shielded by the state action exemption. The Ninth Circuit's characterization of the alleged violation of state policy as an ordinary error or occasional abuse seems insufficient to insulate the municipality from liability for action that restrains competition." Kern Tulare Water Dist. v. City of Bakersfield, 108 S. Ct. 1752, 1753 (1988) (White, J., dissenting), *denying cert. to* 828 F.2d 514 (9th Cir. 1987).

would be left to whatever administrative (or perhaps judicial) review process the state had established. This approach wrongly assumes that the issue of whether the action is within the legislative mandate is identical to the issue of whether it is pursuant to a clearly articulated state policy. State review may conclude that a restraint is within the broad outlines of the state policy; but that conclusion does not establish that the restraint is within a clearly articulated policy to displace competition by the type of regulation at issue.

The power to interpret the policy without review by the federal courts amounts to the power to articulate the policy itself. To recognize such a power undermines the clear articulation requirement. The federal courts cannot in principle abandon the responsibility of determining the issues of immunity and, if necessary, liability.[69] That task involves, first, an interpretation of the policy itself to determine if the alleged conduct was contemplated by the legislature. If it was, then the conduct is immune. If, however, as in *Patrick*, it was not, then the court must determine if the regulatory action was, as alleged, actually a violation of the antitrust laws. This issue may be similar to the issue of whether the regulatory action is consistent with the legislative criteria, an issue state law may give to administrative or judicial review. A federal court may therefore properly consider the reasoning of any state body that reviews the regulatory action for consistency with the legislative standard. But it cannot be bound by that body's conclusions on the ultimate issue of whether a violation occurred.

---

[69] The federal courts should not, for example, be bound by the decision of the state supreme court that the administrative action at issue was within the legislative mandate. *See* Consolidated Gas Co. of Florida v. City Gas Co. of Florida, 880 F.2d 297, 303, *vacated pending rehearing en banc*, 889 F.2d 264 (11th Cir. 1989). *But see* Consolidated Television Cable Serv., Inc. v. City of Frankfort, 857 F.2d 354, 360 (6th Cir. 1988), *cert. denied*, 109 S. Ct. 1537 (1989) (accepting state supreme court's determination that municipality's CATV activities were within state constitutional and statutory delegation of authority to franchise or operate utilities).

B. The definition of agreement

In *Fisher v. Berkeley*[70] the Court upheld a municipal price-fixing program without any showing that it was authorized by a legislatively enacted policy. *Fisher* upheld a municipal rent control scheme against an antitrust challenge by landlords, not because it was exempt, but because it did not involve the requisite agreement. When proposals were made to a rent stabilization board, and the board then issued orders establishing rent ceilings, there was no "meeting of the minds" because the board—presumably acting in the public interest—merely listened to the proposals and made an *independent* decision concerning what prices to set;[71] the decision of landlords to follow the price orders was coerced and reflected no agreement with their terms. These conclusions followed, the Court said, regardless of the level of government at which the orders were formulated.[72] It was not necessary, then, that the price-setting activity of the rent stabilization board be pursuant to a policy clearly articulated by the legislature.[73]

Fisher is very much a child of the active supervision requirement. It defines "unilateral" action as simply action that a public body actively supervises; by the same token, it defines nonunilateral, or "hybrid" state action, by reference to *Schwegmann*[74] and *Midcal*, as action in which the state enforces an unsupervised private choice. In the resale price maintenance cases, it said, since there was no independent regulatory review of the privately set

---

[70]   475 U.S. 260 (1986). For discussion, *see* Wiley, *The Berkeley Rent Control Case: Treating Victims as Villains*, 1986 SUP. CT. REV. 157.

[71]   475 U.S. at 266–67.

[72]   *Id.* at 265.

[73]   Justice Powell's concurrence, *id.* at 270–74, and Justice Brennan's dissent, *id.* at 279–81, reached the clear articulation issue and resolved it in opposite ways.

[74]   Schwegmann Bros. v. Calvert Distillers Corp., 341 U.S. 384 (1951).

prices by regulators, there was an agreement, presumably between the government, which enforced the prices, and the wholesalers who set them. The Court also suggested that if regulators were simply to do what represented interests wanted, without the independent exercise of discretion, the meeting of the minds requirement could be satisfied.[75]

Fisher is potentially more damaging than the unvarnished active supervision requirement, because its logic applies regardless of the level of government at which the independent bureaucratic discretion is applied. It therefore threatens to displace altogether the clear articulation requirement, which requires that policies inconsistent with antitrust be adopted by sovereign state bodies. Fortunately, however, *Fisher* has had little practical impact.

The absurdities of *Fisher* are the direct result of the presumption, first expressed in *Hallie* that administrative and municipal action is in the public interest. Under that assumption, interest-group pressures on agencies do not result in agreements to act in ways the group urges but in an independent, dispassionate evaluation of the public interest separate from the preferences of their constituents.[76] But it is more consistent with our democratic traditions to view government as a mechanism by which constituents make collective choices.[77] If we adopt this view, all govern-

---

[75]   The Court termed this type of conduct "corruption." 475 U.S. at 269. This notion of "corrupt" official action closely resembles the "conspiracy exception" to the *Parker* doctrine. Under that rarely invoked rule, immunity is unavailable where municipalities act "solely to further the competitive commercial purposes of private parties." Omni Outdoor Advertising, Inc. v. Columbia Outdoor Advertising, Inc., 1989-2 Trade Reg. Rep. (CCH) ¶ 68,872, at 62,572 (4th Cir.). The majority and dissenting opinions in *Omni* well illustrate the difficulties involved in distinguishing such conduct from ordinary successful lobbying. *See also* Bolt v. Halifax Hospital Medical Center, 891 F.2d 810 (11th Cir. 1990).

[76]   *See* J. BUCHANAN & G. TULLOCK, THE CALCULUS OF CONSENT 11 (1965).

[77]   *Id*. at 13.

mental action is the result of an agency relationship with represented interests, and therefore involves an agreement.

The antitrust issue, then, is not whether there is an agreement, but whether the agreement constitutes a cartel or an exclusionary practice. This issue may be complex, since the institutional structures of restraints that involve public action may differ from the conventional categories of antitrust offenses. In cases in which the restraint is within the legislature's clearly articulated policy, of course, the issue need not be pursued, since the conduct is immune. In other cases, however, courts should not circumvent the issue by artificial distinctions between public and private conduct.

V. Supervision and participation

Professor Thomas Jorde has argued that the active supervision requirement can be justified as promoting a value independent of the clear articulation requirement: the interest in citizen participation.[78] Active supervision provides at least an opportunity for citizen participation in regulatory decisionmaking, while unsupervised private conduct does not. He says "although the public is able to participate in the initial decision to delegate regulatory authority, that is not the critical point at which decisions are made about whether and how to supplant competition with regulation."[79]

Properly interpreted, the clear articulation requirement presumes that the critical decision to displace competition with regulation is made by a sovereign state body in which all interests are represented. That process exhausts any legitimate federal concern about citizen participation. This is particularly so because a requirement of active supervision forecloses some forms of regulation entirely. It therefore undermines the more significant form of citizen participation in the legislative process in favor of a very dubious form of participation at the level of

---

[78]   Jorde, *supra* note 1, at 249-50.

[79]   *Id*. at 250.

regulatory implementation. At that level, the quality of participation permitted by the agency or municipality is unpredictable and quite likely to be weighted heavily toward regulated interests. The fact that the supervision requirement forecloses regulatory options also implies that it undermines other values of federalism that Professor Jorde recognizes, including those of experimentation and diffusion of power.

Professor Jorde notes that the active supervision requirement may not be much of a hurdle if *Southern Motor Carriers* is an instance of adequate supervision.[80] But the requirement does mandate a bureaucratic regulatory structure, even if it does not mandate actual review of every private action. To that extent, it both limits the state's regulatory flexibility and undermines the role of clear articulation.

Of course, Professor Jorde's argument in support of active supervision presupposes a weakened clear articulation requirement,[81] and so attempts to accomplish some of the objectives of my interpretation of the clear articulation requirement. I nonetheless believe that the active supervision requirement is ill suited to that task.

VI. Conclusion

Until *Patrick*, it appeared that the main practical effect of the active supervision requirement was to invalidate resale price maintenance in liquor distribution. If that were the only shortcoming of the requirement, one could hardly be very concerned about it. The only objection would be that it forecloses a regulatory option of relatively small practical importance. But it is increasingly apparent that the requirement has a far more important negative effect in its use of the existence of a bureaucratic regulatory structure as a criterion of legitimacy in regulation. This emphasis has now become so strong, it threatens to displace the clear articulation requirement as an indicator of valid

---

80 *Id.*

81 *Id.* at 242–44, 247–48.

state policy. The Court should abandon its concern with supervision—the mere existence of a regulatory structure—and refocus the state action doctrine on the nature of the state's legislative choice. Necessarily, this formulation of the doctrine presumes that the courts must evaluate some actively supervised conduct—such as municipal rent control and peer review—under substantive antitrust standards.

22
State antitrust remedies: lessons from the laboratories

BY RALPH H. FOLSOM*

Justice Brandeis once praised the diversity of legal experiments undertaken in the American states acting as "laboratories" of social and economic change.[1] In recent years, the states have been reviving their antitrust laws in the best of laboratory traditions, largely ignoring the Uniform State Antitrust Act.[2] A sense of the

---

* Professor of Law, University of San Diego.

[1] New York Ice Co. v. Liebmann, 285 U.S. 262 (1932) (Brandeis J., dissenting).

[2] Arizona and North Dakota have adopted the Uniform State Antitrust Act [USAA]. Michigan has adopted an antitrust law which is substantially similar to the USAA, but which includes criminal penalties. The USAA was drafted in 1963. *See* Arnold & Ford, *Uniform State Antitrust Act: Toward Creation of a National Antitrust Policy*, 15 CASE W. RES. L. REV. 102 (1963). It was approved by the National Conference of Commissioners on Uniform State Laws in August of 1973. Several commentators have negatively assessed the USAA in part because it omits criminal sanctions and creates a discretionary treble damages remedy. *See* Rubin, *Rethinking State Antitrust Enforcement*, 26 FLA. L. REV. 653 (1974); Note, *Reviving State Antitrust Enforcement: The Problems of Putting New Wine in Old Skins*, 4 J. CORP. LAW 547 (1979).

diversity of the experiments involved, especially in antitrust remedies, can easily be seen in the appended indexes.[3] A sense of the revival can be had from the table, a statistical compilation of state antitrust litigation reported in CCH Trade Cases from 1980–1988. After surveying the causes for the revival of state antitrust law, this article reviews state antitrust experiments with an eye toward lessons from the laboratories. Many of these lessons are drawn from a comparison of the statistical evidence on levels of state antitrust litigation with the presence or absence of particular state antitrust remedies.

The revival of state antitrust law

Thirteen states adopted antitrust statutes prior to the first federal law, the Sherman Act of 1890.[4] Most states legislated on antitrust by the early 1900's: Today, only Vermont and Pennsylvania do not have primary antitrust statutes.[5] Early state antitrust laws often prohibited "trusts" (combinations in restraint of trade). A few states, *e.g.*, California and New York, still retain such prohibitions as their basic antitrust law. After an active and moderately successful period in the late 1800's and early 1900's,[6] state antitrust law entered a period of decline. In 1949, for example, the California Cartwright Act was described

---

[3]   All of the indexes appended cover the basic state antitrust statutes on restraints of trade and monopolization unless otherwise indicated. State laws governing unfair practices (sales below cost, etc.) are generally omitted. Little FTC Acts are generally included.

[4]   15 U.S.C. § 1 *et seq. See* Rubin, *supra* note 2, at 657, for a discussion of the origins of state antitrust law.

[5]   Pennsylvania relies on the common law of restraint of trade and monopolies. Vermont has a Little FTC Act, which has been construed to broadly prohibit restraints of trade. *See* State v. Heritage Realty Co., 407 A.2d 509 (Vt. 1979).

[6]   *See generally* May, *Antitrust Practice and Procedure in the Formative Era: The Constitutional and Conceptual Reach of State Antitrust Law, 1880-1918*, 135 U. PA. L. REV. 495 (1987).

by one author as a "sleeping beauty."[7] By 1982, however, another commentator announced with reference to the California Little FTC Act that the "sleeping giant had awakened."[8] This reversal of perspective is indicative of the widespread revival of state antitrust law in recent years. Indeed, former Antitrust Division chief, Professor William Baxter, has declared that by 1996 antitrust law "will be primarily enforced by the states. . . ."[9]

There are a number of reasons for the recent revival of state antitrust law. First, the courts have removed doubts surrounding the constitutionality of state antitrust laws (which generally operate in harmony with federal law). Second, there has been an expansion by the courts of concurrent state antitrust jurisdiction. Third, the federal government (mostly under the Carter administration) provided financial, evidentiary and remedial support to state antitrust authorities. Fourth, interstate cooperation through the National Association of Attorneys General (NAAG) coupled with a desire to fill the gap created by Reagan administration antitrust policies has spurred state antitrust law enforcement. Fifth, there has been a wave of new "modern" state antitrust legislation enacting diverse state antitrust remedies. Each of these developments is discussed below.

Constitutional and complementary law

During the early years of antitrust, there was considerable doubt as to the constitutionality of state laws. Many arguments were made that Congress intended to exclusively "occupy the field" of antitrust with its federal statutes. It was also argued that since state antitrust laws could substantially conflict with federal

---

7   Note, *The Cartwright Act—California's Sleeping Beauty*, 2 STAN. L. REV. 200 (1949).

8   Papageorge, *The Unfair Competition Statute: California's Sleeping Giant Awakens*, 4 WHITTIER L. REV. 561 (1982).

9   *What Will Be the State of Antitrust Law in the Year 1996?*, 1 ANTITRUST 32 (Fall, 1986).

law they should not be tolerated.[10] To a very large extent these arguments have been rejected by the courts.[11] State and federal antitrust enforcement have been consistently seen as *complementary*. State antitrust law is, therefore, no longer in constitutional limbo. Private plaintiffs and state and local prosecutors know they are dealing with valid statutes and have moved forward with renewed confidence.

The perception of the courts that state and federal antitrust law are complementary is affirmed by recent legislative developments. Many modern state antitrust statutes are essentially paraphrases of their federal counterparts. Furthermore, most states follow federal case law in interpreting their state statutes. Thirty-two states require such adherence by express provision in their basic antitrust statutes and Little FTC Acts.[12] The remainder

---

[10] *See generally* Rubin, *supra* note 2; *Reviving State Antitrust Enforcement, supra* note 2; May, *supra* note 6.

[11] *See, e.g.*, Speegle v. Board of Fire Underwriters of the Pacific, 29 Cal. 2d 34, 172 P.2d 867 (1946) (California Cartwright Act of 1907 constitutional); Pounds Photographic Labs, Inc. v. Noritsu America Corp., 818 F.2d 1219 (5th Cir. 1987) (Texas Free Enterprise and Antitrust Act of 1983 constitutional).

[12] State statutory provisions on following federal antitrust law: ALASKA STAT. § 45.50.545 (Little FTC Act only); DEL. CODE 6, § 2113; D.C. CODE § 28-4515; FLA. STAT. § 542.32; FLA. STAT. § 501.204 (Little FTC Act); HAW. REV. STAT. § 480-3 (includes Little FTC Act); ILL. REV. STAT. 38, § 60-11; ILL. REV. STAT. 121½, § 262 (Little FTC Act); IOWA CODE § 553.2; ME. REV. STAT. 5, § 207 (Little FTC Act); MD. CODE § 11-2022(A) (1)-(2); MASS. GEN. L. 93, § 1; MASS. GEN. L. 93A, § 2 (Little FTC Act); Michigan Antitrust Reform Act § 14; MO. REV. STAT. § 416.141; MONT. REV. CODE § 30-14-104 (Little FTC Act); NEB. REV. STAT.§ 59-829; NEV. REV. STAT. § 598A.050; N.H. REV. STAT. § 356:14; N.H. REV. STAT. § 358-A:13 (Little FTC Act); N.J. REV. STAT. § 56:9-18; N.M. STAT. § 57-1-15; OR. REV. STAT. § 646.715(2); R.I. GEN. L. § 6-36-2; S.C. CODE § 39-5-20 (Little FTC Act); S.D. CODIFIED LAWS § 37-1-22; TEX. BUS. & COM. CODE § 15.04; UTAH CODE § 76-10-926; VT. STAT. 9, § 2453 (Little FTC Act); VA. CODE § 59.1-9.17; WASH. REV. CODE § 19.86.920; W.V. CODE § 47-18-16.

generally follow federal precedent as a matter of case law.[13] Consequently, state antitrust laws rarely conflict in a significant way with federal antitrust law and are rarely preempted.[14]

This is not to say that variations on antitrust themes do not emerge at the state level. State law functions *within reasonable limits as determined by the courts* differently from federal antitrust law. For example, state statutes on sales below (full) cost,[15] per se restraints of trade,[16] territorial price discrimination,[17] and

---

[13] *See, e.g.*, California case law: Corwin v. Los Angeles Newspaper Service Bureau, Inc., 4 Cal. 3d 842, 484 P.2d 953 (1971); Chicago Title Insurance Co. v. Great Western Financial Corp., 69 Cal. 2d 305, 444 P.2d 481 (1968).

[14] State antitrust laws are generally preempted in the field of professional interstate sports. Application of state law in this area has been held an undue burden on interstate commerce. *See, e.g.*, Partee v. San Diego Chargers Football Co., 128 Cal. App. 3d 501, 180 Cal. Rptr. 416 (1982) (football); HMC Management Corp. v. New Orleans Basketball Club, 375 So. 2d 700 (La. App. 1979) (basketball); State v. Milwaukee Braves, Inc., 31 Wis. 2d 699 (1966) (baseball).

[15] Sales below full cost statutes: Ark. Stat. § 70-303; Cal. Bus. & Prof. Code § 17043; Col. Stat. § 6-2-105; Haw. Rev. Stat. § 481-3; Idaho Code § 48-404; Ky. Stat. § 365.030; La. Rev. Stat. 51,§§ 422, 423; Me. Rev. Stat. 10, § 1201; Md. Code § 11-404; Mass. Gen. L. 93, § 14F; Minn. Stat. § 325D.04; Mont. Rev. Code § 30-14-209; N.D. Cent. Code § 51-10-03, 51-110-04; Okla. Stat. 15, § 598.3; Pa. Stat. 73, § 213; R.I. Gen. L. § 6-13-3; S.C. Code § 39-3-150; Tenn. Code § 47-25-203; Utah Code § 13-5-7(a); W.V. Code § 47-11A-2; Wis. Stat. § 100.30(3); Wy. Stat. § 40-4-107.

[16] *See* Index A.

[17] Territorial (locality) price discrimination statutes: Ark. Stat. §§ 70-301, 70-120; Cal. Bus. & Prof. Code §§ 17040, 17031; Col. Stat. § 6-2-103(1); Del. Code 6, § 2504; Fla. Stat. § 540.01; Haw. Rev. Stat. § 481-1; Iowa Code §§ 551.1, 551,2; Kan. Stat. § 50-149; Ky. Stat. § 365.020; La. Rev. Stat. 51, § 331; Minn. Stat. § 325D.03; Miss. Code § 75-21-3; Mont. Rev. Code §§ 30-14-207, 30-14-208; Neb. Rev. Stat. §§ 59-501, 59-502; N.M. Stat. § 57-14-3; N.D. Cent. Code § 51-09-01; Okla. Stat. 79, §§ 2, 81; Or. Rev. Stat. § 646.040; S.D. Codified Laws § 37-1-4 through 6; Utah Code § 76-10-903; Wyo. Stat. §§ 40-4-101, 40-4-106.

exclusive dealing[18] vary somewhat from federal statutory law. In recent years, these variations have usually been upheld by the courts.[19] Another important example is state legislative repudiations of the U.S. Supreme Court decision in *Illinois Brick*.[20] Such repudiations exist in about a dozen states, and are a major source of litigation under California antitrust law.[21] The Ninth Circuit rejected the authority of the states to authorize indirect purchaser actions for damages.[22] The U.S. Supreme Court unanimously reversed.[23] The Supreme Court reaffirmed that state antitrust laws are not expressly or indirectly (by virtue of an intent to occupy the field) preempted. It also reasoned that nothing in *Illinois Brick* suggests that it would be contrary to congressional purposes to allow indirect purchaser actions for damages under state antitrust laws. In the Supreme Court's opinion, state indirect

---

18   Some states have extended their statutory equivalents of section 3 of the Clayton Act to cover services and/or real estate transactions, not just goods. *See, e.g.*, CAL. BUS. & PROF. CODE § 16727 (services included).

19   *See, e.g.*, William Inglis & Sons v. ITT Continental Baking Co., 668 F.2d 1014 (9th Cir. 1981) (California prohibition against sales below *full* cost not preempted by contrary federal monopolization law). *Accord*, Hartsock-Fisher Candy Co. v. Wheeling Wholesale Grocery Co., 328 S.E.2d 144 (W. Va. Sup. Ct. App. 1984). *See also* Louisiana Power and Light Co. v. United Gas Pipe Line Co., 493 So. 2d 1149 (La. 1986); Dussouy v. Gulf Coast Investment Corp., 660 F.2d 594 (5th Cir. 1980) (federal law on intraenterprise conspiracies not followed).

20   Illinois Brick Co. v. Illinois, 431 U.S. 720 (1977).

21   *See* Index I; R. H. FOLSOM & R. C. FELLMETH, CALIFORNIA ANTITRUST LAW AND PRACTICE § 55 (1983); McDavid, *The California Experience: A Hole in the* Illinois *Brick Wall?*, 1 ANTITRIST 16 (Winter, 1987). In states where indirect purchaser damages actions were permitted, a higher than average level of litigation prevailed. *See* table.

22   *In re* Cement and Concrete Litigation, 817 F.2d 1435 (9th Cir. 1987).

23   California v ARC America Corp., 490 U.S. 93, 109 S. Ct. 1661, 104 L. Ed. 2d 86 (1989). NAAG has drafted a model statute implementing state indirect purchaser remedies.

purchaser statutes do not unnecessarily complicate federal antitrust proceedings. Nor do they reduce the incentives of direct purchasers to bring federal treble damages actions. Moreover, the Supreme Court concluded that state indirect purchaser claims do not contravene any federal policy against imposing state liability for damages in addition to federal antitrust liabilities.

Expansive concurrent jurisdiction

State and federal antitrust laws are concurrently applicable to most American trade and commerce. Under recent law, there is very little subject matter covered exclusively by either federal or state antitrust law. This result has been achieved by expansive federal and state judicial interpretations and statutory amendments in the field of antitrust jurisdiction.

Federal antitrust laws, for the most part, now apply to all American business activities, however *local* in nature, *affecting* interstate commerce. The activities involved can be in production or marketing and can involve goods or, in most cases, services. This "effects test" approach has greatly expanded the jurisdictional reach of the Sherman Act, the anticompetitive mergers prohibition of the Clayton Act (specifically amended to adopt this approach in 1980[24]) and the FTC Act (also specifically amended to adopt this approach in 1975[25]). Thus, for example, even local real estate sales have been held by the U.S. Supreme Court to affect interstate commerce and subject to federal antitrust law.[26]

Only the Clayton Act prohibitions against price discrimination, exclusive dealing and tying, and interlocking directorates remain subject to the narrower "in the flow of commerce" test of federal antitrust jurisdiction. This test generally requires that

---

[24] 15 U.S.C. § 18.

[25] 15 U.S.C. § 45.

[26] Goldfarb v. Virginia State Bar, 421 U.S. 773 (1975); McLain v. Real Estate Board of New Orleans, Inc., 444 U.S. 232 (1980).

goods be in transit across state borders or be produced for interstate markets before these statutes apply.[27]

The expansive "effects test" approach to federal antitrust subject matter jurisdiction has also been applied at the state level. This is consistent with the general tendency of state law to follow federal precedent. Under this approach, state antitrust jurisdiction extends to all American business activities, however *national* in nature, that *affect* the commerce of the state.[28] Several states have legislated this approach.[29] California has even held that its Cartwright Act can reach United States foreign commerce in appropriate circumstances.[30] There must, of course, also be a constitutional basis for asserting state personal jurisdiction over the defendants under the "minimum contacts" rule of the 14th amendment.[31] Most states broadly apply the minimum contacts rule under their "long-arm statutes."[32]

---

[27]   *See* Gulf Oil Co. v. Copp Paving Co., 419 U.S. 186 (1974) (price discrimination on intrastate sales of asphalt for interstate highways within California not in the flow of interstate commerce—only state antitrust remedies available).

[28]   An excellent analysis of the demise of strict territorial limits to state antitrust jurisdiction and the emergence of this expansive approach is presented in Hovenkamp, *State Antitrust in the Federal Scheme*, 58 IND. L.J. 375 (1983). *See, e.g.*, Pounds Photographic Labs, Inc. v. Noritsu America Corp., 818 F.2d 1219 (5th Cir. 1987) (Texas antitrust law governs interstate transactions implicating Texas commerce); St. Joe Paper Co. v. Superior Court, 120 Cal. App. 3d 991, 175 Cal. Rptr. 94 (1981) discussed in text at note 33, *infra. Compare In re* Wiring Device Antitrust Litigation, 498 F. Supp. 79 (E.D.N.Y. 1980) (dated South Carolina antitrust statute not applicable to interstate commerce).

[29]   *See* FLA. STAT. § 542.31; ILL. REV. STAT. 38, § 60-7.9; MINN. STAT. § 325D.66; N.M. STAT. § 57-1-13; and TEX. BUS. & COM. CODE § 15.25 (fact that activities also affect interstate or foreign commerce no barrier to state antitrust actions under state law).

[30]   *See* Amarel v. Connell, 202 Cal. App. 3d 137, 248 Cal. Rptr. 276 (1988).

[31]   *See* International Show Co. v. Washington, 326 U.S. 310 (1945).

[32]   *See, e.g.*, CAL. CODE CIV. PROC. § 410.10 (personal jurisdiction may be exercised on any basis not inconsistent with the California or United States constitutions).

A good example of the expansive approach to state antitrust jurisdiction is the California case of *St. Joe Paper Co. v. Superior Court.*[33] California purchasers bought corrugated containers from out-of-state manufacturers through out-of-state wholesalers for delivery in California. The purchasers sued in the superior court under the Cartwright Act, alleging a nationwide price-fixing conspiracy and seeking treble damages. The manufacturers unsuccessfully moved to quash process, asserting lack of sufficient contacts for personal jurisdiction under the California long-arm statute. The court of appeal held that sufficient minimum contacts were established via proof of the manufacturers' election to serve the California market indirectly, proof that the sales to wholesalers were made with the expectation of resale to the California purchasers, and proof of economic benefit from deliveries in California. Activities taking place in other states that entail foreseeable effects in California may be sufficient to satisfy the minimum contacts requirement. Actual physical activity of the defendants in California was not required.

The court of appeal indicated that when a corporation purposely avails itself of the privilege of conducting activities within California it has clear notice that it is subject to state suits, and can act to alleviate the risk of burdensome litigation by procuring insurance, passing the expected costs on to customers, or, if the risks are too great, severing its connection with California. Hence, if the sale of a product of a manufacturer or distributor is not simply an isolated occurrence, but arises from the efforts of the manufacturer or distributor to serve, directly or indirectly, the market for its product in California, it is not unreasonable to subject it to a California antitrust suit. Even an *isolated act of economic activity*, such as the making and performance of a contract in California, may be sufficient to accord state jurisdiction over the defendant when the cause of action is related to that isolated act.

---

[33]   120 Cal. App. 3d 991, 175 Cal. Rptr. 94 (1981).

Federal support and remedies

From 1977–79, under the Carter administration, the federal government provided financial grants[34] to the states for the purpose of developing antitrust expertise within the offices of the state attorneys general. Many states took this opportunity to create their first "antitrust divisions" or "units" within their attorney general's office. California, for example, now has about a dozen full-time state antitrust prosecutors and several active county district attorney antitrust units at the county level. Public enforcement actions at the state level doubled from approximately 200 to 400 prosecutions during the 1977–79 grants period. This initial seed money has continued to bear fruit during the 1980's. State antitrust public prosecutions have been increasing.[35]

Federal statutory amendments have given state antitrust authorities greater incentives to file damages actions in federal court. Amendments to the Clayton Act adopted by Congress in 1976 (sections 4 C–H) allow the state attorneys general to file treble damages actions on behalf of natural citizens of their states injured by Sherman Act antitrust violations. In such parens patriae actions, the attorneys general represent the victims (typically consumers) of antitrust violations.[36] Parens patriae actions

---

[34]   15 U.S.C. § 3739. Pub. L. No. 94-503, § 116, 90 Stat. 2415 (October 15, 1976). These grants and their impact are discussed in *Reviving State Antitrust Enforcement, supra* note 2, at 593.

[35]   *See* table.

[36]   15 U.S.C. § 15C-H. The attractiveness of parens patriae actions to the attorneys general was seriously undermined by the U.S. Supreme Court decision in *Illinois Brick*. Illinois Brick Co. v. Illinois, 431 U.S. 720 (1977). In that decision, the Supreme Court disallowed recovery of treble damages under the Clayton Act to all but direct purchasers. Indirect purchasers, such as the ordinary consumers often represented by attorneys general in parens patriae actions, were generally barred from recovering price-fixing surcharges as a matter of federal antitrust law.

(footnote 36 continued)

resemble class actions: individuals may opt out of them (but rarely do) to pursue their own relief. The most common parens patriae actions involve allegations of price fixing when consumers pay surcharges. Monetary relief granted in such actions may be subject to a variety of "fluid recovery mechanisms" allowing individual consumers to recover small claims. Settlements of parens patriae actions must be court approved. Many state antitrust statutes also incorporate parens patriae remedies.[37]

In parens patriae or proprietary governmental actions, the attorneys general benefit from section 5(a) of the Clayton Act which provides that final judgments or decrees in Justice Department actions create prima facie evidence of antitrust violations in related suits for damages.[38] In 1980, section 5(a) was amended to specifically allow parties seeking federal antitrust damages relief to argue that a *conclusive* presumption of a violation flows from the doctrine of offensive collateral estoppel after final Justice Department judgments or decrees are obtained.[39] If such arguments prevail, it is hard for the state attorneys general to lose.[40]

The attorneys general have attempted to overcome the effects of *Illinois Brick* by alleging vertical price-fixing conspiracies between retailers and suppliers in parens patriae actions. This is an attempt at invoking the co-conspirator exception to the bar of *Illinois Brick*. The practical impact of such allegations is to create substantial pressures from the retailers on their suppliers to settle such actions. *See* Wilson, *Defending an Antitrust Action Brought by a State AG*, 1 Antitrust 10 (Winter, 1987).

[37] *See* Index H. State attorneys general may also file individual or class actions for treble damages on behalf of state and local government units injured by federal antitrust violations. This especially is done after federal authorities file price-fixing suits when state and local units have purchased the product in question (*e.g.*, hospital purchases of pharmaceuticals).

[38] 15 U.S.C. § 16(a).

[39] *Id.*: "Nothing contained in Section 5(a) shall be construed to impose any limitation on the application of collateral estoppel. . . ."

[40] *See* Parklane Hosiery Co. v. Shore, 439 U.S. 322 (1979). *Compare* GAF Corp. v. Eastman Kodak Co., 519 F. Supp. 1203 (S.D.N.Y.

Federal statutory amendments have also given state antitrust authorities greater rights of access to federal evidence of antitrust violations. Section 4F of the Clayton Act, adopted in 1976, obligates the Justice Department to share its investigative files with state antitrust law-enforcement officials in order to facilitate state antitrust actions in federal court.[41] In 1980, amendments to the FTC Act gave the Commission authority to release its confidential investigative records to state agencies for law enforcement purposes.[42] There is, however, considerable argument that the federal authorities under the Reagan administration did not honor these statutory commitments.[43] And the courts have specifically held that the Justice Department and the FTC may deny state access to premerger informational filings required under the Clayton Act.[44]

In 1983, the U.S. Supreme Court ruled that state attorneys general must show a "particularized need" for federal grand jury materials in order to obtain their release.[45] In 1985, rule 6(e) of the Federal Rules of Criminal Procedure was amended to allow

---

1981) and Argus, Inc. v. Eastman Kodak Co., 552 F. Supp. 589 (S.D.N.Y. 1982) (offensive collateral estoppel allowed) *with* Southern Pacific Communications Co. v. American Tel. & Tel. Co., 740 F.2d 1011 (D.C. Cir. 1984) and Jack Foucett Assoc., Inc. v. American Tel. & Tel. Co., 603 F.2d 552 (D.C. Cir. 1984) (offensive collateral estoppel denied).

[41]   15 U.S.C. § 15F(b).

[42]   15 U.S.C. § 46(f).

[43]   *See* Constantine, *An Inside Look at Current Trends in State Antitrust Enforcement*, 1 ANTITRUST 6 (Winter, 1987) at nn. 4-6: "Those [federal] agencies now generally oppose disclosure, press courts to adopt constructions which limit disclosure and when disclosure is unavoidable, often reduce the investigative files to a point where they are incomprehensible."

[44]   Mattox v. FTC, 752 F.2d 116 (5th Cir. 1985); Lieberman v. FTC, 771 F.2d 32 (2d Cir. 1985) (state access to premerger notification filings denied).

[45]   Illinois v. Abbott & Assocs., Inc., 460 U.S. 557 (1983).

state authorities access to federal grand jury materials if a violation of state criminal law might be revealed.[46] This change could provide more federal support to state antitrust enforcement.

NAAG versus the Reagan administration on antitrust

In recent years, the National Association of Attorneys General, a group principally comprised of the 50 state attorneys general, has led the opposition to many Reagan administration antitrust policies. NAAG has promoted the enforcement of state antitrust law through: (1) seminars; (2) the sharing of information, expertise, and evidence; (3) coordinated investigations, prosecutions, interventions, and amicus briefs; and (4) the development of common antitrust policy guidelines and statutory proposals. Several examples of coordinated legal action are notable and harbingers of the future. A remarkable 46 states joined in an amicus brief filed in connection with *Monsanto Co. v. Spray-Rite Service Corp.*[47] A total of 37 states, led by New York and Maryland, instituted coordinated resale price maintenance litigation in federal courts against the Minolta Corporation.[48] State antitrust filings were collaborated by nine states in the *Copper Water Tubing* litigation.[49] These states pooled their settlement

---

[46]   18 U.S.C. rule 6(e).

[47]   465 U.S. 752 (1984). *See* Constantine, *Current Antitrust Enforcement Initiatives By State Attorneys General*, 56 ANTITRUST L.J. 111, 116 (1987).

[48]   One prosecutor described *Minolta* as follows:

"We did that in a nice way, in a very organized fashion. That was because it was the first national governmental resale price maintenance case in many years. We eschewed criminal penalties in that case because we felt that, in a sense, the business community had been lulled and tricked into thinking that resale price maintenance was no longer illegal. I suggest that the next time we may not be so lenient." *See* Constantine, *supra* note 47, at 115.

[49]   *See, e.g.*, Delaware v. Anaconda Co., Civ. No. 7272 (Ch. Ct. 1983); Maine v. Phelps Co., No. CV-83-370 (Sup. Ct. Me. 1983); New Hampshire v. Cambridge Lee Industries, Inc., 83-E-195 (Sup. Ct. N.H. 1983).

recoveries in accordance with a prearranged formula benefiting smaller states. All 50 states agreed upon the State Attorneys General Antitrust Improvements Act of 1987, which contains a lengthy listing of proposed federal antitrust amendments.[50]

NAAG has adopted Vertical Restraints Guidelines (1985) and Horizontal Mergers Guidelines (1987). The NAAG Guidelines represent common statements of prosecutorial policies that openly "counter" current Department of Justice guidelines in the same fields.[51] NAAG has also adopted a Voluntary Pre-merger Disclosure Compact (1988) and a Model State Statute Governing Pre-Merger Notification (1988). Under this compact, NAAG serves as a clearinghouse for state attorneys general seeking access to federally notified data and documents of corporations contemplating mergers. The states then review these mergers under their antitrust laws.[52]

For nearly 100 years federal and state antitrust law have, for the most part, peacefully coexisted. Under the Reagan administration, however, new tensions emerged—notably in the areas of resale price maintenance, nonprice vertical restraints of trade, and mergers. Federal antitrust enforcement policies of the Justice Department and FTC were altered to become more "laissez faire" in outlook than in any administration since the 1920's. Moreover, the Reagan administration systematically reduced antitrust law enforcement resources. Between 1980 and 1985, for example, the number of employees at the Antitrust Division of

---

[50]   *See* Constantine, *supra* note 47, at 118.

[51]   For example, NAAG takes the position that the Justice Department Vertical Restraints Guidelines "do not accurately reflect the judicial interpretation of the federal antitrust laws with regard to nonprice vertical restraints of trade, vertical price-fixing agreements, the relevance of intrabrand competition, the application of per se rules, tying arrangements, the distinction between horizontal and vertical restraints, and the liability of corporations for acts of responsible corporate employees." NAAG Resolution issued with Vertical Restraints Guidelines, December 4, 1985.

[52]   *See* text at notes 71–76, *infra*.

the Justice Department declined by 35%. Even larger reductions in staff took place at the FTC. The state attorneys general committed themselves to "filling the gap" created by Reagan administration antitrust policies by increasing their state antitrust prosecutions. A federal district court antitrust award in 1988 of over $500,000 to NAAG will no doubt help finance this effort.[53]

New legislation and diverse remedies

The revival of interest in state antitrust law and a realization that many antitrust offenses are local in character has nurtured a wave of new and diverse state antitrust legislation. Twenty-five state legislatures, the Virgin Islands and the District of Columbia have adopted major new antitrust laws since 1970.[54] These "modern" antitrust statutes typically prohibit restraints of trade and monopolization, much like sections 1 and 2 of the Sherman Act. Surprisingly few of them or their predecessors prohibit the four Clayton Act[55] offenses (price discrimination,[56] exclusive dealing

---

53 New York v. Dairylea Cooperative, Inc., No. 81 Civ. 1891 (S.D.N.Y. 1988).

54 Major state antitrust legislation since 1970: Alaskan Antitrust Law of 1975; Arizona Uniform State Antitrust Act of 1974; Connecticut Anti-Trust Act of 1971; Delaware Antitrust Act of 1980; District of Columbia Antitrust Act of 1981; Florida Antitrust Act of 1980; Iowa Competition Law of 1976; Kentucky Consumer Protection Act of 1976; Maryland Antitrust Act of 1972; Massachusetts Antitrust Act of 1978; Michigan Antitrust Reform Act of 1984; Minnesota Antitrust Law of 1971; Missouri Antitrust Law of 1974; Montana Unfair Trade Practices and Consumer Protection Act of 1973; Nebraska Consumer Protection Act of 1974; Nevada Unfair Trade Practice Act of 1975; New Jersey Antitrust Act of 1970; New Mexico Antitrust Act of 1979; North Dakota Antitrust Law of 1987; Oregon Antitrust Statute of 1975; Rhode Island Antitrust Act of 1979; South Dakota Antitrust Laws of 1977; Texas Free Enterprise and Antitrust Act of 1983; Utah Antitrust Act of 1979; Virgin Islands Anti-Monopoly Law of 1973; Virginia Antitrust Act of 1974; West Virginia Antitrust Act of 1978.

55 15 U.S.C. § 12 *et seq.*

56 Prohibitions comparable to Clayton Act, § 2 (15 U.S.C. § 13): CONN. GEN. STAT. § 35-45; IDAHO CODE § 48-202; MD. CODE § 11-

and tying arrangements,[57] anticompetitive mergers,[58] and interlocking directorates).[59] Furthermore, in recent years, 18 states
have passed "Little FTC Acts" which prohibit unfair methods of
competition, as is done in section 5 of the Federal Trade Commission Act [FTC Act].[60]

Half the states have not yet modernized their basic antitrust
statutes or have only partially modernized them. The panorama
of state antitrust statutory law in 1990 is thus quite diverse. This
is well illustrated by the review in Index A of statutory restraint
of trade law: With some overlap, 32 states and the District of
Columbia prohibit restraints of trade in terms comparable to
section 1 of the Sherman Act, 4 states prohibit "trusts" (combinations in restraint of trade), 3 states prohibit unreasonable

---

204(a)(3)-(5); N.M. STAT. § 57-14-1 *et seq.*; OR. REV. STAT. §§ 646.040,
646.050; 646.090; UTAH CODE § 13-5-3; VA. CODE § 59.1-9.7; WIS. STAT.
§ 133.04.

[57]   Prohibitions comparable to Clayton Act, § 3 (15 U.S.C. § 14):
ALASKA STAT. § 45.50.566; CAL. BUS. & PROF. CODE § 56727; CONN.
GEN. STAT. § 35-29; HAW. REV. STAT. § 480-5; ILL. REV. STAT. 38, § 60-
3(4); KAN. STAT. § 16-112; LA. REV. STAT. 51, § 124; MD. CODE § 11-
204(a)(6); MASS. GEN. L. 93, § 6; MO. REV. STAT. § 416.031; NEB. REV.
STAT. § 59-1605; N.C. GEN. STAT. § 75-5-(b)(2) (no requirement of
anticompetitive intent); R.I. GEN. LAWS § 6-36-6; TEX. BUS. & COM.
CODE § 15.05(c).

[58]   Prohibitions comparable to Clayton Act, § 7 (15 U.S.C. § 18):
ALASKA STAT. § 45.50.568; HAW. REV. STAT. § 480-7; ME. REV. STAT.
§ 1102-A; NEB. REV. STAT. § 59-1606; TEX. BUS. & COM. CODE
§ 15.05(d); WASH. REV. CODE § 19.86.060.

[59]   Prohibitions comparable to Clayton Act, § 8 (15 U.S.C. § 19):
ALASKA STAT. § 45.50.570; HAW. REV. STAT. 480-8; WIS. STAT. § 133.06.

[60]   Prohibitions comparable to Federal Trade Commission Act, § 5
(15 U.S.C. § 45): ALASKA STAT. 45.50.471; CAL. BUS. & PROF. CODE
§ 17200; CONN. GEN. STAT. § 42-110b; FLA. STAT. § 510.204; HAW. REV.
STAT. § 480-2; ILL. REV. STAT. 121½, § 262; LA. REV. STAT. 51, § 1405;
ME. REV. STAT. 5, § 207; MASS. GEN. L. 93A, § 2; MONT. REV. CODE
§ 30-14-10; NEB. REV. STAT. § 59-1602; N.C. GEN. STAT. § 75-1.1; S.C.
CODE § 39-5-20; UTAH CODE § 13-5-2.5; VT. STAT. 9, § 2453; WASH.
REV. CODE § 19.86.020; W.V. CODE § 46A-6-104; WIS. STAT. § 100.20.

restraints of trade, 11 states specifically prohibit bid rigging, and a surprising 21 states have codified per se illegal restraints of trade (*e.g.*, price fixing). State statutory provisions governing monopolization (Index B) are also diverse: 24 states and the District of Columbia have prohibitions comparable to section 2 of the Sherman Act, 11 states prohibit monopolies (typically only those undertaken to exclude competition or fix prices), and 15 states possess no prohibition against single-firm monopolization.

Private plaintiffs have often been surprised by the generally powerful nature of modern state antitrust remedies, *e.g.*, automatic double or treble damages,[61] costs and attorneys' fees,[62] and liberal class action rules.[63] However, some states make multiple damages awards discretionary with the court, often conditioning such awards upon a showing of flagrancy or willfulness.[64] A few states do not allow any private damages relief for antitrust violations.[65] But, unlike Federal Trade Commission law, some states permit private actions for damages under their Little FTC Acts.[66]

Public prosecutors have generally treated the wave of new state antitrust laws as statements of legislative purpose in favor of increased antitrust enforcement. Some state antitrust statutes, *e.g.*, the California Cartwright and Little FTC Acts, even permit local (city or county) as well as state enforcement. Prosecutors

---

[61]　*See* Index C.

[62]　Most states provide that prevailing state antitrust plaintiffs shall recover their costs and attorneys' fees. *See, e.g.*, CAL. BUS. & PROF. CODE § 16750(a). A few states allow such recoveries to defendants, if there was no basis in law or fact for the suit. *See, e.g.*, FLA. STAT. § 542.22(1).

[63]　*See, e.g.*, California class action rules applied in antitrust cases analyzed in R. H. FOLSOM & R. C. FELLMETH, *supra* note 21, at §§ 217 & 218.

[64]　*See* Index C.

[65]　*Id.*

[66]　*See* Index D.

(and defendants) have sometimes found that public remedies under state antitrust law are more severe than under federal law, *e.g.*, civil penalty actions[67] and forfeitures of corporate rights to do business within the state.[68] State criminal sanctions, on the other hand, are more likely to be misdemeanors instead of felonies as under the Sherman Act.[69] And a surprising number of states have not criminalized or decriminalized their basic antitrust laws.[70]

Public antitrust enforcement at the state and local levels is often perceived as "paying for itself." In many instances this is quite literally true. The moneys expended by state attorneys general and district attorneys on antitrust enforcement are often recouped through settlements, criminal fines and civil penalties. In a minority of states, *e.g.*, Missouri and Washington, modern antitrust statutes establish "revolving antitrust funds." These funds are special accounts from which public officials draw moneys to conduct investigations and bring antitrust actions. They are funded by state and local recoveries in antitrust litigation. In most instances, such recoveries are paid into state and/or local treasuries. Either way, the self-supporting nature of state antitrust law enforcement tends to generate substantial political and budgetary good will.[71] It also provides a ready argument for

---

67   *See* Index E. *See* text at notes 71–76, *infra*.

68   *See* Index F. These forfeitures were sought quite often by attorneys general in the early years of state antitrust law. *See* May, *supra* note 6, at n. 49. The severity of removing corporate charters and business privileges has made them a rare remedy today. In the extreme, the automatic revocation of business privileges and the interdiction of others from doing business with antitrust violators is constitutionally suspect. *See* New Jersey v. New Jersey Trade Waste Ass'n, 1983-2 Trade Cas. (CCH) ¶ 65,645 (N.J. Super. 1983) (interdiction penalty amounts to cruel and unusual punishment).

69   *See* Index G.

70   *Id.* Some of these states, *e.g.*, Arizona, Georgia and Pennsylvania, have made bid rigging a criminal offense.

71   *See generally*, *Reviving State Antitrust Enforcement*, *supra* note 2, at 588.

defense counsel that state antitrust enforcement actions are brought to fill the coffers of public prosecutors. Connecticut's revolving antitrust fund was terminated in part because of such arguments.[72]

Lessons from the laboratories

A number of tentative lessons have begun to emerge from the experiments in antitrust law conducted by the states in recent years. Some of the most interesting of these lessons concern state antitrust remedies.

LESSON ONE   There does not appear to be any magic formula for a viable state antitrust enforcement program. Almost regardless of their content,[73] state antitrust statutes and remedies are being construed liberally to cover most major antitrust offenses, reach distant offenders, and provide effective relief. The U.S. Supreme Court's affirmation of state indirect purchaser remedies has already been discussed. Mergers' remedies provide another example. Only six states have a legislative equivalent of section 7 of the Clayton Act.[74] Yet a significant number of attorneys general are busy scrutinizing local, regional and some national mergers that the Reagan administration either ignored or even approved.[75] The legal basis for such reviews is often the power of

---

[72]   *See* Langer, NAAG ANTITRUST & COMMERCE REPORT (February 1988), at 4.

[73]   *But see* California v. Texaco, Inc., 46 Cal. 3d 1147, 252 Cal. Rptr. 221 (1988) (Cartwright Act prohibition against "trusts" does not reach mergers).

[74]   *See* note 14, *supra.*

[75]   *See, e.g.,* California v. Texaco, Inc., 193 Cal. App. 3d 8, 219 Cal. Rptr. 824 (1985) (FTC consent order bars application of California mergers law), *aff'd on other grounds,* California v. Texaco, Inc., 46 Cal. 3d 1147, 252 Cal. Rptr. 221 (1988); California v. American Stores Co., 872 F.2d 837 (9th Cir. 1989) (FTC approval of merger no bar to state challenge under federal law); Texas v. Coca-Cola Bottling Co., 1985-2 Trade Cas. (CCH) ¶ 66,765 (Tex. Ct. App. 1985) (Texas equiva-

the states, in parens patriae, to obtain injunctive and divestiture relief under the federal antitrust laws.[76] This *federal* remedy has become an effective part of many state antitrust enforcement programs, and recently received the imprimatur of the entire U.S. Supreme Court.[77] Mergers scrutiny is being taken seriously by corporate counsel, who sometimes negotiate settlements in order to remove the risks of a formal state antitrust challenge.[78]

One possible end result is the Balkanization of American mergers law. Will it occur? Perhaps not if NAAG acts as an effective coordinator of state activities, or federal antitrust mergers enforcement becomes more vigorous. But what if the Maine and Massachusetts attorneys general cannot agree on an important regional merger? The law on conflict of state antitrust laws is uncharted. One important commentator argues that while such conflicts are theoretically possible, they are unlikely in practice.[79] Indeed, NAAG is planning to create an "Antitrust Division" with "business review" powers under its Horizontal Mergers Guidelines. Mergers decisions by NAAG Antitrust Division will effectively bind all states.[80] Such procedures, it is suggested, will

---

lent to section 7 of Clayton Act not preempted—soft drink merger challenged); City of Pittsburgh v. May Department Stores Co., 1986-2 Trade Cas. (CCH) ¶ 67,304 (W.D. Pa. 1986) (divestiture obtained by Pennsylvania while federal premerger filings under review by FTC).

[76]   15 U.S.C. § 26. *See* Georgia v. Pennsylvania Railroad Co., 324 U.S. 439 (1945).

[77]   California v. American Stores, Co., 495 U.S. 271, 100 S. Ct. 1853, 109 L. Ed. 2d 240 (1990)

[78]   *See, e.g.*, proposed settlement of state antitrust charges by the attorneys general of Massachusetts, Maine and New Hampshire concerning Campeau Corporation's hostile takeover bid for Federated Department Stores, Inc., 54 Antitrust & Trade Reg. Rep. (BNA) 502 (1988); proposed settlement of New York charges by divestiture if R.H. Macy & Co. instead acquired Federated Department Stores. *Id.*

[79]   *See* Constantine, Panel Discussion, 56 Antitrust L.J. 145 (1987), at 145-47.

[80]   *Id.*

State Antitrust Litigation as Reported in CCH Trade Cases, 1980–1988*

State	Private actions	Pendent private claims in federal court	Litigated public investi-gations	Criminal prose-cutions	Public civil actions	Public consent settle-ments	Total
Alabama	—	—	—	—	—	—	0
Alaska	3	—	1	—	1	1	6
Arizona	5	4	2	—	4	15	30
Arkansas	1	—	—	—	—	—	1
California	50	47	1	1	6	4	109
Colorado	1	2	1	1	2	4	11
Connecticut	6	5	2	—	3	17	33
Delaware	—	—	—	—	—	3	3
District of Columbia	—	—	—	—	—	—	0
Florida	9	7	2	—	—	1	19
Georgia	3	—	—	1	—	—	4
Hawaii	2	6	—	—	—	3	11
Idaho	2	1	—	—	—	—	3
Illinois	16	19	1	2	8	2	48
Indiana	5	3	—	—	—	—	8
Iowa	—	5	2	—	4	1	12
Kansas	1	2	—	—	—	—	3
Kentucky	2	1	—	—	—	—	3
Louisiana	2	8	—	1	—	—	11
Maine	—	—	—	—	—	7	7
Maryland	4	6	—	—	1	3	14
Massachusetts	1	3	—	—	1	10	15
Michigan	7	7	—	4	—	1	19
Minnesota	7	7	1	—	2	3	20
Mississippi	3	6	—	—	—	—	9
Missouri	5	8	—	—	1	2	16
Montana	1	3	1	1	1	—	7
Nebraska	2	—	—	—	1	1	4
Nevada	—	—	—	—	—	1	1
New Hampshire	4	2	—	—	—	—	6

* Excludes cases concerning covenants not to compete. Little FTC Act litigation not reported.

Table (Cont'd.)

State	Private actions	Pendent private claims in federal court	Litigated public investi- gations	Criminal prose- cutions	Public civil actions	Public consent settle- ments	Total
New Jersey	10	4	—	6	2	6	28
New Mexico	4	3	—	2	2	1	12
New York	28	40	16	10	5	2	101
North Carolina	8	10	—	—	—	—	18
North Dakota	—	1	—	—	—	—	1
Ohio	4	22	1	—	1	—	28
Oklahoma	4	1	—	—	—	—	5
Oregon	5	3	—	—	—	11	19
Pennsylvania	3	—	—	—	—	—	3
Rhode Island	—	3	1	—	3	2	9
South Carolina	4	4	—	—	—	—	8
South Dakota	1	2	1	—	—	—	4
Tennessee	5	1	2	—	1	2	11
Texas	5	10	1	—	2	7	25
Utah	—	2	—	1	—	1	4
Vermont	—	—	—	—	—	—	0
Virginia	2	20	—	—	1	3	26
Washington	10	7	—	—	4	9	30
West Virginia	2	5	—	—	—	—	7
Wisconsin	8	6	—	—	1	1	16
Wyoming	—	—	—	—	—	—	0
Totals	245	296	36	30	57	124	788
(Percentage)	(31.09%)	(37.56%)	(4.57%)	(3.81%)	(7.23%)	(15.73%)	(100%)

* Excludes cases concerning covenants not to compete. Little FTC Act litigation not reported.

provide uniformity and predictability to state mergers law enforcement.[81]

LESSON TWO   The existence of multiple damages remedies significantly affects the level of private antitrust litigation in particular states. For example, when Index C is correlated with the table, the 12 states allowing actual damages relief or disallowing damages relief entirely reported a mere 8% of all private state

---

[81]   *Id.*

antitrust litigation from 1980 through 1988. In the states where treble damages are not automatic, but rather discretionary with the court (typically a showing of willfulness or flagrancy is required), 18% of all private damages actions were reported. The 26 states and the District of Columbia awarding automatic double or treble damages reported 74% of all such cases. Furthermore, when the table is correlated with the availability of indirect purchaser remedies, nearly double the average level of state antitrust litigation is revealed in the 11 states and the District of Columbia with such remedies.[82]

Several proposals were made by the Reagan administration, and by commentators, to alter the federal treble damages antitrust remedy.[83] The state correlations presented above suggest that repeal or erosion of the automatic federal treble damages remedy would substantially decrease the volume of private federal litigation and, consequently, the significance of federal antitrust law. Similarly, the state correlations suggest that federal repeal of *Illinois Brick*[84] (which has often been proposed) would probably have the opposite impact.

LESSON THREE   State codifications of per se illegal restraints of trade do not appear to have had a major impact on private litigation levels. Reported private antitrust actions in states with codified per se rules are slightly less than in all states. States with

---

[82]   The 50 states and the District of Columbia averaged 10.6 private state antitrust actions during 1980-88. States with indirect purchaser remedies averaged 17.0 actions.

[83]   *See generally* C. H. Easterbrook, *Detrebling Antitrust Damages*, 28 J. L. & ECON. 454 (1985); A. M. Polinsky *Detrebling versus Decoupling Antitrust Damages: Lessons from the Theory of Enforcement*, 74 GEO. L. J. 1231 (1986); Salop & White, *Treble Damages Reform: Implications of the Georgetown Project*, 55 ANTITRUST L. J. 91 (1986); W. BREIT & K. G. ELZINGA, ANTITRUST PENALTY REFORM: AN ECONOMIC ANALYSIS (1986).

[84]   *See note 59, supra.* Repeal of *Illinois Brick* is proposed in the State Attorney Generals Antitrust Improvements Act of 1987, discussed *supra* at note 43.

automatic treble or double damages remedies *and* per se codifications averaged only a slightly higher number of private antitrust actions.[85] However, these results could reflect the disutility of litigating such specific statutory prohibitions.

The presence of an automatic treble damages remedy, as previously discussed in Lesson Two, correlates with significantly higher state antitrust litigation levels. Thus, one possible inference is that treble damages, not per se codification, is a more important incentive to private antitrust litigants.

LESSON FOUR The table indicates that approximately one-third of all reported state antitrust litigation is initiated by public prosecutors. Assuming that this is a representative figure, there is clearly more reliance on public enforcement actions at the state versus the federal level.[86] This may be attributable to a number of factors. In part, it is a response by the state prosecutors to reduced Reagan administration antitrust law enforcement. On the private side, the absence of a uniform, automatic treble damages remedy diminishes the amount of litigation. Finally, the lower levels of awareness of state antitrust law among all attorneys also contribute to this result. Lesson Two is reinforced: with reduced private enforcement, public actions generate much of the practical significance of antitrust law.

LESSON FIVE Criminal antitrust prosecutions at the state level, as under federal law, are rare and generally limited to horizontal price fixing and bid-rigging activities. Only New Jersey, New York and Michigan have reported notable numbers of criminal prosecutions in the table.[87]

---

[85] The 50 states and the District of Columbia averaged 10.6 private state antitrust actions during 1980–88. The 21 states with codified per se rules averaged 8.6 actions. The 12 states with codified per se rules and automatic damages remedies averaged 10.7 actions.

[86] Private federal antitrust actions amount to approximately 85% to 90% of all federal actions. *See* Salop & White, *supra* note 83.

[87] A prominent New York prosecutor sees a "pronounced trend" in the states toward criminal prosecution. *See* Constantine, *supra* note 43, at 6.

It has been argued that the absence of felony criminal antitrust penalties at the state level renders state antitrust remedies inadequate.[88] It has been suggested, therefore, that the states be given the power to enforce section 1 of the Sherman Act in state or federal courts.[89] This creative proposal relies excessively on criminal law deterrence as the measure of adequacy of public remedies. It seems more appropriate to inquire whether state antitrust laws provide for criminal fines or civil penalties that are not de minimis. By this measure, very few states have inadequate public antitrust remedies.[90] It is also worth remembering that even the threat of a misdemeanor jail term for white-collar antitrust offenders can have significant deterrence.

LESSON SIX   The preferred public remedy of many state prosecutors is the civil penalty action. It is a remedy that is virtually unknown at the federal level.[91] One of its major attractions is the avoidance of constitutional and statutory rules of criminal procedure. Most state antitrust statutes create some form of public civil penalty relief, and a majority of them provide for more than lump-sum penalties. State prosecutors especially favor this remedy when state law permits a cumulation of such penalties per violation,[92] per diem[93] or per victim.[94] In California, for example,

---

[88]   *See Reviving State Antitrust Enforcement, supra* note 2, at 644.

[89]   *Id.* at 646.

[90]   *Compare* Indexes E and G. There are no states entirely without criminal or civil penalty remedies under their restraint of trade statutes.

[91]   There are no public civil penalty remedies for violations of the Sherman, Clayton or Federal Trade Commission Acts. Violation of an existing FTC cease and desist order or consumer protection rule can result in civil penalties. *See* 15 U.S.C. § 49(l)-(m).

[92]   *See* Index E.

[93]   *Id.*

[94]   *See* People v. Superior Court, 96 Cal. App. 3d 181, 157 Cal. Rptr. 628 (1979) (each victim constitutes a violation for purposes of cumulating civil penalties under California's Little FTC Act).

very large sums have been recovered in state antitrust public civil penalty actions.[95] Most modern state antitrust statutes create public civil penalty relief,[96] and the states' experience invites consideration of this remedy at the federal level either as an alternative *or* in addition to existing federal remedies.

States are also beginning to append civil penalty claims to federal causes of action. In a decision of first impression, the U.S. District Court for the Eastern District of New York ruled that it had jurisdiction to enforce the civil penalty provisions of New York's Donnelly Act.[97] The court allowed a judgment for civil penalties to the state in addition to confirming a jury verdict of nearly $8 million in treble damages under the Clayton Act. The amount of the treble damages recovery must be taken into consideration in fixing the civil penalty.[98]

LESSON SEVEN   The different overall volumes of state antitrust litigation reported in the table do not correlate with distinct patterns of state statutory or case law. States that have "modernized" their antitrust statutes are spread across the spectrum of significantly, moderately and insignificantly active states measured by reported litigation volumes. This suggests that major statutory revisions are not always a prelude to revitalization of state antitrust law.

As perhaps might have been expected, California and New York are the most active state antitrust jurisdictions. The table further indicates a second tier of significantly active states: Arizona, Connecticut, Illinois, New Jersey, Ohio and Washington. A third tier of moderately active states includes: Colorado, Florida, Hawaii, Iowa, Maryland, Massachusetts, Michigan,

---

[95]   *See* People v. National Association of Realtors, 155 Cal. App. 3d 578, 202 Cal. Rptr. 243 (1984).

[96]   *See* Index E.

[97]   New York v. Amfar Asphalt Co., 1987-1 Trade Cas. (CCH) ¶ 64,417 (E.D.N.Y. 1986).

[98]   *Id.*

Minnesota, Missouri, New Mexico, North Carolina, Oregon, Tennessee, Texas, Virginia, and Wisconsin. At the other end of the spectrum, there are jurisdictions with virtually no reported antitrust litigation: Alabama, Arkansas, District of Columbia, Nevada, North Dakota, Rhode Island, Utah, Vermont and Wyoming. These different levels of reported litigation activity provide a rough indicator of the degree of potential antitrust risk in each state.

There are so many variables (including size and sophistication) that could explain the different litigation levels reported in the table that it is difficult to generalize about contributing factors. However, California and New York, the most litigious states, have the following in common: (1) active state and local public prosecution antitrust units; (2) automatic treble damages remedies; (3) a case law tradition of following federal antitrust precedent; and (4) old and only partly modernized antitrust statutes.

On the other hand, California and New York antitrust law and practice differ in many important respects. California prosecutors predominantly utilize public civil penalty relief actions. This remedy is available in New York, but criminal prosecutions are generally favored. California has a Little FTC Act that is commonly pleaded in the alternative with Cartwright Act complaints in both public and private actions. No such act exists in New York. California allows private indirect purchaser actions by statute,[99] but New York case law rejects them.[100] These differences help to explain why there is more public litigation in New York than in California. Furthermore, New York case law has proliferated Donnelly Act exemptions;[101] California case law has limited

---

[99] *See* R. H. FOLSOM & R. C. FELLMETH, *supra* note 21, at §§ 165 & 177.

[100] Russo & Dubin v. Allied Maintenance Corp., 95 Misc. 2d 344, 407 N.Y.S.2d 617 (Sup. Ct. N.Y. Cty. 1978). *See* text at note 54.

[101] "The Donnelly Act is perhaps as well known for those activities it does not apply to as for those that it does," International Services Agencies v. United Way of New York State, 108 Misc. 2d 305, 437

and even reversed Cartwright Act exemptions.[102] This may partially explain the somewhat lower level of antitrust litigation under New York law.

Conclusion

The American states have been conducting a wide range of antitrust law experiments. For some of these experiments the results are not yet known. For others, especially variations on the theme of remedies in antitrust law, the states already offer some important though tentative lessons. One conclusion seems certain: there will be more experiments worth watching in the future.

N.Y.S.2d 533-535 (Sup. Ct. Albany Co. 1981). The court went on to state: "It has been held not to apply to: (1) the systematic and deliberate practice of price discrimination by oil companies in the sale of gasoline to dealers (State of New York v. Mobil Oil Corp., 38 N.Y.2d 460, *supra*); (2) the practice of law (*Matter of Freeman*, 34 N.Y.2d 1); (3) the medical profession (People v. Roth, 100 Misc. 2d 542, *aff'd* 74 A.D.2d 1008); (4) labor unions and farmer and dairy co-operatives (General Business Law, Sec. 340, sub'd 3); (5) professional sports teams (American League Baseball Club of N.Y. v. Pasquel, 187 Misc. 230); (6) television rights (Matter of Sullivan County Harness Racing Ass'n v. Glasser, 68 Misc. 2d 579, *aff'd* 38 A.D.2d 690, *rev'd on other grounds* 39 N.Y.2d 269); (7) public utilities (Matter of Attorney General v. Interborough-Metropolitan Co., 125 App. Div. 804); and (8) the operation of private social clubs despite allegations that such clubs exist to foster commercial activity (Kiwanis Club of Great Neck v. Board of Trustees of Kiwanis Int., 83 Misc. 2d 1075, *aff'd* 52 A.D.2d 906, *aff'd* 41 N.Y.2d 1034, *cert. denied* 434 U.S. 859)." The court also held that the Donnelly Act does not apply to not-for-profit charitable corporations and associations.

[102]   *See* Cianci v. Superior Court, 40 Cal. 3d 903, 710 P.2d 375 (1985) (prior Supreme Court cases creating "learned professions" exemption from Cartwright Act expressly overruled).

INDEX A

State Provisions on Restraints of Trade

Prohibitions Comparable to Sherman Act, Section 1

Alabama Code Sec. 8-10-3
Alaska Statutes Sec. 45.50.562
Arizona Revised Statutes Sec. 44-1402
Colorado Statutes Sec. 6-4-101
Connecticut General Statutes Sec. 35-26
Delaware Code 6 Sec. 2103
District of Columbia Code Sec. 28-4502
Florida Statutes Sec. 542.18
Hawaii Revised Statutes Sec. 480-4(a)
Idaho Code Sec. 48-101
Iowa Code Sec. 553.4
Kentucky Statutes Sec. 367.175
Louisiana Revised Statutes 51 Sec. 122
Maine Revised Statutes 10 Sec. 1101
Massachusetts General Laws 93 Sec. 4
Michigan Compiled Laws Sec. 28.70(2)
Missouri Revised Statutes Sec. 416.031
Nebraska Revised Statutes Secs. 59-801, 59-1603
New Hampshire Revised Statutes Sec. 356:2
New Jersey Revised Statutes Sec. 56:9-3
New Mexico Statutes Sec. 57-1-1
North Carolina General Statutes Sec. 75-1
North Dakota Century Code Sec. 51-08.1-02
Oklahoma Statutes 79 Sec. 1
Oregon Revised Statutes Sec. 646.725
Rhode Island General Laws Sec. 6-36-4
South Dakota Codified Laws Sec. 37-1-3.1
Texas Business and Commerce Code Sec. 15.05(a)
Utah Code Sec. 76-10-914(1)
Virginia Code Sec. 59.1-95
Washington Revised Code Sec. 19.86.030
West Virginia Code Sec. 47-18-3
Wisconsin Statutes Sec. 133.03

Codified Per Se Categories of Restraints of Trade

Alabama Code Sec. 8-10-1 (price fixing)

Arkansas Statutes Sec. 70-101 (price fixing)

Colorado Statutes Sec. 6-4-101 (price fixing)

Connecticut General Statutes Sec. 35-28 (price fixing, market division, group boycotts)

Hawaii Revised Statutes Sec. 480-4(a) (price fixing)

Idaho Code Sec. 48-101 (price fixing)

Illinois Revised Statutes 38 Sec. 60-3(1) (horizontal price fixing, horizontal market division)

Indiana Code Sec. 24-1-2-1 (price fixing)

Kansas Statutes Sec. 50-112 (price fixing)

Michigan Compiled Laws Sec. 750.151 (price fixing)

Minnesota Statutes Sec. 325D.51 (horizontal price fixing, horizontal market division, selected group boycotts)

Montana Revised Code Sec. 30-14-205 (price fixing)

Nevada Revised Statutes Sec. 598A.060 (price fixing, horizontal market division, tying practices)

New Hampshire Revised Statutes Sec. 356:2 (price fixing, market division, group boycotts)

North Carolina General Statutes Sec. 75-5 (price limitations, territorial restraints, tying practices)

Ohio Revised Code Sec. 1331.02 (price fixing)

Oklahoma Statutes 79 Sec. 3 (price fixing)

South Carolina Code Secs. 39-3-10, 39-3-130 (price fixing)

Tennessee Code Sec. 47-25-101 (price fixing)

West Virginia Code Sec. 47-18-3 (price fixing, market division)

Wyoming Statutes Sec. 40-4-101 (price fixing)

"Trusts" (Combinations in Restraint of Trade)

California Business and Professions Code Sec. 16726, 16720

Kansas Statutes Sec. 50-101, 50-102

Mississippi Code Sec. 75-21-1, 75-21-3

Ohio Revised Code Sec. 1331.01

Special Prohibitions Against Bid-Rigging

Arizona Statutes Sec. 34-251 *et seq.*
Georgia Statutes Sec. 16-10-22
Indiana Code Sec. 24-1-2-3
Minnesota Statutes Sec. 325D.51
Mississippi Code Sec. 75-21-15
Montana Revised Code Sec. 30-14-205
New Hampshire Revised Statutes Sec. 356:2
North Carolina General Statutes Sec. 133-24
Pennsylvania Statutes Sec. 73-1611 *et seq.*
Vermont Statutes 29 Sec. 908
Virginia Code Sec. 59.1-68.7

Other

Georgia Statutes Sec. 13-8-2(a)(2) (contracts in general restraint of trade)
Illinois Revised Code 38 Sec. 60-3(2) (unreasonable restraints of trade)
Maryland Code Sec. 11-204(A)(1) (unreasonable restraints of trade)
Minnesota Statutes Sec. 325D.51 (unreasonable restraints of trade)
New York General Business Law Sec. 340(1) (combinations to maintain monopolies or restrain trade)
Wyoming Statutes Sec. 40-4-101 (combinations to prevent competition)

No Prohibition

Pennsylvania
Vermont

INDEX B

State Provisions on Monopolization

Prohibitions Comparable to Sherman Act, Section 2

Alabama Code Sec. 8-10-3
Alaska Statutes Sec. 45.50.564
Connecticut General Statutes Sec. 35-27
District of Columbia Code Sec. 28-4503
Florida Statutes Sec. 542.19
Hawaii Revised Statutes 480-9
Idaho Code Sec. 48-102
Indiana Code 24-1-2-2
Kentucky Statutes Sec. 367.175
Louisiana Revised Statutes 51 Sec. 123
Maryland Code Sec. 11-204(A)(2)
Massachusetts General Laws 93 Sec. 5
Minnesota Statutes Sec. 325D.52 (monopoly power)
Mississippi Code Sec. 75-21-3
Missouri Revised Statutes Sec. 416.031
Nebraska Revised Statute Secs. 59-802, 59-1604
New Jersey Revised Statutes Sec. 56:9-4
New Mexico Statutes Sec. 57-1-2
Oregon Revised Statutes Sec. 646.730
South Dakota Codified Laws Sec. 37-1-3.2
Texas Business and Commerce Code Sec. 15.05(b)
Utah Code Sec. 76-10-915
Virginia Code Sec. 59.1-9.6
Washington Revised Code Sec. 19.86.040
Wisconsin Statutes Sec. 133.03

Monopolies

Arizona Revised Statutes Sec. 44-1403
Arkansas Statutes Secs. 70-105, 70-106
Illinois Revised Statutes 38 Sec. 60-3(3)
Iowa Code Sec. 553.5
Michigan Compiled Laws Sec. 28.70(3)

Montana Revised Code 30-14-205
New Hampshire Revised Statutes Sec. 356:3
North Dakota Century Code Sec. 51-08.1-03
Rhode Island General Laws Sec. 6-36-5
South Carolina Code Secs. 39-3-120, 39-3-110
West Virginia Code Sec. 47-18-4

States Without a Prohibition Against Single Firm Monopolization

California	North Carolina
Colorado	Ohio
Delaware	Oklahoma
Georgia	Pennsylvania
Kansas	Tennessee
Maine	Vermont
Nevada	Wyoming
New York	

INDEX C

State Provisions on Private Damages Relief

Treble Damages Automatic

Arizona Revised Statutes Sec. 44-1408B
California Business and Professions Code Sec. 16750(a)
Connecticut General Statutes Sec. 35-35
District of Columbia Code Sec. 28-4508
Florida Statutes Sec. 542.22(1)
Hawaii Revised Statutes Sec. 480-13(a)-(b)
Idaho Code Sec. 48-114
Illinois 38 Revised Statutes Sec. 60-7(2) (per se offenses)
Indiana Code Sec. 24-1-2-7
Kansas Statutes Sec. 50-801
Louisiana Revised Statutes 51 Sec. 137
Maine Revised Statutes 10 Sec. 1104, Para. 1
Maryland Code Sec. 11-209(b), (c)
Minnesota Statutes Sec. 325D.57
Missouri Revised Statutes Sec. 416.121
Montana Revised Code Sec. 30-14-222
Nevada Revised Statutes Sec. 598A.210
New Jersey Statutes Sec. 56:9-10(a)
New York General Business Law 340(5)
North Carolina General Statutes Sec. 75-16
Oklahoma Statutes 79 Sec. 25
Oregon Revised Statutes Sec. 646.780
Rhode Island General Laws Sec. 6-36-11
South Dakota Codified Laws Sec. 37-1-14.3
Utah Code Sec. 76-10-919
West Virginia Code Sec. 47-18-9
Wisconsin Statutes Sec. 133.18

Treble Damages Discretionary With Court

New Mexico Statutes Sec. 57-1-3
Washington Revised Code Sec. 19.86.090

Treble Damages Conditional Upon Willful or Flagrant Violation

Alaska Statutes Sec. 45.50.576
Illinois 38 Revised Statutes Sec. 60-7(2) (non-per se offenses)
Massachusetts General Laws 93 Sec. 12
Michigan Compiled Laws Sec. 28.70(8)(2)
New Hampshire Revised Statutes Sec. 356:11
North Dakota Code Sec. 553.12(1)
Texas Business and Commerce Code Sec. 15.21(a)
Virginia Code Sec. 59.1-9.12

Double Damages Automatic

Ohio Revised Code Sec. 1331.08

Double Damages Conditional Upon Willful or Flagrant Violation

Iowa Code Sec. 553.12(1)

Actual Damages

Alabama Code Sec. 6-5-60
Colorado Statutes Sec. 6-4-108
Georgia (Case Law)
Mississippi Code Sec. 75-21-9
Nebraska Revised Statutes Secs. 59-821, 59-1609

No Private Damages Relief

Arkansas
Delaware
Kentucky
Pennsylvania
Tennessee (recovery of consideration)
Vermont
Wyoming

INDEX D

States Providing Private Damages Relief Under Little FTC Acts

Alaska Statutes Sec. 45-50-531 (discretionary treble damages)
Connecticut General Statutes Sec. 42-110g
Florida Statutes Sec. 501.207
Hawaii Revised Statutes Sec. 480-13 (treble damages)
Illinois Revised Statutes 121½ Sec. 270a
Louisiana Revised Statutes 51 Sec. 1409
Massachusetts General Laws 93A Secs. 9, 11 (discretionary treble damages)
Montana Revised Code Sec. 30-14-133
Nebraska Revised Statutes Sec. 59-1609
New Hampshire Revised Statutes Sec. 358-A:10
North Carolina General Statutes Sec. 75-16 (treble damages)
South Carolina Code Sec. 39-5-140 (treble damages)
Utah Code Sec. 13-5-14 (treble damages)
Washington Revised Code Sec. 19.86.090
West Virginia Code Sec. 46A-6-106
Wisconsin Statutes Sec. 100.20 (double damages)

INDEX E

State Provisions on Public Civil Penalty Relief

Per Violation Penalties

Alaska Statutes Sec. 45.50.551(b) (Little FTC Act)
Arizona Revised Statutes Sec. 44-1407
California Business and Professions Code Sec. 17206 (Little FTC Act)
Connecticut General Statutes Sec. 42-1100(b) (Little FTC Act)
Delaware Code Title 6 Sec. 2107
Florida Statutes Sec. 542.21
Maine Revised Statutes 10 Sec. 1104, Paras 2, 3 (per course of illegal conduct)
Massachusetts General Laws 93 Sec. 9 (per course of illegal conduct)
Massachusetts General Laws 93A Sec. 4 (Little FTC Act)
Michigan Compiled Laws Sec. 28.70(7)
Mississippi Code Sec. 75-21-7
Montana Revised Code Sec. 30-14-142(1)
Nebraska Revised Statutes Sec. 59-1614(2) (Little FTC Act)
New Hampshire Revised Statutes Sec. 356:4-a
New Hampshire Revised Statutes Sec. 358-A:4
North Carolina General Statutes Sec. 75-15.2 (Little FTC Act)
Oregon Revised Statutes Sec. 646.760(1)
Rhode Island General Laws Sec. 6-36-10
South Carolina Code Sec. 39-5-110
South Dakota Codified Laws Sec. 37-1-14.2
Utah Code Sec. 76-10-918
Virginia Code Sec. 59.1-9.11
Washington Code Sec. 19.86.140 (Little FTC Act)
West Virginia Code Sec. 47-18-8

Per Diem Penalties

Arkansas Statutes Sec. 70-102
Kentucky Statutes Sec. 367.990(8)
New Jersey Statutes Sec. 56:9-10(c)
Ohio Revised Code Sec. 1331.03

Lump Sum Penalties

Connecticut General Statutes Sec. 35-38
Illinois 121½ Revised Statutes Sec. 267 (Little FTC Act)
Illinois 38 Rev. Stat. Sec. 60-7(4)
Iowa Code Sec. 553.13
Minnesota Statutes Sec. 325D.56, subd. 1
Nebraska Revised Statutes Sec. 59-1614(1)
Nevada Revised Statutes Sec. 598A.170
New Mexico Statutes Sec. 57-1-7
New York General Business Law Sec. 342-a
Oklahoma Statutes 79 Sec. 27
Texas Business and Commerce Code Sec. 15.20
Washington Code Sec. 19.86.140
West Virginia Code Sec. 46A-7-111
Wisconsin Statutes Sec. 133.03

INDEX F

State Provisions on Forfeitures of Corporate Rights

Arkansas Statutes Secs. 7-103, 70-111
California Business and Professions Code Secs. 16752, 16753
Connecticut General Statutes Sec. 35-36a
Connecticut General Statutes Sec. 42-110p (Little FTC Act)
Illinois 121½ Revised Statutes Sec. 267 (Little FTC Act)
Indiana Code Sec. 24-1-2-5
Idaho Code Secs. 48-107, 48-108
Iowa Code Sec. 553.12(1)
Kansas Statutes Secs. 50-103, 50-104, 50-105
Kentucky Statutes Sec. 367.200
Louisiana Revised Statutes 51 Sec. 139
Maryland Code Sec. 11-209(a)
Massachusetts General Laws 93A Sec. 8 (Little FTC Act)
Minnesota Statutes Sec. 325D.60
Mississippi Code Sec. 75-21-19
Montana Revised Code Sec. 30-14-223
Montana Revised Code Sec. 30-14-141 (Little FTC Act)
Nebraska Revised Statutes Secs. 59-809, 59-810, 59-811, 59-813,
    59-1615
Nevada Revised Statutes Secs. 598A.180, 190
New Hampshire Revised Statutes 358-A19
New Jersey Statutes Secs. 56:9-7, 9-8
Ohio Revised Code Secs. 1331.07, 1331.11, 1331.12
Oklahoma Statutes 79 Secs. 26, 31
Oregon Revised Statutes Sec. 646.760(2)
Rhode Island General Laws Sec. 6-36-17
South Carolina Code Secs. 39-3-20, 39-3-160, 39-3-170
Tennessee Code Sec. 47-25-104
Vermont Statutes 9 Sec. 2458 (Little FTC Act)
Washington Revised Code Sec. 19.86.150
Wisconsin Statutes Sec. 133.12

INDEX G

State Provisions on Criminal Offenses

Felonies

California Business and Professions Code Sec. 16755(a)
Colorado Statutes Sec. 6-4-107
Florida Statutes Sec. 542.21
Hawaii Revised Statutes 480-16
Illinois 38 Revised Statutes Sec. 60-6 (per se offenses)
Louisiana Revised Statutes 51 Secs. 122, 123
Maine Revised Statutes 10 Secs. 1101, 1102
Minnesota Statutes Sec. 325D.56, subd. 2
Nebraska Revised Statutes Sec. 59-801, 59-802, 59-805
Nevada Revised Statutes Sec. 598A.280
New Mexico Statutes Sec. 57-1-6
New York General Business Law Sec. 341
North Carolina General Statutes Sec. 75-1
Ohio Revised Code Sec. 1331.99
Rhode Island General Laws Sec. 6-36-16
South Dakota Codified Laws Secs. 37-1-3.3, 37-1-7
Tennessee Code Sec. 47-25-103
Texas Business and Commerce Code Sec. 15.22
Utah Code Sec. 76-10-920
Wisconsin Statutes Sec. 133.03

Misdemeanors

Alabama Code Secs. 8-10-1, 8-10-2, 8-10-3
Alaska Statutes Sec. 45.50.578
District of Columbia Code Sec. 28-4506
Idaho Code Secs. 48-101, 48-102
Indiana Code Secs. 24-1-2-1, 24-1-2-2
Iowa Code Sec. 553.14
Kansas Statutes Secs. 50-106, 50-114, 50-132
Maryland Code Sec. 11-212
Massachusetts General Laws 93 Sec. 10
Michigan Compiled Laws Sec. 28.70(9)

Mississippi Code Sec. 75-21-1
Missouri Revised Statutes Sec. 416.051(1)
Montana Revised Code Sec. 30-14-224
New Hampshire Revised Statutes Sec. 356:4 (corporate
  violations are felonies)
New Jersey Statutes Sec. 56:9-11
Oklahoma Statutes 79 Sec. 27
Oregon Revised Statutes 646.990(3)
Wyoming Statutes Sec. 40-4-104

No Criminal Sanctions

Arizona	Kentucky	Vermont
Arkansas	North Dakota	Virginia
Connecticut	Pennsylvania	Washington
Delaware	South Carolina	West Virginia
Georgia		

INDEX H

State Parens Patriae Remedies

California Business and Professions Code Sec. 16760
Connecticut General Statutes Sec. 35-32(c)-(d)
Delaware Code Title 6 Sec. 2108(b)-(g)
District of Columbia Code Sec. 28-4507(b)-(e)
Florida Statutes Sec. 542.22(2)-(3)
Florida Statutes Sec. 501.2075 (Little FTC Act)
Hawaii Revised Statutes Sec. 480-13(c) (includes Little FTC Act)
Massachusetts General Laws 93 Sec. 9
Nebraska Revised Statutes Sec. 84-212
Nevada Revised Statutes Sec. 598A.160
Oregon Revised Statutes Sec. 646.775
Rhode Island General Laws Sec. 6-36-12
South Dakota Codified Laws Secs. 37-1-23 through 31
Virginia Code Sec. 59.1-9.15
West Virginia Code Sec. 47-18-17

INDEX I

States Allowing Indirect Purchaser Actions for Damages

Alabama Code Sec. 6-5-60
California Business and Professions Code Sec. 16750(a)
District of Columbia Code Sec. 28-4509
Hawaii Revised Statutes Sec. 480-14
Illinois Revised Statutes 38 Sec. 60-7(2)
Kansas Statutes Sec. 50-801
Maine Revised Statutes 10 Sec. 1104
Michigan Compiled Laws Sec. 28.70(2)
Minnesota Statutes Sec. 325D.57
Mississippi Code Sec. 75-21-9
New Mexico Statutes Sec. 57-1-3
South Dakota Codified Laws Sec. 37-1-33
Wisconsin Statutes Sec. 133.18

23
Antitrust principles and regulatory needs

BY ALMARIN PHILLIPS*

I. Introduction

This article provides a critical review of the recent "procompetitive" policies for regulated industries. Innovative applications of the antitrust laws and, more generally, a variety of deregulatory actions are covered. Section II looks at the intellectual scenery up to about 1965, emphasizing the growing tensions between regulation, the regulators and academic critics. The early responses to these criticisms, including those of the regulators, legislators, and the courts, are treated in section III. Private actions as well as cases brought by the Antitrust Division of the Department of Justice [DOJ] are examined.

Section IV looks at the same areas after the deregulation movement got into full swing. Section V looks more closely at three industries, evaluating the efficacy of the new policies and raising questions about remaining or emerging regulatory needs. The industries dealt with in this section are commercial aviation, electric power and telecommunications. Section VI summarizes the findings.

*   Hower Professor of Public Polity and Professor of Economics and Law, University of Pennsylvania.

AUTHOR'S NOTE: *Carole Phillips and Richard Schmalensee provided helpful comments on an early draft.*

II. The intellectual scenery to 1965

The intellectual underpinnings of the recent moves toward deregulation trace back for several decades. Horace Gray published a stinging condemnation of regulation in 1940.[1] The same theme was updated when Walter Adams joined Gray in a 1955 volume, *Monopoly in America.*[2] Adams and Gray charged that "Among all the devices used by government to promote monopoly, public utility, or public interest, regulation is . . . perhaps the worst."[3] They opined further that "The prospects for restoring market competition, while limited by technological factors, are more numerous and more attractive than are commonly supposed. . . . The goal of public policy should be to get all the competition we can under the circumstances— to make competition do as much of the world's work as possible. . . ."[4]

Adams and Gray noted that similar views had been expressed by Henry Simons[5] and Eugene Staley,[6] both of whom had in turn been cited "with approval" by Frank Graham.[7] Paul Douglas—later Senator Douglas—was similarly critical of public utility regulation.[8] Adams and Gray found sympathy as well in a 1954 legal analysis by Louis B. Schwartz.[9] In that piece—a reaction to Justice Frankfurter's decision upholding the primary jurisdiction of the Federal Maritime Board in the *Far East Conference* case[10]—Schwartz argued that, in suits brought under the antitrust laws, the courts should enunciate a policy to the

---

[1] Gray, *The Passing of the Public Utility Concept,* 16 J. LAND & PUBL. UTIL. ECON. 8 (1940).

[2] W. ADAMS & H. M. GRAY, MONOPOLY IN AMERICA: THE GOVERNMENT AS PROMOTER (1955).

[3] *Id.* at 39.

[4] *Id.* at 71.

[5] H. C. SIMONS, A POSITIVE PROGRAM FOR LAISSEZ-FAIRE (1934).

[6] E. STALEY, WORLD ECONOMY IN TRANSITION (1939).

[7] F. D. GRAHAM, SOCIAL GOALS AND ECONOMIC INSTITUTIONS (1942).

[8] P. DOUGLAS, ETHICS IN GOVERNMENT (1954).

[9] Schwartz, *Legal Restriction of Competition in the Regulated Industries: An Abdication of Judicial Responsibility,* 67 HARV. L. REV. 436 (1954).

[10] Far East Conference v. U.S., 342 U.S. 570 (1952).

effect that "free enterprise ought to prevail to the maximum extent consistent with the . . . objectives of the applicable legislation."[11]

Still, these early protagonists of procompetitive, deregulatory policies found few others in their camp. The "academic scribblers" from whom "madmen in authority"[12] distilled the subsequent frenzy of deregulatory actions came later. Until at least the mid-1960's, the advocates of deregulation were few in number and selective in the industries they studied. Keyes,[13] Caves[14] and Levine[15] prepared early and influential attacks on the Civil Aeronautics Board [CAB] and the airlines. Coase,[16] Levin[17]

---

[11] Schwartz, *supra* note 9, at 475. For contextual discussion, *see* Zimmerman, *The Legal Framework of Competitive Policies Toward Regulated Industries*, in PROMOTING COMPETITION IN REGULATED MARKETS (Almarin Phillips ed. 1975) and Areeda, *Antitrust Laws and Public Utility Regulation,* 3 BELL J. ECON. & MGMT. SCI. 42 (1972). Related work critical of regulation includes M. BERNSTEIN, REGULATING BUSINESS BY INDEPENDENT COMMISSION (1955); J. M. LANDIS, REPORT ON REGULATORY AGENCIES TO THE PRESIDENT-ELECT (Senate Committee on the Judiciary, 86th Cong., 1960); P. W. MACAVOY, THE ECONOMIC EFFECTS OF REGULATION (1965); and Trebing, *Toward the Incentive System of Regulation*, PUB. UTIL. FORTNIGHTLY, July 18, 1963, at 22.

[12] J. M. KEYNES, THE GENERAL THEORY OF EMPLOYMENT MONEY AND INTEREST 383 (1936). A more complete quote is: "The ideas of economists and political philosophers, both when they are right and when they are wrong, are more powerful than is commonly understood. Indeed, the world is ruled by little else. Practical men, who believe themselves to be quite exempt from any intellectual influences, are usually the slaves of some defunct economist. Madmen in authority, who hear voices in the air, are distilling their frenzy from some academic scribbler of a few years back.I am sure that the power of vested interests is vastly exaggerated compared with the gradual encroachment of ideas."

[13] L. S. KEYES, FEDERAL CONTROL OF ENTRY INTO AIR TRANSPORTATION (1951) and *Reconsideration of Federal Control of Entry into Air Transportation*, 22 J. AIR L. & COM. 92 (1955).

[14] R. E. CAVES, AIR TRANSPORT AND ITS REGULATORS: AN INDUSTRY STUDY (1962).

[15] Levine, *Is Regulation Necessary? California Air Transportation and National Regulatory Policy*, 74 YALE L.J. 1416 (1965).

[16] Coase, The Federal Communications Commission, 2 J.L. & ECON. 1 (1959).

[17] Levin, *Workable Competition and Regulatory Policy in Television Broadcasting*, 34 LAND ECON. 101 (1958).

and Steiner[18] raised fundamental questions about the Federal Communications Commission's [FCC's] regulation of the broadcasting industry. The surface transportation industries and their regulation were scrutinized in 1959 by Meyer, Peck, Stenason and Zwick.[19] David A. Alhadeff provided a seminal study of the monopolistic aspects of bank regulation in 1954;[20] this was followed by a myriad of related studies on banking markets including some pioneering quantitative studies.[21] There were also some early commission studies of the effects of regulation on banking markets, including that of the Commission on Money and Credit[22] and the Heller Committee.[23]

The regulation of securities markets was similarly analyzed in the early period by various groups and commissions. Some of the studies were sponsored by public bodies,[24] some by the af-

---

[18] Steiner, *Programming Patterns and Preferences, and the Workability of Competition in Radio Broadcasting,* 55 Q.J. ECON. 194 (1952).

[19] J. R. MEYER, M.J. PECK, J. STENASON & C. ZWICK, THE ECONOMICS OF COMPETITION IN THE TRANSPORTATION INDUSTRIES (1959).

[20] D. A. ALHADEFF, MONOPOLY AND COMPETITION IN BANKING (1954). *See also* David & Alhadeff, *Recent Bank Mergers,* 69 Q.J. ECON. 503 (1955) and Alhadeff, *A Reconsideration of Restrictions on Bank Entry,* 76 Q.J. ECON. 246 (1962).

[21] For example, Edwards, *Concentration in Banking and Its Effect on Business Loan Rates,* 46 REV. ECON. & STATISTICS 294 (1964); G. J. Benston, A Statistical Study of the Cost of Banking Operations (Ph.D. dissertation, University of Chicago, 1963); P. M. Horwitz, *Economies of Scale in Banking,* in COMMISSION ON MONEY AND CREDIT, PRIVATE FINANCIAL INSTITUTIONS (1963). Phillips, *Competition, Confusion and Commercial Banking,* 19 J. FIN. 32 (1964) is nonquantitative, but evoked considerable reaction.

[22] Report of the Commission on Money and Credit, Money and Credit: Their Influence on Jobs, Prices and Growth (1961).

[23] Report of the Committee on Financial Institutions to the President of the United States (1963).

[24] In particular, SECURITIES AND EXCHANGE COMMISSION, REPORT OF THE SPECIAL STUDY OF SECURITIES MARKETS (1963); I. FRIEND, F. E. BROWN, E. S. HERMAN & D. VICKERS, A STUDY OF MUTUAL FUNDS, H. REP. No. 2274, 87th Cong., 2d Sess. (1962).

fected industry groups,[25] and there were a few apparently independent studies.[26] Electric utilities were the subject of a good deal of discussion of optimal *regulated* rates, but were not favored with many early proposals for deregulation. Adams and Gray did not wholly ignore them,[27] and Hughes presented what may be the first economic analysis of pooling, a phenomenon essential to many subsequent schemes for deregulating the generation phase of the industry.[28] Stigler and Friedland wrote a provocative criticism of regulation, with electric power used as the example.[29]

In the same year that Stigler and Friedland presented theoretical and empirical evidence of the ineffectiveness of regulation, Averch and Johnson [A-J] published their influential analysis of regulatorily induced inefficiencies.[30] This article led to a swarming of academic output critical of the regulatory process.[31] At the same time, interest in marginal cost pricing and peak load pricing was tweaked

---

25   I. Friend, G. W. Hoffman & W. J. Win, The Over-the-Counter Securities Market (1958).

26   *For example,* Stigler, *Public Regulation of the Securities Market,* 37 J. Bus. 117 (1964); W. J. BAUMOL, THE STOCK MARKET AND ECONOMICS EFFICIENCY (1965).

27   Adams & Gray, *supra* note 2, at 186–87. *See also* Adams, *The Role of Competition in Regulated Industries,* 48 AM. ECON. REV. 527 (1958).

28   Hughes, *Short-Run Efficiency and the Organization of the Electric Power Industry,* 76 Q.J. ECON. 592 (1962).

29   Stigler & Friedland, *What Can Regulators Regulate? The Case of Electricity,* 5 J.L. & ECON. 1 (1962).

30   Averch & Johnson, *Behavior of the Firm Under Regulatory Constraint,* 52 AM. ECON. REV. 1052 (1962).

31   The A-J literature is too vast to provide even a sampling here. A useful guide for clarifying what is and what is not the "proper" A-J effect is in Baumol & Klevorick, *The A-J Thesis: Input Choices and Rate of Return Regulation: An Overview of the Discussion,* 1 BELL J. ECON. & MGMT. SCI 162 (1970). An analysis of the sensitivity of the A-J conclusions to alternative assumptions can be found in E. E. BAILEY, ECONOMIC THEORY OF REGULATORY CONSTRAINT (1973).

by the experiments undertaken by Électricité de France under the ingenious Marcel Boiteux.[32] Again, the electric utilities received the greatest attention, and little of it was friendly. This discussion evolved into considerations of optimal departures from marginal cost pricing (Ramsey pricing), although this development comes after 1970 in the United States.[33] While a good deal of the A-J and optimal pricing materials can be seen as arguments in favor of—or at least not inconsistent with—efficient regulation, they appeared at a time of growing discontent with regulation and seem often to have been used to show how bad in practice regulation really was.

III. The early responses to proposals for increased competition in the regulated industries

It turned out that there were only limited areas in which antitrust principles could be applied to regulated industries in the absence of legislative change.[34] Early on—well before the deregulation discussion had become anything like a "movement"— the Antitrust Division and others had opposed the approval by the Interstate Commerce Commission [ICC] of the merger of seven

---

[32]   Boiteux, *La tarification au coût marginal et les demands aléatoires,* CAHIERS DU SÉMINAIRE D'ECONOMÉTRIE (1951) and, by the same author, *Peak Load Pricing,* 33 J. Bus. 157 (1960). English translations of several of the French contributions appear in MARGINAL COST PRICING IN PRACTICE (J. R. Nelson ed. 1964). Bailey & White, *Reversals of Peak and Off-Peak Prices,* BELL J. ECON. & MGMT. SCI. 75 (1974) contains a good bibliography of contributions to that date.

[33]   The original paper is Ramsey, *A Contribution to the Theory of Taxation,* 37 ECON. J. 47 (1927). The French treatment began with Boiteux, *Sur la question des monopoles public: astrients à l'équilibre budgetaire,* 24 ECONOMETRICA 22 (1956). The American literature begins generally with Baumol & Bradford, *Optimal Departures from Marginal Cost Pricing,* 60 AM. ECON. REV. 265 (1970).

[34]   The following discussion will not attempt to make clean distinctions between exempted industries and regulated industries. Matters relating to labor, agricultural cooperatives, insurance, other so-called exempt activities will not be addressed, however. Similarly, no attention will be given to possible immunities arising from state actions or to Noerr-Pennington issues.

large motor carriers.[35] The Interstate Commerce Act made such consolidations lawful when authorized by the ICC and enumerated the factors the Commission was to consider in making its "public interest" decisions. In rejecting the Department's appeal against the commission order, the court held that:

> ... there can be little doubt that the commission is not to measure propos-als for . . . consolidations by the standards of the antitrust laws. . . . No other inference is possible than that . . . the preservation of competition among carriers, although still a value, is significant chiefly as it aids in the attainment of the objectives of national transportation policy.[36]

Despite accumulating arguments that increased intra- and inter-modal competition would be in the public interest,[37] the immunity from antitrust actions against ICC-approved consolidations was up-held by the Court in subsequent cases.[38] Even in the most contro-versial of the cases, competition played a limited role and smaller carriers seemed important only insofar as they stood to receive some of the spoils.[39] In fact, rather than altering the law to permit antitrust standards to apply, Congress passed the Railroad Revital-ization and Regulatory Reform Act of 1976[40] which continued to

---

[35] McLean Trucking Co. v. U.S., 321 U.S. 67 (1944).

[36] *Id.* at 85–86.

[37] For example, President Kennedy's Transportation Message of April 5, 1962—the 75th birthday of the ICC—proposed that "practices by carriers . . . be covered by existing laws against monopoly and predatory trade practices" [as quoted by Peck, *Competitive Policy for Transportation*, in PERSPECTIVES ON ANTITRUST POLICY (A. Phillips ed. 1965) at 245–46]/

[38] Minneapolis and St. Louis Ry. v. U.S., 361 U.S. 173 (1959); Seaboard Air Line R.R. v. U.S., 382 U.S. 154 (1965); U.S. v. ICC, 396 U.S. 491 (1970) (the "Northern Lines" case). Baltimore and Ohio R.R. v. U.S., 386 U.S. 372 (1967). The Court remanded on other grounds. In Denver & Rio Grande W.R.R. v. U.S. 485 (1967), the Court extended the *McLean* holding to the public interest test applicable to the issuance of stock even though no express exemption appeared in the governing section of the Interstate Commerce Act.

[39] Penn-Central Merger and N&W Inclusion Cases, 389 U.S. 486 (1968).

[40] 90 Stat. 31 (Feb. 5, 1976). This act did permit greater rate freedom for rail carriers and established a variable cost standard for rate minima (section 202(b)).

list the competitive effects of a merger as but one of several factors to be considered. The consolidation of railroads into a small number of large systems, not the preservation or creation of competition, was the policy goal of the period for the railroads.

The Federal Aviation Act also provided for approval of mergers among air carriers by the CAB under "public interest" standards.[41] The immunity thus created withstood strong challenges; indeed, the Supreme Court upheld dismissal of an antitrust complaint filed by the Department of Justice against Pan Am's exercise of its partial ownership of Panagra to prevent the latter from applying for route authorizations competitive with Pan Am's. The deciding point was not so much that an express statutory exemption existed but rather that the CAB was entrusted with measuring the public interest. The Court refused "to hold that there are no antitrust violations left . . . to enforce," but did hold that it would "be odd to conclude that an affiliation . . . that passed muster [under the Federal Aviation Act] should run afoul of the antitrust laws."[42] Justice Douglas, who delivered the opinion, had not yet received the deregulation message as it related to air carriers.[43]

Curiously, at about the same time the Court was reading antitrust standards out of air carrier cases, it assured a role for the Clayton Act in mergers among regulated natural gas companies affected by stock acquisitions.[44] Similarly, and with what many observers believed to be a tortured interpretation of the Act and of the facts, the Court extended Clayton Act standards to bank merg-

---

41   The Airline Deregulation Act of 1978, discussed below, originally provided for transfer to the DOJ of the CAB's authority under 408 (consolidation, merger, acquisition of control), 409 (interlocking relationships), and 412 (poolings and agreements), but legislative amendments resulted in retention of that authority by the Department of Transportation until January 1989.

42   Pan American World Airways, Inc. v. U.S., 371 U.S. 296 (1963).

43   Justice Douglas also delivered the opinion in Hughes Tool v. Transworld Airlines, Inc., 409 U.S. 363 (1973), in which immunity based on the CAB's pervasive regulatory overview was found.

44   California v. F.P.C., 369 U.S. 483 (1962). This case reached the Court as U.S. v. El Paso Natural Gas, 376 U.S. 651 (1964).

ers, despite prior regulatory approval under the Bank Merger Act of 1960.[45] Repeal of the antitrust laws would be implied only when there was plain repugnancy between the antitrust and regulatory provisions: "The fact that banking is a highly regulated industry," said the Court, "makes the play of competition not less important but more so." The decisions in this and parallel bank merger cases turned out to be the primary reason for passage of the Bank Merger Act of 1966, the terms of which largely overruled the Court so far as application of the Clayton Act is concerned.

Private antitrust actions were also making inroads into the regulatory area, although not always with the desired consequences. Thus, when it was held that rate bureaus constituted conspiracies under the antitrust laws[46]—even though for damage purposes the Commission-approved tariffs reached thereby may not be set aside.[47]—Congress responded with the Reed-Bullwinkle Act negating the import of the decision.[48] The *Silver* case[49] was widely hailed as an antitrust victory over regulation, although the decision in fact hinged on a finding that the challenged conduct was not within the jurisdiction of the Securities and Exchange Commission [SEC]. In subsequent cases, the primary jurisdiction of the SEC in regulating the securities markets withstood antitrust attacks.[50] Here, however,

---

[45]   U.S. v. Philadelphia National Bank, 374 U.S. 321 (1963).

[46]   Georgia v. Pennsylvania R.R., 312 U.S. 439 (1945).

[47]   This is the result of Keough v. Chicago and N.W.R. Co., 260 U.S. 156 (1922).

[48]   In this, Congress followed the pattern it set after U.S. v. Southeastern Underwriters' Association, 322 U.S. 533 (1944). The latter case gave rise to the McCarran-Ferguson Act partially exempting the business of insurance.

[49]   Silver v. New York Stock Exchange, 373 U.S. 341 (1973). Earlier, however, in Thill Securities Corp. v. New York Stock Exchange, 433 F.2d 264 (7th Cir. 1970), *cert. denied,* 401 U.S. 994 (1971), an appeals court had denied immunity with respect to an antirebate rule without finding a lack of regulatory jurisdiction.

[50]   Gordon v. New York Stock Exchange, 422 U.S. 659 (1975); U.S. v. N.A.S.D., Inc., 422 U.S. 694 (1975). *See also* the related Ricci v. Chicago Mercantile Exchange, 409 U.S. 289 (1973), where action under the antitrust laws was stayed until relief was sought from the Commodity Exchange Commission.

the SEC—with prodding from Congress[51]—at last took action to phase-out fixed commission rates.

The Department of Justice successfully attacked market-sharing agreements approved by state regulators in the *Florida Power* case.[52] Monopolistic practices—refusals to wheel power accompanied by other overt actions against municipalities seeking to operate their own distribution systems—were held violative of the Sherman Act in *Otter Tail*.[53] The Federal Power Commission [FPC] (later Federal Energy Regulatory Commission [FERC]) itself began actions against power companies whose rates might result in "price squeezes" detrimental to independent electricity distribution operations.[54] In a somewhat different vein, no immunity was found for electric utilities that engage in activities beyond those expressly permitted by statute even when the activities were approved or even required by a state regulator.[55]

There were early cases involving antitrust and regulation in broadcasting, as well. The applicability of the Sherman Act to certain conspiratorial and coercive uses of affiliation arrangements in connection with station exchanges was established by 1959.[56] A monopolization case—motivated, it seems, more by political than economic concerns—was brought against the three networks in

---

51   Securities Act Amendments of 1975. For prior analysis urging such action, *see* Baxter, *NYSE Fixed Commission Rates: A Private Cartel Goes Public,* 22 STAN. L. REV. 675 (1970).

52   U.S. v. Florida Power Corp. and Tampa Electric Co., 1971 Trade Case. (CCH) pp 73,637 (settled by consent decree).

53   Otter Tail Power Co. v. U.S., 410 U.S. 366 (1973).

54   FPC v. Conway, 426 U.S. 271 (1976). A series of cases, discussed briefly below, involve this aspect of price discrimination. For the FPC's antitrust responsibilities, *see* Gulf States Utilities Co. v. FPC, 411 U.S. 747 (1973).

55   Castor v. Detroit Edison Co., 428 U.S. 579 (1976). The regulatorily mandated tying of "free" electric light bulbs to sales of electricity was involved.

56   U.S. v. Radio Corporation of America, 358 U.S. 334 (1959).

1972 and withstood claims that the matters had been the subjects of extensive FCC proceedings.[57]

On the telecommunications side, the FCC has been engaged in problems relating to noncarrier provided customer premise equipment since shortly after World War II.[58] This hardly reflected an interest in competition on the part of the Commission, however. In the *Hush-A-Phone* matter, the FCC at first upheld the carriers' "foreign attachment" tariff provisions, backing away from this position only on remand from the court of appeals.[59] The famous *Carterfone* case came to the Commission from a private antitrust case. The trial court, while retaining jurisdiction, deferred to the FCC "to resolve all questions related to the justness, reasonableness, validity and effect of the tariff and practices complained of."[60] The Commission's subsequent decision in *Carterfone*[61] and a complicated succession of events gave rise to several other private antitrust actions and eventually to a largely unregulated terminal equipment and interconnect industry.

The course toward deregulation in interexchange telecommunications services was similarly initiated by cases thrown onto the Commission, not by the Commission's having adopted a procompetitive policy stance.[62] The *Above 890,*[63] *MCI,*[64] and *Specialized Common Carriers*[65] cases arose because of applications to the

---

[57] U.S. v. NBC, Civ. No. 72–819 (C.D. Cal. 1972) (settled by consent decree). There were first amendment difficulties that caused the case as initially brought to be dropped and the case to be entered anew.

[58] Use of Recording Devices, 11 F.C.C. 1033 (1947).

[59] Hush-A-Phone Corp., 20 F.C.C. 391 (1955); Hush-A-Phone Corp. v. U.S., 238 F.2d 266 (D.C. Cir. 1956); Hush-A-Phone Corp., 22 F.C.C. 112 (1957).

[60] Carter v. AT&T, 250 F. Supp. 188, 192 (N.D. Tex. 1966).

[61] Carterfone, 13 F.C.C. 2d 420 (1968).

[62] *See* Hinchman, *Intercity Telecommunications Competition—By Design or Default?*, TELEMATICS (Oct. 1984), at 3.

[63] Allocation of Frequencies in the Bands Above 890 Mc., 27 F.C.C. 359 (1959).

[64] Microwave Communications, Inc., 18 F.C.C. 2d 953 (1969).

[65] Specialized Common Carriers, 29 F.C.C. 2d 870 (1971).

Commission and the Commission attached important limitations to the operating authority it believed it was granting in each of these decisions.[66] It was some years later—and after court intervention[67] that the FCC consciously sought to create rivalry in ordinary, switched message toll service. Of far more consequence, the DOJ brought the new *U.S. v. AT&T* case in 1974, alleging both that AT&T's responses to these events were anticompetitive and that the FCC was unable to regulate AT&T effectively.[68]

IV. Deregulation and antitrust after 1975

A. Transportation

The most notable example of deregulation and increased reliance on market competition is, of course, that of air transportation. Save for the carriers themselves, there were by 1975 few arguing for the continuance of regulation.[69] In fact, one of the more interest-

---

66 Without detail, these decisions prevented "sharing" (*i.e.*, no resale), "piece-out" (*i.e.*, no partial use of the public network) and, it was thought, the provision of switched services.

67 MCI Communications Corp. v. AT&T, 369 F. Supp. 1004 (E.D. Pa. 1973), *rev'd*, 496 F.2d 214 (3d Cir.1974); Bell System Tariff Offerings, 46 F.C.C. 2d 413 (1974) concern certain private line services that include limited use of local switching facilities. MCI Telecommunications Corp., 60 F.C.C. 2d 25 (D.C. Cir. 1976); MCI Telecommunications Corp. v. F.C.C., 561 F.2d 365 (1977); Petition of American Telephone and Telegraph Co. for a Declaratory Ruling and Expedited Relief, 67 F.C.C. 2d 1455 (1978); MCI Telecommunications Corp. v. F.C.C., 580 F.2d 590 (D.C. Cir. 1978), *cert. denied*, 439 U.S. 980 (1978) concern MCI's Execunet service, which featured general access to local switching facilities.

68 U.S. v. AT&T, Civ. No. 74–1698 (D.D.C. 1974), ended by modification of final judgment in U.S. v. Western Electric Co., Civ No. 82–0192 (D.D.C. 1982).

69 "It was probably fair to say that [by the mid-1970's] no impartial academic observer of any standing doubted that the airline business, if unregulated, would reach something more or less resembling a competitive equilibrium." Levine, *Airline Competition in Deregulated Markets: Theory, Firm Strategy and Public Policy*, 4 YALE J. ON REG. 393, 394 (1987). This article provides a reasonable, extensive bibliography of materials appearing after those cited notes 13, 14, and 15, above.

ing aspects of airline deregulation is that CAB acted to hasten its own demise. The provisions of the Airline Deregulation Act of 1978 are well known; its consequences on industry structure and performance are discussed below.

In some respects the structure of the trucking industry resembles that of commercial aviation, and some of the deregulation fervor for the latter rubbed off on trucking.[70] The Supreme Court prodded the ICC to pay more attention to competitive factors in its 1974 *Bowman* decision.[71] The Commission thereafter issued new policy directives[72] and generally supported the thrusts of the Motor Carrier Act of 1980. This Act provided for increased pricing and operating freedoms. Rate bureau actions are somewhat circumscribed, but a large measure of antitrust immunity remains. Mergers among trucking firms continue to be scrutinized by the ICC in terms of previously existing public interest standards. Antitrust zealots can give no more than one-and-a-half cheers for their progress here.

In rail transportation, changes brought by the Railroad Revitalization and Regulatory Reform Act of 1976 were augmented by the Staggers Rail Act of 1980. The Act declared that it was government policy "to allow, to the maximum extent possible, competition . . . to establish reasonable rates . . . and to minimize the need for . . . regulatory control over the rail transportation system."[73] The establishment of new lines and the abandonment of old lines were made easier and greater pricing flexibility was permitted (though with special provisions for carriers with market dominance). As is true of the Motor Carrier Act, antitrust immunity is retained for

---

[70] Literature prior to 1975 is referenced in Moore, *Deregulating Surface Freight Transportation*, in Promoting Competition in Regulated Markets, *supra* note 11, at 55. An early classic is A. F. Friedlaender, The Dilemma of Freight Transport Regulation (1969).

[71] Bowman Transportation v. Arkansas Zest Freight System, 419 U.S. 281 (1974).

[72] Policy Statement on Motor Carrier Regulation 44 Fed. Reg. 60,296 (1979).

[73] 49 U.S.C.A. 10101a (Supp. V, 1981).

many collective railroad rate bureau activities. Increased attention to possible anticompetitive effects—particularly regional effects—is required in Commission consideration of rail mergers, but immunity from the antitrust laws is provided here as well.

B. Financial markets

The most remarkable aspect of deregulation in banking and financial markets is the extent to which it has occurred in the absence of guiding regulatory or legislative actions. Market forces took over, with the courts assuming a leading role through accommodating re-interpretations of the law.[74] The regulatory agencies were forced by market developments to begin the gradual relaxation of controls on deposit interest rates. The phasing-out of these controls was mandated by the Deposit Institution Deregulation and Monetary Control Act of 1980. This Act, along with the Garn-St. Germain Act of 1982, broadened the lines of business, types of deposits and chartering options available to the deposit institutions.

The anticompetitive—but, because of state actions and court decisions, increasingly irrelevant—McFadden Act and Douglas amendment restrictions on interstate branching and holding companies have withstood all attacks to date; so have the Glass-Steagall provisions of the Banking Act of 1933, although here, too, the decision of the courts have somewhat reduced their significance. No major changes have occurred in the applicability of the antitrust laws, although the Financial Regulatory Act of 1978 does add competitive tests for the approval of changes in control of insured banks and bank holding companies. The current Savings and Loan crisis seems to be giving deregulation a bad name, although it is closer to the truth to blame regulation (and regulators) for the Savings and

---

74   For a detailed survey of the role of the courts, see in particular Langevoort, *Statutory Obsolescence and the Judicial Process: The Revisionist Role of the Courts in Federal Banking Regulation*, 85 MICH. L. REV. 672 (1987); for the earlier period, including references, *see* Phillips, *The Metamorphosis of Markets: Commercial and Investment Banking*, 1 J. COMP. CORP. L. & SEC. REG. 227 (1978).

Loan problems. Nonetheless, the Financial Institutions Reform, Recovery, and Enforcement Act of 1989 re-instituted constraints on the powers of thrift institutions.

C. Energy

The energy area has not been immune from deregulation efforts. Both legislation and regulatory actions have stressed greater reliance on the market. The Department of Energy Organization Act of 1977 supplanted the old FPC with the FERC, an agency within the Department of Energy [DOE]. FERC continues to regulate both the natural gas industry and interstate oil pipelines, but with an orientation somewhat different from that of the FPC. The Natural Gas Policy Act of 1978 and the Outer Continental Shelf Lands Act Amendment of 1978 were intended, *inter alia*, to increase competition in gas and crude oil.[75]

Antitrust has been applied quite directly. A decision by the Nuclear Regulatory Commission [NRC] under the Atomic Energy Act that ruled against a utility on the basis of probable antitrust violation was upheld on appeal.[76] Following the doctrine of *Otter Tail*, the Public Utilities Regulatory Policy Act of 1978 apparently gives limited authority to FERC to order wheeling when that would be in the public interest. In yet other contexts, the per se rule has been used against electric utilities engaged in price-fixing and market-sharing agreements.[77] What may become an uncontrollable series of private antitrust actions and regulatory proceedings is emerging from the "price squeeze" aspects of the *Conway* case.[78] Again, more is said below about antitrust and the electric power industry.

---

75   See INCREASING COMPETITION IN THE NATURAL GAS MARKET: SECOND REPORT REQUIRED BY SECTION 123 OF THE NATURAL GAS POLICY ACT OF 1978 (Report No. DOE/PE–0069, January 1985) and OIL PIPELINE RE-REGULATION: REPORT OF THE U.S. JUSTICE DEPARTMENT (Antitrust Division, Department of Justice (May 1986)).

76   Alabama Power Co. v. N.R.C., 692 F.2d 1362 (11th Cir. 1982).

77   Gainesville Utility Dept. v. Florida Power and Light Co., 573 F.2d 292 (5th Cir. 1978).

78   F.P.C. v. Conway Corp., 426 U.S. 271 (1976). For a detailed discussion of this and subsequent cases, *see* Lopatka, *The Electric Utility Price Squeeze as an*

D. Communications

There have been a few legislative changes and numerous unsuccessful proposals for further legislation in the areas subject to FCC regulation. Amendments to the Communications Act in 1981 and 1982 allow lotteries in deciding among license applicants and provide for longer terms between license renewals. The Cable Communications Policy Act of 1984 seems to be giving mixed results. On the one hand, it protects the renewal rights of existing operators so long as their service has been reasonable. This policy flies in the face of Demsetz' proposal for competitive bidding.[79] On the other hand, the Act does limit the prerogatives of local franchising authorities in ways broadly consistent with deregulation objectives. Consumer complaints about price increases for cable services are causing Congress seriously to consider re-regulation legislation.

The Commission, for its part, considered for a time the abolition of its financial interest and syndication rule [FISR]. It later abandoned this course despite the conclusions of a special study group that showed that the FISR was anticompetitive.[80] As this is being written, it seems that the Commission is again considering abolishing the FIRS.

The Commission has deregulated small cable companies,[81] terminated regulation of content in radio broadcasting,[82] eliminated syndicated program exclusivity rules,[83] and authorized direct satel-

---

Antitrust Cause of Action, 31 UCLA L. REV. 563 (1984), and Note, *Antitrust Jurisdiction and Remedies in an Electric Utility Price Squeeze,* 52 U. CHI. L. REV. 1090 (1985).

[79] Demsetz, *Why Regulate Utilities?* 11 J.L. & ECON. 55 (1968).

[80] FCC NETWORK INQUIRY SPECIAL STAFF, AN ANALYSIS OF TELEVISION PROGRAM PRODUCTION, ACQUISITION AND DISTRIBUTION (June 1980). For discussion and references, *see* Fisher, *The Financial Interest and Syndication Rules in Network Television: Regulatory Fantasy and Reality,* in ANTITRUST AND REGULATION: ESSAYS IN MEMORY OF JOHN J. MCGOWAN (Franklin M. Fisher ed. 1985).

[81] 79 F.C.C. 2d 652 (1980).

[82] Deregulation of Radio, 73 F.C.C. 2d 457 (1979).

[83] *Id.*

lite broadcasting.[84] It has taken other actions in the broadcasting area that may or may not be regarded as procompetitive. These include increasing from seven to twelve the number of stations of any type a single owner may possess,[85] repeal of a rule aimed at reducing the trading of stations,[86] and eliminating time constraints on advertising.[87]

On the telecommunications side, the FCC followed its *Carterfone* decision by preempting state regulatory authority over interconnection of customer premise equipment.[88] The Commission then instituted a registration program and set forth requirements for standard plug and jack interfaces to render unnecessary any tariffed "special requirements pertaining to the installation of registered equipment."[89] Initially PBXs, key telephone systems, main station telephones, coin telephones, and party line equipment were excluded from the registration program, but by 1978 these had been included as well.[90]

It was really after court intervention in *Execunet II*[91] that the FCC began consciously to pursue competitive policies in switched,

---

84   Direct Broadcast Satellites, 45 Fed. Reg. 72,719 (1980).

85   100 F.C.C. 2d 74 (1984).

86   55 Rad. Reg. 2d (P&F) 1081 (1982).

87   98 F.C.C. 2d 1076 (1984). For a highly critical view of the F.C.C. under Chairman Mark Fowler, *see* Ferrall, Jr., *The Impact of Television Deregulation on Private and Public Interests*, 39 J. Comm. 8 (1989).

88   Telerent Leasing Corp., 45 F.C.C. 2d 204 (1974), *aff'd sub nom.* North Carolina Utility Commission v. FCC, 537 F.2d 787 (4th Cir. 1976), *cert. denied,* 429 U.S. 1027 (1976).

89   Docket No. 19,528, *First Report and Order,* 56 F.C.C. 2d 593 (1975).

90   There is a long and complex course of regulatory and court action involved. The *Third Report and Order* under the same docket is at 67 F.C.C. 2d 1255 (1978); the *Fourth Report and Order,* at 70 F.C.C. 2d 1808 (1979). The conduct of AT&T through this period is a critical part of plaintiff's case in Litton Systems, Inc. v. AT&T, 700 F.3d 785 (2d Cir. 1983) and several other private antitrust suits.

91   MCI Telecommunications Corp. v. FCC, 580 F.2d 590 (1978), *cert. denied,* 439 U.S. 980 (1978).

Message Telecommunications Service-like interexchange services. These policies were inordinately complicated by the perhaps unanswerable question of the proper rate to charge the "other common carriers" [OCCs] for interconnections with the local exchanges. A docket was opened to deal with this question in 1978, but the matter has yet to be fully resolved.[92] A partial solution was achieved by transferring a major portion of local exchange cost recovery from the interexchange carriers (i.e., from toll rates) to the local exchange carriers (i.e., to local "access" charges). Interstate customer access charges were announced in 1983, with phasing-in beginning in 1984.[93]

The FCC's actions were accompanied by requirements under the Modification of Final Judgment [MFJ] in U.S. v. AT&T that the local Bell companies provide equal access to the OCCs by certain dates. The FCC has also ruled under Computer Inquiry III that AT&T and the Bell exchange carriers must provide "open network architecture" or, temporarily, "comparably equal interconnection" so that competition among interexchange carriers, exchange carriers and noncarrier providers of enhanced services would be facilitated.[94] More is said of this in the next section.

V. Competition and deregulation: does it always work?

It is clear that the deregulation movement gained wide support in the late 1970's and 1980's. Regulation, it turned out, was extended in the 1930's and 1940's to areas in which it caused more problems than it cured. It is possible that there is now a full turn of the screw—that deregulation and antitrust have been applied in areas in which they are the inappropriate remedy?

The bases for this possibility are easy to identify. If deregula-

---

[92]   CC Docket 78–72, MTS-WATS Market Structure—Access Charges. Important Reports and Orders and Notices of Inquiry appear at 67 F.C.C. 2d 757 (1978); 71 F.C.C. 2d 440 (1979); 77 F.C.C. 2d 224 (1980); 90 F.C.C. 2d 6 (1982).

[93]   CC Docket 78–72, 93 F.C.C. 2d 241 (1983).

[94]   CC Docket 85–229, F.C.C. 86–252 (released June 16, 1986).

tion is attempted in areas where there are discernible reasons to suspect "market failure," it ought come as no surprise that the deregulation efforts are less than fully successful. Even in such instances, deregulation may produce improvements—temporary or long lasting—over the hitherto existing regulation, since regulation, too, is imperfect. There is, that is, "regulatory failure"[95] as well as market failure. These caveats aside, however, it could still be the case that the consequences of market failure are worse than those of regulatory failure.

The most obvious cause of market failure is cost subadditivity or, more popularly, the cost conditions of "natural monopoly."[96] If two or more firms behave competitively in such circumstances, only one can eventually survive. If the firms are regulated so as to assure the survival of both, one can hardly describe the results as "competition." Moreover, social costs are not minimized.

Another cause of market failure is externalities. Here the problem may be that a firm (or, more properly, a product) that ought to exist does not. The more general problem is that too little or too much of a good is produced. The socially beneficial (positive externality) or the socially detrimental (negative externality) "neighborhood effects" of activities are not properly reflected in the calculus of profit-maximization by individual firms and consumers.

Markets may also fail because of transactions cost considerations or, stated another way, because of inefficient organizational structures. Market-mediated exchanges among separate entities are not always superior to transactions governed by interorganizational conventions and fiats.[97] It may thus be possible to encounter circumstances in which what were thought to be procompetitive industrial reorganizations to correct regulatory failure result instead in

---

95   Wolf, *A Theory of Non-Market Failures,* THE PUBLIC INTEREST, no. 55 (Spring, 1979), at 114.

96   The seminal article is Baumol, *On the Proper Cost Tests for Natural Monopoly in a Multiproduct Industry,* 67 AM. ECON. REV. 809 (1977).

97   *See* generally O. E. Williamson, MARKETS AND HIERARCHIES: ANALYSIS AND ANTITRUST IMPLICATIONS (1975).

market failures. This is particularly likely when (1) the transactions require large investments in assets that are highly specific to a particular use; (2) the number of actual and potential buyers and/or sellers is small; (3) substantial periods of time and/or repetitive transactions are involved; (4) there is uncertainty about complex and ungovernable factors that may significantly affect the outcome of the transactions and, hence, when comprehensive, contingent contracts are impossible to write; and (5) there are differences in the completeness and the nature of the relevant knowledge possessed by the parties.[98]

More generally, markets may fail because of the "existence" problem; nothing resembling competitive equilibria may exist. This is the case, of course, when natural monopoly cost conditions prevail and, in a different sense, when the costs associated with market-mediated transactions induce inefficiencies. There are, however, more vexing questions for which theory offers far less guidance. Once the theoretical domain of homogeneous goods and "price-taking" firms is abandoned, it becomes more than a remote possibility that no stable equilibria exist for some combinations of market structures and firm behavior.[99] For example, the responses by individual firms to an initial condition of disequilibrium may involve a collective "over-shooting" of price or nonprice reactions, with consequent oscillating, dynamic disequilibria. Markets in which complementary goods appear may be more prone to such instabilities than are those in which all goods are substitutes. Product differentiation, cost differences, differential locational effects on costs and/or demand, varying expectations and imperfect information may similarly give rise to stability problems.

Some faith in the existence of stable markets can be derived from observations common to us all—markets that are "falling apart" are

---

98 *Id.*, and by the same author, *Transaction-Cost Economics: The Governance of Contractual Relations*, 22 J.L. & Econ. 233 (1979).

99 Market failure due to the nonexistence of equilibria is discussed briefly in Bator, *The Anatomy of Market Failure*, 72 Q.J. Econ. 351 (1958). More extended, but not easily fathomed, discussions appear in L. G. Telser, Competition, Collusion and Game Theory (1972), especially at 162–72; 250–71.

not day-to-day occurrences. On the other side of the coin, it is difficult to assess precisely which market characteristics are critical to stability in particular cases. It is not impossible that some of the conditions necessary for the existence of an equilibrium might appear to be harmful market imperfections or unnecessary regulatory intrusions. That deregulation in some instances may yield unstable market structures and market performance that does not converge toward the competitive ideal ought not be lightly dismissed.

A. Commercial aviation

Arguments to the effect that deregulation and procompetitive policies are not completely successful are likely to be misunderstood. This will be particularly the case with the deregulation of commercial aviation where, as noted, essentially all "impartial academic observers" were convinced that a competitive market was possible.[100] If, as seems likely, this conclusion turns out to have been wrong, it need not follow that the abandonment of the old regulatory regime was an error. It may mean, however, that further policy actions are needed.

The affection economists developed for deregulation of air transportation was premised on two principal points. First, it was concluded that natural monopoly cost conditions did not exist and, second, it was assumed that airline markets were highly contestable.[101] Growing evidence shows that the degree of contestability was highly exaggerated.Entry is not as easy as had been thought, and exit is far from costless.[102] It seems as well that even though

---

[100]   Levine, *supra* note 69.

[101]   *See, for example*, Kahn, *Deregulation of Air Transportation: Getting from Here to There*, in REGULATING BUSINESS: THE SEARCH FOR AN OPTIMUM (1978). The experience of intrastate carriers was also influential. *See* W. JORDON, AIRLINE REGULATION IN AMERICA: EFFECTS AND IMPERFECTIONS (1970) and Keeler, *Airline Regulation and Market Performance*, 3 BELL J. ECON. & MGMT. SCI. 399 (1972).

[102]   A brief survey of such evidence appears in Levine, *supra* note 69. *See also* Statement of Roger B. Andewelt, Deputy Assistant Attorney General, Antitrust Division, before the Subcommittee on Antitrust, Monopoly, and Business Rights, Committee on the Judiciary, United States Senate, *Mergers and Competition in the Airline Industry* (March 25, 1987).

classic natural monopoly cost conditions do not prevail, peculiar networking effects mean that an incumbent carrier often has distinct advantages for certain expansions in service.[103] These structural conditions imply that a substantial degree of market power remains in some unregulated airline markets. The conditions have also made mergers attractive, augmenting the problems of market power.

The structural conditions are accompanied by other industry characteristics that make questionable the existence of a stable, multifirm, competitive equilibrium. There are interdependencies between the supply (cost) functions and demand functions of air carriers that are highly unusual. One of the strongest criticisms of the old form of regulation rested on one such interdependence. Increases in flight frequency are tantamount to price reductions on the demand side, but they have the effect of increasing cost per passenger mile on the supply side.[104] With regulation, it was said, frequency competition (and other forms of nonprice competition) gave rise to lower load factors, higher costs and higher fares. Regulation caused the carriers to engage in a negative-sum game and to rely on occasional regulatory responses by the CAB to bail them out.

Frequency competition remains as a strategic tool in the deregulated environment. It is not the only form of rivalry that affects costs as well as demand, however. Advertising, whether general or route-specific, stimulates demand but increases costs. So do frequent flyer programs and qualitative aspects of service used by customers to make comparative evaluations.[105] When one carrier initiates cost-increasing, demand-stimulating moves, the other carriers must follow or make other competitive responses if they are not to lose market share. None gains much revenue relative to the others, but all face higher costs.

---

[103]   That is, the differences between incremental revenues and incremental costs for the expansion among the carriers give rise to "rents" for the carrier best positioned to provide that service. *See* Bailey & Williams, *Sources of Rent in the Regulated Airline Industry*, 31 J.L. & ECON. 173 (1988).

[104]   Douglas & Miller, III, *The CAB's Domestic Passenger Fare Investigation,* 5 BELL J. ECON. & MGMT. SCI. 205 (1974).

[105]   Safety may not be among these—as long as major accidents are infrequent events.

This puts great pressure on reducing those operating costs that do not cause direct reductions on demand—perhaps including safety-related items such as maintenance, flight crew training and crew size. The same thing goes on with respect to fares, where downward moves are practically universally met, but upward moves are not.[106] Unilateral efforts by one carrier to control or reduce such rivalry may go unmatched by others. In fact, the more *some* others follow the leader to improve *joint* profitability, the greater the temptation for another not to follow or, having followed, subsequently to "cheat."

The market-directed way to avoid these adverse results typically involves more concentrated markets and the creation of higher barriers to entry. The "hub-and-spoke" network configurations now popular with carriers reduce time delays between flights and produce operating economies by concentrating traffic from several lower density routes onto higher density routes. Passengers—or many of them, at least—benefit from "on-line feed" and improved flight frequency. As individual carriers have come to dominate particular major hubs, however, the number of alternative carriers from whom customers can conveniently opt is often significantly reduced. Reductions in nonstop flights have increased *scheduled* flight times for many travelers and, as it has turned out, the unscheduled delays caused by air traffic congestion and other factors associated with hub-and-spoke networking have increased travel times even more. There is increasing evidence that prices are significantly higher at hubs dominated by one carrier.[107]

At least 75 carriers have entered interstate commercial service since 1978.[108] This makes the view that air carrier markets are con-

---

[106] This argument rests on no more than a generalized "kinked-demand curve" concept. *See* Stigler, *The Kinky Oligopoly Demand Curve and Rigid Prices*, 55 J. Pol. Econ. 432 (1947) for a contribution and reference to earlier work.

[107] *See* Hurdle, Johnson, Joskow, Werden & Williams, *Concentration, Potential Entry and Performance in the Airline Industry*, 38 J. Indus. Econ. 119 (1989).

[108] *See* R. Bowles & G. Mercer, FAA Method for Forecasting Commercial Traffic (APO–110, Federal Aviation Administration, February 2, 1987) for these and related data.

testable seem credible. The fact that at least 44 of these have either returned to commuter status or otherwise ceased operations does not, by itself, detract from contestability arguments. On top of this, however, are a series of horizontal, vertical and complementary mergers that have increased concentration significantly since 1978. Not surprisingly, several of the larger mergers have involved "failing firms." That this led to their being unopposed by the Department of Transportation, despite apparent anticompetitive effects, is also not surprising. Of far more importance, concentration at major hubs increased dramatically with mergers of carriers whose operations were complementary.

Efforts to reduce labor costs have taken a heavy toll on union power, with mergers as well as bankruptcies used as strategic weapons against organized labor. Unlike advertising, frequent flyer programs and flight frequency competition, this is an area in which cost reductions do not immediately spell reductions in demand. Whether the longer term reductions in the quality of service that is almost certain to result will be good or bad for the carriers and the public is yet to be seen.

The critical question—and there can be no definitive answer— is whether, absent regulation, the structural changes that have occurred were not inevitable.[109] Could the industry, without the CAB, possibly have remained competitively structured and yet achieve sustainable fares, operations and profits? Has it even now, with a more monopolistic structure, achieved those conditions? Or, more problematically, is there here a set of markets for which the structure and performance of competitive markets cannot simultaneously exist? The old regulations seem to have failed, and so may the experiments in fully market-determined results.

B. Electric power

As noted in section III, the electric power industry has been the subject of proposals for deregulation and innovative applications of

---

109   An early suggestive piece to this effect is Phillips, *Airline Mergers in the New Regulatory Environment*, 129 U. PA. L. REV. 856 (1981).

antitrust law. The deregulation proposals range from suggestions for complete deregulation of the industry as currently structured to those advocating full vertical disintegration and deregulation of only wholesale power transactions.[110] In a growing number of states, some form of competitive bidding is required for electric generating capacity and FERC appears to be headed in the same direction.[111]

The central problem with the disintegration and competitive bidding proposals is that transactions in the industry are "characterized by uncertainty, complexity, asset specificity and sunk costs." Vertical disintegration would mean that "market transactions must replace internal organization," with the result that "complex long-term contracts"[112] would appear as the transactions-governance mechanism. "These contractual relationships are not likely to be any more efficient and may well be less efficient than conventional regulation of franchised monopolies. Indeed [so far as transmission and distribution are concerned] the difference between a regulatory agency here and an authority to administer a short-term franchise contract through competitive bidding is likely to be only a matter of semantics."[113] And an unregulated transmission company would likely possess substantial market power with respect to both generating and distribution companies.

Do the characteristics of the industry mean that competitive markets—in the full sense of the term—would not work even at the

---

[110]   For detail, *see* P. L. JOSKOW & R. SCHMALENSEE, MARKETS FOR POWER: AN ANALYSIS OF ELECTRIC UTILITY DEREGULATION (1983).

[111]   *See* D. J. DUANA, R. E. BURNS, D. N. JONES & M. EIFERT, COMPETITIVE BIDDING FOR ELECTRIC GENERATING CAPACITY: APPLICATION AND IMPLEMENTATION (National Regulatory Research Institute, Nov. 1988) and Howard & Westfall, *The FERC Opens Pandora's Box: Increased Competition and Heightened Antitrust Exposure for Electric Utilities*, PUB. UTIL. FORTNIGHTLY, March 3, 1988, at 22. A moderate view appears in THE TRANSMISSION TASK FORCE'S REPORT TO THE COMMISSION; ELECTRICITY TRANSMISSION: REALITY, THEORY AND POLICY ALTERNATIVES (Federal Energy Regulatory Commission, Oct. 1989).

[112]   P. L. JOSKOW & R. SCHMALENSEE, *supra* note 110, at 120, with similar discussion throughout.

[113]   *Id.* at 125.

generation stage? Probably, yes, they mean just that. Efficient generation requires that generating facilities be interconnected into a coordinated regional system. That system must include a dispatching mechanism that instantaneously matches load with generation, including provision for scheduled maintenance and unscheduled breakdowns of individual facilities. A mechanism for meeting peak load and bulk power demands must also exist.

Bilateral short-term contracts that specify prices, quantities and delivery schedules for just the contracting parties are grossly insufficient. It may be possible to develop a degree of competition in wholesale transactions if this competition develops in the context of a coordinated (and regulated) transmission system and if regulation at the distribution level is properly harmonized with the rest of the industry. It is at this point that antitrust enters the picture. The necessary harmonization of the distribution end has, it seems, been given too little attention.

One type of antitrust action derives from the *Otter Tail* case.[114] The circumstances surrounding the refusals by Otter Tail to wheel power for independent municipal distribution companies were complex. Otter Tail apparently wanted to acquire such systems and engaged in a variety of practices in addition to its refusals to wheel. The extension of *Otter Tail* to other wheeling cases requires care, nonetheless. It is sometimes possible for one or several distribution utilities to arrange to buy power from a third party with which they are not interconnected at wholesale rates below those being charged by their current supplier. The new source is most often a federal power project. The historic source is probably, like Otter Tail, a large, partially or wholly integrated investor-owned utility [IOU], while the distribution systems are likely to be a small cooperative or municipal operation. The distribution utility requests that, for a fee, the IOU accept power onto its transmission facilities from their new source and deliver the same amount of power to their systems. That is, they want the IOU to wheel power for them.

Requests for wheeling are obviously predicated on rate differentials. If wheeling were required, it appears that competition at the

---

[114] Otter Tail Power Co. v. U.S., 410 U.S. 366 (1973).

generating level would be stimulated. Still, it is far from clear that wheeling is universally in the public interest. Note first that whether the transmission grid is operated under a pooling agreement or by a single company, there is no identification of the electricity that goes into the transmission grid at one point and the electricity that comes out at any other. Further, as noted, there has to be an instantaneous balancing of overall generation with overall load. Thus, in a physical sense, the wholesale contract for which the distribution utility requires wheeling represents only a switching among alternative generation sources. then, too, the reason for the rate differential may be with federal power project pricing policies, not with real economies.

As viewed by the operator of the transmission system, each wheeling contract reduces the degrees of freedom it has in coordinating the system's operations, including centralized dispatching choices aimed at minimizing overall costs. Of greater consequence, the contracts for wheeled power are often not for the total and varying requirements of the distribution utility, but rather for a fixed, bulk amount that is less than even the minimum actual load of the distribution utility. The transmission utility which, on the one hand, may be forced to wheel the bulk of the power to the distribution utility is, on the other hand, left with the obligation to supply the residual, highly varying load requirements, including the peak load. The distribution utility (usually the plaintiff in an antitrust action) acts on the presumption that the rates charged for the power needed to satisfy the new, lower but more variable, power requirement will be those existing prior to the newly arranged deals with third parties. To provide residual and peak requirements on this basis would almost certainly entail losses for the original supplier.

While the motive for the kind of "rate arbitraging" involved in wheeling are clear, it is not obvious that generalized rules fashioned under antitrust principles will be conducive to increased efficiency in the electric power industry. Transferring the logic of the "essential facilities" doctrine as it applies to a football stadium[115] to the

---

115   Hecht v. Pro-Football, 444 F.2d 931 (D.c. Cir. 1971). For an excellent discussion in the context of regulated industries, *see* Tye, *Competitive Access: A Comparative Industry Approach to the Essential Facility Doctrine,* 8 ENERGY L.J. 337 (1987).

case of electric transmission facilities is hazardous. The problems inherent in forecasting demand and the long lead times involved in constructing generating capacity are themselves cautions against increasing the uncertainties and reducing the rewards to those charged with meeting peak demands.

Following *Otter Tail*, the Supreme Court imposed a "price-squeeze" antitrust obligation on the FERC;[116] the doctrine has since been successfully used in other civil litigation.[117] The same cast as that in the wheeling cases continues, with the large IOU and the small municipals, but here the latter charge that increases in the IOU's wholesale rates (subject to FERC regulations) narrow the spread between the prices at which the municipals buy power and the rates at which they sell power (subject to state regulation). This price-squeeze could—but need not—be part of the tactics used by the IOU to get the municipal's franchise. The squeeze could arguably be part of the IOU's efforts to compete for large industrial customers. It could also be nothing more than the consequences of uncoordinated, dual federal-state regulation.

Joskow argues correctly that it is difficult to ascribe a predatory intent to IOU's in these circumstances.[118] Such an intent requires the foregoing of short-term profits in the expectation that, with less competition downstream after the action, subsequent recoupment is possible. The regulatory character of the electric power industry and the limited possibilities for retail competition make this expectation a remote one. "The price-squeeze doctrine as applied to the electric power industry represent a body of antitrust law in search of a real anticompetitive problem."[119]

---

116   FPC v. Conway Corp., 426 U.S. 271 (1976).

117   City of Mishawake v. American Electric Power Co., 616 F.2d 976 (7th Cir. 1980). For additional cases and a legal critique, *see* Lopatka, *supra* note 78 and Note, *supra* note 78. An economic analysis appears in Joskow, *Mixing Regulatory and Antitrust Policies in the Electric Power Industry: The Price Squeeze and Retail Market Competition*, ANTITRUST AND REGULATION, *supra* note 80.

118   Joskow, *id.*

119   *Id.* at 186.

All-in-all, the competitive problems of the electric power industry seem better left to the regulators than to the antitrust courts.

C. Telecommunications

BACKGROUND   There has been tension between regulation and antitrust in telecommunications dating from the infancy of the industry. And AT&T discovered early that agreements restricting the scope of its operations might facilitate the resolution of serious legal difficulties. Thus, the early struggle between Western Union and AT&T over patents (and markets) was resolved by an 1879 compact that kept AT&T out of the telegraphy business and Western Union out of telephony.[120]

State regulation of telephone service began in Connecticut and Missouri in 1879 and 21 additional states had some form of regulation governing telephones by 1900.[121] Federal regulation began with the Mann-Elkins Act of 1910, which vested power in the ICC to declare unlawful rates that were not "just and reasonable." By 1910, however, Theodore Vail had expressly accepted the quid pro quo of regulation for monopoly, aiming AT&A toward the goals of "One policy, One System, Universal Service."[122]

Vail's dream of noncontentious relations between AT&T and governmental agencies was short-lived. As AT&T acquired more and more of the independent telephone companies that had sprung up since the 1870's, strong opposition arose with respect to its becoming *the* monopoly server and concerning its conduct toward the independents. The Justice Department brought an antitrust case in 1913[123] and, to settle the matter, AT&T made its "Kingsbury

---

120   G. W. BROCK, THE TELECOMMUNICATIONS INDUSTRY (1981), at 89–99; A. STONE, WRONG NUMBER: THE BREAKUP OF AT&T (1989), at 36–37; G. D. SMITH, THE ANATOMY OF A BUSINESS DECISION: THE ACQUISITION OF WESTERN ELECTRIC AND THE ORIGINS OF THE BELL TELEPHONE SYSTEM (1982) at 34–54, 92–98.

121   U.S. v. AT&T, Defendants' Third Statement of Contentions and Proof, v. 1, p. 137; Plaintiff's Third Statement of Contentions and Proof, v. 2, p. 1795.

122   STONE, *supra* note 120, at 44–48.

123   U.S. v. AT&T Co., Eq. No. 6082 (D.c. Ore. 1913).

Commitment." The accord with the government rested on AT&T's agreeing, *inter alia*, to "refrain from acquiring competing independent telephone companies," to make arrangements so that the independents could "secure for their subscribers toll service over the lines of the . . . Bell System"[124] and to dispose of its controlling stock interest in Western Union.

What might now be called the procompetitive policy approach undertaken through the Kingsbury Commitment was reversed with passage of the Willis-Graham Act in 1921. That Act rested squarely on the proposition that "telephoning is a natural monopoly," a monopoly that "ought exist in the interest of economy and good service in the public welfare" and one "which must be promoted instead of being forbidden." It was, according to a Member of the House, "silly to believe that there can be competition either in service or charges."[125] Further consolidations—subject to ICC approvals—were forthcoming, but as many as 2,000 (mostly noncompeting) independents remained by the end of the decade. Government ownership rather than competition was proposed by some as the remedy for perhaps ineffectual federal regulation.[126]

The emergence of radio in the 1920's again presented the question of AT&T's scope of operations. A 1926 agreement left radio to RCA and, of course, kept RCA out of the telephone business.[127] The Communications Act of 1934 provided new federal regulations for both radio and telephone. It provided also a vehicle for an intensive investigation of AT&T. One consequence was that AT&T elected to abandon its Electrical Research Products subsidiary and with it, experiments in the commercialization of telephotography, televi-

---

[124] Defendants' Third Statement, *supra* note 121, at 163–66. AT&T entered a Consent Decree in 1914 that incorporated some of the provisions of the Kingsbury Commitment. It nonetheless continued to acquire many independents with the approval of the DOJ.

[125] *Id.* at 169–71.

[126] Plaintiff's Third Statement, *supra* note 121, at 1832–33.

[127] Reich, *Research, Patents, and the Struggle to Control Radio: A Study of Big Business and the Uses of Industrial Research*, 51 BUS. HIS. REV. 208, 229–30 (1977).

sion transmission, stereophonic sound and talking motion pictures.[128] Another consequence was that, while neither the 1938
"Walker Report" nor the 1939 FCC report questioned the natural
monopoly characteristics of telecommunications, the seeds of the
1949 antitrust case were planted.Indeed, Holmes Baldridge, an attorney who worked on the Walker Report is said to have pressed
the 1949 case after joining the Antitrust Division because of failing
to get what he wanted from the Commission.[129]

The 1956 decree was a repetition of AT&T's practice of resolv-
ing problems by agreeing to limit its scope of operations. So far as
AT&T and the Bell Operating Companies [BOCs] were concerned,
the limitation was to "the furnishing of common carrier communication services." For Western Electric, the restriction was against
manufacturing for sale or lease "any equipment which is of type not
sold or leased . . . to Companies of the Bell System, for use in
furnishing common carrier communication services."

As was true of the Kingsbury Commitment, it was not long
before the inflexible provisions of the 1956 antitrust decree con-
flicted with changing FCC policies and, indeed, with the objectives
of AT&T itself. With advances in technology, distinctions between
communications, data processing, and information services became
blurred. The growth of the computer industry—particularly after the
introduction of distributed processing in the middle and late 1960's—
caused rapidly increasing demand for the transmission of data among
the nodes at which it was generated, used, stored, or processed. This
gave rise to ideas for data networks and "computer utilities," the implementation of which required terminal equipment and network services that AT&T was unable or unwilling to provide. Specialized
common carriers [SCCs] were envisioned, and data transmission was
prominent among the services proposed in their applications.[130]

---

128   STONE, *supra* note 120, at 66.

129   *Id.* at 73–74.

130   This section relies on A. Phillips, *New Technologies and Diversified
Telecommunications Services: Policy Problems in an ISDN Environment* in
DEREGULATION AND DIVERSIFICATION OF UTILITIES 107–25 (M. Crew ed. 1989).

Data processing and transmission required new kinds of terminal equipment. The "foreign attachment" provisions of existing tariffs prevented others from providing that equipment so that the new services could be carried on the network. Market reality and the 1956 decree made it clear that AT&T and the other carriers could not provide the required array of devices. Yet it was equally clear that entry by the SCCs and interconnect terminal equipment suppliers was inevitable if the growing needs for data transmission could not be accommodated on the networks of the existing common carriers.

The FCC began its *Computer Inquiry [CI-I]* in 1966. In a 1971 Final Decision (modified in 1973), the FCC distinguished between regulated communications services and unregulated data processing services in the same way as had been done in the 1956 decree. Regulated common carriers were permitted to engage in unregulated data processing services only through separate corporate entities. This ruling was of no avail to AT&T, however, because of the provisions of the 1956 decree.

It soon became apparent that the distinctions between regulated telecommunications and unregulated data processing were not clear. In an effort to clarify policy, the *Second Computer Inquiry [CI-III]* was opened in 1976. A 1980 CI-II ruling produced a dichotomy of "basic services" and "enhanced services." "Basic service" was defined as the offering of transmission capacity to move information from one place to another; "enhanced services," those that utilize computer technology to alter the content or to provide subscriber interaction with stored information. All enhance services—along with all customer premises equipment [CPE]—were deregulated. The FCC also used the rationale that AT&T was subject to potential regulation in an attempt to circumvent the restrictions of the 1956 decree.

Despite the experience with the Kingsbury Commitment and the 1956 decree, AT&T entered yet another such agreement in 1982. The MFJ presented the court with a document that barely considered enhanced services, ongoing technology, and the role of network carriers in providing information services. The events on which the MFJ was based took place in the 1950's, 1960's, and

1970's, and were primarily concerned with ordinary telephone service and the terminal, transmission, and switching equipment involved in producing that service.

The DOJ's Competitive Impact Statement and the court recognized that changes in technology might in time alter the economic significance of the (BOCs') apparent access bottleneck. And the court, it appears, was less concerned than the DOJ about the BOC's providing both regulated and unregulated services so long as there were not significant adverse competitive effects. Even so, there were severe restrictions against BOC offerings of information services, particularly electronic information services. No service involving the "generating, acquiring, storing, transforming, processing, retrieving or making available information . . . conveyed via telecommunications" could be offered by the BOCs. Further, the telecommunications services of the BOCs could make no changes "in the form or content" of information "as sent and received." In short, while the MFJ appeared to remove the vestiges of the 1956 decree for AT&T, the BOCs could neither provide the generic interfacing that would facilitate others' use of the network to deliver information services not themselves provide such services.

The FCC continued its work on enhanced services without particular reference to the provisions of the MFJ. The commission embarked on a "multiple vendor" policy approach based on its CI-II determinations. In this approach the Commission adopted a policy that it calls "procompetitive" but that may more accurately be described as "hands-on deregulation."[131] This attempt at blending competition and regulation may be the worst of all worlds.

A *Third Computer Inquiry [CI-III]* was opened in 1985. In a May 1986 Phase I Order, the FCC recognized that the inefficiencies and costs associated with structural separation for carrier provision of enhanced services may often outweigh the benefits. While main-

---

[131] *See* V. Goldberg & A. Phillips, Efficiency and Governance in Alternative Regulatory Regimes: Hands-On Deregulation in Telecommunications (unpublished manuscript).

taining the basic/enhanced service definitions of CI-II, the Commission adopted new regulations to govern the offerings of enhanced services. Separate subsidiaries would no longer be required. The Commission has recently reiterated the position after an appeals court overthrew its CI-III order.[132]

Dominant carriers (*i.e.*, AT&T and the BOCs) were required to provide comparably efficient interconnection [CEI] to apparent competitors for any enhanced services the carriers are permitted to offer. They were also required to file plans for open network architecture [ONA]. Any basic service used in the offering of an enhanced service must be tariffed and available to others on an "unbundled and functionally equal basis." Beyond this, the carriers were required to file detailed accounting plans and to receive approval for the methods used in allocating joint and common costs. A *Report and Order* under Docket No. 86–111, released in February 1987, provides guidelines for that purpose. Cross-subsidization is again the underlying issue; the order aims at inhibiting "carriers from imposing on ratepayers for regulated . . . services the costs and risks of unregulated ventures."

Phase II orders under *CI-III* established that protocol processing is an enhanced service which, if offered by AT&T or a BOC, must satisfy nonstructural safeguards set forth by the Commission. The latter specify types of access to end offices, interfaces, transmission, and transport networks that must be made available to value-added network competitors and the network rate elements for which tariffed rates must be available. At least one Commissioner has recognized that the "regulatory cleavage between basic and enhanced services is a relic of the past."[133] At the same time, a docket was opened to consider the carriers' ONA plans. These plans were approved in principle in 1989 and 1990.

As might have been expected, shortcomings in the 1982 MFJ

---

[132] California v. FCC, Case No. 87–7230 (9th Cir., 6 June 1990); CC Docket No. 90–368, In re: Computer III Remand Proceedings (6 August 1990).

[133] Commissioner Patricia Diaz Dennis, as quoted in TELECOMMUNICATION REPORTS, January 18, 1988, at 5.

were becoming apparent shortly after it was entered. The MFJ required triennial reports (after the 1984 divestiture) to the court. The first such report was filed in February 1987 and made what many regarded as rather startling recommendations.[134] These include a lifting of the ban on BOC provision of interexchange services for areas outside their own local exchange areas, removal of all restrictions on BOC manufacturing and distribution of telecommunications equipment and CPE, removal of restrictions on nontelecommunications businesses, and—most relevant to this discussion—removal of the ban on BOC provision of information services.

The court's initial reaction to the proposals was distinctly negative. While Judge Greene was prepared to exempt the transmission of information generated by others and did repeal the restriction on BOC entry into nontelecommunications businesses, his September 1987 opinion emphasized the ancient antitrust factors—the pervasiveness of local exchange bottlenecks and the dangers that these would be used anticompetitively if the restrictions on information services were relaxed. Six months later, Judge Greene clarified the meaning to be attached to the exemption for the "transmission of information generated by others." It was made clear that the BOCs are foreclosed from the "generation of information content." The court reaffirmed, however, that data transmission, address translation, protocol conversion, billing management, and introductory information content are "transmission functions." The restriction against "electronic publishing," as defined in the MFJ, was explicitly continued.

The definition of "electronic white page" information services was clarified to make more evident what the court regarded as permissible "gateway service" transmission of introductory information content. Similarly, the court indicated that it is now prepared to accept "kiosk" billing by the BOCs, so long as nothing

---

[134] "Report and Recommendations of the United States concerning the Line of Business Restrictions Imposed on the Bell Operating Companies by the Modification of Final Judgement," U.S. v. Western Electric Co., Civil Action No. 82–0192 (February 1, 1987). The DOJ position is based in large measure on THE GEODESIC NETWORK: 1987 REPORT ON COMPETITION IN THE TELEPHONE INDUSTRY, prepared by Peter Huber, a Consultant to DOJ.

more than minor and "technical" revenue sharing is involved. The adoption of any sort of protocol conversion services would be allowed so long as they do not involve manipulation of content. The court appears to have concluded that the generic capability to convert individual users' protocols for electronic mail services does not constitute a change in content.

Perhaps the most surprising of the recent modifications to the MFJ are those concerning voice storage and retrieval, voice messaging, and more particularly, electronic mail services by the BOCs. After a careful probing of alternatives, the court concluded that "the risk of anticompetitive activity is small" and permitted the BOCs to participate in these markets—again subject to the prohibition against their providing or manipulating information content. In other places in the opinion, the court indicates a willingness to defer to FCC decisions pertaining to enhanced services and to accept the procedural safeguards set forth by the Commission. Still, "if it appears [to the court] that the Regional Companies are abusing the authority granted . . . and that FCC control is insufficient to curb violations, the court will take the requisite enforcement action."

TENSION BETWEEN COMPETITION AND REGULATION: REMAINING POLICY PROBLEMS   An extremely difficult set of problems arises because of the probable existence of significant economies of scale and scope in the switched network.While some have argued that these economies are limited to size ranges much below those of the United States network, the bulk of the credible evidence shows no evidence of diseconomies throughout the network sizes thus far experienced.

The economies of scale in the old system were not restricted to interexchange services. They undoubtedly arose in part from the integral provision of local exchange and interexchange services. Here the arrangements required by the MFJ entail inefficiencies in the forced and arbitrary separation of functions. Indeed, the provision by the BOCs of equal trunk-side access to an indefinite and changing number of interexchange carriers is far from costless. The costs of providing CEI (or ONA) for the multiple vendors of enhanced services in today's environment may reach such proportions that the general public will benefit little from them.

Scope economies probably result from the common use of local facilities to produce a variety of enhanced services. Protocol conversion, standing alone, as well as in conjunction with a "gateway service" for many individual enhanced service offerings are good illustrations of where common usage should be associated with cost complementarities and scope economies.

The nature of the FCC's concerns under its *CI-III* rules makes it clear that there are enormous problems inherent in maintaining multiple vendor offerings of enhanced services. The conditions attached to the Commission's recent approval of voice mail services [VMS] by BOCs[135] make one wonder whether the non-structual safeguards of *CI-III* are not worse than the structural separation required by *CI-II*.

A CEI plan is required to show that the carriers would "provide interconnection opportunities to others . . . to insure that basic facilities are available to other enhanced service providers and users on an unbundled and functionally equal basis." The plans had to cover "interface functionality, unbundling of basic services, resale, technical characteristics, installation, maintenance and repaid, end-user access, CEI availability, minimization of transport costs, and recipients of CEI."

To satisfy the equal interface functionality requirement, the carriers' own VMS offering have to interconnect with the network "in the same way and on the same terms and conditions available to all voice mail providers." The basic services that support the carriers' VMS must be "unbundled from other basic service offerings and associated with a specific rate element." The carriers may "not use network functions that are not available to all providers in an unbundled tariffed form." Indeed, the carriers "purchase" the CEI elements "at the same tariffed rates, terms, and conditions as other voice mail providers," thus making resale of its services easily

---

[135] For example, In the Matter of Pacific Bell and Nevada Bell Plan for Voice Mail Services, Memorandum Opinion and Order, FCC 88–11 (Released: February 18, 1988). Quotes in text are from this source.

possible. An installation, maintenance and repair system is setup to prevent discrimination. Any end user access system (*e.g.*, abbreviated dialing) made available to the carriers' VMS subscribers must be made available to "competitors."

The foregone advantages are precisely the sort of efficiencies that led the Commission to abandon its earlier *CI-II* "separate facilities" requirement. Here, however, since the carriers charge themselves the same tariffed rates as it charges all other VMS providers, the Commission's view is that "it achieves the procompetitive goals" of CEI requirements. The goal of protecting competitors—not preserving competition—is what really drives this "hands-on deregulation."

There are pricing inefficiencies in the FCC's approach, too. Standard economic theory for static surplus maximization for a multiproduct natural monopoly calls for pricing the services according to the familiar Ramsey-Boiteux inverse elasticity rule. In the case of telecommunications, modifications are required to account for network externalities and non-zero cross-demand elasticities. Historically, the prime example of such pricing appeared in connection with basic subscription (access) and toll (usage) rates. It was recognized early that low access rates made subscription more attractive, led to an increase in the proportion of households and businesses having telephones, and consequently, increased the demand for telephone usage. Thus, despite low price elasticity in the demand for access, the more profitable and publicly acceptable strategy for the carriers was to keep those rates relatively low so long as the consequent increases in penetration and toll traffic more than offset the losses.

The present situation is more complicated. A large array of interactive telecommunications services can be provided with the networks now in place and the potential is growing. In addition to improved telephone service, new networks services may include voice storage and retrieval, centrex, interactive data-based videotex, telefax, teletex (electronic mail), fast and slow moving pictures services (picture phone), high resolution picture services, general protocol and speed conversion services, and services based on fast and slow packet switching. And, as has been evidenced, both the FCC and the court now see merit in permitting the BOCs to provide at least the broadly defined transmission services on which these are based.

While below-cost rates for access to ordinary voice telephone service are now less easy to justify because of near-universality in service, universality obviously does not extend to enhanced services. Indeed, with respect to most enhanced services, penetration rates are as low as they were for telephone services in the very early years of this century. The multiplicity of possible services and the complexity of the demand interrelationships among them make coordinate pricing strategies even more relevant, however. In the context of modern technology, the demand for one service by the class of customers depends not just on the price of that service, but as well on the menu of available services—that is, the number and type of service providers—and on the number of other subscribers to those services. And as was the case for the telephone years ago, low rates for access may initially be necessary to stimulate demand growth, greater universality, and a broader array of service. Without such pricing, the new services may be available only to large users and then largely through specialized terminal equipment rather than through the network and central office switching equipment [COSE].

Despite Judge Greene's recent liberalization in the permissible enhanced service offerings of the BOCs, the modified MFJ still prevents the patterns of pricing necessary to bring enhanced services to the general public. And this is not oversight: the court explicitly rejects pricing structures that even hint at cross-subsidization. The FCC's *CI-III* requirements are formidable obstacles as well. The unbundled, tariffed offering of each element involved in each enhanced service, with rates based on fully distributed costs, simply obviates the possibility of efficient pricing. Scope economies will necessarily be foregone, and, indeed, the whole purpose of permitting the integrated use of COSE and the network in providing enhanced services will be thwarted. "Competitors" may be benefited, but the public will not be.

Unfortunately, even if the MFJ were further modified and even if the FCC adopted an explicit net revenue test (with revenue sharing) for enhanced services, there would be enormous difficulties in establishing nationwide (or areawide) service systems in the United States. With a unified structure, it is possible to internalize the sharing of costs and revenues among many activities. It is not necessary to set rates and share costs and revenues in ways that assure the profitability of arbitrarily separated components of the system. More specifically, the revenues from local exchange and transport services in each of the many exchange areas need not cover some arbitrary measure of the full costs of the system assigned to those services in those areas. The same thing is true across services as well as across geographic areas.

Given the now fractionalized structure, contractual and regulatory means have to be developed to share costs and revenues among large numbers of participants. This was not easy to do in the former settlements and division of revenues process for plain old telephone service; it appears hopelessly complicated in the new structure with new services. There are the 22 BOCs, 1,500 other local exchange companies, three substantial facilities-based, nationwide interexchange carriers, and an indeterminate and changing number of resale carriers. Literally tens of thousands of information service providers would have to be accommodated, some with only local reach and others with regional, national, and international orientations.

The transactions costs involved in the combined regulation of and contracting among these parties in order to create a nationwide, enhanced service system are probably prohibitive. Even if contracts (within the context of a permissive regulatory system) could be defined, the idiosyncratic nature of some of the investments as well as the number and heterogeneity of the participants would expose the parties to the dangers of post-contractual opportunistic behavior. *Ex ante* commitments for participation would lack full credibility. Free-riding among the interexchange carriers would be possible, particularly in the light of MFJ and other regulatory requirements mandating equal access, CEI and ONA.

The transition to the "information society" in the United States may be a rapid one for a small number of select, high volume users;

it will not be rapid in the putting into place of a nationwide network available to the general public. Indeed, the failure in the United States to recognize the infrastructural importance of a modern telecommunications system, including the need for integrated pricing decisions and nonproprietary standards for ubiquitous user interfacing, may slow progress not only in the use of information itself but also in the other industrial, commercial, and service sectors that will be increasingly dependent on information processing and information flows.

The "procompetitive" telecommunications policies that have developed in the United States during the past two decades will not result in intolerable inefficiencies in plain old telephone service. The big problems will emerge in connection with new telecommunications technologies. If the policies continue to insist and enlarge on competitive solutions, including competitive solutions to problems of standardization, and if the services and pricing policies of local exchange carriers continue to be restricted as they now are, a public network for new services operation on common carrier principles for the benefit of the nation at large will not become available.

Putting AT&T back together again is not the answer. We must, nevertheless, appreciate that proposals for various forms of integrated service offerings may rebound to the public benefit. We need recognize, too, that competition and efficiency are incompatible in many telecommunications services, particularly when the concept of efficiency pays proper attention to the bestowing of benefits to the general public.

VI. Conclusions

At one time there appeared to be a consensus that market failure signaled the need for regulatory response. Some entity— some commission or agency—was seen as a necessary ingredient to correct such situations. That the market itself might effect a cure was largely overlooked.

Recent years have witnessed a reversal from the earlier reliance on regulation. The reversal, it seems, has gone to the extreme that now regulatory needs tend to be ignored. In many instances, markets do work well when governed by no more than antitrust principles and a judicial system that assures the efficiency of private contracting. But sometimes there is a need for regulation.

The right mix of regulation and competition is not easily determined. What works for one industry may not work in another. What works well at one point in time may not work well at another. Thus, when antitrust principles are applied to markets that are—perhaps of necessity—partially regulated, the application must be done with care. The peculiar circumstances that dictate regulatory needs caution against the use of per se rules and heavy reliance on stare decisis.

Good policy decisions turn more on common sense than on the unthinking transference of precedents. Certainly emotional attachments to either free markets or to regulatory processes stand in the way of good policy decisions. The most sagacious of us will err, and it is well that we occasionally acknowledge mistakes and plot new courses.

Part III
Economic Perspective

24
Economic perspective: an introduction

BY WILLIAM J. CURRAN III*

The Sherman Act's 100-year history—a complex, intriguing story of clashing political values and contrasting economic ideals—must be understood if we are to enter the next century with our democracy intact and our economy in the service of our nation's citizens.

Articles collected in this section reflect the ambivalence we all feel in the absence of clear consensus. We share a strong impulse to work toward consensual solutions that will harmonize conflicting ideals and eliminate confusion when values clash. We want policies that consistently produce right results and that alleviate our anxious world's ambivalent choices and possibilities. We may declare democracy our politics of choice, but we actually choose a far different system that makes choices for us through institutions that delimit options *and* opportunities. We must learn to live amid difference and diversity before we can hope to devise policies that will serve us both politically and economically.

Authors assembled here search for single right answers or construct broad syntheses that unite policy with the world in its complexity. The authors who seek final, right answers embrace

---

*Admitted to practice, New York, Pennsylvania, and Nebraska and the editor of The Antitrust Bulletin.

economics and its singular answers, while the others apply history's lessons liberally. The authors—those who read history and those who eschew it for economics—form two camps of old antagonists. Out of this conflict may emerge some new insights for the future in this second century of the Sherman Act.

Most articles collected for this section discuss antitrust's future, as well as explore its history and examine past policy failures. Yet, with the single exception of Professor D. T. Armentano, all authors support the Sherman Act, believe its successes outnumber its failures, and prophesy a strong nation and vibrant economy under antitrust vigilance. Indeed, Armentano would repeal the Sherman Act—for weakening the economy and destroying political liberties—on both economic and legal grounds. Judge Douglas H. Ginsburg, in a rejoinder to Armentano, argues against repeal and against all grounds Armentano treads. Armentano and Ginsburg can find no common fields to till and leave us to plow history's grounds anew for answers to difficult questions.

The Armentano and Ginsburg pieces remind us that the Sherman Act's 100-year history reflects this nation's preference for economic and free enterprise solutions to social problems, but that the nation fears any economic change which might threaten traditional social values. The Sherman Act—as a historical product of values and ideals debated democratically—changed slowly during its first 80 years but changed cataclysmically during the last 20 years, without regard to its social impact. Questions of justice and fairness, once central to antitrust analysis, have been all but eliminated from judicial, prosecutorial, and legislative consideration now that the Sherman Act is in the service of economics. Policy makers' embrace of economics—with the Supreme Court's endorsement and encouragement—has destroyed the long but tenuous balance that had existed between politics and economics; and, in the absence of this fundamental historical accord, there can be no reconciliation of the views that Armentano and Ginsburg represent.

Most other authors in this section share policy views. They would agree that the antitrust goals of increased industrial productivity and efficiency will enhance consumer welfare, that consumer welfare is economically valid, and that a broad consensus supports most current interpretation and enforcement. They would, however, differ on enforcement stratagems necessary to accomplish such goals.

Donald F. Turner, in a remarkable article—the capstone to many years of scholarship and service to the nation—questions some of his own policy decisions, tackles antitrust's most vexing issues, and proposes some basic procedural reforms. He reasons toward solutions that complement prevailing economic wisdom by assuming the liberty-enhancing benefits of efficiency, but he never seriously addresses the political implications of this wisdom. With characteristic lucidity, he never wavers in his rationalistic support of antitrust as the great regulator of the world's greatest economy, while he strains to conceal the historical clash with equity and justice.

Another grand historical traditionalist, Hans Thorelli, together with James M. Patterson, at first surprise with their nouvelle scientific jargon, with their ahistorical and "flexible" Sherman Act views, and with their apparent tolerance for "collective" global market restraints. Ultimately, however, they do succumb to history and attempt its synthesis with science, but—unlike Turner—they do not sacrifice liberties to further their economic vision. They attempt to identify some approximate equality between buyers and sellers in "open markets" and search for an analytical point at which they would interdict collectives that restrain individual economic liberties. They may dress their analysis in modern scientific garb, but they cannot conceal their heartfelt sympathies for justice and equity.

Articles by former Congressman Peter W. Rodino, Jr. and Professor William G. Shepherd assiduously attack the Chicago School underpinnings of current federal enforcement. Shepherd bemoans the dearth of section 2 monopolization actions against large firms' market dominance. He broadly puts forth targets for a federal campaign for enforcers who currently reject section 2 enforcement and attacks their intellectually weak justifications for the economic status quo. He exposes the logical fallacies of the Chicago School, points out that Chicago Schoolers mistake market dominance for efficiency and "success," and, heartened by section 2 enforcement history, recommends action against "relatively few" targets that do not cross a "broad range of U.S. industry." Ironically, a Chicago policy of neglect might well constitute the most responsible and effective approach toward large dominant firms if they are "few" and if one only seeks to achieve—as Shepherd does—their "shrinkage."

Congressman Rodino recognizes economics' political component and would save antitrust for responsible legislative action. That a legislature cannot achieve rational policies does not trouble Rodino, who sees himself as antitrust's trusted guardian against heretical Chicago School enforcers. He finds popular antitrust support for vigorous enforcement, for an open, free-moving economy, and for democratic values and a commitment to free markets. Whether these "democratic values" can be found in our economy plagues antagonists in their arguments over justice and economics, but he leaves such questions for us.

Rodino and Shepherd—as unyielding in their rectitude as Chicago Schoolers—do not find common grounds from which consensus policies might emerge. Antitrust has become a partisan political football—devoid of solid intellectual groundings—to be booted around by whoever occupies the White House and by whatever party dominates Congress. What preoccupies policy makers today is not that they be intellectually correct, but that they maintain unyielding power and control.

Antitrust's political distortion began with World War II, with America's exportation of "values" and continues today with the export of such concepts as deregulation and privatization. These values— purely and culturally Americana—reflect no great intellectual thought, only our need as the world's great nation—with the most profound beliefs in individualism, free enterprise, and minimal government—to affect world events. Other nations, to their credit, have rejected our political views for greater economic justice, while we nonetheless continue trading freely in the world's marketplace of political values without an understanding of history or cultural diversity.

Joel Davidow reviews America's post–World War II exportation of antitrust, as well as the world's circumspect adoption of

American values and ideals. Clearly, America has influenced others; but, as Davidow shows, these views have far less saliency and influence than we might imagine. The world—at least the highly industrialized European nations—might have adopted American policies immediately after the war, but most nations established their own unique judicial institutions and competitive policies in keeping with their histories and their needs in the last half of this century. Davidow maps America's few global export successes; he diplomatically ignores America's failure to influence the world and Third World nations in basic economic equity and justice, and he deftly draws comparisons between American policies and those of other industrialized states that have rejected equity for efficiency.

Certainly, the most important disciples of American ideals are the member nations of the European Community. Professor Valentine Korah does not deny the intellectual discipleship, nor the debt of member nations to America's leadership, but she does show how American values were blended with European perspectives to achieve economic and political institutions unique to these nations. Professor Korah recognizes that a single nation's competitive policies cannot be universal to the world and must reflect a particular nation's needs, historical experiences, and political traditions. She explains how the Community's understanding of efficiency concepts might evolve historically, but it is not always clear from her article whether American views will be heard above rising Western European and United Kingdom voices as they struggle with eastern nations to ease the great financial burden of converting to capitalism.

It is interesting to compare Professor Korah's retelling of Europe's untidy policy developments with Richard Steuer's neat legal formulations. America, unlike the Community, may have wholly absorbed efficiency concepts that dictate how goods and services will be distributed; yet as the law tailors efficiency to fit the risks, uncertainties, and perils facing modern business, it also compromises efficiency's ability to yield predictably competitive solutions to legal disputes. Thus, by tailoring efficiency realistically, the law actually negates predictability and defeats efficiency's greatest strength. Steuer does not despair. He aptly notes the law's resilient growth and adaptation to both commercial realism and efficiency and its rational accommodation of both as principles evolve. The law, as a human enterprise, will reflect complex historical articulations of social needs and aspirations, no matter how economics might struggle scientifically to reduce reality to manageable and objective rearticulations.

We study history's great themes to help illuminate the past and to help us meet the future. Great themes captured the nation 100 years ago, and themes of democracy and economics occupy a larger world today. How the world responds will change how we view justice and how we feel about democracy. Economics may fast-freeze us in current time, but the Sherman Act will thaw before the fires that fan global change.

Authors in this section extol antitrust values and virtues; but, writing in the present from the past, they see societal change through 19th-century history and science while ignoring the future's promise. We must leave the past's powerful grip and prepare to emerge this century into the light and fire of the next—freed of old divisions and antagonisms, imbued with democracy's liberating possibilities—to face diversity and to formulate policies tolerant of these new social forces. From past conflict emerges the insight that policies must expand to account for the differences that we will all face in a world rapidly growing diverse in its attitudes and approaches to life and to law.

25
Time to repeal antitrust regulation?

BY D. T. ARMENTANO*

Antitrust regulation has enjoyed a widespread popular and intellectual support throughout most of its history. The general reason for that support is not difficult to discern. Antitrust law appears to be a straightforward public-interest attempt to promote business competition and control the abuses familiarly associated with monopoly power. "Competition" implies economic efficiency, growth, and industrial fairness. "Monopoly" implies economic inefficiency, restricted innovation, and the power of the few over the many. A law that intends to promote business competition and restrain monopoly power would appear to make intelligent sense from a public-interest perspective.

Since at least 1974, however, various antitrust theories and policies have come under sustained criticism.[1] An increasing number of theoretical and empirical studies have now appeared that have been severely critical of "traditional" antitrust policy.[2] Some analysts have even questioned the legitimacy of the alleged

---

*   Professor of Economics, University of Hartford.

[1]   INDUSTRIAL CONCENTRATION: THE NEW LEARNING (H. Goldschmid, H. M. Mann & J. F. Weston, eds. (1974).

[2]   The most influential critical study was R. BORK, THE ANTITRUST PARADOX: A POLICY AT WAR WITH ITSELF (1978). *See also* Y. BROZEN, CONCENTRATION, MERGERS, AND PUBLIC POLICY (1982).

public-interest origins of the Sherman Act.[3] The general thrust of the critical literature (the new learning) is that much of the traditional antitrust enforcement effort (*i.e.*, restricting mergers to prevent concentration) has been misguided, and has likely hampered both industrial efficiency and consumer welfare. This (revisionist) view still appears to be a minority position among academic economists.[4] Yet it was persuasive enough with policy makers to have contributed to a modest shift in the administration of the federal antitrust laws in the 1980's.

Antitrust policy in the 1980's

Federal antitrust enforcement in the 1980's was far more relaxed than in previous periods. The traditional antitrust concern over the growth of big companies and over industrial concentration was reduced. Business arrangements whose sole probable effect was to expand market output (regardless of the effect on particular competitors) were excluded generally from antitrust scrutiny. Conglomerate and vertical mergers, and even many horizontal consolidations (within certain liberalized merger guidelines) were permitted without objection. Price discrimination cases were abandoned and vertical nonprice agreements were seen by many analysts as promoting market efficiency. Finally, the antitrust authorities—especially the Federal Trade Commission—began a modest challenge of various state and local regulations and ordinances (taxicab and cable TV licensing) that represented *legal* barriers to entry and competition.[5]

These changes in the administration of the antitrust laws, however, have not led to any *general* abandonment of the antitrust mission. Many business mergers and tying agreements

---

3   DiLorenzo, *The Origins of Antitrust: An Interest-Group Perspective*, 5 INTERNATIONAL REV. L. & ECON. 73-90 (1985).

4   Economists still overwhelmingly appear to support traditional antitrust notions. *See* Kearl, Pope, Whiting & Wimmer, *A Confusion of Economists?* 69 AMER. ECON. REV., PAPER & PROC. May 1979, at 30.

5   *See* Muris, *Antitrust and the FTC*, 6 CATO POLICY REP., Sept./ Oct. 1984, at 18-19.

are still regulated by the antitrust authorities under a rule of reason approach. Horizontal price agreements and resale price maintenance remain illegal per se. Various cooperative agreements (*i.e.*, joint ventures) between domestic and foreign companies still remain under close antitrust scrutiny. So-called predatory practices—both price and nonprice—remain illegal, while both private antitrust litigation (which constitutes more than 90% of all antitrust litigation) and state antitrust regulation remain active. No substantive section of the antitrust laws—even including the blatantly anticonsumer Robinson-Patman Act of 1936—has been repealed or even reformed, and the Reagan administration's 1986 legislative attempt to reform the Clayton Act went nowhere with the Congress.[6] In short, antitrust still remains a very important regulatory paradigm with strong political and intellectual support. This will likely continue into the 1990's.

An important reason for the survival of the antitrust paradigm is that both the important critics *and* the supporters of traditional antitrust regulation still believe that some antitrust regulation is necessary to preserve competition and prevent socially harmful restraints of trade.[7] Both groups agree that it is both legitimate and necessary to regulate large horizontal mergers and most interfirm price agreements. In addition, both the antitrust critics and the traditionalists share the same welfare standard and the same economic theory of monopoly power.[8] The traditionalists would certainly go farther in their employment of antitrust regulation. Yet neither group supports the entire abandonment of public and private antitrust policy.

---

[6] For a discussion of the Reagan antitrust proposals see Washington Post, Jan. 19, 1986, at H1, 4 and Washington Post, Feb. 20, 1986, at E1. Major portions of that proposal stalled in the Congress. *See* THE ECONOMIST, Aug. 23, 1986, at 25.

[7] *For example, see*, R. BORK, *supra* note 2. *See, also*, Easterbrook, *The Limits of Antitrust*, 63 TEX. L. REV. 1-40 (1984).

[8] *See, for example*, Liebeler's discussion of monopoly power in *Intrabrand Cartels under GTE Sylvania*, 30 UCLA L. REV. 13-17 (1982).

There are two general reasons to prefer that all antitrust regulation be repealed rather than additionally reformed. The first reason is strategic. The recent administrative reforms may only be temporary and they could be undone by different administrators (and judges) with different antitrust philosophies. The second reason is more fundamental. It will be argued below that the theoretical and practical case against antitrust regulation is now substantial enough to rationalize complete repeal.

The case for repeal

The case for antitrust repeal can be summarized: First, traditional enforcement of the antitrust laws is based on *equilibrium* theories of competition and monopoly, and such theories are simply irrelevant for policy purposes.[9] Business competition is a dynamic discovery process and a firm's market share is an indication of its relative efficiency and not of its market power or of any resource misallocation. Resource-misallocating monopoly, by contrast, can be associated with *legal* restraints on business competition or cooperation. All such legal restraints should be repealed.

Second, the nonlegal "barriers to entry" literature in industrial organization is hopelessly confused and the bulk of it must be ignored for antitrust purposes. Most of these traditional barriers represent specific efficiencies (scale economies, technological advantages, good will) that some business organizations have earned in open-market competition with other firms. Such earned efficiencies are not harmful to consumers (on the contrary they are advantages *for* consumers), do not misallocate economic resources, and should not be of concern to the antitrust authorities.

Third, the actual history of both public and private antitrust enforcement is replete with cases brought against business organizations that were engaged in an intensely competitive market process. The indicted firms were often expanding production,

---

[9]   D. T. ARMENTANO, ANTITRUST POLICY: THE CASE FOR REPEAL (1986).

lowering costs and prices, and engaging in rapid technological development. Yet antitrust, both public and private, has been employed repeatedly against such firms; the overall effect has been to stifle and restrict the competitive process. Antitrust regulation, like tariffs, has been protectionist of the existing market structure of business organizations, and that is the ultimate irony (and cost) of traditional antitrust enforcement.[10]

Fourth, the continuing antitrust regulation of mergers and the flat prohibition of interfirm price agreements assumes that the antitrust regulators can discover and evaluate the social costs and benefits associated with such activity. But such utilitarian, cost-benefit calculations are impossible since the data cannot be known to outside observers or aggregated across different individuals or firms. Antitrust regulation of mergers and other interfirm agreements is an example of government planning and social engineering, and is fully subject to the "pretense of knowledge" criticism that has frequently been made of other government regulatory policies.[11]

Finally, efficiency considerations aside, antitrust regulation violates the natural rights of property owners (or their trustees) to make decisions concerning the peaceful use of their own property. Such laws, as Adam Smith remarked, cannot be made "consistent with liberty and justice."[12]

Competition and equilibrium

Antitrust regulation assumes that monopoly power can misallocate economic resources and reduce social welfare. This allocative inefficiency is caused by a reduction in market output and an

---

[10] McChesney, *Law's Honour Lost: The Plight of Antitrust*, 31 ANTITRUST BULL. 359-83 (1986). *See also*, Baumol & Ordover, *Use of Antitrust to Subvert Competition*, 28 J. L. & ECON. 247 (1985).

[11] D. LAVOIE, NATIONAL ECONOMIC PLANNING: WHAT IS LEFT? (1985).

[12] A. SMITH, THE WEALTH OF NATIONS 128 (Modern Library ed. 1937).

increase in market price due, say, to business collusion or merger. It is this precise behavior, antitrust supporters assert, that ought to be the primary focus of any "rational" antitrust policy.

Yet there are important difficulties with this simple theory of output restriction and resource misallocation. For instance, what is the precise state of the market prior to the exercise of monopoly power? It is traditional in microeconomics to assume that monopoly power spoils some competitive equilibrium where market price and marginal cost are *already* equal. But why assume that the market process has already reached an equilibrium? In a dynamic business world this static assumption would appear completely unwarranted. Yet, it is a necessary assumption in order to conclude that a restraint of trade misallocates anything, or that antitrust regulation can improve allocative efficiency.

The dependence of antitrust policy on static equilibrium assumptions can be illustrated by reference to the figure. The standard approach in microeconomic theory is to assume that a competitive equilibrium already exists at Q_2 and that the exercise of monopoly power restricts output to Q_1. The monopolist is said to have "driven a wedge" between price and marginal cost and some allocative inefficiency (the welfare-loss triangle ABC) is evident.[13] Yet, if the initial market situation is some *disequilibrium* output level such as Q_3, a voluntary restriction of market output to Q_2 need not generate (any) allocative inefficiency. On the contrary, such a restriction in supply could improve allocative efficiency since it would tend to narrow the gap between marginal cost and market price (P_3). Indeed, any antitrust interference with this restraint of trade would, itself, be socially inefficient under strict neoclassical assumptions. Thus, the orthodox antitrust policy conclusion, *i.e.*, that restraints of trade misallocate resources, appears ambiguous in the absence of information concerning a preexisting competitive equilibrium.

---

[13]   This is the standard analysis in microeconomics. See any microeconomics text, or *see* H. R. VARIAN, INTERMEDIATE MICROECONOMICS: A MODERN APPROACH 420–24 (1987).

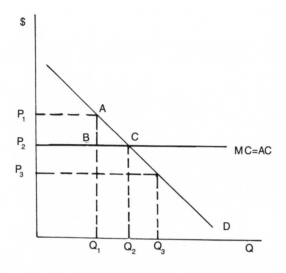

Figure

The competitive market process and efficiency

Many of the theoretical problems associated with antitrust policy stem directly from the assumption that competition is an *equilibrium* condition where all relevant market information is already known and constant. *If* market competition were an end-state equilibrium condition, then any reduction in output could be socially inefficient and the antitrust mission might be relatively unambiguous. (It would still be ambiguous since countervailing efficiencies associated with any output restriction would have to be taken into account.) But actual business competition is a dynamic discovery process under conditions of uncertainty; it is not a static state-of-affairs.[14] During that process, business organ-

---

[14] F. A. HAYEK, INDIVIDUALISM AND ECONOMIC ORDER 92–106 (1972). On the development of the historical distinction between the competitive

izations are continually attempting to discover and adapt to market information concerning costs and prices, information that equilibrium theory assumes market participants already have. This disequilibrium discovery process can involve increases or decreases in market output (as we have already shown). It can involve product differentiation (since consumer tastes are differentiated), advertising (since market information is not perfect), and the failure of specific rivals—activities that are always "inefficient" from a strict competitive equilibrium perspective. It can encompass interfirm cooperation as well as interfirm rivalry. All of these activities are part and parcel of a disequilibrium process in which firms attempt to discover and exploit uncertain opportunities for profit at the lowest cost.

The recognition that competition is a discovery process under conditions of uncertainty appears to create important difficulties for the traditional antitrust perspective. The traditional theory of competition as an end-state equilibrium assumes the existence of zero transactions costs, perfect knowledge, and constant preferences; unsurprisingly, it concludes that output restrictions can lower social welfare and justify some antitrust intervention.[15] But since the actual competitive process always occurs in the context of positive transactions costs, imperfect information, and changing preferences, it is not obvious why any static equilibrium condition should serve as the relevant efficiency (or welfare) standard. Indeed, since the equilibrium condition is irrelevant to the problem that must be solved by the competitive process, *i.e.*, the *discovery* of market information and the *adjustment* to market uncertainty, it ought not to serve as the relevant efficiency benchmark. (A more relevant benchmark would be an institutional setting that maximized the opportunity for generating, disseminating, and using information.) Without that specific benchmark, output restrictions—even if successful—would not necessarily lower social welfare (even assuming for the sake of argument that "social" welfare could be measured) and the role of antitrust regulation would become extremely ambiguous.

---

process and the competitive *equilibrium*, *see* McNulty, *Economic Theory and the Meaning of Competition*, 82 Q. J. ECON. 639-56 (1968).

[15]   J. HIRSHLEIFER, PRICE THEORY AND APPLICATIONS (2d ed. 1980).

Monopoly and equilibrium

Unwarranted equilibrium assumptions also create difficulties for the traditional economic analysis of "monopoly power." Let us assume for the moment that the actual market output *is* at Q_2 in the figure, and that monopoly power (created through merger or collusion) does cause market output to be restricted and market price to be increased from P_2 to P_1. Clearly this situation is imaginable; just as clearly, however, it is *not* a true equilibrium condition. With market price now above cost (with normal returns treated as a cost), it would appear that there are strong incentives for entrepreneurs to attempt to expand market output. The normal market process, in short, would continuously work to exploit these potentially profitable opportunities, and this process would work (other things remaining the same) to elimi- nate any allocative inefficiency.

Importantly, this entrepreneurial process of discovery and adjustment is exactly the same one that occurs in any competitive disequilibrium, a disequilibrium that might arise due, say, to changes in consumer demand or factor costs. Indeed, a competi- tive disequilibrium (with market price above cost) is theoretically indistinguishable from the alleged "monopoly power" situation assumed here. In a free market there is no unique monopoly power or price; there are only prices that are higher (or lower) than some theoretical equilibrium price. Thus, the alleged ineffi- ciency under "monopoly" is thoroughly contrived out of unwar- ranted equilibrium assumptions. Again, the role of any rational antitrust policy becomes completely ambiguous.

Let us assume, for instance, that there exists an industrial market with no legal barriers to entry. Business organizations will enter that market and prosper if they can produce products and services and allocate resources in an efficient manner. The firms that grow and accumulate market share will have earned their market positions through exceptional long-run performance, and advancing that market position will depend upon a continuously exceptional performance. Market share and market position (at any moment in time) will be (objective) evidence of a firm's (subjective) relative efficiency.

On the other hand, firms that misallocate resources (from a consumer perspective) will tend to lose market position relative to more efficient business organizations. Firms with relatively higher costs, restricted outputs, higher prices, poor quality products, repressed innovation, and generally restrictive practices, will experience lower profits and will lose market share to relatively more efficient rivals.[16]

What beneficial role can antitrust regulation play in this discovery and adjustment process? To employ antitrust against the successful firms would clearly be anticonsumer and destructive of incentives and of industrial efficiency. Yet to employ antitrust against the firms that perform poorly would be unnecessary since strong economic incentives exist for such firms to change their behavior, or, given failure, for the market process to reallocate resources away from such organizations. Thus, any regulatory antitrust would be either harmful, premature, or redundant. In the absence of an intelligent theory of how the equilibrating process might be continually subverted (in open markets), the justification for traditional antitrust regulation appears to evaporate entirely.

Barriers to entry

In an effort to salvage traditional antitrust enforcement, it has been argued that nonlegal barriers to entry protect business organizations with monopoly power from the competitive process. On analysis, however, much of the barriers to entry doctrine simply self-destructs. Most of the so-called barriers turn out to be economic advantages and efficiencies that leading business organizations earn in the marketplace.[17] For instance, certain large

---

[16]   Demsetz, *Industry Structure, Market Rivalry, and Public Policy*, 16 J. L. & ECON. 1–70 (1973).

[17]   *See* R. BORK, *supra* note 2, at chap. 16. Also see Demsetz, *Barriers to Entry*, 72 AMER. ECON. REV. 47–57 (1982).

firms enjoy economies of scope and scale that often permit low-cost production, distribution and sale. Certain firms enjoy an excellent reputation for high-quality products and service built up over many decades. Certain firms successfully differentiate their product, successfully advertise their product, and successfully engage in research and development to keep a continuous flow of products available to accommodate the ever-changing tastes of consumers.

From a competitor's perspective, all of these business achievements would represent economic "barriers" that unfairly serve to "limit competition." It should be obvious, however, that from the relevant consumer perspective, these barriers represent economic values and advantages that consumers willingly support and sustain. To attack these advantages with antitrust policy would be to attack the very virtues that the competitive market process serves to discover and perpetuate. Thus, the (nonlegal) barriers-to-entry discussion (and the more recent nonprice predation discussions) represent the final bankruptcy of conventional antitrust theory.

There may be some justification for the use of antitrust policy against strictly *legal* barriers to entry created by state and local government. Legal barriers cannot be legitimized by a competitive market process in which lower costs, improvements in technology, and better products restrain the entry of less efficient suppliers. Indeed, legal barriers are often employed to protect existing business organizations from newer, low-cost suppliers with a more efficient technology. Legal barriers to entry can prevent entrepreneurs from exploiting profit opportunities generated by the market process itself. Thus, there is little question that the economic system is made less efficient by this exercise of governmental power.

Some analysts are sympathetic to the use of antitrust against legal barriers.[18] Several caveats are in order, however. First, this is the *only* use of antitrust that can be justified. Second, the

---

[18] Armentano, *Towards a Rational Antitrust Policy*, in *Hearings Before the Joint Economic Committee, Antitrust Policy and Competition* 23–33 (1984).

possible dangers from antitrust abuse—*i.e.*, attacking purely voluntary cooperative agreements rather than strictly legal restrictions—may overwhelm the marginal benefits associated with prosecuting legal monopoly. Third, most legal monopoly at the state and local level is already immune from antitrust attack under the so-called state action and *Parker* doctrines.[19] Given these legal difficulties, it would appear more realistic to work to repeal both antitrust regulation and all other legal restrictions on competition or cooperation.

Do dominant firms restrain trade?

The alleged public interest purpose of antitrust regulation is the prevention of socially inefficient restraints of trade. Trade is restrained whenever firms with monopoly power reduce market output and raise market price. If antitrust is to promote the public "welfare," it must be employed to thwart such behavior.

Yet much of the actual history of antitrust enforcement—both public and private—is sharply at odds with this alleged social purpose. Many of the business organizations that have been indicted and convicted under the laws were *not* restraining market output. Indeed, a reasonable inference would be that they were attempting to *expand* market output, and that they were frequently engaged in an intensely competitive market process.[20] Indeed, it was this precise competitive behavior (and not any sort of monopolization) that likely precipitated the antitrust legal action against them. In many landmark antitrust cases, therefore, it was the antitrust laws themselves that served to restrain trade.

In the *Standard Oil* case,[21] market outputs for kerosene expanded enormously throughout much of the late 19th century and prices for kerosene declined substantially. The price of

---

[19]   Parker v. Brown, 317 U.S. 341 (1945).

[20]   D. T. ARMENTANO, ANTITRUST AND MONOPOLY: ANATOMY OF A POLICY FAILURE (2d ed. 1990).

[21]   Standard Oil Company of New Jersey v. U.S., 221 U.S. 1 (1911).

kerosene decreased from 30 cents a gallon in 1869, to 9 cents in 1880, and to 7.4 cents in 1890. The average price of kerosene (at retail) in 1897 was approximately 6 cents per gallon.

The price and output scenario is similar in the *American Tobacco* case.[22] The district court had noted that tobacco outputs had expanded greatly between 1890 (when the American Tobacco Company was formed) and 1907 (when American Tobacco was indicted for illegal monopolization).[23] A few tobacco product prices did increase during the period, but the price of cigarettes and little cigars were both substantially lower in 1907 than they had been in the 1890's. Moreover, these price reductions were accomplished during a period in which the basic input, leaf tobacco, had become increasingly expensive.

In neither of these classic antitrust cases was the leading firm able to erect inefficient barriers to competition, nor was it able to "monopolize" any trade. There were at least 147 independent oil refiners in the U.S. petroleum market in 1911, prior to the legal divestiture of the Standard Oil company.[24] And in the tobacco industry, despite the many mergers (over 250) of the American Tobacco company, there were many *thousands* of rival tobacco firms (cigars, smoking tobacco, snuff, cigarettes) offering wide product choices to consumers.[25] In the absence of legal barriers to entry, the competitive market process flourished in both industries.

It could not be reasonably maintained in *Alcoa* that the company had restrained trade by attempting to reduce market output and raise market price.[26] Aluminum ingot prices declined from $5.00 per pound in 1887 to 38 cents per pound in 1910 to 22

---

[22]   U.S. v. American Tobacco Company, 221 U.S. 106 (1911).

[23]   U.S. v. American Tobacco Company, 164 F. 700 (D.C. 1908), esp. 712 and 726.

[24]   D. T. ARMENTANO, *supra* note 20, at 67.

[25]   *Id.* at 89.

[26]   U.S. v. Aluminum Company of America, 148 F.2d 416 (2d Cir. 1945).

cents per pound in 1937, the year Alcoa was indicted for illegal monopolization. The Alcoa company produced and sold approximately 500 million pounds of aluminum ingot in 1937. Indeed, the appeals court (1945) complained, revealingly, not about any restraint of production but about the fact that Alcoa had efficiently "doubled and redoubled" its productive capacity to meet any new market demand that might arise for its product.[27]

The explicit attack on industrial efficiency and expanded outputs—and not on any restraint of trade—is even more obvious in the private antitrust cases. Here there is little pretense that it is the "public interest" that is being served or that output restraint is the concern. In these cases the plaintiff is usually a disgruntled rival who is unhappy with the particular outcome of an open-market competitive process, a process that frequently generates new products for consumers and additional market outputs.[28] In *Berkey* for instance, reversed on appeal in 1979,[29] the plaintiff (Berkey) argued that the successful innovation of Kodak's new Instamatic camera (and film) was unanticipated, and thus hindered unfairly the plaintiff's ability to compete. Ignored throughout the lower court decision was the fact that the Instamatic camera expanded the market enormously, and that Kodak's camera-film innovation was made successful only by the willing choices of consumers. Thus, it was the open-market competitive process itself that had tended to exclude less innovative rivals such as Berkey, and antitrust regulation was employed in an attempt to thwart and hinder that market process.

Given our earlier theoretical discussion, it is easy to understand why antitrust regulation is frequently employed in such a perverse manner. The traditional structure-conduct-performance perspective in industrial organization tends to associate "compe-

---

[27] U.S. v. Aluminum Company of America, 148 F.2d at 430–32.

[28] *See* F. M. FISHER, J. W. MCKIE & R. B. MANKE, IBM AND THE DATA PROCESSING INDUSTRY: AN ECONOMIC HISTORY, esp. 448–49 (1983).

[29] Berkey Photo Inc. v. Eastman Kodak Co., 603 F.2d 263 (2d Cir. 1979), *cert. denied*, 444 U.S. 1093 (1980).

tition'' with the purely competitive equilibrium condition. That particular condition, as we have noted, is continuously threatened by changing tastes and preferences, and by business organizations that are relatively more efficient than their rivals. Such firms innovate, and advertise, and differentiate their products, and tend to gain market share as a direct consequence of their market performance. During this competitive process, old market structures change and new market structures emerge to reflect the changing relative performance of these firms. Yet this entire equilibrating process is inconsistent with the strict competitive equilibrium condition. Thus, in the name of preserving "competition," *i.e.*, the equilibrium condition, antitrust regulation is often employed, perversely, in an attempt to restrict the equilibrating process itself. Poor theorizing leads, inevitably, to poor policy.

Horizontal agreements

The most important remaining area of strict antitrust enforcement is horizontal business agreements. The traditional position on nonprice horizontal agreements is that they should be permitted when their probable social benefits exceed their probable social costs. The social benefits would include economies of scope and scale in production, advertising, financing, and transportation, as well as specific economies associated with joint research and development. The social costs associated with horizontal agreements would relate to the probability that the agreement might restrict market output and raise market price. Under this approach, small horizontal mergers, for example, would be allowed since there would be little threat of any increased market power; larger mergers and joint ventures, however, would be regulated on a case-by-case basis and some would be prohibited.

Interfirm price agreements are treated even more severely than mergers and joint ventures. According to the traditional perspective, price fixing should be illegal per se since it intends only to restrict output and raise prices. Since there is no "integration" of productive facilities in a "naked" price agreement, there is likely to be little, if any, offsetting social benefit associated with such an agreement. Thus, price agreements between firms can be flatly prohibited.

These positions are now open to debate. The most general criticism is that it is unclear how antitrust regulators (or courts) can rationally calculate the probable social advantages and costs associated with proposed agreements that have not yet taken place. The fundamental problem here is to explain how outside observers (regulators, economists, judges) can have access to economic information (concerning costs and benefits) that can only be known to the market participants themselves.[30] In the absence of any general equilibrium condition, opportunity costs and utility are fundamentally subjective notions; they don't lend themselves to interpersonal aggregation and comparison. And since regulators (or courts) cannot have such knowledge or do such calculations, it is unclear how any rule of reason or per se prohibition is to be scientifically defended.

There are at least three perspectives that might be employed to defend the per se *legality* of horizontal interfirm agreements. The first is that if these agreements are truly harmful to consumers, there will be strong economic incentives for specific firms to break the agreements and restore competitive rivalry. Historically, it would appear that inefficient price agreements (unenforceable in the courts) tend to break apart and generally prove unworkable in the long-run.[31] Antitrust is unnecessary to dissolve inefficient agreements that would tend to dissolve naturally.

A second position on interfirm price agreements is that there may be significant efficiencies and economies associated with them. (Importantly, these efficiencies may be easier to realize through contract than through merger since contracts provide more flexibility and selectivity with less risk than complete merger.) Interfirm price agreements may reduce uncertainty and

---

[30]   J. M. Buchanan, *Introduction: L.S.E. Cost Theory in Retrospect*, in L.S.E. ESSAYS ON COST 14–15 (J. M. Buchanan & G. F. Thirlby eds. 1981).

[31]   For a general discussion of the unworkability of implicit and explicit collusion, see Y. BROZEN, *supra* note 3, at chap. 6.

transactions costs, and this may lead to an increase in long-run market output.[32] Market-division agreements between firms may end wasteful cross-hauling and advertising. The employment of rate bureaus in the trucking industry may reduce information and transactions costs for motor carriers that employ their services.[33] Cooperative interfirm agreements and joint ventures on research and development may lower innovation costs and improve overall efficiency. Since the antitrust regulators cannot know beforehand which interfirm agreements *will* actually reduce costs—that information is only discovered during the cooperative process itself— and since they cannot "total up" aggregate cost and benefits for comparison, any antitrust regulation of interfirm agreements is without sufficient scientific foundation.

Antitrust and liberty

A final reason for permitting horizontal interfirm agreements was outlined briefly by Adam Smith in *The Wealth of Nations* more than 200 years ago. Smith was confident that businessmen often gathered to fix prices and conspire against the public, but he was insistent that no law "consistent with liberty and justice" could prohibit such activity.[34] The fact remains that antitrust law prohibits voluntary agreements that do not *in themselves* involve a violation of anyone else's rights. Within a natural rights framework, for instance, owners of property (or their trustees) have the absolute right to make any contract or agreement for the exchange of that property on any terms mutually acceptable. Price fixing, tying agreements, and price discrimination—though unpopular—are all voluntary arrangements, and don't involve

---

[32] Dewey, *Information, Entry and Welfare: The Case for Collusion*, 69 AMER. ECON. REV. 587–94 (1979).

[33] *See, for example,* J. A. Hausman, Information Costs, Competition, and Collective Rate Making in the Motor Carrier Industry (paper prepared for the Motor Carrier Ratemaking Study Commission, August 16, 1986).

[34] A. SMITH, *supra* note 12, at 128.

any violation of rights from this perspective.[35] Indeed, the anti-trust laws themselves must violate rights since they directly interfere with the liberty of property owners to make certain voluntary agreements or contracts.

In addition, antitrust law has proven unusually vague and fluid in practice, and its arbitrary enforcement over the years has consistently violated strict principles of due process of law.[36] What, for instance, does it mean to "reduce competition substantially"? What are "reasonable" and "unreasonable" restraints of trade, apart from what any court has said in any particular case? Can anyone know the "relevant market" in any antitrust legal action *prior to* the initiation of said legal action? Can prices that are high, low, and equal all be illegal under the antitrust laws? Most students of antitrust enforcement—especially the enforcement of the Robinson-Patman Act—will agree that antitrust has been a civil liberties and due-process nightmare. Adam Smith's insight into the dangers to individual liberty inherent in such a law have proved to be sadly prophetic.

Conclusions

The economic and normative case for free markets without any antitrust regulation grows stronger. Since the laws inevitably interfere with the discovery and dissemination of market information, they must tend to make the competitive market process less efficient. And since the laws inevitably interfere with individual property rights and voluntary exchange, they must restrict liberty and freedom. In short, antitrust regulation appears to have lost all of its claim to political legitimacy. In a rapidly changing information and technological world, with an inevitable internationalization of markets, the burden of proof is clearly now on those who would retain the law to demonstrate why all antitrust regulation should not be abolished.

---

[35] Pilon, *Corporations and Rights: On Treating Corporate People Justly*, 13 GA. L. REV. 1245–1370 (1979).

[36] This has been most obvious in Federal Trade Commission enforcement of the Robinson-Patman Act. *See* D. T. ARMENTANO, *supra* note 20, at chap. 6.

26
Rationalizing antitrust: a rejoinder to Professor Armentano

BY DOUGLAS H. GINSBURG*

In his case for repeal of the antitrust laws, Professor Armentano[1] launches a sweeping attack both on historical patterns of antitrust enforcement and on the power of microeconomics as a guide for current policy makers. Though I largely agree with Armentano's critique of historical experience, I am more sanguine than he is about current antitrust policy and about whether it can and should be preserved. I discuss, in turn, the two fundamental propositions of Armentano's argument: first, that the economic case for repeal is compelling and, second, that repeal is necessary to prevent a return to the misguided antitrust enforcement policies that have characterized much of the century since passage of the Sherman Act.

---

* Judge, United States Court of Appeals for the District of Columbia Circuit; Assistant Attorney General, Antitrust Division, United States Department of Justice, 1985–86.

[1] Armentano, *Time to Repeal Antitrust Regulation?* 35 ANTITRUST BULL. 311 (1990) [hereinafter Armentano].

I. Equilibrium theories

Armentano observes that in order to conclude with scientific rigor that a particular restraint of trade will produce an inefficient allocation of resources, antitrust regulators must make the assumption that the exercise of market power "spoils some purely competitive equilibrium where market price and marginal cost are *already* equal."[2] He then attacks that assumption on the ground that competition is not an end-state equilibrium but, instead, "a dynamic discovery process."[3] Although Armentano does not acknowledge it, his critique is, at bottom, a restatement of the theory of the second-best: Because not all resources are allocated efficiently *ex ante*, one cannot determine whether a particular reallocation will enhance or reduce efficiency *ex post*. This criticism of antitrust law proves far too much, however, as it would render untenable all economic regulation.

Antitrust regulation carries no less justification (Armentano might say "and no more") than many other government actions designed to make markets more efficient. Consider a classic case for government intervention: suppression of a market externality, such as air pollution. It is by now familiar wisdom that:

> The key to achieving the social optimum where there are externalities is to induce private profit-maximizers to restrict their output to the socially optimal, not privately optimal, point. This is done by policies that cause the firm to operate along the social marginal cost curve rather than along the private marginal cost curve. When this is accomplished, the externality is said to have been "internalized" in the sense that the private firm now takes it into consideration.[4]

Were policy makers to insist upon the level of certainty demanded by Armentano concerning the effects of regulatory intervention, the result would always be inaction. Although one can never guarantee that the secondary effects of a particular action will not produce unforeseen consequences such that regulation will be

---

2   *Id.* at 316. (Emphasis in original.)

3   *Id.* at 314.

4   R. Cooter & T. Ulen, Law and Economics 46 (1988).

inefficient in a global sense, one still may exercise an informed guess concerning the local effects of government intervention. For instance, one can say with confidence that measures compelling producers to internalize the social costs of their activities will reduce a significant impediment to the operation of accurate price signals in the market, wholly apart from any other consequences that such measures might have. To insist, more broadly, upon a defense of the global effects of such actions, as does Armentano, is to posit a test that few, if any, public policies could pass.

Like the case for regulation of air pollution, the core case for antitrust regulation rests upon the control of an externality; in antitrust, the externality is the exercise of market power by which a producer—or a group of producers—may increase price and reduce quantity, resulting in a transfer of wealth from consumers to producers as well as a deadweight loss to society. There are two basic methods by which firms may acquire market power: mergers and collusion.[5] A merger involves an integration of corporate structure such that the merged firm will be able to control price and quantity decisions in the relevant market. Collusion produces the same result through cooperation rather than common corporate control. While one must carefully distinguish the analysis of mergers from that of collusion, the common origin of our concern with both practices lies in the observation that each involves the generation of an externality, and is thus fundamentally indistinguishable from air pollution and similar regulatory problems.

---

[5] There is considerable doubt about whether vertical restraints can facilitate a significant exercise of market power. *See generally* DEPARTMENT OF JUSTICE, GUIDELINES FOR VERTICAL RESTRAINTS (1985). Resale price maintenance and various types of selective distribution arrangements may so rarely be inimical to consumer interests, and the risk of Type I diagnostic error may be so great, that regulators should rely upon the self-correcting force of market entry. *See* Posner, *The Next Step in the Antitrust Treatment of Restrictive Distribution: Per Se Legality*, 48 U. CHI. L. REV. 6 (1981). In any event, one could hardly justify pursuit of vertical restraint cases if one could not answer Armentano's attack on the regulation of the core antitrust cases involving horizontal mergers and collusion, which is the burden of this essay.

The justification for control of externalities also renders problematic Armentano's later statement that, "[w]ithin a natural rights framework, . . . owners of property . . . have the absolute right to make any contract[s] . . . on any terms mutually acceptable."[6] Although Armentano correctly observes that, as between the parties who voluntarily enter into such arrangements, neither mergers nor collusion "involve any violation of rights,"[7] he ignores the impact of such actions on third-party consumers; therein lies the externality. The reduction in quantity and increase in price occasioned by such agreements will have two effects: first, marginal consumers will no longer purchase products that they would otherwise buy in a competitive market; second, inframarginal consumers will have to submit to a transfer of wealth, in the form of supracompetitive prices paid to producers. Such involuntary impositions upon third parties are consistent with a "natural rights framework" only if that framework is so specified. In another observer's regime of natural rights, however, consumers may be entitled to a "fair price" for the goods they need.[8]

Apart from these broader issues, Armentano's own example does not support his criticism of "the standard approach in microeconomic theory." He correctly posits that "if the initial market situation is some *disequilibrium* output level such as Q_3 [in his figure], a voluntary restriction of market output to Q_2 . . . could improve allocative efficiency since it would tend to narrow the gap between marginal cost and market price P_3."[9] Though not entirely clear, Armentano's example appears to contemplate a reduction in quantity resulting from an agreement among producers in an otherwise competitive market.

First, the premise of this illustration seems inconsistent with Armentano's assumption of dynamic competition, since disequi-

---

6   Armentano at 327.

7   *Id.* at 327–28.

8   *See, e.g.*, J. MARITAIN, RIGHTS OF MAN AND NATURAL LAW 113 (1971).

9   Armentano at 316. (Emphasis in original.)

librium does not persist for any significant time in such a market. Second, it is extremely unlikely that a consortium of producers in a dynamically competitive market would ever know where the equilibrium quantity, Q_2, lies at any moment; only by making independent, atomistic adjustments of price and quantity in response to dynamic market conditions can the market as a whole even approximate the efficient level of output. Third, and most important, Armentano neglects to note that a legal regime that would permit an agreement among producers to move from Q_3 to Q_2 would, in addition, have to accept an agreement to move from Q_2 to Q_1—by definition, an inefficient allocation. Any attempt to limit such agreements to the efficient Q_2 level would founder for want of centralized knowledge of where that point lies.

Armentano appears to have reached his peculiar conclusion by taking literally the concepts of equilibrium price and quantity underlying the microeconomic model, to the exclusion of any other consideration. He forgets that the model is merely a simplifying abstraction, which must be supplemented if it is to be applied usefully to real world markets. For example, the equilibrium model assumes perfect knowledge, but Armentano makes no suggestion—nor would any antitrust policy maker—that the market operates with such omniscience. If one took literally the model's assumptions of perfect knowledge and zero transactions costs, then regulation of mergers and of collusion would indeed be superfluous; potential competitors would have perfect awareness of profit opportunities and could costlessly enter the market to drive price down to marginal cost.

II. Monopolization and market entry

The possibility of market entry often makes it possible for antitrust regulators to countenance a merger between firms with high market shares; if their postmerger exercise of market power would attract competition quickly and at low cost—an empirical question—then the merged firm will not find it profitable to exercise that power in the first place. In Armentano's view, however, the theoretical possibility—not the empirically realistic probability—of market entry justifies outright repeal of the prohibitions on the creation of monopoly power through either mergers or collusion. That market entry will restrain such action in some instances, however, does not make it a panacea; indeed, even Armentano is sensitive to the legal barriers that may inhibit entry into some markets.[10] Nonetheless, his prescription for repeal necessarily assumes away not only legal barriers to entry but also the transaction costs of entry and the losses incurred prior to such entry.

That entry will occur in the long run says little about the time period required for such action, which may be substantial, depending upon the difficulty of assembling the necessary resources. If government officials knew that a particular merger would create a firm with market power, then it would be perverse for them to permit the merger on the ground that the resulting price increase will eventually induce competitive entry to force prices back down at some future date. In the interim, while the merged firm has restricted output and increased price, there is an immediate and irretrievable loss of consumer welfare and of allocative efficiency. The losses from the merger are certain and present, whereas future entry, if and when it occurs, merely restores competitive pricing and prevents further losses.

Armentano's discussion unfortunately fails adequately to differentiate between mergers and collusion. In the latter case, however, the time period necessary for entry—if entry ever occurs—is both uncertain and further prolonged for an additional reason: firms involved in collusion do not publicize their activities. Even if there were no legal sanction to make secrecy essential to successful collusion, the desire not to attract market entry would still lead firms to collude only furtively. Unlike alterations in market structure via merger, which are visible to potential entrants, cartels do not advertise the profit opportunities they create for potential entrants. Unless potential entrants are able nonetheless to infer from the cartel price that collusion has indeed taken place, they would not have any special reason to enter the market; even if they do conclude that the market is

---

[10]   *Id.* at 321.

cartelized, entry may remain unattractive due to the possibility that the colluding firms could at any moment revert to competitive pricing, either because of a falling out amongst themselves (cartels being unstable in the long run) or specifically in order to defeat imminent entry.

If entry does eventually occur, however, then the result would be not only restoration of competitive pricing but also excessive investment in productive facilities. If the productive capacity of the industry as a whole was sufficient to supply the efficient quantity, Q_2, before inauguration of an agreement to restrict output, then any subsequent entry attracted by the cartel's pricing will occasion an avoidable social cost in the form of excess capacity. Specifically, the transaction costs of investing and then disinvesting in the excess capacity—as well as the losses attributable to plant and equipment that cannot be converted to other uses—will be deadweight social costs.

III. Horizontal agreements

Focusing on the acquisition of market power through collusion, Armentano advances three principal arguments for the repeal of the prohibition on horizontal agreements, such as price-fixing agreements, currently deemed unlawful per se. First, Armentano contends that regulators cannot "calculate the probable social advantages and costs associated with proposed agreements that have not yet taken place." Specifically, regulators are unlikely to have access to "economic information (concerning costs and benefits) that can only be known to the market participants themselves." Since "opportunity costs and utility are fundamentally subjective" and "don't lend themselves to interpersonal aggregation and comparison," Armentano doubts that "any rule of reason or per se prohibition" can be "scientifically defended."[11]

To support this claim, Armentano cites, without elaboration, to James Buchanan's discussion of the nature of costs.[12] In the

---

[11]   *Id.* at 326.

[12]   *Id.* at n.30.

cited portion of that essay, Buchanan contends that one should understand cost as "that which the decision-maker sacrifices or gives up when he selects one alternative rather than another.[13] A regulator cannot measure cost, thus conceived, "since there is no way that [the] subjective mental experience [of the decision-maker] can be directly observed."[14] As I understand him, Buchanan is merely refining the familiar concept of opportunity cost, not advancing the far broader proposition, offered by Armentano, that the subjectivity of cost renders impossible all economic comparisons.

With respect to any horizontal agreement, the relevant comparison is between the cost to consumers and the benefit to producers. This question turns upon the nature of the agreement selected, and its impact upon third parties (generally consumers), not solely upon the other options foregone by "the people who actually make the business decisions."[15]

Here, too, Armentano's critique is not unique to antitrust regulation. In the world of subjective costs and benefits that he seems to posit—in which a dollar may provide greater utility for one person than another—one could not justify any form of regulation on the ground that it would make society better off; one could never determine whether the collective gains will outweigh the subjective reduction in utility for those upon whom regulation exerts coercive power. Armentano's position would mean that government could never effect a nonconsensual transfer, or prevent a consensual transfer, in the furtherance of collective goals. Such a principle would sound the death-knell not only for the antitrust laws but also for all efforts to control externalities, for taxation, and for government transfer payments. Once again, at bottom, Armentano has done no more than reiterate the theory of the second-best.

---

[13]   J. M. Buchanan, *Introduction: L.S.E. Cost Theory in Retrospect*, in L.S.E. ESSAYS ON COST 3, 14 (J. M. Buchanan & G. F. Thirlby eds. 1981).

[14]   *Id.* at 15.

[15]   *Id.* at 17.

Second, Armentano contends that horizontal agreements with anticompetitive consequences will "tend to dissolve naturally."[16] This argument, like its counterpart regarding mergers, overlooks that the time period necessary for dissolution may be long indeed.[17] During my tenure in antitrust enforcement, for example, the average life span of price-fixing conspiracies uncovered by the Justice Department seemed to be about 10 years.

Third, Armentano argues that horizontal agreements may contribute to market rationalization by, for instance, reducing risk, lowering "wasteful cross-hauling and advertising," and facilitating joint ventures. For this claim, Armentano relies upon Donald Dewey's "Information, Entry, and Welfare: The Case for Collusion."[18] Dewey makes clear, however, that these beneficial consequences of horizontal agreements depend upon the existence of special circumstances,[19] a significant qualification that Armentano ignores. Dewey, furthermore, cautions readers that "it seems best to refrain . . . from asserting or implying that the analysis of this paper has shown that legalizing collusion will increase economic welfare."[20]

Armentano concludes that, absent the ability to ascertain the costs and benefits of horizontal agreements, regulation of such agreements is "without sufficient scientific foundation."[21]

---

[16] Armentano at 326.

[17] *See* DeBow, *What's Wrong With Price Fixing*, 12 REG. 46 (1988).

[18] 69 AM. ECON. REV. 587 (1979).

[19] Dewey, for example, underscores that his conclusions rest upon an assumption of free entry into the cartelized industry. *Id.* at 593. For further discussion, *see* DeBow, *supra* note 17, at 47.

[20] Dewey, *supra* note 18, at 594. With respect to research joint ventures, moreover, the National Cooperative Research Act of 1984, 15 U.S.C. §§ 4301–4304 (Supp. 1984), permits firms to obtain immunity from treble damage liability for cooperative activities enumerated in filings with government agencies. If other types of joint ventures are being inhibited, then broader application of the NCRA scheme would seem a more targeted response to the problem than is wholesale repeal of the ban on anticompetitive joint ventures.

[21] Armentano at 327.

Although I think this claim beside the point for the reasons outlined above, I add that, even if one could not determine the costs and benefits associated with particular agreements, one could still try to compare the cost of prohibiting certain types of horizontal agreements, such as price fixing, with the benefits claimed from allowing all such agreements, the efficiency-reducing and the efficiency-enhancing alike. The first-best regulatory regime, of course, would discriminate perfectly between efficient and inefficient horizontal agreements. Realistically, however, one must make an informed guess as to whether disallowing some or allowing all agreements provides the superior policy.

IV. Historical enforcement practice

Apart from economic theory, Armentano rests his case upon enforcement practices in the first few decades of the antitrust era. I share his conclusion that early antitrust policy tended to perceive as barriers "economic advantages and efficiencies that leading business organizations earn in the marketplace";[22] the fruits of prior investments made to suit consumer preferences, such as lucrative patents, good will, and product differentiation, should not be taxed away by antitrust policy. Armentano likewise points to such familiar—though hardly recent—cases as *Standard Oil* (1911),[23] *American Tobacco* (1911),[24] and *Alcoa* (1945)[25] as examples of the prosecution of single firms that had not, in fact, restrained output. I would go as far as to say that from its early stages through the 1960's, and to a lesser degree as recently as the 1970's, antitrust law was too frequently the mechanism by which less enterprising firms or latecomers could, with the aid of the government, deprive their more successful predecessors of the benefits of innovation and risk taking.

---

[22]   *Id.* at 320.

[23]   Standard Oil Co. v. U.S., 221 U.S. 1 (1911).

[24]   U.S. v. American Tobacco Co., 221 U.S. 106 (1911).

[25]   U.S. v. Aluminum Co. of America, 148 F.2d 416 (2d Cir. 1945).

Armentano correctly traces the downfall of this approach to the emergence in the early 1970's of a reformist scholarship that criticized this historical experience and counseled reduced attention to concentration and to absolute firm size. Armentano, however, sees the reformist critique as producing only "modest changes" in policy. I believe that this conclusion seriously understates the transformation of antitrust law that has occurred in the last decade or two.

In the 1980's, the government did not bring any single-firm antitrust prosecution on a theory of market dominance. With regard to merger control, only transactions posing a palpable threat of creating significant market power were targeted for interdiction. Since revision of their merger guidelines in 1982, the Department of Justice and the Federal Trade Commission have avoided inquiry into industrial concentration as a concern in itself.[26] Discarding simple concentration ratios, such as the market shares of the four leading firms, in favor of the Herfindahl-Hirschman index, for example, shifted attention from size per se to the probable ability of the merged firm to exercise market power.[27] The guidelines also direct the antitrust agencies to estimate the time period necessary for distant geographic markets, new entry, and technologically related markets to bring forth additional supply in response to a hypothetical price increase in the merging firms' market.[28] Such focused standards guide enforcement officials in distinguishing between those mergers for which potential entry will serve as an adequate restraint and those that are likely to inaugurate a substantial period in which producers may exercise market power. The courts, likewise, have held enforcement agencies to account for why competitive entry will not solve the problems associated with a challenged merger.[29]

---

[26] UNITED STATES DEPARTMENT OF JUSTICE, MERGER GUIDELINES (1984) (hereinafter DOJ Guidelines); UNITED STATES FEDERAL TRADE COMMISSION, STATEMENT CONCERNING HORIZONTAL MERGERS (1982).

[27] DOJ Guidelines at § 3.1.

[28] *Id.* at §§ 2.1–2.3.

[29] *See, e.g.*, United States v. Waste Management, Inc., 743 F.2d 976 (2d Cir. 1986); United States v. Calmar, Inc., 612 F. Supp. 1298 (D.N.J. 1985).

In short, the "structure-performance-conduct" model that the reformist scholars called into question has largely disappeared as a part of antitrust policy for the last decade. The reform scholarship of the 1970's became both the conventional wisdom and the prevailing government policy of the 1980's. Gone are the once-familiar calls for deconcentration legislation, such as the Neal Commission Report of 1969.[30] In a recent discussion of vertical restraints, William Baxter—a member of the Neal Commission who later served as President Reagan's first Assistant Attorney General for the Antitrust Division—argued that antitrust law should restrict inquiry to "the exercise or formation of market power."[31] Charles F. Rule, the last Reagan appointee to head the Antitrust Division, likewise stated that "antitrust law is, and should be, focused solely on the condemnation of conduct that threatens to restrict output and raise price and that does not generate offsetting efficiencies."[32] Even Robert Pitofsky, who has not always agreed with the reformist scholarship,[33] recently acknowledged that "hawks as well as doves must learn the lessons of economics if they are to establish sensible [antitrust] policies."[34]

---

[30]   *See* Task Force Report on Antitrust Policy ("Neal Commission Report"), CCH Trade Reg. Rep., Supp. to No. 415 at A-1 (1969) (proposal for Concentrated Industries Act).

[31]   Baxter, *The Viability of Vertical Restraints Doctrine*, 75 CALIF. L. REV. 933, 948 (1987).

[32]   Charles F. Rule, *On Being Head of the Antitrust Division: The World View of a Soon-To-Be Former Assistant Attorney General*, Remarks Before the Antitrust Law Section of the New York State Bar Association 7 (Jan. 18, 1989).

[33]   *See* Pitofsky, *The Political Content of Antitrust*, 127 U. PA. L. REV. 1051, 1075 (1979): "[T]he trend toward use of an exclusively economic approach to antitrust analysis excludes important political considerations . . . [such as] the fear that excessive concentration of economic power will foster anticompetitive political pressures, the desire to reduce the range of private discretion by a few in order to enhance individual freedom, and the fear that increased governmental intrusion will become necessary if the economy is dominated by a few . . . ."

[34]   Pitofsky, *Does Antitrust Have a Future?* 76 GEO. L.J. 321, 326 (1987).

Notwithstanding these developments, Armentano favors outright repeal of the antitrust laws in part for a "strategic" reason: Reforms in administrative policy may be short lived due to changes in the political climate.[35] It is indeed reasonable to be concerned about the possibility of retrogression in enforcement policy, but for that matter, if the politics are favorable to a misguided policy, then even repeal is no guarantee against its reenactment.

I should think that whether repeal is preferable to reform, however, depends upon whether anything about the nature of antitrust enforcement makes it inherently prone to use in furtherance of economically ill-advised policies. I concede that the answer is to some degree yes, for reasons related to the incentives of the antitrust enforcement agencies to over-enforce the laws placed under their control, and not for reasons arising from any inherent inadequacies in antitrust theory. Greater enforcement activity increases the budget and staff of the antitrust agencies, as well as the importance of agency officials; they also benefit from enhanced post-government employment opportunities brought about by the increased need for experienced insiders to defend private clients against future agency enforcement actions.

If the political appointees entrusted with enforcement of the antitrust laws do not appreciate the importance of recent developments in antitrust theory, then there will be a significant risk that they will be captured by their staffs, whose incentives—quite naturally—run toward increased involvement in glamorous, high-profile enforcement activities. The antitrust statutes, as currently framed, do little to control this risk; indeed, in ignorant or ambitious hands, the central provisions of the Sherman and Clayton Acts are potentially dangerous weapons, as their broad terms invest enforcement agencies with necessarily wide discretion. The incentive and the ability to embark upon an efficiency-reducing enforcement program form a hazardous combination. This problem can be remedied, however, short of repeal, by reforms that narrow the antitrust laws so that they can reach only appropriate targets. The argument for wholesale repeal, by con-

---

[35] Armentano at 314.

trast, must disregard the core case for regulation based upon suppression of the externalities that the creation of market power engenders.

Elsewhere, I have set forth the case for one particular such reform: the proposed Merger Modernization Act[36] would amend § 7 of the Clayton Act, by narrowing the present prohibition of mergers whose effect may be "substantially to lessen competition, or to tend to create monopoly" so that it would reach only mergers that "increase the ability to exercise market power," defined as "the ability of one or more firms profitably to maintain price above competitive levels for a significant period of time."[37] Enactment of such a measure would go far toward institutionalizing the recent changes in enforcement policy with respect to mergers.

V. Conclusion

Armentano begins with the observation—hardly contestable in light of recent scholarship—that the antitrust laws have too often produced perverse consequences. Antitrust enforcement policy has periodically pandered to antibusiness or antibigness political sentiment, and when it has done so, its principal victims have been economic efficiency and, as a result, consumers. But this account does not accurately describe antitrust enforcement in the 1980's, which concentrated on two major areas: mergers likely to create a firm with the ability to exercise market power over a substantial period of time, and collusive activities—such as horizontal price-fixing agreements—which are not likely to have any socially redeeming value.

Armentano understandably expresses concern over the perils of leaving in place the same laws that spawned inefficient enforcement action over most of the last century. I do not fear,

---

[36] *Merger Law Reform: Hearings on S. 2160 Before the Senate Comm. on the Judiciary*, 99th Cong., 2d Sess. 24-60 (1986).

[37] *Id.* at 15-17, *reprinting* S. 2160, 99th Cong., 2d Sess. §§ 2(a) & (d) (1986).

and I am not sure that he fears, that enforcement officials will actually become more ignorant with time and, for that reason, revert to the old ways. But the concatenation of political forces may yet again elicit enforcement activity that is economically inefficient, and that regulators will seek to justify on grounds apart from the legitimate, efficiency-enhancing purpose of antitrust law. For example, antitrust regulators of the future might prevent a merger that does not threaten to create market power, in order to preserve, for a time, redundant jobs that an efficiently scaled single firm would eliminate. This would be considerably less likely if the antitrust statutes were reformed to aim more precisely at the creation of market power through mergers and its exercise by collusion among nominal competitors. In the absence of legislative reform, recent enforcement policies have accomplished the same objective, and no evidence has yet been produced to show that those policies have occasioned any increase in market power at the expense of consumers.

In the area of mergers, the current agenda should focus not upon repeal of the antitrust laws, but upon research into the price behavior of industries in which significant mergers were permitted under modern enforcement policy. With regard to collusion, recent empirical evidence indicates that prices have fallen in the wake of government-initiated indictments. For example, the price of federally assisted highway construction, which had been elevated about 10 percent by price-fixing agreements in many locales, reverted to competitive levels after a major enforcement initiative against that industry. An examination of stock prices associated with firms indicted for horizontal price-fixing conspiracies from 1962 to 1980 estimates the benefits to consumers from the elimination of monopoly rents at a present value of approximately \$2 billion.[38] Through continued research along these lines, we may better document the consequences of the recent transformation in enforcement policy and thereby build the case for the reforms necessary to assure for the second hundred years a more rational law of antitrust than we had for most of the last century.

---

[38]   Bosch & Eckard, The Benefits of Antitrust Enforcement: Some Evidence from Federal Price Fixing Indictments (unpublished manuscript, Aug. 1987).

27
A reply to Judge Ginsburg

BY D. T. ARMENTANO*

Since there is at least a general agreement between Judge Ginsburg and myself concerning the historical misuse of antitrust
policy, let me turn, instead, to our areas of theoretical disagreement.

I maintained, in brief, that competition was a dynamic process and not an end-state equilibrium condition; that antitrust
regulators were incapable (theoretically and practically) of distinguishing an "inefficient" restraint of trade from an "efficient"
restraint; that economic information concerning the costs and
benefits of mergers (or cooperative agreements) was subjective
and did not lend itself to rule of reason analysis; and that
consumer-harmful "restraints" would prove unworkable. I also
noted that voluntary cooperative agreements did not violate
property rights in any strict sense and, therefore, should be
allowed in a free society.

In his rejoinder, Judge Ginsburg argues that microeconomic
models are not to be taken literally; that regulators can (and
should) make an "informed guess" concerning the effects of
antitrust intervention; that business disequilibriums are unlikely

---

* Professor of Economics, University of Hartford.

because dynamic competition exists; and that my argument against antitrust regulation (a second-best argument) proves too much and can invalidate *any* government intervention. He also notes that my natural rights argument is not consistent since collusive agreements can have negative third-party effects on consumers.

I concede that my theoretical criticism of antitrust regulation is broad and can be used to invalidate all economic regulation. If private costs and benefits are subjective and cannot be aggregated, and if we live in a disequilibrium economic world, then regulatory "guesses" are hardly "informed," and decision making is best left to market participants. But rather than deal with the full implications of my criticism, Ginsburg dismisses it as simply "proving too much."

Ginsburg asserts that my assumption of both dynamic competition *and* disequilibrium appears inconsistent. Indeed, he holds that the assumption of dynamic competition implies that "disequilibrium does not persist for any significant time." I disagree. It seems far more reasonable to assume that the existence of dynamic competition and the passage of time imply a continuously disequilibrium world, but one in which there are important equilibrating forces at work. We can reasonably "assume" the existence of equilibrating forces—which is all that I do—but not of the equilibrium condition itself (which is what Ginsburg does).

Judge Ginsburg accuses me of taking the microeconomic models too literally in my criticism of the concept of market power. The models are only a "simplifying abstraction" that must be supplemented if they are to be made useful in real-world market situations. But this is a curious criticism to say the least. If we don't take the models literally, what does the concept "market power" mean? What is a competitive condition "literally," and when is market output actually restrained? Judge Ginsburg asserts that the models are a simplifying abstraction, but of what? The fact remains that the models—taken literally— assume a competitive (equilibrium) condition that monopoly power is said to distort. If this competitive equilibrium does not exist, and if the private "restraint" itself does not establish a monopoly equilibrium condition, the standard conclusions concerning allocative inefficiency and antitrust intervention simply don't follow.

Judge Ginsburg criticizes me for holding that consumer-harmful agreements tend to dissolve naturally over time. He notes that during his tenure in antitrust enforcement, the average life span of discovered price-fixing conspiracies was 10 years. But the length of an interfirm cooperative agreement and the existence of *effective output restraint* are not identical situations. *Attempts* at effective conspiracy may last for years, even decades, but where is the unambiguous evidence that private cartels can exercise monopoly power in markets legally open to competitive entry? Additionally, any evaluation of interfirm cooperative agreements would have to take into account any possible cost savings associated with agreement. If the restraints had a negligible effect on output and if there were cost savings, it is not obvious that "society" benefited from the legal prohibition of price agreement.

Finally, I don't believe that the existence of negative wealth effects on consumers (presumably from an output restraint) invalidates my natural rights framework. The consumer decision to purchase (at the higher price) is just as voluntary as the price agreement between the suppliers. There has been no involuntary restriction of the property rights of third parties as Judge Ginsburg asserts. Their rights to their property (their money income) are fully intact both before and after any price change. If this were not so, any and all negative externalities (capital losses, for example) would be "rights violating" and would then justify regulation or prohibition. On the other hand, *non*rights violating negative externalities (such as those created by cooperative agreements) must be carefully distinguished from *rights-violating* externalties—such as harmful pollution—which are clearly invasive of someone's private property and should be "regulated" on that basis alone (and *not* on the basis of any "efficiency" consideration).

28
The virtues and problems of antitrust law

BY DONALD F. TURNER*

U.S. antitrust law has plainly made significant beneficial contributions to the performance of the U.S. economy, by prohibiting such plainly anticompetitive agreements as naked horizontal price-fixing and monopolization of markets by mergers or by conduct unrelated to efficiency, product innovations and similar procompetitive actions. It is equally clear that retention of antitrust law limitations on anticompetitive conduct will continue to be a highly important feature of public economic policy.

However, unsound interpretations of antitrust laws have adverse economic effects. Court-formulated rules have varied from time to time over the years since antitrust statutes were passed, and the scope of antitrust prohibitions were either enlarged or reduced. While there are extensive disputes as to what the precedents' defects have been and are, it is generally recognized that antitrust law has had and still has some undesirable features that the courts or Congress should correct.

And, given the existence of defects, it is a proper approach of government enforcement agencies not to bring cases solely on the

---

* Professor of Law, Georgetown University Law Center.

basis that they would be upheld because of past precedents, but on the basis that they should be upheld because they rest on interpretations of antitrust law that reflect a clearly sound economic analysis of the competitive pros and cons of the conduct in question. For the same reason, government agencies, at least after a decent interval, should bring cases for the purpose of persuading the Supreme Court to reverse precedents that mistakenly held certain restrictive conduct to be lawful.

These were my views while Assistant Attorney General in charge of the Antitrust Division. I rejected a number of staff-recommended complaints that, in my opinion, rested on unacceptable theories based on court precedents that I believed had gone too far—a disturbing feature of several decisions in the preceding years. I also sought dismissal of a few pending government cases which I thought ill-based. But, I also filed a few cases in which success would depend on reversal or limitation on the scope of prior precedents, or on the creation of a new or expanded prohibitory rule. In retrospect, I made some mistakes. For example, I should not have appealed the *Von's Grocery*[1] merger case to the Supreme Court; and my 1968 merger guidelines were too severe.

I also believe it is a vitally important function of the Antitrust Division to arrange for the filing of amicus briefs, particularly to the Supreme Court, in private antitrust cases involving important issues—either supporting or opposing the plaintiff's or defendant's legal theories. Here was another mistake I made—not requesting the Solicitor General to file amicus briefs objecting to plaintiffs' claims in *Utah Pie* and *Albrecht*.[2]

I now turn to brief discussions of the following subjects: (1) the goals of antitrust law; (2) the problems faced by courts in formulating suitable rules, and how they should be met; (3) a brief discussion of a few examples of the substantive rules that should be reformulated; and (4) the appropriateness of eliminat-

---

[1]   United States v. Von's Grocery Co., 384 U.S. 270 (1966).

[2]   Utah Pie Co. v. Continental Baking Co., 386 U.S. 685 (1967); Albrecht v. Herald Co., 390 U.S. 145 (1968).

ing mandatory treble damages and jury trials in private antitrust suits. My discussion is largely drawn from my longer article to be published in a special issue of the *California Law Review*, which covers papers presented at the November 1986 conference sponsored by the New York City Bar Association.

I. Goals of antitrust law

Antitrust law is characterized as a procompetition policy. The economic goal of a procompetition policy is to improve the economy and promote consumer welfare through increased efficiency in the use and allocation of resources, and through the development of new and improved products, new productive, distributional and organizational techniques that further put economic resources to more beneficial use. A corollary is that the primary function of antitrust law is the protection and promotion of such procompetitive conduct, not protection of competitors as such. The legislative history of the Sherman Act and other antitrust laws did suggest "populist" goals as well—social and political reasons for limiting business size and preserving large numbers of small businesses and business opportunities. However, economics-based antitrust law serves those goals to a substantial extent by preventing agreements, mergers, and unilateral conduct that eliminate or reduce competition without economic benefits. And, possibly excepting the secondary-line feature of the Robinson-Patman Act, there is no reasonable basis for presuming from the legislative history that the courts must give weight to populist goals where serving them would interfere with competitive pricing, efficiency or progressiveness gains, and hence consumer welfare. Moreover, incorporating populist goals is questionable even where there is no such apparent conflict, as inclusion would broaden the proscription of business conduct having no significant anticompetitive effects, increase vagueness in the law, and discourage conduct involving efficiencies not easily recognized or proved.[3]

---

[3] For an extended discussion concerning antitrust goals, *see* 1 P. AREEDA AND D. TURNER, ANTITRUST LAW 103-12 (1978), and 4 P. AREEDA AND D. TURNER, ANTITRUST LAW ¶¶ 903-904 (1980).

II. Problems in formulating rules

With populist goals set aside, the function of courts is to formulate antitrust rules promotive of economic competitive goals. Ideal rules are those that are both clearly predictable in their application, and economically rational, in that they render unlawful conduct that is anticompetitive, but not conduct that is economically beneficial. There are areas where economic analysis strongly supports a clear simple rule. For example, it is generally agreed that naked horizontal price-fixing or market-sharing agreements—unrelated to such legitimate forms of cooperation as joint ventures—are properly held to be unlawful per se.

However, it is often difficult to formulate rules that are both clear and economically rational. The problem arises in several circumstances. First, there may be gaps in economic theory, such as the absence of economic analysis of novel practices. Second, there may be conflicts among economists as to the competitive effects of particular practices. Third, economic analysis often indicates that assessment of the effects of particular conduct requires consideration of several market factors, and both short-run and long-run effects. This points in the direction of complex rather than simple rules. But, it may be difficult to get and assess adequate facts for deciding individual cases where the outcome depends on assessing various factors and balancing anticompetitive and procompetitive effects.

There have been various approaches to such problems. In some decisions, the Supreme Court suggested that difficulties in economic analysis or obtaining relevant facts warrant adopting a simple rule of illegality.[4] However, recognizing that this approach may well have undesirable economic consequences, the Court has tended in recent years to take into account factors that are highly relevant to a rational assessment of the conduct concerned. Even so-called per se rules have qualifications. In *BMI* and *NCAA* the Court recognized that the per se approach to horizontal price-

---

[4] Standard Oil Co. v. U.S., 337 U.S. 293, 307–11 (1949); U.S. v. Philadelphia Nat'l Bank, 374 U.S. 321, 371 (1963); U.S. v. Topco Assocs., 405 U.S. 596, 609–10 (1972).

fixing or similar competition-reducing agreements is not appropriate where the practice is in the context of cooperation that has economic justification.[5] The so-called per se rule, as to the illegality of tying arrangements, rests on a finding of market power over the tying product. And, the Court in *Northwest Wholesale Stationers* recognized that there are limitations on the scope of collective refusals to deal that are subject to the rule of so-called per se illegality.[6]

The extreme alternative to the per se approach is the "rule of reason" requiring examination of all facts bearing on whether the conduct is on balance anticompetitive or procompetitive. But, the problems posed by such an approach—vagueness, unpredictability, costs of litigation, and difficulties in obtaining facts—have in some instances led to modified versions of the rule of reason, creating presumptions of illegality on the basis of certain findings, such as that the legitimate objective of defendants were achievable by less restrictive alternatives. In short, as the Supreme Court noted in the *NCAA* case, "there is often no bright line separating *per se* from Rule of Reason analysis."[7] In other words, use of "per se" "rule of reason" labels has been confusing.

The question, therefore, is what approach the courts should take in endeavoring to clarify and improve substantive antitrust rules. Professor Areeda has supplied an excellent analysis and a sound proposal.[8] The key is the formulation of presumptions, the selection and sequence of which depends on the nature of the conduct concerned; plus resting burdens of proof as to each specified issue on either plaintiffs or defendants.

Economic analysis problems do not warrant a severe cut-back on the scope of antitrust law. The ability of judges to assess them

---

[5] *BMI*, 441 U.S. at 19–23 (1979); *NCAA*, 468 U.S. at 98–104 (1984).

[6] 105 S. Ct. 2613, 2621 (1985).

[7] 468 U.S. at 104, n.26.

[8] 7 P. AREEDA, ANTITRUST LAW, ch. 15 (1986).

has improved over time, and the Supreme Court has demonstrated a growing and sound tendency to review, clarify, modify or overrule past precedents that are economically irrational.

I now turn to a few examples of substantive rules that should be revised.

III. Revision of substantive rules

A. Vertical resale restraints

1. *Albrecht v. Herald Co.*,[9] holding maximum resale price to be unlawful per se, plainly should be reversed. Apart from vertical integration, which could be economically unavailable or more costly, such a restraint may be the necessary device for insuring that the efficiency or other benefits from exclusive territorial or customer distributorships are passed on to consumers.

2. *Continental T.V. v. GTE-Sylvania*[10] was clearly correct in reversing *Schwinn* and subjecting territorial and customer restrictions on distributors to the rule of reason; but mistakenly suggested that legality be tested by weighing the adverse effects on intrabrand competition against the beneficial effects on interbrand competition. Even a monopolist may have efficiency or other justifications for territorial or customer restrictions, and reversing *Albrecht* would enable such a firm to achieve such gains without losing them from monopoly pricing by the distributors.

Although it may involve some proof assessment problems, a sensible rule would be that territorial or customer restrictions are presumptively lawful, and unlawful only if plainly attributable to dealer coercion.

---

9   390 U.S. 145 (1968).

10   433 U.S. 36 (1977).

3. It is arguably proper to maintain the presumptive illegality of minimum resale price maintenance restrictions that do not have all the efficiency potentials, such as scale economies, attributable to nonprice resale restrictions, and may be adopted by a producer solely to encourage distributors to push its product over those of competitors. But, such restriction may have a competitive justification in some circumstances. For example, where the product involved is a complex product requiring costly presale services, but sales maximization requires a plurality of dealer outlets in retail markets, minimum resale price maintenance may be the only way to eliminate the free-rider problem.

4. The *Colgate* doctrine, preserved by *Monsanto* despite the recognition that it may have the same undesirable competitive effects as resale restriction agreements, is questionable.[11] Dealer acquiescence to the producer's stated resale policy, in response to the threat of termination if failure to acquiesce, may accurately be described as an agreement.

B. *Tying contracts*

Under present law, tying the sale of separate products (or services) is classified as unlawful per se where the seller has "market power" over the tying product and the tying covers a "not unsubstantial" dollar volume of sales of the tied product. A few lower court decisions have qualified the rule with a "good will" defense, *i.e.*, proof that requiring purchase of the tied product or service was critical to high performance of the tying product. But, Supreme Court opinions have stated the view that such a purpose is normally served by the less restrictive alternative of defining the specifications of the product to be used with the tying product.

There are reasons for concluding that the law's coverage is too broad. First, the Supreme Court was wrong in stating that "tying arrangements serve hardly any purpose beyond the suppression of

---

[11]   Monsanto v. Spray-Rite Serv. Corp., 465 U.S. 752, 761 (1984), *reaffirming,* U.S. v. Colgate & Co., 250 U.S. 300 (1919).

competition.''[12] There are a number of purposes that are either procompetitive or devoid of anticompetitive intent.[13] Second, the "market power" predicate is mistakenly assumed to be met where the tying product is patented, copyrighted, or distinctive from products offered by competitors. Third, a substantial dollar amount of sales of the tied product does not show foreclosure of a substantial share of the tied product market; a fortiori it does not indicate a tendency to monopoly. In short, present antitrust prohibition extends to tying arrangements having no significant anticompetitive effects.

Tying can have such effects where the seller has a high degree of market power in the tying product market and the tying leads to monopoly or near-monopoly of the tied product. The latter consequence is a fortiori bad if it either eliminates the leading potential entrants into the tying product market, or raises barriers to such entry. Therefore, prohibition of tying should not be totally abandoned.

But, it would make sense to limit presumptive illegality at least to cases where plaintiff has proved that (1) the seller has substantial market power in the tying product market, *e.g.*, at least a 50% market share; and (2) a substantial share—*e.g.*, 15% to 20%—of the tied product market is foreclosed. And even in such cases, illegality should be subject to negation by proof (1) that tying is the least costly and most effective way of insuring efficient functioning of the tying product; (2) that tying of servicing to sale or lease of a complex product facilitates product improvement; or (3) of substantial cost savings from joint production of the tied products (though perhaps that gain can be achieved by the superficially less restrictive alternative of lowering the aggregate price if the buyer purchases both).

---

[12] Standard Oil Co. v. U.S., 337 U.S. 293, 305–306 (1949).

[13] Such purposes include: tying a complementary product to insure high performance of the tying product; tying servicing to the sale of a product in order to generate information leading to product improvements; cost savings from joint production or distribution; and use of tying as a vehicle for indirect price competition in an oligopoly market.

C. *Monopolizing conduct: "leveraging"*

It is vitally important to the promotion of efficiency, innovations, and other procompetitive benefits, that the Supreme Court eliminate the overly broad implications of decisions concerning the alleged abuse of monopoly power. For example, in *Griffith* the Court stated that "the use of monopoly power, however, lawfully acquired, to foreclose competition, to gain a competitive advantage, or to destroy a competitor, is unlawful."[14] Taken literally, this appears to wipe out the right of the holder of a potential proposed product or low-cost production process to use its advantage to drive out competitors. It also appears to preclude consideration of efficiency or other economic benefits that may result from a firm with monopoly power engaging in vertical integration, integration into complementary products or services, or tying arrangements.

The Supreme Court decision in *Aspen Skiing*,[15] while arguably a correct result in light of the unusual facts, also contains some dangerously broad language. The district court had instructed the jury that it had to consider whether the defendant had used its power "by anti-competitive *or* exclusionary means or for anti-competitive *or* exclusionary purposes" (emphasis added); and that Aspen Skiing's refusal to deal with the competitor was unlawful if there were no "valid business reasons" for the refusal. As a predicate for its review analysis, the Supreme Court stated that:

> If a firm has been "attempting to exclude rivals on some basis other than efficiency," it is fair to characterize its behavior as predatory.[16]

This proposition may imply that a firm with monopoly power has a duty to assist competitors, *e.g.*, by supplying them with superior product components or perhaps even licensing a superior

---

[14]   U.S. v. Griffith, 334 U.S. 100, 107 (1948).

[15]   Aspen Skiing Co. v. Aspen Highlands Skiing Corp., 105 S. Ct. 2847 (1985).

[16]   *Id*. at 2859.

production process, where competitors need such assistance in order to compete effectively.

Thus, *Aspen Skiing* invites a plethora of section 2 refusal-to-deal cases by competitors against a rival whose alleged monopoly power is based on narrowly defined markets, and may lead to a cut-back on the basic principle that it is no violation of section 2 for a firm to acquire or maintain monopoly power through self-developed productive process efficiency or superior product components. It may also discourage vertical integration and integration into complementary products by firms with monopoly power, which is often economically beneficial.

IV. Other issues

The potential adverse economic effects of antitrust law need to be reduced not only by efforts to clarify and revise some substantive rules, but also by a reassessment and revision of rules applicable to private antitrust suits.

It is appropriate to retain private rights of action as a supplement to governmental enforcement. It is extremely unlikely that government agencies would ever be given sufficient resources to investigate, detect, and bring suits against all violations. Moreover, elimination of private actions would deprive courts of the power to prevent undue cut-backs in the scope of antitrust law enforcement by government agencies. However, there are problems with private actions that need to be dealt with. A substantial number of private antitrust cases are ill-founded, brought in hopes of obtaining substantial cash settlements from defendants seeking to avoid the costs of litigation and the risk that bits of evidence—such as damaging but unauthorized employee statements—will lead to adverse jury verdicts.

Thus, in my opinion, antitrust law would be improved and its costs reduced by (1) eliminating the mandatory treble-damage rule, (2) eliminating jury trials of private suits (or if not, continuing the trend toward expanded scope of summary judgment).

A. *Treble Damages*

Treble damages provide a powerful financial incentive for parties to detect and sue for violations of antitrust law, and discourage illegal conduct by increasing the cost to the violator.

On the other hand, the mandatory treble damages rule has the countervailing adverse effects of encouraging baseless or trivial suits brought in hopes of coercing settlements, and of discouraging legitimate competitive behavior in the gray rule of reason areas of the law. Moreover, mandating treble damages over the whole range of antitrust law is inconsistent with the customary standards for punitive damages, which are similar to those applied to criminal sanctions. Treble damages seem plainly unfair where antitrust rules are vague or where illegality is a close question, resting on complex facts not fully available to defendants at the time their actions took place, or on balancing of anticompetitive and procompetitive effects. Thus, the mandatory treble-damage rule should be eliminated.

The more difficult issue is how the scope of trebling should statutorily be defined. The appropriate general approach is that, at most, treble damages should be limited to "clear" violations, namely cases in which:

a. the law was clear at the time the conduct occurred; and

b. the factual predicates for liability, including *inter alia* the anticompetitive nature of the conduct and the plain absence of any procompetitive justification, are clear.

But, the statutory provision should perhaps be more specific, both to lower the decision-making burden on courts and diminish the adverse consequence of vagueness.[17]

---

[17] One precise formulation would be to limit treble damages to buyer or seller harms from naked horizontal price-fixing or market-sharing agreements. Such a rule may well make sense, but if deemed too narrow, could be extended to other specified violations.

Such an approach may tend to discourage private actions in complicated rule of reason areas. However, lowering of incentives to bring close cases in the rule-of-reason areas—where there are significant procompetitive probabilities—would not lead to significant consumer harm. Indeed, by lowering firms' disincentives to engage in economically beneficial behavior, the consequence may well be a net consumer gain.

B. Elimination of jury trials

There would be significant gains from eliminating jury trials in private antitrust actions. First, it would reduce the private and public costs of antitrust litigation. Jury trials involve procedures (such as jury selection, oral presentation of documentary evidence, and formulation of jury instructions) not required in court trials. Moreover, trial to judges would facilitate narrowing of issues put to full trial and also facilitate summary judgment.

More importantly, elimination of juries would increase the probability of accurate results. Juries cannot easily absorb and retain all of the evidence presented in the typical antitrust case. There are procedural devices that would help in this regard, but they do not solve the problem that the nature and complexity of the factual and legal issues raised in most antitrust cases are beyond the competence of most jurors to understand and to reason through to a rationally based conclusion. (Even in a case alleging a horizontal price-fixing agreement, absent direct evidence of agreement, whether or not there was a conspiracy requires an analysis of economic and business factors beyond the competence of most jurors.) Consequently, there is a high likelihood that jury decisions will be influenced by emotional and other irrational factors, thus inviting distorted case presentation and legal argument.

Moreover, unlike judges, who are, or typically feel, obligated to spell out the reasons behind their fact findings and ultimate conclusions of law, juries, even when required to submit special verdicts, do not have to explain how they reached their results. As a result, corrective appellate review would be facilitated by eliminating jury trials. Full district court opinions and the greater scope of appellate review would lead to greater clarification and rationalization of substantive antitrust rules and to greater consistency of results.

I see no overriding disadvantages. Judges as well as juries might be biased, but judges are more constrained because they have to explain their decisions and are concerned with the prospects of appellate reversal. Some judges may be unfamiliar with antitrust law when they first get an antitrust case, but they do have to learn it, and over the years their learning and understanding accumulate.

The problem, of course, with this proposal is raised by the seventh amendment to the Constitution, which provides that "[i]n Suits at common law, where the value in controversy shall exceed twenty dollars, the right of trial by jury shall be preserved."[18] Although the language is limited to common law actions, the Supreme Court expanded its coverage to action enforcing statutory rights "if the statute creates legal rights and remedies, enforceable in an action for damages in ordinary courts of law."[19] However, the Court has opened the door by indicating the right to jury trial hinges, among other things, on "the practical abilities and limitations of juries."[20] While this test was offered with reference to issues, not cases as a whole, there have been a few lower court decisions denying jury trial in antitrust cases of high complexity. And, the Third Circuit has held that the seventh amendment is overridden by the due process clause where:

> the complexity of a suit [is] so great that it renders the suit beyond the ability of a jury to decide by rational means with reasonable understanding of the evidence and applicable legal rules. . . .[21]

---

[18] U.S. CONST., amend. VII.

[19] Curtis v. Loether, 415 U.S. 189, 194 (1974).

[20] Ross v. Bernard, 396 U.S. 531, 538 n.10 (1970).

[21] *In re* Japanese Electronics Products Antitrust Litigation, 631 F.2d 1069 (3d Cir. 1980).

Moreover, since antitrust law is a vitally important national public policy, and private rights of action were created not merely to enable recovery of damages, but also to supplement governmental enforcement, it seems to me that a strong argument can be made that a congressional statute eliminating jury trial of private antitrust actions would be constitutional, given the importance to antitrust policy of accurate results, clarification of the law, and minimizing disincentives to procompetitive behavior.

Indeed, there are good reasons for the Supreme Court to conclude that the seventh amendment does not cover federal statutory actions generally.[22]

---

[22] *See* Note, 95 YALE L.J. 1459 (1986).

29
Longer live the Sherman Act!

BY HANS B. THORELLI* and JAMES M. PATTERSON**

I. Introduction

Our focus is on restraints of trade by two or more firms. A concept of firm autonomy—vertical as well as horizontal—is implicit in the centenary Sherman Act and subsequent antitrust laws. Yet modern marketing and organization theories emphasize that the border between the typical firm and its environment (including, notably, other firms) is becoming increasingly blurred. This development introduces new issues in the interpretation of the law in several instances of collective restraints on competition, whether they are horizontal or vertical. In any number of situations the very distinction between collective and single-organization restraints is apt to become more obscure. Nonetheless, in the interests of consumers, equal opportunity to engage in commerce, and open market policy, we believe that collective restraints constitute the nexus of antitrust policy.

The key questions addressed are two: Does a policy against collective restraints have a mission to fill at present and in the foreseeable future, taking us into the 21st century? If so, are the

* The E. W. Kelley Professor of Business Administration, Graduate School of Business, Indiana University.

** Professor of Marketing, Graduate School of Business, Indiana University.

Sherman Act, and relevant parts of ancillary legislation, flexible and purposeful enough to fill the mission?

What is presented is essentially a statement of political economy and philosophy rather than a review of cases and trends in interpretation. The environmental background prompting our statement is developed in the next two sections of the paper, on the ecology of markets and consumer policy. In the following section, collective restraints are seen as examples of a broader trend in the direction of networking, that is, the systematic development of standing relationships between firms. The remaining part of that section is devoted to horizontal restraints, followed by an examination of vertical ones.

Although we use specific issues for illustrative purposes in examining horizontal and vertical restraints, we make no claim to full coverage of relevant aspects of antitrust. On the other hand, although antitrust is essentially concerned with the seller side of the marketplace, "it takes two to tango." This point brings consumer policy into purview. We outline a philosophy of consumer policy, based on the premise that the purpose of such policy is to bring about a reasonable degree of equality between buyers and sellers in the market. We do claim that such equality is an indispensable feature of the truly open market system.

It would be unpardonable to neglect the internationalization of business in the age of interdependence. In fact, we challenge the United States to take new initiatives to promote open markets not only in international trade but also in other countries, and notably the Third World.

In the final section we outline a philosophy of antitrust regarding collective restraints, an approach which may be labeled alternativism. Several of its implications are reflected in specific recommendations for the extension—or reinterpretation—of the rule of reason in this area.

The analytical point of departure may best be described as organizational ecology. Organizational ecology has much in common with biological ecology, but it is distinct in emphasizing that human beings and their organizations need not take their environments as given.[1] They may adopt strategies to change their environment rather than being subservient to it. Society itself may be viewed as a metaorganization, so it follows that antitrust (as any other public policy) is ecologically conditioned. Firms, markets, governments— all live in continuous involvement with their environments. Strategies and policies, public and private, symbolize our attempts to cope with the environment of our tasks.

II. The ecology of markets

The nature and balance of those twin primeval forces of cooperation and competition seem to be changing in the United States. The picture is probably a dynamic one in other parts of the world as well, but the change is not always in the same direction. This seems due in part to a change in values in this country favoring greater cooperation, and in part to changes in technology (notably those changes which embrace telecommunications, word and data processing, and robotics) and related economies of scale. Institutional developments and changes in the situation of the consumer in the marketplace have also played a role. Detailed somewhat in this section, these trends seem likely to extend into the foreseeable future.

Cooperation has been strengthened actively by the structural change in values just referred to and passively perhaps also by a certain relaxation in the work ethic. Some observers have stressed that communications technology will facilitate concentration and centralization (current example: airline reservation systems), but it is obvious that it can also facilitate decentralization and competition by making data more widely available.[2] Its prime impact of interest

---

[1] For a fuller statement see Thorelli essays in STRATEGY + STRUCTURE = PERFORMANCE: THE STRATEGIC PLANNING IMPERATIVE (H. Thorelli ed. 1977). Due to the intervention of chance and events of nature, or due to devious strategies, etc., there is, of course, no assurance of "the survival of the fittest" (except if the shibboleth is purely tautological). Thus organizational ecology is generically different from the Social Darwinism popular at the time the Sherman Act was passed; *cf.* H. THORELLI, THE FEDERAL ANTITRUST POLICY— ORIGINATION OF AN AMERICAN TRADITION 109–17 (1955).

[2] Thorelli, *New Informatics Technologies and Consumer Interests*, 10 J. CONSUMER POL'Y 203–10 (1987).

here most likely is not on horizontal structures but rather on vertical distribution systems. A ready example is food distribution, where the information generated by supermarket scanners is of interest to stores, chains, and manufacturers alike, stimulating cooperation and coordination.

Technology is promoting cooperation in at least two other major respects. One is in the areas of marketing research and new product and process development. In the first area we now find such agencies as Information Resources of Chicago working with consumer panels, chain stores, cable television companies, and manufacturers in coordinated fashion to study advertising effectiveness as well as product movements. Perhaps the most telling example in the R&D area is the SEMATECH venture, a joint effort by U.S. manufacturers to do the basic homework to compete with future generations of Japanese semiconductors and memories. The other point of cooperation-promoting impact is in the growing field of systems marketing, whether the systems are orchestrated by a single firm or a consortium of firms. It seems to be a simple fact that in many spheres the resource requirements are becoming "bigger than both of us" (or even larger).

Changes in the nature of competition are perhaps even more significant. The space between products in the marketplace is increasingly being filled by other new products. For instance, in music reproduction we may have our choice between TV, radio, stereo, tape recorders, VCRs, and compact disk players. We are gradually approaching a continuous spectrum of products. In some markets, cross-product and intertype (lap-top vs. table-top computers) competition may be even stronger than the rivalry between different brands of the same product. Further, the huge accumulation of discretionary income in the hands of middle-class people has brought a new intensity of competition among such separate kinds of offerings as cars, fur coats, and travel to Europe or the Orient.

New varieties of competition stem from new types of organizational arrangements among sellers. Examples include far-ranging franchising arrangements and such other varieties of vertical systems as supermarket chains and direct marketing by telephone, tele-

vision, and video tape, posing new challenges to traditional distribution channel systems. Large retailers, such as Sears, K-Mart,
Wal-Mart and The Limited, inject a new element of competition by
usurping from many manufacturers their old role of governing distributive relationships. And although we agree with Corwin Edwards[3] that modern conglomerates may represent a concentration of
economic power greater than the parts of which they are composed
and that frequently there resides in this power the potential of monopolistic abuse, we would also emphasize that in many markets
conglomerates have added a new dimension of actual or (and this
may be no less significant) potential competition.

We also count ourselves among the growing number of observers who maintain that frequently competition among the few can be
more beneficial to society than competition among the many. Oligopoly has reigned in the chemical, drug, and computer industries,
all of which seem to have made rapid progress to the ultimate
benefit of consumers. Conversely, the textile, shoe, and sawmill
industries here, as in several other countries, are represented by
scores or hundreds of firms—and yet the only major "happening" in
these industries often seems to be that they are becoming increasingly depressed relative to other parts of the economy. The point is
that atomistic competition in the Chicago textbook sense seems less
and less worthwhile as an ideal aim of public policy. On the other
hand, there is clearly no guarantee that every oligopoly will yield
constructive competition.

International competition in the last two or three decades has
become a more pervasive element of the ecology of markets than
ever before in the history of humankind. In our view, this is not
primarily due to increasing differences in comparative advantage in
the classic sense, but rather to dramatic improvements in international flows of information as well as personal travel. Superior
communications, in turn, have everywhere (and especially outside
this country) generated a new awareness of international opportunities (especially in this country) and a new willingness to bridge

---

3 Edwards, *The Significance of Conglomerate Concentration in Modern
Economies*, in DIE KONZENTRATION IN DER WIRTSCHAFT (H. Arndt ed. 1971).

differences in culture and other trade barriers. Although the claims of Levitt[4] and other heralds of the globalization of all markets are misleading, it is true that a number of markets are worldwide due to the inherent characteristics of the products involved, as in the case of industrial equipment or soft drinks. Furthermore, a major comparative study directed by Thorelli[5] revealed the existence of a cosmopolitan, cross-cultural segment in all industrialized countries, an elite group of opinion-leading consumers labeled the Information Seekers. This finding has been confirmed in later research. Average consumers, on the other hand, are the bearers of local values and lifestyles. Typically, however, this major segment may be reached by international competitors by adaptation of one or several elements of marketing strategy.

Though the proliferation of products has vastly intensified interproduct and intertype competition, it is also true that it has resulted in a great fragmentation of consumer markets. Meanwhile, higher levels of education and income are increasing consumer sophistication and aspirations. Higher standards of living are typically accompanied by greater individualization of lifestyles, in turn shown in different consumption profiles. In the United States the result seems to be extreme standardization based on economies of scale ("one size fits all"), some moderation in price (and reduction in quality, based on "value analysis" and similar techniques) on the one hand, and extreme segmentation by lifestyle groups on the other.

In the markets of consumer durable products and such services as fast-food restaurants one senses a certain trivialization of competition, in that the differences between competing offerings are less than sellers make them out to be. This might be part of the recent managerial syndrome of maximizing stockholder wealth in the short run, a trend seemingly more characteristic of this country than others. The phenomenon is well illustrated by the oft-heard complaint that with regard to R&D we have too much of the D and too

---

4   Levitt, *The Globalization of Markets*, 61 HARV. BUS. REV. 93–102 (1983).

5   H. THORELLI, H. BECKER & J. ENGLEDOW, THE INFORMATION SEEKERS: AN INTERNATIONAL STUDY OF CONSUMER INFORMATION AND ADVERTISING IMAGE (1975).

little of the R. Critics also maintain that the feedback from consumers through marketing research often provides answers to the firms' questions but fails to depict actual consumer preferences.

In recent industrial organization literature[6] it has again become popular to emphasize the creation of entry, mobility, exit, and reentry barriers (IBM's System 2 PCs might be an example of the latter) as important elements of business strategy. Whether or not such barriers are perceived as important enough by executives to be deliberately included in strategic planning (to "keep the rascals out" or in), the fact of the matter appears to be that technology is helping in barrier demolition in at least two significant ways. First, modern technology permits the same function or feature in a product or process to be attained in many different ways with strikingly similar efficiency. The typical patent can be worked around, and the typical design can be imitated in short order. Second, thanks to robotics, flexible manufacturing systems, mini steelmills, etc., the economies of production these days work in favor of smaller-scale operations about as often as they point to large. With the true globalization of capital markets and the rise of venture capital funds, finance seems no longer to be quite as formidable a bottleneck as it used to be. These days such marketing-related features as company image and reputation and brand loyalty and trust are probably the source of the most important entry barriers. Yet it must be remembered that although goodwill may take years to build, it is a highly delicate source of advantage, one which can easily be lost overnight.

What we have said concerning barriers and individualization of lifestyles, taken together with the enormous needs for specialized services of all kinds, strengthens our belief that there is no immediate danger of further concentration of the economy as a whole. In the last decade big businesses have become bigger, and small businesses have become more numerous—a trend which is likely to continue.

Competition and cooperation are undergoing continual change. The balance between them shifts from time to time; currently coop-

---

6 M. PORTER, COMPETITIVE STRATEGY (1980); G. YIP, BARRIERS TO ENTRY (1982).

eration seems to be making some gains. As we have seen, competition is indeed far from dead—but it still needs nurturing. Contrary to observations by Bork[7] and Brozen[8], public policy (and we add consumer policy to antitrust) is not irrelevant in this context. This is perhaps never so obvious as when one or the other industry or trade association spends its bundle on lobbying for antitrust exemption!

III. Consumer policy: Twin of antitrust

Consumer policy may be defined as measures promoting consumer interests taken by others than the individual consumer acting alone. Thus, consumer policy makers include consumer organizations and many other citizen groups, business, government, educational institutions, and the mass media. Broadly speaking, the emergence of consumer policy is a phenomenon of the last 30 years. Its emergence stems from the fact that total and automatic satisfaction of consumer interests can take place (if at all) only in the dreamworld of atomistic competition, and from the related realization that the time-worn doctrines of caveat emptor reduced the consumer to a secondary position in the marketplace. The origins of "consumerism" as a philosophy or movement need no detailed review here; the single most important factor explaining its relatively recent origin is probably the increasing complexity of modern products and markets, combined with the rising aspiration levels of more sophisticated consumers.

A philosophy of consumer policy in a complementary and synergistic relationship with our antitrust policy will stress consumer emancipation ("help to self-help"), strengthen open markets, encourage pluralist and voluntarist solutions, stimulate decentralization and experimentation, and establish a balance between caveat emptor and caveat venditor.[9] Government agencies should have

---

7   R. BORK, THE ANTITRUST PARADOX: A POLICY AT WAR WITH ITSELF (1978).

8   Y. BROZEN, CONCENTRATION, MERGERS, AND PUBLIC POLICY (1982).

9   Thorelli & Engledow, *Information Seekers and Information Systems*, J. MARKETING, 44, 9–27 (1980); H. THORELLI & S. THORELLI, CONSUMER INFORMATION SYSTEMS AND CONSUMER POLICY (1977).

clearly defined standby obligations in cases where voluntarist-pluralist solutions prove insufficient to safeguard consumer rights. (A significant minority of laggard sellers might refuse to join a voluntary consumer complaint arbitration system, for instance.) The relative emphasis on policy elements flows naturally from these premises; the priority order is information, education, and protection-regulation.

The protection route is given low priority for two reasons. First, it would appear that in the last quarter-century we have established a minimum acceptable threshold of regulatory measures in such key areas as product safety and health. Second, too much protection of the hand-holding variety fosters too much dependence, that is, too much in the sense that it undermines consumer sovereignty and discourages individual judgment. At the other extreme, product information facilitates consumer decision making and increases market transparency. In this manner the sellers providing superior offerings will be more amply rewarded than the others. After all, this is what the competitive enterprise system is all about. To understand the significance of the open market system and the role of market information, to develop a schedule of acquisitions priorities as well as buying criteria for particular products, and to train judgment as a consumer, the citizen needs consumer education. The three prongs of consumer policy clearly overlap; the present context calls only for a general awareness of the differences among them.

Open markets presuppose a substantial equality of power among buyers and sellers as well as a high degree of transparency of the marketplace. Thus consumer policy is not only the logical but the indispensable complement of antitrust in an overall open market policy. Unceasing vigilance on behalf of consumer rights is—and must remain—a hallmark of market improvement policy. At the same time, the pendulum must not be allowed to swing all the way from letting the buyer beware to letting the seller alone do so. Sooner or later, this would lead to market replacement substituting for market improvement. In a democratic society, rights are inextricably linked to responsibilities. This does not mean that all consumers have to exercise their rights and/or responsibilities all the time;

it does mean that at least some of us exercise them at least some of the time. In the figure, key consumer rights and responsibilities are shown in a matrix involving the three principal aspects of consumer policy. Note that the traditional rights indicated presuppose the existence of a basic freedom to consume. There are obvious opportunities for both synergies and tradeoffs among the policy measures exemplified in the cells of the matrix. Such opportunities for reenforcement and substitution also exist among the consumer policy makers who logically constitute a third dimension of the figure.

There is no need to look with pessimism upon the condition of the consumer in the emerging order. Owing to increasing discretionary income and education levels, there can be no doubt that consumer power has increased markedly at the macro level. More has to be done, however, to implement consumer rights at the micro level. The celebrated instruments of Voice and Exit simply are not sufficient. Voice calls for resource commitments in terms of time and nervous energy, which many consumers are not prepared to spend. Exit is of little help where no acceptable substitutes are available (the situation with regard to U.S.-made cars in the last 10 years, in the eyes of many). And ample experience in the Western world indicates that self-regulation by industry is insufficient; indeed, with few exceptions meaningful (if not sufficient) self-regulation everywhere seems to require at least a perceived presence of the Big Stick of the government.

Scanning the environment, we find there is a reasonably solid foundation of consumer protection. Amendments and extensions will be needed as times and values change, but far-reaching reform in this area does not seem called for in the near term. It might unduly divert attention from more urgent priorities in the consumer policy area. Such a priority is obligatory consumer education, currently in force in only a handful of states. Combinable with such courses as economics and civics, consumer ed is easily as important as either of these. The citizen as consumer provides an excellent vantage point to examine the open market system and, beyond it, our economy and society as a whole.

The top priority is reserved for consumer information. The ob-

Figure

Consumer Policy and Consumer Rights and Responsibilities

CONSUMER POLICY	CONSUMER RIGHTS			
	1. CHOOSE FREELY	2. BE INFORMED	3. BE HEARD	4. BE SAFE
A. EDUCATION	decision-making budgeting; nature of market economy, rights and responsibilities	generic product and materials data, information sources	how to assert consumer rights	importance of health and safety, user manuals and training
B. INFORMATION	buying criteria buying advice	models and brands data, independent consumer info programs	market research, two-way market dialog	safety certification, care and maintenance data
C. PROTECTION	maintain open markets, antitrust; stop hi-pressure and deceptive tactics	truly informative advertising, product claims substantiation	complaints-handling machinery	minimize health and accident risks
	CHOOSE WISELY	KEEP INFORMED	SOUND OFF	SAFETY FIRST
	CONSUMER RESPONSIBILITIES			

A third dimension of the matrix would show the makers of consumer policy. These policy-makers include consumer organizations, other citizen groups, business, government, educational institutions and the mass media. (copyright: H. B. Thorelli)

jection is often made that there is already an astounding wealth of such information in the marketplace. But this is also the very reason why a consumer information system (CIS) is so urgently needed. The information is incredibly fragmented and, typically, highly opinionated by seller hype, our friends' prejudices, and our own casuistic experiences. Nowhere (with the possible exception of *Consumer Reports*) is consumer information available in reasonable detail, presented in a reasonably objective fashion, or much less, delivered in a reasonably systematic and comparable manner. Unfortunately, as our Information Seeker research demonstrates,[10] *Consumer Reports* can never be expected to reach more than a small, albeit influential, minority of consumers. Yet it should be obvious that consumers need their CIS as urgently as managers need their MIS.

Having assigned top priority to product information among consumer policy measures, we shall briefly outline a prototype computer-based CIS. The technology for its design is already at hand, evidenced by the diagnostic data banks available to doctors, lawyers, and real estate operators, as well as the advance reservation systems of several airlines. In Canada, Great Britain, France, and Germany, CIS experimentation has proceeded farther than in this country. The problems retarding development are financial and administrative (or at least perceived to be such). To be viable and— equally important—credible, such a CIS needs pluralist sponsorship, including consumers and producers, distributors and dealers, standardization and testing bodies, academics, and governments. In keeping with democratic tradition, and as business support in updating myriads of data is necessary in any case, the program should be voluntary in nature. A national CIS has the potential of adding local price, service, and availability data—of special importance in nonmetropolitan markets. Its dialog feature permits the incorporation of both optional educational background (what is meant by decibel, signal-to-noise ratio etc.) and custom-tailored information.

Start-up expenses would likely have to be financed by foundations, businesses, and government. Once in place, operating expenses of the consumer information utility might well be covered by user fees and by voluntary submission of updated information by businesses, Consumers Union, the National Bureau of Standards, and so on. All information would be "tagged" by origin, enabling consumers to evaluate data credibility. Misleading data would be

---

10   H. THORELLI, H. BECKER & J. ENGLEDOW, *supra* note 5.

subject to the same sanctions as misleading advertising. The system would be accessible by telephone, by interactive video and cable, by personal computers, and by terminals in libraries, stores, and airports.

Should the computerized information utility fail to meet with the degree of voluntary cooperation needed for success, a unified point of purchase–oriented informative labeling and quality certification program might be considered as a substitute. Outlined by Thorelli and Engledow,[11] such a program should be voluntary in principle, though mandatory participation might be considered in markets where data are not readily accessible or where product characteristics and performance are beyond advance inspection by the customer.

In retrospect, one might ask why consumer policy was not directly linked to antitrust from the outset. First, we should note that most people still do not perceive the linkage. Second, a century ago most Americans still believed that competition and equal opportunity among sellers in and of themselves were sufficient to protect the interests of the buying public. Third, the idea of letting the buyer beware—already more than a millennium old at the time— was still reigning supreme for all practical purposes.

IV. Networking—between markets and hierarchies

The term "network" here refers to two or more firms or business organizations involved in long-term relationships.[12] For expository purposes we may think in terms of a spectrum of arrangements, from loose to tight, from arms'-length bargaining to total integration, from spot transactions via standing relations to the internalization of markets. At one end of the spectrum is what we may call the open market. At the other we find the firm that is relatively self-sufficient in terms of vertical or functional integration. In some ways these distinctions are analogous to

---

[11] Thorelli & Engledow, *supra* note 9.

[12] Thorelli, *Networks: Between Markets and Hierarchies*, 7 STRATEGIC MGMT. J. 37–51 (1986).

Williamson's[13] markets and hierarchies, although he would likely include as part of "markets" a number of in-between forms where we would rather apply the generic term "networks."

We should emphasize that networks are not the same as "administered markets," for a network may constitute only a small part of one or several markets. In most markets one would typically find a number of competing networks. Although networking is especially important in industrial and services marketing and in international business operations, examples of standing associations and "relational marketing" are increasingly found in most parts of the economy of this country. Japanese executives all seem to be networkers—which may well be another clue to understanding their success!

Between markets and hierarchies, networks also represent a mix of internalization and externalization of functions and activities. Although network maintenance cost is not negligible, networks are created to reduce transactions costs and opportunistic behavior on the part of members—primarily by increasing the level of trust and predictability. Personal contacts are indispensable here.

Utilities, money, power, information, and social contacts flow along the links of the network. While customarily one finds elements of competition both within and between networks, they may be viewed as instruments of "maintaining cooperation." As exclusionary and power characteristics are inherent in networks, there must be both "good" ones and "bad" ones from the viewpoint of antitrust and open market philosophy. Most Americans would regard OPEC as an offensive cartel and regard Underwriters' Laboratories, on the whole, as a meritorious organization. The key challenge in this and the following section is to provide some guidelines for acceptable and nonacceptable networking.

Strategic issues often resolved in a networking context include:

> new product development,
> marketing channels and franchising,

---

13   O. WILLIAMSON, MARKETS AND HIERARCHIES: ANALYSIS AND ANTITRUST IMPLICATIONS (1975).

patent and trademark licensing,

standardization,

turnkey contracts and "systems selling,"

make-lease-or-buy decisions,

diversification,

barter and reciprocal trading,

internationalization,

developing suppliers,

banking arrangements.

For antitrust purposes we identify three major categories of networking, involving competitors in a given industry, suppliers and customers in industrial marketing, and vertical systems (marketing channels), respectively. Vertical systems are treated in the next section. Vaguely related to such systems are networks comprising one or several suppliers and customers (notably original equipment manufacturers) in industrial marketing. Generally, industrial marketing networks do not represent an area of great excitement to antitrust. It is true that by preempting vertical integration by the parties, such arrangements may reduce potential competition. Reciprocity, often practiced between industrial firms, is a somewhat questionable practice, as it implies that at least one of the parties is in doubt as to whether his sale would have made it under open market conditions. There may certainly be abuses of power, though in the industrial marketing context such abuses rarely see the light. On the other hand, industrial marketing networks can be of great benefit in joint product or process development, technology transfer, systems selling, and so on. To the extent that antitrust concerns enter this picture, evaluation should be based on an application of the rule of reason to the "total setting" rather than to isolated instances of restraint of trade.

Perhaps the single most vital area of antitrust application involves horizontal arrangements, that is, networking among competitors. The last quarter-century has witnessed the rapidly increasing spread of horizontal arrangements, many of which bear little or no resemblance to the classic trade association. Essentially, this is to be seen as an institutional response to a dynamic environment characterized by increasing complexity in technology and products, a need for standardization seen by buyers and sellers alike, the internationalization of business, the inroads by Japanese and other overseas competitors on U.S. markets, and scale economies as well as bargaining power obtainable by joint buying or contracting-out of certain functions. Perhaps the most important driving force has been the massive information needs of increasingly "professional" management all the way from General Motors to the swelling numbers of households run more or less like firms.

The Reagan administration adapted to these trends actively by its "broad-minded" Business Review program and tacitly by allowing a multitude of newfangled cooperative arrangements to go unchallenged. In some respects it probably went overboard in assimilating Chicago-style thinking that "what is, is right." Nevertheless, on balance this type of "soft" response, permitting considerable experimentation, was probably better than a policy of "stonewalling" in an era of institutional dynamics. We do see as a healthy sign the somewhat more rigorous approach relative to restrictive business practices taken by the Bush administration.

A summary overview of the horizontal arrangements field is helpful in developing guidelines for evaluating networking among competitors. Initial observation is that price and output-restricting cartels remain per se illegal under the Sherman Act. Significant infringements of both competition and consumer sovereignty, such agreements are properly regarded as conspiracies against the public. With regard to most other species of (horizontal) networking, it will be seen that we prefer the extended application of the rule of reason.

This includes specialization agreements that generally have been regarded as ipso facto illegal in the past. In some mature markets where all competitors try to be everything to everybody, for example, agreements to specialize in certain product versions or market segments might be more beneficial than harmful, taking all interests into account. (Admittedly, most firms should be able to derive the benefits of specialization by pursuing a "nichemanship" strategy on their own.)

A more clear-cut case of ambiguity (calling for the rule of reason) is that of standardization. The benefits of standardization are obvious, including minimum quality requirements, interchangeability, scale economies, and transactions cost savings. Yet it has been abused both here and in other countries for exclusionary purposes, a weapon directed both at domestic competitors and at imports. Standards may also restrain competition when they are not realigned with technological progress or changing demands of the marketplace. Purchasing directors on standards committees are powerful enough to keep industrial product standards customer oriented. On the other hand, such standards bodies as ASTM, ANSI, and even Underwriters' Laboratories have been more producer- than user-oriented in venturing into consumer product standards. Evaluation of the adequacy of consumer representation should be a significant part of the continued application of the rule of reason to standards groups.

A special problem area is ethical standards developed by professional groups. When codes of ethics restrain competition unduly they should be stricken down or reprehensible parts eliminated. In such a context client-oriented provisions might also be prescribed. Why is there no Patients' Bill of Rights in the codes of ethics of the medical profession?

The administration of data banks has been a classic trade association activity since the dawn of the century. Antitrust judges have developed a series of rules of reasonableness in evaluating such organized information exchanges among competitors, notably as they pertain to pricing data. Exchanges are more acceptable to the extent that they limit price reports to past transactions, preserve the anonymity of individual competitors, and make data available to buyers as well as sellers. They are less acceptable to the extent that they concern future prices, identify traders, withhold information from buyers, and carry recommendations or "loaded" comments on current or future price and production policies. In the *Container Corp.* case (1969)[14] the Court also reserved the right to look at such program details in their setting, that is, in the context of the struc-

---

14   U.S. v. Container Corp. of America, 393 U.S. 333 (1969).

ture of the industry. Asymmetric information among competitors, or among sellers and buyers, is not conducive to open markets.

It is clear that in the age of technological communication and increasing application of professional techniques in management the use of data banks and exchanges of all kinds will accelerate. As a commendable example we mention the PIMS Program [Profit Impact of Market Strategies], operated by the Strategic Planning Institute [SPI]. In effect, this is a nonprofit organization of which any firm in any industry can become a member, provided it pays the fee and is willing to submit data for at least 5 years of operation. PIMS is by far the most sophisticated data bank relating to structure-strategy-performance relationships among lines of business (strategic business units) in existence anywhere in the world. Members can get the benefit of comparing themselves with the entire set of 3,000+ businesses or with as few as the dozen businesses looking most like themselves (often active in other industries) but performing significantly better or worse on a number of criteria. In addition, at least a score of scholarly books and doctoral theses and a hundred articles in professional journals have been written by a large number of academics whose projects have been found worthwhile by SPI.[15]

More controversial examples of recent developments are collective credit reporting agencies and airline reservation systems based on the cooperation of individual airlines and voluntary groups of travel agencies. A rule of reason might imply that collective credit reporting programs are more acceptable the more it is true that any firm (at least in the industry concerned) can subscribe, that subscribers are free to acquire supplementary data elsewhere, and that firms or persons reported on may have access to relevant data about themselves and the opportunity to voice any objections. The airline-travel agency reservation systems, which handle most flight ticket sales, are really vertical distribution networks as well as data banks. American and United, whose systems dominate the market, provide agents with computerized listings of the flights of all airlines and

---

15   For an excellent bibliography on PIMS and its findings, *see* R. BUZZELL & B. GALE, THE PIMS PRINCIPLES (1987).

arrange for the bookings. Other airlines, which pay transaction fees for tickets booked through one of the systems, have complained that those fees are too high, that the contracts binding agents to the systems are too restrictive, and that the systems give the airlines operating them an unfair advantage. At least until recently, apparently the American and United systems consistently listed the flights of the system airline first. The battle over the several systems has been joined but not yet resolved. The nature of the complaints provides some clues for criteria in applying the rule of reason to the situation.

The relationship between research and development and antitrust traditionally has been an uneasy one. By spurring competition antitrust may be expected to stimulate innovation, yet patents confer a temporary monopoly on their owners. There is no doubt that, if properly applied, antitrust and patent policy can coexist, and many apparent inconsistencies have been ironed out over the years. Of interest here is the pooling of R&D efforts. Like other pooling arrangements, joint R&D constitutes a potential restraint on competition among participants and, in addition, may be used for exclusionary purposes. Yet it is true that in electronics, aerospace, and other areas of modern technology R&D is sufficiently resource-demanding that many companies hesitate to "go it alone." Also, Japan seems to have set a tantalizing example of the potential benefits of coordinated research efforts. Other examples are provided by the European Community.

Spurred by such developments the U.S. government in the last decade has taken an increasingly favorable view toward joint R&D. An early and striking example was the Microelectronic and Computer Technology Corporation, which, when founded, comprised most of the leading semiconductor and computer manufacturers of the country except IBM. For various reasons not very successful, that venture has been followed by the SEMATECH consortium for semiconductor development. The National Cooperative Research Act of 1984 positively encourages similar ventures and goes on to specify that their legality under the antitrust laws is to be evaluated by applying the rule of reason. One criterion mentioned in this context is the availability of licenses to outside parties. Other criteria might include the following:

> In the absence of the joint effort, would the activity be undertaken by individual firms acting independently?
>
> Do ancillary restraints limit continued independent activity?
>
> Is the joint venture open to all members of the industry?
>
> Are members representing different industries, providing potential synergy?
>
> If all members are from the same industry, how concentrated is that industry? Are small firms represented as well as large ones?

According to the Commerce Department, more than 100 cooperative research ventures have already been registerd. The Webb-Pomerene Act of 1918 represented the first antitrust exemption for export cartels. A condition was that such ventures not restrain competition in domestic commerce—an obviously illusory notion. The problem is, rather, whether the disadvantages of such restraint are outweighed by the advantages of collective action by U.S. exporters in international markets, where cartels are typically not interfered with. It is estimated that in 1979 less than 2 percent of U.S. exports were handled by W-P associations.[16] Largely in response to the success of the Japanese export trading companies (*sogo shosha*), Congress in 1982 passed the Export Trading Company (ETC) Act, to ease further antitrust constraints for exporters, permitting banks to invest in ETCs and instructing the Commerce Department to promote the development of such companies. The 1918 exemption for export cartels was retained. Although less than a resounding success to date, the ETC Act may well become more important in the future. In addition to the effect on domestic competition of ETC possibly emerging international rules conflicting with the 1982 or 1918 laws should be taken into account in the evaluation of antitrust implications.

In international trade the rule of reason should also be applied

---

[16] Kaikiti, *The Export Trading Company Act: A Viable International Marketing Tool*, 27 CALIF. MGMT. REV. 59–64 (1984).

to collective efforts to restrain piracy of product design, trademarks, computer software, and other intellectual property.

Cooperative buying arrangements furnish a major example of competitive networking to be evaluated by the rule of reason. Such schemes may be entered into to establish a service otherwise difficult to obtain (such as insurance for underground oil tanks) or to prevail upon economies of scale and attendant bargaining power, as in the case of voluntary chains or joint procurement of freight and travel services. Cooperative selling is inherently a more doubtful proposition. This is so even when a group of drug wholesalers, each active in a different region of the country, get together to bid on national accounts otherwise dominated by a handful of national vendors. It may well have been a mistake by the Department of Justice to approve such an arrangement in 1987.[17] On the other hand, consortia representing companies in different industries jointly selling an entire system or turnkey project would often be legitimate.

V. Vertical marketing networks

No area of antitrust enforcement has given the courts more difficulty than the regulation of vertical marketing networks. This is primarily due to the acceptance of the standard view of the marketing channel that regards vertical networks as a series of successive competitive markets and hence sees vertical channel relationships as relationships between buyers and sellers or between independent competitors. It is a view ill suited for evaluating modern-day vertical marketing systems.

The autonomy of vertically linked units often results in wasteful duplication and high intrasystem transaction costs, while the fragmentation of the network sacrifices potential scale economies. Consequently, the centrally coordinated vertical marketing system has become the dominant mode of distribution. In fact, the entire vertical system, rather than constituent firms, has become the meaningful unit of competition.

---

17 *See* U.S. Department of Justice, Press Release AT 202–633–2016, May 21, 1987.

Just as a high degree of interorganizational coordination is required within a marketing channel if that channel is going to have a long-run impact on the markets it serves, so too, functional specialization is essential for effective channel performance. It is the way that scale economies and professional expertise are brought to bear on the distribution process. Functional specialization results, however, in even greater operational interdependence. This functional interdependence increases still further the need for centralized coordination and administration. In effect, the channel network becomes an overarching organization of organizations.

Anytime there is an interdependency relationship, the seeds of conflict are present. Conflicts arise within distribution channels over how much inventory should be carried by various members, who has the right to represent a particular product within a given territory, whether prices are being maintained at reasonable levels, why distributors and dealers are sometimes bypassed via direct selling, and the like. In fact, most public and private antitrust activity directed at contractual channels arises from these internal channel conflicts generated by channel interdependence.

Antitrust interpretation is based on an economic view of market behavior. Hitherto this view has tended to exclude organizational analysis to determine whether and how various structures and arrangements will affect the public interest. Although other interests are present, the overriding purpose of antitrust enforcement is to maintain competition as the principal regulator of business behavior, channels of distribution included. Conclusions as to how this purpose is to be implemented may differ, depending on the perspective applied.

Economic theory views the relationships between levels of distribution primarily as relationships between buyers and sellers, that is, as market relationships. And, of course, in a competitive market these vertical relationships are defined largely by price, which in turn is governed by the interaction of supply and demand. Moreover, assuming that the vertical markets are competitive, or should be, no one buyer or seller would be large enough or in a strategic enough position to influence price. No participant stands in any significant relationship to any other. Power is absent; each participant is free from the influence of any other.

This view of the channel situation ignores the near universal conditions of mutual dependency and power relations that severely limit and possibly disqualify the market mechanism as the appropriate model for guiding public policy in this area. The typical distributive market is clearly imperfectly competitive. Each imperfection partially frees distributors and manufacturers from market constraints. To the extent that they are thus freed, they have some bargaining power over those with whom they deal. Thus a manufacturer who has created consumer preference for his brands enjoys a bargaining advantage in his dealings with distributors, just as a dealer who benefits from consumer habit and from location is strengthened in his relations with wholesalers. Monopolistic and oligopolistic elements in horizontal competition add uncertainties to vertical relationships and cause their outcome to rest in part on relative bargaining strengths. Furthermore, even the increase in size associated with mass distribution has added to the importance of bargaining power.

The conditions of dependency and control characteristic of modern distribution thus vitiate much of the economic analysis of distribution's vertical conflicts. Power is essential for vertical marketing networks to function effectively, but power is not really compatible with classic economic analysis. While there never existed absolute equality of bargaining power on opposite sides of distributive markets, the enormous increase in the size of both manufacturers and retailers and the attraction of mass markets have changed much of modern distribution from a flow through a series of largely autonomous markets to a single movement dominated by manufacturers, large wholesalers, or key retailers. Moreover, dominance by a manufacturer often reflects a calculated strategy on his part to shift the selective function to the consumer or end user and away from intermediate markets. Many manufacturers now compete more for the patronage of the final buyer than for that of the wholesaler. In such cases, the bargaining position of the independent wholesaler is weakened still further, since he now stands between the manufacturer and the retail level, where the competitive success of the "pull" strategy is determined. Such manufacturers must and do control both the wholesale level and the retail level. Texaco and General Motors cannot afford to let their retail dealers operate at arms' length. If the pull strategy is to work, the retail presentation must be carefully orchestrated. In such cases, the wholesaler either integrates into the manufacturer's system or is bypassed. It may not always be possible to bypass the independent wholesaler due to the discrepancy of assortments, but often the independent retailer can be reached directly.

The net result of all of these developments in contemporary distribution is that power has come to rival strictly economic factors as the governing element in the vertical relationships in a channel of distribution. And yet, the courts' mode for analyzing antitrust issues in the channel area assumes either that power does not exist or that when it does, it is an "imperfection" which must be eliminated.

Modern competition is no longer simply defined by horizontal relationships. Increasingly, the relevant unit of competition is the entire network of interrelated institutions and agencies, even when distributors in any given geographic area handle the product lines of more than one manufacturer. Disregarding the realities, the enforcement of the antitrust laws continues to seek to preserve large numbers of independent decision makers at all levels of distribution. As a consequence, many manufacturers and franchisors are finding it difficult, short of integration under common ownership, to exert influence on the independent businessmen who deal in their products and in the markets where their products are sold. In these cases the network may not be strong enough to secure the synergy and scale benefits of a well-organized channel system.

The contradiction between the legal norm (or fiction) and reality reached its zenith in the 1967 *Schwinn* decision.[18] In that decision, the Court sought to reconcile the irreconcilable by resorting to a gimmick, namely the ancient doctrine of "restraints on alienation." The result was chaos. If taken literally, the *Schwinn* decision

---

18   U.S. v. Arnold Schwinn & Co., 338 U.S. 365 (1967).

outlawed much of what was going on in modern marketing. As a consequence, it took only a few years for *Schwinn* to be radically modified. The controlling decision is now *GTE Sylvania*.[19] This 1977 case backed away from the alienation doctrine and returned the law to the relativism of the 1963 *White Motor* case,[20] which had held that much of the substance of distributive relations needed to be subjected to a rule of reason analysis and that most vertical restrictions were not illegal in and of themselves without first looking at their competitive consequences.

Sylvania was not an endorsement of vertical restrictions. In *Sylvania*, the Court merely rejected the application of the per se rule to certain vertical restrictions. There is still a latent presumption in favor of autonomy in the language used; it is just no longer an unqualified presumption.

Vertical restrictions tend to reduce intrabrand competition. Obviously, customer-group and territorial restrictions seek to eliminate intrabrand competition for the same customers. Location restrictions have the same effect, due to practical constraints on the effective marketing area of retail outlets. Incidentally, it should be noted that the Sherman Act does not distinguish between interbrand competition and intrabrand competition. This distinction has come from the *White Motor* case.

Indirectly, however, vertical restrictions may actually promote interbrand competition by allowing the manufacturer to achieve certain efficiencies in the distribution of his products, vis-à-vis his competitors. For example, new entrants can induce dealer investment, and established firms can induce distributor promotion and point of purchase support.[21]

The creativity of marketers in developing "legal" ways to achieve vertical control of distribution is boundless. As the law hems in what can be done in the way of conventional vertical re-

---

19   Continental T.V., Inc. v. GTE Sylvania, 433 U.S. 36 (1977).

20   White Motor Co. v. U.S., 372 U.S. 253 (1963).

21   *Sylvania*, 433 U.S. 36 (1977) at 54.

strictions, managers of contractual networks have responded with novel arrangements that achieve essentially the same result, but in an ambiguous manner.

The marketing of gasoline provides an excellent example of this process of finding ways around restrictions on tying, exclusive dealing, and vertical price-fixing. As the control of the retail setting became more and more important after World War I, and as the power of well-located independent retailers began to increase at the expense of the refiners who were forced to bid for their customers, most majors began to integrate forward into retailing to a significant extent. The way to guarantee that a prime location would carry your brand without having to pay a premium or grant other concessions was to control the retail property.[22]

Later, as depression-plagued states began to impose chain-store taxes and as unions sought to organize company-operated stations, and for other reasons, Amoco developed its "Iowa plan," which shifted the operation of its stations from company employees to franchised lessee-dealers, an arrangement copied by most other major refiners in short order.[23]

To check the threat of a lessee-dealer selling a competitor's products, the industry adopted the practice of lending but not licensing or selling the signs, pumps, and tanks at the leased station. Technically, the lessee-dealer was free to sell competing brands, but not through the pumps and tanks or under the sign of the landlord-refiner. Because the station was leased with pumps, signs, and tanks in place, a short-term lessee would have to secure his supplier-landlord's permission to remove the present pumps and tanks and change all architectural identification, signs, and logos before he could sell a competing brand. This proceeded under the real threat of nonrenewal of the short-term station lease and the obligation to restore the property to its original condition. By such prac-

---

22   F. ALLVINE & J. PATTERSON, COMPETITION LTD.: THE MARKETING OF GASOLINE 27 (1973).

23   J. McLEAN & R. HAIGH, THE GROWTH OF THE INTEGRATED OIL COMPANIES 270 (1954).

tices major refiners were able to achieve the same results as though they had tied the product to the lease of the station and had then required an exclusive dealing agreement from the lessee.[24] Short-term leases were also used to "motivate" certain behavior from lessee-dealers. Station hours and appearance, sales of "unfriendly" tires, batteries, and accessories (after-market items), pricing, and the like could be controlled by a frank discussion of renewal prospects.[25]

Some of these practices have subsequently been found to be surrogates for traditionally prohibited practices, and thus illegal. But many still persist as proof of the fact that contractual vertical marketing systems do possess imperatives that must be accommodated if they are to remain viable competitors to integrated systems.

In the days before the soft drink bottlers were able to persuade Congress to exempt them from antitrust regulations governing vertical territorial restrictions, Pepsi bottlers were restricted by the terms of their franchises to store-door as opposed to warehouse delivery. This effectively confined their geographic market to the limited area that could be effectively served by driver salespeople making small-scale drops. Location clauses and area of primary responsibility provisions served the same end in other industries.

In the case of package-goods manufacturers, the use of free display racks given to retailers on the condition that they not be used to display products of competing manufacturers tends to achieve much the same end as an exclusive dealing agreement. This is especially true if the category is characterized by low turns yet must be carried by all full-fledged drug or food stores. In many cases, the free rack is designed to use all of the allotted space for a particular category and hence serves to completely block all competing brands. Foot care and pet care products are examples of this practice.

---

24   Bogosian v. Gulf Oil Corp., 561 F.2d 434 (3rd Cir. 1977); *cert. denied*, 434 U.S. 1086 (1978).

25   U.S. Federal Trade Commission, Report on Anticompetitive Practices in the Marketing of Gasoline (mimeographed, 1967); Phillips v. Crown Cent. Petrol. Co., 602 F.2d 616 (4th Cir. 1979); *cert. denied*, 444 U.S. 1074 (1980).

In recent years, national or house accounts have been used creatively in an attempt to circumvent the per se rule against vertical price-fixing.[26] For example, some oil companies have declared discount chains to be house accounts in order to prevent their jobbers from selling them motor oil at wholesale prices, which would allow the discounter to undercut the price of motor oil sold through traditional service station channels. Once the discount chains were designated house accounts, they received no more sales calls from either the jobber or the refiner.

The leading manufacturer of automatic rollover car washes, 80 to 90% of which are sold to service stations, achieved a system of de facto vertical price control. By declaring all major oil companies and their branded stations to be national accounts, they were required to be sold at specified national account prices, despite the fact that the actual sale, installation, and subsequent service of the account were the responsibility of the local distributor.[27] In other product areas, manufacturers have used profit passover or warranty reimbursement plans to confine distributors to their assigned territory.[28]

These are a few of the many instances that show the need to control and coordinate contractual vertical marketing networks is seemingly irresistible. As one loophole or backdoor practice is closed, managers discover new methods. The problem is clear: The law is out of tune with reality and needs to be rethought in this area.

In this context it is to be noted that the resurrection of "reasonableness" as the basis for judging vertical nonprice restraints poses a number of problems in addition to deciding what general factors are to be considered. Obviously, in any given case the courts will

---

26   See Capital Temporaries of Hartford, Inc. et al. v. Olsten Corp., 383 F. Supp. 902 (1974); Greene v. General Foods, Corp., 517 F.2d 635 (5th Cir. 1975); cert. denied, 424 U.S. 942 (1976); Bostick Oil Co. v. Michelin Tire Corp., 702 F.2d 1207 (1983); Ryko Mfg. Co. v. Eden Services, 759 F.2d 671 (8th Cir. 1985).

27   Ryko Mfg. Co. v. Eden Services, 759 F.2d 671 (8th Cir. 1985).

28   Eiberger v. Sony Corp., 622 F.2d 1068 (2nd Cir. 1980); Ohio-Sealy Mattress Mfg. Co. v. Sealy, Inc., 585 F.2d 821 (7th Cir. 1978).

have to decide what priority to give these factors and how to make them operational and give them relative weights. What is needed is a new theory of channel competition, consistent with the realities of modern marketing, to guide judges and other policy makers in their assessment of the competitive implications of networked channel arrangements. Without this, enforcement will often work at cross-purposes with the basic objectives of antitrust.

In the meantime, some considerations and questions of relevance to antitrust interpretation of vertical networks may be offered. One justification for the interest in intrabrand competition is that significant product differentiation reduces the effectiveness of interbrand competition as a check on intrabrand market power while increasing this intrabrand market power. If it is possible for a buyer to substitute freely a different brand of the same product without a significant sense of deprivation, little is lost from a lessening of intrabrand competition. But if, because of product differentiation, such substitution is not free and easy, the importance of intrabrand competition increases, and the justification for restricting it becomes a matter of concern.[29]

A related question is whether we should bother to distinguish between ownership integration, achieved by internal growth or merger, and integration achieved through agreement. Traditionally, under the Sherman Act, ownership integration has been judged on the basis of market size, and questions about the lessening of intrabrand competition are ignored. By contrast, contractual integration is treated quite differently and more stringently, despite the fact that contractually linked vertical marketing systems are more flexible than are ownership channels. Often the only distinction between the two is the one of title, a distinction that many feel to be irrelevant for antitrust purposes.[30] Obviously, when assessing the validity of a business practice, what effect the practice has on competition is of primary concern and not the legal form in which it is cast.[31]

---

[29] P. AREEDA, ANTITRUST ANALYSIS: PROBLEMS, TEXT, CASES 71 (2d ed. 1974).

[30] Bork, *The Rule of Reason and the Per Se Concept: Price Fixing and Market Division II*, 75 YALE L. J. 373, 472 (1966).

[31] Greene v. General Foods Corp., 517 F.2d 635 (5th Cir. 1975), *cert. denied*, 424 U.S. 942 (1976).

If the treatment of contractual integration should continue to be more restrictive than the treatment of ownership integration, the ultimate result might be to undermine contractual integration, including franchising, as a means for the independent merchant to become an efficient and effective competitor of large integrated firms. This would, then, weaken the competitive system.

Basically, the theory underlying the law of contractual integration holds that actual or potential intrabrand competition between channel members at the same level or at vertically adjacent levels of the channel can be injured in two different ways:[32]

> by eliminating competition between two consenting parties, that is by agreement; and
>
> by injuring intrabrand rivals.

This concern for preventing vertical agreements that may injure competition between potential intrabrand rivals underlies those sections of the antitrust law that regulate exclusive dealing agreements, customer and territorial restrictions, and price fixing.

The second proposition above, namely that overly aggressive competition can injure intrabrand rivals, underlies those areas of antitrust law that deal with price discrimination, tying and reciprocity, requirements contracts, vertical and conglomerate mergers, and market foreclosure methods generally.

Even after *Sylvania*, many commentators argue that the law's present theory of contractual vertical restrictions still operates on incorrect assumptions concerning the purposes and effects of these contractual restrictions and that these assumptions are in turn causing the law to attack efficiencies as well as restraints. This is a key issue for public policy to address. Is it properly the purpose of antitrust to compel competition among dealers of a particular manufacturer's brand?[33] Will the consuming public and the freedom

---

[32]   Bork, *Contrasts in Antitrust Theory*, 65 COLUM. L. REV. 400 (1965).

[33]   Posner, *Antitrust Policy and the Supreme Court*, 75 COLUM. L. REV. 297 (1975).

of enterprise actually benefit from such enforced intrabrand competition? Should the theory that guides horizontal relations in conventional markets be used to guide the development of the law of vertical relations? How can we distinguish between positive and negative vertical restrictions? Should all vertical restrictions be legal, as some hold? Should they all be per se illegal?[34] Perhaps there is a workable rule of reason approach, such as that advocated by Justice Powell in his *Sylvania* decision—that is, the view taken in this article.

VI. Global open market policy

Time was when the huge U.S. domestic market operated in splendid semi-isolation from the rest of the world. No longer. In recent decades our dependence on imports has been growing steadily, and more and more American companies are dependent on sales and direct investment abroad. Currently we are the world's Number One debtor nation. Equally important, competition by international companies in U.S. domestic markets is growing more intense every day. Assuming that Americans will still want to increase their standards of living, it is a prediction tantamount to fact that we shall be much more dependent on international trade, for three solid reasons. We shall have growing imports of raw materials and energy at competitive cost, imports of technology (no longer can a single nation get her arms around this "object" exploding in *n*-dimensional space), and imports of consumer luxury goods (providing the "individualization of lifestyles" accompanying higher living standards). We must also relearn how to pay for these imports.

The United States needs to pursue a global open market policy more aggressively and more consistently than it has for the last 10 years. The overriding reason for such a policy is that to regain international competitiveness we need an open market at home. But there are other solid reasons. American businesses will need freedom of action abroad for the many initiatives that must be taken.

---

[34] *See, e.g.*, Comanor, *Vertical Territorial and Customer Restrictions: White Motor and Its Aftermath*, 81 Harv. L. Rev. 1419 (1968).

American consumers should not have to subsidize inefficient industries for indefinite periods to the tune of many billions of dollars a
year. Furthermore, an open external market tends to be a prerequisite for open domestic markets. By now, developing nations (such
as the People's Republic of China)—if not most development economists—are finally beginning to realize that a viable open market
sector is indispensable to economic development.[35] This is due to
the motivating effect of the open sector on entrepreneurship and,
even more importantly, on the entire population, as it takes advantage of newfound freedom of choice and the shift from sellers' to
buyers' markets. As the largest donor and lender to developing
countries, this nation has a major interest in the emergence of viable
open market sectors in the Third World.

Three prongs of a global open market policy are of special
concern here. First, we must work indefatigably toward the reduction of trade barriers, visible and invisible, established by other
governments. Parallel efforts must aim at retaining and broadening
the GATT agreement and providing it with some teeth of enforcement. Second, we must set an example by liberalizing our own
trade policy at a pace preferably ahead of other nations. We must
also learn to make use of time-specific mechanisms of deescalation
(sunset). For example, as an industry matures and requires restructuring, the impact of global competition may be softened by barriers
scheduled in advance to be stepped down progressively to zero over
a 5-year period, allowing the industry to get its house in order.

Third, we need to renew our initiative of 40 (!) years ago aimed
at the creation of a universal agreement regarding restrictive business practices in international trade. As the globalization of industries continues, it is obvious that the temptation to augment public
trade barriers (or, indeed, to substitute for the elimination of such
barriers) with private ones will sometimes be irresistible. It seems
reasonable to assume, for example, that joint ventures, "strategic
alliances," and licensing agreements may restrain as well as promote competition (or, in some cases, do both). Similarly, attempts

---

35   Thorelli, *What Can Third World Countries Learn from China?*, 1 J.
GLOBAL MARKETING, 69–84 (1987).

at dividing the market of the European Community along national lines by local competitors—in obvious contravention of the community idea—occur from time to time. Clearly, the control of restrictive business practices in international trade calls for multinational effort. To "extend the long arm" of our own antitrust policy beyond confines acceptable in international law constitutes a reprehensible invasion of the sovereignty of other nations. (A preliminary step in the direction of limiting extraterritorial application was taken in the Foreign Trade Antitrust Improvements Act of 1982.) For the same reason, the United States has no business trying to force Japanese semiconductor manufacturers to raise their prices in third countries. Neither should we forget that many a strategic alliance has been formed to help head off or jump over governmental protectionist barriers (for example, U.S.–PRC joint ventures in China and Japanese-American ones in the United States).

VII. Epilogue

It is time to return to our initial questions. Horizontal and vertical networks of cooperation are the order of the day, in many instances an obvious response to powerful environmental imperatives. There is much rivalry between networks and oftentimes even within them. Yet to varying degrees all networks constitute virtual congeries of restraints on competition. Concerned with maintaining—and improving—open markets, we see some networks as good, others as bad; it would thus seem obvious that a policy regarding collective restraints has a mission to fill in the foreseeable future, a mission probably even more important than merger and monopoly policy. Many collective restrictions serve a useful social purpose. This may be the case, for instance, when demonstrably they have substituted oligopolistic competition of the constructive variety for the kind of inert competition that may be found in some fragmented markets. Clearly, prohibition of all agreements between members of horizontal and vertical networks is inappropriate.

Collective price-fixing is, however, sufficiently repugnant to the open market system to be held per se illegal. With regard to horizontal price cartels, this simply means the future extension of established doctrine. We are also recommending the continued application of the per se rule to collective output restraints. In the vertical area we disapprove of recent enforcement vacillations regarding resale price maintenance (RPM), and we argue that the outright prohibition of RPM agreements in interstate commerce should stand. One would also hope that states will minimize encroachments of RPM in intrastate commerce. Being quite familiar with three-quarters of a century of debate on the pros and cons of this matter, we say this mainly because such agreements so easily substitute for price cartels and invite other restraints.

On the other hand, we would take a more "businesslike" approach to suggested prices. A manufacturer (or a wholesaler) reasonably might refuse to deal with a distributor (or dealer) who cut such prices if the manufacturer (etc.) could demonstrate that the distributor (etc.) had viable interbrand alternatives and the consumer, viable intrabrand alternatives. The burden of proof would be shifted due to the critical nature of any practice smacking of price-fixing. Apart from the shifted burden of proof, this would be an example of our overall philosophy of alternativism and rule of reason applied to vertical networks.

Public policy regarding vertical restraints also poses troublesome issues of equity and power. When options are limited and dependence is great, the tendency is to convert economic and marketing disputes into political issues and to seek to resolve them through political means. The politicization of vertical networks may well negate the justification for allowing the structure of agreements to emerge in the first place. It is the old issue of hierarchies versus markets that has long troubled us in economic and political affairs. Edward Mason once described the issue as a search for "that degree of market power which is necessary to an efficient conduct of business but beyond which there is an inevitable divergence between the particular and the general interest."[36]

Questions of equity and power also have an impact on the party

---

[36]   E. MASON, THE CORPORATION IN MODERN SOCIETY 7 (1961).

whose satisfaction is the ultimate rationale of the market system: the consumer. We emphasize that consumer policy is the indispensable other side of the antitrust coin. Without a reasonable degree of equality of buyers and sellers we shall never have a truly open market. A philosophy and agenda of consumer policy was outlined. Cognizant of the globalization of business operations, we also see the elimination of distorting public and private barriers to international trade as a crucial element in future open market policy.

Because collective restraints may be "good" as well as "bad," it is clear that they have to be evaluated by the extended use of the rule of reason. But as the range of restraints is almost endless in variety and intensity, any attempt at identifying a set of suitable guidelines that are in themselves reasonable must be based on a common philosophy. Ours may be labeled alternativism. It specifically takes into account that freedom of enterprise, decentralization of power, and the maintenance of competition were cardinal objectives as much as economic efficiency in the passage of the Sherman Act—objectives we believe are as valid today as they were a century ago.[37] Generally, we see the maintenance of a substantially open market system as the ideal of antitrust. An indispensable part of contemporary and future interpretation, therefore, must be the freedom of choice and information and other key consumer rights. The alternatives of buyers need safeguarding as much as do those of sellers.

The application of the alternativist view presupposes an ecological analysis, that is, an analysis in which the total situation is taken into account in the evaluation of restraints of trade, whether they occur singly or concurrently. Such analysis notably includes the effects produced in the interaction of the institutional arrangements, strategies pursued, and market structure at hand, focusing on the role of the restraints being challenged. A natural sequel is that the Antitrust Division and the courts need to make much more use of the expertise of not only economists but marketing people, organization theorists, and—why not?—technologists as well in the evaluation of collective restraints.

---

[37] THORELLI, FEDERAL ANTITRUST POLICY, supra note 1.

It would lead us too far in this context to go further into guidelines for the evaluation of particular restraints than we did by exemplification in the sections on horizontal and vertical restraints above. The alternativist perspective, however, allows us to derive some rule of reason criteria of varying degrees of generality:

If the restrictive practice is allowed to stand, to what extent does it allow for independent action of the parties involved?

How does it affect the alternatives—and sources of supply—of actual and potential competitors?

Will the relevant segment of end consumers still have viable alternatives?

If data or other intellectual property are generated by the collective arrangement, are these outputs available to competitors on reasonable terms? What about the general public?

Is the arrangement subject to active competition by individual firms (domestic or foreign) or by other collective arrangements in the same market?

To what extent are independent make-lease-or-buy decisions foreclosed?

Does the arrangement markedly increase the concentration of economic power in the market and/or the relative power among participants to the arrangement?

Has the arrangement demonstrably increased economic efficiency and/or demand for the generic product (as compared to any specific brand directly involved)?

To what extent have consumers shared in increased productivity? Have the productivity gains resulted in restriction of the freedom of choice?

What are the effects on interbrand as well as intrabrand competition?

If more than one type of restraint is involved, is the cumulative impact of the restraints still reasonable?

Will the restraints on hand likely stimulate other restrictive behavior?

We are now in a position to answer the second introductory question: Yes, the Sherman Act (and relevant parts of ancillary legislation) is flexible and purposeful enough to meet the mission of evaluating collective restraints of trade today and in the foreseeable future. In the pull of social forces, competition still needs legal, political, and philosophical endorsement, a type of "Magna Carta of the economy." Moreover, in the complex, technocratic, and persuasion-saturated markets of today the consuming public—the second but most important party in open market systems—needs policy support, as we have developed in some detail.

America's key gift to the world of political economy is the federal antitrust policy. At a time when cooperation in both constructive and odious forms is all the rage, the centenarian Sherman Act's vital significance is its emphasis on competition as the prime mover in every open market system. This lesson should not be lost in the economic reforms of socialist and Third World countries— nor in the contemporary U.S. debate. Longer live the Sherman Act!

30
Section 2 and the problem of market dominance

BY WILLIAM G. SHEPHERD[*]

Antitrust is the United States fundamental industrial policy, which reaches throughout most of the economy. For nearly a century, these policies have been unique on the world scene. They have raised the degree of competition and enhanced the level of performance in many U.S. markets.

Section 2 is the central tool in this policy set. By providing a method for reducing existing market dominance, it makes U.S. antitrust both complete and sufficient. Section 2 has had a checkered history, marked by inactive intervals, and its strictest actions (such as toward Standard Oil and American Tobacco in 1911, Alcoa in 1945, and A.T. & T. in 1982) have been few.[1]

---

[*]   Professor of Economics, University of Massachusetts, Amherst, Mass.

AUTHOR'S NOTE: *I am indebted to Walter Adams, Donald I. Baker, Kenneth E. Boyer, William S. Comanor, Henry W. de Jong, J. Denys Gribbin, Takeo Nakao, and Don E. Waldman for discussion on these issues. I have also benefited from graduate students and seminar participants at the University of Amsterdam, the University of Massachusetts, the University of Michigan, Nankai University, and the University of Southern California.*

[1]   See S. N. WHITNEY, ANTITRUST POLICIES (1958); A. D. NEALE & D. G. GOYDER, ANTITRUST LAWS OF THE UNITED STATES (3d ed. 1984); and W. G. SHEPHERD, PUBLIC POLICIES TOWARD BUSINESS (8th ed. 1991).

Also, section 1's bar to collusion may well have had wider, more sustained effects in the economy than have section 2's specific actions in a relatively few industries.

Even so, section 2 has caused significant changes and discouraged the growth and abuses of dominance. Yet since 1980 section 2 has been stopped cold by antitrust officials, with virtually no cases filed or in prospect.[2] This lapse is more severe than the moderate fluctuations that had been familiar in earlier decades.

Conceivably section 2's own past effectiveness, plus the more general spread of competition since 1960, has removed all important cases of market dominance. Or possibly the Chicago school "efficiency" doctrine is correct, that any cases of market dominance merely reflect superior performance by the dominant firm; in that view, it should be endorsed rather than sued.[3] Or perhaps section 2 cases have become too unwieldy to prosecute successfully.

---

[2]   There is no single best summary of the reduction in antitrust enforcement after 1980, but an interesting set of articles on that subject is provided in two special issues titled *A Retrospective Examination of the Reagan Years*, 33 ANTITRUST BULL. 201–415 (1988) and 33 ANTITRUST BULL. 429–613 (1988).

[3]   For statements of the "efficiency school" view, *see* Harold Demsetz's and John S. McGee's chapters in HARVEY J. GOLDSCHMID, H. MICHAEL MANN & J. FRED WESTON, INDUSTRIAL CONCENTRATION: THE NEW LEARNING (1975); and *Smirlock, Gilligan & Marshall, Tobin's q and the Structure-Performance Relationship*, 74 AM. ECON. REV. 1051 (1984). The approach is assessed in Schmalensee, *Collusion Versus Differential Efficiency: Testing Alternative Hypotheses*, 34 J. IND. ECON. 399 (1987); IOANNES N. KESSIDES, INTERNAL VS. EXTERNAL MARKET CONDITIONS AND FIRM PROFITABILITY: AN EXPLORATORY MODEL (Working Paper, Department of Economics, University of Maryland, December 1987); and Shepherd, *Three "Efficiency School" Hypotheses About Market Power*, 33 ANTITRUST BULL. 395 (1988).

For a critical assessment of the "efficiency school" and its antitrust lessons, *see* Fox & Sullivan, *Antitrust—Retrospective and Prospective: Where Are We Coming From? Where Are We Going?* 62 N.Y.U. L. REV. 936 (1987).

This article maintains instead that, on economic grounds, section 2 actions against dominance can and should be renewed. There are significant candidates for treatment, which are not immunized by possible superior efficiency; and action toward them can be effective. The economic analysis that follows in part I will show that market dominance involves ineffective competition, because parity and mutual pressure among rivals are lacking.

Part II notes that past section 2 actions have mostly provided high yields, even in the most recent cases (including the Antitrust Division's 1970's case against IBM, which was withdrawn in 1982). Part III reconsiders a main barrier to section 2 action: the view that monopoly positions and high profits must be accepted as a necessary stimulus to superior performance. Competition is a superior stimulus, I will suggest, and so a return to the mainstream application of section 2 is appropriate.

This article is based on the mainstream of research on industrial organization, as it has cumulated over more than five decades. Despite current vogues for certain doctrines that favor monopoly, the research foundations of a strict section 2 policy are firm. Moreover the candidates are relatively few, so that a revived section 2 policy would be compact and manageable.

I. The economics of market dominance

A. *The role of competitive parity*

It is important to begin with the essential nature of competition. Effective competition involves a mutual striving among comparable rivals, on a basis of *competitive parity*.[4] At each point in the ongoing sequence of competitive episodes, the rivals

---

4   This is clear in the standard dictionary definitions of the term "competition," which refer to rivalry among comparable competitors. In the industrial organization literature, *see* JOE S. BAIN, INDUSTRIAL ORGANIZATION (rev. ed. 1968); GEORGE J. STIGLER, THE ORGANIZATION OF INDUSTRY (1968); W. G. SHEPHERD, THE ECONOMICS OF INDUSTRIAL ORGANIZATION (3d ed. 1990); and F. M. SCHERER & DAVID ROSS, INDUSTRIAL MARKET STRUCTURE AND ECONOMIC PERFORMANCE (3d ed. 1990).

need to be (approximately) on par with each other, so that they can exert strong mutual pressure. Being on par, they each can use the same array of competitive weapons, and they each have approximately the same prospects of coming out ahead in each episode. When competitive parity exists, there need be no concern about the tactic used in the competitive battle, because all firms will be capable of asserting and defending themselves effectively.[5]

If parity is maintained in the series of competitive episodes, then effective competition continues to mutually constrain all firms' prices toward costs. Accordingly, the firms' capitalized values (as embodied in the market values of their stock) are held down approximately to the cost of their investments (apart from the effects of unusual degrees of efficiency or innovation).[6] Any firm's efforts to defeat any or all of its competitors will be absorbed by the totality of competitors, without causing any efficient ones to fail. Each competitive episode, therefore, proceeds as a meaningful interaction, with mutual pressure, and winning occurs by superior effort or skill.

Competitive parity is therefore fundamental for effective competition in markets, just as it also is in healthy sports competition. To be superior means to have lower costs or better products. When there is parity and effective competition, then

---

[5]   This is shown in Shepherd, *Assessing "Predatory" Actions by Market Shares and Selectivity*, 31 ANTITRUST BULL. 1 (1986). For contrast, *see* Areeda & Turner, *Predatory Prices and Related Practices Under Section 2 of the Sherman Act*, 88 HARV. L. REV. 697 (1975); and the discussion and sources in SCHERER & ROSS, *supra* note 4, at 335-40.

[6]   The ratio of the current *market value* of the company to the *book value* has come to be known among economists as "Tobin's *q*." A high ratio means that investors have made large capital gains. A high Tobin's *q* ratio reflects the firm's ability to gain high profits, which may in turn reflect market power, or superior efficiency or innovation, or some combination. The ratio can of course be misused in debate, and it is usually hard to measure in practice. But it does focus on the capital gains that are the ultimate aim of gaining monopoly power.

For a compact economic and statistical discussion of this topic, *see* Shepherd, *Tobin's* q *and the Structure-Performance Relationship: A Comment*, 76 AMER. ECON. REV. 1205 (1986).

only scale economies, higher product quality (compared to price), faster innovation, or greater strategic genius will enable a firm to win in any episode or any series of episodes. The rewards for success in each episode are scaled in the form of differential rates of profitability, which correspond to the scaling of prizes in a sports event.

But each episode is only one event, like one game in a season and one season in a continuing series of seasons. The competitive process is an ongoing sequence of such encounters, and for competition to remain effective there must be a continual renewing of parity among the rivals during the series of episodes.

A comparison with sports competition is instructive on this point.[7] Sports leagues use elaborate rules and structures, intended precisely to maintain parity among the athletes or teams during the competitive process. These rules are constantly adjusted as needed, and the emergence of any "dynasty" (as when one team dominates its league even for a moderate time, such as a season or two) is seen as a lapse from real competition. Competition ceases to occur meaningfully; unbalanced contests lack drama and mutual pressure.

Industrial markets should receive the same degree of concern about parity, for unbalanced competition between mismatched firms can be as weak and meaningless as it is between mismatched boxers in different weight classes, or between football teams with different numbers of players.

B. *Market dominance prevents effective competition*

Whenever parity is absent and firms are not comparable, then competition is not effective. In the standard situation of market dominance, the leading firm has over 40%–50% of the market, and there is no close rival.[8] The dominant firm is capable of

---

[7]   For a review of the main research issues, *see* ROGER G. NOLL, GOVERNMENT AND THE SPORTS BUSINESS (1974).

[8]   Market dominance has been a prominent topic since the formation of scores of trusts in major U.S. industries during 1890–1905,

eliminating any small rival it chooses, at any given time, or possibly all of the rivals. It may choose not to do so from moment to moment, but its relative power to do so exists and, of course, is much greater than whatever lesser power the little rivals may possess. The dominant firm is able to deploy competitive weapons unavailable to the little rivals, particularly the strong use of selective pricing and promotion. Its costs of capital are commonly lower, and its profits are usually more stable, with a lower degree of risk. Therefore its financial resources are larger and of higher quality.

The mainstream literature of industrial organization from 1890 to 1960 brought out these differences in detail.[9] But much of the "new" post-1970 writing reflects an ignorance of this literature and an aversion to real-market research. This is often reinforced by a dedication to Chicago-school doctrines, or to pure theory as the best method for researching industrial economics. This limited set of research values has permitted much of the field to deny the imperfections that can favor dominant firms.

---

followed by the series of investigations and antitrust actions. It fell into neglect after 1920, as action ceased and the 1930's interest in oligopoly boomed. On the rather sparse recent literature on dominance, *see* SCHERER & ROSS, *supra* note 4.

W. G. SHEPHERD, THE TREATMENT OF MARKET POWER (1975), considers some policy treatments for dominance; DENNIS C. MUELLER, PROFITS IN THE LONG RUN (1986), offers important new empirical evidence about the persistence and effects of dominance; and for an emphasis on "new" theory, *see* THE ECONOMICS OF MARKET DOMINANCE (Donald Hay & John Vickers eds., 1987).

[9]   As a small selection, *see* RICHARD T. ELY, TRUSTS AND MONOPOLIES (1907); WILLIAM Z. RIPLEY, TRUSTS, POOLS, AND CORPORATIONS (rev. ed. (1915); the 21 REPORTS and extended Hearings of the Temporary National Economic Committee, 1939–41; CARL KAYSEN, THE UNITED SHOE MACHINERY CASE (1959); S. N. WHITNEY, *supra* note 1; JOE S. BAIN, *supra* note 4; JOHN M. BLAIR, ECONOMIC CONCENTRATION (1972); W. G. SHEPHERD, *supra* note 8; and F. M. SCHERER & DAVID ROSS, *supra* note 4.

The little rivals are commonly placed in a submissive posture.[10] The incentives for the little firms to take aggressive actions are actually high; small firms *could* gain high profitability by succeeding aggressively against dominant firms, and this does happen in some real instances. But usually the little firms face a danger of overwhelming reactions by the dominant firm, which can apply superior force and competitive devices, such as extensive selective pricing. The little rivals usually survive by not challenging the dominant firm across the board, instead seeking to find market niches, which do not threaten the dominant firm.

In short, the dominant-firm setting involves a steep variation in competitive pressure: the small firms must endure extreme degrees of pressure and risk, while the dominant firm faces only light pressure. Competition is unbalanced, and it is weak over a majority of the market (that is, it exerts weak pressure upon the dominant firm itself). The leader is not forced to perform well, either in cost efficiency, in keeping prices down to costs, or in vigorous innovation. Meanwhile the extreme pressure on the little firms will tend to reduce their morale, effort and performance, even if it does not actually induce them to leave the market.

The dominant-firm setting therefore lacks the creative tension and striving of balanced competition.[11] Competition is ineffective,

---

[10]   Some writers on dominant firms have assumed the opposite: that the fringe firms are aggressive while the dominant firm is passive to their actions; *see, for example*, Worcester, Jr., *Why Dominant Firms Decline*, 65 J. Pol. Econ. 338 (1957). For strong counter-evidence, *see* Dennis C. Mueller, *supra* note 8; Geroski, *Do Dominant Firms Decline?* in The Economics of Market Dominance, *supra* note 8; and W. G. Shepherd, *supra* note 8.

[11]   Joseph A. Schumpeter was much too optimistic, in asserting that dominant firms will be subject to powerful threats and pressures for displacement. His charming "creative destruction" phrase merely represents hope and clever word usage, rather than thorough and reliable research, either before 1942 or since. *See* his Capitalism, Socialism and Democracy (1942); and compare with the sources in notes 5 and 10, *supra*.

and performance is inferior. A principal lesson of this analysis is *that the dominant firm's market share must usually decline below 40%–50% if competition is to become effective.* That fact is denied by officials and experts for the dominant firms, especially in cases of deregulation where a former monopolist (such as A.T. & T. in long-distance telephone service) seeks to retain its dominance over the market amid a group of small rivals. Those rivals are said to exert tight pressure, but the reality is usually the opposite.

Indeed, the imbalance may continue or even grow more severe, rather than tend to correct itself. Dominance yields excess profits, which provide resources for the firm to reinforce and enlarge its dominance in the future.[12] The higher the dominant firm's current profitability, the less likely it is that the dominance will fade under attack by superior and/or better financed rivals. Dominant-firm markets may have an underlying instability, in which the flow of excess profits enlarges the dominance. The degree of this structural instability depends on at least several factors, including the scale of profit-rate rewards to higher market shares.

Against this, it is of course true that actual cases of dominance are usually subject to some tendency to decay, from a variety of market forces. On the rate of decay, there has been remarkably little research. My own estimates are that market shares above 60% may tend to decline naturally at about one point per year, on average.[13] Possibly the rate has risen since 1960 in the U.S., as the general degree of competition in the economy

---

[12] This effect of excess profits holds whether the profits arise from pure market power, or from superior performance, or from some mix of the two.

[13] *See* SHEPHERD, *supra* note 8, at 113–25; confirmatory evidence is offered in DENNIS C. MUELLER, *supra* note 8, and Geroski, *supra* note 10. Geroski finds a rate of decay of only about one-half of a point per year.

increased during 1950 to 1980.[14] But the rate may have fallen again since 1980, particularly in major markets with high advertising intensity.[15] In general, there are numerous major cases of dominance lasting more than five decades, so that no general confidence that it will naturally decline seems justified.[16]

C. *"Efficiency-school" doctrine, as a last resort*

Dominance therefore remains an economic topic of great interest and importance. Yet in the literature of industrial economics and antitrust, competitive parity has become an oddly neglected topic. Indeed, some current arguments deny its importance outright. One such view is the "efficiency school," which takes the Chicago-school position to the extreme: all dominance is claimed to represent superiority. This extreme approach has gained a certain degree of popularity in the 1980's, particularly in Washington during the Reagan administration.[17]

Yet, in fact, the Chicago school has been defeated on every major issue since the 1950's. First, Stigler and others asserted in the early 1950's that competition was nearly ubiquitous in the

---

[14]   This rise is assessed in Shepherd, *Causes of Increased Competition in the U.S. Economy, 1939–1980,* 64 REV. ECON. & STAT. 613 (1982).

[15]   Industries with little advertising have declined in concentration, on average, since 1954, while advertising-intensive industries have shown markedly rising concentration. On the general effects of advertising, *see* Comanor & Wilson, *The Effect of Advertising on Competition: A Survey,* 17 J. ECON. LIT. 453 (1979).

[16]   The cases include *IBM, Eastman Kodak, Campbell Soup, Gillette,* and *Procter & Gamble,* for example; see W. G. SHEPHERD, *supra* note 1, and Geroski, *supra* note 10.

[17]   As Fox and Sullivan note, the view has prevailed only in the Reagan administration, rather than in the research community, where it is still a (vigorous) minority; *see* Fox & Sullivan, *supra* note 3.

U.S. economy.[18] That was disproven.[19] Then they asserted that any actual monopoly power will tend to decay rapidly.[20] That was shown to be an exaggeration.[21] Then they said that the economies of scale are large enough to justify all important cases of market dominance.[22] Bain, Scherer, Pratten, Weiss and others disproved that general claim.[23] Chicagoans also tried to deny that market structure is related to profitability: instead, econometric research has continued to show market shares to be strongly related to profit rates and other measures of monopoly gains.[24]

Lacking a research basis for their views, Chicagoans eventually offered a kind of last-ditch approach. In the 1970's,

---

[18]   *For example, see* GEORGE J. STIGLER, FIVE LECTURES ON ECONOMIC PROBLEMS (1949); and G. WARREN NUTTER, THE EXTENT OF ENTERPRISE MONOPOLY IN THE UNITED STATES: 1899-1939 (1951).

[19]   *See* JOE S. BAIN, INDUSTRIAL ORGANIZATION (1958); THE STRUCTURE OF AMERICAN INDUSTRY (Walter Adams, ed., 2d ed. 1959); W. G. SHEPHERD, MARKET POWER AND ECONOMIC WELFARE (1970); and JOHN M. BLAIR, *supra* note 9.

[20]   *See, for example,* GEORGE J. STIGLER, *supra* note 4; and Gort, *Analysis of Stability and Change in Market Shares*, 7 J. POL. ECON. 51 (1963).

[21]   *See* JOHN M. BLAIR, *supra* note 9; W. G. SHEPHERD, *supra* note 19; and F. M. SCHERER & DAVID ROSS, *supra* note 4.

[22]   *See* Stigler, *The Economies of Scale*, 1 J.L. & ECON. 54-71 (1958); GEORGE J. STIGLER, *supra* note 4; Peltzman, *The Gains and Losses from Industrial Concentration*, 20 J.L. & ECON. 229 (1970).

[23]   *See* F. M. SCHERER & DAVID ROSS, *supra* note 4, especially the review and summary of data at 111-41.

[24]   Attention originally focused on 4-firm concentration ratios; *see* Leonard W. Weiss's survey chapter of concentration-profits patterns, in HARVEY J. GOLDSCHMID, et al., *supra* note 3. On the more complete study of several structural elements, including market share, concentration, and entry barriers, *see* Shepherd, *The Elements of Market Structure*, 54 REV. ECON. & STAT. 25 (1972); Shepherd, *supra* note 6; Ravenscraft, *Structure-Profit Relationships at the Line of Business and Industry Level*, 65 REV. ECON. & STAT. 22 (1983); and DENNIS C. MUELLER, *supra* note 8.

Demsetz, McGee, and Brozen suggested the *possibility* that dominant firms might have gained their dominance by a series of periods of superior performance (in the form of lower costs, better innovations, etc.).[25] That is an interesting point, and it may apply in some degree to some cases. But this possibility soon came to be asserted to be a *certainty* by Bork and others. All cases of existing dominance were claimed to reflect, and to be normatively justified by superior efficiency.

In this view, monopoly does not in fact really exist: any high market shares merely embody efficiency.[26] Since competition is meant to provide superior efficiency, monopoly really is competition. All monopoly profits are relabeled as only "rents," reflecting "differential efficiency." Firms supposedly do not try to attain dominance or monopoly, as many of their officials would privately admit they do. Instead, they only "seek rents." Any constraints placed on such dominant firms or on their profits are declared to be antiefficient, because they would "penalize superiority."

Little credible research has been offered that these possibilities are frequently borne out in real markets.[27] Yet they have attracted a number of judges and antitrust officials. Efficiency-school assertions have blocked most section 2 actions since the middle 1970's. Yet they remain as merely a last-resort claim. They seek to convert the familiar, occasional problem of reconciling compe-

---

[25] *See* Shepherd, *On the Core Concepts of Industrial Economics*, in MAINSTREAMS IN INDUSTRIAL ORGANIZATION (Henry W. de Jong & W. G. Shepherd, 1986). In Shepherd, *supra* note 3, I note that the view that all dominance reflects superiority is based on a logical contradiction and is untenable on logical grounds.

[26] *See* Shepherd, *On the Mainstream Concepts of Industrial Economics*, *supra* note 25; Fox and Sullivan (*supra* note 3) provide an excellent review of the new Chicago-school lexicon and its reversal of the mainstream concepts and research findings.

[27] Virtually the only research item is Peltzman, *supra* note 22; Scherer effectively rebutted it in his *The Causes and Consequences of Rising Industrial Concentration*, 22 J.L. & ECON. 191 (1979).

tition with a fair reward for good performance, into an absolute bar against any constraint.

The 1880's extremism of William Graham Sumner and Jeremiah Jenks is here resurrected by the efficiency school as if it were new and different, but it is not. The possibility of superiority remains an interesting insight, which may apply to some cases, but it is merely speculation. Moreover, the existence of any past superiority would not change the current existence of the dominance, with its harmful effects on economic performance. The efficiency-school claim is that the good actions exceed any monopoly effects, a factual claim needing evidence. But no really significant evidence has been provided.

D. *"Contestability" (ultrafree entry)*

A second approach seeking to exonerate dominance is the "contestability school," which since 1982 has carried the idea of potential entry to the theoretical extreme.[28] The analysis is pure, in a static context using highly abstract Cournot-Nash models, with the maximization of consumer surplus as the only criterion of efficiency.

In a contestable market, there is perfectly free entry and exit (a better term for the situation is "ultrafree entry").[29] In such a model, potential entry can be so absolute that it totally dominates the firm or firms already established inside the market. No existing firm, even a complete monopolist, can raise its price

---

[28]   The leading writings are WILLIAM J. BAUMOL, JOHN C. PANZAR & ROBERT D. WILLIG, CONTESTABLE MARKETS AND THE THEORY OF INDUSTRY STRUCTURE (1982); and Baumol & Willig, *Contestability: Developments Since the Book*, OXFORD ECONOMIC PAPERS (November 1986).

[29]   For the reasons to avoid the term "contestability," in favor of "ultrafree entry," *see* Shepherd, *"Contestability" versus Competition*, 74 AM. ECON. REV. 572 (1984), which also offers a critique of the "contestability" approach. For extensive further criticism on the core logic of the Baumol-school approach, *see* Schwartz, *The Nature and Scope of Contestability Theory*, OXFORD ECONOMIC PAPERS (November 1986).

above minimum cost without inviting certain, instant and total displacement by an entrant. By definition, ultrafree entry forces even a monopolist to adopt competitive behavior. Dominance therefore ceases to be a problem, because it has been assumed away.

This tautology was offered with strong self-praise by its authors. For example, it is "a unifying framework for a pure theory of industrial organization where none was available before" in a literature that was "generally disconnected." The theory "will transform the field and render it far more applicable to the real world," with contributions that are "fundamental." Also its authors have testified in a number of important antitrust and regulatory cases, claiming that the theory is widely accepted and can settle practical issues decisively.[30]

Yet the field has largely rejected the theory as a help in understanding real-world conditions. Ultrafree entry is seen as offering little more than interesting insights, with minimal relevance for antitrust policy. The theory probably does not fit any important real markets. And when tested simply at the level of logical consistency, the theory contains important flaws; it rests on two assumptions that are mutually contradictory.[31]

---

[30] Thus Baumol testified at length in 1984–85 in favor of the attempted merger of the Santa Fe and Southern Pacific railroads. Though the merger would have created a single monopoly railroad in the southwestern corridor between Texas and southern California, Baumol argued that trucks provided virtually perfect contestability, which would absolutely prevent any possible monopoly effects. In fact, half of the railroads' freight volume was known to be large-scale, uniform cargoes, for which trucking costs are about twice as high as railroad costs. The merger was rejected by the Interstate Commerce Commission in 1986.

Baumol has also offered his theory to defend United Airlines and American Airlines' strategies in using their dominant computer reservation systems (Apollo and Sabre) to reduce competition from other airlines. The theory was again presented as firmly established.

[31] *See* Shepherd, *supra* note 29. One key assumption is that entry is total, instant and overwhelming. Another is that entry is so negligible

Whatever validity the theory may have, it exists only in the pure, extreme case. Schwartz and others have shown that the theory is not robust, when the assumptions are diluted, and therefore contestability probably adds little to the mainstream concepts and knowledge of competition. The previous voluminous knowledge of entry is still valid, even if the contestability version of entry has little validity. Potential entry can matter in many real markets, as Bain and others have long stressed. But entry usually will be a secondary matter, compared to *actual* competition among firms already established in the market.

Accordingly the two "new" schools defending dominance are generally vacuous. They have not displaced the central logic of the neoclassical theory of monopoly, as applied in many hundreds of markets during the last century. Market dominance does usually impose the familiar costs of monopoly (regardless of any good actions that may have helped to create the dominance). And careful study in each case is needed, in order to determine if the dominance actually has arisen from scale economies or sustained superiority.

Even where superiority has been involved in some degree, the true scope of that superiority needs to be assessed. A small superiority, combined with skillful use of market imperfections, can enable a firm to capture high and lasting dominance, with large social costs. Yet the dominant firm's officials will demand a blank check to retain the dominance and its excess profits, even though the original "good" actions may have been small. This question of the "efficient rewards" required for deserving monopolists occupies section II below.

---

that the established firm does not regard it as significant. The mutual contradiction could hardly be more direct. And both assumptions are required if the theory is to reach its critical conclusion: that "contestability" guarantees a competitive result even when competitive conditions do not obtain inside the market. Therefore the theory is vacuous, as a matter of logic.

E. *The mainstream continues*

Altogether, the main issues are little changed from earlier decades. Monopoly is still defined mainly by market shares, and its various social harms are significant. Most of the post-1970 new concepts have actually been long familiar, even prior to 1900. And some recent technical "advances" in analysis have tended to divert attention from the central conditions, rather than to improve scientific understanding.

Some recent theoretical discussions have been valuable. But the field has found it difficult to maintain a grasp on the core issues, amid the proliferation of mathematical tools that yield definite conclusions but only under rarified assumptions. While many analysts have been modeling short-run duopoly choices under various permutations of Cournot-Nash assumptions, the urgent matters of real markets have lost focus. That has made it easier for the efficiency-school and contestability writers to offer vacuous assertions that monopoly has little or no existence or social cost.

It is important to be cautious about these issues and the use of antitrust. But because the new economic exonerations of market dominance are logically flawed and lacking in empirical support, the supposed economic case against section 2 is largely weightless. The basic issues, and the impacts of monopoly, remain largely unchanged. There may be fewer cases ripe for treatment now than in 1905 or 1935, but the economic basis for dealing with them is firm.

II. Yields of past section 2 cases

Have the past section 2 cases actually yielded positive economic results? Each case has been controversial, involving claims and legal theories that are open to debate. But what matters ultimately is whether the cases improved efficiency and innovation: that is, whether their benefits clearly exceeded their costs. By evaluating that, and by assessing the conditions of the cases, we can gain hints whether further section 2 cases are likely to offer favorable yields.

A. Three waves of section 2 actions

Section 2 actions have come in three waves, during 1905–1920, 1938–1952, and 1968–1984.[32] They are summarized in table 1, which shows the leading cases, the time intervals involved, and the main outcomes. Each surge in section 2 activity followed a major wave of mergers. Some such stimulus appears to be important in stimulating and supporting large-scale section 2 actions.

Table 1 indicates that section 2 activity has at times been extensive. The first wave, in particular, reached very far, touching virtually every major case of high market share at the time, as table 2 suggests. Actions were taken toward an actual majority (Standard Oil, U.S. Steel, American Tobacco, International Harvester, American Sugar, General Electric, and Corn Products) of the ten largest dominant firms, as shown in table 2.[33] No comparable broadside has occurred subsequently, and none is conceivable now.

Although conviction and restructuring were obtained in only a few cases, there were significant changes in Standard Oil, American Tobacco, and Du Pont.[34] Little direct relief was gained in most of the other actions, but after 1920 there were implicit merger constraints in effect on such firms as U.S. Steel and International Harvester. There was also a series of lost opportunities. For example, it is widely agreed that if U.S. Steel and the

---

[32]   See WHITNEY, supra note 1; Shepherd, supra note 1; and A. D. NEALE & D. G. GOYDER, supra note 1.

[33]   For excellent listings of the largest firms at various times beginning in 1909, see A. D. H. KAPLAN, BIG ENTERPRISE IN A COMPETITIVE SYSTEM (rev. ed. 1965).

[34]   See S. N. Whitney, supra note 1; on Standard Oil, see GEORGE W. STOCKING, THE OIL INDUSTRY AND THE COMPETITIVE SYSTEM (1925).

leading meatpackers had been restructured along competitive lines in 1920, their later performance would probably have been much more efficient and innovative.[35]

The second wave of section 2 actions was confined to firms ranking much lower on the national lists (compare table 1 with table 3). Even so, these firms included many of the major firms with market shares over 50%. The more important cases (such as *Western Electric* and *IBM*) were aborted after 1952, and others reached only modest results (*Alcoa*, for instance).[36]

By the late 1960's, several main dominant firms were candidates for treatment, including IBM, A.T. & T., General Motors, Eastman Kodak, Campbell Soup, Xerox, and Gillette. Government cases were in fact developed and filed against IBM, A.T. & T., and Xerox; they formed the crest of the 1970's third wave of section 2 cases. But much attention in the 1960's and 1970's was diverted to the "tight-oligopoly question."

Ultimately the only action on this front was the Federal Trade Commission's case filed in 1972 against the leading cereals companies. The harms to competition it alleged were significant, though it was experimental as a strictly legal matter.[37] The case

---

[35]   U.S. Steel continued to decline in market share right through to the 1970's, because of a widely recognized inefficiency and slow innovation; *see* THE STRUCTURE OF AMERICAN INDUSTRY (W. Adams, ed. various eds. 1951–1986). The meatpackers lingered on as sluggish oligopolists, missed the major technological changes of the 1930's–1960's, were then swallowed up by conglomerates, and have virtually disappeared.

[36]   On *Alcoa*, *see* MERTON J. PECK, COMPETITION IN THE ALUMINUM INDUSTRY (1961); on *Western Electric* and *IBM*, *see* RALPH NADER & MARK GREEN, THE CLOSED ENTERPRISE SYSTEM (1973), and *Economic Concentration: Hearings by the Hart Committee, Senate Subcommittee on Antitrust and Monopoly* (1974–75).

[37]   On the case's rationale, *see* R. Schmalensee, *Entry Deterrence in the Ready-to-Eat Cereals Industry*, 9 BELL J. ECON. 305 (1978); and Scherer, *The Welfare Economics of Product Variety: An Application to the Ready-to-Eat Cereal Industry*, 28 J. INDUS. ECON. 113 (1979).
On the political elements in handling of the case, *see* MICHAEL PERTSCHUK, FTC REVIEW: 1977–84, A REPORT TO THE HOUSE SUBCOMMITTEE ON OVERSIGHT AND INVESTIGATIONS esp. 56–57 (September 1984).

Table 1
Major Section 2 Cases, 1905 to 1984

Cases	Time between Monopolization and Remedy		Time between Beginning and End of Action*		Outcome
	Years	Interval (years)	Years	Interval (years)	
1905 to 1920					
American Tobacco	1890-1916	26	1906-12	6	Dissolution into three main firms.
Standard Oil	1875-1918+	43+	1905-12	7	Dissolution into about a dozen regionally dominant firms.
Du Pont (gunpowder)	1902-13	11	1906-12	6	Mild dissolution; reversed quickly by effects of World War I.
Corn Products	1897-1920	23	(1910)-19	(12)	Slight changes from a consent decree.
American Can	1901-	—	(1909)-20	(11)	No change.
U.S. Steel	1901-	—	(1907)-20	(13)	Acquittal. Informal limits on further mergers.
AT&T	1881-	—	(1909)-13	(4)	Compromise. AT&T retained its position; agreed to interconnect and avoid further mergers.
Meatpackers (Armour, Swift, Wilson, Cudahy)	1885	—	(1905)-1920	(12)	Compromise. Packers agreed to stay out of adjacent markets and to cease coordination.
American Sugar	1890-	—	1908-14	6	No action. American Sugar's position had slipped already.
United Shoe Machinery	1899-		(1908)-18	10	USM leasing restrictions were modified.
International Harvester	1902		1906-18	12	Compromise. Trivial divestiture.

1938 to 1952

Alcoa	1903-(1953)	(50)	1934-50	16	War plants sold to new entrants.
National Broadcasting Company	1926-43	17	1938-43	5	"Blue Network" divested (became American Broadcasting Corp.).
Pullman	1899-1947	(65)	(1937)-1947	(10)	Divestiture of sleeping car operation. Manufacturing monopoly was not directly changed.
Paramount Pictures	1914-48	34	(1935)-1948	(13)	Vertical integration removed.
American Can	1901-(1955)	(54)	(1945)-1950	(5)	Compromise: certain restrictive practices stopped, to foster entry.
Du Pont (GM holdings)	1918-61	43	(1945)-1961	(16)	Divestiture.
United Shoe Machinery	1899-1970	71	(1945)-1969	(61)	Share reduced to 50 percent.
United Fruit	1899-1970	71	1948-70	22	Moderate divestiture.
American Tobacco	(1920)-	—	1938-46	8	Conviction but no significant remedy.
Du Pont (cellophane)	1925-	—	(1945)-1956	(11)	Acquittal.
Western Electric	1881-	—	1946-56	10	Case effectively abandoned.
IBM	(1925)-	—	1947-56	9	Case effectively abandoned.

1968 to 1984

IBM (1969 case)	(1925)-	—	1965-82	17	Dropped.
Cereals (1972 case)	(1950)-	—	1970-82	12	Acquittal.
Xerox (1973 case)	1961-	14	1970-75	6	Compromise. Some opening of access to patents.
AT&T (1974 case)	1881-	—	1965-84	19	Substantial divestiture.

* Based on evidence of the start of official investigation and the end of official action. Parentheses indicate estimates.

SOURCE: W. G. SHEPHERD, PUBLIC POLICIES TOWARD BUSINESS 186-87 (7th ed. 1985).

Table 2

Changes in Market Position, Leading Dominant Firms, 1910–1935

Asset rank among all industrial firms in 1910		Estimated assets, 1909–10 ($ millions)	Estimates for 1910		Estimates for 1935	
			Market share (percent)	Entry barriers	Market share (percent)	Entry barriers
1	United States Steel	1,804	60	Medium	40	Medium
2	Standard Oil (New Jersey)	800	80	Medium	35	Medium
3	American Tobacco	286	80	Medium	25	Medium
6	International Harvester	166	70	High	33	Medium
7	Central Leather	138	60	Low	—	—
8	Pullman	131	85	High	80	Medium
10	American Sugar	124	60	Low	35	Low
13	Singer Manufacturing	113	75	Medium	55	Low
16	General Electric	102	60	High	55	High
19	Corn Products	97	60	Low	45	Low
21	American Can	90	60	Medium	51	Medium
25	Westinghouse Electric	84	50	High	45	High
30	Du Pont	75	90	Medium	30	Low
34	International Paper	71	50	Low	20	Low
37	National Biscuit	65	50	Low	20	Low
55	Western Electric	43	100	High	100	High
59	United Fruit	41	80	Medium	80	Medium
61	United Shoe Machinery	40	95	High	90	High
72	Eastman Kodak	35	90	Medium	90	Medium
*	Alcoa	35	99	High	90	Medium

* Not available.

SOURCE: W. G. SHEPHERD, PUBLIC POLICIES TOWARD BUSINESS 179 (7th ed. 1985).

eventually was dismissed in 1981; by then the Commission, including the legal and economic staffs, were being shifted to the

Table 3

Changes in Market Position, Leading Dominant Firms, 1948–1978

Asset rank among all industrial firms in 1948		Estimated assets, 1948 ($ millions)	Estimates for 1948		Estimates for 1973	
			Market share (percent)	Entry barriers	Market share (percent)	Entry barriers
2	General Motors	2,958	60	Medium	55	High
9	General Electric	1,177	50	High	50	High
20	Western Electric	650	100	High	98	High
29	Alcoa	504	80	High	40	Medium
33	Eastman Kodak	412	80	Medium	80	Medium
38	Procter & Gamble	356	50	Medium	50	Medium
47	United Fruit	320	80	Medium	60	Medium
60	American Can	276	52	Medium	35	Low
69	IBM	242	90	Medium	70	High
76	Coca-Cola	222	60	Medium	50	Medium
*	Campbell Soup	149	85	Medium	85	Medium
*	Caterpillar Tractor	147	50	Medium	50	Medium
*	Kellogg	41	50	Medium	45	Medium
*	Gillette	78	70	Medium	70	Medium
*	Babcock and Wilcox	79	60	Medium	50	Medium
*	Hershey	62	75	Medium	70	Low
*	Du Pont (cellophane)	(65)	90	High	60	Medium
*	United Shoe Machinery	(104)	85	High	50	Low

* Not available.

SOURCE: W. G. SHEPHERD, PUBLIC POLICIES TOWARD BUSINESS 180 (7th ed. 1985).

Chicago-school persuasion. The tight-oligopoly topic drained action from the dominant-firm cases, which outranked tight oligopoly as an economic problem.

The third section 2 wave can be said (with one large exception: A.T. & T.) to have been a failure, even a fiasco. The *IBM* case was abandoned, the cereals action was dismissed, and the Xerox settlement was mild and came mere months before the invasion by new Japanese imports began. These cases appeared to validate the growing belief that section 2 cases were too complex, easily stalled, and weak in remedies.

The *A.T. & T.* case proved just the opposite. Though it was easily the biggest of the cases in inherent complexity, it was moved rapidly along after 1977 by an effective judge and brought to a relatively clear and coherent conclusion, applying surgery that was much more radical than had previously seemed conceivable.[38] Moreover, the outcome is increasingly recognized as economically sound, because the new strong competition has followed predictable lines that had long been suggested by specialists.[39]

In short, the long history of section 2 had seen a seeming decline in scope and vigor, perhaps also reflecting a shrinkage in feasible candidates for action. But the *A.T. & T.* case reversed these lessons, showing that virtually any section 2 outcome is still possible, even with very large and complex situations.

B. *Yields of section 2 actions*

But have the cases been efficient, in economic and social terms? A legal victory may cause economic harm *or* good, or neither, and so there is a need for research on the effects of section 2 actions. In fact, little empirical study has been done on

---

[38]   Among the numerous recent books on the A.T. & T. divestiture, *see* PETER TEMIN, THE FALL OF THE BELL SYSTEM (1987); ALVIN VON AUW, HERITAGE AND DESTINY: REFLECTIONS ON THE BELL SYSTEM IN TRANSITION (1983); and BREAKING UP BELL (David S. Evans ed. 1983). *See also* MacAvoy & Robinson, *Winning by Losing: The AT&T Settlement and Its Impact on Telecommunications*, 1 YALE J. REG. 1 (1983).

[39]   One such earlier analysis is W. G. Shepherd, *The Competitive Margin in Communications*, in TECHNOLOGICAL CHANGE IN REGULATED INDUSTRIES (William M. Capron ed. 1971). Even earlier is Sheahan, *Integration and Exclusion in the Telephone Equipment Industry*, 70 Q. J. ECON. 249 (1956).

the issue. In 1975 I offered a modest set of estimates comparing the costs and benefits of major section 2 cases.[40] It has no predecessors, and to my knowledge it has not been followed by similar studies.[41]

The estimates involve an element of speculation, but they are based on reasonable assumptions about (1) the rate at which market shares would have declined in the absence of antitrust action; (2) the average effects of market power on profits, costs and innovation; (3) the presence or absence of scale economies; and (4) the likely costs of the antitrust actions.

As given in table 4, the estimates are probably close to the true values, and they probably do not have major biases. If anything, they may tend to understate the yields of the cases.

The net yields appear to have been high, especially for the earlier cases. Benefit-cost ratios over 5 must be considered substantial, and most of the case yields are higher than that. The one lower-yield case, *United Shoe Machinery*, was a rather small company by the 1960's, which was ripe for treatment in the first wave. It suggests also that the scale economies of legal actions favor focusing on the larger dominant firms. In fact, the main conditions affecting section 2 yields are the size of the firm, the quickness of action after the original monopolization, and the closeness of control of the firm. The ideal case has been a large-scale recent (or incipient) monopoly still in the original monopolizers' hands.

Altogether, the evidence, including the recent *A.T. & T.* case, indicates that section 2 has had high economic yields and can still

---

[40] It is presented and explained in W. G. SHEPHERD, *supra* note 8, at 184–91 & appendix C.

[41] One earlier study by George J. Stigler dealt with other effects of the laws—on concentration and collusion—not with cost-benefit comparisons of their economic yields; moreover, his conclusions were rather vague, or "meagre and undogmatic," in his words. See his *The Economic Effects of the Antitrust Laws*, 9 J.L. & ECON. 225 (1965). Other studies have sought to show effects on behavior, but again with no strong findings.

Table 4

Estimate of Costs and Benefits, Major Treatments Under Section 2

Company	Public agency costs[a]	Private adjustment costs[a]	Sum of costs[a, b]	Sum of benefits	Ratio of benefits to costs
Standard Oil	20	25	45	3,021	67.1
American Tobacco	10	5	15	312	20.8
International Harvester	15	0	15	331	22.1
Corn Products Refining	5	1	6	46	7.7
United States Steel	25	2	27	636	23.6
Alcoa	25	0	25	470	18.8
American Can	15	3	13	96	7.4
United Shoe Machinery	20	5	20	93	4.7

[a] $ millions.

[b] Adjusted to 1947–49 values using the U.S. Bureau of Labor Statistics wholesale price index.

SOURCE: W. G. SHEPHERD, THE TREATMENT OF MARKET POWER 319 (1975).

provide them. The natural forces of decay still operate too, in reducing dominance, as shown by the decline of General Motors during 1978–88 from 48% to 37% of U.S. sales of new automobiles. But a number of other major dominant firms still persist, such as IBM, Eastman Kodak, Campbell Soup, Gillette, and Procter & Gamble, and still others are emerging in newer markets.[42] Because the recent doctrines defending dominance have little substance, section 2 remains as an important and under-used policy device.

---

[42] Space prohibits any substantive discussion here of the best section 2 treatments for these possible candidates. The main need is to reactivate the discussion of the economic merits of such cases.

C. Other lessons

Three other categories of lessons are also worth noting.

1. SEVERITY OF REMEDIES The remedies were actually moderate, even in the big 1911 cases: Standard Oil merely separated into its parts, which continued cooperating with each other into and through the 1920's, and American Tobacco sacrificed only a minor part of its capacity.[43] Moreover, the severity of remedies abated sharply after 1911, and it dwindled further in the second wave. Since 1913 there has been scarcely any direct dissolution or divestiture at all in the manufacturing industry, *except* for the massive A.T. & T. action in 1984.[44] Conduct remedies have also been moderate throughout section 2's history.

2. DURATION Table 1 shows that the duration of section 2 actions—from the initial study through to a final remedy—has lengthened, from about 6 years to about 20 (again, with *A.T. & T.* as the exception, at about 12 years). The average interval from the *original monopolization* to remedy, which was already over 20 years in 1911 (35–40 years for *Standard Oil*), has grown much longer. In the two major 1911 cases, *Standard Oil* and *American Tobacco*, the remedy was applied two or more decades after the monopoly was created, and only after the firm's market position was already weakening. In no case has an incipiency treatment been applied quickly enough to intercept a rising position of market power.[45]

---

43 *See* GEORGE W. STOCKING, *supra* note 34; and S. N. WHITNEY, *supra* note 1.

44 There has been an enormous flow of divestiture by firms since 1969, as conglomerate firms have shed subsidiaries in the effort to improve profitability by returning to their main lines of production. Divestiture is a familiar occurrence in U.S. industry, so that its policy uses, as in the A.T. & T. divestiture of 1984, can proceed in an orderly fashion.

45 Such an incipiency case was attempted in the FTC's action toward the Du Pont company in the "titanium dioxide" case, begun in 1978 and decided in 1981; *see* part III *infra* for a summary and evaluation of that case.

3. ORIGINAL OFFENDERS   Actions have never removed much or most of the capitalized monopoly gain from the original monopolizers. The capitalized monopoly gains of the Rockefeller, du Pont, Duke, and other major family fortunes was virtually untouched by the early actions, and the effective amnesty for monopoly wealth has been even more complete since then.

D. Conditions for success

The two necessary preconditions for bringing suit have been a high market share and a high degree of profitability. There were virtually no suits against oligopolists and/or against firms with average or depressed rates of return.

There have been five main elements of a legal victory:

1. There must be a well-conceived and thorough economic case for action, based on extensive research on the critical economic elements of the dominant firm and of the remedy. The old Bureau of Corporations provided this research in the first wave of cases. It was often lacking in later cases, but the recent *A.T. & T.* case benefited from a massive study by the Federal Communications Commission.

2. There must be widespread grass-roots support, both in the political arena and in the form of private and state-level legal actions against the dominant firm. This was true as early as 1880–1904 for the *Standard Oil* case, and during 1969–1984 for the *A.T. & T.* case.

3. There must be skillful handling of the case, by the prosecutors and the courts, particularly to prevent delay by overwhelming the agencies and courts with irrelevant documents and by procedural stalling and detours. There is a sharp contrast, for example, between the delays of the 1970's *IBM* case and the brisk, focused handling of the *A.T. & T.* case.

4. It helps if the defendant is caught by surprise, or is complacent or inept, or has displayed flagrantly abusive actions and markedly excess profits. Standard Oil, American Tobacco and A.T. & T. fit most of those patterns.

5. A specific, feasible basis for remedy must be available, so that the seeming absence of a clear cure will not chill the case from the start.

After a legal victory, there must still be an effective remedy. A genuine cure has been more probable under four conditions:

1. There needed to be a technical basis for dividing the firm, such as decentralization, an origin in recent mergers, or a set of distinct subsidiaries.

2. It helps if the firm's products were relatively simple and standardized, so that innovation or national military concerns were not involved.

3. If only a moderate weakening in the monopolist's total position was involved—so that the company's stock price was not sharply reduced by the remedy—then action was more likely. The *Standard Oil, American Tobacco, Alcoa,* and *A.T. & T.* cases fit this pattern.

4. If the stock was closely held, then the expected or actual impact was not a matter of widespread anxiety, and direct action was more likely. Standard Oil illustrated that in 1913.

In brief, section 2 has worked best against a fading but still profitable dominant firm, which has committed evident abuses and is inept in its defense, when the prosecution and judges are unusually competent, and when a clear and "easy" basis for remedy exists. Few cases make it through these screens, especially in the face of skillful delaying tactics and the mobilizing of political intervention (through Congress, military officials, or other government departments). In fact, section 2 actions must overcome strong biases in information, manipulation of public attitudes, limited antitrust resources, judicial conservatism, and delay.[46]

---

[46] For the first general economic cost-benefit framework for analyzing efficient antitrust choices, *see* W. G. SHEPHERD, *supra* note 8, at chap. 3. The role of the main biases that may distort these choices is framed and analyzed at 71–85. For more recent theoretical discussions, *see* Schwartz, *An Overview of the Economics of Antitrust Enforcement,* 68 GEO. L.J. 1075 (1980); and Noll, *Comment: Settlement Incentives and Follow-on Litigation,* in PRIVATE ANTITRUST LITIGATION: NEW EVIDENCE, NEW LEARNING 371–79 (Lawrence J. White ed. 1988). These recent discussions are aimed mainly at predicting litigation activity, rather than framing the normative issues of efficient policies.

In 1975 I noted that these conditions had caused a de facto repeal of section 2.[47] The law's prohibition on dominance had been diluted in practice, while the agencies were left without sufficient resources to research the cases, carry them to trial, and supervise the remedies. The 1980's have reinforced these problems by withdrawing enforcement efforts.

The *A.T. & T.* case provides an immense exception, which reestablishes the value of section 2. Many of the usual preconditions for success were absent. The firm was the largest firm in the world, and it extended deeply into the economic and political fabric of the country, giving it high degrees of political influence. Its technology and services were complex and (at least before 1969) had a generally high popular reputation (reinforced by extensive A.T. & T. self-advertising) for quality. Like IBM, A.T. & T. could claim to be a high-technology leader that could be harmed by judicial tampering.

Moreover, A.T. & T. stock was very widely held, so that millions of citizens might fear for their savings and pension funds.[48] The possibilities for delay were great (as IBM was demonstrating concurrently during the 1970's in defending against its antitrust case). The needed divestiture was not mild, and so it could be portrayed as a radical remedy. Finally, the monopoly elements were deeply ingrained in A.T. & T.'s fabric and culture, so that any change (after repeated antitrust failures in earlier attempts) seemed inevitable. Nonetheless, a combination of favorable conditions, including skillful handling by a forceful judge, made the impossible entirely possible.

It is instructive to compare this result with the *IBM* case, which was abandoned in January 1982, simultaneously with the announcement of the *A.T. & T.* settlement. IBM presented a

---

[47] In W. G. SHEPHERD, *supra* note 8, at chap. 7.

[48] But stockholders actually benefited from the divestiture, as the stocks of A.T. & T. and the Baby Bells rose after 1983; *see* TEMIN, *supra* note 38.

classic situation of pervasive price discrimination, comparable to a public utility.[49] Its new 360 family of computers in the 1960's pooled overhead costs among computer lines ranging from small to very large. IBM targeted varying profit rates among those models, systematically in line with competitive pressures.

Discrimination also occurred horizontally, among individual purchasers of identical models, as special concessions were given in order to win contracts. When new competition arose in peripheral equipment in the late 1960's, IBM also adopted deep price discrimination to repel that incursion. Finally, IBM rushed out two money-losing "fighting ship" lines to repel superior computers of small rival firms.

Some of these actions were "predatory" even by the strict cost standard popularized by Areeda and Turner after 1975.[50] That alone should have led to conviction, as an abuse by a dominant firm. But the larger discriminatory pattern was even more pervasively anticompetitive, smothering competition in ways comparable to those cited in the convictions of *Standard Oil* and *United Shoe Machinery*. The main economic evidence for this was compact, clear and incontestable, since it came from the crucial top-management pricing decisions for the entire 360 line.[51] IBM's own chairman, Thomas J. Watson, Jr., in his recent memoirs has described the case as sound and justified.

---

[49]   *See* W. G. SHEPHERD, *supra* note 19, which discusses the horizontal and vertical price discrimination in some detail; it is based directly on IBM pricing information. *See also* RICHARD T. DeLAMARTER, BIG BLUE (1986), for an extensive coverage of the pricing and strategic issues as they were presented in the Antitrust Division's case.

[50]   *See* Areeda & Turner, *supra* note 5.

[51]   During 1967–68 I was Special Economic Assistant to Donald F. Turner, Jr., the head of the Antitrust Division. A prime task was to develop the IBM case for possible filing. One of my more successful activities was the location and analysis of these crucial pricing documents.

But IBM was able to divert attention to two other issues: (1) market definition, and (2) Areeda-Turner tests of "predation."[52] Its lawyers asserted an extremely large relevant market, including all items used in any way with computers (for example, at times IBM's market definition included *all* equipment sales made by the Western Electric subsidiary of A.T. & T., even though Western made almost no computers for open sale). And IBM asserted that only proven "predation" could be used as an element of violation of section 2.

IBM also argued that its market share was dropping rapidly, and it claimed that its high rates of return were not a true indicator of monopoly power. And it urged that potential entry into the industry was easy and that much entry had in fact occurred.

Moreover IBM used stalling relentlessly, by a variety of procedural devices, so as to slow the case and to create complexities. The Antitrust Division staff was plagued by turnover, inexperience and certain errors in tactics: for one example, the case should have been kept compact and pointed. The judge let actual trial of the case plod on from 1975 to 1981, an unfortunate experience that may have shown Judge Greene what to avoid in the *A.T. & T.* case.

Finally in 1982 William Baxter, Reagan's new antitrust chief (who earlier had consulting experience and financial support from IBM), withdrew the case entirely, citing delay and a lack of proof. The action appeared to be an astute political move, balanced by the *A.T. & T.* settlement, and there were claims that an unleashed A.T. & T. would guarantee effective new competition for IBM, and vice versa. In fact A.T. & T. has had little

---

[52]   For a lengthy presentation of IBM's view of the case, as developed by its chief economic expert, *see* FRANKLIN M. FISHER ET AL., FOLDED, SPINDLED AND MUTILATED: ECONOMIC ANALYSIS AND US VERSUS IBM (1983).

The Areeda-Turner test for predation became pivotal, requiring proof that prices actually were set below costs. It narrowed the focus and diverted attention from the larger pattern of behavior that IBM had followed.

success in computers, and as of 1990 IBM is reported (without challenge) to retain 80 percent of the mainframe computer market. IBM's main threat is from its own internal rigidity and bureaucracy, also widely reported in the business press during 1984–88. These internal inefficiencies led it in early 1988 to launch a drastic reorganization.

The *IBM* case therefore embodied much that can go wrong in section 2 cases, and it created estoppel, which will probably prevent any further antitrust treatment of IBM during the rest of this century. But the case's failure was mainly one of people, not of the policy instrument itself.

In contrast, the *A.T. & T.* case indicates that virtually any section 2 action is possible, even of great scale or complexity, if the case is handled competently. Moreover the A.T. & T. episode has suggested that section 2 can accomplish important gains in efficiency and innovation. There were complaints and doubting of the outcome during the transition years of 1984–85, and there are still inconveniences. Yet the changes were accomplished with less disruption than might have been expected for the largest corporate reorganization in history, without interrupting the functioning of the telephone system.

Even more impressive has been the general acceptance of the wisdom of the entire action. Baby Bells now choose equipment suppliers freely, and they seek forcefully to compete against their old parent. Equipment innovation is recognized to be much faster than the old Bell System would have provided. There is virtually no support for restoring the pre-1984 Bell System, even if it were possible.

The *A.T. & T.* case has legitimized section 2 again. It was a much more difficult case than *Standard Oil* and *American Tobacco*. Rather than an outmoded, fading policy, section 2 can best be seen as an effective, powerful instrument that is capable of restoring competition in virtually any market.

III. Efficient rewards for monopolists: or, why section 2 need not "punish success"

There are important lingering inhibitions about section 2. One of the most influential recent arguments against section 2 actions has been that they will "stifle incentives" and "punish success." That argument needs to be addressed here in some detail.[53] If, as I will suggest, the argument has little merit, then an important barrier to renewed section 2 actions could be set aside.

The argument is an ancient one. A firm attains dominance after a series of actions, some of them possibly innovative, others merely designed to raise market share. The firm then asserts that its dominance reflects only its many "good" actions and is therefore justified by them. Any restraint on the firm's market position, or on the resulting high profits, will "punish success," cut its incentives to continue performing well, and eliminate other firms' incentives toward excellence. The monopolist demands the right to an open capture of unrestricted monopoly rewards and continued market dominance.

Such an incentive-reward mechanism has intuitive appeal and, indeed, some logical validity, and it has long been a common point in antitrust defenses. Prospective rewards do stimulate performance throughout much of human activity. But the interesting questions are ones of degree: How large do the rewards need to be, compared to the scope of the good actions? Do monopoly-profit rewards exert stronger incentives than competitive-profit rewards?

The issue involves comparing benefits (from the good performance) with costs (the monopoly profit and the attendant social burdens of monopoly). The necessary choice is between an *open-capture* basis and a finite *efficient-reward* basis. Under effective competition, those two bases are likely to give similar or identical results; but under monopoly, they may differ sharply.

---

[53]   The main points in part III are given in more detail in Shepherd, *Efficient Profits Versus Unlimited Capture, as a Reward for Superior Performance: Analysis and Cases*, 34 ANTITRUST BULL. 121 (1989).

The issue involves some simple economic theory, which relates directly to real cases. I will first explore the concepts, in order to define the efficient reward and contrast it with the unlimited reward that emerged in the case law and was used to stop section 2 actions in the 1980's. Then I will note several of the major cases (the *FTC Du Pont* "titanium dioxide" case, *Berkey Photo v. Eastman Kodak*, the *FTC Xerox* case, *US v. International Business Machines Corp.*, and the *FTC cereals* case) that helped to establish the policy precedents.

The simple lesson will be that the efficient reward is a meaningful concept that can be defined with some precision: *in most cases it is the competitive profit rate, adjusted for risk and other factors.* It involves a finite reward, rather than the open-ended capture of profits as commonly demanded by the officials of dominant firms. The efficient reward is usually, of course, much smaller than the unlimited amounts accepted by the recent case decisions. Estimating such rewards could become part of the treatment of section 2 cases, though it would usually be an inexact practical exercise. It would address the issue coherently, replacing the casual, often empty remarks in the recent case decisions with sound and careful economic appraisals.

A. *Concepts of efficient incentives*

Suppose that a firm has done certain "good" actions in the course of attaining dominance: perhaps preparing a cheaper production method for producing the whitener titanium dioxide; or a sharper photographic film; or a better copying machine; or a faster computer; or a wider variety of breakfast cereals. Suppose too that the *net* social contribution of those actions can be identified, by comparing the value of the new products or cost savings with those that other firms would have done. Only the net gains matter, and they are often modest because other firms would have done the good actions nearly as well and as soon.

For that net contribution, what size of reward is efficient? The reward is, by itself, costly to society, because it raises prices above costs and imposes the various well-known monopoly impacts, such as higher costs, slower innovation, and reduced freedom of choice. The social aim is to obtain the benefits of the good actions, while minimizing the social costs that are imposed by the monopoly rewards. Therefore the efficient reward for the dominant firm should be identified and the actual reward should not go above that level.

Because the benefits are finite, the efficient reward will always be finite in amount, rather than unlimited. Therefore an open-capture basis for rewards can be immediately rejected. It has no place in an efficient economy, operating in line with neoclassical economic theory. There, all factors are paid finite amounts, related to the value of their contributions to production. Only a *finite* reward to dominant firms is consistent with that efficient system.

The profit-maximizing firm will instead demand an unlimited capture of market share and profits. It will present its gross contribution as the proper basis for reward, rather than the smaller net gain, as defined above. The dominant firm may overstate its own contribution and exaggerate how strongly the rewards in this episode will influence its future performance. It will say that "winners" deserve to "take the spoils," and it will deny that society has a stake in defining the net contribution and minimizing the efficient reward.

Therefore, small (or imaginary) net contributions can become a basis for claiming carte blanche to monopolize large industries and draw unlimited monopoly profits.

The correct efficient reward derives instead from mainstream neoclassical theory of efficient markets, and it can be summarized simply. *The performance-maximizing reward is provided by the competitive rate of return.* Competitive markets evoke a maximum of effort and performance, in the struggle to survive and thrive. Inferior performance carries a death sentence. Competition therefore applies strong compulsion to perform well. The pressure will usually be at least as strong as it is from monopoly rewards.[54]

Intuition is also instructive. Millions of firms attempt to live under the pressures of effective competition, in thousands of U.S. markets, routinely performing at the limits of possibility in cost-cutting and innovation. Their expected and actual rewards are usually limited to the competitive rate of return. Competition consistently "stifles" these firms' monopoly-profit incentives for superior performance. Yet these firms continue exerting maximum performance levels.

Therefore a competitive rate of return is usually sufficient to evoke maximum performance. Moreover, by limiting the profits to the levels necessary to sustain the firm, this competitive standard prevents the firm from accruing extra funds that can then be used to prevail in the future by exploiting market imperfections. Thus the efficient-reward standard helps to renew effective competition, by intercepting the dominant firm's efforts to extend its monopoly power.

The competitive rate of return may not be precisely known, but a sizable literature has developed over the last six decades concerning the rates of return under utility regulation.[55] It permits one to specify the competitive rate as being near the going interest rate, such as approximately in the range of 8% to 12% in recent years.

Several adjustments may be appropriate:

One is for risk; in many cases a risk premium of one to three points above the competitive rate of return may be suitable. But note that for a dominant firm with market power, the degree of

---

[54]   For an analysis comparing competitive and monopoly incentives, *see id.*

[55]   *See* ALFRED E. KAHN, THE ECONOMICS OF REGULATIONS (1971); RICHARD SCHMALENSEE, THE CONTROL OF NATURAL MONOPOLIES (1979); among others.

risk is likely to be low, rather than above average. If so, then the proper risk adjustment would *subtract* from the standard rate of return, not add to it.

An adjustment for "second best" may also be needed. If profit rates in other related markets are markedly above the average rates of return in the economy, then they influence the opportunity cost of capital in the market in question. New projects by the dominant firm may need to match those higher rates of return. Of course, the reverse would also hold, if profits in adjacent markets are unusually low.

Other adjustments may also be appropriate. But all adjustments can be discussed, specified and then estimated, even if only roughly. The result is an estimated competition-related profit rate that sets the limit on the needed "incentive" or "deserved" profit rate. As a definite, moderate reward, it will be seen to be sufficient and fair, in line both with business experience and intuition, and with fundamental economic theory.

This criterion is all the stronger if one compares the incentive power of competitive and monopoly profits. If the open-capture approach were to be valid, *then monopoly profits must always exert greater incentive power than do competitive profits, even up to extremely high profits.* This is quite unlikely, as noted above. Superior performance to obtain monopoly profits is optional, while performance to attain competitive profits is compulsory. Optional actions are unlikely to exceed those done under the full pressure of competition.

Moreover, the monopoly–profit-induced actions are likely to be subject to diminishing responses to profits, as is true of economic behavior in other contexts. Even if a modest degree of monopoly profits might conceivably stir extreme efforts in some firms, any additional profit rewards are likely to encounter diminishing responses. That would pull them even further below the competition-stimulated levels.

To summarize, the conditions needed for monopoly profits to add to industrial performance are not credible or likely. Logic, research and business experience indicate that competitive profits are the more powerful and sufficient stimulus, and they are free of the monopolist's usual tendencies toward internal slack and retarded innovation. Conceivably, monopoly profits might in some cases and over limited ranges, exert a stronger stimulus to performance than competitive profits do. But the burden of proof is against that possibility, and so affirmative evidence would be needed to establish and define those conditions.

The efficient incentive level of rewards is finite, at the level of adjusted competitive profits. Open capture is acceptable only when competition is so tight that profits are constrained to be near to the adjusted competitive rate in any event. Dominance is precisely the situation where effective competition does not exist.

B. Leading antitrust cases

Dominant firms have been using the incentive defense successfully in the last decade, so much that it has become a precedential barrier to section 2 actions. Dominant firms have won not only the legal basis to continue but also to make an unlimited capture of excess profits on into the indefinite future.

None of these case decisions has examined the actual benefits and costs, nor articulated the correct standard, nor recognized that an explicit standard is needed. Not only has the wrong logic been used, but also the judges have indulged in casual, naive comments about the firms' supposedly large past contributions and the absolute need, as they acquiesce in it, to avoid any dilution of incentives.

The five cases are summarized in table 5. They include some of the leading dominant-firm positions of the 1960's and 1970's, and IBM, Kodak, Du Pont, and the cereals firms continue to hold those positions at this writing. Space does not permit a detailed discussion of each case, though that would help to clarify the extent of the judicial indifference to the crucial incentive-response conditions. The best that can be done here is a compact review of the main points.

Table 5
Conditions in Five Recent Cases Involving Market Power

Case	Defendant's probable market share at the alleged violation	Defendant's claimed "good" actions	Defendant's alleged anti-competitive actions	Defendant's return on investment during the period of alleged market power or monopoly control	Decision in the case
FTC: Du Pont (titanium dioxide)	30% in 1972, rising toward 50% during the 1970's.	Developing the chloride method (using ilmenite ore), 1940's–1960's. Building a large new plant. Kept price low during 1972–1982.	Attempting to monopolize by deliberate strategy, combining pricing policies and a refusal to license the technology.	12% during 1972–1982; over 20% expected after 1982.	Dismissal by the FTC in 1981.
Berkey Photo v. Eastman Kodak	Over 65% in amateur film; over 40% in film developing.	Innovation of improved films and cameras, since 1890.	Designing and introducing the Instamatic II camera and film; one objective apparently was to disadvantage competitors.	Over 20% in recent decades.	Most claims decided favorably to Kodak in 1981; remainder subsequently settled.
FTC: Xerox	100% of plain-paper copiers 1961–1970; about 90% until 1975.	Development and innovation of xerography; rapid growth during the 1960's.	Exclusion of competition by refusal to license; price discrimination; lease-only policy; and tying of supplies.	Over 27% during 1961–1970; stock price rise over 100-fold.	Settlement, opening access to three Xerox patents in 1975.

U.S. v. IBM	Over 70% of mainframe computers in the 1960's.	Innovations in computer products. Rapid growth.	Excluding competitors by "fighting ship" programs. Price discrimination. Lease-only policies. Bundling of services. Actions against peripheral equipment firms. Design changes to make obsolete competitors' peripheral attachments.	A steady 18% return during 1960–1977.	Withdrawal of the case by the Antitrust Division after trial but before decision in 1982; IBM successful in most parallel cases.
FTC: Cereals (Kellogg's, General Foods, General Mills)	Combined share of about 80% during 1955–1982.	Developing a wide variety of cereals products.	"Packing the product space," so as deliberately to prevent entry. Jointly stopping the offerings of premiums in 1957.	Over 20% since 1955 for Kellogg's; probably over 20% for the others.	Dismissal by FTC in 1982.

SOURCE: Shepherd, *Efficient Profits Versus Unlimited Capture, as a Reward for Superior Performance: Analysis and Cases*, ANTITRUST BULLETIN, 34 (spring 1989), pp. 121–52.

1. THE DU PONT TITANIUM DIOXIDE CASE[56] In this case, Du Pont used a carefully designed pricing strategy, based on a partly fortuitous 15% cost advantage, to raise its market share from 30% to over 60%. Rather than license its better technology, or permit others to develop it, Du Pont established an apparently permanent dominance.

In exonerating Du Pont, the FTC said that any constraint would "unduly penalize" the firm for its innovation. Even requiring (profitable) licensing would have harmed incentives: "Imposition of a duty to license might serve to chill the very kind of innovative process that led to DuPont's cost advantage." (*FTC* decision, at 747–48).

2. BERKEY PHOTO VERSUS EASTMAN KODAK[57] Since 1890 the Eastman Kodak Company has dominated the market for amateur photographic supplies, especially for film (with 80% to 90% of that market). In the 1970's it was sued by Berkey Photo, a much smaller firm, for allegedly monopolizing the market. Berkey won at trial but then lost on all important counts in the appeals court.

Berkey charged that Eastman had deliberately designed and introduced its Instamatic II camera and matching film so as to

---

[56] For the more detailed issues and evidence in this case, see the extensive case materials in U.S. Federal Trade Commission, In the Matter of E.I. du Pont de Nemours & Co., Docket No. 9108, filed 1978, decided 1981; and in Shepherd, *Testimony* in that case, ANTITRUST LAW & ECONOMICS REVIEW vol. 11, no. 4 (1979), and vol. 12, nos. 1 & 4 (1980). I was the expert witness on economic issues called by the FTC staff in the case.

[57] For summaries of this and earlier antitrust cases affecting Eastman Kodak, *see* Brock, *Structural Monopoly, Technological Performance, and Predatory Innovation: Relevant Standards Under Section 2 of the Sherman Act*, 21 AM. BUS. L.J. 291 (1983); and Brock, *Persistent Monopoly and the Charade of Antitrust: The Durability of Kodak's Market Power*, 14 U. TOL. L. REV. 653 (1983).

For details of the case itself, *see* Berkey Photo v. Eastman Kodak Co., 603 F.2d 263 (2d Cir. 1979), *cert. denied*, 444 U.S. 1093 (1980).

maximize the harm to Berkey and other competitors in the film developing market. That fact was proven at the trial.

Yet the appeals court concluded that Eastman had attained its dominance in earlier decades by virtue of its innovations. Such dominant firms, it said, have the right to engage in "hard" competition against all competitors. To limit "hard" competition would discourage innovation:

> If a firm that has engaged in the risks and expenses of research and development were required in all circumstances to share with its rivals the benefits of those endeavors, this incentive would very likely be vitiated. . . . Because . . . a monopolist is permitted, and indeed encouraged, by [the Sherman Act] to compete aggressively on the merits, any success that it may achieve through "the process of invention and innovation" is clearly tolerated by the antitrust laws. . . .[58]

Both the monopoly profits ("any success") the "aggressive competition" were approved, without any limit.

Like the FTC in the *Du Pont* case, the appeals court here made no effort to assess the incentives function, the costs or the social benefit values for any of Eastman's innovations, or to compare them with Eastman's profits. If an efficient-reward basis had been applied instead, the resulting efficient profit values for this secure dominant firm would probably have been far below the actual profits that had already been obtained by Eastman over many decades.[59] Therefore it would not have stifled incentives to have set reasonable limits on the manner in which Eastman introduced products so as to harm its small competitors.

3. FTC: XEROX CORPORATION   In the 1960's Xerox Corporation held a complete monopoly on plain-paper copiers, owing mainly to crucial patents it had obtained from Chester Carlson and

---

[58]   *Berkey*, 603 F.2d at 281.

[59]   The profits after taxes averaged about 19% of equity capital during the 1960–75 period, more than double the probable cost of capital to the firm. This rate of return was for the entire Eastman Kodak company; the rate of return on just film operations would probably have been higher than that.

developed during the 1950's. Its profits averaged over 27% on equity during the 1960's, and its stock price rose over a hundred-fold. By 1971 Xerox's continuing overwhelming dominance appeared secure. It rested on complex strategies of overlapping patents, discriminatory pricing, a lease-only policy, and a tying policy that required customers to use Xerox toner and ink.

An FTC action against Xerox was filed in 1973, seeking to limit these strategies and to increase competition.[60] But after brief negotiations, the FTC and Xerox reached a compromise in 1975 that was relatively moderate: it opened up various Xerox patents, but applied no penalties. Evidently Xerox's past technological reputation (based on actions taken in the 1950's and 1960's) protected it from a stricter treatment. Xerox's very high profit rates and extraordinary investors' gains were implicitly approved as a reward for innovation, and Xerox was given a free hand to capture further future profits.

The FTC's reasoning reflected the doctrine of maximum capture, as a necessary incentive for good actions. Though Xerox's degree of risk-taking in the 1950's was high, the commitment of funds by the firm was quite limited. The later excess profits and investors' capitalized gains, at many billions of dollars, were several orders of magnitude greater.

4. U.S. VERSUS INTERNATIONAL BUSINESS MACHINES CORPORATION[61]   IBM attained approximately a 70% share of the emerging U.S. computer market in the 1950's, by building on its sales network and 90% share in the tabulating machines industry.[62]

---

60   In the Matter of Xerox Corp., decision and order, 86 F.T.C. 364 (1975). *See also* Blackstone, *Restrictive Practices in the Marketing of Electrofax Copying Machines and Supplies*, 23 J. INDUS. ECON. 189 (1975).

61   U.S. v. International Business Machines Corp., 69 Civ. 200 (S.D.N.Y. complaint filed January 17, 1969).

62   Recall SHEPHERD, *supra* note 19; and R. T. DELAMARTER, *supra* note 49. I was involved in the Antitrust Division's 1967–68 investigations of IBM, and I helped to design the heart of the suit's original economic approach to IBM's pricing policies. But I did not participate in the case after 1969.

In 1964–68 IBM took several bold steps in introducing and defending the several lines of its new 360 computer family. In 1969 it reacted so sharply to new, innovative competition against part of its product line that it lost money while driving out important competitors (including General Electric and RCA). In 1969–72, it adopted further "hard" competitive tactics against small new competitors in the "peripheral equipment" market.

IBM was sued by the Antitrust Division in January 1969, for monopolizing the main computer market and, soon after, by numerous small competitors for its actions in peripherals markets. IBM eventually won virtually all of those cases, and the Division's case was voluntarily withdrawn in 1982, just before the court reached a decision (widely expected to be a conviction of IBM). The underlying reasoning in all the cases: IBM had been a vigorous innovator. That earned IBM its market dominance, and so it should be free to conduct vigorous, "hard" competition, in harvesting the rewards for its good actions.

This is the open-capture doctrine once more, reflecting a deep aversion to appear to discourage this large firm with its progressive reputation. Yet IBM's actual degree of net contribution has not been addressed or compared with the monopoly costs. IBM has often followed innovations, rather than led them, and many innovations have come from outside the industry.

In short, the simple notions of good actions and incentives (unsupported by specific facts about costs and needed incentives) have validated IBM's capture of past profits and given it official approval to maximize its future market power and profits.

5. FTC: THE CEREALS PRODUCERS CASE Kellogg, General Mills, and General Foods have long been the leading ready-to-eat cereals producers, with market shares of about 44%, 20%, and 18% respectively.[63] Advertising is intensive, absorbing about 10% of revenues, and profit rates have averaged over 20% of equity for three decades and more.

---

63 *See* Schmalensee, *supra* note 37; Scherer, *supra* note 37.

An experimental FTC action toward these firms was begun in 1972, ran a difficult course, and ended with an exoneration of the firms in 1982.[64] The case charged a "shared monopoly," in which the firms proliferated new brands of cereals so as to "pack the product space" to make new entry difficult.

The only relevant fact here is that brand proliferation was, in the end, held to be a *positive* sign of innovativeness, rather than, as the FTC staff charged, a tactic for creating monopoly power. The proliferation justified the firms' combined dominance and high profit rates, both past and future.

To summarize, these five decisions have invoked an incentive function as crucial, while avoiding both a coherent discussion of its elements and a serious assessment of its nature. They have assumed the needed rewards to be unlimited, and no comparisons of efficient rewards with actual and prospective profits have been made. The decisions have created an unwarranted bias in favor of dominant firms in the precedents now governing section 2 cases.

IV. In conclusion

Section 2 has long been the more liberal element of U.S. antitrust policy. There have been some major cases, which have been valuable in preserving the sense of pressure against market dominance. But the whole accomplishment of section 2 has (except for the important A.T. & T. case) been moderate and often delayed.

Since 1980, the role of section 2 has virtually disappeared. This change has little basis in mainstream economic concepts and empirical research. Instead it reflects a current popularity of extreme claims, based in part on unrealistic theories. The errors have gotten lodged in many economists' views, as well as in the antitrust agencies and a proportion of the federal judiciary. Restoring section 2 against those views may be difficult.

---

[64]   Federal Trade Commission, In the Matter of Kellogg's et al., 99 F.T.C. 8 (1982) (complaint dismissed).

But the case for a revival is strong, based on economic analysis. Moreover, the shrinkage in the ranks of large dominant firms should make the revival easier to mount, because the candidates for treatment are relatively few. A revived section 2 would not overreach, threatening a broad range of U.S. industries.

The century point of the Sherman Act is a particularly appropriate time to revive section 2. That might not only restore competitive parity to a series of major markets, but also put antitrust policy back into balance.

31
The future of antitrust: ideology vs. legislative intent

BY PETER W. RODINO, JR.*

Advocating an [antitrust] enforcement agenda based on vague populist concerns and which yields results that reduce consumer welfare is fundamentally at odds with the principle of separation of powers. . . . Only the Legislative Branch, and then only through constitutionally enacted statutes, can override the consumer welfare focus of the current statutes.

Assistant Attorney General, Charles F. Rule[1]

If the legislature enacts into statutory law a common law concept, as Congress did . . . in the Sherman Act, that is a clue that the courts are to interpret the statute with the freedom with which they interpret a common law principle—in which event the values of the framers may not be controlling at all.

Judge Richard Posner[2]

---

* Former Chairman, Committee on the Judiciary, U.S. House of Representatives. Representative Rodino was first elected to the House in 1948.

[1] Antitrust, Consumers and Small Business, Remarks Delivered at the 21st New England Antitrust Conference, Cambridge, Massachusetts 8 (Nov. 13, 1987).

[2] *Statutory Interpretation—in the Classroom and the Courtroom*, 50 U. CHI. L. REV. 800, 818 (1983).

*There are literally thousands of statutes out there that are
being interpreted by the courts day in and day out. The notion
that Congress could possibly keep track of the interpretations
. . . , let alone promptly intervene and surgically change
those particular ones of which they disapprove, does not seem
to me to bear much relationship to the world with which I'm
familiar.*

Assistant Attorney General, William F. Baxter[3]

I have been fortunate to watch the continuing evolution of
antitrust over the past 40 years from the perspective of an elected
member of the U.S. Congress. Throughout that period, the
antitrust laws have remained the primary system of laws for
insuring competition, fairness, and vitality in our distinctive
American free enterprise system. I am convinced that the overwhelming majority of Americans are strong, though frequently
silent supporters of these goals of antitrust. But for antitrust to
survive the next 100 years, the enforcement scheme must remain
responsive to the needs of this broad, pluralistic constituency.

The principal provisions of the antitrust laws have been
written with the constitutional generality of an economic charter.[4]
Interpretations of sections 1 and 2 of the Sherman Act and
section 7 of the Clayton Act have shifted over the years with
changing economic and social philosophies. This adaptability
may be a survival tool; but it is also subject to abuse. Flexibility,
as recent experience shows, can be a license to pursue an ideologically driven policy with little regard for the established body of
case law built upon a mainstream, consensus approach to antitrust. An essential check on such departures is the congressional
intent underlying the statutory language.

---

[3]   *Antitrust Division and Office of Legal Counsel of the Depart-
ment of Justice: Oversight Hearings, House Comm. on the Judiciary,
Subcomm. on Monopolies and Commercial Law*, 98th Cong., 1st & 2d
Sess. 136 (1986).

[4]   In the United States v. Topco Associates, Inc., 405 U.S. 596, 610
(1972), the Court described the antitrust laws as the "Magna Carta" of
free enterprise.

Ironically, the interpretive liberty assumed by antitrust enforcers in recent years could have the effect of constraining the interpretive discretion of those who follow. There are indications that radical departures from congressional intent may push Congress to legislate with greater specificity, removing much of the interpretive latitude that has characterized antitrust over the past century. Congress, as the branch most directly answerable to the electorate, has a special constitutionally delegated responsibility to use its oversight and lawmaking powers to insure that antitrust retains its relevance and effectiveness in a constantly evolving economic world. But Congress itself is severely (and unconstitutionally) constrained in performing that task if those who enforce the antitrust laws do not adhere to legislative intent.

Legislative intent and the Reagan antitrust "revolution"

Beginning in 1981, antitrust enforcement officials have demonstrated an uncommon dedication to a simple and at least superficially appealing measure of antitrust—that enforcement action should be taken only when private conduct undercuts the overall efficient allocation of society's limited resources.[5] To put it another way, if private conduct does not reduce society's overall economic output, it should be permitted. For some observers, this means that absent the power to limit output in a particular market, a business should be freed of virtually all antitrust restraints.[6] The increased producer profits flowing from market power are, according to former Assistant Attorney General for Antitrust, Charles F. Rule, not an antitrust concern in and of themselves because "producer surplus provides that incentive for risk-taking, innovation, and other fixed investments."

---

[5] Straining the antitrust laws through the esoteric filter of "allocative efficiency" theory is long removed in language and substance from Senator Sherman's view that the antitrust laws "will be a warning that all trade and commerce, all arguments, all struggles for money and property, must be governed by the natural law that the public good must be the test for all." 21 Cong. Rec. 2457 (1890).

[6] R. Bork, The Antitrust Paradox: A Policy at War With Itself 20–21 (1978).

Moreover, even if the profits are not spent for innovative activity, the Assistant Attorney General has suggested that the company and its stockholders (possibly "the proverbial widows and orphans") may be more deserving of the profits than consumers.[7]

Current policy substantially curtailing antitrust enforcement also carries a "libertarian" undertone that all government interventions are inherently suspect and threatening to individual liberties. The last chief of the Antitrust Division under the Reagan administration, charged with enforcing the primary set of laws designed to prevent the abuse of private economic power, argues that the greatest threat to individual liberty "is not private power, economic or otherwise, but rather the 'government' power to coerce."[8] He has said that any interpretation of antitrust's goals going beyond "consumer welfare" is a "prescription for tyranny" and amounts to "central planning by lawyers."[9]

There is, of course, nothing unusual about an administration putting its own "spin" on antitrust. Ideological debate about antitrust policy was well underway in 1890, when the "economic Darwinists" argued against enactment of any antitrust law.[10] But the impact of current ideologically driven policy shifts has been more severe than any within the past 40 years. In its execution, President Reagan's policies brought a reduction in the size of the Antitrust Division to slightly more than half its 1980 size, the

---

[7]   Rule, *supra* note 1, at 5.

[8]   *Id*. Contrast Mr. Rule's views with the goal of the Sherman Act's sponsors to limit what they felt were dangerous accumulations of private power. In Senator Sherman's words, if "we will not endure a king as a political power we should not endure a king over the production, transportation, and sale of any of the necessaries of life." 21 CONG. REC. 2457 (1890).

[9]   Rule, *supra* note 1, at 5.

[10]   Clark, *The "Trust,"* 51 NEW ENGLANDER & YALE REV. 223, 228–29 (1890); Gunton, *The Economic and Social Aspects of Trust*, 3 POL. SCI. Q. 385, 403 (1888).

elimination of virtually all enforcement activity other than classic cartel cases and a vastly diminished flow of merger cases,[11] an extensive campaign to curtail private enforcement (executed through amicus interventions and departmental guidelines), and proposed legislation designed to further curtail private enforcement and codify its own scaled-back merger enforcement policy.[12]

This far-reaching cutback in antitrust has generally been cast as the natural and rational implementation of new economic learning. To be sure, it is widely conceded in retrospect that antitrust policy during the 1960's may have been insufficiently sensitive to potential inefficiencies created by certain classes of enforcement action. Well before 1980, the courts had begun responding to this criticism in decisions that extended the range of lawful behavior.[13] Although this "moderated" enforcement policy met with widespread acceptance, the more extreme and ideological approach now being pursued has pushed well beyond consensus.

Historians, writing before the ideological debate over consumer welfare goals had seized center stage, concluded that Congress had a variety of goals in enacting the Sherman Act, each of them centered around protecting the process of competition. These goals were to keep prices low for consumers, to maintain efficiency, to preserve an opportunity for all who would compete in a business or trade, and to maintain a balanced

---

[11] Categories of enforcement wholly or largely ignored include vertical restraints, predatory pricing, and, since Mr. Baxter resigned in 1983, monopolization.

[12] This record is detailed in *Oversight Hearings of the Antitrust Division, Subcomm. on Monopolies and Commercial Law, House Comm. on the Judiciary*, 100th Cong., 2d Sess. (February 24, 25, and March 3, 1988) Serial No. 126.

[13] *See*, Continental T.V., Inc. v. GTE Sylvania Inc., 433 U.S. 36 (1977); United States v. General Dynamics Corp., 415 U.S. 486 (1974). The courts were responding to criticism that had begun in the 1960's. Bork, *Legislative Intent and the Policy of the Sherman Act*, 9 J.L. & Econ. 7 (1966).

industrial structure less conducive to corruption and abuse of power.[14]

There are various views about which, if any, of these goals Congress intended to be preeminent. Based upon his extensive analysis of legislative history and popular and scholarly writings during the period leading up to 1890, Thorelli concluded that the immediate intended beneficiary "was in all probability the small business proprietor or tradesman whose opportunities were to be safeguarded."[15] Professor Lande made his own extensive analysis of the legislative history and concluded that Congress' primary purpose was to prevent " 'unfair' transfers of wealth from consumers to firms with market power."[16] In his view, Congress intended to challenge market power that raised prices to consumers even in instances in which enforcement might undercut efficiency.

Among the various interpretations of congressional intent, there is only one—that embodied in what has now become colloquially known as the Chicago school of economics—that is consistent with key aspects of current antitrust policy. The Justice Department has embraced the Chicago school's viewpoints declaring that "consumer welfare and economic efficiency" are now the "mainstream" of antitrust.[17] Have the Chicago school and the Justice Department, writing almost a century after Congress enacted the Sherman Act, made a major breakthrough in understanding the congressional intent that had been misinterpreted for all these years? Are they advancing a well-documented and empirically sound case, or is their analysis simply result-driven revisionism with little regard for the historical record?

---

[14] H. THORELLI, THE FEDERAL ANTITRUST POLICY 226-27 (1954); R. HOFSTADTER, THE PARANOID STYLE IN AMERICAN POLITICS AND OTHER ESSAYS 199-200 (1965).

[15] THORELLI, *supra* note 14, at 226-27.

[16] Lande, *Wealth Transfers as the Original and Primary Concern of Antitrust: The Efficiency Interpretation Challenged*, 34 HASTINGS L.J. 65, 68-69 (1982).

[17] Rule, *supra* note 1, at 9-10.

From my perspective, the Chicago school's interpretation of legislative intent is highly implausible. Anyone familiar with the legislative process knows that among the elected Members of Congress, there are widely diverse interests, levels of understanding, and motivations that accompany any vote on major legislation. Even among the members of the House and Senate Judiciary Committees—those likely to have been most familiar with the Sherman Act—it is impossible to show that a consensus of legislative intent had coalesced around an arcane economic concept ("allocative efficiencies") that apparently was not widely discussed in economic writings in this country before the 1930's.[18] Indeed, the Sherman Act was primarily the product of committee deliberations and mark-ups in which economists had no evident role.[19]

Nor is the view that allocative efficiencies alone are to be the linchpin for antitrust interpretation founded on any immutable economic learning. In fact, underlying the exclusive focus on allocative efficiencies are a number of fundamental questions of analysis and application as to which economists and antitrust experts differ widely. For example—

1. Once an analyst moves past the libertarian assumption that antitrust enforcement will always produce a less efficient allocation of resources, than the unencumbered, private exercise of power, actual measurement of efficiencies becomes a difficult and frequently subjective exercise (it is still more difficult to predict their future occurrence). To be blunt, how precisely is a judge to determine allocative efficiencies?

2. Professor Scherer has calculated that the adverse impact of market power on the consumer comes far more from a wealth transfer to the "monopolist" than from an adverse allocation of resources.[20] Is the court to ignore this major wealth transfer to the detriment of

---

18   Lande, *supra* note 16, at 88–89 and n.97.

19   R. HOFSTADTER, *supra* note 14, at 200.

20   Scherer, *Antitrust, Efficiency, and Progress*, 62 N.Y.U. L. REV. (1987).

consumers simply because the additional market power might be marginally more efficient?

3. Will the increased profits attained by a more efficient producer that has substantial market power be squandered in increased benefits for management or employees and defensive behavior to protect its market position?[21]

4. Schumpeter argued that innovation efficiencies may be far more important to economic development than production efficiencies.[22] What if industry structure or behavior that may marginally increase production and allocative efficiencies is likely to discourage aggressive innovation?[23]

5. As Judge Learned Hand wrote in 1945: "it is possible, because of its indirect social or moral effect, to prefer a system of small producers, each dependent for his success upon his own skill and character, to one in which the great mass of those engaged must accept the direction of a few."[24] Should attaining or preserving allocative efficiencies, no matter how small or uncertain, override such social goals set out by the Congress?

These questions do not lend themselves to simple answers based on empirical observation. An individual's answers will vary depending upon economic, political, and social philosophy. The Chicago school view that society will benefit if allocative efficiencies are the sole calculus for determining antitrust policy is the product of individual political and economic preferences that are by no means consensus choices of other experts or of the American electorate at large. But more importantly, this analysis either ignores or consciously separates itself from the written

---

[21]   *See* the discussion and sources cited in Lande, *supra* note 16, at 78–79 and nn. 52–56.

[22]   J. A. SCHUMPETER, CAPITALISM, SOCIALISM AND DEMOCRACY, 83 (1942).

[23]   Professor Scherer has concluded that "relatively small firms and 'outsiders' appear to originate a disproportionate fraction of the most radical inventions." Scherer, *supra* note 20.

[24]   United States v. Aluminum Company of America, 148 F.2d 416, 427 (2d Cir. 1945).

ledger or congressional intent that, absent constitutional imperatives, must guide statutory interpretation and enforcement policy.

Legislative intent—the last 40 years (1948–1988)

Of course, proper interpretation of the Sherman Act does not
end with an examination of the original intent of its framers. The
Sherman Act has been amended and supplemented by a number
of major antitrust provisions enacted since 1890. Through enactment of these provisions and of authorization and appropriation
measures for the antitrust agencies, and through the oversight
process, Congress is constantly expressing its views as to antitrust
policy and the nature and level of enforcement.

Among the most important amendments or additions to the
Sherman Act are the Clayton Act and Federal Trade Commission
Act, each enacted in 1914. The legislative history of these provi-
sions, discussed by other commentators,[25] is not addressed here.
Instead I have chosen to focus on relatively more recent expres-
sions of congressional intent during my tenure as a Member of
Congress.

The first major antitrust legislation for which I voted was the
Celler-Kefauver Act of 1950.[26] The 1950 legislation was enacted to
make clear that section 7 of the Clayton Act, which referred to
stock acquisitions, also covered acquisitions of the assets of a
target company.[27] According to an FTC witness, the Commission
had been urging legislative action to close the loophole for 23
years.[28] Political support for the Commission's recommendation

---

[25]   *See* Lande, *supra* note 16, at 106–30, and sources cited therein.

[26]   P.L. 81-899, 64 Stat. 1125 (1950).

[27]   The interpretation of section 7 limiting its application to stock
acquisitions was established by court decisions in the 1920's and 1930's.
Arrow-Hart & Hegeman Electric Co. v. FTC, 291 U.S. 532 (1934); FTC
v. Western Meat Co., 272 U.S. 554 (1926).

[28]   *Amending Sections 7 and 11 of the Clayton Act: Hearing Before
Subcomm. No. 3 of the House Comm. on the Judiciary*, 81st Cong., 1st
Sess. 11 (1949), Statement of FTC General Counsel William T. Kelley
[hereinafter 1949 House Hearings].

began to grow in the 1940's as concern with economic concentration mounted. In his January 1947 state of the Union address, President Truman expressed concern with the "growing concentration of economic power and the threat to free competitive enterprise." The President concluded that "during the war, this long-standing tendency toward economic concentration was accelerated."[29] This theme was carried forward in both the Democratic and Republican platforms in 1948, both of which stressed the importance of antitrust enforcement for small business.[30]

In the years during and immediately following World War II, Americans were especially sensitive to the close tie between antitrust and democratic values. Attorney General Tom Clark told a House subcommittee in 1949 that "the strength of the United States depends on the maintenance of a vigorous economy, free from the domination either of private greed or political dictatorship, but resting firmly on equality of opportunity in a competitive market." According to Clark, the first symptom of weakness was "unhealthy economic concentration which if

---

[29]   The President made similar remarks in his 1948 state of the Union address. See the letter of July 8, 1949, from President Truman to House Judiciary Chairman Emanuel Celler, *reprinted in Study of Monopoly Power: Hearings Before the Subcomm. on the Study of Monopoly Power, House Comm. on the Judiciary*, Serial No. 14, Pt. I, 81st Cong., 1st Sess. 68–69 (1949) [hereinafter Hearings on Monopoly Power]. The House report on Celler-Kefauver indicated that both President Hoover and President Franklin Roosevelt had previously urged a tightening of the Sherman and Clayton Acts. H.R. REP. No. 1191, 81st Cong., 1st Sess. 13 (1949).

[30]   As quoted by House Judiciary Committee Chairman Emanuel Celler, the Democratic Platform read: "We recognize the importance of small business in a sound American economy. It must be protected against unfair discrimination and monopoly and be given equal opportunities with competing enterprises to expand its capital structure. We advocate the strengthening of existing antitrust laws by closing the gaps which experience has shown have been used to promote the concentration of economic power." 1949 House Hearings, *supra* note 28, at 17.

allowed to progress, furnishes a fertile field for Communist doctrine.''[31]

Concern for small business and the trend toward concentration was echoed in testimony of numerous government and private witnesses[32] and was prominently mentioned in both the House and Senate reports on the Celler-Kefauver Act. The House report stressed that acquisitions "have a cumulative effect." The amendment was designed to allow intervention in the "cumulative process" even when the effect of an individual acquisition was insufficient to trigger the Sherman Act.[33] The report also pointed to other changes in the wording intended to make clear that section 7 applied to "all types of acquisitions, vertical and conglomerate as well as horizontal."[34] The Senate report stated that the "enactment of the bill will limit further growth of monopoly and thereby aid in preserving small business as an important competitive factor in the American economy."[35] Picking up a House theme, the Senate report stressed that the intent of the amendment "is to cope with monopolistic tendencies in

---

[31] Hearings on Monopoly Power, *supra* note 29, at 92–93. Along the same line, Professor Adolf Berle, Jr. of the Columbia Law School told the same subcommittee that "bigness, when it goes out of bounds, apparently leads to socialism, or at least it has in practically every other country in the world." *Id.* at 251.

[32] *E.g.*, 1949 House Hearings, *supra* note 28, at 26–27, 31 (testimony of Assistant Attorney General Herbert Bergson and Council of Economic Advisers Member John D. Clark); Hearings on Monopoly Power, *supra* note 29, at 129–43, 228–29 (testimony of Morris L. Ernst and Prof. Adolph Berle).

[33] H.R. REP. No. 1191, 81st Cong., 1st Sess. 8 (1949). This approach was consistent with the testimony of FTC General Counsel William T. Kelley, 1949 House Hearings, *supra* note 28, at 11.

[34] H.R. REP., *supra* note 29, at 11.

[35] S. REP. No. 1775, 81st Cong., 2d Sess. (1950).

their incipiency" before they reach the point of violating the Sherman Act.[36]

The Celler-Kefauver Act passed both Houses by a substantial and bipartisan majority.[37] With this amendment, section 7 became the key provision for controlling anticompetitive mergers and acquisitions. Congress' major goals expressed during the deliberations that led to enactment—halting monopolistic tendencies in their incipiency, maintaining opportunities for small business, and maintaining a balanced industrial structure compatible with democratic values—are consistent with the goals of the Sherman Act's framers 60 years earlier. They cannot be genuinely reconciled with the view that antitrust is to be guided solely by its impact on allocative efficiencies.

The expressions of legislative intent accompanying the 1950 legislation are by no means isolated. The Hart-Scott-Rodino Act of 1976 provided a critical premerger reporting system and was accompanied by strong congressional support for merger enforcement designed to prevent concentration before it develops.[38] Even in instances in which legislation has limited the reach of the antitrust laws (*e.g.*, the Export Trading Company Act enacted in

---

[36]   *Id.* The House report cited with approval language on section 7 from the 1914 Senate report that stressed the need "to arrest the creation of trusts, conspiracies, and monopolies in their incipiency and before consummation." H.R. REP., *supra* note 33, at 4, *citing* S. REP. No. 698, 63d Cong., 2d Sess. 1 (1914).

[37]   H.R. 2734 passed the House on August 15, 1949, by a vote of 223 to 92 and the Senate on December 13, 1950, by a vote of 55 to 22.

[38]   The House report on the Hart-Scott-Rodino Act, citing language in the preamble to the original Clayton bill, described the purpose of section 7 as to "prohibit certain trade practices which . . . singly and in themselves are not covered by the Sherman Act . . . and thus to arrest the creation of trusts, conspiracies and monopolies in their incipiency and before consummation." H.R. REP. No. 1373, 94th Cong., 2d Sess. 7 (1976). The report also restated Congress' concern that "democracy can be preserved only by dispersing and decentralizing economic and financial power." *Id.*

1982[39] and the Shipping Act enacted in 1984[40]), Congress has continued to specify that small businesses and competitors are protected groups.

The Export Trading Company Act contains a provision limiting the jurisdictional reach of the Sherman Act and the Federal Trade Commission Act to conduct that has a "direct, substantial, and reasonably foreseeable" impact on the commerce of the United States. A major concern underlying this legislation was a possible misperception among businessmen, "especially small businessmen, that antitrust law prohibits efficiency-enhancing joint export activities."[41] Although much of this legislation is consistent with the view that the antitrust laws are intended to protect consumers, one clause of this bill demonstrates Congress' continuing concern with fairness to competitors: it retains U.S. antitrust jurisdiction over export opportunities of U.S. firms even if injury to such export opportunities is the *only* impact in the U.S. (i.e., there is *no* discernible impact on U.S. consumers).[42]

The 1984 Shipping Act, another bill that limits application of the U.S. antitrust laws, specifically preserves antitrust jurisdiction over transportation "within or between" foreign countries if there is a "direct, substantial and reasonably foreseeable effect on the commerce of the United States."[43] This provision was originally added by the House Judiciary Committee, which was concerned that U.S. firms not be unfairly excluded by other U.S. firms from competing for a share of such foreign transportation. Once again, Congress provided for this protection for U.S.

---

[39] Pub. L. 97-290, 96 Stat. 1233, 15 U.S.C. §§ 6a, 45(a)(3).

[40] 98 Stat. 67, 46 U.S.C. §§ 1701 et seq.

[41] H.R. Rep. No. 686, 97th Cong., 2d Sess. 4 (1982).

[42] Section 7(1)(B) of the Sherman Act, 15 U.S.C. § 6a. This provision provides that if jurisdiction lies only because conduct has a "direct, substantial, and reasonably foreseeable effect" on a U.S. person's export trade or commerce, then the Sherman Act "shall apply to such conduct only for injury to export business in the United States." *Id.*

[43] 46 U.S.C. § 1706(a)(3).

competitors despite the lack of any apparent threat to U.S. consumers in such situations.[44]

These and other examples[45] of more recent expressions of legislative intent by no means suggest that Congress is unconcerned with the potential negative impact that overzealous antitrust enforcement might have on allocative efficiencies. But they strongly affirm Congress' continuing resolve that antitrust enforcement address antitrust goals beyond such efficiencies. Attempts to read such goals out of the antitrust laws must confront not only 100-year-old legislative history from the original Sherman Act debates but Congress' repeatedly demonstrated Jeffersonian resolve to protect small business and values of dispersed economic power and fairness to competitors.

Legislative intent and current policy

For an antitrust expert, keeping informed of new developments is a time-consuming endeavor. On an almost daily basis, there are new judicial interpretations, antitrust guidelines issued by federal and state authorities, and evolving economic and legal analyses. In the midst of this flurry of nonlegislative activity, one could easily conclude that the legislative intent behind the Sherman or Clayton Acts is antiquated[46] if not wholly irrelevant.[47] To be sure, there is ample room within the conceptual framework of these provisions for debate, discussion, and analysis that, in the long term, will benefit our understanding of antitrust and help to

---

[44] The House report cited with approval Pacific Seafarers, Inc. v. Pacific Far East Line, Inc., 404 F.2d 807 (D.C. Cir. 1968), *cert. denied*, 393 U.S. 1093 (1969). H.R. REP. No. 53, Pt. 2, 98th Cong., 1st Sess. 32–33 (1983). In *Pacific Seafarers*, the court held that the Sherman Act did apply to protect a U.S. firm's right to compete against other U.S. firms for U.S. government-financed cargoes transported between Taiwan and South Vietnam.

[45] See the discussion of resale price maintenance accompanying notes 48–59, *infra*.

[46] Baxter, *supra* note 3.

[47] Posner, *supra* note 2.

reshape enforcement policy. But unless we are to destroy our constitutional framework in which legislative responsibilities are assigned to the Congress, legislative intent must be abided.

There is another aspect to the role of Congress. As the branch most responsive to the people, the Congress brings to the antitrust laws a perspective that, over time, reflects the views of the electorate. While there is no constitutional obligation on the executive to follow every antitrust whim of every legislator, collectively Congress can be a fairly accurate barometer of American public opinion. If the President, or his delegated agents in the executive branch, ignores strongly held views of the electorate, public frustration can lead to other responses inconsistent with the free-enterprise underpinnings of our economy.

In some instances, as for example in the area of resale price maintenance, Congress has spoken recently and with directness, leaving little doubt as to the preferred interpretation and enforcement policy. The conflict in this area was foreshadowed in 1981 when former Assistant Attorney General William Baxter told the Monopolies Subcommittee that "there is no such thing as a harmful vertical restraint."[48] In 1982, the Justice Department intervened as an amicus in *Monsanto Co. v. Spray-Rite Service Corp.*[49] to argue that the per se rule against resale price maintenance should be overturned. In January of 1985, the Department issued vertical restraint guidelines that sought to enlarge the area of vertical restraints treated under the rule of reason at the expense of the per se rule governing resale price maintenance.[50]

---

[48] *Oversight Hearings on the Antitrust Division of the Department of Justice: Subcomm. on Monopolies and Commercial Law, House Comm. on the Judiciary*, 97th Cong., 1st and 2d Sess. 7 (1983).

Mr. Baxter told the subcommittee subsequently that "if there is no concentration either at the upstream level or at the downstream level, the agreement cannot possibly have anticompetitive consequences." *Oversight Hearings on the Antitrust Division, Subcomm. on Monopolies and Commercial Law, House Comm. on the Judiciary*, 98th Cong., 1st Sess. 131 (1986).

[49] 465 U.S. 752 (1984).

[50] Department of Justice, Vertical Restraints Guidelines, January 23, 1985.

The Justice Department's approach to vertical restraints is consistent with an overall libertarian philosophy and, arguably, with the view that enforcement should occur only when there is proven harm to allocative efficiencies.[51] The Department's position, however, fails to account for the need to maintain competition at all levels of the distribution system, including the retail level.[52] In their key role as the final leg in the distribution system, retailers determine whether the consumer receives the benefits of efficiencies generated at more distant production and distribution levels. As Professor Comanor points out, multiline retailers achieve economies of scope that could not be achieved by a manufacturer-owned retailer selling a single line of goods. Moreover, according to an FTC study cited by Comanor, consumers rely on large or well-estalished outlets as a certification of quality, giving such outlets substantial leverage over manufacturers.[53]

Over the years, Congress has remained an active participant in framing policy toward vertical restraints. In 1937, Congress enacted legislation that permitted states to establish fair trade laws authorizing resale price maintenance; this authority was extended in 1952.[54] But in 1976, the Consumer Goods Pricing Act[55] removed even this exception from the general rule and reaffirmed the Supreme Court's longstanding precedent that

---

[51]   Resale price maintenance would not further allocative efficiencies if, as Professor Comanor believes, it results in consumers being forced to pay for information and services that they do not need or desire. Comanor, *Vertical Market Restrictions, and the New Antitrust Policy*, 98 HARV. L. REV. 983, 990–1000 (1985).

[52]   H.R. REP. No. 421, 100th Cong., 1st Sess. 11–13 (1987).

[53]   *Oversight Hearings on the Antitrust Division of the Department of Justice: Subcomm. on Monopolies and Commercial Law, House Comm. on the Judiciary*, 100th Cong., 2d Sess. (Feb. 24, 1988) (testimony of Prof. William Comanor).

[54]   50 Stat. 693, *amending* 15 U.S.C. § 1; 66 Stat. 632, *amending* 15 U.S.C. § 45.

[55]   89 Stat. 801, *amending* 15 U.S.C. §§ 1, 45(a) (1976).

resale price maintenance is per se illegal.[56] Following the Department's 1982 amicus intervention in *Monsanto*, Congress began placing riders on Justice Department appropriation bills to bar the use of appropriated funds for the purpose of seeking a judicial reversal or narrowing of the per se rule against resale price maintenance.[57] And Congress responded to the Vertical Restraints Guidelines by enacting a resolution in December of 1985 that called upon the Attorney General to withdraw the Guidelines.[58] These strong and virtually unprecedented congressional statements regarding antitrust policy have been ignored by the Department, which, in the last 8 years, has yet to bring a single vertical price-fixing case.[59]

Merger enforcement is another area in which enforcement policy has failed to adhere to legislative intent. The current relaxed policy toward mergers and acquisitions has helped to stimulate a record-breaking surge in merges and acquisitions.[60] In

---

[56] Dr. Miles Medical Co. v. John D. Park & Sons, Co., 220 U.S. 373 (1911). The Supreme Court has repeatedly affirmed this holding, most recently in 324 Liquor Corp. v. Thomas Duffy, 107 S. Ct. 720 (1987).

[57] The history of the appropriations and authorization riders is detailed in H.R. REP. No. 421, *supra* note 52, at 5-6.

[58] The resolution noted that the Guidelines do not have the force of law, do not accurately state current case law, and "shall not be considered by the courts of the United States as binding or persuasive." P.L. 99-180 (605, 99 Stat. 1169).

[59] The debate over antitrust policy toward resale price maintenance was most recently fought over H.R. 585, the Freedom from Vertical Price Fixing Act, as passed by the House of Representatives in November 1987. The bill would have clarified the evidentiary burden confronting a retailer who seeks to prove resale price maintenance and would codify the per se rule against resale price maintenance. The Senate version of this bill, S. 430, was reported by the Senate Judiciary Committee during the 100th Congress.

[60] Statistics compiled by the House Judiciary Committee show that both the frequency and the size of reported acquisitions have increased dramatically over the past 8 years:

(footnote 60 continued)

the face of this surge, merger enforcement has actually decreased as a percentage of cases reported under the Premerger Notification Program.[61] It is widely acknowledged that current enforce-

(60 cont) *Year*	*Number of acquisitions announcements*	*Total reported value (in billions)*	*Number of takeovers >$1 billion*	*Reported value of takeovers >$1 billion (in billions)*
1976	1145	$ 20.0	1	$ 2.17
1977	1209	$ 21.9	1	$ 1.57
1978	1452	$ 34.2	0	0
1979	1526	$ 34.18	3	$ 6.22
1980	1565	$ 33.06	3	$ 6.50
1981	2326	$ 66.96	8	$20.55
1982	2295	$ 60.39	9	$23.97
1983	2345	$ 52.25	7	$10.39
1984	3064	$125.23	19	$55.19
1985	3165	$139.13	26	$60.82
1986	4022	$190.0	34	$68.76
1987	3701	$167.5	30	$62.20

SOURCE: Information published in MERGERS & ACQUISITIONS (1976–87).

61   Additional Requests and Enforcement Actions as a Percentage of Reported Transactions

Year	*Premerger notifications received*	*Number of additional requests*			*Rate of additional requests*	*Number of enforcement actions*			*Rate of enforcement actions*
		DOJ	*FTC*	*Tot.*		*DOJ*	*FTC*	*Tot.*	
1979	868	51	58	109	12.6%	10	10	20	2.3%
1980	824	38	36	74	9.0%	10	13	23	2.8%
1981	1083	33	46	79	7.3%	4	14	18	1.7%
1982	1144	24	26	50	4.4%	9	7	16	1.4%
1983	1128	20	28	48	4.3%	3	3	6	.5%
1984	1400	37	40	77	5.5%	7	6	13	.9%
1985	1749	53	31	84	4.8%	4	5	9	.5%
1986	2406	40	42	82	3.4%	7	4	11	.5%
1987	2254	36	26	62	2.8%	6	8	14	.6%

SOURCE: Information supplied in Annual Premerger Notification Reports and by the FTC and Department of Justice. Additional request and enforcement rates computed as a percentage of premerger notifications.

ment standards allow many acquisitions with market shares that would have been challenged a decade ago.

The principle that acquisitions resulting in high market shares are presumptively anticompetitive has its roots in section 7 of the Clayton Act and in the Celler-Kefauver Amendment to that provision. *United States v. Philadelphia National Bank*, 374 U.S. 321, 363 (1963). This "structural" presumption was incorporated in the Justice Department's 1968 Guidelines[62] and, although in somewhat diluted form, has been carried forward in the 1984 version.[63] Most economists continue to believe that the presumption is well grounded in economic theory.[64] But many acquisitions involving the highest category of concentration under the 1984 Guidelines are being approved, apparently because no significant barriers to entry are perceived,[65] because anticipated efficiencies from the combination are expected to outweigh any anticompetitive effects,[66] or because the market share numbers for some other reason are believed to overstate the anticompetitive potential of the acquisition.[67]

---

[62] Department of Justice, Merger Guidelines (1968), 2 Trade Reg. Rep. (CCH) ¶ 4510.

[63] Department of Justice Merger Guidelines, 49 Fed. Reg. 26,823 (1984).

[64] Schmalensee, *Ease of Entry: Has the Concept Been Applied Too Readily?* 56 ANTITRUST L.J. 41, 42–43 (1987).

[65] Department of Justice Merger Guidelines, *supra* note 63, at § 3.3. United States v. Waste Management, Inc., 743 F.2d 976 (2d Cir. 1984); United States v. Calmar Inc., 612 F. Supp. 1298 (D.N.J. 1985); Echlin Mfg. Co., 3 Trade Reg. Rep (CCH) ¶ 22,268 (June 25, 1985).

[66] Department of Justice, 1984 Merger Guidelines, *supra* note 63, at § 3.5.

[67] *Id.* at §§ 3.2–3.45. United States v. General Dynamics, 415 U.S. 486 (1974). The Guidelines have been criticized because their methodology may result in broadly defined markets that will overlook many potential anticompetitive problems. Harris & Jorde, *Market Definition in the Merger Guidelines: Implications for Antitrust Enforcement*, 71 CALIF. L. REV. 464, 476–86 (1983).

Enforcement officials have been quick to condemn those Supreme Court decisions of the 1960's that they contend place too much weight on values other than allocative efficiency.[68] Although some of this criticism may be warranted, decisions such as *Von's Grocery* and *Brown Shoe*[69] contained fundamentally accurate descriptions of the legislative intent underlying the Celler-Kefauver Act. Disagreement with the result in a case such as *Von's* should not be a basis for discarding the incipiency doctrine enunciated by the Court based upon its careful reading of the animating concerns underlying the Act.[70]

Concerns with incipiency are very much alive today. Acquisitions among competing firms tend to occur in waves. One can surmise that the top management of a firm whose major competitor has just enlarged its market share through acquisition feels substantial pressure to make a similar acquisition.[71] It is no surprise that within a few days after Pepsi Cola announced its decision to acquire Seven-Up, Coca Cola announced a planned acquisition of Dr. Pepper.[72]

---

[68]   Andrew J. Stenio, Jr., FTC Commissioner, Looking at Antitrust Merger Enforcement With 30/30 Vision, Remarks Delivered at the 39th Conference on Economics, Business Management, and Government 3–5 (Washington, D.C., December 4, 1986).

[69]   Brown Shoe Co. v. United States, 370 U.S. 294, 317 (1962), involved a combination of the nation's third and eighth largest sellers of shoes. United States v. Von's Grocery Co., 384 U.S. 270 (1966), involved two Los Angeles retail grocers with a combined market share of 7.5%.

[70]   384 U.S. at 274–77.

[71]   As economist Alan Ferguson expressed it, "mergers do beget mergers." *Mergers and Competition in the Airline Industry: Hearings Before the Subcomm. on Monopolies and Commercial Law, House Comm. on the Judiciary*, 99th Cong., 2d Sess. 109 (1987) [hereinafter Airline Industry Hearings].

[72]   Those acquisitions in a very concentrated soft drink industry were blocked by the Federal Trade Commission over the opposition of Chairman Oliver. Wall Street J., June 23, 1986, at 2, col. 2.

A more dramatic example of this phenomenon has occurred recently in the airline industry. In 1985, the Department of Transportation approved United Airline's acquisition of the Pacific Division of Pan American World Airways despite the opposition of the Department of Justice and competing airlines. As Professor Kahn has pointed out, whether or not the United acquisition in itself threatened serious anticompetitive consequences, its approval left the Department of Transportation in a difficult position to stop the chain of acquisitions that followed.[73] United's major U.S. competitor in the Pacific market, Northwest Airlines, immediately sought to acquire Republic Airlines despite the extremely high market shares of the two airlines on routes to and from Minneapolis and Detroit. Northwest argued that it needed Republic's feeder routes to successfully compete against United in the Pacific.[74] Once again, the Department of Transportation allowed the merger to proceed. A rash of further acquisitions followed. The national market share of the five largest airlines rose from 58% in 1985 to 74% in 1987.[75] The levels of concentration for individual city-pair markets, the markets most relevant to the traveling consumer, are sure to be far higher. A large percentage of U.S. airports are now dominated by one or two airlines.[76]

---

[73] *Authorization for the Antitrust Division of the Department of Justice: Oversight Hearings of the Subcomm. on Monopolies and Commercial Law, House Comm. on the Judiciary*, 99th Cong., 2d Sess. 15–17 (1988) (testimony of Alfred Kahn).

The same view was expressed by another expert witness. Airline Industry Hearings, *supra* note 71, at 109 (testimony of Alan Ferguson).

[74] Testimony of Alfred Kahn, *supra* note 73, at 16–18.

[75] Market shares computed based on scheduled revenue passenger miles of domestic routes. Information compiled by the General Accounting Office for the House Judiciary Committee.

[76] According to the Wall Street Journal, in 15 of the nation's top airports, over 50% of the business is now carried by a single carrier or over 70% by the two largest carriers. Wall Street Journal, July 20, 1987, at 1, col. 6. Since the Journal statistics were published, the U.S. Air acquisition of Piedmont Airlines further increased concentration in several east coast airports.

Had the Departments of Transportation and Justice acted to stop this merger wave early on, the domino-like series of mergers would probably not have occurred. Instead, having allowed the first few mergers to proceed, officials were confronted with a fairness argument ("my competitor was allowed to merge, so why can't I?"). If a decisionmaker fails to adhere to the legislative intent to stop a trend toward concentration in its incipiency, it becomes difficult to stop that trend at a later point when questions of fairness are raised in defense.[77]

The airline mergers of the past few years also illustrate the substantial risk of ignoring the presumption that high market shares will be anticompetitive. Airlines were touted as a classic example of an industry with low entry barriers.[78] But if this assumption was once valid, it is illusory today. Among the widely recognized barriers confronting a new entrant today are (1) obtaining landing slots and terminal facilities in busy airports; (2) obtaining equitable access to a computer reservation system (frequently controlled by a competitor); (3) obtaining new-generation aircraft that meet noise pollution requirements (there is frequently a long wait for obtaining delivery of such aircraft); (4) entering with a major presence in one or two "hub" cities sufficient to sustain a competitive system; and (5) overcoming customer loyalties built up through frequent-flier programs.[79]

While there is widespread expert support for the notion that low entry barriers are a basis for overcoming the presumption against high–market-share mergers, any assessment of the impact of barriers is necessarily subjective.[80] Economic theorists who

---

[77] Testimony of Alfred Kahn, *supra* note 73, at 16–17.

[78] Airline Industry Hearings, *supra* note 71, at 4, 100, 103 (testimony of Alan Ferguson and Gregory S. Dole, Associate General Counsel, Department of Transportation).

[79] Airline Industry Hearings, *supra* note 71, at 18–25, 114–20, 134–37.

[80] Professor Schmalensee would agree that, in theory, low entry barriers negate the effect of high concentration. But he points out that

conclude that entry into a particular market will be easy do not necessarily have the same information (or react the same way to it) as a real-world businessman. The example of the airline industry demonstrates the danger in discounting or discarding the presumption. Studies of the airline industry appear to show that routes on which actual competition exists are likely to have lower fares than those on which competition is "potential"—based on the possibility of entry by another carrier.[81]

Legislative intent as a dynamic process

Those who have passed by the headquarters of the Federal Trade Commission on Washington, D.C.'s Pennsylvania Avenue will recall the massive concrete sculpture of a muscular man restraining a rebellious workhorse. The vision of this 1940's sculptor was of government and industry as two distinct figures straining to reach an equilibrium. The artist obviously did not see government as a single, overpowering figure symbolizing state ownership or control of the means of production, nor did he envision a wholly equine scene in which the horses of private enterprise ran unrestrained. The role of government was as a moderating (but not dominating) force.

The bipartisan coalition that has supported antitrust enforcement, beginning with men such as Republican Senator John Sherman, has cast antitrust as a moderate and politically acceptable path for maintaining a free-market system. It is this broad political purpose of antitrust, as valid today as it was in 1890, that has too frequently been ignored in recent debates about antitrust policy. To those concerned with the rise and fall of nations and civilizations, the dynamism, innovation, and political balance that comes from diffused economic as well as political power may legitimately be held above the attainment of short-run

---

there are "real barriers to entry in most real markets." He further stresses that, with respect to entry barriers, "there is theoretical dispute, there are measurement debates, and there are no ready benchmarks." Schmalensee, *supra* note 64, at 42–43.

[81] Testimony of Alfred Kahn, *supra* note 73, at 18.

efficiencies. The most efficient economic institution is of little value if it contains the seeds of its own destruction.

Proponents of measuring antitrust solely by allocative efficiencies argue that any other measure will be unwieldy and sacrifice certainty in the law.[82] But aside from the certainty that comes from the libertarian presumption against any enforcement, allocative efficiencies, as I have pointed out, do not provide a certain measure for judges.[83] Congress and antitrust policymakers have before them a continuing challenge to spell out the goals of antitrust provisions in any situation in which uncertainty can bring socially undesirable results. In recent years, Congress has demonstrated its willingness to reexamine antitrust questions and to legislate with greater specificity when the situation warrants.[84] There is no reason to believe that Congress is unwilling to continue to work with the enforcement agencies, through further amendments or administrative guidelines, to spell out various areas of the law where uncertainty has deterred socially beneficial conduct.

A narrow antitrust focus, which looks solely at allocative efficiency, offers little hope of addressing the broad range of competitive concerns that Congress and the nation must confront in guiding our industrial organization into the next century. For the most part, these will not be new concerns, but familiar ones adjusted to changing international circumstances.

I believe that antitrust has a critical role to play in the coming battle for international competitive survival, but only if vigorous competition is maintained on the domestic front. To adopt the

---

[82] Assistant Attorney General Rule recently argued: "In the past, uncertainty over where the line would be drawn between efficient and unlawful practices, combined with automatic treble damages liability, has chilled the development of more efficient business practices." Rule, *supra* note 1, at 12.

[83] Notes 20–24 and accompanying text, *supra*.

[84] National Cooperative Research Act of 1984, P.L. 98-462, 98 Stat. 1815; Local Government Antitrust Act of 1984, P.L. 98-544, 98 Stat. 2750.

view that fairness to competitors and equity to consumers has no place in our economic system will only sap the American economy of its vitality and diversity and replace it with either a government-directed policy or a set of monolithic core industries. In either case, innovation will be stifled and public confidence in our distinctive American system of free enterprise—already shaken by nonstop takeover wars and insider trading scandals—will continue to erode. If efficiency theorists see no danger in this scenario, then, in my view, they have followed a false "scent" leading them above the "timberline," far removed from the consensus view of the American people and its closest governmental representative, the Congress.

Conclusion

In the century since passage of the Sherman Act, it was never Congress' mission to simply "protect" the antitrust laws as if they were some kind of immutable set of principles important in and of themselves. Quite the contrary, the competition statutes stand not as a testament to congressional action but, rather, as a tribute to the strongly held, consensus views of their real progenitors, the American people. Preserving the congressional intent behind the antitrust laws is to protect the goals that they are designed to accomplish. Should the popular support behind the antitrust laws waver, reverse its course, or cease to exist, Congress will surely take note and undoubtedly take action. But as yet, such popular support for an open and free-moving economy has not weakened, nor has popular opinion embraced an oversimplified view of the diverse forces that shape our competitive free-market system.

The enforcement agencies would do well to remember these simple facts. For, while the enforcement arm of the government will remain the primary "micromanager" of antitrust policy, that role in no way vests these agencies with original policymaking power that can move at odds with congressional choices reflective of the popular will.

The current economic debate surrounding the antitrust laws is, as always, illuminating but hardly new and original. For a hundred years, the "allocative efficiency" proponents have promoted a singular emphasis on one variable of analysis at the expense of the multiple goals that animated Senators Sherman and Hoar and others to strike out against illegal restraints of trade that threatened to harm the diversity and vitality of the economic system. That system was the locomotive that led America, first, to meeting the challenges of the industrial age, and now, to the demands of the "post-industrial" society of high technology and a burgeoning service-oriented economy.

And yet, even in the midst of a changing world marketplace, a belief that our economic system should continue to reflect democratic values and commitment to free markets appears to persist. Until such time as abstract economic models can provide the type of empirically based data to support a wholesale change in congressional policy, until such time as the American people take comfort in a theoretical system that is not alarmed by undue concentration in core industries or in the elimination of small and mid-sized firms that traditionally have provided innovative spur to competitive pricing and the widest selection of goods and services, the congressional view of antitrust as the ultimate guarantor of economic liberty and progress will likely continue.

32
The worldwide influence
of U.S. antitrust

BY JOEL DAVIDOW*

By now, the story has been oft told how U.S. antitrust law was exported to most of the Free World in the quarter century after 1944.[1] Decartelization of Japan and Germany was a war aim of the United States during World War II and was in fact carried out by American experts during the period of occupation.[2] Both Germany and Japan were influenced to adopt national antitrust laws which generally followed the U.S. pattern, though with variations.[3] France, the Philippines, and other countries aided by the

---

* Partner, Ablondi, Foster & Sobin; Adjunct Professor George Mason University.

[1] *See* Kintner, Joelson & Vaghi, *Groping for a Truly International Antitrust Law*, 14 VA. J. INT'L. L. 75 (1974).

[2] *See* E. HADLEY, ANTITRUST IN JAPAN 125–26 (1970).

[3] *See* Bock, Korsch & Wolner *Germany,* in ANTITRUST LAWS (W. Friedmann ed. 1956); Osakdani, *Japan,* in ANTITRUST LAWS, *id.* at 238; *see also A Comparative Analysis* in ANTITRUST IN LAWS, *id.* at 525.

United States during that period were also induced to adopt similar laws.[4]

American experts encouraged and aided the development of antitrust rules in the European Coal and Steel Community (ECSC) treaty and later, more indirectly, the Common Market treaty.[5] The United States created the OECD Committee of Experts on Restrictive Business Practices in 1961.[6] In that year, only 8 of the 24 Free World member nations had strong enough laws in place or interest in the subject to participate in the work of the Committee.[7] By the mid-1970's, almost all of the OECD member countries had enacted full-scale antitrust legislation and participated in the general work of the Committee.[8]

The United States was the original sponsor of a United Nations antitrust code which would have been included as a chapter of the 1948 "Havana Charter" for an International Trade Organization but which died when the broader project was aban-

---

4 *See* Castel, *France,* in ANTITRUST LAWS, *supra* note 3.

5 Richard Hamberger discusses the origins of the ECSC rules in *International Conference on Restraints of Competition,* CARTEL AND MONOPOLY IN MODERN LAW 243–61 (1960). Treaty Establishing the European Economic Community, Mar. 25, 1957, 298 U.N.T.S. 11 [hereinafter EC Treaty] (entered into force Jan. 1, 1958). The Common Market rules are examined in Rahl, *European Common Market Antitrust Laws,* 40 ANTITRUST L.J. 810 (1971).

6 *Restrictive Business Practices,* OECD OBSERVER, Oct. 1963, at 16; ORGANIZATION FOR EUROPEAN ECONOMIC COOPERATION, THE ORGANIZATION FOR ECONOMIC COOPERATION AND DEVELOPMENT 35 (1960). The name of the Committee was recently changed to Committee on Competition Law and Policy. *See* OECD, LIST OF BODIES OF THE ORGANIZATION MANDATES MEMBERSHIP OFFICERS 165 (1988).

7 *See* Zisler, *Work of the OECD Committee of Experts on Restrictive Business Practices,* 19 ANTITRUST BULL. 289, 291 (1974).

8 The OECD GUIDE TO LEGISLATION ON RESTRICTIVE BUSINESS PRACTICES (4th ed. 1978) lists 20 Western nations with antitrust laws. *See also* Zisler, *supra* note 7, at 291.

doned.[9] U.S. antitrust officials contributed heavily to a draft 1952–1953 United Nations antitrust code which was rejected in 1954, largely because of business opposition in the United States.[10] Ultimately, in 1980 the United Nations, responding to a developing country initiative, did adopt a Set of Principles and Rules for the Control of Restrictive Business Practices which in its content largely reflected American approaches but did include certain European concepts (such as "abuse of a dominant position") and a small amount of developing country rhetoric and priorities.[11]

All of these broad developments relate to the adoption of an antitrust law, creation of a basic system of enforcement, and willingness (even if limited) to engage in some degree of international cooperation and exchange of information. This trend itself was not without its ups and downs. Some foreign antitrust laws have arguably been weakened rather than strengthened over the years.[12] Many countries that were prepared to adopt and enforce their own antitrust laws were not willing to allow U.S. antitrust laws to be applied to business transactions origi-

---

[9] *See* U.S. DEPARTMENT OF STATE, Pub. No. 3117, Commercial Policy Series 113, HAVANA CHARTER FOR AN INTERNATIONAL TRADE ORGANIZATION OF THE UNITED NATIONS (1947); U.S. DEPARTMENT OF STATE, Pub. No. 3206, Commercial Policy Series 114, HAVANA CHARTER FOR AN INTERNATIONAL TRADE ORGANIZATION OF THE UNITED NATIONS (1948); *see also* Davidow, *The Seeking of a World Competition Code: Quixotic Quest?* in COMPETITION IN INTERNATIONAL BUSINESS 362 (O. Schachter & R. Hellawell eds. 1981); Davidow, *International Antitrust Codes and Multinational Enterprises*, 2 LOY. L.A. INT'L. & COMP. L. ANN. 17, 18 (1979).

[10] *See Report of the Ad Hoc Committee on Restrictive Business Practices,* 16 U.N. ESCOR Supp. 11, U.N. Doc. E/2380/A.C. 37/3(1953); Timberg, Restrictive Business Practices as an Appropriate Subject for United Nations Action, 1 ANTITRUST BULL. 409 (1955).

[11] U.N. Doc. TD/RBP Conf. 10/Rev.L. (1980). *See* Oesterle, *United Nations Conference on Restrictive Business Practices*, 14 CORNELL INT'L. L.J. 1 (1981).

[12] Canada, for instance, has decriminalized much of its antitrust approach, for practical and political reasons. *See* Green, *Mergers in Canada and Canada's New Merger Law* 32 ANTITRUST BULL. 253, 254 (1987). Italy had resisted having any antitrust law, though it did pass antitrust legislation on September 27, 1990. *Discussed in Italy Enacts First Statute to Establish Antitrust Regime*, ANTITRUST & TRADE REG. REP. (BNA No. 1485), at 518 (Oct. 4, 1990).

nating in their countries or even to cooperate in U.S. investigations of such practices.[13] Over the past three decades England, France, Canada, Australia, the Netherlands, and other nations adopted various forms of "blocking legislation" or "clawback statutes" to prevent cooperation with U.S. antitrust prosecutors or plaintiffs and to block or negate the enforcement of treble damage awards.[14]

The process of U.S. influence has been much more complex than a simple pattern of American law being strengthened, followed by emulation abroad. The United States itself has had second and even third thoughts about the wisdom of some of its own stricter antitrust initiatives. There have therefore been occasions on which foreigners have begun to adopt U.S. approaches from a previous decade while American government officials or academics were actively seeking to discourage such emulation on the ground that doctrine being copied was now viewed by many in the United States as having been substantially mistaken.

For instance, France, Ireland, and other countries became fascinated with the problem of buying power in the 1960's and with the preservation of small grocery stores, bakeries, and other food shops threatened by supermarkets or other mass market competitors.[15] The European solution was adoption or consideration of legislation, rather like the Robinson-Patman Act, forbidding price favoritism to large buyers, as well as certain other promotional

---

13   *See* Petit & Styles, *International Response to the Extraterritorial Enforcement of U.S. Antitrust Laws,* 37 Bus. Law. 697 (1982); *see also* 1 B. Hawk, UNITED STATES COMMON MARKET AND INTERNATIONAL ANTITRUST: A COMPARATIVE GUIDE 13–15 (2d ed. 1986).

14   *See* B. HAWK, *supra* note 13, at 13–15; Griffin, *U.S. Antitrust Laws and Transnational Business Transactions: An Introduction,* 21 INT'L. LAW. 307, 308–09 (1987); Gordon, *Extraterritorial Application of U.S. Economic Laws: Britain Draws the Line,* 14 INT'L. LAW 151 (1980).

15   OECD, BUYING POWER: THE EXERCISE OF MARKET POWER BY DOMINANT BUYERS 10–17 (1981) [hereinafter BUYING POWER]. Some countries began studying the issue of buying power much earlier. For example, Canada published a study on buying power as early as 1955. *Id.* at 11. Australia, France, and Ireland began studying the problem in the early 1960's. *Id.* at 13–16. Germany, Great Britain, and Switzerland studied buying power in the mid-1970's. *Id.* at 14–16.

practices.[16] By that time, most U.S. antitrust scholars had become highly critical of legislative bans on price discrimination, and the Antitrust Division had published a monograph calling for repeal of the Robinson-Patman Act.[17]

Similarly, in the 1960's and 1970's the U.S. Antitrust Division developed a list of patent licensing restrictions which it said should be treated as presumptively unlawful.[18] These were sometimes called the "nine no-nos."[19] In 1978 the European Commission pub-

---

[16] Canada amended the Combines Investigation Act in 1960 to prohibit suppliers from offering discounts on promotional items to large purchasers. BUYING POWER, *supra* note 15, at 11. Australia enacted the 1965 Trade Practices Act, which discouraged dominant buyers from seeking favorable prices. *Id.* at 13. Ireland had existing legislation which it began to actively enforce in the 1970's. *Id.* at 16, 51. Ireland strengthened its existing law with the Restrictive Practices Act of 1972, which allows the Restrictive Practices Commission to investigate discriminatory practices between buyers and sellers. *Id.* at 51. In France, the Act of 27th December, 1973, prohibits unjustified discriminatory prices and terms of sale. *Id.* at 69. Although Germany studied the problem of buying power, it did not enact specific legislation to deal with price discrimination because the German government determined that a ban on discrimination must be conditional on market strength. *Id.* at 14–15.

[17] *See* Paul, *The Robinson-Patman Act Revisited in Its 50th Year: Introductory Remarks*, 55 ANTITRUST L.J. 133 (1986); Hansen, *Robinson-Patman Law: A Review & Analysis*, 51 FORDHAM L. REV. 1113 (1983); Liebeler, *Let's Repeal It*, 45 Antitrust L.J. 18 (1976).

[18] *See* Lipsky, *Current Antitrust Division Views on Patent Licensing Practices*, 50 ANTITRUST L.J. 515 (1981).

[19] *See* Wilson, Law on Licensing Practices: Myth or Reality? (speech before the American Patent Law Association, Washington, D.C., Jan. 21, 1975) (according to the nine "no-nos," a licensor may not (1) condition the license on purchase of unpatented materials; (2) require assignment to the licensor or related patents later issued to the licensee; (3) restrict purchasers in the resale of licensed products; (4) restrict a licensee's freedom to deal in products or services not within the scope of the patent; (5) agree with a licensee to deny further licenses without the licensee's consent; (6) condition the license on taking an entire license "package"; (7) condition the license on royalties not reasonably related to the licensee's sales of the licensed products; (8) restrict a licensee's sale of products made by use of the patented process; and (9) require adherence to any minimum price respecting sale of the licensed products).

lished a draft regulation on patent licensing, setting forth a "black-list" of licensing practices to be avoided which was quite similar to the nine no-nos.[20] But by 1981 a more conservative U.S. adminis-tration was openly critical of the nine no-nos list, concluding that almost none of the practices was deserving of presumptive illegal-ity.[21] By 1985 the European Commission swung toward the newer, more permissive American position, altering its draft regulation on patent licensing so as to permit many of the practices on its original blacklist.[22] The European Commission also adopted a permissive reg-ulation on know-how licensing restrictions.[23]

A complex pattern of emulation, deviation, and even conflict about antitrust policy thus evolved. The element of conflict was fueled by major political disputes over jurisdiction and extraterrito-rial enforcement of U.S. law.[24] Moreover, many crucial aspects of U.S. antitrust and its enforcement, such as private treble damage actions, broad pretrial discovery, and class actions, were never embraced by most other free market nations.[25] Merger control was resisted for years but was finally adopted by Canada[26] and

20   See V. KORAH, AN INTRODUCTORY GUIDE TO EEC COMPETITION LAW AND PRACTICE, 72–73 (1978).

21   See Lipsky, *supra* note 18, at 516–17; B. HAWK, *supra* note 13, at 376–77.

22   See COMMISSION OF THE EUROPEAN COMMUNITIES, FIFTEENTH REPORT ON COMPETITION POLICY 38 (1986); OECD COMPETITION POLICY IN OECD COUN-TRIES: 1984–1985, at 241–43 (1987).

23   Commission Regulation 418/85, 28 O.J. Eur. Comm. (No. L 53) 5 (1985) [hereinafter EC Block Exemption Law].

24   See B. HAWK, *supra* note 13, at 13–15; Griffin, *supra* note 14, at 308–10.

25   See OECD, COMPETITION LAW ENFORCEMENT (1984); Jacobs, *Civil En-forcement of EEC Antitrust Law*, 82 MICH. L. REV. 1364, 1371 (1984). Re-cently, France has authorized a limited form of consumer class action.

26   Can. Stat. ch. 26 (1986), which is divided into two parts. Part I is the Competition Tribunal Act. Part II, the Competition Act, amends Can. Rev. Stat. ch. C–23 (1970), *amended by* Can. Rev. Stat. ch. 10 (Supp. 1, 1970), Can. Rev. ch. 10 (Supp. 2, 1970), *further amended by* ch. 76, 1974–76 Can. Stat. and ch. 28, 1976–77 Can. Stat. [hereinafter Canadian Merger Control Law].

the EC[27] in the late 1980's. It is useful, therefore, to review the premises of antitrust at this point in the discussion, in order to highlight the differences between acceptance of basic elements of the policy and adoption of ancillary laws and remedies.

Generally, the two most basic tenets of antitrust are that horizontal cartel arrangements are unacceptable[28] and that intentional monopolization achieved by means of leverage or exclusionary tactics should also be prohibited.[29] These two principles are largely followed abroad. However, the United States supplemented its antitrust laws in 1914[30] and 1950[31] by creating and strengthening a system of merger control, and again in 1936[32] by adopting legislation to prohibit many forms of price discrimination.[33] The U.S. statutory arsenal also includes a prohibition of interlocking directorates,[34] state antitrust laws,[35] and franchisee or dealer protec-

---

[27]   Council Regulation 4064/89, 32 O.J. Eur. Comm. (No. L 395) 1 (1989) (entered into force in September 1990) [hereinafter EC Merger Control Regulation].

[28]   *See* H. HOVENKAMP, ECONOMICS AND FEDERAL ANTITRUST LAW § 4.1 (1985); L. SULLIVAN, HANDBOOK OF THE LAW OF ANTITRUST § 59 (1977); Clark, *Antitrust Comes Full Circle—The Return to the Cartelization Standard,* 38 VAND. L. REV. 1125 (1985).

[29]   H. HOVENKAMP, *supra* note 28, at § 5.5; L. Sullivan, *supra* note 28, at § 7; Clark, *supra* note 28, at 1126, 1136.

[30]   Clayton Act of October 15, 1914, ch. 323, § 7, 38 Stat. 730 (current version at 15 U.S.C. § 18 (1982)).

[31]   Celler-Kefauver Act of December 29, 1950, ch. 1184, 64 Stat. 1125 (current version at 15 U.S.C. § 18 (1982)).

[32]   Robinson-Patman Act of June 19, 1936, ch. 592 1, 49 Stat. 1526 (current version at 15 U.S.C. § 13(a) (1982)).

[33]   15 U.S.C. § 13(a).

[34]   Section 8 of the Clayton Act, 15 U.S.C. § 19. *See* SCM Corp. v. FTC, 565 F.2d 807 (2d Cir. 1977).

[35]   *See* R. FOLSOM, STATE ANTITRUST LAW & PRACTICE (1990); *see also* L. SULLIVAN, *supra* note 28, at § 238.

tion laws.[36] Many of these provisions have no counterparts abroad.[37]

The United States has a uniquely strong and varied set of antitrust remedies. Americans chose to make the antitrust laws both criminal and civil, and applicable both to companies and to natural persons.[38] The enforcement of U.S. laws is entrusted both to a specialized commission, the Federal Trade Commission, and to a division within the Department of Justice, the Antitrust Division.[39] Besides state enforcement, the United States also allows the bringing of private actions for damages or injunctive relief,[40] which actions are not dependent on there being a prior government prosecution or conviction.[41] Private actions are encouraged by a statutory guarantee of treble damages, plus costs and attorneys' fees, to the successful plaintiff.[42] Antitrust plaintiffs also have the advantage of the very liberal pretrial discovery provisions of the Federal Rules of Civil Procedure.[43]

When one studies the extent to which these characteristic elements of U.S. antitrust enforcement have been adopted abroad, one finds that the U.S. system has not been widely followed in regard to many of its special elements, particularly in regard to private damage actions. The body of this paper will look particularly at a few

---

36   *See* 3 G. GLICKMAN, FRANCHISING (1990) (incorporating an extensive compilation of primary source material, including federal and state statutes); *see also* R. GIVENS, ANTITRUST: AN ECONOMIC APPROACH § 11 (1988).

37   *See* ANTITRUST LAWS, *supra* note 3, at 522–27.

38   *See* Continental Ore Co. v. Union Carbide & Carbon Corp., 370 U.S. 690 (1962); United States v. Aluminum Co. of America, 148 F.2d 916 (2d Cir. 1945).

39   *See* L. SULLIVAN, *supra* note 28, at §§ 240–41, R.GIVENS, *supra* note 36, at § 26.01.

40   15 U.S.C. 15; 15 U.S.C. § 26.

41   15 U.S.C. § 15.

42   15 U.S.C. § 15.

43   *See* Hoopes v. Union Oil Co., 374 F.2d 480 (9th Cir. 1967); Paramount Film Distributing Corp. v. Center Theatre, 333 F.2d 358 (10th Cir. 1964); Schenley Industries, Inc. v. N.J. Wine & Spirit Wholesalers Ass'n, 272 F. Supp. 872 (D.N.J. 1967).

major topics, namely merger control, private enforcement, and deregulation, and will analyze the reasons why the American versions of these trends have varied widely in their influence abroad. The discussion will also note the development of a countertrend, namely, the adoption by the United States of the European idea of notification.

I. Merger control

There are a number of different rationales concerning why merger control is a useful or even vital supplement to antitrust rules prohibiting cartels and monopolies. The most obvious rationale is that horizontal mergers perforce eliminate competition—permanently.[44] However, this rationale has seldom been sufficient in itself, since it is also clear that mergers produce efficiencies, may increase the ability of the merging firms to compete with larger rivals, and will not have any major monopolistic or price effects if there remains effective competition outside the merger.[45]

The second rationale stems from the theory of oligopolistic competition, to the effect that industries with small numbers of competitors (usually fewer than eight, perhaps four or even two) are less likely to have fluctuating prices, low profit margins, innovation, and efficiency than are industries with larger numbers of competing firms.[46]

A third theory, that some mergers create significantly increased opportunities for tacit collusion, is much like the second; however, it assumes further that oligopolies perform badly not simply because of their structure but because the fewness of firms facilitates

---

[44] *See* H. HOVENKAMP, *supra* note 28 at § 11.1; T. BRUNNER, T.KRATTENMAKER, R. SKITOL & A. WEBSTER, MERGERS IN THE NEW ANTITRUST ERA 6–8 (1985) [hereinafter T. BRUNNER].

[45] *See* Merger Guidelines of Department of Justice, 2 Trade Reg. Rep. (CCH) § 4490 (June 14, 1984) [hereinafter 1984 Merger Guidelines]. *See also* H. HOVENKAMP, *supra* note 28, at § 11.2; T. BRUNNER, *supra* note 44, at 36–38; Clark, *supra* note 28, at 1162.

[46] *See* H. HOVENKAMP, *supra* note 28, at § 4.2.

consciously parallel pricing and other strategies designed to avoid vigorous competition.[47]

The United States did not adopt a specific merger control statute until 1914.[48] The original statute was flawed and was of little use until it was amended and strengthened in 1950.[49] Full-scale surveillance of mergers and prevention of those thought to be anticompetitive were not possible until passage of legislation in 1976 requiring prior notification of all large acquisitions involving acquiring firms with more than $100 million in sales or assets and acquired firms with more than $10 million in assets. This mandates that the transaction may not be consummated until a government investigation can be completed.[50]

The substance of American merger-antitrust rules has also undergone substantial development and refinement, a process that could be viewed as involving an ebb and flow. During the early 1960's the government was fully or partially successful in challenging a wide variety of mergers, acquisitions, and even joint ventures.[51] Horizontal mergers involving firms accounting for less than 10% of market sales were held illegal in the context of trends toward concentration.[52] Vertical mergers involving foreclosures of less than 5% were also held illegal.[53] Both conglomerate mergers and joint ventures were held to be prohibited if they eliminated substantial potential competition between the parties to the transac-

---

47   *See id.* at §§ 4.2, 11.1; Clark, *supra* note 28, at 1163.

48   Clayton Act, ch. 323 § 7, 38 Stat. 730 (1914) (current version at 15 U.S.C. § 18 (1982)).

49   The Celler-Kefauver Act strengthened the merger control provisions of the original Clayton Act provision. 15 U.S.C. §18.

50   Hart-Scott-Rodino Antitrust Improvements Act of 1976, 15 U.S.C. §§ 1, 8, 15c, 18a, PL 94-435, 90 Stat. 1383 (1976).

51   *See, e.g.,* United States v. Von's Grocery Co., 384 U.S. 270 (1966); United States v. Philadelphia National Bank, 374 U.S. 321 (1963); Brown Shoe Co. v. United States, 370 U.S. 294 (1962).

52   *See, e.g.,* United States v. Pabst Brewing Co., 384 U.S. 546 (1966); *Von's Grocery Co.,* 384 U.S. 270.

53   Pabst Brewing Co., 384 U.S. 546; *Brown Shoe Co.,* 370 U.S. 294.

tion.[54] It was also suggested in certain opinions that efficiency was not a factor justifying a merger and even that efficiencies resulting from a merger might be reasons to view the merger as an illegal threat to smaller competitors.[55] In that era, market definition was carried out in a way best summarized by the statement that a merger is illegal if it lessens competition in the market least favorable to it.

Eventually, U.S. merger control reached a peak and receded. A major turn came when new Justice Department merger guidelines in 1982 and 1984 increased to between 14% and 18% the threshold market share below which a horizontal merger would clearly not be challenged.[56] Second, the concept of low barriers to entry was used in the new guidelines and in cases to hold that mergers consolidating even up to 48% of a "market" could be tolerated if new rivals might easily enter.[57] Third, the new guidelines made it clear that vertical and conglomerate mergers would seldom be challenged, regardless of their size.[58]

The Justice Department recently argued that it has not ignored its obligation to challenge mergers but rather has limited its intervention in the market to "those situations where there is a significant likelihood of harm to consumer welfare."[59] The Department

---

[54] United States v. Falstaff Brewing Corp., 410 U.S. 526 (1973); United States v. Penn-Olin Chemical Co., 378 U.S. 158 (1964).

[55] *See, e.g., Brown Shoe Co.*, 370 U.S. at 316 (quoting United States v. Aluminum Co. of Am., 148 F.2d 416, 429 (2d Cir. 1945)).

[56] 1984 Merger Guidelines, *supra* note 45, at § 4490; Merger Guidelines of Department of Justice, 2 Trade Reg. Rep. (CCH) § 4500 (June 14, 1982) [hereinafter 1982 Merger Guidelines].

[57] *See, e.g.*, United States v. Waste Management, Inc., 743 F.2d 976 (2d Cir. 1984).

[58] 1984 Merger Guidelines, *supra* note 45, at § 4.21. The Guidelines require a plaintiff to show extensive vertical integration between the markets, significant barriers to market entry, and structural characteristics of the market which will produce noncompetitive activity. *Id.*

[59] Remarks of C. Rule, Assistant Attorney General, Antitrust Division, U.S. Department of Justice, at the 21st New England Antitrust Conference 11 (Nov. 13, 1987) (transcript released by Department of Justice).

further contends that its revised merger guidelines have injected a measure of certainty into the antitrust enforcement arena by setting clear standards of conduct for businesses.[60]

Merger control in Europe has varied considerably from jurisdiction to jurisdiction.[61] Merger controls are a relatively recent development. Until 1972, only the United States, Canada, Great Britain, and Japan had significant merger control laws in force.[62] The Canadian law was never employed successfully and had to be amended in 1986 to become effective.[63] The Japanese law was seldom employed at all.[64] The EC adopted a strong but limited ($5 billion size limit) merger control system in late 1989.[65] Today, many developed countries have adopted merger control laws.[66] For the most part, these laws are either based on a competition test[67] or are analyzed on a case-by-case basis.[68] West Germany, the nation most influenced by U.S. approaches, had a merger notification provision in sec-

---

60   *Id.* at 12.

61   *See* OECD, GUIDE TO LEGISLATION ON RESTRICTIVE BUSINESS PRACTICES (1979) [hereinafter OECD Legislation Guide]; OECD, MERGER POLICIES AND RECENT TRENDS IN MERGERS (1984) [hereinafter OECD MERGER POLICIES]; *see generally* Davidow, *Antitrust, International Policy and Merger Control*, 15 J. INT'L. L. & ECON. 519, 520 (1981).

62   OECD MERGER POLICIES, *supra* note 61, at 7.

63   Canadian Merger Control Law, *supra*, note 26. For 20 years, the Canadian Parliament had failed to accept reform proposals; *see* Green, *supra* note 12, at 253.

64   For the Japanese legislation, *see* Act. No. 214 of 1949, §§ 1–4 *partially amended* and § 5 *deleted by* Act. No. 259 of 1953 (concerning the prohibition of particular mergers and requirements for filing).

65   EC Merger Control Regulation, *supra* note 27, at art. 1(2)(a).

66   Germany, Australia, New Zealand, France, Ireland, and Sweden have enacted merger control laws in the past 15 years. OECD MERGER POLICIES, *supra* note 61, at 7.

67   Canada, Germany, Japan, the United States, and the ECSC employ a competition test. *Id.* at 11.

68   France, Ireland, New Zealand, Sweden, and Great Britain use the case-by-case approach. *Id.*

tions 22–24a of the Act Against Restraints of Competition, implemented in 1957.[69] Germany amended the Act in 1973 to give the Federal Cartel Office the power to prohibit a merger if it is likely to create or strengthen a dominant market position.[70]

In recent years Germany has actively enforced its merger laws. For example, in 1985 the German Federal Cartel Office prohibited a proposed joint venture of the five leading German cable companies to produce fiber optic cable on the grounds that the venture would strengthen the market position of the five firms while blocking the market to competitors.[71] A major difference between German law and U.S. law is the right of the Minister of Economic Affairs to overrule the Federal Cartel Office and allow certain mergers in light of broader politico-economic needs of the nation.[72] The major example of this involved the combination of Germany's two major petroleum firms. The rationale for exemption was the need to compete worldwide with still-larger major oil companies.[73]

---

[69] *See* Act Against Restraints of Competition, German Federal Republic, §§ 22–24a, *amended* April 16, 1980 by the Fourth Amendment of the Law Against Restraints of Competition, BGB1.I.S. 458, printed in OECD LEGISLATION GUIDE, *supra* note 61.

[70] OECD MERGER POLICIES, *supra* note 61, at 25–26.

[71] OECD, *supra* note 22, at 111. Germany amended the Act against Restraints of Competition twice since 1973. The 1976 amendment set forth specific merger provisions for the publishing industry, and the 1980 amendment lowered the threshold for exempted mergers. *See* OECD MERGER POLICIES, *supra* note 61, at 26–27. The 1980 amendment was enacted in response to three earlier mergers that were exempt from control: an energy firm acquired 65 medium-sized firms, and two electrical firms each acquired 50 small firms. *Id.* at 27.

[72] *See* Markert, *Merger Control in Western Europe: National and International Aspects* in COMPETITION IN INTERNATIONAL BUSINESS 293, 294–96 (O. Schachter & R. Hellawell eds. 1981). The Federal Cartel Office will prohibit a merger which creates or strengthens a dominant market position unless the merging firms prove that the merger will enhance competition. *Id.* at 295. The participant firms may request a public interest exemption from the Minister for Economic Affairs. *Id.* at 296. Both the decision of the Federal Cartel Office and the decision of the Minister for Economic Affairs are subject to judicial review. *Id.*

[73] *Id.* at 296.

In the United Kingdom, referral of larger acquisitions to the Monopolies and Mergers Commission has been carried out for many years. Oddly, the British employ a public interest standard rather than a pure competition test.[74] This has meant that the Commission has had to consider objections to mergers on grounds such as that the acquirer is foreign, the takeover is hostile, or the combined firm would not treat unions well.[75] The United Kingdom has recently adopted a new and streamlined merger control system which includes a voluntary prenotification procedure using a standard form.[76]

French merger control was not authorized until 1977.[77] It has seldom been used. The horizontal merger standard referred to a combined market shape of about 40%, more than twice as high as the present U.S. standard.[78] In 1985 France stiffened its merger control law to apply to firms with a combined 25% of a relevant

[74]   *Id.* at 299–301. The Fair Trading Act of 1973 contains merger control laws. *See* OECD LEGISLATION GUIDE, *supra* note 61, at vol. 2. The Secretary of State refers proposed or consummated mergers to the Monopolies and Mergers Commission. Markert, *supra* note 72, at 299. The Commission makes an independent decision as to whether the merger would operate against the public interest. *Id.*

[75]   *Id.* at 300.

[76]   The Companies Act of 1989, Ch. 40 § 146 (effective Apr. 1, 1990), *discussed in* COMMISSION OF THE EUROPEAN COMMUNITIES, NINETEENTH REPORT ON COMPETITION POLICY 161(1990); *U.K. Unveils New System for Pre-Merger Notification of Mergers,* Antitrust & Trade Reg. Rep. (BNA No. 1460), at 504 (Apr. 5, 1990).

[77]   Control of Economic Concentration, Government of France, Act No. 77–806, July 19, 1977. Under French law, the Minister for Economic Affairs, Finance and the Budget has discretionary power to prohibit or dissolve a merger if the Competition Commission finds that the merger would give the directors of one enterprise the power to influence management of another enterprise and would prevent adequate competition in the market. Markert, *supra* note 72, at 301. The merger law does not require prenotification but contains strong incentives for firms to voluntarily notify the minister of proposed mergers. *Id.* at 302.

[78]   Control of Economic Concentration, Government of France, Act No. 77–806, July 19, 1977. *See* Markert, *supra* note 72, at 301.

market, as opposed to the previous threshold of 40%.[79] However, only one merger has actually been challenged.[80]

The decision by a country to adopt antitrust merger control legislation and to screen mergers does not necessarily mean that any significant percentage or appreciable number of mergers will actually be challenged or prohibited. In fact, the percentages are low everywhere. In 1985, for instance, U.S. antitrust authorities screened more than 17,000 and challenged nine.[81] In the same year, West Germany screened 700 mergers and challenged seven, a higher percentage than in the United States.[82] On the other hand, the Japanese FTC screened 1,000 mergers and challenged none of them.[83] Australia in 1984 screened about 100 mergers and challenged one of them.[84] In 1985 the United Kingdom screened approximately 200 mergers and challenged none.[85] Sweden had approximately the same record as the United Kingdom.[86]

Canada in 1986 adopted its first system of civil merger control (the earlier criminal law approach had proved infeasible), combined with a premerger notification system patterned after that of the United States.[87] Recent prosecutions and settlements of major cases

---

[79]   *See* OECD, COMPETITION POLICY IN OECD COUNTRIES: 1985–1986 110 (1987).

[80]   In 1984 the Commission found two mergers that would restrain competition. The Minister authorized the first merger, which resulted in an 80% market share, after the Commission found that the merger significantly contributed to economic and social progress. The Minister prohibited the second merger, however, after the Commission found no offsetting public interest benefits to the resulting restraint on competition. OECD, *supra* note 22, at 102–03.

[81]   *See* OECD, *supra* note 79, at 240.

[82]   *Id.* at 125–27.

[83]   *Id.* at 146–47.

[84]   OECD, *supra* note 22, at 39.

[85]   OECD, *supra* note 79, at 216–17.

[86]   *Id.*

[87]   Canadian Merger Control Law, *supra* note 26; OECD, *supra* note 79, at 67–69.

indicate that the system is being enforced seriously and will have significant effect.

After seeking merger control authority unsuccessfully for 13 years, the European Commission stated in 1987 that it would seek to apply Articles 85 and 86 of the EC Treaty to proposed mergers without new rules or authorization.[88] That policy was facilitated by a decision of the European Court of Justice upholding the applicability of the existing Treaty provisions to merger and acquisition transactions.[89] These developments led the Council of the EC finally to announce that it would adopt a merger control regulation in 1989, including premerger notification of very large transactions.[90]

The Common Market merger control system adopted in December 1989 includes strong power to halt mergers and review them. If, as expected, the size limits are reduced to perhaps $2 billion, it may become a significant regulatory system. Even then, the reference in the legal standard to creation or expansion of a

---

[88] The competition commissioner threatened to use Articles 85 and 86 if member countries did not approve merger controls. *See Competition Rules,* Financial Times, Nov. 30, 1987, at 1:22. Articles 85 and 86 of the EEC Treaty govern anticompetitive practices in all industries except coal, steel, and atomic energy. *See* E. KINTNER & M. JOELSON, AN INTERNATIONAL ANTITRUST PRIMER, 194–224 (1974).

[89] The court upheld a Brussels decision that Article 85 applied to change of control agreements and Article 86 applied to situations where a firm exercises control over a competitor. *See EC Court Decision on Merger Regulation Under Rome Treaty Generates Uncertainty*, Antitrust & Trade Reg. Rep. (BNA No. 1343), at 863 (Dec. 3, 1987).

[90] *See EC Commission Unveils Revisions of Draft Merger Control Regulation*, Antitrust & Trade Reg. Rep. (BNA No. 1356), at 408 (Mar. 10, 1988). The draft proposal, endorsed by all but one EC member country, is based on four broad principles. First, the regulation applies only to large transnational mergers. Second, firms planning a merger are required to notify and seek approval from the Commission before the merger. Third, mergers resulting in strengthening or establishment of dominant market position are prohibited with certain exceptions. Fourth, the Commission will review proposed mergers on an expedited basis. *Id.* at 408. The only member country opposing the proposal is Great Britain. *See France Backs Plans for EC Takeover Controls,* Financial Times, June 23, 1988, at 2, col. 1.

dominant position would seem to prevent the application of the new law to most oligopoly situations.

II. Private actions and treble damages

One of the most important and characteristic features of U.S. antitrust has been private treble damage action. Over the decade 1974 to 1983, an average of about 1,400 antitrust cases a year were filed in the United States.[91] Of the 1,400 cases, only about 100 were typically government prosecutions, while the other 1,300 were private actions.[92]

However, although private actions were and are much more numerous than government prosecutions in America, they have never been as important. Nearly all major national or international cartel cases were discovered by government prosecutors and first sued by the Justice Department.[93] In many instances, such as the heavy electrical equipment bid-rigging cases, a few government prosecutions led to hundreds of private "follow-on" cases seeking and recovering large damages.[94] Virtually all industry restructuring stemmed from government actions. Prominent examples include the dismantling of Standard Oil,[95] United Shoe Machinery,[96] and AT&T,[97] and the attempted breakup of IBM.[98]

---

[91] *See* Salop & White, *Treble Damage Reform: Implications of the Georgetown Project*, 55 ANTITRUST L.J. 73, 78 (1986).

[92] *Id.* For a detailed analysis of Department of Justice Antitrust Enforcement in the 1970's, *see* Wallace, *Antitrust Enforcement in the Seventies*, 30 CATH. U. L. REV. 431 (1981).

[93] *See* Clark, *supra* note 28, at 1184; Wallace, *supra* note 92.

[94] *See* Wallace, *supra* note 92, at 435.

[95] Standard Oil Co. v. United States, 221 U.S. 1 (1911).

[96] United States v. United Shoe Machinery Co., 247 U.S. 32 (1918).

[97] United States v. American Telephone & Telegraph Co., 552 F. Supp. 131 (D. D.C. 1982).

[98] The government's case against IBM was dismissed in 1982. United States v. IBM, No. 69 Civ. 200 (S.D.N.Y. dismissal filed Jan. 8, 1982).

Almost all cases preventing mergers have been government actions. Government actions are also enormously more successful than private actions. Statistically, it appears that the government wins a much higher percentage of the cases it brings than do private plaintiffs. The Justice Department and Federal Trade Commission have prevailed in more than 70% of the actions they have instituted since 1950, while private plaintiffs have won fewer than 20%.

Private actions have performed four major functions in the U.S. market.[99] First, they have allowed victims of price-fixing schemes or monopolies to recover their losses from overcharges. Awards in the hundreds of millions of dollars have been granted and sustained to whole classes of purchasers or even to a single injured competitor.[100] Second, they have served as a partial check on arbitrary cutoffs of distributors, especially when the disfavored distributor has been a price-cutting maverick complained about by rival distributors. Third, they have been the main instrument for enforcing the statutory rules regarding price discrimination. Fourth, they have provided a remedy against predatory forms of unfair competition, particularly when carried out by a dominant firm or a small group of firms.

The history of private antitrust actions outside the United States is virtually nonexistent. In England, France, Germany, and the like, the number of private actions ever litigated appears to be less than a dozen.[101] In two cases, one in Germany and one in England, appellate courts have held that damages can be sought in private actions challenging violations of Common Market anti-

---

[99]   For a survey of private actions in the United States, *see* Salop & White, *Economic Analysis of Private Antitrust Litigation*, 74 GEO. L.J. 1001, 1002–04 (1986). *See also* Cavanagh, *Contribution, Claim Reduction, and Individual Treble Damage Responsibility: Which Path to Reform of Antitrust Remedies?* 40 VAND. L. REV. 1277, 1282–83 (1987).

[100]   *See* Milstein, Birrell & Kessler, *S. 1300—H.R. 4831—An Overdue Antitrust Reform*, 31 ANTITRUST BULL. 955, 958–61 (1986).

[101]   *See* Jacobs, *supra* note 25, at 1366.

trust rules.[102] Damages have yet to be awarded in a litigated case.[103] However, one British damage action against a bid-rigging conspiracy was settled for more than £9 million.[104]

Japan's one significant private action, a consumer action against price-fixing oil companies, was only minimally successful.[105] Germany also has only one famous case.[106] The Common Market antitrust regulations, the most important body of antitrust law in Europe, do not provide for private actions or damage actions.

The causes of the lack of private antitrust actions outside the United States are generally known. No other country has provided

---

[102] Under German law, a private plaintiff can recover damages for breach of a duty created by statute only if the duty was created for the plaintiff's benefit. Jacobs, *supra* note 25, at 1366. In the *BMW* case, the German Federal Supreme Court held that Article 85 of the Treaty of Rome imposes a duty for the benefit of a private plaintiffs. *BMW Car*, 1980 EEC 213 (W. Ger.); *see* Jacobs, *supra* note 25, at 1366. Under English law, the House of Lords held in *Garden City Foods Ltd. v. Milk Marketing Board* that violation of Article 86 of the Treaty of Rome gave rise to a private course of action and a remedy in damages. 38 COMMON MKT. L. REV. 43 (1983); *see* Jacobs, *supra* note 25, at 1366.

[103] Courts in EC member states have regularly enforced Articles 85 and 86 of the EC Treaty. *See* Jacobs, *supra* note 25, at 1364. As of 1984, there was no case where a private plaintiff recovered damages under either EC treaty law or state law. *Id.*

[104] *See* Korah, *supra* note 20, at 49–50. The UK government soon plans to introduce new laws to curb restrictive practices, cartels, and monopolies. *Supra* note 76. The laws include a provision which will allow private individuals for the first time to bring an action against cartels. *Id.*

[105] Kai v. Nippon Sekiyu, K.K., 1005 Hanrei jiho 32 (Tokyo High Ct., July 17, 1981); *discussed in* Ramseyer, *The Costs of the Consensual Myth: Antitrust Enforcement and Institutional Barriers to Litigation in Japan*, 94 Yale L.J. 604, 618 (1985). In Sato v. Sekiyu Renmei, 997 Hanrei jiho 18 (Yamagata Dist. Ct., Mar. 31, 1981), a related case arising from the same activities as Kai, the plaintiffs chose to sue under the general tort damage provisions of the Japanese Civil Code; Ramseyer at 623.

[106] *Supra* note 102. Germany does not allow private challenges to mergers. *See* Markert, *supra* note 72.

for multiple damages, so the incentive to sue is less.[107] Contingency fee arrangements by lawyers are generally not accepted abroad, so it is not possible to have prominent or aggressive attorneys finance such litigation.[108] Class actions are rare abroad, and thus it is harder for small purchasers to pool their claims.[109] Liberal pretrial discovery is rare, so uncovering violations is much more difficult and unlikely.

All this is not to say that Europeans or Asians are indifferent to the welfare of antitrust victims.[110] Common Market law provides that an injured party may demand that the EC Commission challenge a restrictive practice that is injuring him, and the complainant may sue the Commission if it fails to respond.[111] No such right exists in the United States. The Commission has established its right to emergency injunctive relief to prevent the cutoff of a complaining dealer or purchaser.

The United States itself has begun to reexamine the worth of private enforcement and of treble damages. American courts increasingly have held that a plaintiff must allege public injury in order to seek relief from a competitor's unfair business practices under section 1 of the Sherman Act.[112] The Export Trading Company Act of 1982[113]

---

107 *See* Jacobs, *supra* note 25, at 1371; *see also* E. KINTNER & M. JOELSON, *supra* note 88, at 193. Even single damage awards in the United States are significantly higher than damage awards in foreign nations. *See* Note, *Foreign Plaintiffs and Forum non Conveniens: Going Beyond Reyno*, 64 TEX. L. REV. 193, 203–04 (1985).

108 *See* Note, *supra* note 107, at 197–99.

109 *See id.* at 199–201.

110 EC antitrust law does not cap antitrust fines at $10 million, as does the United States, but limits the award to 10% of aggregate turnover based on worldwide sales; EC Merger Control Regulation, *supra* note 27, at art. 14(2).

111 The Commission of the EC has the duty to enforce antitrust infringements of the Treaty of Rome against individuals and companies. *See* Jacobs, *supra* note 25, at 1365. The Commission has no authority to compensate a victim. *Id.* at 1367. Private rights created by community law are enforced by national courts, and the available remedy depends on national law. *Id.* at 1368; *see* E. KINTNER & M. JOELSON, *supra* note 88, at 192–94.

112 *See, e.g.*, Stifel, Nicolaus & Co. v. Dain, Kalman & Quail, Inc., 578 F.2d 1256 (8th Cir. 1978).

113 PL 97–290, 96 Stat. 1233 (codified at 15 U.S.C. §§ 4001 et seq. (1982)).

allows only single damages to those who successfully challenge the conduct of a registered export company.[114] An unsuccessful plaintiff may have to pay the attorneys' fees of the defendant.[115]

In the recent Structural Impediments Initiative (SII)[116] negotiations, the United States persuaded Japan to strengthen both public and private antitrust enforcement[117] and to authorize its FTC to aid private plaintiffs.

III. Guidelines and notification: a study in cross-fertilization

The issue of notification of transactions for antitrust clearance, combined with guidelines for non-notification or for presumptive legality, provides an interesting example of reverse influence, or perhaps cross-fertilization. These elements help to create what might be called an administrative approach to antitrust enforcement. Between 1890 and 1976, U.S. antitrust was a fairly pure prosecutorial, case law system involving no guideline or notification provisions except for export associations, which had to be registered with the Federal Trade Commission. In the 1940's, both the FTC and the Justice Department developed procedures for providing answers to specific submitted transactions.[118]

---

[114] 15 U.S.C. § 4016(b)(1).

[115] 15 U.S.C. § 4016(b)(4).

[116] Antitrust & Trade Reg. Rep. (BNA No. 1470), at 931 (June 14, 1990). *Interim Report of U.S. and Japanese Delegations on Talks under Structural Impediments Initiative, Released April 5, 1990, reprinted in* Int'l. Trade Rep. (BNA No. 15), at 527 (Apr. 11, 1990). *Key Elements of U.S.-Japan Structural Impediments Initiative Report Released by the Office of the U.S. Trade Representative on June 28, 1990, reprinted in* Antitrust & Trade Reg. Rep. (BNA No. 1473), at 28 (July 5, 1990).

[117] Wall Street Journal, Jan. 14, 1991, at A10, col. 6.

[118] For a current discussion of these procedures, *see In re* Cowles Comm., Inc., 80 F.T.C. 997, 999 (1972). Current versions of these provisions are codified at: Department of Justice Antitrust Division Business Review Procedure, 28 C.F.R. § 50.6 (1990), Federal Trade Commission Business Review Procedure, 16 C.F.R. §§ 1.1–1.4 (1990).

In Europe, the notification idea was older and much stronger. In England, domestic cartels had to be notified, and could in some instances be justified. When the Common Market began antitrust enforcement in 1962, it created strong incentives for notification.[119] Thousands of agreements, particularly distribution and licensing agreements, are notified to the Commission each year.[120] So many come in that most are not ruled on for years. The Commission recently had to develop a "negative clearance" procedure to deal with transactions requiring a quick, if tentative, answer.[121]

A key element of Common Market law has been the group exemption.[122] By listing what kinds of agreements or restrictions need not be registered because they are unlikely to be anticompetitive, the Commission creates a "guidelines" body of law that is easy to follow.[123] Usually, the exemptions feature a "white list," a "gray list," and a "black list," setting forth contractual clauses that are, respectively, always acceptable, acceptable only if submitted and examined, or almost never acceptable.[124]

In the past dozen years, the United States has moved closer to the guidelines/notification approach to enforcement. In 1968 the Antitrust Division issued a first set of Merger Guidelines, setting forth market share figures under which it normally would not challenge a merger.[125] In 1976 merger enforcement was supplemented with a major premerger notification system, created by the Hart-Scott-Rodino Act.[126] The

---

119   *See* Robbins & Donck, *Common Market Law Influences Indiana Firms with Business Overseas,* 7 IND. BUS. J., Nov. 10, 1986, at A29.

120   *Id.*

121   Council Regulation No. 17/62, 5 O.J. Eur. Comm. (No. 13) art. 2 (1962); *See also* Robbins & Donck, *supra* note 119.

122   EC Block Exemption Law, *supra* note 23.

123   *Id.*

124   *See EEC Competition: Papering Over the Cracks,* Financial Times, Nov. 14, 1985, at 2:27.

125   Merger Guidelines of Department of Justice, 2 Trade Reg. Rep. (CCH) ¶ 4510 (May 30, 1968).

126   Hart-Scott-Rodino Antitrust Improvements Act of 1976, 15 U.S.C. §§ 1, 8, 15c, 18a, PL 94–435, 90 Stat. 1383 (1976).

Act itself, combined with FTC regulations, created defined classes of transactions (for example, under $15 million) that need not be notified.[127]

In 1980 the Antitrust Division responded to criticism that fear of prosecution was inhibiting U.S. foreign or export business ventures by publishing an antitrust guide for international operations.[128] The guide eschewed market share or size criteria and instead used hypothetical cases to clarify controversial points of law and enforcement policy.[129]

In 1982 and 1984, the Antitrust Division issued revised versions of its Merger Guidelines.[130] The new Guidelines allowed mergers of close to 20% of markets.[131] In addition, the Guidelines suggested that mergers necessary to achieve efficiency might be justified and that the Department would consider potential foreign competition when defining markets.[132]

Also in 1982, the United States enacted the Export Trading Company Act,[133] which granted partial antitrust immunity and single damage treatment to registered export ventures cleared by the Justice Department and the FTC. In 1984, legislative on cooperative research granted similar protection to research joint ventures but did not require any form of review.[134] The legislation was enacted in response to the general consensus that although smaller R&D firms were more innovative than larger firms, certain projects—like de-

---

[127]   *See* Griffin, *supra* note 14, at 340.

[128]   *Antitrust Division, U.S. Department of Justice, Antitrust Guide Concerning Research Joint Ventures* (1980).

[129]   *Id.*

[130]   1984 Merger Guidelines, *supra* note 45; 1982 Merger Guidelines, *supra* note 56.

[131]   1984 Merger Guidelines, *supra* note 45, at § 4.134.

[132]   *Id.*

[133]   Export Trading Company Act of 1982, PL 97–290, 96 Stat. 1233 (codified at 15 U.S.C. §§ 4001 et seq. (1982)).

[134]   National Cooperative Research Act, 15 U.S.C. § 4301 (Supp. III 1985).

velopment of supercomputers—might require large-scale cooperative research and that antitrust laws tended to discourage such a cooperative venture.[135]

Shortly after the United States enacted legislation protecting most joint research from antitrust prosecution, the European Commission issued regulations accomplishing the same thing.[136] This imitation was clearly traceable not only to a desire to ape the United States but also to the perceived need to compete better with Japan by facilitating research and development with important trade implications, such as developing semiconductors.

IV. Deregulation and privatization

Almost everyone who takes an interest in antitrust policy soon comes to realize that it is very closely related to the broader subject of competition policy. Antitrust law regulates the behavior of competing firms in sectors of the economy where the state allows competition to play the major allocative and incentivizing role. Antitrust law, as such, does not dictate what sectors or percentage of the economy should be organized competitively. The two primary alternatives are economic regulation (usually of entry price and output) or state ownership. The latter could coexist with competition and antitrust regulation, but usually the reasons justifying state ownership also justify restraints on the ability of private firms to compete with the state-owned entity.

Antitrust enforcement is primarily justified by economic analysis and empirical observation indicating that private firms subject only to antitrust rules are more flexible, efficient, innovative, consumer sensitive, and internationally competitive than are regulated or state owned entities. This analysis has thus logically led not only to support for antitrust enforcement as such but also to advocacy for deregulation and privatization.

In the United States, privatization as such has seldom been a

---

135   *See* S. Rep. No. 427, 98th Cong., 2d Sess. 1–4 (1984).

136   OECD, *supra* note 22, at 13; *see* Adweek, June 6, 1988.

significant issue, since extremely few U. S. firms are government owned. Deregulation, however, has been a more important, bipartisan trend during the last two decades than has antitrust enforcement itself.[137] Repealing the legacy of the New Deal and earlier, the United States has opened entry in trucking,[138] airlines,[139] and telephones.[140] Prices have been deregulated in regard to brokerage commissions[141] and legal fees,[142] as well as railroad and other transportation changes.[143]

In Europe in the 1960's, this U.S. trend was viewed with skepticism if not outright derision. Much of the trend was seen as inconsistent with the high degree of social policy Europeans expected from their public utilities or even their heavy industries. But by the 1980's the London Stock Exchange followed the New York Stock Exchange out of the era of fixed commission rates,[144] as did the Tokyo exchange. British steel was privatized.[145] Key aspects of

---

137 *See generally* Brown, *New Concepts for a Changing International Economy,* 11 WASH. Q. 86 (1988).

138 *See Trucking Decontrol Ball Begins,* Facts on File World News Digest, Dec. 31, 1978, § C1, at 1007 (available on Nexis); *see also Trucking: The Squeeze Gets Tighter,* TRANSPORTATION & DISTRIBUTION, April 1988.

139 *See Picking up Congress's Ball,* 10 NAT'L. J. 2081 (1978). The U.S. passenger airplane industry took an important step toward deregulation with the termination of the Civil Aeronautics Board at the end of 1984.

140 *See Suddenly Everybody Wants Small Phone Companies,* FORBES, July 9, 1979, at 114.

141 *See Farewell Xanadu,* BUSINESS MONTH, May 1988, at 26.

142 *See* Goldfarb v. Virginia State Bar, 421 U.S. 773 (1975).

143 U.S. railroads were deregulated by the Railroad Revitalization and Regulatory Reform Act, PL 94–210, 90 Stat. 31 (1976) and by the Staggers Rail Act, PL 96–448, 94 Stat. 1895 (1980).

144 *See* OECD, *supra* note 22, at 185; *see also* AM. BANKER, Nov. 3, 1986, at 20; Yassukovich, *Life After Big Bang: The Future,* 16 INT'L. BUS. LAW. 11 (1988).

145 Recently the EC decided to deregulate the steel industry. *See EC Agrees to Scrap Steel Controls,* Financial Times, June 25, 1988, at 20; *Europe's Steel Rejoins the Free World,* Financial Times, June 24, 1988, at 18.

telecommunications in Japan[146] and Germany[147] were opened up to new entrants and technologies.[148] European Communities antitrust began pushing for the deregulation of Common Market airline competition—a goal vastly complicated by the continued prevalence of government ownership in that field.[149]

New Zealand enacted the Commerce Act of 1986[150] to promote competition in deregulated markets. The Act effectively eliminated fixed brokerage fees for stockbrokers and real estate agents.[151]

Clearly, deregulation has been as much the great success story of American economic policy influence abroad in the last 20 years as anticartel policy was the major success of the previous 20.

V. Conclusion

A primary difficulty in assessing the success of the exportation of U.S. antitrust principles in the last two decades is the changing conception of what antitrust policy is. If antitrust is viewed as synonymous with populism—with opposition to business and industrial power as such—then it must be said that it has not been much

---

[146]   *See* Brown, *supra* note 137.

[147]   *See West German Foreign Minister Tells Reagan of Plan to Open Telecommunications Markets*, Int'l. Trade Rep. (BNA No. 4), at 104 (Jan. 27, 1988). The Federal Cartel Register and the Register of Competition Rules were abolished in 1985 as part of a government policy to minimize regulation and bureaucratic constraints. COMMISSION OF THE EUROPEAN COMMUNITIES, FIFTH REPORT ON COMPETITION POLICY 124 (1986); *see also European Telecommunications,* Financial Times, May 11, 1988, at 1.

[148]   For an overview of the European Telecommunications Industry, *see European Telecommunications,* Financial Times, May 11, 1988, at 1.

[149]   *See Coming: Massive Consolidation of European Airlines,* Business Month, June 1987, at 16.

[150]   New Zealand Commerce Act 1986, No. 5, 1 1986 N.Z. Stat. 69(repealing Commerce Act of 1975).

[151]   *See* R. MILLER, PRICE SETTING AND THE COMMERCE ACT 8 (1987). The Commerce Act 1986 eliminates price-fixing and restrictive trade covenants. *Id.* at 1.

adopted in recent years in the major industrialized countries. At most, there has been a gradual spread and strengthening of merger control legislation. Such legislation, however, has been carefully tailored generally to permit all but the largest and most horizontal of mergers and acquisitions.

As is discussed below, the United States has become a somewhat cautious and selective exponent of antitrust doctrine. American officials have probably spent more time in the last two decades warning their allies about the dangers of overly populist antitrust doctrines than they have urging the emulation of particular U.S. enforcement rules.

This survey also indicates that resistance to the U.S. approach to private treble damage actions abroad remains very strong. No other nation has adopted the treble damage approach. In no other nation has the private damage action become a common occurrence. Although it appears that the United States will adhere to the essence of its treble damage approach, there are some signs of retreat and reconsideration.

The grounds for winning treble damages have been considerably narrowed by conservative court decisions. The number of cases being filed has declined significantly. In regard to a number of specialized types of defendants, such as export trading companies, joint research associations, and local governments, treble damages or all damages have been prohibited.

It does seem certain that the United States will adhere to its view that classic cartel practices—that is, price-fixing, bid-rigging, market and customer allocation, and boycotts—are almost always unacceptable when not integral parts of legitimate business activities such as sports leagues, stock exchanges, or other joint ventures. It appears that the same view has become fairly well entrenched in most free market countries.

The largest issue of antitrust policy in the last decade has been that of deregulation. This is an area which U.S. policy and analysis have been very influential. However, even deregulation is a broad concept which covers some very distinct subparts.

In the United States, the major aspect of economic deregulation has been the removal of government controls limiting entry, pricing, and profits in common carrier industries such as airlines and trucking, where it came to be presumed that effective competition would result from normal market forces, including intermodal competition. This trend has also occurred in Europe, but it has been complicated by the greater prevalence there of state ownership of the competing carriers themselves.

In Europe, a major element of deregulation has been "privatization," that is, the selling off to private shareholders of companies the state had previously owned. This has not been frequent in the United States, because government ownership has always been very rare in America. In Europe, privatization has often been the necessary first step to later, more extensive forms of deregulation.

Second, there has been the concept that when antitrust rules interfere with vertical practices or legitimate forms of business integration, then antitrust itself becomes a form of unnecessary regulation, such that the way to achieve deregulation is to reinterpret or repeal certain very strict aspects of antitrust doctrine.

Third, in order not to condemn their own activities, states have always taken the position that antitrust condemns only unauthorized private cartels. This formulation leads to legal decisions holding, for instance, that OPEC is not an antitrust violation and that the U.S.–EC steel quota system involves no antitrust violation. Nevertheless, this approach is not helpful in determining whether state sponsorship of quota arrangements should be viewed as consistent or inconsistent with antitrust policy and whether deregulation should include giving up the sponsorship of such arrangements. At a lesser level, there remain difficult questions concerning how much deference a state should give to a cartel injurious to its interests which is approved or tolerated by the exporting state but which does not involve direct state participation or compulsion.

It is very difficult to generalize at this time concerning whether state-sponsored cartel activities, particularly in the trade and natural resources field, are really becoming less frequent or less defensible because of the deregulation movement. In many states it appears that antitrust authorities are waging a quiet civil war with practical-minded politicians and trade officials who favor quota solutions to international competition problems, particularly because "voluntary" arrangements are technically not subject to retaliation under the GATT.

In sum, competition policy and antitrust law are likely to remain highly debatable and controversial subjects in each of the major market economy nations. Considerable national variation in approach is to be expected. U.S. thinking and U.S. approaches willprobably continue to have a more significant influence than will those of any other nation, but they will certainly not always be decisive, especially since these issues have recently been reopened and critically reexamined in the United States itself.

33
From legal form toward economic efficiency—article 85(1) of the EEC treaty in contrast to U.S. antitrust

BY VALENTINE KORAH*

I. Objectives of EEC competition law

Even if economic efficiency defined in terms of consumer welfare be the only objective of antitrust, there are problems in applying the policy to factual situations. In the European Economic Community [EEC], it is clear that there are other aims to be pursued. The preamble to the EEC Treaty mentions objectives that Chicago would consider too vague to provide a basis for law:[1] social factors such as improving the working conditions of the peoples of Europe

---

* Barrister, Professor of Competition Law, University College, London.

AUTHOR'S NOTE: *I shall not bore readers by describing the U.S. rules or philosophy. I shall merely try to describe the attitudes in Europe in a way that contrasts with those in the United States.*

[1] *E.g.,* R. BORK, THE ANTITRUST PARADOX 7, et seq. (1978). "A consideration of the virtues appropriate to law *as* law demonstrates that the only legitimate goal of antitrust is the maximization of consumer welfare. Current law lacks these virtues precisely because the Supreme Court has introduced conflicting goals, the primary one being the survival or comfort of small business."

and reducing the differences in prosperity between the regions; fair competition; peace and liberty.[2]

The mechanism by which the improved standard of living and other objectives are to be achieved is the integration of the market, and, in the field of competition, this has been elevated to an independent aim. The competition rules set out in articles 85 and 86 of the EEC Treaty[3] start by providing that certain kinds of restrictive conduct are prohibited as "incompatible with the common market." The abolition of tariffs and quotas imposed by government on trade between member states[4] should not be counteracted by agreements between undertakings to keep national markets separate.

Nevertheless, efficiency is an important objective. The reason for abolishing governmental barriers between states was to enable European industry to obtain economies of scale similar to those achieved in North America, without creating unduly concentrated markets. Firms which efficiently produce what consumers want to buy should grow at the expense of other firms and industries. Efficiency is, however, not the only, or even the most important, objective.

II. Barriers to entry perceived as pervasive

Europe is divided by legal and cultural factors in a way that the United States is not. In Europe, intellectual property rights are national, not Community-wide. Most taxation is levied nationally and at different rates and on different bases in each member state. In some countries, price control, which is not illegal under EEC law if it does not bear more heavily on imports, has led to substantial differences between prices in different member states. There are also more entry barriers (in the strict sense of keeping out an

---

2 For a fuller analysis, *see* 2 B. HAWK, UNITED STATES, COMMON MARKET AND INTERNATIONAL ANTITRUST: A COMPARATIVE GUIDE chap. 7, 7 et seq. (2d ed. 1987).

3 See the Appendix to this article for some of the pertinent EEC Treaty provisions.

4 Before the establishment of the Common Market, the main form of protection between European countries was quotas.

equally efficient firm, whose cost of entry will exceed that of the incumbent) in Europe than in the United States. Member states have been adept in devising rules, apparently to insure safety or consumer protection, that exclude products and firms from other member states. These are now being attacked in the Community Court on an automatic basis by the Commission of the European Communities. Moreover, article 30 of the Treaty,[5] which prohibits measures that may restrict trade between member states, overrides the national laws in national courts, as do other provisions dealing with the free movement of services and the right of establishment. Nevertheless, many such barriers remain, and the fear of prosecution under national laws that infringe the rules of free movement, even if reduced by the prospect of a Euro-defense, may deter all but the bravest importer from other member states.

In the Common Market, entry barriers are perceived as pervasive. Any obstacle a new firm faces in entering a market is treated as a barrier, even if the incumbent firms had to invest as much to overcome it.[6] If the competition rules are intended to protect small

---

[5] Article 30 prohibits between member states all quotas, including a nil quota, and measures of equivalent effect. This is a fundamental principle of the treaty and not merely a rule, so it has been interpreted widely by the Community Court to forbid any measure, legislative or administrative, that bears more heavily on goods imported from another member state than on domestic products, and the derogations from its application provided in article 36 are narrowly construed.

[6] In Europemballage and Continental Can v. Commission, (6/72) [1973] E.C.R. 2151; [1973] C.M.L.R. 199; Comm. Mkt. Rep. (CCH) 8171, for instance, the Community Court treated the capital investment and technology needed to make metal cans as entry barriers. Markets for empty cans are geographically small, because of the high relative cost of transport, but a new entrant can usually build a plant at a distance from those of existing suppliers, so the minimum efficient scale, though large in relation to the local market, would not be looked on as an entry barrier by most economists. It usually costs a new entrant less to obtain access to technology than it cost the incumbent to develop it. The important recent innovation in can making—the two-piece can—had not been developed at the time of the judgment, and there were two main sources of licenses, Continental Can and American Can.

The Court quashed the decision for not considering whether the maker of cylindrical cans or canners might have started making the odd-shaped ones

firms that would like to enter or stay in the market,[7] the extended definition of entry barrier may be appropriate. Potential competition may restrain a firm with a large share of a market from imposing poor bargains on consumers and suppliers, but only actual entry will satisfy the other objectives, although satisfying these other objectives may be at the cost of efficiency.

Moreover, many people dispute whether potential competition is as effective as is accepted by Chicago. The market for corporate control[8] and the willingness of firms to enter new markets depend on outsiders' having sufficient knowledge of the incumbent firm's profits.[9] These are seldom known soon enough or in sufficient detail. Moreover, apart from London and Frankfurt, the capital markets in Europe are less developed than are those in the United States.

It used to be said that, in the absence of regulation, air routes between two cities were contestable markets, even if they supported

---

traditionally used for fish and meat products. It did not consider the possibility of a completely new entrant making cans with a technology license from American Can.

In Stergios Delimitis v. Henninger Brau, (C243/89) judgment Feb. 28, 1991, not yet reported, however, the Court looked to entry barriers that would keep out equally efficient firms, such as the licensing laws that make it difficult to open a new pub, or the rules that make it difficult to make a successful hostile bid for a company in some countries.

7   Even in the United States, Fox, *The Modernization of Antitrust, A New Equilibrium,* 66 CORNELL L. REV. 1140 (1981), criticizes the view that the only goal of antitrust has ever been or should be efficiency. In her view, the goal of preserving economic opportunity for small firms seldom conflicts with efficiency and should be respected when it does not. This is a possible justification for the Supreme Court's judgment in Aspen Skiing Co. v. Aspen Highlands Skiing Corp., 472 U.S. 585 (1985).

8   *See* Manne, *Mergers and the Market for Corporate Control,* 73 J. POL. ECON. 110 (1965), where he shows how this market functions as an efficient constraint on the inefficiency of incumbent management.

9   Regulation, such as the Williams Act 1968 that regulates tender offers in the interest of shareholders in the target company, may also interfere unduly with the market for corporate control. *See* Fischel, *Efficient Capital Market Theory, the Market for Corporate Control and the Regulation of Cash Tender Offers,* 57 TEX. L. REV. 1 (1978).

only a single flight each day. An entrant did not have to sink his capital into equipment that had no other use. Once the incumbent began to charge more than the costs of a normally efficient operator, another would bring a plane from another route, and compete.[10] Such hit-and-run entry, however, has not occurred since deregulation in the United States. The sunk costs of acquiring slots and a hub may be greater than had formerly been realized. Recent developments in this industry have made some believe that entry barriers may be higher and more prevalent than previously thought. In the Common Market, air transport is heavily regulated, and price-fixing and quotas are only just beginning to be restrained by the EEC competition authorities. No one seriously suggests that the regulated European market for air transport is contestable.

The Community institutions have analyzed markets in the short term. In *Michelin v. Commission*[11] the Community Court admitted the relevance of the cross elasticity of supply as well as of demand but stated that the possibility of Michelin's market share being eroded by the erection of a new factory was irrelevant because it would take too long.

---

[10] *See* Baumol, *Contestable Markets: An Uprising in the Theory of Industrial Structure,* 72 AMER. ECON. REV. 1982; expounded at greater length by W. J. BAUMOL, J. C. PANZAR & R. D. WILLIG, CONTESTABLE MARKETS AND THE THEORY OF INDUSTRIAL STRUCTURE (1982).

[11] In Nederlandsche Banden-Industrie Michelin v. Commission, (322/81) [1983] E.C.R. 3461; [1985] 1 C.M.L.R. 282; Comm. Mkt. Rep. (CCH) 14,031 at ¶ 41, the Community Court stated: "The final point which must be made is that there is no elasticity of supply between tyres for heavy vehicles and car tyres owing to significant differences in production techniques and in the plant and tools needed for their manufacture. The fact that time and considerable investment are required in order to modify production plant for the manufacture of light vehicle tyres instead of heavy vehicle tyres or vice versa means that there is no discernible relationship between the two categories of tyre enabling production to be adapted to demand on the market."
    If product markets are defined in a way that reflects this view, markets will be narrow, and firms with no power over price will be treated as dominant. Many practices that are unlikely to harm consumer interests will be seen as exclusionary. Only firms that could enter the market with minor adaptation to existing plant are treated as potential competitors.

Markets are viewed far more statically in Europe than they are by the Department of Justice in the United States. In its *Ninth Report on Competition Policy*, 1980, the Commission, which enforces the competition rules in the EEC, asserted that:

> It is an established fact that competition carries within itself the seed of its own destruction. An excessive concentration of economic and financial commercial power can produce such far-reaching structural changes that free competition is no longer able to fulfill its role as an effective regulator of economic activity. Consequently, the second fundamental object of the Community's competition policy must be to ensure that at all stages of the Common Market's development there exists the right amount of competition in order for the Treaty's requirements to be met and its aims achieved. (p. 10)

The Commission perceived the first objective as keeping the Common Market open and unified, the second as insuring fairness in the marketplace, and the third as protection of the legitimate interests of workers, users, and consumers.

The passage is profoundly disturbing. Efficiency is not mentioned. Indeed, all three objectives alleged may decrease it. The Commission presupposes that entry barriers are so high that no one will compete with the incumbent firm once it ceases to be efficient or begins to take monopoly profits. Who is to decide how much competition is right? My hope and impression, however, is that such a passage would not be accepted by those who are currently in charge of competition policy.

III. Bifurcation between article 85(1) and (3)

Unlike section 1 of the Sherman Act, article 85(1), which prohibits, as incompatible with the Common Market, agreements that have the object or effect of restricting competition within the Common Market and which may affect trade between member states, is qualified by article 85(3), which provides for exemption where an agreement contributes to improving production or distribution, or promoting economic or technical progress, provided that a fair share of the benefits is passed on to consumers and competition is not eliminated.[12] The possibility of exemption has made it seem less vital to interpret article 85(1) in a way that does not prohibit cooperation that increases efficiency.

In the early days, when the first implementing regulation, No. 17/62, was adopted, the Commission deliberately took power itself to control the application of article 85. National courts with diverse traditions might be expected not to follow any consistent path. So, to assure uniform interpretation and application and to reduce uncertainty for businessmen, the Commission took exclusive power[13] in article 9(1) of regulation 17 to grant exemptions under article 85(3); and, from its earliest decisions in 1964, it treated any restriction on conduct that was likely to have important consequences on the market as restricting competition contrary to article 85(1).[14] Exclusivity, for instance, is normally found by the Commission to restrict competition because it restrains the other party from dealing with outsiders, although the Commission has granted group exemptions for categories of exclusive distribution and franchising agreements and for patent and know-how licenses because of their procompetitive effects! Frequently, the Commission exempts agreements on the ground that without the protection of exclusivity the dealer would not provide the services required by the supplier.

---

12   Article 85(3) is set out in the Appendix to this article.

13   Although the regulation was adopted by the Council of Ministers—that is, with the agreement of all the member states—it was drafted and proposed by the Commission.

14   The law in the former West Germany was based on the restriction of freedom, though in relation to vertical agreements a market analysis must also be made and free-rider arguments are accepted. Occasionally the Community Court has also treated restrictions of conduct as restrictions of competition without making a market analysis, for instance, in Societé de Vente de Ciments et Bétons de L'Est v. Kerpen & Kerpen, (319/82) [1983] E.C.R. 4173; Comm. Mkt. Rep. (CCH) 10,043; and *Windsurfing,* (193/83) [1986] 3 C.M.L.R. 489; Comm. Mkt. Rep. (CCH) 14, 271. *Windsurfing* has been subjected to devastating criticism by Venit, *In the Wake of* Windsurfing: *Patent Licensing in the Common Market,* FORDHAM CORPORATE L. INST. 521 (1986).

On other occasions the Court has cleared, as not infringing article 85(1), ancillary restraints needed to support some procompetitive transaction or network of transactions. *See* note 21 *infra.*

When applying article 85(3) the Commission does attempt to make a market analysis but, until recently, has seldom been willing to do so when applying article 85(1) in individual decisions. This is said to make it easier for officials and businessmen to know when to notify an agreement with a request for exemption.

A. Invalidity

The difference between an exemption granted under 85(3) and a clearance from article 85(1) is important. A national court is required by article 85(2) of the EEC Treaty to treat as void, restrictions of competition that infringe article 85, and it has no power to exempt agreements under article 85(3). It may adjourn the case for the Commission to grant an individual exemption,[15] but it is doubtful whether it can enforce the restrictive provisions until they have been exempted.[16] To obtain an exemption the parties must notify the agreement to the Commission,[17] and the exemption cannot be retroactive to a date earlier than that of notification. Indeed, if the agreement does not merit exemption as it stands, the Commission has usually required the parties to amend the agreement and has granted the exemption only from the date of the amendment.

---

15 Brasserie de Haecht v. Wilkin (no. 2), (48/720) [1973] E.C.R. 77; [1973] C.M.L.R. 287; Comm. Mkt. Rep. (CCH) 8170. It has recently been decided that the Commission is required by article 5 of the EEC Treaty to assist national courts. Stergios Delimitis v. Henninger Brau, cited at note 6 *supra*.

16 In de Norre v. Concordia, (47.76) [1977] E.C.R. 65 at pp. 82–83; [1977] 1 C.M.L.R. 378; Comm. Mkt. Rep. (CCH) 8386, the Commission suggested in relation to the fifth question that a national court might enforce an agreement that the Commission's practice demonstrates would be exempt: There would then be little chance of conflicting decisions. The Court never dealt with this issue, which became irrelevant owing to its decision on others, but the Advocate General rejected it at p. 109 as inconsistent with BRT v. SABAM, (127/73) [1974] E.C.R. 51 & 313; [1974] 2 C.M.L.R. 238; Comm. Mkt. Rep. (CCH) 8268 & 8269. The general tenor of the judgment in Stergios Delimitis suggests that a national court must wait for the Commission to exempt.

17 Regulation 17, article 9(1).

The most important disadvantage of the Commission's practice of seldom making a realistic market analysis under article 85(1) is that it has actually to exempt agreements which increase competition but which are found to come within the prohibition of article 85(1), and it has the resources to adopt few such decisions each year.[18] More often it sends a comfort letter to the parties, few of which are published. One saying that the agreement is not caught by the prohibition of article 85(1) is helpful, because a national court may take it into consideration when deciding whether to enforce the provision,[19] although if this is stated to be because of the firm's small market share, under 5% in any member state, it will not be much use if the transaction is successful and the market share rises substantially. A letter stating that the agreement merits exemption but that the Commission is closing the file has the drawback of implying that the agreement is caught by the prohibition. This may make it more difficult to enforce the agreement in national courts. Many lawyers specializing in competition cases say that they have been able to obtain letters of the former type. Currently, however, the Commission is more likely to state that it is closing its file, without giving any reasons. Such a letter is of little value when enforcing an agreement, although, if the notification was proper, it must make it impossible for the Commission to impose fines for conduct based on its letter.

B. *Practical solution*

What many of the best lawyers frequently recommend is to clean up the agreement before negotiations are finalized, so that the

---

[18] It managed 10 in 1988, the most in any year. Since regulation 17 applies to almost all sectors of an economy with a population of some 320 million (rising to 340 million with the reunification of Germany), a legal adviser can be almost sure that the agreement his clients are negotiating will not receive an individual exemption.

[19] Procureur Publique v. Giry & Guerlain, (253/78) [1980] E.C.R. 2327; [1981] 2 C.M.L.R. 99; Comm. Mkt. Rep. (CCH) 8714; comment, Korah, 7 EUR. L. REV. 221 (1981).

Commission is unlikely to impose any fines,[20] and to persuade their clients to establish a file, while the appropriate managers are still available, showing that any restrictions accepted are the minimum necessary to make the transaction viable. On occasion the Court has adopted the view that restrictions without which a transaction that requires investment would not be viable do not, in themselves, restrict competition,[21] and reliance is placed on this doctrine of ancil-

---

20   Article 15(2) Regulation 17/62 enables the Commission to impose fines of up to 10% of each firm's aggregate turnover worldwide and for all products the year before, for an intentional or negligent infringement of articles 85 or 86. Admittedly, the Commission has probably not gone beyond 4%, and often it is the turnover for the particular product that is taken. When there is substantial likelihood of fines, for instance, for an agreement dividing markets or fixing prices, it is probably better to stop implementing the agreement, and so informing the other parties, than to notify it. Notification does not preclude the imposition of fines for earlier periods, and abrogation of the agreement may be more impressive mitigation than notification.

21   La Technique Minière v. Maschinenbau Ulm, (56/65) [1966] E.C.R. 235; [1966] C.M.L.R. 357; Comm. Mkt. Rep. (CCH) 8047, in respect of exclusive distribution when this is necessary to penetrate the market of another member state. In Nungesser v. Commission, (258/78) [1982] E.C.R. 2015; [1983] 1 C.M.L.R. 278; Comm. Mkt. Rep. (CCH) 880; Korah, *Exclusive Licenses of Patent and Plant Breeders' Rights under EEC Law after Maize Seed,* 28 ANTITRUST BULL. 699(1983), the Court held that an open exclusive license of plant breeders' rights—that is, one that does not grant absolute territorial protection but restrains the licensor from granting further licenses for the territory, or selling there himself—does not in itself restrict competition. In *Coditel (2),* (262/81) [1982] E.C.R. 3381; [1983] 1 C.M.L.R. 49; Comm. Mkt. Rep. (CCH) 8865, described in the text to note 34 below, and Louis Erauw-Jacquery v. La Hesbignonne (27/87) [1988] E.C.R. 1919, [1988] 4 C.M.L.R. 576, [1989] 2 C.E.C. 637, described in the text to note 35 below, the Court went further and ruled that exclusivity did not in itself restrict competition even when, in the circumstances, it would confer absolute territorial protection. The precedent may well be limited to licenses of performing rights and plant breeders' rights. Other cases are: *Pronuptia,* (161/84) [1986] 1 C.M.L.R. 414; Comm. Mkt. Rep. (CCH) 14,245 in relation to distribution franchising; and Remia and Nutricia v. Commission, (42/84) [1985] E.C.R. 2545; [1987] 1 C.M.L.R. 1; Comm. Mkt. Rep. (CCH) 14,217 in relation to a covenant not to compete with a business sold as a going concern. In all these cases the Court stressed that in the circumstances, the restriction was needed to induce investment and

lary restraints.[22] The main reason for not notifying the agreement is the likelihood that the Commission would require some alteration to be made before sending a comfort letter or granting an exemption. Such an amendment of the agreement would require the consent of both parties, enabling either party to renegotiate the whole deal, even if the actual change required did not affect the balance of commercial advantage and even if one party had improved its relative bargaining position as a result of investment by the other.

The Commission has taken various steps to reduce the drawbacks of its refusal to analyze the effects of restrictions realistically under article 85(1). It has granted group exemptions for the more common vertical agreements as well as for specialization agreements whereby each party agrees to make one range of products and sell them exclusively through the other in a specified area, thereby increasing the scale of operations of each, provided that the parties' market shares are under 20%. These group exemptions are of some help, but most of the regulations apply only to a narrow range of agreements. They include a blacklist of provisions and, sometimes, of conditions that prevent the application of the exemption. Some of these are unduly restrictive or unclear in their operation. For instance, article 3(3) prevents the application of the exemption for exclusive patent licenses[23] where:

---

in *Remia* that the Commission has a wide discretion in applying article 85(1).

The Commission has been less willing to use the ancillary restraint doctrine where the Court has not required it to do so. Most of its officials are jurists, though a few have studied economics.

22 The doctrine is not identical with that formulated by Judge Taft in U.S. v. Addyston Pipe and Steel Co., 85 Fed. 271 (6th Cir. 1898), *aff'd*, 175 U.S. 211 [1899]. It seems that there is no need to balance the severity of such restrictions against the procompetitive effect of the transaction as a whole. On the other hand, the doctrine may be narrower in that it seems that the restrictions must be shown to be necessary and not merely reasonably necessary. The EEC doctrine may not apply in relation to the excess when the restrictions are wider than necessary, *Nutricia*, O.J. 1982, L 376/22; [1984] 2 C.M.L.R. 165; Comm. Mkt. Rep. (CCH) 10,567.

23 Under Regulation 2349/84, note 32 *infra*. The group exemption for research and development granted by Regulation 418/85, O.J. 1985, L 369/5,

one party is restricted from competing with the other party, with undertakings connected with the other party or with other undertakings within the common market in respect of research and development, manufacture, use of sales, . . . without prejudice to an obligation on the licensee to use his best endeavors to exploit the licensed invention.

Unless the proviso for "best endeavors" prevents the basic clause from having any application, the regulation will seldom apply. A patentee may hesitate to grant an exclusive license for good technology, if the licensee is likely to look into competing ways of overcoming a technical difficulty. Moreover, it would be difficult to establish that the licensee was not misusing the licensed know-how when developing competing technology. Such clauses in the blacklists encourage firms to distort their agreements or to integrate forward or backward and avoid the need for restrictive agreements.

Many officials in the Commission believe that patent licenses are horizontal once both parties have started to produce and sell, even if the territories are so far apart that the goods could not travel and even if the licensee could not have entered the market without a license.[24]

Instead of relying on broad concepts that are helpful to economic analysis, such as the distinction between naked and ancillary restraints, or between horizontal and vertical agreements, the EEC rules are far more legalistic. Even when the Community Court has ruled that certain ancillary restraints do not restrict competition, it has stated that others, equally necessary to make the transaction viable, do.

In Europe, many lawyers study economics, but macroeconomics more often than price theory. Many officials would not find it easy to apply such broad tests and think that lawyers advising business would find similar difficulty. In practice, however, in-house

---

hardly ever applies, for the reasons I tried to explain in Korah, *Research and Development, Joint Ventures and the European Economic Community Competition Rules,* 3 INT'L. J. TECHNOLOGY MGMT. 7 (1988).

[24] *See* Venit's perceptive comment, *supra* note 14.

lawyers are usually very quick to see the commercial and economic consequences of their firm's agreements, and specialist competition lawyers soon pick up the skill and are continually educated by their clients. Only recently have a few British universities started to teach the economics of law. We are far behind the learning in North America.

IV. Rules becoming less formalistic

To avoid the need to apply such broad economic concepts under article 85(1), officials have devised and the Court has sometimes accepted formalistic pigeonholes. Of course, all laws are pigeonholes, but some respond to the economic considerations better than others do.

A. Exclusive purchasing agreements by dealers

Until recently the Commission thought that exclusive purchasing obligations almost always restricted competition if they were common in a particular trade. In *Stergios Delimitis v. Henninger Brau,*[25] however, the Court indicated the narrow conditions in which an exclusive purchasing agreement between a single beer house and a brewery in Germany foreclosed other brewers from entering the market or expanding. In the context of other ties, were there real and concrete possibilities of entry or expansion?

There would be if the free trade were sufficient to provide an outlet for the production of a firm of minimum efficient scale, or if the ties were not of long duration. The Court added that the national court asked to enforce the contract should take into account the possibility that a new or expanding brewery might acquire a brewery already on the market with a chain of tied beer houses, or of avoiding the ties by opening up new beer houses.

To this end, the national court should take into consideration the regulations and agreements concerning the acquisition of companies and the establishment of outlets, as well as the minimum number of outlets

---

[25] *Supra* note 6.

needed for profitable exploitation of a system of distribution and the existence of untied wholesalers. [Author's translation of the Court's transcript in French]

In other words, only if it were difficult to make a hostile bid for a company or if licensing requirements made it difficult to open new outlets would there be foreclosure. These would constitute entry barriers even to Chicago thinkers.

It added that even if there were foreclosure, only those agreements that contributed significantly thereto were illegal and void. Those of short duration, even by the larger brewers, might not infringe article 85(1), while long-term ties by even a small brewery might infringe it.

On the basis of this judgment it may not be necessary to bring exclusive purchasing agreements within the group exemption, unless there are national or regional licensing requirements that make it difficult for new or expanding firms to establish new outlets.

It is not yet clear how far this judgment will be applied widely outside the field of exclusive purchasing agreements to other vertical agreements or joint ventures.

B. Selective distribution

I have tried to analyze the formalistic rules, reminiscent of those in *Schwinn*,[26] used when judging whether a vertical restriction as to those to whom a dealer may resell infringes upon article 85(1),[27] and I suggested that since *Villeroy & Boch*,[28] "the Commis-

---

26 U.S. v. Arnold, Schwinn & Co., 388 U.S. 365 (1967).

27 Korah, *The Relationship between Article 85(1) and (3) of the EEC Treaty—Selective Distribution*, 2 INT'L. J. FRANCHISING & DISTRIBUTION L. (1988).

28 O.J. 1985, L 376/15; [1988] 4 C.M.L.R. 461; Comm. Mkt. Rep. (CCH) 10,758. The decision is, however, not easy to reconcile with the Court's judgments in Metro v. Commission, (26/76) [1977] E.C.R. 1875; [1978] 2 C.M.L.R. 1; Comm. Mkt. Rep. (CCH) 8435; and Metro v. Commission (No. 2), (75/85) [1986] E.C.R. 3021; [1987] 1 C.M.L.R. 118; Comm. Mkt. Rep. (CCH) 14,326.

sion has moved from those formal rules toward a view that where the market is competitive, it should be left to judge whether such systems should flourish." This enables a brand owner to impose restraints where the market is competitive and may help to increase efficiency by enabling retailers who invest in ways that promote the brand as a whole to reap the fruit of their investment.

Unfortunately, in its recent decisions the Commission seems to have returned to the earlier, formalistic case law.[29]

C. Exclusive licenses of intellectual property rights

Since 1972 the Commission has habitually held that where the holder and his licensees obtain a substantial market share by the time the Commission starts to investigate the matter, an exclusive patent license restricts competition because it restrains the licensor from granting a license to someone else for the same territory, and such a hypothetical licensee might then have exported to another member. This is a per se rule, although the Commission has often said that it does not apply per se rules. The Commission has also treated a license to produce and sell under, say, a French patent as a license to manufacture anywhere in the Common Market, subject to a contractual ban on making or selling elsewhere, which is subject to control under article 85.[30] Recently, however, the Court has been

---

[29] See Yves Saint Laurent Parfums, O.J. 1990, C320/11, where the Commission persuaded a brandowner in a competitive market to establish a system for approving retailers who satisfied its qualitative criteria. The cost of this seems to be disproportionate to the benefit, as there is no duty on anyone to supply such approved retailers. The Commission takes the view that restraining dealers from supplying any qualified dealer is anticompetitive.

See also Vichy, O.J. 1991, L75/57, subject to appeal, (T–2/91) O.J. 1991, C116/12, where the Commission withdrew the immunity from fines gained by notification from a restriction on dealers supplying anyone other than a pharmacy with its cosmetics, although the decision did not reintroduce the possibility of fines for a restraint on selling to outlets where no pharmacist was present. From the press release, but not the decision, it appeared that the agreement was horizontal. If it was purely vertical, the market should have sufficed to punish a distribution system if it was unduly restrictive.

[30] This is the basis on which the draft group exemption for patent licenses was drafted.

prepared to look more closely at the facts and, in *Nungesser v. Commission*,[31] it ruled that in view of the investment made by both licensor and licensee in developing and propagating an important new variety of maize seed that would grow in the colder climate of Northern Europe, an "open exclusive license," one under which the licensor promised not to grant further licenses for the territory nor to exploit it directly did not, in itself, infringe article 85(1).[32] This is in marked contrast to the Commission's decision in *Davidson Rubber*[33] that once the exclusive sales license was made nonexclusive, the exclusive manufacturing one should be exempted on the ground that without granting exclusivity, Davidson would not have had its process exploited in Europe in 1959. If it needed to grant exclusivity, the other licensee to whom it might have granted a nonexclusive license was purely hypothetical. In this context, the Court has adopted the concept of ancillary restraints: Without a limited amount of territorial protection, the new variety of maize would not have been developed and sold in the Federal Republic—consequently, that amount of territorial protection did not restrict competition. Unfortunately, there was no analysis as to the amount of territorial protection needed. Even in the United States, however, the rule of reason seldom results in balancing competitive pros and cons: According to a truncated analysis under the rule of reason, if the restriction of conduct may have positive effects on interbrand competition it is unlikely to infringe section 1 of the Sherman Act unless the supplier's or grantor's market share is substantial.

Nevertheless, the Court did not go all the way in *Nungesser*.

---

31   Cited in note 21 *supra*.

32   Even so, its decision that absolute territorial protection for the licensee clearly went too far for an exemption to be granted is formalistic. Open exclusivity gives considerable protection for bulky objects of little value, such as open-top cans before they are filled, but very little for items of greater value in relation to their weight and bulk. In relation only to a license of performing rights or of plant breeders' rights in basic seed has the Court ruled that absolute territorial protection does not, in itself, infringe article 85(1). *Coditel (2)* and *Louis Erauw-Jacquery, supra* note 21.

33   O.J. 1972, L 143/31; [1972] C.M.L.R. D52; Comm. Mkt. Rep. (CCH) 8444.

Even when considering the Commission's refusal to grant an exemption under article 85(3), it stated that absolute territorial protection goes far too far, and as both parties had endeavored to prevent the French licensees' customers from selling in the Federal Republic, the Commission was right to refuse an exemption. The Court did not attempt the difficult task of deciding how much protection from parallel imports was necessary to persuade Nungesser to invest in cultivating and obtaining approval for the new variety. It seems more likely that the judges did not agree: Some determined the tenor of the part of the opinion relating to open exclusivity, and others, the rest.

In *Coditel (2)*[34] the Court went further in permitting even absolute territorial protection in relation to performing rights, the free movement of which is dealt with under different provisions from goods. The case came before the Court under article 177 of the EEC Treaty, under which the Court does not decide the case but interprets the treaty and subordinate legislation in abstract terms, leaving application of the law to the national court that asked for a ruling. The Community Court did not have to decide whether the exclusive licenses to perform the film granted to a different licensee in each member state infringed article 85(1). It ruled that exclusivity does not do so in itself, but reminded the Belgian court to determine

> whether the exercise of the exclusive right to exhibit a cinematograph film does not create artificial, unjustified barriers, having regard to the requirements of the film industry, or the possibility of royalties exceeding a fair remuneration for the investments made, or an exclusive right for a period which is excessive by reference to these requirements, and whether generally the exercise of such right within a specified geographical area is not likely to prevent, restrict or distort competition.

The Court prescribed an impossible balancing process to be performed by the Belgian court but did not have to decide itself how great was the protection required to induce sufficient investment in making a film or by the distributor in bringing it to the market. Since the Court did not have to apply the test it indicated, it

---

[34] *Supra* note 21.

had less incentive to take the simple line that when there is competition between film makers, the market can be relied upon to reduce the resources controlled by those who make bad decisions as to the amount of protection to be given to distributors.

In *Louis Erauw-Jacquery*[35] the Court cleared even an export ban in an agreement between the holder of plant breeders' rights and the propagator who grew the certified seed from the basic seed supplied to him. Basic seed ceases to be protected by plant breeders' rights if it ceases to be distinct, uniform, and stable, so the holder relies on the propagator to handle it with care. He is, therefore, permitted to control propagators far more carefully than dealers or other licensees.

The Court has moved a long way in the field of licensing intellectual property rights from the Commission's view that exclusive licenses automatically infringe article 85(1) but that an exclusive manufacturing license may be exempted when all the licensees may sell throughout the Common Market and an exclusive license for manufacture is needed to induce the relevant investment. Open exclusivity is not caught by article 85(1), when it can be justified because of the need for risky investment by licensor and licensee. In the case of plant breeders' rights and the cinema industry, even absolute territorial protection may be justified. Although it is a vast improvement on the Commission's earlier cases, the extent of territorial protection still has elements of rigidity. Open exclusivity may give considerable protection when a protected product, such as an open-top can before it is filled, is of little value in relation to the cost of transporting it. It may give very little protection to small, complex items.

Soon after *Nungesser* and *Coditel (2)*, the Commission adopted a regulation granting a group exemption for exclusive patent licenses. It has perceived licenses as horizontal, at least by the time the licensee is producing and selling the product in competition with the licensor, even if the licensee could not have gotten into the

---

[35]   (27/87) [1988] E.C.R. 1919; [1988] 4 C.M.L.R. 576; [1989] 2 C.E.C. 637.

market without the licensed technology. Consequently, the early published draft of the block exemption[36] contained a very long blacklist of provisions that would prevent the application of the exemption. After the Court's decision in *Nungesser,* and under pressure from business[37] supported by member states, the draft was considerably liberalized before adoption.[38]

Exclusivity and associated territorial restraints were permitted between licensor and licensee, but only to a limited extent between licensees. Moreover, the regulation did not permit any export limitations to be placed on buyers from the manufacturers, so if, for one reason or another such as price control in some member states or high costs associated with sparse population in the territory, prices were lower in some other countries, there was no way of taking advantage of the regulation while deterring sales in the high-priced country by purchasers from the manufacturer in the low-priced area. The blacklist still prevents many other clauses which used to be common in patent licenses and which the U.S. Department of Justice would not think restrictive of competition unless the licensee could have manufactured without the benefit of the license.

After the regulation was adopted, there were two Commission decisions on licenses of patents and plant breeders' rights that were very rigid and formalistic—*Velcro/Aplix* and *Plant Breeders' Rights.*[39] Since then, however, there have been one case on a patent

---

36 O.J. 1979, C 58/12; [1979] 1 C.M.L.R. 478.

37 Business was becoming increasingly concerned that the formalistic view of the Commission was deterring the negotiation of efficient contracts that competitors in the United States and Japan were able to make.

38 Regulation 2349, O.J. 1984, L 219/15, with corrections O.J. 1985, C 113/2; comment, Venit, *EEC Patent Licensing Revisited: The Commission's Patent License Regulation,* 30 ANTITRUST BULL. 457 (1985).

39 O.J. 1985, L 233/22; [1989] 4 C.M.L.R. 157; Comm. Mkt. Rep. (CCH) 10,719; comment Korah, [1985] EIPR 296.

O.J. 1985, L 369/9; [1988] 4 C.M.L.R. 193; Comm. Mkt. Rep. (CCH) 10,757.

Provisions, such as a strong grant-back clause, that are blacklisted in the group exemption for patent licenses were condemned without analysis, even

and know-how license, one on a know-how license to a joint venture to which the licensor was party, and several on pure know-how agreements.

In *Boussois-Interpane,*[40] the Commission ensured that the group exemption should rarely apply. Some provisions were cleared as not restricting competition contrary to article 85(1), such as a non-exclusive feed and grantback clause, the obligation to keep the know-how secret, various payments to be made up front by the licensee, and the obligation to pay royalties as long as the patents remained in force and Boussois was using them. The Commission found, however, that the know-how license did infringe article 85(1) in relation to the exclusive territory and associated export bans. The licensee agreed to produce in a factory built for it by the licensor in France and, for a little more than 5 years, not to sell in the territory allocated to other exclusive licensees who might be appointed. Because there were patents in only some of the places that might be protected, this protection went beyond that exempted by the group exemption. Moreover, only the method actually being used was protected by patent anywhere, so the Commission stated that the know-how was not ancillary to the patent license, and the group exemption did not apply.

Nevertheless, the Commission exempted these restrictions on conduct on the ground that they made the holder of important technology more willing to license and Boussois more inclined to invest in manufacture, use, and putting on the market. Consequently, they helped to disseminate and further develop a new product. The Commission still did not accept in a formal decision under article 85(1) that without such bans there might be less licensing and that the Common Market

---

when the reasons recited in the regulation or in the earlier case law did not apply. The contract in *Velcro/Aplix* provided that a reasonable sum should be paid to the licensee for improvements and that the licensee should have the benefit of improvements by other licensees, so the provision neither was unfair on the licensee nor did it remove its incentive to innovate.

Contrast the attitude to the blacklist in *Fluke/Philips*, O.J. 1990, C188/2; [1990] 4 C.M.L.R. 682. Officials are no longer stating that they will treat blacklisted clauses as necessarily invalid.

40   O.J. 1987, L 50/30; [1988] 4 C.M.L.R. 124.

might be even more fragmented than it is at present. I shall postpone consideration of *Mitchell Cotts*[41] until the end of the next topic.

Even when the Court has held that open exclusive licenses do not infringe article 85(1), it has only twice cleared the agreements before it if there were export limitations. Nevertheless, the Commission's attitude to licenses in cases that do not proceed to a decision is becoming more liberal than is apparent from the case law. The group exemption for know-how licenses granted by regulation 556/89 is far more generous than was that for patent licenses, with important provisos attached to the blacklist of provisions that prevent the application of the exemption. True, the group exemption was adopted under article 85(3), but it applies automatically, so intervention by officials in specific cases will not be required to render a contract valid.

D. Joint ventures

The Court has not yet delivered any judgments relating to joint ventures, apart from *Philip Morris,*[42] so it has not applied the doctrine of ancillary restraints to such cooperation. Nevertheless, the Commission has recently been clearing aspects of joint ventures that it would have exempted 5 years ago.

Until 1985 the Commission habitually held that joint ventures in concentrated industries, even for sophisticated research and development, were caught by article 85(1). It adopted the analysis of the U.S. Supreme Court in *Penn-Olin*[43] and consistently held that

---

[41] Text to note 51 *infra*. O.J. 1987, L 41/31; [1988] 4 C.M.L.R. 111; Com. Mkt. Rep. (CCH) 10,852.

[42] (142 & 156/84), BAT v. Commission, [1987] E.C.R. 4487; [1988] 4 C.M.L.R. 24; Comm. Mkt. Rep. (CCH) 14,405. The judgment is important in bringing within the scope of article 85 agreements to acquire shares that lead to power to influence the commercial policy of a competitor. The Court, however, decided only that, given its limited willingness to review decisions made by the Commission, it would not quash a decision to close a file, on the ground that the acquisition did not enable Philip Morris to control Rothmans' commercial policy and thus did not restrict competition.

[43] U.S. v. Penn-Olin Chem. Co., 378 U.S. 158 (1964).

no party with a substantial equity in a joint venture was likely to compete with it, whether or not express restrictions were accepted. It also found that the parties were potential competitors even when, in applying article 85(3), it accepted that neither firm would, on its own, perform the functions entrusted to the joint venture. One example should suffice.

In *Vacuum Interrupters,*[44] AEI and Reyrolle Parsons produced a great variety of heavy electrical equipment, including switchgear apparatus, in competition with each other. Switchgear includes a circuit breaker to interrupt the electrical current. In theory, interrupters operating in a vacuum have a great technical advantage in preventing the current from arcing over the break, but in practice great difficulties were encountered in their development. Considerable work had been done over 20 years, and patents were acquired in the United States and the United Kingdom, some of which had expired. Serious work started in the United Kingdom some 10 years before the decision, when the parties separately started to work on the problems. Each found the difficulties so great that the cost was not likely to be recovered commercially without collaboration.

So, in 1968, they formed a joint company, Vacuum Interrupters Ltd., in which AEI held 60% and Reyrolle Parsons 40% of the equity, to develop, design, and make vacuum interrupters to be incorporated in switchgear. They agreed to make their technology available to it and not to compete with it. After various mergers and reconstructions affecting the parties, the agreement was renewed in 1970 and notified to the Commission.

The joint venture succeeded in making interrupters capable of operating at low voltages. By the time of the decision, it had spent a million and a half pounds. Vacuum interrupters were being made also in the United States and Japan by other firms. Sales by the joint venture had been only for experimental purposes and not on a commercial scale.

The Commission held that the parties, which had experience in

---

[44] *Vacuum Interrupters*, O.J. 1977, L 48/32; [1977] 1 C.M.L.R. D67; Comm. Mkt. Rep. (CCH) 9926.

the field of heavy electrical equipment and making components for it, were potential competitors of the joint venture. The object and effect of the transaction, therefore, was to restrict competition. The agreement would probably also discourage other manufacturers in the Common Market from developing such switchgear, so it affected trade between member states and infringed article 85(1) of the treaty. This finding was purely hypothetical because, when considering article 85(3), the Commission accepted that each party had decided to stop developing vacuum interrupters.

The Commission exempted the agreement on the ground that it had led to some success, and each parent had previously given up individual research. The joint venture was free to sell interrupters to anyone, and not merely to its parents.[45] Its operations were confined to the development, production, and sale of vacuum interrupters and had not spread into other fields. There were no restrictions not indispensable to the cooperation.

After some time, the joint venture succeeded in producing a few interrupters for low voltages, but the problems again proved to be too great. The research would have been abandoned had not Bush, a user of switchgear, offered to contribute both know-how relating to switchgear and funds to the joint venture. Again, although the Commission found that the relevant market was interrupters in general and not just vacuum interrupters, it exempted rather than cleared the revised agreement,under which 20% of the shares in the joint venture were transferred to a new party.[46] It stated that the addition of a new party automatically brought its old exemption to an end and that the joint venture made it less likely that the parties would compete.

In its *Thirteenth Report on Competition Policy,* however, the Commission promised in future to look more realistically before

---

45   Now the Commission is anxious to ensure that there is more than one seller in the market, and it may insist that the joint venture should sell only to the parties, in order to ensure that there are no joint sales.

46   *Vacuum Interrupters* (No. 2), O.J. 1981, L 383/1; [1981] 2 C.M.L.R. 217; Comm. Mkt. Rep. (CCH) 10,296.

finding that the parties were potential competitors. It said that the relevant factors included access by each party to finance, its capacity, technology, and distribution facilities, its ability to bear the risk, and the size of the demand.

We rejoiced that the Commission was going to appraise agreements *ex ante*, from the viewpoint of the parties deciding whether to undertake commitments to invest, and we hoped for clearance, rather than exemption of agreements between those with complementary resources, where the risk was too great for one firm, and so forth. The next two decision did not, indeed, find that the parties were potential competitors, but in the first, *BP/Kellogg*,[47] the Commission found that ancillary restrictions, which, when dealing with article 85(3), it described as reasonable and necessary, restricted competition and required exemption.

In *Optical Fibres*,[48] Corning Glass had developed and obtained patents for producing optical fibers. This was a revolutionary innovation, completely ousting the previous technology. Corning exploited its technology in the United Kingdom and the Federal Republic of Germany through licenses to a joint venture with a large cable maker in each country. The Commission found that each joint venture considered separately did not restrict competition but that the network of joint ventures, with a common technology provider in markets that were concentrated at the level to which the joint ventures sold, did restrict competition and required exemption.[49] The theory seems to be that Corning might refuse to expand

---

47   O.J. 1985, L369/6; [1986] 2 C.M.L.R. 619; Comm. Mkt. rep. (CCH) 10,747.

In *BP/Kellogg*, BP had discovered a catalyst that might be useful for making ammonia and agreed to develop a process to use it with help from Kellogg, a builder of process plants. The restrictions consisted of limited exclusivity: BP would not sell its catalyst except to Kellogg's customers, and Kellogg would not enter into research and development of other processes for making ammonia without telling BP and giving it an opportunity to terminate the agreement.

48   *Optical Fibres*, O.J. 1986, L 235/30; Comm. Mkt. Rep. (CCH) 10,813.

49   *Optical Fibres*, O.J. 1986, L 235/30; [1988], Comm. Mkt. Rep. (CCH) 10,813 at ¶¶ 46 and 48, respectively; comment, Korah, *Critical Com-*

capacity at one of the joint venture plants in order to protect prices in the territory of another joint venture. The Commission, therefore, granted the exemption only after ensuring that Corning's control of each joint venture was reduced, that either party should be able to expand the capacity of a joint venture's plant at its own expense if the other did not want to do so jointly, and that territorial protection between the joint ventures was reduced. It also ensured that market information did not pass from the joint ventures to the parents or to other joint ventures.[50]

In *Mitchell Cotts/Sofiltra,*[51] Mitchell Cotts had been buying sophisticated filter papers from Sofiltra but entered into a joint venture to which Sofiltra granted a know-how license that enabled the joint venture to make the key component of the filter. The Commission held that it was irrelevant that Sofiltra had only a minority holding, owing to its influence over the joint venture as the provider of key technology and its power to veto specified matters on the board. Nevertheless, the joint venture did not in itself restrict competition in the market for the finished product because Mitchell Cotts lacked the technology and research capability to make the key component. Consequently, it was not a potential competitor of Sofiltra in manufacture even of the finished product. The Commission clearly accepted that there was no loss of potential competition if not more than one party could have done on its own the task entrusted to the joint venture.

The Commission then referred to the number of competitors and the parties' small market shares and concluded that third parties were not foreclosed from similar joint ventures. Nevertheless, Sofiltra and the joint venture competed in the sale of complete filters, so the Commission found that Sofiltra's covenant not to

---

ments on the Commission's Recent Decisions Exempting Joint Ventures to Exploit Research That Needs Further Development, 12 EUR. L. REV. 18 (1987).

[50] The Commission has been strongly influenced by the article by Brodley, *Joint Ventures and Antitrust Policy*, 95 HARV. L. REV. 1523 (1982). It has also been influenced by B. HAWK, *supra* note 2.

[51] *Supra* note 41.

make or license others to make similar filters in the territory did infringe article 85(1), and it exempted it until 1994, by which time the joint venture may be using all its capacity and Sofiltra should be free to start manufacture in the territory. It held that the other provisions did not infringe article 85(1).

In 1990, for the first time, the Commission cleared two joint ventures when it considered that the parties were not potential competitors. In *Odin,*[52] the parties had complementary technology, so neither of them could have achieved on its own the task of the joint venture, to develop a carton with a replaceable metal lid.The parties did not compete in other fields, so there was no spillover effect. There were other firms with experience of making cardboard cartons laminated with plastic, and others making metal cans, so the joint venture did not foreclose others from collaborating in competition with Odin. The ancillary restraints were very minimal and considered necessary to make the collaboration viable. In both decisions, the Commission appraised the situation *ex ante,* from the time when the parties undertook commitments to invest.

Unfortunately, in several other recent decisions[53] the Commission appraised the position *ex post* and exempted agreements which do not seem to me to have restricted any competition that was possible without the joint venture. Recently, there seems to have been little coordination of Commission decisions. It is hoped that this will improve shortly and that future appraisals will be carried out *ex ante,* but it is difficult to persuade officials to cease working in the way they have worked for decades.

At least the Commission has accepted, in two formal decisions,

---

52   O.J. 1890, L209/15; [1990] 2 C.E.C. 2066. *See also ECR Konsortium,* O.J. 1990, L228/31; [1990] 2 C.E.C. 2082.

53   *BBC Brown Boveri/NGK,* O.J. 1988, L301/61; [1989] C.M.L.R. 610; *Cekacan* O.J. 1990, L299/64; [1990] 2 C.E.C. 2099; *KSB/Goulds/Lowara/ITT,* O.J. 1991, L19/25; *Alcatel Espace/ANT Nachrichtentechnic* O.J. 1990, L23/19; [1991] 4 C.M.L.R. 208; [1990] 1 C.E.C. 2096. In *Alupower-Chloride* O.J. 1990, C152/3; [1990] 4 C.M.L.R. 739, the proceedings were terminated by an informal comfort letter, and it is not clear whether it stated that the agreement was exempted or outside the scope of article 85(1).

that ancillary restrictions necessary to make a procompetitive transaction viable can be cleared. This is important because it does not have the resources to make more than six to ten decisions a year granting exemptions. Nevertheless, those who specialize in EEC competition law have quite often persuaded officials to issue a comfort letter stating that in its view the joint venture does not restrict competition. The drawback of this practice is that it is known only to a comparatively small number of specialists. Nevertheless, it has the great advantage of reducing the risk of each party being unable to appropriate to itself the benefits of its investment in the joint venture without undue use of the Commission's resources. Even to obtain such a comfort letter, however, the parties have to take the trouble to notify, which requires the preparation by senior management, under the guidance of specialized lawyers, of annexes explaining the market and the need for the joint venture.

V. Conclusion

During the 1960's the Commission ensured that the difficult decisions—whether an agreement that may lead to efficiencies infringes article 85—should be made only by it, through its exclusive power to grant exemptions, and through habitually finding that any restriction on the parties' freedom of conduct that has important effects on the market restricts competition. In the 1970's it developed various legalistic rules and block exemptions, and legal advisers had to advise their clients to distort their agreements to come within one of the permitted areas, even if, in so doing, they were making the market less efficient and less competitive. Firms interested in having only retailers who could provide point of sale services arranged to sell directly to retailers and selected them carefully, because if a wholesaler were allowed to sell only to approved retailers, the restriction would be caught by article 85(1) unless all retailers who qualified under objective criteria were appointed. This distorted markets, by deterring the brand owner from using independent wholesalers who might have supplied competing products and achieved scale efficiencies.

In this article I have tried to trace, in rather general terms, the history of exclusive technology licenses and joint ventures for research and development. There has been a marked and increasing change over the last few years. Many restrictions are being found not to restrict competition contrary to article 85(1), on the ground that they are necessary to induce certain transactions and investment. The Court has cleared open exclusive licenses, and the Commission has permitted considerable territorial restrictions in its group exemption for patent licenses.[54] Nevertheless, it has not gone all the way and cleared any important joint ventures. It is no good holding that the joint venture itself is not caught by article 85(1), if the ancillary restrictions necessary to make it viable, such as exclusivity, are found to require exemption.

Appendix: Antitrust Components of the EEC Treaty

Article 85 of the EEC Treaty provides:

1. The following shall be prohibited as incompatible with the common market: all agreements between undertakings, decisions by associations of undertakings and concerted practices which may affect trade between Member States and which have as their object or effect the prevention, restriction or distortion of competition within the common market, and in particular those which:

(a) directly or indirectly fix purchase or selling prices or any other trading conditions;

(b) limit or control production, markets, technical development, or investment;

(c) share markets or sources of supply;

(d) apply dissimilar conditions to equivalent transactions with other trading parties, thereby placing them at a competitive disadvantage;

(e) make the conclusion of contracts subject to acceptance by

---

[54] *Supra* note 38.

the other parties of supplementary obligations which, by their nature or according to commercial usage, have no connection with the subject of such contracts.

2. Any agreements or decisions prohibited pursuant to this Article shall be automatically void.

3. The provisions of paragraph 1 may, however, be declared inapplicable in the case of:

—any agreement or category of agreements between undertakings;

—any decision or category of decisions by associations of undertakings;

—any concerted practice or category of concerted practices;

which contributes to improving the production or distribution of goods or to promoting technical or economic progress, while allowing consumers a fair share of the resulting benefit, and which does not:

(a) impose on the undertakings concerned restrictions which are not indispensable to the attainment of these objectives.

(b) afford such undertakings the possibility of eliminating competition in respect of a substantial part of the products in question.

Article 86 provides:

Any abuse by one or more undertakings of a dominant position within the common market or in a substantial part of it shall be prohibited as incompatible with the common market insofar as it may affect trade between Member States. Such abuse may, in particular, consist in:

(a) directly or indirectly imposing unfair purchase or selling prices or other unfair trading conditions;

(b) limiting production, markets or technical development to the prejudice of consumers;

(c) applying dissimilar conditions to equivalent transactions with other trading parties, thereby placing them at a competitive disadvantage;

(d) making the conclusion of contracts subject to acceptance by the other parties of supplementary obligations which, by their nature or according to commercial usage, have no connection with the subject of such contracts.

The objectives of the Common Market and the way they are to be achieved are stated in articles 2 and 3.

Article 2 provides:

The Community shall have as its task, by establishing a common market and progressively approximating the economic policies of Member States, to promote throughout the Community a harmonious development of economic activities, a continuous and balanced expansion, an increase in stability, an accelerated raising of the standard of living and closer relations between the States belonging to it.

Article 3 provides, *inter alia,* that

For the purposes set out in Article 2, the activities of the Community shall include, as provided in this Treaty and in accordance with the timetable set out therein:

(a) the elimination, as between Member States, of customs duties and of quantitative restrictions on the import and export of goods, and of all other measures having equivalent effect;

(b) the establishment of a common customs tariff and of a common commercial policy towards third countries;

(c) the abolition, as between Member States, of obstacles to freedom of movement for persons, services and capital; . . .

(f) the institution of a system ensuring that competition in the common market is not distorted; . . .

34
The turning points in distribution law

BY RICHARD M. STEUER[*]

Discounters across the United States waited with anticipation for the Supreme Court's 1988 decision in *Business Electronics Corp. v. Sharp Electronics Corp.*[1] So did their suppliers. The case presented an opportunity for the Court to address some of the latest analytical initiatives developed by the lower courts in antitrust cases involving distribution, and either apply the brakes or open the throttle. as it turned out, *Sharp* would be the capstone of the "Reagan Revolution" in antitrust, making it more difficult for dealers to recover against their suppliers. But over the hundred years that antitrust has been with us, the law of distribution never progressed in a straight line, and even as *Sharp* was being decided, other voices were being heard.

Aficionados of antitrust know that what commonly is called the Reagan Revolution in antitrust really began years before President Reagan took office. A shift in philosophy first appeared in the mid-1970's, in some pivotal decisions of the United States Supreme

---

* Partner in the firm of Kaye, Scholer, Fierman, Hays & Handler, New York, New York.

1   108 S. Ct. 1515 (1988).

Court and the lower federal courts. These decisions, notably *Generally Dynamics*[2] in the field of mergers, and then *Sylvania*[3] in the field of distribution, signaled an end to the "go-go" era of antitrust that had begun in the 1960's.

Today, we again are experiencing some rumblings in the philosophical bedrock, and the parallels with the mid-1970's invite comparison. Is there a "counterrevolution" under way, as some argue,[4] or merely a few aberrations? Will *Sharp Electronics* squelch any counterrevolutionary tendencies, or is it triggering an even broader ideological backlash? Can a practical set of rules be formulated that will reconcile the seemingly contradictory approaches that have been emerging and integrate the new theories with the realities of today's markets?

The focus here will be on antitrust law as applied to distribution and marketing, including dealer terminations and vertical restraints imposed by manufacturers and other suppliers upon their wholesale and retail distributors.[5] In 1963 the Supreme Court observed that we had acquired too little experience in judging vertical restraints—that we know "too little of the[ir] actual impact" on competition or the "economic and business stuff out of which these arrangements emerge."[6] Twenty-five years and hundreds of cases later it safely can be said that no area of antitrust jurisprudence has been exposed to more scrutiny than the relationships between suppliers and their distributors. Inexperience will no longer serve as an excuse. We continually will learn more, of course, but the body of experience

---

2   United States v. General Dynamics Corp., 415 U.S. 486 (1974).

3   Continental T.V., Inc. v. GTE Sylvania Inc., 433 U.s. 36 (1977).

4   *See* Fox & Sullivan, *Antitrust—Retrospective and Prospective: Where Are We Coming From? Where Are We Going?* 62 N.Y.U. L. Rᴇᴠ. 936, 970 n.3 (1987) [hereinafter *Retrospective*].

5   "Restraints imposed by agreement between competitors have traditionally been denominated as horizontal restraints, and those imposed by agreement between firms at different levels of distribution as vertical restraints." *Sharp*, 108 S. Ct. 1515, 1522–23 (footnote omitted).

6   White Motor Co. v. United States, 372 U.S. 253, 261, 263 (1963).

and learning available today is as much as anyone has a right to expect as an empirical basis for formulating rules of law.

Before we can begin assessing the current standards, however, it is necessary to review how we got here—observing antitrust's centennial—and where, exactly, we are. The former will be familiar to the aforementioned aficionados, but the latter may hold a few surprises.

I. The legacy of *Sylvania*

The law governing restraints on distribution has undergone a remarkable amount of kneading and pounding over the last hundred years. Following passage of the Sherman Act in 1890,[7] and even prior to that under the common law, most restraints on the distribution of goods, except for resale price maintenance, were subject to the rule of reason and were generally upheld as lawful.[8] The standards of liability began to grow stricter in the 1940's, however, starting with *United States v. Bausch & Lomb Optical Co.*[9] Then, in the early to mid 1960's, it seemed all at once that every distribution restraint had become suspect, and many were found to be illegal per se.[10] Within the space of about 10 years, the Supreme Court decided *Schwinn,*[11] *Sealy,*[12] *Parke, Davis,*[13] *Albrecht,*[14] *Simpson,*[15] *Brown*

---

7 Ch. 647, §§ 1–8, 26 Stat. 209, 209–10 (1890) (codified as amended at 15 U.S.C. §§ 1–7 (1982).

8 *E.g.,* Fowle v. Park, 131 U.S. 88 (1889); Denison Mattress Factory v. Spring-Air Co., 308 F.2d 403, 407–10 (5th Cir. 1962); Snap-On Tools Corp. v. FTC, 321 F.2d 825, 830–33 (7th Cir. 1963); Sandura Co. v. FTC, 339 F.2d 847 (6th Cir. 1964). *See* ABA ANTITRUST SECTION, VERTICAL RESTRICTIONS LIMITING INTRABRAND COMPETITION 7 n.14 (Monograph No. 2, 1977) [hereinafter ABA Monograph No. 2].

9 321 U.S. 707, 721 (1944).

10 *See* ABA Monograph No. 2, *supra* note 8, at 7–8.

11 United States v. Arnold, Schwinn & Co., 388 U.S. 365 (1967).

12 United States v. Sealy, Inc., 388 U.S. 350 (1967).

13 United States v. Parke, Davis & Co., 362 U.S. 29 (1960).

14 Albrecht v. Herald Co., 390 U.S. 145 (1968).

15 Simpson v. Union Oil Co., 377 U.S. 13 (1964).

Shoe,[16] *Fortner,*[17] *Northern Pacific*[18] and *Klors.*[19] These dramatic decisions touched off a torrent of government and private litigation, the effect of which was to strike down a broad array of distribution practices and significantly expand the range of per se illegality.[20] They also provoked intense response from the business community and academia, prompting a number of highly influential articles[21] built upon the pioneering work of Aaron Director, Lester Telser and other proponents of the Chicago school of economics.[22] The prime target was *Schwinn,*[23] which set the tone for the decade by extending the per se rule to vertical restraints on territories and customers, holding categorically that "it is unreasonable without more for a manufacturer to seek to restrict and confine areas or persons with whom an article may be traded after the manufacturer has parted with dominion over it.[24]

A swing back toward the rule of reason came abruptly, beginning with the Supreme Court's 1977 decision in *Sylvania,*[25] which overturned *Schwinn* and embraced the economic approach of the Chicago school commentators. In rapid succession, *Monsanto*[26] replaced *Parke, Davis* as the governing authority on refusals to deal (making it more difficult to infer conspiracy from communications between suppliers and dealers); *Jefferson Parish*[27] replaced *Fortner*

---

16   FTC v. Brown Shoe Co., 384 U.S. 316 (1966).

17   Fortner Enters. v. United States Steel Corp., 394 U.S. 495 (1969).; *See also* United States Steel Corp. v. Fortner Enters., 429 U.S. 610 (1977).

18   Northern Pac. Ry. v. United States, 356 U.S. 1 (1958).

19   Klor's Inc. v. Broadway-Hale Stores, Inc., 359 U.S. 207 (1959).

20   *See* ABA Monograph No. 2, *supra* note 8, at 7–8.

21   *See, e.g.*, Continental T.V., Inc. v. GTE Sylvania, Inc., 3433 U.S. 36, 48 n.13 (1977) (collecting articles).

22   Telser, *Why Should Manufacturers Want Fair Trade?* 3 J.L. & Econ. 86 (1960). [Posner article on Chicago school.]

23   United States v. Arnold, Schwinn & Co., 388 U.S. 365 (1967).

24   *Id.* at 379.

25   Continental T.V., Inc. v. GTE Sylvania Inc., 433 U.S. 36 (1977).

26   Monsanto Co. v. Spray-Rite Serv. Corp., 465 U.S. 752 (1984).

27   Jefferson Parish Hosp. Dist. No. 2 v. Hyde, 466 U.S. 2 (1984). The law of tying has continued to become more flexible since *Jefferson Parish*. Some

as the controlling precedent on tying (limiting per se illegality only to some, not all, tie-ins); and *Northwest Wholesale Stationers*[28] replaced *Klors* as the leading pronouncement on boycotts (limiting per se illegality only to boycotts designed to disadvantage competitors of the boycotters themselves). At the same time, *J. Truett Payne*[29] and *Falls City Industries*[30] narrowed the reach of the Robinson-Patman Act,[31] and *Broadcast Music*[32] and *NCAA*[33] re-defined the law on horizontal agreements. Meanwhile, important lower court decisions fenced in the consignment rule of *Simpson*,[34] narrowed the reach of *Sealy* and *Topco*,[35] and re-

---

courts have relied upon the concurring opinion of Justice O'Connor in that case, calling for application of the rule of reason to all tying cases. *See* Hand v. Central Transp., Inc., 779 F.2d 8 (6th Cir. 1985).

[28] Northwest Wholesale Stationers, Inc. v. Pacific Stationery & Printing Co., 472 U.S. 284 (1985).

[29] J. Truett Payne Co. v. Chrysler Motors Corp., 451 U.S. 557 (1981).

[30] Falls City Indus. v. Vanco Beverage, Inc., 460 U.S. 428 (1983).

[31] Ch. 592, 1, 49 Stat. 1526 (1936).

[32] Broadcast Music, Inc. v. Columbia Broadcasting Sys. Inc., 441 U.S. 1 (1979).

[33] NCAA v. Board of Regents, 468 U.S. 85, 115 n.55 (1984) (suggesting that *Sylvania* can govern certain forms of collective action).

[34] *E.g.*, Mesirow v. Pepperidge Farm, Inc., 703 F.2d 339 (9th Cir.), *cert. denied*, 464 U.S. 820 (1983); Hardwick v. Nu-Way Oil, 589 F.2d 806, 809 (5th Cir.), *cert. denied*, 444 U.S. 836 (1979); Janush v. U-Haul Co. of Detroit, 1981-1 Trade Cas. (CCH) ¶ 64,070 (E.D. Mich. 1981); Action Towing & Rental v. U-Haul International, 507 F. Supp. 987 (E.D. La. 1981); Everhart v. United Refining Co., 1980-81 Trade Cas. (CCH) ¶ 63,788 (N.D. Ohio 1980).

[35] United States v. Sealy Corp., 388 U.S. 350 (1967); United States v. Topco Assoc., 405 U.S. 596 (1972). The *Topco* rule against dealer-instigated restraints may be ready to topple, even though it was cited as good law in *Sylvania*. The *Topco* rule came in for close scrutiny in Rothery Storage & Van Co. v. Atlas Van Lines, Inc., 792 F.2d 210, 226 (D.C. Cir. 1986), *cert. denied*, 107 S. Ct. 880 (1987), where Judge Bork wrote: "[T]o the extent that *Topco* and *Sealy* stand for the proposition that all horizontal restraints are illegal per se, they must be regarded as effectively overruled [by *BMI* and *NCAA*]." This

fined the exclusive dealing standards of *Tampa Electric*[36] and *Brown Shoe*.[37]

The arrival of the Reagan administration at the Justice Department brought with it calls for further change, particularly with respect to the per se rule against resale price maintenance. These appeared in speeches[38] and in amicus briefs that the Department files in a number of significant cases.[39] Other recommendations advanced by the Department focused on general tests under which vertical restraints should be analyzed. These proposals eventually found their way into a set of Vertical Restraints Guidelines issued by the Antitrust Division in 1986.[40] The most prominent features of the Guidelines were market power "screens" exempting vertical restraints imposed on brands with only a small share of the market,[41] and a "vertical restraints index" measuring the impact of restraints based on the structure of the relevant industry.[42] There also were some general observations labeling certain restraint such as location clauses as virtually per se lawful.[43] The most controversial passage in the Guidelines, however, was the stated intention not to

---

view apparently is consistent with that of the Justice Department, which has given clearance to a variety of dealer-initiated arrangements in recent years that would have been considered highly suspect, if not per se illegal, in the past. *See, e.g.*, PPG Indus., Inc. business review letter, Dec. 22, 1986; U.S.D. Corp. business review letter, April 22, 1985.

36   Tampa Elec. Co. v. Nashville Co., 365 U.S. 320 (1961).

37   Brown Shoe Co. v. United States, 370 U.S. 294 (1962). Under *Tampa Electric* the focus had been on "quantitative substantiality," but the *Beltone* case introduced the balancing approach of *Sylvania* into exclusive dealing analysis. *See* Beltone Electronics Corp., 100 F.T.C. 68, 204, 209–10 (1982).

38   For example, in 1982, FTC Chairman Miller remarked that resale price maintenance "can be a procompetitive tool," and should not be subject to a per se standards. 42 Antitrust & Trade Reg. Rep. (BNA) 234 (Jan. 28, 1982).

39   *See, e.g.*, Monsanto Co. v. Spray-Rite Serv. Corp., 465 U.S. 752, 761–62 n.7 (1984).

40   U.S. Dep't of Justice Vertical Restraints Guidelines, 50 Fed. Reg. 6263 (1985), *reprinted in* 48 Antitrust & Trade Reg. Rep. (BNA) No. 1199 (Spec. Supp. Jan. 24, 1985) [hereinafter Vertical Restraints Guidelines].

41   Vertical Restraints Guidelines, *supra* note 40, at 4.1.

42   *Id.* at 4.1 n.25.

43   *Id.* at 2.5.

treat restraints on resale prices as per se illegal if they were coupled with nonprice restraints.[44]

More detailed descriptions of the changes wrought over the past decade appear in a number of sources,[45] and it is not the purpose here to provide more than a quick synopsis so that particular analytical doctrines that were developed during that era may be placed in context. Overall, the effect of the last 10 years has been to reverse the tide of the 1960's and to replace it with a sharply different outlook. Today, vertical restraints—other than outright resale price maintenance—are rarely viewed with disapprobation by the courts. More often it is the motivation of the challenger of such restraints that is suspect.[46] Moreover, dealers have been denied recovery to the extent that their damages turn out to be nothing but the lost fruits of "free riding" on the efforts of other dealers, without regard to whether or not the particular restraints they are challenging have anticompetitive effects.[47]

Such is the climate today that one court recently expressed the broad generalization that "a classic vertical arrangement . . . tends to promote interbrand competition by encouraging greater capital investment and advertising by the [dealer]."[48] Compare this to *Schwinn,* where little over 20 years ago the Supreme Court stated

---

[44] *Id.* at 2.3 ("[I]f a supplier adopts a bona fide distribution program embodying both nonprice and price restrictions, the Department will analyze the entire program under the rule of reason if the nonprice restraints are plausibly designed to create efficiencies and if the price restraint is merely ancillary to the nonprice restraints").

[45] *E.g., Retrospective, supra* note 4.

[46] *See* Mozart Co. v. Mercedes-Benz of North America, Inc. 833 F2d 1342, 1349–50 (9th Cir. 1987); Original Appalachian Artworks, Inc. v. Granada Electronics, Inc., 816 F.2d 68, 74 (2d Cir. 1987), *cert. denied,* 108 S. Ct. 143 (1987); Local Beauty Supply, Inc. v. Lamaur Inc., 787 F.2d 1197, 1201–03 (7th Cir. 1986).

[47] Original Appalachian Artworks, Inc. v. Granada Elecs., Inc., 816 F.2d 68 (2d Cir. 1987), *cert. denied,* 108 S. Ct. 143 (1987); Local Beauty Supply, Inc. v. Lamaur, Inc., 787 F.2d 1197, 1203 (7th Cir. 1986); Disenos Artisticos E Industriales, S.A. v. Work, 676 F. supp. 1254 (E.D.N.Y. 1987).

[48] Philadelphia Fast Foods, Inc. v. Popeyes Famous Fried Chicken, Inc., 647 F. Supp. 216, 224 (E.D. Pa.), aff'd mem., 806 F.2d 253 (3d Cir. 1986).

that territorial and customer restraints—"classic vertical arrangements" if ever there were any—"are so obviously destructive of competition that their mere existence is enough" to constitute a per se violation of the Sherman Act.[49] Times have changed to the point that by 1986, Judge Posner, writing for the Seventh Circuit, went so far as to comment: "Many thoughtful people believe that vertical restraints are as a rule beneficial to consumers and ought not be condemned lightly *or ever*."[50] There was little doubt that the Reagan Revolution in antitrust had become mainstream.

II. Other voices

Equipoise was not to be, however. Even as the Justice Department, the courts and the commentators were putting the finishing touches on the new orthodoxy, a series of events began to unfold:

1. Congress strongly criticized the Justice Department's amicus program, and cut off funding in 1983 to put an end to it.[51]

2. Congress condemned the Justice Department's Vertical Restraints Guidelines in an unusual joint resolution in 1985.[52]

3. Congress commenced hearings in April 1987 on proposed legislation to rewrite the rule of *Monsanto*, and to codify the per se rule against resale price maintenance.[53]

---

[49]   388 U.S. at 379.

[50]   Illinois Corporate Travel, Inc. v. American Airlines, Inc., 806 F.2d 722, 728 (7th Cir. 1986) (emphasis added).

[51]   *See* Departments of Commerce, Justice, and State, the Judiciary, and Related Agencies Appropriations Act, 1984, Pub. L. No. 98–166, 510, 97 Stat. 1071, 1102–03 (1983). *See also* Departments of Commerce, Justice, and State, the Judiciary, and Related Agencies Appropriations Act, 1987, Pub. L. No. 99–500, 605, 100 Stat. 1783, 1783–93 (1986); Departments of Commerce, Justice, and State, the Judiciary, and Related Agencies Appropriations Act, 1988, Pub. L. No. 100–202, 605, 101 Stat. 1329, 1329–38 (1987).

[52]   *See* Vertical Restraints Guidelines Resolution, S. Con. Res. 56, 99 Stat. 1136, 1169–70 (1985).

[53]   *See* section III(C), *infra*.

4. State attorneys general began investigating instances of resale price maintenance and other vertical restraints, and started filing complaints.[54]

5. Some courts began to reject the market power screen.[55]

6. Commentators began to point out exceptions to the Chicago school generalizations and shortcomings in its premises.[56]

7. The decline of the dollar against other currencies drove up the prices of most imported goods, creating pressure to keep retail prices in check.[57]

8. The stock market collapse of October 1987, on the heels of a series of insider trading revelations, served to undermine the public's trust in the business community.[58]

9. Macy's and Campeau vied to acquire Federated Department Stores, sparking charges that retailing was becoming too concentrated and prompting a congressional investigation.[59]

---

[54] E.g., Maryland v. Minolta Corp., 51 Antitrust & Trade Reg. Rep. (BNA) 298 (D. Md. 1986) (consent decree) (cameras) (cases also brought by New York and other states); Oregon v. White's Electronics, Inc., 50 Antitrust & Trade Reg. Rep. (BNA) 644 (Ore. Cir. Ct., 1986) (consent decree) (metal detectors); California v. Robert Bosch Corp., 48 Antitrust & Trade Reg. Rep. (BNA) 972 (Cal. Super. Ct. 1985) (consent decree) (stereo equipment); California v. Kaypro Corp., 48 Antitrust & Trade Reg. Rep. (BNA) 510 (Cal. Super. Ct. 1985) (consent decree) (computers).

[55] *See* section VI, *infra.*

[56] Comanor, *Vertical Price-Fixing, Vertical Market Restrictions, and the New Antitrust Policy,* 98 Harv. L. Rev. 983 (1985) (disputing theory that vertical restraints always add to consumer welfare; distinguishes between new customers and old customers with different demand curves); *compare* Marvel & McCafferty, *Resale Price Maintenance and Quality Certification,* 15 Rand J. Econ. 346 (1984) (quality certification); Steiner, *The Nature of Vertical Restraints,* 30 Antitrust Bull. 143 (1985); Fox, *The Modernization of Antitrust: A New Equilibrium,* 66 Cornell L. Rev. 1140, 1182 (1981).

[57] *See, e.g.,* Washington Post, Jan. 5, 1988, at C1; *N.Y. Times,* Dec. 3, 1987, at D4, col. 4.

[58] *See, e.g.,* Washington Post, Dec. 3, 1987, at C1.

[59] *See* Commonwealth v. Campeau Corp., 1988–1 Trade Cas. (CCH) ¶ 68,093 (D. Mass. 1988). *See also* City of Pittsburgh v. May Dep't Stores Co., 1986–2 Trade Cas. (CCH) ¶ 67,304 (W.D. Pa. 1986).

10. Judges—and Chicago school antitrust experts—Bork and Ginsburg each lost the opportunity to influence the Supreme Court from within.[60]

11. The Reagan administration drew to a close.

The cumulative impact of these developments has been to cast a cloud of uncertainty over antitrust. Some commentators have concluded that a "counterrevolution" is under way, and the battle lines have been drawn.[61] Predictability is in jeopardy again. In the highly charged atmosphere of Washington, both discounters and suppliers have sent armies of lobbyists trekking up and down Capitol Hill to press their case on the future of distribution law, and have sent legions of lawyers across to the Supreme Court toting green-covered amicus briefs. To assess whether anything of substance really is changing, however, it is necessary to take a closer look at the law of distribution being applied today.

In essence, four major changes in the manner in which distribution cases are analyzed under the antitrust laws have emerged from the Reagan Revolution. The first is a marked change, initiated by *Monsanto*, in the standards for finding conspiracies between suppliers and dealers to terminate other dealers and to impose vertical restraints. The second is change in the definition of the offense of per se illegal resale price maintenance, announced in *Sharp Electronics*. The third is the presumption that vertical restraints create efficiencies and combat free-rider problems in the absence of proof to the contrary, an approach that also finds support in *Sharp*. The fourth is the widespread adoption by the courts of the market power "screen" device for applying the rule of reason. Together, these four changes have resulted in dramatically different patterns of analysis, and of litigation strategy, than existed a decade ago. All are important, but the most publicized of these changes have been those concerning the conspiracy standards, making this the place to begin.

---

60   *See, e.g.*, N.Y. Times, Nov. 8, 1987, 1 (Main), p. 1.

61   *See, e.g.*, Statement of Chairman Oliver, 57 ANTITRUST L.J. 235, 241–42 (1988).

III. Trend no. 1: conspiracy

Monsanto had a profound effect on the standards for inferring both conspiracy between a supplier and a dealer to terminate another dealer, and conspiracy between a supplier and a dealer to fix resale prices or adopt other vertical restraints. Both of these changes will be discussed in the sections that follow.

A. Conspiracies to terminate dealers

The law on dealer terminations has undergone intellectual convulsions in recent years. The seminal *Colgate*[62] decision in 1919 held that absent a purpose to monopolize, the Sherman Act "does not restrict the long recognized right of trader or manufacturer . . . freely to exercise his own independent discretion as to parties with whom he will deal."[63] This freedom was severely constrained in the immediately ensuing years by the Court's decisions in *Schrader's,*[64] *Frey*[65] and *Beech-Nut,*[66] which held that although a supplier can refuse to deal with anyone, including discounters, it cannot take additional steps to bring about adherence by its dealers to fixed qresale prices.

In 1960, in the *Parke, Davis* decision,[67] the Supreme Court returned to this subject and ruled that when a supplier goes "beyond mere announcement of his policy and the simple refusal to deal, and he employs other means which effect adherence to his resale prices . . . he has put together a combination in violation of the Sherman

---

[62] United States v. Colgate Co., 250 U.S. 300 (1919).

[63] 250 U.S. at 307.

[64] United States v. A. Schrader's Son, Inc., 252 U.S. 85 (1920).

[65] Frey & Son, Inc. v. Cudahy Packing Co., 256 U.S. 208 (1921).

[66] FTC v. Beech-Nut Packing Co., 257 U.S. 441 (1922).

[67] United States v. Parke, Davis & Co., 362 U.S. 29 (1960).

Act."[68] The Court held that if a supplier is "unwilling to rely on . . . voluntary acquiescence . . . , and takes affirmative action to achieve uniform adherence . . . , the customers' acquiescence is not then a matter of individual free choice. . . ."[69]

Subsequently, in a line of cases culminating in the Third Circuit's decision in *Cernuto*,[70] the lower courts held that termination of one dealer at the behest of another dealer was per se illegal because it had "horizontal effects," even if it was not, strictly speaking, a horizontal agreement. Other cases, most notably the circuit court opinion in *Monsanto*,[71] held that if a complaint from another dealer *preceded* the termination chronologically, it properly could be inferred by the trier of fact that the termination was at the complaining dealer's behest and therefore the product of a conspiracy.

The Supreme Court overturned this approach in its own decision in *Monsanto*,[72] ruling that an agreement to terminate a dealer may not be inferred simply from the fact that the manufacturer received complaints from other dealers prior to the termination. Under the Supreme Court's standard, "there must be evidence that *tends to exclude the possibility* that the manufacturer and non-terminated distributors were acting independently."[73] The Court explained that "distributors are an important source of information for manufacturers," and that "[a] manufacturer and its distributors have legitimate reasons to exchange information about the prices and the reception of their products in the market."[74] The Court observed that if an inference of conspiracy could be drawn from "highly ambiguous evidence"—like the fact that a complaint preceded the

---

68   362 U.S. at 44.

69   *Id.* at 46–47.

70   Cernuto, Inc. v. United Cabinet Corp., 595 F.2d 164 (3d Cir. 1979).

71   Spray-Rite Service Corp. v. Monsanto Co., 684 F.2d 1226 (7th Cir. 1982).

72   Monsanto Co. v. Spray-Rite Service Corp., 465 U.S. 752 (1984).

73   465 U.S. at 764 (emphasis added).

74   *Id.* at 762, 763.

termination—this important exchange of information would be chilled, and the doctrines of *Sylvania* and *Colgate* would be eroded.[75]

Monsanto was interpreted by the lower courts to raise by several notches the standard for proving agreements between suppliers and dealers to terminate other dealers, even though in *Monsanto* itself the Supreme Court found that sufficient evidence of conspiracy had been presented to support liability and a $10.5 million judgment. Indeed, most of the subsequent cases applying *Monsanto* have granted summary judgment to the defendants, ruling that no conspiracy could be inferred once the supplier has advanced legitimate reasons for effecting the termination.[76] The case that attracted

---

[75] *Id.* at 763.

[76] Illinois Corporate Travel, Inc. v. American Airlines Inc., 806 F.2d (7th Cir. 1986) denial of plaintiff's motion for preliminary injunction aff'd) (court rejected plaintiff's theory that airline refused to deal with it in order to protect other discounters); Garment District, Inc. v. Belk Stores Services, Inc., 799 F.2d 905 (4th Cir. 1986) (directed verdict for defendants aff'd) (supplier permitted to refuse to deal with one dealer to avoid being dropped by a larger, complaining dealer; no price-fixing conspiracy proved), *cert. denied*, 107 S. Ct. 1728 (1988); McCabe's Furniture, Inc. v. La-Z-Boy Chair Co., 798 F.2d 212 (8th Cir. 1986) (judgment for plaintiff after jury verdict rev'd) (no unambiguous evidence of price-fixing conspiracy although there was sufficient evidence of conspiracy; plaintiff had proceeded on per se theory only), *cert. denied*, 108 S. Ct. 1728 (1988); Morrison v. Murray Biscuit Co., 797 F.2d 1430 (7th Cir. 1986) (judgment for defendant after bench trial on documents) (no proof that termination was pursuant to price-fixing conspiracy where complaining broker did not set his own prices and had been granted exclusive right to serve customer in dispute); Pink Supply Corp. v. Hiebert, Inc., 788 F.2d (8th Cir. 1986) (summary judgment for defendants aff'd) (no admissible evidence of agreement); Pumps and Power Co. v. southern States Industries, Inc., 787 F.2d 1252 (8th Cir. 1986) (judgment for plaintiff after jury trial rev'd) (failure of proof that manufacturer and distributor conspired to refuse to supply customer with components for assemblies that all three sold in competition with one another); Business Electronics Corp. v. Sharp Electronics Corp., 780 F.2d 1212 (5th Cir. 1986) (plaintiff must prove a resale price maintenance agreement between supplier and another distributor for the per se rule to apply; per se instruction held erroneous) (judgment for plaintiff after jury trial rev'd), *aff'd*, 108 S. Ct. 1515 (1988); National Marine Electronic Distributors, Inc. v. Raytheon Co., 778 F.2d 190 (4th Cir. 1985) (directed verdict for defendant aff'd) (mail order dealer termination; conspiracy could not be inferred); Burlington Coat Factory

the most attention has been *Garment District, Inc. v. Belk Stores Services, Inc.,*[77] in which the Fourth Circuit Court of Appeals held that no conspiracy could be inferred where the supplier showed that it had refused to deal with a discounting dealer in order to avoid

---

Warehouse Corp. v. Esprit De Corp., 769 F.2d 919 (2d Cir. 1985) (summary judgment for defendants aff'd) (retailer's speech to 600 other retailers insufficient to prove conspiracy with supplier); Terry's Floor Fashions, Inc. v. Burlington Industries, Inc., 763 F.2d 604 (4th Cir. 1985) (summary judgment for defendants aff'd) (carpet transshipper terminated; no evidence excluding the possibility of independent action); Landmark Development Corp. v. Chambers Corp., 752 F.2d 369 (9th Cir. 1985) (summary judgment for defendant aff'd) (defendant demonstrated legitimate business motives); Magid Manufacturing Co. v. U.S.D. Corp., 654 F. Supp. 325 (N.D. Ill. 1987) (defendant's motion for summary judgment granted) (plaintiff, a nationwide distributor, did not fit into supplier's new territorial plan); Proctor v. General Conference of Seventh-Day Adventists, 651 F. Supp. 1505 (N.D. Ill. 1986) (judgment for defendants after bench trial) (no conspiracy proven); Philadelphia Fast Foods, Inc. v. Popeyes Famous Fried Chicken, Inc., 647 F. Supp. 216 (E.D. Pa. 1986) (plaintiff's motion for j.n.o.v. denied) (no evidence of competition among licensees; conspiracy not proven); Cutters Exchange, Inc. v. Durkoppwerke GmbH, 1986–1 Trade Cas. (CCH) ¶ 67,039 (M.D. Tenn. 1986) (defendants' motion to dismiss granted) (supplier took over its own distribution; no proof of conspiracy; section 2 claims not dismissed); Empire Volkswagen, Inc. v. World-Wide Volkswagen Corp., 627 F. Supp. 1202 (S.D.N.Y. 1986) (defendant's motion for summary judgment granted) ("A plaintiff must . . . prove that the manufacturer sought the retailer's agreement to maintain prices, and that the retailer communicated its agreement to do so to the manufacturer"), aff'd, 814 F.2d 90 (2d Cir. 1987); Computer Connection, Inc. v. Apple Computer Corp., 621 F. Supp. 569 (E.D. La. 1985) (defendants' motion for summary judgment granted) (valid business reasons for termination shown; unauthorized sales of "Lisa" units; plus sworn denials of conspiracy); C.E.D. Mobilephone Communications, Inc. v. Harris Corp., 1985–1 Trade Cas. (CCH) ¶ 66,386 (S.D.N.Y. 1985) (defendant's motion for summary judgment granted) (no effect on relevant market proved); Gilchrist Machinery Co. v. Komatsu America Corp., 601 F. Supp. 1192 (S.D. Miss. 1984) (plaintiff's motion for preliminary injunction denied) (plausible business explanations offered; conspiracy would not be inferred). *See also* Hennessy Industries Inc. v. Solar Industries, Inc., 779 F.2d 402 (7th Cir. 1985) (defendants' motion to dismiss granted) (patent licensee convinced licenser not to continue licensing competing licensee except at higher fee; interbrand competition eliminated; but no per se offense; no injury to competition was alleged).

77   799 F.2d 905 (4th Cir. 1986), *cert. denied*, 108 S. Ct. 1728 (1988).

being dropped by a much larger dealer that had complained about the discounter. As the court put it, the supplier merely "sought to retain many dealers by sacrificing one."[78]

Garment District at first was dismissed by some observers as a sport, but other courts soon followed suit. In *The Jeanery, Inc. v. James Jeans, Inc.*,[79] a major full price dealer, JJ's, complained about price cutting by a discounter, The Jeanery. A representative of the supplier, James Jeans, promised to "take care of things," and The Jeanery eventually was terminated. A jury awarded damages, but the district court granted judgment n.o.v. and the Ninth Circuit affirmed upon the following analysis:

The Jeanery's evidence consists of (1) competitor's complaints about The Jeanery's persistent price cutting; (2) a strongly phrased complaint by JJ's, a major customer of James Jeans', coupled with James Jeans' statement that it would "take care of things"; (3) allegedly coercive tactics used by James Jeans to enforce adherence to its pricing policy; and (4) the alleged absence of a plausible business justification for James Jeans' decision to terminate The Jeanery. Taken as a whole, *this evidence is insufficiently probative of a conspiracy to permit the case to go to a jury.*[80]

The court held that, taken together, this evidence showed "nothing more than an effort by a manufacturer to calm an angry customer," and did not "tend to prove an agreement to terminate a retailer who had failed to follow the alleged resale price maintenance scheme."[81]

Likewise, in *Parkway Gallery Furniture, Inc. v. Kittinger/Pennsylvania House Group, Inc,*[82] the district court granted summary judgment to a supplier who had terminated two dealers following

---

78 799 F.2d at 910.

79 849 F.2d at 1148 (9th Cir. 1988).

80 849 F.2d at 1157.

81 *Id.* at 1158.

82 1988–1 Trade Cas. (CCH) ¶ 67,970 (M.D.N.C. 1988), *aff'd,* 878 F.2d 801 (4th Cir. 1989).

complaints from other dealers that the two had violated a policy against mail and telephone solicitation of customers in other marketing areas. Borrowing a phrase from *Garment District* the court held that the supplier "merely sought to retain many dealers by sacrificing [two dealers], if necessary, because of non-compliance with [the solicitation restriction]."[83] Similarly, in *McCabe's Furniture, Inc. v. La-Z-Boy Chair Co.,*[84] *Winn v. Edna Hibel Corp.*[85] and several other cases,[86] courts refused to find conspiracies to terminate where the evidence showed that the supplier had terminated a discounter in order to placate a complaining dealer.

And in *Westman Commission Co. v. Hobart International, Inc.,*[87] a case that began in the *Schwinn* era and continued through the Reagan era, the Tenth Circuit held that a so-called limited distributorship is as legitimate an arrangement as an exclusive distributorship, so that if one of several dealers in an area asks its supplier to terminate another dealer in order to create a "limited," though not exclusive, distributorship in the area, this should not be per se illegal.[88] Previously, it had been recognized in such cases as *Packard*[89] and *Oreck*[90] that a request by one dealer to eliminate all

---

83   1988–1 Trade Cas. (CCH) ¶ 67,970 at 57,943.

84   798 F.2d 323 (8th Cir. 1986), *cert. denied*, 108 S. Ct. 1728 (1988).

85   1988–2 Trade Cas. (CCH) ¶ 68,300 (11th Cir. 1988).

86   National Marine Electronic Distributors, Inc. v. Raytheon Co., 778 F.2d 190 (4th Cir. 1985); Dunnivant v. Bi-State Auto Parts, 851 F.2d 1575 (11th Cir. 1988); The Sample, Inc. v. Pendleton Woolen Mills, Inc., 1989–1 Trade Case. (CCH) ¶ 68,405 (S.D.N.Y. 1989).

87   796 F.2d 1216 (10th Cir. 1986), *cert. denied*, 107 S. Ct. 1728 (1988).

88   796 F.2d at 1229. Lomar Wholesale Grocery, Inc. v. Dieter's Gourmet Foods, Inc., 627 F. Supp. 105 (S.D. Iowa 1985) (defendant's motion for summary judgment granted) ("de facto" exclusive distributorship; also, not enough proof to infer conspiracy to fix prices), *aff'd,* 824 F.2d 582 (8th Cir. 1987), *cert. denied*, 107 S. Ct. 707 (1988).

89   Packard Motor Car Co. v. Webster Motor Car Co., 243 F.2d 418 (D.C. Cir.) *cert. denied*, 355 U.S. 822 (1957).

90   Oreck Corp. v. Whirlpool Corp., 579 F.2d 126 (2d Cir.) (en banc), *cert. denied*, 439 U.S. 946 (1978). *Accord*, Crane & Shovel Sales Corp. v. Bucyrus-Erie Co., 1988–2 Trade Cas. (CCH) ¶ 68,166 (6th Cir. 1988).

other dealers in the area in order to create an exclusive distributorship normally would be legal; but no recent decision explicitly had held that a request by one dealer to terminate another dealer *without* creating an exclusive dealership, and for no reason other than reducing the number of dealers competing in the area, would be legal. The Tenth Circuit, however, observed that "[r]esponding to the possibility of the loss of an existing distributor's loyalty is analytically no different from ensuring distributor loyalty in advance by the granting of an exclusive distributorship."[91]

The effect of these decisions was to move the law beyond *Monsanto* by holding that not only is "something more" than evidence of complaints preceding termination necessary in order to prove an agreement, but the "something more" must go beyond evidence that the supplier carried out the termination for the specific purpose of satisfying the complaining dealer, who was threatening to drop the line. At the same time, it must be noted that other courts have held that this kind of evidence *can* be sufficient to raise the inference of conspiracy.[92] These divergent lines of cases have made this an area of persisting uncertainty, and that uncertainty will be explored in greater detail later.

B. Combinations and conspiracies to impose vertical restraints

Monsanto's reworking of the law of conspiracy was not confined to the standard of proof of an agreement to terminate a dealer. The Court went on to hold that to prove a price-fixing conspiracy (or, presumably, a conspiracy to adopt any other vertical restraint) within a distribution network, a plaintiff must offer more than merely "a showing that the distributor conformed" to the supplier's suggestions.[93] There must be (1) proof that the manufacturer (or other supplier) sought "acquiescence or agreement" from the dis-

---

91   796 F.2d at 1229.

92   *See* section VII(A), *infra.*

93   465 U.S. at 764 n.9.

tributor,[94] and (2) proof that the distributor "communicated" its acquiescence or agreement to the manufacturer.[95] In the Court's words: "[E]vidence must be presented both that the distributor communicated its acquiescence or agreement, and that this was sought by the manufacturer."[96]

There was no precedent cited for this proposition, which seemed to narrow the definition of a "combination or conspiracy" to maintain resale prices or adopt other vertical restraints. Previously, the law on proving such conspiracies had followed a progression from *Colgate* through *Parke, Davis*. This line of cases, together with some language from *Simpson*,[97] *Schwinn*,[98] and *Albrecht*,[99] had been relied on as authority in a series of lower court decisions holding that evidence of "coercion" of dealers by a supplier, either by terminations or threats of termination, could be enough to establish conspiracy even without any "communicated" acquiescence or agreement.[100]

---

94   Id.

95   Id.

96   Id.

97   Simpson v. Union Oil Co., 277 U.S. 13, 17 (1964) ("We made clear in [*Parke, Davis*] that a supplier may not use coercion on its retail outlets to achieve resale price maintenance. We reiterate that view, adding that it matters not what the coercive device is. [*Colgate*], at explained in [*Parke, Davis*], was a case where there was assumed to be no agreement to maintain retail prices.").

98   United States v. Arnold, Schwinn & Co., 388 U.S. 365, 372 (1967) ("Schwinn has been 'firm and resolute' in insisting upon observance of territorial and customer limitations by its bicycle distributors and upon confining sales by franchised retailers to consumers, and that Schwinn's 'firmness' in these respects was grounded upon the communicated danger of termination").

99   Albrecht v. Herald Co., 390 U.S. 145, 149 (1968) ("[In *Parke, Davis* it was] held that an illegal combination to fix prices results if a seller suggest[s] resale prices and secures compliance by means in addition to the 'mere announcement of his policy and the simple refusal to deal. . . .' ").

100   *See generally* ABA, REFUSALS TO DEAL AND EXCLUSIVE DISTRIBUTORSHIPS 14–20 (Monograph No. 9, 1983); Russell Stover Candies, Inc., 100 F.T.C. 1,

In *Monsanto*, however, the Court seemed to close the door on the "coercion" theory, stating: "Under *Colgate*, the manufacturer can announce its resale prices in advance and refuse to deal with those who fail to comply. And a distributor is free to acquiesce in the manufacturer's demand in order to avoid termination."[101] By requiring "communicated" acquiescence or agreement on the part of the distributors, the Court rejected the more expansive interpretations lower courts had given to *Parke, Davis* and *Albrecht* in the "coercion" cases, which required only acquiescence itself, without any communication.[102]

With the decline of the coercion theory, suppliers began to enjoy greater latitude in influencing resale prices. Even before *Monsanto*, a supplier could suggest resale prices without creating any agreement or combination. Similarly, it could refuse to take on new dealers who it anticipated would not adhere to its suggested prices. It probably could announce to its existing dealers in advance that it intended to terminate any dealer who did not follow those prices—although there was disagreement on this point.[103] And, it could actually terminate dealers if their prices did not conform. Since *Monsanto*, it has been clarified that a supplier may demand acquiescence from its dealers in maintaining specific retail prices. None of these actions will result in a "meeting of the minds" or "a common scheme," even though prior to *Monsanto* demands for acquiescence might have provided sufficient evidence of "coercion" to make out a combination or conspiracy.

34–35 (1982), *rev'd*, 718 F.2d 256 (8th Cir. 1983); Yentsch v. Texaco, Inc., 630 F.2d 46, 53 (2d Cir. 1980); Russell Stover was vacated by the Eighth Circuit, but *Yentsch* remained on the books, and was subsequently cited by Judge Posner. *See* Roland Mach. Co. v. Dresser Indus., 740 F.2d 380, 393 (7th Cir. 1984); Jack Walters & Sons Corp. v. Morton Bldg., Inc., 737 F.2d 698, 707 (7th Cir.), *cert. denied*, 469 U.S. 1018 (1984).

101   465 U.S. at 761.

102   *But see* Black Gold, Ltd. v. Rockwool Indus., Inc., 732 F.2d 779, 780 (10th Cir.) ("we do not construe *Monsanto* as a retreat from those cases holding that a combination occurs between a seller and buyers 'whose acquiescence in [the seller's] firmly enforced restraints was induced by "the communicated danger of termination." ' "), *cert. denied*, 491 U.S. 854 (1984).

The dealer, for its part, may "acquiesce in the manufacturer's demand" and "[conform] to the suggested price" under *Monsanto* without creating any agreement.[104] But it may not "communicate" its acquiescence to the supplier. This is where *Monsanto* drew the line between unitary action and a meeting of the minds.

Lower courts have applied this formulation since *Monsanto* in a number of cases to determine whether there has been any agreement to adopt vertical restraints. In *The Jeanery,*[105] for example, described in the previous section, there was evidence that the supplier actually had threatened to withhold shipments from discounters who did not adhere to "keystone pricing"—*i.e.*, a 100% markup. As one dealer testified about the supplier's admonition regarding discounting: "what was said to me was, 'Orders could be lost, could be shipped to the wrong destination, or just never processes.' "[106] This did not persuade the court:

> Certainly . . . a manufacturer may advise a dealer that its policy is to terminate a dealer who does not sell at keystone, or to favor filling orders placed by complying dealers. This is *legitimate pressure* to get a dealer to sell at keystone. No inference of antitrust conspiracy can be drawn from such evidence.[107]

The court concluded that this evidence fell "far short of establishing an agreement to fix prices between the manufacturer and the complaining retailer," and that "regardless of [the supplier's] conduct, to establish an agreement it takes two to tango."[108]

The dissent in *The Jeanery* drew parallels between the evidence of a price-fixing agreement and the evidence found sufficient to

---

103   *See* Russell Stover Candies, Inc., 100 F.T.C. 1 (1982), *rev'd* 718 F.2d 256 (8th Cir. 1983).

104   *Monsanto*, 465 U.S. at 764 n.9.

105   The Jeanery, Inc. v. James Jeans, Inc., 849 F.2d 1148 (9th Cir. 1988).

106   849 F.2d at 1159.

107   *Id.* (emphasis added).

108   *Id.* at 1160.

prove such an agreement in *Monsanto* itself.[109] The dissent pointed out that the evidence of a conspiracy between the supplier and the complaining dealer, JJ's, to terminate The Jeanery was "at least compelling circumstantial evidence of the existence of an underlying arrangement to maintain resale prices. . . ."[110] JJ's specific complaint had been that "we've got a guy right across from me that's selling your product for $5.50 off all the time," strongly suggesting that JJ's and the supplier both understood that JJ's had been adhering to keystone pricing, according to the dissent. The majority replied that in *Monsanto* there had been evidence that the supplier had pressured a dealer into charging the fixed price, while neither The Jeanery nor JJ's had ever agreed to James Jeans' retail pricing scheme.[111] In the course of its discussion, the majority recognized the "coercion" theory, but held that it actually required "demands or threats," as distinguished from "mere exposition, persuasion, argument or pressure."[112] The court specifically held that threats to delay shipments to discounters fall only into the category of "legitimate pressure."[113]

In *Parkway Gallery*,[114] the district court similarly recognized that the coercion theory exists, but took the position that it requires a court to find "that the defendant *coerced* the plaintiff's adherence to a policy *by seeking and obtaining assurances of compliance*."[115]

---

[109]   *Id.* at 1163–64.

[110]   *Id.* at 1164.

[111]   *Id.* at 1160.

[112]   *Id.* at 1158.

[113]   *Id.* at 1159.

[114]   Parkway Gallery Furniture, Inc. v. Kittinger/Pennsylvania House Group, Inc., 1988–1 Trade Cas. (CCH) ¶ 67,970 (M.D.N.C. 1988), *aff'd,* 828 F.2e 801 (4th Cir. 1989).

[115]   *Id.* at 57,945 (first emphasis in original; second emphasis added). *See also* Isaksen v. Vermont Castings, Inc., 825 F.2d 1158, 1163 (7th Cir. 1987) ("The fact that [a dealer] may have been coerced into agreeing is of no moment; an agreement procured by threats is still an agreement for purposes of section 1."), *cert. denied,* 107 S. Ct. 1728 (1988); Beer Wholesalers, Inc. v. Miller Brewing Co., 426 N.W. 2d 438, 443 (Minn. Ct. App. 1988) ("Evidence that a distributor changed its prices in response to coercion may meet [the *Monsanto*] standard.").

This, in effect, modifies the coercion theory by engrafting onto it *Monsanto*'s requirement of "communicated" acquiescence. Other cases likewise have held that mere acquiescence to coercion is not enough to prove a legally cognizable agreement.[116]

The result of these cases has been to elevate evidence of "communication" of acquiescence or agreement to a restraint to a critical position in any vertical case. Without it, a plaintiff will be hard pressed to fashion a cause of action that will meet the *Monsanto* test. Whether the coercion theory is dead or simply modified beyond recognition, the fact remains that coercion without some "communicated acquiescence" will not prove an agreement.

C. Proposed legislation

Reaction to *Monsanto* in Congress came swiftly. In 1986, Representative Seiberling introduced a bill in the House to undo the changes that *Monsanto* had set into motion.[117] The bill never was

---

116   *See* International Logistics Group, Ltd. v. Chrysler Corp., 1989–2 Trade Cas. (CCH) ¶ 68,744 at 61,908 (6th Cir. 1989) ("Current legal precedent supports the conclusion that a conspiracy may not evolve under circumstances where a dealer or distributor involuntarily complies to avoid termination of his product source"); Link v. Mercedes-Benz of North America, Inc., 788 F.2d 918, 924–26 (3d Cir. 1986) (no error where court refused to instruct jury that mere acquiescence by dealer to manufacturer's price guide constituted illegal price fixing); Curry v. Steve's Franchise Co., 1985–2 Trade Cas. (CCH) ¶ 66,877, at pp. 64,368 (D. Mass. 1985) (plaintiff's inaction in the face of personal visit from defendant's agent at which time agent physically changed plaintiff's posted prices was insufficient basis from which to infer agreement); *cf.* Sorisio v. Lenox, Inc., 1989–1 Trade Cas. (CCH) ¶ 68,502 (2d Cir. 1988), *aff'd* 1989–1 Trade Cas. (CCH) ¶ 68,503, at 60,764 (D. Conn. 1988) (coercion theory rejected where plaintiff failed to prove compliance; "[a]bsent evidence of some agreement, actual compliance is crucial to an inference of a combination"); Purity Products, Inc. v. Tropicana Products, Inc., 1989–1 Trade Cas. (CCH) ¶ 68,420 (D. Md. 1988) (evidence of surveillance insufficient to prove conspiracy).

117   H.R. 5293, 99th Cong., 2d Sess. (1986).

reported out of committee, but in the next Congress, Representatives Rodino and Hyde introduced a successor "Monsanto Bill."[118] Their bill would have permitted a resale price maintenance conspiracy to be inferred from evidence that (1) a supplier "received . . . a communication regarding price competition" from one of its dealers, and (2) "in response to" that communication terminated or refused to supply another dealer.[119] The bill explicitly limited the meaning of the phrase "in response to," specifying that a termination or refusal to supply should be considered "in response to" a communication only "if such communication is a *substantial contributing cause* of such termination or refusal to supply."[120]

At the same time, Senators Metzenbaum, Rudman, Simon and Bradley introduced a similar bill in the Senate.[121] Hearings were conducted in both Houses, with testimony presented by representatives of discounters and of suppliers.[122] Testimony also was submitted by the Department of Justice, which maintained that the legislation was unnecessary.[123]

Prior to the House vote, a report was released to accompany the House bill which capsulized many of the criticisms that had been leveled at *Monsanto*.[124] The report took issue with both of the es-

---

[118] H.R. 585, 100th Cong., 1st Sess. (1987) (the "Freedom From Vertical Price Fixing Act").

[119] *Id.* at 2(a).

[120] *Id.* (emphasis added).

[121] S. 430, 100th Cong., 1st Sess. (1987) (the "Retail Competition Enforcement Act").

[122] *See Retail Competition Enforcement Act: Hearings on S. 430 Before the Comm. on the Judiciary,* 100th Cong., 1st Sess., 100–436 (1987) [hereinafter *S. 430 Hearings*]. On April 2, 1987, the House conducted hearings on the portion of H.R. 585 dealing with the proper evidentiary standards to be applied in dealer termination cases. The transcripts of these hearings have not yet been published, but copies of the witnesses' prepared statements are available from the House Subcommittee on Monopolies and Commercial Law. Copies also are on file with the author.

[123] *See S. 430 Hearings, supra* note 122, at 159–88.

[124] H.R. Rep. No. 100–421, 100th Cong., 1st Sess. (1987) [hereinafter *H.R. 585 Report*].

sential holdings of *Monsanto*, including the holding that in order to prove a conspiracy between a supplier and a dealer to cut off another dealer, "something more" than evidence of prior complaints by the first dealer is required—specifically, that there must be evidence "that tends to exclude the possibility that the manufacturer and nonterminated distributor were acting independently."

The report observed that this requirement imposes a "double-barrel" burden upon plaintiffs that does not exist in other kinds of antitrust cases:

> Not only must a plaintiff seeking to reach the jury *prove* a conspiracy, but he also must *disprove* the existence of any or all hypothetical explanations for the manufacturer's conduct that "might justify a dealer termination." To many observers, such a test appears to be unnecessary and unfairly harsh.[125]

The report took the position that under "accepted law," a plaintiff need not introduce evidence "excluding all possible circumstances that would defeat liability, provided that the evidence that is produced is sufficient to permit a reasonable reference [sic] supporting liability."[126] The report continued:

---

[125]   *Id.* at 14 (emphasis in original). The same language appears in the 1990 Report, H.R. Rep. No. 101–438, 101th Cong., 2d Sess. at 14 (1990). The *H.R. 585 Report* was just as hard on lower court decisions which have sought to apply this holding: "In the Ninth Circuit, and at least one decision in the Southern District of New York, the rule now appears to be that proof of a legitimate reason for termination will justify entry of summary judgment or a directed verdict against a terminated dealer unless the plaintiff comes forward with 'strongly persuasive' evidence of conspiracy running counter to the alleged conspirators' economic self-interest." *Id.* at 22–23. The *H.R. 585 Report* complained that the phrasing of this test implies that even if there is a genuine issue of material fact regarding conspiracy, defendant may still be granted summary judgment "if the plaintiff is not 'strongly persuasive.' " *Id.* at 23.

The *H.R. 585 Report* may have been too hasty in remarking that this burden does not exist in other kinds of antitrust cases, as *Monsanto*'s "exclude the possibility" requirement has begun to appear in antitrust conspiracy cases of all kinds, including cases that do not involve dealer terminations.

[126]   *Id.* at 17 (citing Lavendar v. Kurn, 327 U.S. 645, 652–53 (1946).

The Court's result would not have been disturbing if it were limited to the conclusion that evidence of a termination *following* price-related complaints by other distributors is not, standing alone, necessarily sufficient to create a jury inference of conspiracy. That view generally prevailed in the courts of appeal prior to *Monsanto*. The Court's additional statement that even evidence that a termination was "in response to" such complaints is not sufficient to go to the jury, however, rests on much weaker ground. Most appellate courts considering the latter question prior to *Monsanto* had difficulty in finding sufficiency.[127]

The standard proposed in the House bill would have required a plaintiff opposing a summary judgment motion to show that a supplier had received a complaint from a dealer, and "in response to" that complaint had terminated a rival dealer.[128] The House Report explained that the phrase "in response to" was not meant to cover "situations where a termination was simply subsequent in time" to a complaint, but rather "instances where the termination was *causally related*" to the complaint.[129] The Senate used the term "because of" rather than "in response to" in its bill, but the intent appears to have been the same—as the Senate Report explained, "the price commu-

---

[127] *Id.* at 18 (emphasis in original). The *H.R. 585 Report* added that the *Monsanto* approach "stands in stark contrast to other areas of the law" such as Title VII employment discrimination actions. In those cases, according to the *H.R. 585 Report,* proof that a plaintiff was qualified but rejected for a position, while the employer continued to seek applicants with similar qualifications, is sufficient to go to a jury, and actually mandates an inference of discrimination, even though it does not preclude the possibility of finding that plaintiff was rejected for nondiscriminatory reasons. *Id.* at 17–18 n.61.

[128] *Id.* at 26.

[129] *Id.* at 27 (emphasis in original). The *H.R. 585 Report* added: "The phrase 'in response to' was thus designed to connote the requisite 'but for' causation needed to demonstrate that a termination or refusal to supply was the result of a price complaint, and was not simply the result of independent action by the supplier. Beyond this causative formula, the elusive 'something more' factor, alluded to in *Monsanto*, was not needed, since causation already implies that 'something more' is involved than a mere in-time sequence of unconnected events." Id.

nication [would have to have been] a 'major contributing cause' of the termination or refusal to supply."[130]

The House Report also took issue with *Monsanto*'s other essential holding, that to prove a vertical conspiracy to fix prices (or to adopt other vertical restraints) there must be evidence "both that the distributor communicated its acquiescence or agreement, and that this was sought by the manufacturer." The report commented that "[a]lthough the Court did not define its terms, the remark suggests that something akin to a formal offer and acceptance is necessary."[131]

The report was highly critical of this "communication" requirement, observing that it served to "increase the plaintiff's burden establishing a conspiracy," making it impossible for a dealer to prove unlawful combination by showing that he or other dealers had been coerced into compliance with the restraint.[132] The report favored dropping the communication requirement and returning to the former coercion test, pointing out that "[p]recedent for allowing compliance by dealers to establish that a tacit agreement exists" can be found in the Supreme Court's decision in *Perma Life*.[133]

The minority views submitted with the Senate Report disputed the assessment that *Monsanto* had created confusion, and asserted

---

130   S. Rep. No. 100–280, 100th Cong., 2d Sess. 11 (1988) [hereinafter *S. 430 Report*].

131   *H.R. 585 Report, supra* note 124, at 16. *See also* H.R. Rep. No. 101–438, 101st Cong., 2d Sess. at 16 (1980) (same language).

132   The *H.R. 585 Report* stated: "The underlying rationale behind this [communication] requirement is not immediately apparent. Certainly, the 'contract, combination . . . or conspiracy' language of the Sherman Act does not dictate this result. The Court would not have strained common usage or precedent if it had found instead that a manufacturer's refusal to deal with a distributor, or its threat of such action resulting in a distributor's compliance with announced policy, constituted concerted action. Similarly, economic analysis cannot explain this result because there is no difference in economic effect between a distributor's compliance and his entering into a formal agreement." *H.R. 585 Report, supra* note 124, at 16.

133   *Id.* at 17 n.59.

that even if some confusion had resulted, "the more appropriate way to correct the situation is through the judicial process."[134] The minority report dismissed the contention that *Monsanto* had threatened the very existence of discounters, noting that "[t]he discount trade industry is flourishing, even after the *Monsanto* decision in 1984." It cited a report that in 1987 "there were some 57 publicly traded discount companies, including K-Mart, Wal-Mart, Federated Department Stores, and Burlington coat."[135] The minority concluded that legislation was entirely unnecessary.

The House bill was passed on November 9, 1987, but the Senate bill was not brought to a vote in the 100th Congress. In the 101st Congress, however, new versions of both bills were soon introduced—H.R. 1236 and S. 865—and more hearings were held.

The new Senate bill added a proviso specifying that the request, demand or threat made by the complaining dealer must be "the major contributing cause" of the termination or refusal to supply. This was changed to "the major cause," however, to make clear that where there are multiple causes for the termination, the demand or threat need not have been the sole cause but must have been the major cause.'[136] The House bill continued to use the phrase "a substantial contributing cause" indicating that a court would not be required to find "that the price communication was the sole, primary, or even at least 50 percent of the cause of the termination."[137]

New reports were issued by both the Senate[138] and the House,[139] although much of the commentary was borrowed from the earlier

---

134   *S. 430 Report, supra* note 130, at 15.

135   *Id.* at 16–17.

136   S. Rep. No. 101–251, 101st Cong., 2d Sess. at 13 (1990).

137   H.R. Rep. No. 101–438, 101st Cong., 2d Sess. at 34 (1990). The dissenters recommended that a "but for" test, like that in the Senate bill, be substituted. *Id.* at 44.

138   S. Rep., *supra* note 136.

139   H.R. Rep. *supra* note 137.

reports. The new material focused largely on the *Sharp* case, which had been decided after the previous reports were issued. The House Report, like the earlier House Report, also included a detailed account of the history of distribution, beginning with *Dr. Miles*.[140]

On April 18, 1990, the House approved the bill by a vote of 235 to 157, giving the opponents sufficient votes to sustain a presidential veto. The Senate bill was voted out of the Senate Judiciary committee on February 22, 1990 by a vote of 7 to 6, but at this writing that bill has not been brought to the floor for a vote of the full Senate. As before, both bills were opposed by the Justice Department.

Puzzled? The debate on conspiracy standards leaves the law polarized, with the proposed legislation and strongly worded reports from Congress, juxtaposed against *Monsanto* and the post-*Monsanto* decisions in the lower courts. This has made for ample uncertainty, plenty of tension and no clear guideposts as to where the line between conspiracy and unilateral activity is to be drawn. With the search for certainty proceeding in two different directions at once, it is no wonder that it has not been found. But solutions are addressed at the end of this article; first, the remaining megatrends will be examined, beginning with changes in the law of resale price maintenance.

IV. Trend no. 2: resale price maintenance

The law on resale price maintenance has undergone considerable expansion followed by considerable erosion over the years. For example, the fixing of *maximum* resale prices was ruled per se illegal by the Supreme Court at the height of the *Schwinn* era in *Albrecht*,[141] but courts today almost always find a way to avoid finding illegality in these cases. Each court has discovered its own rationale for refusing to impose liability, holding that there was

---

140   *Id.* at 7–10.

141   Albrecht v. Herald Co., 390 U.S. 145 (1968).

insufficient proof of causation, or of agreement, or of injury.[142] This approach is likely to be encouraged further by the Supreme Court's recent decision in *Atlantic Richfield Co. v. USA Petroleum Co.*[143] There, the Court did not reach the question whether maximum resale price maintenance should remain per se unlawful, but included this rather tentative footnote: "We assume, *arguendo*, that *Albrecht* correctly held that vertical, maximum price-fixing is subject to the *per se* rule.[144] The Court then went on to observe that "[t]he procompetitive potential of a vertical maximum price restraint is more evident now than it was when *Albrecht* was decided, because exclusive territorial arrangements and other nonprice restrictions were unlawful *per se* in 1968."[145]

Another departure from the *Schwinn* era has been the discard of the rule embodied in *Pearl Brewing*,[146] which had held that it was per se illegal for a supplier to grant a discount to a dealer on the

---

[142]   Northwest Publications, Inc. v. Crumb, 752 F.2d 473 (9th Cir. 1985) (judgment for counterclaim-defendants aff'd) (no causation because short-term termination clauses would have prevented dealers from raising their prices in any event); Jack Walters & Sons Corp. v. Morton Buildings, Inc., 737 F.2d 698 (7th Cir.), *cert. denied*, 469 U.S. 1018 (1984) (summary judgment for defendant aff'd) (supplier's price advertising, listing dealers' names; persuasion and policing during promotion not illegal; also, no antitrust injury); Curry v. Steve's Franchise Co., 1985–2 Trade Cas. (CCH) ¶ 66,877 (D. Mass. 1985) (defendants' motion for summary judgment granted) (not enough coercion to establish agreement); Martindell v. News Group Publications, Inc., 621 F. Supp. 672 (E.D.N.Y. 1985) (defendant's motion to dismiss after bench trial granted) (supplier's price advertising; no coercion proved). *Cf.* USA Petroleum Co. v. Atlantic Richfield Co., 1988–2 Trade Cas.(CCH) ¶ 68,255 (9th Cir. 1988) (maximum resale price maintenance can amount to predatory pricing); Kowalski v. Chicago Tribune Co., 1988–2 Trade Cas. (CCH) ¶ 68,173 (7th Cir. 1988) (affirming denial of distributor's motion for preliminary injunction). *Compare* City of New York v. Toby's Electronics, 1982–2 Trade Cas. (CCY) ¶ 64,732 (N.Y. City Civil Ct. 1981) (posting of manufacturers' suggested retail prices mandatory under City Code if retailer charges more).

[143]   495 U.S. 328 (1990).

[144]   *Id.* at 335 n.5.

[145]   *Id.* at 343 n.13.

[146]   Pearl Brewing Co. v. Anheuser-Busch, 339 F. Supp. 945 (S.D. Tex. 1972).

condition that the discount be passed along to the dealer's customers. Cases from the 1980's jettisoned that rule completely, and recognized that such a condition is reasonable and in the interest of consumers, as long as the dealer remains free to set its own price, to which the discount is applied.[147]

The post-*Sylvania* cases did not disturb the per se rule against garden-variety resale price maintenance, however, and that rule subsequently was reaffirmed by the Supreme Court in *Midcal*,[148] *Monsanto*,[149] and *324 Liquors*.[150] Nevertheless, as noted earlier, there have been pronouncements on the part of government leaders in recent years urging that resale price maintenance no longer should be treated as per se illegal because it is, in many cases, procompetitive.[151] Not only have there been speeches to this effect by the Assistant Attorney General in charge of the Antitrust Division and the Chairman of the Federal Trade Commission, but in 1981 the Justice Department voluntarily dismissed a pending criminal action against Mack Trucks for resale price maintenance, which had been instituted by the previous administration.[152] The press release issued at the time indicated that Mack's program had "consisted, at most, of vertical pricing arrangement."[153] Without any

---

147 Jack Walters & Sons Corp. v. Morton Buildings, Inc., 737 F.2d 698 (7th Cir.), *cert. denied*, 469 U.S. 1018 (1984) (summary judgment for defendant aff'd) (supplier gave discounts to dealers while advertising special retail prices); Lewis Service Center, Inc. v. Mack Trucks, Inc., 714 F2d 842 (8th Cir. 1983), *cert. denied*, 467 U.S. 1226 (1983); AAA Liquors, Inc. v. Jos. E. Seagram & Sons, Inc., 705 F2d 1203 (10th Cir. 1982), *cert. denied*, 461 U.S. 919 (1983); Bryant Heating and Air Conditioning Corp. v. Carrier Corp., 597 F. Supp. 1045 (S.D. Fla. 1984) (defendants' motion for summary judgment granted).

148 California Retail Liquor Dealers Ass'n v. Midcal Aluminum, Inc., 445 U.S. 97 (1980).

149 Monsanto Co. v. Spray-Rite Service Corp., 465 U.S. 752, 761 (1984).

150 324 Liquors Corp. v. Duffy, 479 U.S. 335 (1987).

151 *See* section I, *supra*.

152 5 CCH Trade Reg. Rep. ¶ 50,431.

153 Id.

evidence of horizontality, this was not enough to persuade the Antitrust Division of its illegality.

In 1983, the Justice Department took the further step of filing an amicus curiae brief with the Supreme Court in *Monsanto*, arguing that the per se rule against resale price maintenance should be abandoned. The brief asserted that "the overboard rule that prohibits all resale price maintenance, without regard to its actual impact in the marketplace, is unwarranted; it disserves consumers by precluding beneficial practices along with those that are pernicious."[154]

The response from Congress to this step was dramatic. Prior to the oral argument in *Monsanto*, Congress inserted a provision in the Justice Department's appropriations bill for fiscal year 1984 prohibiting the further expenditure of funds to advocate discontinuation of the per se rule against resale price maintenance.[155] At the argument the Government did not press the point, and the Court refused to reach it.[156]

This same restriction was included again in the appropriations measures for fiscal years 1987 and 1988,[157] after the Justice Department's Vertical Restraints Guidelines appeared, espousing the controversial position that vertical price restraints could be justifiable if coupled with nonprice restraints.[158] In reaction to the Guidelines, Congress also adopted a resolution stating that the Guidelines "(1) are not an accurate expression of the Federal antitrust laws or of congressional intent . . . (2) shall not . . . be treated by the courts . . . as binding or persuasive; and (3) should be recalled. . . ."[159]

---

[154] Brief for the United States as Amicus Curiae in Support of Petitioner, Monsanto Co. v. Spray-Rite Serv. Co., 465 U.S. 752 (1984) (No. 82–914).

[155] *See* note 51, *supra*.

[156] 45 Antitrust & Trade Reg. Rep. (BNA) 925 (Dec. 8, 1983).

[157] *See id.*

[158] Vertical Restraints Guidelines, *supra* note 40, at 2.3.

[159] Pub. L. No. 99–180, 605, 99 Stat. 1136, 1169–70 (1985). *See also* H.R. Rep. No. 99–399, 99th Cong., 1st Sess. 12–13 (1985) (to accompany H.R. Res. 303) ("Throughout the Guidelines are unsupported notions that work to establish certain larger 'themes' at variance with substantive law and current policy.").

This ongoing controversy over resale price maintenance led to inclusion in the 1987 version of the *"Monsanto* bill" of a separate section explicitly defining resale price maintenance as a per se offense. The section provided that in civil resale price maintenance cases, the

> fact that the seller of a good or service and the purchaser of such good or service entered into an agreement to establish the resale price of such good or service shall be sufficient to establish that such seller and such purchaser engaged in concerted action to set, change, or maintain the prices of such good or service in violation of such section.[160]

But notwithstanding the readiness of Congress to champion continuation of the per se rule against resale price maintenance, criticism of the rule continued, and was not limited to the enforcement agencies. Some courts joined in questioning the rule as well, although they felt constrained to abide by it. In *Isaksen v. Vermont Castings, Inc.,*[161] for example, Judge Posner remarked that a "retail price floor prevents . . . free riding and thus encourages dealers to provide necessary point-of-sale services [but] arguments of this sort have not persuaded the Supreme Court to relax the judge-made rule, now more than 75 years old, that makes resale price maintenance illegal per se under section 1 of the Sherman Act, regardless of the circumstances of its adoption."[162] Indeed, one court went so far as to deny injunctive relief to a terminated discounter that had alleged resale price maintenance on the ground that even if there had been price fixing, the discounter would have been "tak[ing] advantage of inflated prices" occasioned by the price fixing, so its protection was not within the "fundamental purpose of the antitrust laws" and it was not entitled to an injunction.[163]

---

160   Freedom from Vertical Price Fixing Act, *supra* note 118, at 2(b).

161   825 F.2d 1158 (7th Cir. 1987), *cert. denied*, 108 S. Ct. 1728 (1988).

162   825 F.2d at 1162.

163   Local Beauty Supply, Inc. v. Lamaur Inc., 787 F.2d 1197 (7th Cir. 1986). *See* Note, *Standing and the Use of "Antitrust Injury"*: Local Beauty Supply, Inc. v. Lamaur, Inc., 13 J. CORP. L. 169 (1987).

But by far the most explosive development in the law of resale price maintenance since *Sylvania* has been the Supreme Court's decision in *Sharp Electronics,* [164] which redefined the offense itself. The Court restricted per se interdiction to agreements fixing resale prices or price levels, thereby excluding from per se condemnation agreements simply to eliminate price-cutters.

The facts were not complicated. In the early 1970's, Sharp had marketed a line of high-end business calculators, and had two dealers in the Houston area, Business Electronics and Hartwell. Business Electronics was terminated in 1973, after Hartwell complained about it to Sharp for cutting prices. Business Electronics sued, and a jury found that there had been an agreement between Sharp and Hartwell to terminate Business Electronics because of its price cutting. The jury was instructed that such an agreement would constitute a per se violation of the antitrust laws, and it awarded $600,000 in damages, which was trebled.

The Fifth Circuit reversed.[165] It held that the jury instructions had been erroneous, and that there cannot be a per se illegal agreement between a manufacturer and a dealer to fix resale prices unless there is an express or implied agreement to set prices *at some level*—not just to terminate other dealers who are discounters. This decision appeared to be in conflict with decisions of other courts of appeals, particularly the Third Circuit's decisions in *Cernuto*[166] and its progeny.

The Supreme Court granted certiorari,[167] and in a 6 to 2 decision (in which Justice Kennedy did not participate) it affirmed the Fifth Circuit and rejected the *Cernuto* line of cases. In an opinion written by Justice Scalia, the Court held that "an agreement between a manufacturer and a dealer to terminate a 'price cutter,' without a *further agreement* on the *price or price levels* to be charged by the remaining dealer," does not amount to a per se violation of the

---

[164] 108 S. Ct. 1515 (1988).

[165] 780 F.2d 1212 (5th Cir. 1986).

[166] Cernuto, Inc. v. United Cabinet Corp., 595 F.2d 164 (3d Cir. 1979).

[167] 107 S. Ct. 3182 (1987).

antitrust laws.[168] The Court expressed concern that if a per se rule were applied on these facts, any termination of a dealer who "happens to have charged lower prices" would be unreasonably risky, because the manufacturer would find it difficult to prove that its real motivation for terminating the dealer was poor service or some other shortcoming, even if this were true.[169] The Court surmised that dealers who cut prices typically cannot afford to offer the best service, making it hard to establish whether the low prices or poor service provided the impetus for the termination:

> In the vast majority of cases, it will be extremely difficult for the manufacturer to convince a jury that its motivation was to ensure adequate services, since price cutting and some measure of service cutting usually go hand in hand.[170]

The Court concluded that to prove per se unlawful resale price maintenance, a plaintiff should be required to prove an actual agreement between the supplier and a dealer to charge a particular price or adhere to a price level.

Previously, there were some opinions suggesting that in order to prove resale price maintenance, it was sufficient to prove an agreement between a supplier and a dealer to raise prices or prevent prices from being lowered, without necessarily pegging a particular price or a particular minimum price. Cases such as *Parke, Davis,*[171] *Albrecht*[172] and *Socony-Vacuum*[173] seemed to support this conclu-

---

168   108 S. Ct. at 1521 (emphasis added). *Compare* the Justice Department's Vertical Restraints Guidelines at 2.3, limiting per se treatment to "an explicit agreement as to the specific prices at which goods or services would be resold."

169   108 S. Ct. at 1521.

170   Id.

171   United States v. Parke, Davis & Co., 362 U.S. 29 (1960).

172   Albrecht V. Herald Co., 390 U.S. 145 (1968).

173   United States v. Socony-Vacuum Oil Co., 310 U.S. 150 (1940).

sion, as did a number of lower court cases.[174] Under *Sharp*, it is necessary to prove agreement on a price level—however that comes to be defined—or on a particular price.

Prior to *Sharp*, there also were some cases which suggested, contrary to the rule at common law,[175] that proof that a supplier had terminated a dealer at the behest of another dealer, just to get rid of him and for no other demonstrable purpose (such as establishment of an exclusive dealership), would establish an actionable vertical "boycott" or vertical "refusal to deal." *Oreck*,[176] for example, drew a distinction between "true exclusive dealerships" and "two-firm vertical combinations to exclude a distributor from supply." The district court decision in *Westman*, reversed in 1986 after remaining on the books for 8 years, drew the same distinction, asserting that conspiracies to exclude a dealer's competitor from supply are per se unlawful.[177] *Cernuto*[178] also assumed that such combinations would

---

[174] *E.g.*, Lehrman v. Gulf Oil Corp., 464 F.2d 26 (5th Cir.) (price "floor"), *cert. denied*, 409 U.S. 1077 (1972); Sun-Drop Bottling Co. v. Coca-Cola Bottling Co., 604 F. Sup. 1197 (W.D.N.C. 1985) (agreement by retailer not to reduce prices of other brands); United States v. Serta Assocs., Inc., 296 F. Supp. 1121, 1125–27 (N.D. Ill. 1968), *aff'd per curiam*, 393 U.S. 534 (1969) ("all attempts to influence the locally advertised prices of the dealers are illegal, including price restrictions in Serta's cooperative payment program."). *See also* National Ass'n of Attorney's General Vertical Restraints Guidelines (Dec. 4, 1985), *reprinted in* 4 Trade Reg. Rep. (CCH) ¶ 13,400, at 21,153: "An RPM agreement is reached when two or more independent firms agree to fix, raise, lower, maintain or stabilize the price at which goods or services will be resold. There need not be any agreement on specific resale prices."

[175] *See, e.g.*, Dye v. Carmichael Produce Co., 64 Ind. App. 653, 116 N.E. 425 (1917) (dictum) (collecting authorities).

[176] Oreck Corp. v. Whirlpool Corp., 579 F.2d 126 (2d Cir.) (en banc), *cert. denied*, 439 U.S. 946 (1978).

[177] 461 F. Supp. 627 (D. Colo. 1978), *rev'd*, 796 F. 2d 1216 (10th Cir. 1986), *cert. denied*, 107 S. Ct. 1728 (1988). The district court opinion in *Westman* distinguished between a supplier's unilateral refusal to deal and an agreement with a dealer to cut off a competing dealer's source of supply. The court held the latter per se illegal, stating that "a conspiracy to exclude a competitor from the trade is, in and of itself, the substance which the Sherman Act is intended to prohibit. Its pernicious effect is not . . . subject to serious question." 461 F. Supp. at 636.

[178] Cernuto, Inc. v. United Cabinet Corp., 595 F.2d 164 (3d Cir. 1979).

be illegal per se, although it based this assumption on a questionable finding that there were "horizontal effects" implicit in such a scenario. If this had been the rule applied by the Supreme Court, the agreement Hartwell had elicited from Sharp to terminate Business Electronics would have been illegal regardless of whether prices or "discounting" had even been discussed, and regardless of how resale price maintenance was defined.

Both of these notions were exploded by *Sharp*. Under *Sharp* there must be proof of "an agreement on price or price level" to establish per se illegal resale price maintenance, and termination of one dealer at the behest of another, even where an exclusive distributorship does not result, is not per se illegal.

The court's rationale for insisting on proof of an agreement to peg a resale price or resale price level was the proposition (previously advanced by a number of economists) that such an agreement—and only such an agreement—can facilitate price-fixing cartels among suppliers of different brands or among different dealers.[179] If each supplier were able to peg retail prices, it would become easy for suppliers not only to fix prices with one another, but then to *monitor* each other's prices in the marketplace. No one could cheat, because just as under the fair trade laws[180] everyone would know every brand's retail prices with certainty. In contrast, mere agreements to get rid of "discounters," as evidenced in the *Sharp* case, will not achieve the same level of assurance as to the prices that rivals actually are charging, at least according to this theory.

The Court devoted only a footnote to discussion of the possibility of "dominant retail power" becoming a concern in dealer termination cases.[181] The Court dismissed such power as "rare, because of the usual presence of interbrand competition and other dealers,"

---

179 *Sharp*, 107 S. Ct. at 1521.

180 Id.

181 *Id.* at n.2.

and stated that "it should therefore not be assumed but rather must be proved."[182]

A lengthy dissent was filed by Justice Stevens, joined by Justice White.[183] The dissent argued,under an approach much like that taken in *Cernuto*,[184] that the termination of Business Electronics was horizontal in effect, and should have been treated as per se illegal on this basis. The dissent called this a "naked agreement to restrain the trade of [a] third part[y]," which was "the product of coercion by the stronger of two dealers. . . ."[185]

The dissent also pointed out that although the majority took the opportunity to make some broad statements about the desirability of vertical nonprice restraints (such as territorial restrictions), "it does not appear that [Sharp] imposed *any* vertical non price restraints upon either [Business Electronics] or Hartwell."[186] The dissent insisted that the case involved nothing but a "naked agreement to terminate a dealer because of its price cutting," of the kind that has always been per se illegal.[187]

Responding, the majority denied that there was a "naked" restraint, and held that a restraint need not be ancillary to any formal service obligations in order to be reasonable, so long as the economic effect of the restraint holds the *prospect* of enhancing competition.[188] Of course, there was no restraint in *Sharp* at all—no exclusive dealership, no resale price maintenance, nothing but the termination. Why, then, did the Court choose to address the pro-

---

182 *Id.*

183 *Id.* at 1526–37.

184 *Cernuto*, 595 F. 2d at 168.

185 *Sharp*, 108 S. Ct. at 1529.

186 *Id.* at 1528 (emphasis added).

187 *Id.* at 1535.

188 *Id. Cf.* Newberry v. Washington Post Co., 438 F. Supp. 470, 473–76 (D.D.C. 1977) (suggesting that even where there is no interbrand competition at all, territorial restraints still can be reasonable where they promote efficiency and thereby have the potential to enhance interbrand competition if it arises).

competition effects of vertical restraints in this context? Because, it concluded, it would be "perverse" to require suppliers to impose some vertical restraint just to enable them to terminate free riders, since the same justification should apply whether there is a formal restraint or not.[189] Acknowledging that it might be changing the rules, the majority applauded the "dynamic potential" of the term "restraint of trade," and stated that the "changing content of the term . . . was well-recognized at the time the Sherman Act was enacted."[190]

Finally, the dissent parsed both the majority opinion and the Court's earlier decision in *Monsanto*, and concluded that in the future, a terminated dealer in a position like that of Business Electronics will be able to establish liability only by overcoming three separate hurdles:

> First, the terminated dealer . . . must introduce "evidence that tends to exclude the possibility that the manufacturer and nonterminated distributors were acting independently." . . .
> Second, the terminated dealer must prove that the agreement was based on a purpose to terminate it because of its price cutting. . . .
> Third, the manufacturer may rebut the evidence tending to prove that the sole purpose of the agreement was to eliminate a price cutter by offering evidence that it entered the agreement for legitimate, nonprice-related reasons.[191]

This prognostication is likely to be cited routinely in defendants' motions to dismiss and motions for summary judgment.

Sharp provoked an immediate response in Congress, which at the time already was considering the *Monsanto* bill. The proposed legislation included a provision designed to clarify that the offense of per se illegal resale price maintenance should encompass conspiracy "between a supplier and distributor to terminate or cut off supply to a second distributor because of the second distributor's

---

189   108 S. Ct. at 1522 n.3.

190   *Id.* at 1523.

191   *Id.* at 1534–35.

pricing policies."[192] The House Report explained the intent behind this provision:

> Quite simply, if the purpose or effect of concerted activity is to affect or stifle price competition in any manner, then vertical price fixing is at issue; and the per se rule is the applicable test.[193]

Immediately after *Sharp* was decided, Senator Metzenbaum called a news conference to argue that the *Sharp* decision highlighted the need for legislation.[194] An aide to the Senator asserted that in contrast to *Sharp*, the House Report took the position that "proof of a *per se* agreement does not require proof of an agreement to set prices at any particular level."[195] House Judiciary Committee Chairman Rodino remarked in a separate statement that *Sharp* had "refocused attention on the need for Congress to state with unequivocal clarity that all forms of RPM are illegal *per se*."[196]

When the Senate proceeded to debate its bill in June 1988, a month after *Sharp* was decided,[197] it adopted an amendment offered by Senator Metzenbaum to clarify that the proposed legislation would not affect current law on *maximum* resale price maintenance.[198] "The amendment," according to the Senator, "would not change the current rule that maximum vertical price fixing is automatically illegal but the rule would not be codified."[199] This cryptic statement seemed to recognize that while the per se rule against maximum resale price maintenance has never been formally over-

---

[192] *H.R. 585 Report, supra* note 124, at 38.]

[193] *Id.* at 39 (emphasis in original).

[194] 54 Antitrust & Trade Reg. Rep. (BNA) No. 1365, at 816 (May 12, 1988).

[195] *Id.*

[196] *Id.*

[197] 55 Antitrust & Trade Reg. Rep. (BNA) No. 1373, at 4 (July 7, 1988).

[198] *Id.*

[199] *Id.*

turned, it is not being vigorously enforced and today enjoys little support.

The Reagan administration strongly opposed the legislative efforts to overturn *Monsanto* and *Sharp*. The head of the Antitrust Division commented that "[t]he risk of harm to the law of vertical restraints, to the law of conspiracy in general and to the specific legal distinction between unilateral decisions and conspiratorial actions by manufacturers would require the Administration to exert the maximum effort to defeat the legislation."[200]

In the new versions of the House and Senate bills, introduced in 1989, the sections on resale price maintenance have been redrafted to address *Sharp* directly. The House bill provides that in civil resale price maintenance cases,

> the fact that the seller of a good or service and the purchaser of such good or service entered into an agreement to set, change, or maintain the price (other than a maximum price) of such good or service for resale shall be sufficient to constitute a violation of such section. An agreement between the seller of a good or service and the purchaser of such good or service to terminate another purchaser as a dealer or to refuse to supply such other purchaser because of that purchaser's pricing policies shall constitute a violation of such section, whether or not a specific price or price level is agreed upon.[201]

The Senate bill is to the same effect.

The Senate Report in the 101st Congress was particularly critical of lower court decisions applying *Sharp*, particularly *The Jeanery, Inc. v. James Jeans, Inc.*[202] and *Toys "R" Us, Inc. v. R. H. Macy & Co.*[203] The House Report was equally emphatic:

---

200   53 Antitrust & Trade Reg. Rep. (BNA), at 230 (August 13, 1987).

201   H.R. 1236, 101st Cong., 2d Sess. 2(b) (1990).

202   849 F.2d 1148, 1160 (9th Cir. 1988) (*Sharp* "teaches that a manufacturer can agree to terminate a price-cutting distributor in response to a complaint from another dealer").

203   1990–1 Trade Cas. (CCH) ¶ 68,890 (S.D.N.Y. 1990). *See also* Corrosion Resistant Materials Co. v. Steelite, Inc., 1988–2 Trade Cas. (CCH) 68,359 (D.N.J. 1988) (applying *Sharp*).

The effect of *Sharp* has been to set up an almost impenetrable—and certainly unrealistic—barrier for terminated dealers to redress antitrust injury since rarely do conspirators engage in such simplistic practices as actually entering into an explicit agreement to set specific prices.[204]

The House Report concluded that only suppliers with "an extreme degree of business naivete or outright stupidity" will generate evidence of an express agreement to set specific prices, and "slightly more sophisticated resale price fixers should have nothing to fear . . . if Congressional action is not forthcoming.[205]

The Bush administration, like the Reagan administration, has not supported this legislation. At his confirmation hearing in June 1989, Assistant Attorney General James F. Rill agreed with Senator Metzenbaum that resale price maintenance is per se unlawful, but commented that codification of this rule might be unnecessary. Subsequently, both the Department of Justice and the Federal Trade Commission conveyed their opposition.

All this debate leaves the definition of resale price maintenance completely at sea. The *Sharp* definition of setting a "price or price level" is in need of clarification in further decisions, but at the same time Congress has been deliberating a very different clarification of its own. The most rational response to this situation is bewilderment. But one thing seems clear—if *Sharp* stands up for the long haul, the per se rule will apply only to resale price maintenance of the plain vanilla variety. If *Sharp* is overturned by Congress, the definition of resale price maintenance will be anyone's guess.

V. Trend no. 3: presuming efficiencies

In *Sylvania*, the Supreme Court made it clear that under the rule of reason a supplier may justify dealer terminations and nonprice

---

204   H.R. Rep. No. 101–438, 101st Cong., 2d Sess. at 2 (1990).

205   *Id.* at 28.

vertical restraints on the ground that they create efficiencies by combating free-rider problems and thereby encouraging dealers to compete more aggressively against other brands. The Court said,

> Vertical restrictions promote interbrand competition by allowing the manufacturer to achieve certain efficiencies in the distribution of his products. Because of market imperfections such as the so-called "free-rider" effect, . . . services might not be provided by retailers in a purely competitive situation, despite the fact that each retailer's benefit would be greater if all provided the services than if none did.[206]

The "free-rider" effect had been described by Professor Telser 1960, and later by several other economists.[207] It was the basis for a number of lower court decisions prior to *Sylvania*, and has been reexamined and clarified in scores of lower court decisions since.[208]

As in *Sylvania* itself, the defendants in these cases bore the burden of proving the free-rider "defense" as a means of justifying dealer terminations under the rule of reason.[209] Once the plaintiff demonstrated the restraint on competition, the supplier had an opportunity to rebut that evidence with proof that the restraint produced efficiencies, which usually included combating a free-rider

---

206 433 U.S. 36, 54.

207 *See, e.g., Sylvania*, 433 U.S. 36, 48 n.13 (citing Posner, *Antitrust Policy and the Supreme Court, an Analysis of the Restricted Distribution, Horizontal Merger and Potential Competition Decisions*, 75 COLUM. L. REV. 282 (1975)).

208 *See, e.g.*, Three Movies of Tarzana v. Pacific Theatres, Inc., 828 F.2d 1395, 1399–400 (9th Cir. 1987); Westman Comm'n Co. v. Hobart Int'l, Inc., 796 F.2d 1216, 1226–27 (10th Cir. 1986); Davis-Watkins Co. v. Service Merch., 696 F.2d 1190, 1195 (6th Cir. 1982), *cert. denied*, 466 U.S. 931 (1984); Winter Hill Frozen Foods and Servs., Inc., v. the Haagen-Dazs Co., 1988–2 Trade Cas. (CCH) ¶ 68,182, at 59,199–201 750, 757–59 (D. Md. 1980), *aff'd*, 638 F.2d 15 (4th Cir.), *cert. denied*, 454 U.S. 864 (1981).

209 *See, e.g.*, Davis-Watkins Co. v. Service Merch., 696 F.2d 1190, 1195, 1200–01 (6th Cir. 1982), *cert. denied*, 466 U.S. 931 (1984).

problem. More recently, however, several courts have been prepared to presume a free-rider justification, barring evidence to the contrary—an approach that now appears to have been endorsed in *Sharp*, if only in dictum.

For example, in cases like *Magid Manufacturing Co. v. USD Corp.*[210] and *Moffat v. Lane Company, Inc.,*[211] the courts have presumed, in the absence of evidence to the contrary, that the supplier had a legitimate, independent business reason for terminating a dealer—usually the elimination of free riding. In the second *Valley Liquors* decision,[212] the Seventh Circuit undertook to explain this trend, noting that the supplier "does not have to prove that it actually had an independent reason. Under the *Monsanto* standard, it is up to [the terminated dealer] to present evidence 'that tends to exclude the possibility' that [the supplier] acted independently.' "[213] In other words, it should be up to the dealer seeking to avoid summary judgment to present proof that the supplier did not have an independent reason.

The House Reports accompanying the *Monsanto* bills have been sharply critical of this trend. The reports took aim at a number of cases, but none more than *Magid Manufacturing*. The reports commented that "[t]he lasting impression of *Magid* appears to be that so long as the termination would 'theoretically' not be inconsistent with the [supplier's] best interest, no inference of concerted activity can plausibly be shown."[214]

Despite this criticism, the Supreme Court took the opportunity in *Sharp* to embrace exactly this type of approach. The Court did not hesitate to assume that the supplier, Sharp, had valid business

---

210   654 F. Supp. 325 (N.D. Ill. 1987).

211   No. 82–1667–2, slip op. (D. Mass. June 13, 1984) (LEXIS, Genfed library, Dist. file).

212   Valley Liquors, Inc. v. Renfield Importers, Ltd., 822 F.2d 656 (7th Cir. 1987), *cert. denied*, 108 S. Ct. 488 (1988).

213   *Id.* at 664.

214   53 Antitrust & Trade Reg. Rep. (BNA) 770 (Nov. 12, 1987); H.R. Rep. No. 101–438, 101st Cong., 2d Sess. at 25 (1990).

justifications for terminating Business Electronics. At the same time, the Court was unwilling to assume that the complaining dealer, Hartwell, possessed market power, even though the jury had found that Hartwell possessed muscle enough to bring the termination about. Explaining its holding, the Court asserted that "a quite plausible purpose of the restriction [was] to enable Hartwell to provide better services. . . ."[215] Yet there was no proof that this was Sharp's purpose; moreover there *was no restriction* in *Sharp* to begin with—no exclusive dealership,[216] no customer restriction, nothing but the termination, which is not a restriction at all, but a refusal to continue dealing. This readiness to presume efficiencies—specifically, elimination of free riding as a means of encouraging better service—represented an endorsement, albeit in dictum, of the trend already developing in the lower court cases before *Sharp* was decided.

The *Sharp* dictum is tantalizingly vague on this point, however, never quite instructing whether efficiencies should be presumed in all distribution cases or only in some, and never explaining why the Court chose to address this point in the first place. This is a trend in its infancy, and although the Supreme Court appears to have endorsed it, a great deal more case law will be required to gauge where it is heading.

VI. Trend no. 4: market power screens

Not long after *Sylvania* was announced, a number of courts began holding that before it even becomes necessary for a court to undertake weighing the procompetitive and anticompetitive effects of a vertical restraint under the rule of reason, the plaintiff first must be prepared to show that the supplier imposing the restraint has substantial market power. The underlying assumption was that if a brand does not wield sufficient power to influence the prices of

---

215   108 S. Ct. at 1522.

216   Except, arguably, a de facto exclusive analogous to that found in *Oreck.*

other brands in the market, or to exclude other brands from the market altogether, then as a matter of law it should make no difference whether distributors of that brand are subject to vertical restraints. This reasoning developed into a line of cases erecting a market power "screen," similar to that which later would be incorporated into the Justice Department Guidelines.[217] These cases concluded that where a supplier lacks substantial market power, its vertical restraints never can be unreasonable under the rule of reason because such a supplier is powerless to influence the level of prices in the overall relevant market regardless of what restraints it may impose on distributors of its own brand.

This approach was articulated soon after *Sylvania* in *Muenster Butane, Inc. v. Stewart Co.,*[218] where the court held that:

> [P]roof of the antitrust defendant's "substantial" market power should be a preliminary hurdle in all restricted distribution (vertical restraint) cases.[219]

As explained soon after in *Valley Liquors, Inc. v. Renfield Importers, Ltd.:*[220]

> Only if [plaintiff] can allege facts that give rise to an inference that [defendant] had sufficient market power to control . . . prices must we proceed to the first step in the Rule of Reason analysis, which is to balance the effects the vertical restraint has on intrabrand and interbrand competition.[221]

Similarly, in *O.S.C. Corp. v. Apple Computer, Inc.,*[222] the court observed:

---

217 Vertical Restraints Guidelines, *supra* note 40.

218 651 F.2d 292 (5th Cir. 1981).

219 651 F.2d at 298.

220 822 F.2d 6656 (7th Cir.), *cert. denied*, 108 S. Ct. 488 (1987).

221 822 F.2d at 666.

222 601 F. Supp. 1274, 1291 n.8 (C.D. Cal. 1985), *aff'd*, 792 F.2d 1464 (9th Cir. 1986).

Only if a manufacturer so dominates a market as to exert substantial monopoly or market power—"the power to raise prices significantly above the competitive level without losing all of one's business"—is there any danger of harm to competition from an intrabrand vertical restriction. . . . Absent significant market power, a vertical restriction is reasonable as a matter of law.[223]

This approach has become commonplace in cases involving nonprice vertical restraints.[224] The cases establish a market power "screen," which is considerably less complicated than that proposed in the Justice Department Guidelines, under which nonprice vertical restraints will not be further scrutinized under the rule of reason if the brand does not have a substantial share of the market—at least 10% or 20%. The "screen" has been applied in cases challenging territorial restraints,[225] customer restraints,[226] exclusive dealing[227] and tying.[228]

---

223 601 F. Supp. at 1291 n.8.

224 *See* notes 225 through 227, *infra.*

225 Assam Drug Co. v. Miller Brewing Co., 798 F.2d 311 (8th Cir. 1986) (territorial restraint) (summary judgment for defendant aff'd) (low market share; only 19.1%); Carib Aviation & Marine Consultants, Ltd. v. Mitsubishi Aircraft International, Inc., 640 F. Supp. 582 (S.D. granted) (no adverse effect on competition demonstrated; 8% market share); Gilchrist Machinery Co. v. Komatsu America Corp., 601 F. Supp. 1192 (S.D. Miss. 1984) (territorial restraint) (preliminary injunction denied) (small market share); Reborn Enterprises, Inc. v. Fine Child, Inc., 590 F. Supp. 1423 (S.D.N.Y. 1984), *aff'd*, 754 F.2d 1072 (2d Cir. 1985) (territorial restraint) (supplier's voluntary assignment of restricted territories is presumptively more efficient; also, no evidence of market share).

226 O.S.C. Corp. v. Apple Computer, Inc., 792 F.2d 1464 (9th Cir. 1986) (customer restraint; mail order prohibition) (summary judgment for defendant aff'd) (no effect on competition shown); Hayco Systems, Inc. v. Savin Business Machines, 777 F.2d 306 (5th Cir. 1985) (customer restraint; sales to state government) (summary judgment for defendant aff'd) (no market power) *cert. denied*, 479 U.S. 916 (1986).

227 Roland Machinery Co. v. Dresser Industries, Inc., 749 F.2d 380 (7th Cir. 1984) (grant of preliminary injunction rev'd; stimulating dealers; stimulating suppliers; Judge Posner's "screen"); Barnosky Oils, Inc. v. Union Oil of California, 582 F. Supp. 1332 (E.D. Mich. 1984) (summary judgment for defendant granted) (too small a market share).

228 Will v. Comprehensive Accounting Corp., 776 F.2d 665 (7th Cir. 1985) (judgment for defendants after jury trial aff'd) (no market power proved), *cert. denied*, 475 U.S. 1129 (1986).

Some courts are beginning to question this approach, however. In *New York v. Anheuser-Busch, Inc.,*[229] the district court rejected application of the market power screen, which it referred to as a "two-step test."[230] Defendants in that case had argued, on the strength of decisions in the Fifth, Seventh and Eighth Circuits, that a "plaintiff must prove that the defendant has market power" before "the court may begin the balancing of competitive and anticompetitive effects under the rule of reason."[231] The court found it "clear . . . , however, that the Second Circuit has not adopted this two-step analysis."[232] For support, it cited *Eiberger v. Sony Corp.,*[233] a case decided shortly after *Sylvania*, in which the Second Circuit indicated that a nonprice vertical restraint can be considered unreasonable for foreclosing *intra*brand competition, regardless of whether it has any effect on interbrand competition.[234]

In years past, *Eiberger* has found little company as a precedent for the proposition that a nonprice vertical restraint can run afoul of the rule of reason even if its only demonstrable effect is on intrabrand competition. In the *Anheuser-Busch* case, however, the court was citing it to make the somewhat different point that even a supplier with a relatively low market share can have a real impact on interbrand competition. The court asserted that the facts before it demonstrated why a market power threshold is not always appropriate:

---

229 673 F. Supp. 664 (E.D.N.Y. 1987).

230 673 F. Supp. at 667.

231 *Id.*

232 *Id.*

233 622 F.2d 1068 (2d Cir. 1980).

234 The court also cited Copy-Data Systems, Inc. v. Toshiba America, Inc., 663 F.2d 405 (2d Cir. 1981), as a case in which the defendant had only an "insignificant" market share, yet the Second Circuit "made no mention of a need to determine market power prior to applying the rule of reason." In *Copy-Data*, however, the Second Circuit held that the challenged restraint was not unreasonable in any event, so its failure to focus on the defendant's market power assumes less significance.

> Market share alone in the beer industry does not reflect the potential for anticompetitive results. . . . For example, in the beer market one of the competitive characteristics is the high cost of entry into the market. . . . Since relatively few firms share a large percentage of the beer market, high barriers to entry can magnify the effects of industry-wide vertical agreements. . . .[235]

The court concluded that because of the competitive stagnation resulting from high entry barriers, the territorial restraint at issue should not be screened out, and should be subject to a rule of reason inquiry.

Other cases have reached similar conclusions. In *Package Shop, Inc. v. Anheuser-Busch, Inc.,*[236] the court adopted the position that "market share is a poor indicator of firm market power in a product differentiated industry," where customers with strong brand preferences will switch brands only in response to substantial price disparity. Recently, in *Dimidowich v. Bell & Howell,*[237] the Ninth Circuit reversed a summary judgment that had been entered for a supplier and sent a refusal to deal claim back for a rule of reason investigation, even though the supplier's market share was only between 10% and 15%. The court reasoned that where the record includes facts that appear to be out of the ordinary, courts should be reluctant to exclude claims under a simple screen device.

Likewise, in *Redwood Theatres, Inc. v. Festival Enterprises, Inc.,*[238] a California appellate court, applying the Cartwright Act,[239] refused defendants' suggestion that it apply a market power screen in an exclusive distribution case involving the exhibition of first-run pictures in movie theaters. The court held that where products are

---

235   673 F. Supp. at 668.

236   675 F. Supp. 894 (D.N.J. 1987).

237   803 F.2d 1473 (9th Cir. 1986).

238   200 Cal. App. 3d 687, 248 Cal. Rptr. 189 (Cal. Ct. App.), *modified,* 200 Cal. App. 3d 1591b (1988).

239   California's Cartwright Act (Bus. & Prof. Code   16720 *et seq.*) is interpreted like the Sherman Act.

highly differentiated, agreements placing restrictions on competition for distributing each product alone (*i.e.,* on *intrabrand* competition) may be unreasonable:

> [W]here competitive survival [of theater owners] depends on gaining access to a unique product, these [exclusive] agreements may present serious antitrust questions in any well consolidated industry even if it is dominated by no single [supplier].[240]

By analogy, the same argument could be advanced not only about theater owners, but about any dealers in an industry marked by highly differentiated products, where consumers are reluctant to substitute one brand for another. The court concluded that a market share screen would not be a suitable tool of analysis in such circumstances.

This leaves us with a screen test that has been endorsed by a number of courts of appeals, but has been rejected by some courts in cases where products are highly differentiated, where brand loyalty is strong, where new entry is difficult, and where unusual facts suggest that the market might warrant closer scrutiny. Without question, the market power screen would benefit from clarification, both to decide whether it should apply to particular categories of cases, and, if so, to decide what market share percentage should fit through the screen. Despite these uncertainties, the screen clearly has become part of contemporary rule of reason analysis, even though nobody can paint a picture of it yet.

As such, the screen takes its place alongside the presumption of supplier efficiencies, the redefinition of resale price maintenance, and the revision of the conspiracy standards applicable to agreements to terminate and agreements to adopt vertical restraints—together, these are the megatrends of distribution law that have emerged in the years since *Sylvania*. There have been other changes in the standards applicable to particular vertical restraints, of

---

[240] *Redwood Theatres*, 200 Cal. App. 3d at 1591b, *modifying* 200 Cal. App. 3d 687, 707, 248 Cal. Rptr. 189, 201.

course, but these are the changes that have cut across all distribution law. The question today is whether these changes have brought equilibrium to the law, or whether the pendulum again has swung too far.

VII. What standards make sense?

Having survived the roaring sixties, the Chicago school reformation begun in the seventies, and the reaction, if not counterrevolution, of the eighties, as chronicled above, the business community and the judiciary are to be forgiven if they are suffering from motion sickness. The objective of this article is not to reminisce, however. It is to chart a course through the intellectual crosscurrents, and construct a framework for assessing distribution restraints in the nineties.

In theory, everyone is right. In practice, everyone is wrong, at least in certain cases. The reality is that virtually every principle underlying the last 30 years of distribution jurisprudence is applicable in particular instances but inapplicable in others. The problem has been that most of these principles have been advanced as immutable truth. The search has been for nothing less than per se rules of illegality, per se rules of legality, mathematical thresholds and indexes, and unifying principles such as "free riding" applicable to every industry and every locale.

The motivation for this urge to formulate the perfect, transcendent test has been a desire for predictability. Sometimes the underlying notion has been that any bright-line rule would be better than a vague standard of reasonableness on the theory that most judges cannot be trusted to decide antitrust cases without black-and-white, quasimathematical rules—and certainly not juries. There also is a desire for predictability within the business community, whose constituents frequently have voiced the opinion that they can live with almost any set of rules as long as they have some assurance of knowing what the rules are and will be. In other instances, the motivation is simply a matter of espousing some genuine unifying principles to make the task of judging more efficient and more precise.

But none of these principles, as good as they are, can be applied indiscriminately. Each has exceptions, and even principles that seem diametrically opposite one another may both be valid some of the time. Powerful tools of analysis have been developed, but the real truth—the absolute, unimpeachable reality—is that there is no single solution to complex distribution cases, and the task confronting lawyers and judges in each case is to determine which tools properly apply and which do not.

The Supreme Court already has taught that there is no bright line separating per se rules from the rule of reason.[241] By the same token, there are not always bright lines pointing to which of the various tools of analysis properly should be applied in each case. Economists frequently base their theories on the assumption *"ceteris paribus"*—"other things being equal." But in the real world, *ceteris* is almost never *paribus*; each case is different, and each must be judged on its own merits. With this in mind, the remainder of this article will explore the limits of the major principles of analysis and endeavor to harmonize them into a workable guide.

Among the questions posed by the latest cases are those implicit in the trends described above: Should a supplier be able to terminate a dealer in order to keep the peace with another dealer without thereby entering into an "agreement" with the second dealer? Should a supplier be able to convince a dealer to maintain resale prices (or limit its territory or customers) without thereby entering into a combination or conspiracy? Are there limits to when dealers can demand that their suppliers terminate discounters? Should free riding be presumed unless proven otherwise? Should there be a market share screen in vertical restraint cases, or is there too great a danger that this prerequisite will screen out meritorious claims? In the remainder of this article, each of these questions will be addressed, beginning with conspiracy.

---

[241]   NCAA v. Board of Regents, 468 U.S. 85, 104 n.26 (1984).

A. Should "conspiracy" to terminate discounters be easier to prove?

When *Monsanto* was decided in 1982, it was not immediately clear how much of a practical change it would make from *Cernuto* and its progeny—after all, the defendant in *Monsanto* lost that case and wound up facing a $10.5 million judgment. As described above, however, it soon became apparent that the lower courts were relying on *Monsanto* to work some profound changes, dismissing case after case on summary judgment motions that in earlier times would have dragged through discovery.

The immediate question today is not whether *Monsanto*'s "something more" requirement would benefit from further clarification (what precedent wouldn't?), but whether legislation is necessary to rewrite the "*Monsanto* rule." The fact is, supporters of the legislation pending in Congress take issue less with *Monsanto* itself than with subsequent decisions that have interpreted and applied *Monsanto*. If the case law develops further, it may turn out that *Monsanto* will be applied more to the sponsors' liking, making statutory amendment unnecessary.

The original House Report was particularly critical of the *Garment District*,[242] *Magid Manufacturing*[243] and *Moffat*[244] decisions. These cases extended *Monsanto* by granting summary judgment to suppliers even when a terminated dealer had presented evidence that the supplier's reason for carrying out the termination was simply to satisfy the demands of a complaining dealer. These were followed by similar cases such as *The Jeanery*[245] and *Parkway Gallery*.[246] But it is not yet clear how broadly these precedents will

---

[242]   Garment Dist., Inc. v. Belk Stores Servs., Inc., 799 F.2d 905 (4th Cir. 1986), *cert. denied*, 107 S. Ct. 1728 (1988).

[243]   Magid Mfg. Co. v. U.S.D. Corp., 654 F. Supp. 435 (N.D. Ill.1987).

[244]   Moffat v. Lane Co., No. 82–1667–2 (D. Mass. June 13, 1984) (LEXIS, Genfed library, Dist. file).

[245]   The Jeanery, Inc. v. James Jeans, Inc., 849 F.2d 1148 (9th Cir. 1988).

[246]   Parkway Gallery Furniture, Inc. v. Kittinger/Pennsylvania *House Group, Inc.*, 1988–1 *Trade Cas. (CCH)* ¶ 67,970 (*M.D.N.C.* 1988).

apply. The opponents of the bill asserted in the original Senate minority report that *Garment District* was "an anomaly that will probably be corrected as the jurisprudence in this area progresses."[247] Whether or not cases like *Garment District* need to be "corrected"—a point on which there is considerable disagreement—it remains to be seen how they will be applied in suits where different facts are presented.

In a number of cases, notably *Robart*,[248] *American Dermatologists*[249] and *Fragale*,[250] courts have held that a terminated dealer's proof that its termination was caused by another dealer's complaint about its prices was enough to defeat a supplier's motion for summary judgment. For example, in *Robart*, the court held that "proof of a causal nexus between [the complaining dealer's] complaints and plaintiff's termination" could, by itself, "be sufficient to estab-

---

247   *S. 430 Report, supra* note 130, at 15.

248   Robart Manuf. Co. v. Loctite Corp., No. 83-C–7288, slip op. (N.D. Ill. January 9, 1986) (LEXIS, Genfed library, Dist. file).

249   American Dermatologists' Medical Group, Inc. v. Collagen Corp., 595 F. Supp. 79 (N.D. Ill. 1984).

250   Fragale & Sons Beverage Co. v. Dill, 760 F.2d 469 (3d Cir. 1985). *See also* Helicopter Support Systems, Inc. v. Hughes Helicopter, Inc., 1987–1 Trade Cas. (CCH) ¶ 67,593 (11th Cir. 1987) (summary judgment for defendant rev'd) (supplier advised complaining distributor that corrective action had been taken and requested reports of any future discounting; also direct evidence of resale price maintenance abroad); Dimidowich v. Bell & Howell, 803 F.2d 1473 (9th Cir. 1986) (summary judgment for defendant rev'd) (dual distribution; pre-textual refusal to supply replacement parts; despite low market share of supplier (10%–15%), dealer permitted to proceed on conspiracy theory); International Wood Processors v. Power Dry, Inc., 792 F.2d 416 (4th Cir. 1986) (judgment for plaintiffs after jury trial aff'd) (conspiracy between patent licenser and licensee to terminate other licensees); Victorian House, Inc. v. Fisher Camuto Corp., 769 F.2d 466 (8th Cir. 1985) (judgment for plaintiff after jury trial affirmed) (*Cernuto* relied on); Pierce v. Ramsey Winch Co., 753 F.2d 416 (5th Cir. 1985) (judgment for plaintiffs after jury trial aff'd) (transshipping and discounting; issue over jury charge, which was governed by *Monsanto*); Malley-Duff & Associates, Inc., v. Crown Lief Insurance Co., 734 F.2d 133 (3d Cir.), *cert. denied*, 469 U.S. 1072 (1984) (directed verdict for defendants rev'd) (freeze-out of insurance agency; double dealing as evidence of conspiracy).

lish an agreement" to terminate.[251] The court saw "no significant difference between a manufacturer who engages distributors to help police a pricing system and a manufacturer who terminates discounters in response to complaints from distributors."[252] The court further held that the plaintiffs had made an adequate showing of a causal nexus between the complaints and the termination by introducing evidence that the supplier had "told the plaintiffs that the reason for their termination was the complaints by [the other dealer]."[253] The supplier's motion for summary judgment was denied.

The message here is that supporters of the proposed legislation may be too hasty—*Monsanto* is not foreclosing meritorious cases, and if there are instances where it has been misapplied it very well may be "corrected" by the ebb and flow of decisional law. Piecemeal antitrust legislation is inherently undesirable, and ought to be avoided. The antitrust laws have benefited from an elegant simplicity over the years, and efforts to engraft exceptions and clarifications have been turned back time after time (with more than a few exceptions, of course, when necessary). The urge to address particular court decisions like *Garment District* should be resisted as long as possible, to allow the case law to filter the new standards. Legislation should be a last resort, and the courts should be afforded a sufficient opportunity to do their work.

Given this opportunity, the courts should forge a realistic interpretation of the *Monsanto* standard, under which unrebutted evidence that a supplier's principal motive for terminating a discounter was to placate another dealer will constitute sufficient evidence to establish an agreement to terminate. The supplier should be afforded an opportunity to rebut this evidence, of course, and demonstrate its own, independent reasons for the termination. If it succeeds, summary judgment should be granted. On the other hand, if there is a genuine issue as to whether the supplier was merely

---

251   *Robart, supra* note 248.

252   *Id.*

253   *Id.*

knuckling under to a dealer complaint, and if there also is a genuine issue whether this was in support of a conspiracy to fix resale prices or enforce an unreasonable nonprice restraint, summary judgment will not be appropriate. If the law recognizes these distinctions it will maintain its credibility, and not precipitate a legislative resolution.

B. Should conspiracy to adopt vertical restraints be easier to prove?

In *Monsanto* the Supreme Court found evidence of an agreement to adopt resale price maintenance from the fact that the supplier had "approached price-cutting distributors and advised that if they did not maintain the suggested resale price, they would not receive adequate supplies. . . ."[254] When one distributor balked, the supplier pressured its parent company, the parent directed the distributor to comply, and the distributor "informed [the supplier] that it would charge the suggested price."[255] The Court stated that "[e]vidence of this kind plainly is relevant and persuasive as to a meeting of minds."[256] In other words, as the Court put it elsewhere in the opinion, there was "communicated . . . acquiescence or agreement."[257]

How different was this from what transpired in cases like *Garment District* or *The Jeanery*? In *The Jeanery*, the complaining dealers had griped about a discounter's "refusal to retail at 'keystone' "—defined as twice the price paid by the retailer for the goods.[258] There was also evidence that discounters had been threatened with shortages in supply and that these threats actually had been carried out. The evidence showed that the principal complaint

---

[254] 465 U.S. 752, 765.

[255] *Id.*

[256] *Id.*

[257] *Id.* at 764 n.9.

[258] 849 F.2d 1148, 1157.

presented to the supplier, from JJ's, was that "we've got a guy right across from me that's selling your product for $5.00 off all the time."[259] The court held on those facts, however, that there was no evidence of an agreement between the supplier and JJ's "on price or price levels."[260] Judgment n.o.v. for the supplier was affirmed, throwing out the jury verdict.

The dissent in *The Jeanery* did not believe that the *Monsanto* rule was meant to go this far, arguing that in *Monsanto* itself the Supreme Court found an agreement on such similar facts. A principal difference was that in *Monsanto* the supplier had to pressure a dealer into communicating that it would comply with the supplier's pricing recommendations, while in cases like *The Jeanery*, the complaining dealer, on its own initiative, already was telling the supplier to force the discounter to comply with the prevailing price level.[261] In *The Jeanery*, like *Garment District*, the complaining dealer had adopted keystone pricing, and the dissent considered this circumstantial evidence of an agreement to fix prices.[262]

In *Sharp* the facts were less pristine. The evidence showed that Hartwell, the complaining dealer, usually adhered to Sharp's suggested retail prices, but sometimes priced below them. Hartwell suggested to Sharp that its dealers should avoid a "discount" situation and complained that Business Electronics, the discounter, was undercutting him. Hartwell also complained that Business Electronics was free riding on his sales efforts and taking customers away from him after he had developed their interest. Sharp responded that it could not dictate prices to Business Electronics, but when Hartwell gave an ultimatum demanding that Business Electronics be terminated within 30 days, Sharp complied. The Court con-

---

259   *Id.* at 1158.

260   *Id.*

261   Another difference was that in *Monsanto* there was additional documentary evidence of a price-fixing agreement, 465 U.S. at 765–66.

262   849 F.2d at 1164–65. It is worth recalling that in *Albrecht*, the Supreme Court cited the "long accepted rule" that "resale price fixing is a *per se* violation of the law whether done by agreement *or combination*." 390 U.S. 145, 151.

cluded that these facts were not sufficient to prove an "agreement on price or price levels" between Sharp and Hartwell, and therefore the termination was not per se illegal.[263] Instead, the Court affirmed the court of appeals decision, which had "remanded for a new trial."

For practical purposes then, the message of *Sharp* is that where suppliers really have not been entering into agreements with dealers on prices or price levels, complaints from one dealer about another dealer's "discounting" will not be treated as proof that the complaining dealer has communicated its agreement to fix its own resale prices, triggering the per se rule. Before *Sharp*, suppliers in such situations were reluctant to terminate the discounter, even though the discounter had been performing poorly. Suppliers feared that once there were complaints from other dealers, there would be allegations of a price-fixing conspiracy and the threat of per se illegality.[264] Under *Sharp*, suppliers can anticipate that even if an agreement to eliminate discounters is proved, the supplier will be afforded an opportunity to show that it had its own independent reasons for such an agreement, and that no agreement to fix a price or price level ever was part of the deal. If there are no explanations for the agreement other than to protect a complaining dealer from price competition, the rule of reason inquiry will be a short one, but if the supplier really did have reasons for agreeing to eliminate discounters that go beyond curing price competition, the agreement could be held reasonable.

C. How should resale price maintenance be defined?

In the early cases involving terminations of discounters at the behest of other dealers, there was little question as to whether specific prices were being maintained, because the suppliers made no secret of the retail prices they required their dealers to charge.[265]

---

263   108 S. Ct. at 1525.

264   *Id.* at 1521.

265   Frey & Son, Inc. v. Cudahy Packing Co., 256 U.S. 208 (1912); United States v. A. Schrader's Son, Inc., 252 U.S. 85 (1920).

Later, when the law became clear that vertical price fixing was per se illegal, suppliers adopted more subtle means of informing dealers of the prices they were expected to charge.[266] During the *Schwinn* era, the distinction between resale price maintenance and other vertical arrangements that affected resale prices took on less importance because almost all vertical restraints became per se illegal. When *Sylvania* overturned *Schwinn*, the distinction became important once again.

As described earlier, the wisdom of the distinction has been much debated by those who would apply the rule of reason to all vertical restraints, including resale price maintenance. Nevertheless, the fact remains that resale price maintenance is qualitatively different from nonprice vertical restraints such as territorial and customer restraints. Although the latter may eliminate intrabrand competition completely, they do not prevent each dealer from adjusting its own prices in response to competition from other brands. Resale price maintenance, in contrast, removes that discretion from the dealer and leaves it entirely in the hands of the supplier, who may be tempted to refrain from aggressive pricing or even to collude with other suppliers in setting prices. For this reason, resale price maintenance has remained per se illegal, despite all the other changes and all the scholarly debate.

But that does nothing to resolve the question left hanging after *Sharp*: What *is* resale price maintenance? We know that a bilateral

---

266 In *Parke, Davis*, for example, the defendant provided its wholesalers with a catalog containing a "Net Price Selling Schedule" listing suggested minimum resale prices on sales to retailers. 362 U.S. at 32. Retailers were quoted the same prices, but were granted discounts for volume purchases. *Id.* Parke, Davis' suggested minimum retail prices generally provided a 50% markup over cost on products purchased by retailers from wholesalers. a higher markup was provided for products purchased in large quantities by retailers directly from Parke, Davis. *Id.* In response to a query as to how to handle retailers straying from suggested prices, Parke, Davis' attorney advised that the company could lawfully say, "we will sell you only so long as you *observe* such minimum retail prices"; but that it could not say, "we will sell you only if you *agree to observe* such minimum retail prices." *Id.* at 33 (emphasis added).

contract by which a dealer promises his supplier that his retail price will be one dollar per unit will constitute resale price maintenance—but what about a promise to charge between $1.00 and $1.50? To charge 40% over wholesale? To charge the same price as last year? What about an offer from a supplier to pay a rebate at year-end to dealers who have adhered to suggested retail prices? Are these agreements to maintain a price "level"? This much of *Sharp*'s holding will remain a mystery until there are more cases.

Logically, the test should be whether the agreement completely removes the dealer's discretion to charge a price below the set price or price level, even if the dealer is prepared to shoulder any additional costs necessary to maintain its required level of service while operating with slimmer margins. If the agreement removes all such discretion, it should be considered resale price maintenance. If the dealer is constrained only by the fact that it cannot afford to cut prices and still function at the required level of service, the agreement should not be considered resale price maintenance. Once the dealer has genuine discretion, the rule of reason becomes the proper approach.

As for agreements to eliminate discounters, we know that under *Sharp* these are not per se illegal. But this raises an interesting question: What would a rule of reason inquiry consist of where the challenged conduct is an agreement to eliminate discounters? Note that this is different from an agreement to reduce the *number* of dealers, as in *Westman* or *Packard*, and focuses instead on selectively eliminating dealers who cut prices. Presumably, the supplier would be afforded an opportunity to show that such an agreement resulted in efficiencies that outweighed the anticompetitive effects.If the supplier's motive were simply to appease a complaining dealer, however, this would be a hefty burden, much like that which faced the defendants in *Professional Engineers*[267] and *Indiana Federation of Dentists*.[268] In those cases the Supreme Court similarly held that some agreements affecting price may not be illegal per se, yet went on to hold that certain of these agreements are so clearly

---

267 National Soc'y of Prof'l Eng'rs v. United States, 435 U.S. 679 (1978).

268 FTC v. Indiana Fed'n of Dentists, 476 U.S. 447 (1986).

anticompetitive that finding illegality under the rule of reason is "not a matter of any great difficulty." In both cases, the Court held that "[w]hile this is not price fixing as such, no elaborate industry analysis is required to demonstrate the anticompetitive character of such an agreement."[269] Or, as Professor Areeda has put it, in the absence of justification, the court can apply the rule of reason "in the twinkling of an eye."[270]

An agreement to eliminate "discounters" without agreeing on retail prices or price levels to be charged in the future, but for the principal purpose of satisfying a dealer's complaint, would seem to fit this framework. A proven agreement to eliminate discounters that is not buoyed by some genuine justifications is likely to be held illegal under the rule of reason in no time at all. On the other hand, if the facts are more complex, and if the supplier has legitimate reasons for such an agreement, a full scale rule of reason inquiry will be necessary, and under the *Sharp* formulation the agreement could be found reasonable. Moreover, if the agreement turns out to be simply an agreement to reduce the number of dealers in order to create an exclusive dealership or just to thin the herd, as in *Westman*, reasonableness is likely to be easier to establish.

D. Should the free-riding defense be limited?

Identification of the free-rider phenomenon has, without any question, provided an important aid to analyzing distribution cases. No one who has ever shopped for a computer doubts that the potential for free riding is very real where dealers are called upon to provide costly presale services and facilities. Nevertheless, the recent tendency of some courts simply to *assume* the existence of a free-rider problem, and with it the efficiency of vertical restraints as

---

269   476 U.S. at 459 (quoting National Soc'y of Prof'l Eng'rs v. United States, 435 U.S. at 692).

270   P. Areeda, "The Rule of Reason" in ANTITRUST ANALYSIS: GENERAL ISSUES, 37–38 (Federal Judicial Center, June 1981) (*quoted in* NCAA v. Board of Regents, 468 U.S. 85, 109–10 n.39 (1984).

a means of combating the problem, is troublesome.[271] This is particularly so given the boost this trend appears to have been given by the dictum in *Sharp*.

There was a time when some business executives saw vertical restraints as a means of relieving their dealers of the pressure of competition from neighboring dealers. Even in cases where a genuine free-rider problem existed, and the restraint provided an effective means of overcoming it, memos would turn up in the supplier's files suggesting anticompetitive motives for what really were procompetitive arrangements. Eventually, courts became more sophisticated in discerning the existence of free-rider problems and the efficiencies associated with vertical restraints, and began to discount the significance of the loose talk that sometimes found its way into the supplier's documents.[272]

Today, the situation is different. Executives have been made much more aware of concepts like free riding and interbrand competition, and are less likely to attribute their motives for imposing a vertical restraint on a desire to satisfy their dealers' demands to have other dealers fenced in. The challenge courts face in these circumstances is to determine whether the proof of a free-rider justification is credible, or whether it is a pretext.

"Free riding" means taking away customers from other dealers, usually by offering lower prices, without providing comparable services such as promotions and demonstrations that attract customers in the first place[273]—it does not mean taking away customers by offering lower prices while still providing comparable services; it does not mean taking away customers where no significant dealer

---

271   *See* section V, *supra*.

272   *See* McCabe's Furniture, Inc. v. La-Z-Boy Chair Co., 798 F.2d 323 (8th Cir. 1986); H.L. Moore Drug Exch. v. Eli Lilly & Co., 662 F.2d 935 (2d Cir. 1981); A.P. Hopkins Corp. v. Studebaker Corp., 355 F. Supp. 816 (E.D. Mich. 1972), *aff'd*, 496 F.2d 969 (6th Cir. 1974).

273   *See* Continental T.V., Inc. v. GET Sylvania Inc., 433 U.S. 36, 55 (1977); Valley Liquors, Inc. v. Renfield Importers, Ltd., 822 F.2d 656, 663 n.7 (7th Cir. 1987).

services are being offered at all. The latter constitute price competition, not free riding. Courts must endeavor to distinguish between elimination of free riding as a justification for terminations, and elimination of price competition.

In the *Bulova* case,[274] FTC Commissioner Bailey pointed out several years ago that free riding is not a malady to which all industries are equally susceptible. Where there are genuine services being performed by dealers, on which other dealers may try to take a free ride, the problem can be very real. In other markets it may hardly exist at all. As commissioner Bailey put it:

> there are many products whose function or aesthetic appeal is self-evident. Sales of these goods do not require a blandiloquent [*sic*] personal sales effort or major consumer education program. I would put watches (both digital and mechanical) in this category. Authorized and non-authorized watch dealers advertise in the same way. There are no special promotional efforts which are discouraged by transshipping. It follows, then, that the only pre-sale "service" which is fostered by this ban on transshipping is a non-discountable price, which some would say conveys an image of quality. I have never accepted this argument because it leads very logically to the position that resale price maintenance is an even stronger guarantee of that precious "prestige image."[275]

Commissioner Bailey added that even the original Chicago school explanation of the free-rider theory by Professor Telser "limited its applicability to special services 'specific to the commodity and unrelated to the retailers' methods of generally doing business.'"[276]

The willingness of certain courts today to *presume* the existence of a free-rider problem, and the procompetitive nature of vertical restraints, spares suppliers the trouble of explaining why they adopted particular restraints and how those restraints promote competition against other brands. It also forces the plaintiff to prove a

---

274   Bulova Watch Co., 102 F.T.C. 1834 (1983).

275   *Id.* at 1835–36.

276   *Id.* at 1835 n *. (Only footnote in Bailey *Dissent.*)

negative—that there is no free-rider problem and that the restraints in question do not promote competition. Under the more traditional approach, by contrast, it was enough for a plaintiff to show that a vertical restraint reduced intrabrand competition in a magnitude sufficient to have an impact in the interbrand market. It was then incumbent upon the supplier to show that the restraint had procompetitive features and, on balance, was not anticompetitive.

This clearly is not too great a burden—the vast majority of defendants since *Sylvania* have met it.[277] The supplier simply can show a genuine threat of free riding among its dealers, and demonstrate how the vertical restraint helps meet the problem. At that point, the plaintiff will find it necessary to prove that there really is no free-riding problem and that the real reason for the restraint was that the supplier had succumbed to the demands of one or more dealers; alternatively, the plaintiff can try to prove that the supplier's brand has such a dominant share of the market that regardless of whether there is free riding, the restraints cannot possibly serve to promote interbrand competition.[278] This is a heavy burden for the plaintiff already, and the notion of *presuming* free riding and efficiencies makes that burden even heavier. It is true, as the Court pointed out in *Sharp*, that most vertical restraints encourage more dealer services and thereby promote efficiency. But simply to assume these effects is to invite abuse, which ultimately will bring calls to rewrite the rules, threatening the continuation of the very latitude that suppliers now enjoy. Instead, suppliers should continue to be required to prove the reasons for their restraints, something the vast majority of suppliers are easily able to do.

E. Should market power thresholds be retained?

The least controversial of the new trends has been the growing adoption of the market power "screen," permitting courts quickly to dispose of claims that hold no prospect of success. The lingering

---

277 *See supra* note 208.

278 *See* section VII(E), *infra*.

question is exactly where the threshold should be drawn. The Justice Department's Vertical Restraints Guidelines set the threshold at 10% at a minimum, and higher in the context of certain market structures under a set of formulas that cannot be calculated without having a great deal of industry data available.[279] As noted earlier, the courts have begun to employ a simpler straight percentage test, but have chosen a variety of numbers based on the facts before them. Some have held that a market share of under 10% is not enough to warrant further inquiry, while other courts have held that 25% is not enough.

One place to look for clues to the proper threshold is the body of cases in which nonprice vertical restraints previously have been declared unlawful under the rule of reason. If the nonprice vertical restraints of suppliers with as little as x% of the relevant market have been proven unreasonable, it would seem sensible to screen out only those restraints imposed by suppliers with market shares of something less than x. But there are very few of these cases, and they do not provide very good clues.

For example, in *Graphic Products Distributors, Inc. v. Itek Corp.,*[280] decided after *Sylvania* the Eleventh Circuit struck down a territorial restraint in a market where the supplier had a share of over 70%. If there had been a screen of more than 70% in use the court never would have examined the rest of the facts, but this is such a high number as to become meaningless.[281] The fact is, there simply are not enough rule of reason cases in which nonprice vertical restraints have been held unreasonable to provide any meaningful guidance in choosing a threshold.

The next best alternative is to look at cases that have applied the screen to *exclude* claims, to see whether any consensus is develop-

---

279   *See* Vertical Restrictions Guidelines, *supra* note 40, at 4.1.

280   717 F.2d 1560 (11th Cir. 1983).

281   *See also* Kohler Co. v. Briggs & Stratton Corp., 1986–1 Trade Cas. (CCH) ¶ 67,047 (E.D. Wis. 1986) (preliminary injunction for plaintiff—a competing supplier—granted) (defendant had a 62% market share; plaintiff had 8%).

ing. There is precedent for this approach in the field of monopoly law, where over the course of several years the courts gradually built a consensus that a market share under 50% generally would suffice to negate market power.[282]

With vertical restraints, a 10% threshold seems to have considerable support,[283] a threshold between 10% and 20% has several cases to support it,[284] and a threshold of 25% has some support as well.[285] Of course, certain cases described earlier in this article have held that no screen should be applied at all in some circumstances,

---

[282] *See, e.g.*, Domed Stadium Hotel, Inc. v. Holiday Inns, Inc., 732 F.2d 480, 499 (5th Cir. 1984) ("[A]bsent special circumstances a defendant must have a market share of at least fifty percent before he can be guilty of monopolization."); Hiland Dairy, Inc. v. Kroger Co., 402 F.2d 968, 974 and n.6 (8th Cir. 1968) (collecting cases finding violations of Sherman 2; in each case, defendant's market share was at least 70%; court also cited cases refusing to find monopoly where defendant's market share was 50% or less), *cert. denied*, 395 U.S. 961 (1969); Lynch Business Machines, Inc. v. A.B. Dick Co., 594 F. Supp. 59, 67 (N.D. Ohio 1984) (no monopoly power where market share less than 50%); Slocomb Indus. v. Chelsea Indus., 1984–1 Trade Cas. (CCH) ¶ 65,932, at 66,028 (E.D. Pa. 1984) (50% market share insufficient to establish monopoly power).

[283] *See, e.g.*, Ryco Mfg. Co. v. Eden Servs., 823 F.2d 1215 (8th Cir. 1987) (8% to 10% market share and evidence of competition), *cert. denied*, 108 S. Ct. 751 (1988); Rothery Storage & Van Co. v. Atlas Van Lines, Inc., 792 F.2d 210, 217 (D.C. Cir. 1986) (5.1% to 6% market share where largest competitor had 13.3% and 15 largest firms had 70%), *cert. denied*, 107 S. Ct. 880 (1987); Davis-Watkins Co. v. Service Merch., 686 F.2d 1189 1183 (6th Cir. 1982) (18% market share declined to 11% within 1 year due to foreign competition), *cert. denied*, 466 U.S. 931 (1984).

[284] *See, e.g. O.S.C. Corp.*, 601 F. Supp. at 1291 n.8 (20% market share insufficient where substantial evidence of competition), *aff'd*, 792 F.2d 1464 (9th Cir. 1986); *Assam Drug*, 798 F.2d at 311, 318 & n.18 (19.1% market share insufficient where defendant's market share has been declining).

[285] Northwest Power Products, Inc. v. Omark Indus., Inc., 576 F.2d 83, 90–91 (5th Cir. 1978) 25% insufficient where eight firms competed, one larger than defendant), *cert. denied*, 439 U.S. 1116 (1979); Donald B. Rice Tire Co. v. Michelin Tire Co., 483 F. Supp. 750, 761 (D.Md. 1980) 25% insufficient where prices were declining), *aff'd*, 638 F.2d 15 (4th Cir.), *cert. denied*, 454 U.S. 864 (1981); Manufacturers Supply Co. v. Minnesota Mining & Mfg. Co., 688 F. Supp. 303 (W.D. Mich. 1988) (25% share insufficient).

such as situations involving highly differentiated products or high barriers to entry.[286] In addition, there seems to be broad agreement that evidence that the supplier's market share has been declining or increasing significantly should be factored in as well, much as it is in analyzing merger or monopolization claims.[287]

It is impossible to pick a threshold in a vacuum, of course, and unfair to litigants who must have their cases decided while a consensus is in the process of being built. Although 10% appears to be a safe starting point, there may be many cases in which that is too low, depending on the characteristics of the market. All we can say now is that the screen approach makes sense, but that in each case the courts must consider all the variables to make sure that cases are not screened out in which restraints on the distribution of the supplier's brand really do have a meaningful impact on the overall market. Hard as this is, it makes more sense than arbitrarily picking a number. The day may come when we can be more precise, but today, when there is still so much uncertainty over the standards governing vertical restraints, the law is too fluid to settle on a higher threshold with any real confidence.

VIII. Conclusion

For a hundred years the law of distribution has been a contest of extremes, undermining the business community's faith in the ability of the American legal system to formulate consistent, workable rules. And the cases, perplexing as they are, reveal only the tip of the iceberg: For every lawsuit there are thousands of counseling sessions, providing advice that needs to be based not only on the lessons of past precedents but on predictions for the future course of the law.

---

286   *See* section VI, *supra*.

287   *See* Assam Drug Co., Inc. f. Miller Brewing Co., 798 F.2d 311, 318 n.18 (8th Cir. 1986); Business Electronics Corp. v. Sharp Electronics Corp., 780 F.2d 1212, 1221 (5th Cir. 1986) (Jones, J., concurring), *aff'd*, 108 S. Ct. 1515 (1988); *In re* Super Premium Ice Cream Distribution Antitrust Litigation, 1988–2 Trade Cas. (CCH) ¶ 68,162, at 59,087 (N.D. Cal. 1988).

Counselors today can give no guarantees as to how long any given standard in the field of distribution will remain in effect. As long as the lower courts continue to arrive at such divergent interpretations of cases like *Monsanto*, there will be no enduring rules. The time has come to cushion the wild swings of the pendulum and consolidate what has been learned over the past 30 years into a cohesive set of guideposts. Only then can there be some certainty that the rules today, while not necessarily simple or perfectly precise, will still be the rules tomorrow. Absolutism on both extremes must give way to a recognition that the same assumptions will not apply in every case, and that while tools such as per se illegality, the "*Monsanto* test," the free-rider defense and market threshold screens can be very useful, they cannot be applied mechanically or they will become as "wooden" as the old per se test of *Schwinn*.[288] Only by understanding the *premises* behind each of the rules of analysis can we know which ones to apply in each case.

We have reached another turning point. Either the standards announced in *Monsanto* and *Sharp* will be integrated into a fair and realistic analytical approach by the lower courts, or they are going to be thrown out by Congress and replaced with a statute that will need to be interpreted from square one. The challenge is formidable, but only by learning to master all of the tools of analysis, rather than confining analysis to a few pat formulas, can we ever fashion a durable body of law.

---

[288] *See* United States v. Arnold, Schwinn & Co., 388 U.S. 365, 394 (1967) (Stewart, J., dissenting).

Abbreviations

Every accredited law school in the United States publishes at least one journal or law review on a regular basis. Many years ago, the editors of the leading publications agreed on a uniform, abbreviated system of citation which differed from that used in other disciplines. We have utilized this format for *The Antitrust Impulse*. To facilitate checking a footnote, please consider the following example:

X. Smith, *Antitrust Now and Then*, 99 ANTITRUST BULL. 949 (1999).
Author: X. Smith
Article title: Antitrust Now and Then
Journal: *The Antitrust Bulletin*—see explanation below.
Volume: 99
Year of publication: 1999
Page: 949.

The law review abbreviations usually include standard state or university abbreviations. Listed below are some of the less obvious ones and several recurring ones:

ABA (sometimes separated with periods) = American Bar Association

J	=	Journal
L	=	Law
Rev	=	Review
Q	=	Quarterly
U	=	University

Other abbreviations:

AAG	=	Assistant Attorney General
BNA	=	Bureau of National Affairs, Inc.
BOC	=	Bell Operating Company

CAB	=	Civil Aeronautics Board
CCH	=	Commerce Clearing House
CES	=	Center for Economic Studies at the U. S. Bureau of the Census
Cir.	=	Circuit
CIS	=	Consumer Information System
cert.	=	*certiorari*
D	=	District (but see below)
DOE	=	Department of Energy
DOJ	=	Department of Justice
DOT	=	Department of Transportation
EEC	=	European Economic Community
EPO	=	Economy Policy Office at the DOJ (see above)
ETC	=	Export Trading Company (Act)
EWG	=	Executive Working Group on Antitrust
FCC	=	Federal Communications Commission
FERC	=	Federal Energy Regulatory Commission (successor to the FPC)
FPC	=	Federal Power Commission (predecessor of the FERC)
FTC	=	Federal Trade Commission (sometimes referred to as the "Commission")
GATT	=	General Agreement on Tariffs and Trade
HHI	=	Herfindahl–Hirschman Index
HSR	=	Hart Scott Rodino (sometimes referred to as the Antitrust Improvements Act)
ICC	=	Interstate Commerce Commission
LBO	=	Leveraged Buyout
LRD	=	Longitudinal Research Database of the CES (see above)
L.S.E.	=	London School of Economics
MFJ	=	Modification of Final Judgment (usually referring to the AT&T Divestiture settlement)
NAAG	=	National Association of Attorneys General
NIRA	=	National Industrial Recovery Act
NRA	=	National Recovery Administration
NRC	=	Nuclear Regulatory Commission

OECD	=	Organization for Economic Cooperation and Development
R&D	=	Research and Development
RPM	=	Resale Price Maintenance
Reg.	=	Regulation *or* Register
SEC	=	Securities and Exchange Commission
SIC	=	Standard Industry Classification
TNEC	=	Temporary National Economic Committee
U.S.C.	=	United States Code
§	=	Section
¶	=	Paragraph

Index

DATE DUE